Money, Banking and Finance

Money, Banking and Finance

A European Text

P G A HOWELLS AND K BAIN

Addison Wesley Longman Limited
Edinburgh Gate, Harlow
Essex CM20 2JE England
and Associated Companies throughout the world

First published 1998

British Cataloguing in Publication Data
A catalogue entry for this title is available from the British Library

ISBN: 0582-27800-7

Library of Congress Cataloguing-in-Publication Data
A catalog entry for this title is available from the Library of Congress

Set by 36 in 9/12 pt Times
Produced by Longman Singapore Publishers (Pte) Ltd.
Printed in Singapore

Contents

Acknowledgements

Throughout this book we have made use of statistics provided by organizations kind enough to allow their reproduction with acknowledgement of the source. We have, of course, acknowledged each source at the appropriate point but we take this additional opportunity of thanking the Bank of England, the Deutsche Bundesbank, the Institut National de la Statistique et des Etudes Economiques (INSEE), the International Monetary Fund, the UK Office of National Statistics, the Banca d'Italia and the US Federal Reserve Board.

A feature of this book is the guidance it gives students on reading the financial press. We have reproduced extensive material, both tables and reports, from the *Financial Times*. We are pleased to acknowledge that this project would not have been possible without the permission and co-operation of its publishers.

Finally we wish to acknowledge with thanks the innumerable contributions made, wittingly and unwittingly, by students and colleagues at the University of East London. In particular our thanks go to Iris Biefang-Frisancho Mariscal, Murray Glickman and Simon Maggs who many times made helpful suggestions, spotted errors, encouraged and criticized. Any errors that remain are entirely our responsibility.

PGAH
KB

Preface

This book is intended for students taking courses in financial economics, and in money banking and finance. Parts will be of some interest to students of the financial services industry and parts of it may be of some help to students taking courses in monetary economics. The level of analysis is that which we think appropriate, in UK terms, for second and third year undergraduates. As we explain in a moment, the level of difficulty tends to increase in the later parts of the book, but even Parts 1 and 2 assume a basic knowledge of economic theory and at least an acquaintance with statistical theory and elementary notions of finance. It is not therefore suitable for absolute beginners.

The book is divided into six sections. There are many cross-references but a selection of individual sections can be made in order to support courses of varying length, difficulty and content. Parts 1 and 2 provide respectively an introduction to the functions of a financial system and the theory necessary to understand the determination of rates of return, the pricing of assets and the behaviour of asset markets. There is a minimum of institutional detail in Parts 1 and 2 and the theory is essentially that of orthodox economics, albeit with a rather more eclectic view of interest rate determination than usual, and a few questioning words about the rationality of financial markets. Parts 1 and 2 could easily form the basis of a one-semester course which would be students' first exposure to financial economics, divorced from any institutional complexities.

Part 3 focuses on issues related specifically to money and banking. For students specializing in financial economics or financial services this section could be optional though it provides a fuller understanding of the behaviour of interest rates than would be the case without. For students taking units in financial economics as part of a broader economics education, however, Part III is important because it connects the monetary and financial activity, central to this book, with familiar parts of the macroeconomics syllabus. Again, the level assumes a pre-existing knowledge of basic economic theory but students familiar with IS/LM should find it easy to handle. The analysis is fairly orthodox though we accept the endogeneity of money as axiomatic and relegate the base:multiplier account of money supply determination to the status of a curiosity. This view, that central banks can only control interest rates, explains our insistence upon a mixed (market plus administrative) theory of interest rate determination in Part 2. Although Parts 1–3 have recommendations for further reading (as do all parts of the book) references within the chapters are kept to a minimum. This is another reflection of their level and purpose which is to provide a fairly uncontroversial core of theoretical knowledge.

Parts 4 and 5 can be seen in parallel. They both step up the level of analysis and introduce institutional complexities and variations. References, both to further reading and to competing views, are frequently necessary. Either part taken in its entirety could be added to Parts 1 and 2 to make a two-semester course in 'theory and markets' or 'theory and systems', according to choice. A two-semester course covering theory *and* markets *and* systems could, however, be constructed by selecting particular markets for attention and by selecting the systems of just two or three countries for comparative purposes. Unlike the brief treatment of markets in Part 2 (Chapter 5), Part 4 discusses the characteristics of each group of instruments in some detail, distinguishing between different meanings of 'yield' for example. It discusses the use of the instruments and also looks at the trading systems. Differences between practices in major financial centres are highlighted. Part 5 can be seen as the 'institutions' equivalent of Part 4 in that it focuses upon the activities of financial intermediaries. It could have been organized along the lines of Part 4, with chapters devoted to 'banks', 'other deposit-taking institutions', 'insurance companies' and so on, but we felt that this would have been too rigid, repetitive and probably rather descriptive. We also wished to give greater emphasis at some point to the distinctive characteristics of the financial systems of different countries. Our own view is that these are often more strongly reflected in the structure and activities of intermediaries than in markets themselves. Therefore, while each chapter in Part 5 does concentrate upon the activities of inter-mediaries in each country it also raises issues which are relevant to the national financial system itself but which may be peculiar to that system alone.

Part 6, 'Current Issues', almost speaks for itself. It does not have to follow a two-semester course consisting of 'theory and markets' or 'theory and institutions' or 'theory, markets and institutions', but can stand on its own. If, however, such a two-semester course were taken in the second year, then Part 6 would make a one-semester extension in year three for which its level, particularly in the chapters on regulation and innovation, would probably make it more suitable. For good students, however, there could be some logic in a two-semester course in financial economics comprising just 'theory and issues'. Drawing on Parts 1, 2, 3 and 6, such a course would contain little institutional detail but would enable students to concentrate on contemporary debates, equipped with most of the essential monetary and financial theory.

PGAH
KB

Symbols, abbreviations and other conventions

AI	Accrued interest
α	The cash ratio of the nonbank private sector $(= C_p/D_p)$
β	Banks' reserve ratio $(= (C_b + D_b)/D_p)$
β	Beta coefficient (of an asset)
B	The monetary base
BFr	Belgian franc
C	Coupon payment
c	Coupon rate
C_b	Notes and coin held by the banking system
C_c	cost of carry
C_p	Notes and coin held by the non-bank private sector
cy	Current yield
Δ	Change in
d	Rate of discount
d	The Eurobank redeposit ratio
D_b	Deposits of the banking system at the central bank
D_g	Deposits of the government
D_p	Deposits of the non-bank private sector
DM	Deutschmark
Dr	Greek drachma
Ecu	European currency unit
Es	Portuguese escudo
E_F	Forward exchange rate expressed in direct quotation
E_R	Real exchange rate expressed in direct quotation
E_S	Spot exchange rate expressed in direct quotation
FFr	French franc
FM	Finnish markka

Fl	Netherlands guilder
i	Nominal rate of interest
i_d	Domestic interest rate
i_f	Foreign interest rate
$I\pounds$	Irish punt
K	The return on an asset
$\hat{K}$	The expected return on an asset
$\overline{K}$	The required rate of return on an asset
K_m	The rate of return on a 'whole market portfolio'
K_{rf}	the risk-free rate of return
L	Italian lira
L_g	Bank loans to the government
L_p	Bank loans to the nonbank private sector
M	The par or maturity or redemption value of an asset
M_D	Demand for money
M_S	Supply of money
$M1$	$M1$ monetary aggregate
$M2$	$M2$ monetary aggregate
$M3$	$M3$ monetary aggregate
$M4$	$M4$ monetary aggregate
N	Total employment
n	Total number (e.g. of time periods)
n_{im}	Length of time from date of issue to maturity
n_{lc}	Length of time since last coupon payment
n_m	Length of time to maturity
n_{sm}	Length of time from settlement of purchase to maturity
n_{tc}	Length of time to next coupon payment
n_{xc}	Length of time from ex dividend date to next coupon payment
n_{xt}	Length of time between ex dividend date and date of calculation
P	The purchase or market

	price (the price level in the aggregate)
Pm^c	The premium price of a call option
P_s	Spot or cash price
P_x	Strike or exercise price of option
$P_x f$	Discounted option strike price
$\dot{P}$	The rate of inflation
π	The rate of inflation
$\dot{P}^e$	The expected rate of inflation
Pta	Spanish peseta
Q	The number of coupon payments before redemption
r	The real rate of interest
ry	Redemption yield
RR	Required bank reserves
smy	Simple yield to maturity
S_F	Forward exchange rate expressed in indirect quotation
S_f	Shareholders' funds
Sch	Austrian schilling
SDR	Special Drawing Right
SFr	Swiss franc
SKr	Swedish krøne
S_R	Real exchange rate expressed in indirect quotation
S_S	Spot exchange rate expressed in indirect quotation
σ	The standard deviation (of an asset's return), risk
σ^2	The variance (of an asset's return) risk
Σ	summation (of a series)
t	Time period
TR	Total bank reserves
V	Velocity of circulation
Y	Aggregate real output, national income
$\yen$	Japanese yen
$\pounds$	Pound sterling
$\$$	United States dollar

PART 1   Introduction

The role of a financial system

1.1 Introduction

In this chapter we want to provide preliminary answers to the questions posed in the box above: what is a financial system, who uses it, what does it do, does it matter how it does it? Our answers are preliminary in the sense that these questions concern us throughout the book and each later chapter is looking at some aspect of these questions in more detail. The intention here is to provide an introduction – a definition of key terms and the explanation of some basic principles – for readers who have had no prior contact with financial economics, and an overview of the field, as we see it, for all readers.

We begin by defining a financial system as:

a set of markets for financial instruments, and the individuals and institutions who trade in those markets.

The users of the system are people, firms and other organizations who wish to make use of the facilities offered by a financial system. The facilities offered may be summarized as:

- intermediation between surplus and deficit units;
- financial services such as insurance and pensions;
- a payments mechanism;
- portfolio adjustment facilities.

Notice that while different parts of the system may specialize in each of these functions, they all have one thing in common: they all have the effect of channelling funds from those who have a surplus (to their current spending plans) to those who have a deficit. Consider each case in turn. Banks, historically speaking, began as institutions whose function was to accept deposits from those who wished to save and to lend them to borrowers on terms which were attractive to the latter. Only later did they begin to offer a means of payment facility, based initially upon written cheques but now largely electronic. Thus, to have access to the current payments mechanism, one needs to hold bank deposits and these can be on-lent. Similarly, insurance companies and pension funds have a primary purpose which is to offer people a means of managing the risk of some major, adverse event. However, the contributions made by policyholders creates a fund which is usually invested in a wide range of securities. This purchase of securities involves a flow of funds (directly or indirectly) to those who issued the securities as a means of raising funds. The income from the securities goes to meet the expenses of the companies' operations, including some payments to policyholders. Portfolio adjustment facilities have to provide wealth-holders with a quick, cheap and reliable way of buying and selling a wide variety of financial assets. When wealth-holders buy financial assets they are lending (again directly or indirectly) to those who issued the assets. These facilities are obviously supplied by financial markets, but they are also supplied to smaller investors by 'mutual funds' such as unit trusts. Thus, all kinds of financial activity have the effect in some degree of channelling funds from lenders to borrowers.

It is important to bear in mind that economists are usually interested in the way in which a financial system channels funds between the *end users* of the system, that is, between *ultimate borrowers and lenders*, rather than the *intermediate* borrowers and lenders – the financial intermediaries who also borrow and lend but only, as their name implies, in order to channel funds between end users. In developed economies, incomes are generally so high (by world standards) that there are many people who wish to lend; and the state of technology is such that real investment can only be undertaken by borrowing funds to finance its installation and to see firms through the often lengthy period before it earns a return. Given that there is a desire to lend and to borrow, we can get some idea immediately of why modern economies have quite highly developed financial systems.

Faced with a desire to lend or to borrow, the end users of financial systems have a choice between three broad approaches.

Firstly, they can engage in what is usually called *direct lending*. That is to say that they deal directly with each other. But this, as we shall see, is costly, inefficient, extremely risky and not, in practice, very likely.

Secondly, they may decide to use *organized markets*. In these markets, lenders buy the liabilities issued by borrowers. If the liability is newly issued, then the issuer receives funds directly from the lender. To this extent the process has some similarity to direct lending, but dealing in liabilities traded in organized markets has advantages for both parties. Organized markets reduce the search costs that would be associated with direct lending because organized markets are populated by people willing to trade. They also reduce risk since there are usually rules governing the operation of the market which endeavour to exclude the dishonest and the extremely risky. For lenders, there is the big advan-

tage that they can sell their claim on the borrower if, after making the loan, they find they need funds themselves. Indeed, the more typical transaction in organized markets is that where a lender buys, not a newly issued liability, but a liability which was originally bought from the borrower by another lender. In this case the lender is refinancing a loan originally made by someone else, though the borrower is completely unaware of this secondary transaction. The best known markets, of course, are the markets for company shares in Tokyo, London, New York and Hong Kong. But there are organized markets for a vast range of financial instruments, as we shall see in Part 3 of this book.

We have suggested that organized markets may be used by ultimate lenders and borrowers. But they are used also by financial intermediaries who themselves provide a third channel for the transmission of funds between borrowers and lenders. When a lender deals through an intermediary, s/he acquires an asset – typically a bank or building society deposit, or claims on an insurance fund – which cannot be traded but can only be returned to the intermediary. Similarly, intermediaries create liabilities, typically in the form of loans, for borrowers. These too are 'non-marketable'. If the borrower wishes to end the loan, it must be repaid to the intermediary. The advantages of dealing through intermediaries are similar to those of dealing in organized markets: lenders and borrowers are brought together more quickly, more efficiently and therefore more cheaply than if they had to search each other out; and the intermediary is able, through superior knowledge and economies of scale, to reduce the risk of the transaction for both parties. One of the ways in which they do the latter is to hold highly diversified portfolios of assets and liabilities and this involves them as traders in organized markets. Indeed, most markets are probably dominated by intermediaries rather than by end users of the financial system. Figure 1.1 summarizes these three possibilities schematically.

We go next, in Section 1.2, to the question of who the end users are and the supplementary question of what are their motives and interests; in Section 1.3 we shall look at the essential characteristics of financial institutions and their role as intermediaries; in Section 1.4 we look at the broad range of financial

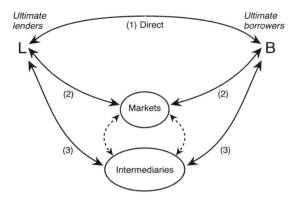

Figure 1.1 The options for lenders and borrowers.

markets and suggest some ways in which they may be ordered and classified as well as introducing some of the basic principles underlying supply and demand in financial markets; in Section 1.5 we look at how all this financial activity relates to the functioning of the 'real' economy.

Remember, as you read these sections, that most issues are dealt with in more detail later in the book. We shall point this out as we go along.

1.2   Lenders and borrowers

In this section we turn our attention to the end users of the financial system – lenders and borrowers – and to their reasons for lending and borrowing. We shall see that these motives differ and in some cases conflict. The role of a financial system is to reconcile these differences, as cheaply and effectively as possible. Remember that lenders and borrowers here are *ultimate* lenders and borrowers. Their motives as lenders and borrowers are different from those of financial intermediaries who are also lending (to ultimate borrowers) and borrowing (from ultimate lenders) and frequently lending and borrowing between themselves. We must not confuse the two.

1.2.1   Saving and lending

As we noted earlier, it is one characteristic of developed economies that incomes are higher than many people require for current consumption. The difference between income and consumption we call *saving*. In these economies, aggregate saving is positive. These savings can be used to buy 'real' capital assets such as machinery, industrial equipment and premises. Savings used in this way are being used for *investment*.[1]

However, many people will be saving at a level which exceeds their real investment spending. Indeed, this is generally true for households whose needs and opportunities for real investment are limited. Many households save without undertaking any real investment. The difference between saving and real investment is their *financial surplus*, and they are often described as *surplus units*. It is this financial surplus that is available for lending and it is this that gives rise to *a net acquisition of financial assets*. Notice that we say 'available for lending'. It does not have to be lent. It is perfectly possible for those with a financial surplus to accumulate what used to be called 'hoards'. That is to say, they could use their surplus to build up holdings of money. Borrowing from the vocabulary of computing, we might say that the accumulation of money holdings is the 'default' setting. This is what happens to those with a financial surplus if they make no conscious decision to do otherwise. They receive their income in money form (usually by the transfer of bank deposits). They use some of that (money) income to make consumption purchases. If consumption is less than income they have positive saving. Assume, for simplicity, that their real investment is zero. Their saving is simultaneously a financial surplus and if they make no positive decision about its allocation it will, by default, accumulate in the form of bank deposits. If they do this, they are not lending.[2]

This distinction between saving and lending, revolving around people's desire to hold money as a

---

1 UK readers need to be careful with the use of the term 'investment'. Economists use the term strictly to refer to the purchase of real, physical, assets whose purpose is to contribute to the production process. The printed and broadcast media, following the financial press, use the term investment to refer to

the acquisition of financial assets. These are quite distinct activities. It is probably too late to insist on the use of 'investment' being confined to its original sense. When there might be any ambiguity, we shall use the term 'real investment' to refer to the purchase of capital equipment.

financial asset, was once a crucial issue in economics. It lay at the centre of contrasting views about the determination of interest rates, as we shall see in Section 3.3.

We can sum up what we have just said in the following identity:

$$(Y - C) - I = NAFA \qquad (1.1)$$

where $(Y - C)$, income minus consumption, is saving; I stands for real investment; and $NAFA$ stands for the *net acquisition of financial assets*. Figure 1.2 summarizes the position more schematically, and also emphasizes the point that the net acquisition of financial assets is equal only to *potential* lending. The accumulation of 'hoards' is an acquisition of financial assets (money) but is not, as we know, lending.

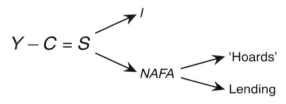

Figure 1.2 Possible uses of saving

What conditions have to be met to induce those with a surplus to lend? As a general principle we shall say that lenders wish to get the maximum *return* for the minimum of *risk*. It is also assumed that lenders have a positive attitude toward *liquidity*. We look at each in turn.

The *return* on a financial asset may take one or more of a number of forms. It may take the form of the payment of interest at discrete intervals. This is the case, for example, with a savings deposit which is, in effect, a loan to a savings institution. Interest is also paid on bonds, though there is also the possibility with a bond of selling at a profit and making a capital gain. With company shares, the attraction of capital gain for some investors is at least as important as the periodic payments, which are variable because

they are ultimately related to the firms' earnings. Some assets, when newly issued, are sold at a discount to the price at which they will later be redeemed, their maturity value. This discount functions, therefore, rather like a capital gain – one pays less for the asset than one receives on its disposal. This discount can be expressed as a fraction (usually of the maturity value) and in this form, known as a *rate* of discount, it can be compared with other rates of return. Discounting is most commonly used in connection with treasury or commercial bills – tradeable securities of short duration. We look at the returns on different types of asset, and at the factors determining those returns, in our discussion of individual markets in Part 4 of this book.

Risk in a financial context is usually taken to refer to the probability that outcomes may differ from what was expected. It takes a number of forms. For the moment we may note that lenders are faced with the possibility of default risk (the borrower fails to repay when expected); income risk (the asset fails to yield the return expected); capital risk (the asset's nominal value differs from what was expected) and inflation risk (the risk that the price level changes unexpectedly, causing a change in the real value of assets). One of the main disadvantages in direct lending, and hence one of the main advantages in using organized markets or specialist intermediaries, is that many lenders would find it impossible to assess accurately the risk of lending to individual borrowers. And if they could, the level of risk to which they found themselves exposed would deter them from lending, perhaps at all or certainly at anything but a very high rate of return.

Other things being equal, lenders are also assumed to prefer opportunities that offer the greatest *liquidity*. By liquidity we mean the ability to retrieve funds quickly and with capital certainty. Notice that two conditions are involved – speed and value. Any asset can be sold quickly – even a house in a depressed housing market – if the seller is prepared to incur a sufficiently large capital loss. The reasons for this positive attitude toward liquidity are quite complex but they are connected with risk and

---

2 Readers who are puzzled by this (because they are tempted to think that the accumulation of money balances, if it is in the form of bank deposits, still results in lending because banks have more deposits to lend) should think carefully and then read footnote 1 in Chapter 3. Definitions of money and details of the money supply process are dealt with in Chapter 6.

uncertainty. In making a loan, a lender is calculating that s/he does not need access to the funds for a given period. In an uncertain world, however, these calculations can go wrong resulting in inconvenience, embarrassment or, for a firm, perhaps even bankruptcy. The ability to retrieve funds quickly, and at a value that can be depended upon, is a positive attraction in any lending opportunity.

1.2.2 Borrowing

At the same time that some people have income which is in excess of their current consumption needs, there will be those – firms, households, public authorities – whose incomes are insufficient for their current spending plans. This will usually be because they are planning to spend on large, expensive, 'real' assets of a kind which lasts for many years. Their need to borrow this year, therefore, may be offset in future by years when saving is the norm. For households, such purchases will typically be major consumer durables, cars or even houses perhaps. For firms, it will be real capital equipment which they hope will add to their cashflow in future and will help them to service and repay the loan. In certain circumstances, however, one can envisage people borrowing in order to purchase financial assets. Notice that this is not likely to be a common situation since it is saying that borrowers can borrow funds at a lower cost than the return that they can get from the financial assets they purchase. This is extremely rare for the personal sector. It is usually much more expensive for individuals to borrow funds than it is for firms or public bodies. A personal loan will cost much more than a firm has to offer on its shares or bonds. But there may have been cases, the Wall Street boom of 1928–9 and the big bull market of the mid-1980s, where people and non-financial institutions have thought, rightly or wrongly, that they could borrow in order to earn a profit from financial assets.

Those who wish to spend (on consumption and real investment) in excess of their income are said to have a *financial deficit* and they are sometimes referred to as *deficit units*. We saw earlier that surplus units must acquire financial assets as a consequence of their financial surplus; deficit units must either shed financial assets (accumulated in the past) or incur financial liabilities (debts). The latter are *borrowers*. Both groups are engaged in the 'net acquisition of financial assets'. The vital difference is that for the former the net acquisition is positive while for the latter it is negative.

The interests of borrowers are mainly twofold. Firstly, they will wish to minimize *cost*. The cost to the borrower is the yield to the lender and may take any one of the number of forms we described above. Notice though that in addition to wanting to borrow at minimum cost, borrowers may also have definite preferences about other terms on which they borrow. For example, a young firm engaged in rapid expansion may prefer to borrow by issuing shares. In the early stages, earnings may be small, a high proportion will be ploughed back into the business and dividend payments will then be small. But shareholders may be willing to hold shares on these terms because they look forward to capital gains as the firm expands. The alternatives, bond issues, for example, mean that the firm commits itself to an outflow of funds right from the start. This cash drain could be critical in the early stages of expansion.

Secondly, and in contrast with lenders, borrowers will wish to maximize the period for which they borrow. This has two benefits. It reduces the risk that the lender will have to be repaid at a time which is inconvenient to the borrower, and also reduces the exposure of the borrower to the risk that the loan might have to be replaced at a time when interest rates have risen.

Table 1.1 summarizes the contrasting interests of lenders and borrowers. A (+) indicates a desire to maximize and a (–) shows a desire to minimize.

Table 1.1: The priorities of lenders and borrowers

Lenders		Borrowers	
Return	(+)	Cost	(–)
Risk	(–)	Length of loan	(+)
Liquidity	(+)		

1.2.3 Lenders, borrowers and the net acquisition of financial assets

Let us summarize. Lenders are a subset of those with a financial surplus. Surplus units are those whose income exceeds consumption and any spending on real capital assets. Their financial surplus ensures that their net acquisition of financial assets is positive. Lending results from the acquisition of financial assets which create loans for borrowers.

Borrowers are a subset of those with a financial deficit. Deficit units have income which is insufficient to meet their planned spending on consumption and real capital assets. Their financial deficit ensures that their net acquisition of financial assets is negative. This 'negative acquisition' may involve disposing of existing financial assets or it may involve acquiring liabilities. Those that take the latter course are borrowing.

We are all familiar with the rule that any asset must be someone's liability. (Even notes and coin, which are sometimes dignified with the special label 'outside money', are technically speaking liabilities of the government.) It follows, therefore, that in the aggregate, financial surpluses and deficits must cancel out. This is simplest to see if we imagine a closed economy. A closed economy is conventionally divided into three sectors: households, firms and the government sector. As a general rule, it is assumed that households run a financial surplus. As we have noted, households spend very little on real investment. By contrast, the business sector is assumed to run a deficit. If the government sector runs a balanced budget, then it follows that the size of the household surplus must match the size of the firms' deficit. If, as frequently happens, the government sector runs a deficit, then the household surplus must match the combined deficits of government and firms. The same principle must hold if we expand the model to incorporate an external sector. *In the aggregate, sector deficits and surpluses must sum to zero.*

In most economies it is possible to find values for all our relevant terms. Figures for income (Y), consumption (C), (S) and real investment (I) can be found in the *national income accounts*. The usual practice is then to transfer the difference between S and I to what are called the *financial accounts*. Capital grants and transfers (KT) are then added in order to yield the financial surplus or deficit and the main function of the financial accounts is to show how sector surpluses or deficits are financed. One of the accounts, for example, will show the household

sector's total sales and purchases of each class of financial asset or liability. The net balance of these sales and purchases matches, in theory, the size of the surplus. Inspection of any country's financial accounts reveals two striking features. The first is that a sector's net transactions in financial assets and liabilities very rarely match the size of the surplus or deficit exactly. There are usually quite large residual errors in financial accounts. The second is that the total volume of transactions (as opposed to their net balance) is much greater than that required to fund a deficit (or dispose of a surplus). The reason is obvious on reflection. People trade in financial assets not just to fund this year's deficit or to dispose of their current surplus. They are, in addition, continually rearranging their financial wealth in response to what they see as important changes in the risk and return characteristics of assets.

1.2.4   Lending, borrowing and wealth

As in all branches of economics, it is important in financial economics to distinguish between stocks and flows. While flows are very important, and it is flows that we have so far been discussing, there are times when stocks matter.

For example, a person with a current financial surplus is adding to his or her stock of financial wealth. A person with a current financial deficit must either run down his or her stock of assets or add to his or her stock of debt. A (flow) surplus leads to an increase in the stock of net financial wealth; a (flow) deficit leads to a reduction in that stock.

Notice that we talk here, as we did with the flows of lending and borrowing, of 'net' positions. People will hold simultaneous debtor and creditor positions. People with mortgages on their home will also hold building society deposits. A firm may have very substantial long-term debt as a result of recent expansion while simultaneously holding a large sum in a high-interest bank account.

This looks strange at first sight. After all, financial intermediaries make their profit by, *inter alia*, charging more to borrowers than they pay to lenders. For some people, many individuals for example, this differential or 'spread' is very large. Surely, one would think, debtors with financial assets would be better off if they disposed of the assets and used the funds to reduce their indebtedness. However, this overlooks the advantages that come from having access to 'ready money'. It ignores the advantages of liquidity. When we discussed the desires of lenders, liquidity was specified as one of the characteristics that lenders preferred in a loan. But the advantages of liquidity apply to everyone, not just to lenders. A net debtor who uses a savings deposit to pay off part of the debt sacrifices the benefit and convenience that liquidity confers – the ability to meet unforeseen demands for payment or the ability to make a purchase at an unforeseen bargain price. When it comes to calculating costs and benefits we should say that our debtor would certainly derive some benefit by using the whole of the deposit to pay off part of the loan. (The benefit would be a saving in interest payments equal to the size of the deposit multiplied by the differential between the borrowing and lending rates.) But this benefit would be accompanied by some cost – the loss of liquidity. The question for the rational debtor is whether he or she values the liquidity services flowing from his or her savings deposit at more or less than the saving in interest payments being currently foregone by holding the savings deposit. There are two important points to draw from this discussion. The first is that financial decisions typically depend upon 'spreads' or differentials between interest rates. However, we are used in economics to the idea that people make decisions on the basis of *relative* prices, so there is nothing new here. The second is that the costs and benefits of financial assets and liabilities are not fully captured by their *pecuniary* characteristics. People hold zero-interest sight deposits because the liquidity benefits outweigh the value of interest that could be had from a time deposit.

Clearly, in making decisions to acquire financial assets and liabilities, people are faced with a very complex choice. The choice is not just about whether to be a borrower or a lender but about the amount of both borrowing and lending that they should undertake. It also involves a choice about the best mix of types of asset and liability for their particular circumstances. When they are making these decisions, people are said to be exercising their *portfolio choice*. As we have seen, exercising portfolio choice involves arranging the portfolio, the mixture of assets

and liabilities, in such a way that, for a given cost, the benefit derived from each asset or liability is equal at the margin. When this is the case, there is no incentive for further rearrangements and investors are said to be in *portfolio equilibrium*. The study of the principles underlying portfolio choice is known as the study of *portfolio theory*. We shall look at these principles in the next chapter.

1.3 Financial institutions

Financial institutions come in lots of different forms and offer a variety of services. Broadly speaking, we may say that financial institutions specialize in one or more of the following functions:

- providing a payments mechanism;
- providing a means of lending and borrowing;
- providing other services, such as foreign exchange, insurance and so on.

Notice, however, that whatever their most obvious function might be, they all have the effect that the institution mediates between those who have a financial surplus and those who have a deficit. Whatever their apparent purpose, they all share the characteristic that they offer many different types of loans to borrowers and create a wide range of assets for lenders. 'Banks' which provide the payments mechanism, for example, do this by accepting deposits which they lend on to borrowers. Other institutions, for example, offer insurance cover or benefits which are paid to the saver conditional upon certain events taking place – the ending of the savings contract or retirement. The firm provides these benefits as a result of investing its clients' contributions in a variety of financial assets. We shall see in Chapter 15 that when we discuss the financial institutions which (together with markets) make up a financial system, we often divide such institutions into two groups. The first is 'banks', or what in most countries we might call 'deposit takers', and 'other' (or non-deposit-taking) financial institutions. The former are discussed in Chapter 6. Discussion of the latter is distributed through the chapters devoted to each country's financial system in Part 5 of the book.

This is partly because banks in any financial system fulfil broadly similar roles and operate in broadly similar ways, while individual countries show wider variation – reflecting their individual histories and development – in non-bank institutions. The major reason for this distinction, however, is that deposit-taking institutions have one peculiar feature which distinguishes them from other financial institutions, and economists regard the distinction as potentially important. This is that their liabilities are used as money. An expansion of bank business, therefore, almost invariably involves an increase in the money supply. We shall see in Section 1.5, and in Chapters 6 and 7, that the creation of money may have particular effects on the economy. This means that banks tend to be subject to special regulation, since a bank failure can have very damaging effects upon the payments mechanism, and also that they are continually affected by the monetary policy that governments choose to pursue. For the rest of *this* section, however, what we say about financial institutions applies equally to banks and non-deposit takers.

1.3.1   Financial institutions as firms

Financial institutions are firms and we can analyse their behaviour in much the same way that economists would analyse the behaviour of any firm. We can imagine them taking various inputs – premises, labour, technology, raw materials – and producing outputs of various kinds. They do this with much the same objectives in mind as any other firm and in the process costs and revenues behave much as they do for other firms. We look at each in turn, noting distinctive features of financial firms where appropriate.

Like most firms, financial institutions hire labour and own or rent specialist premises. In recent years, particularly in the recession of the early 1990s, there have been sharp increases in labour productivity as market pressures have forced firms to cut costs. This has been helped in large measure by technological developments, particularly in computing. Technology has also had its effects upon the 'land' element of inputs. For many years it was accepted, particularly by deposit-taking institutions, that a high street presence was essential to the attraction of customers. This led to large-scale investment in expensive

premises located in prime sites. Indeed, the cost of premises for retail financial institutions was a significant barrier to entry. The past 10 years, however, have seen the rapid growth of telephone banking and 'direct line' insurance companies providing services by telephone and computer terminal and using the cost savings on premises to offer competitive prices to customers.

Where inputs are concerned, the most distinctive feature for non-deposit institutions is the funds that savers wish to lend. These are invested with the institution in order to earn insurance or pension benefits, or to accumulate shares in managed funds of securities. The 'cost' of these inputs consists of the cost of administering the account together with the financial benefits themselves which the institution has to pay out. For deposit institutions the essential input is 'reserves'. We shall see in Chapter 6 how, provided a bank or building society has adequate reserves of notes and coin and its own deposits held usually with the central bank, it has great freedom to create loans and deposits at its own discretion. There is an organized market for these reserves (the 'interbank market' which we shall discuss in Chapter 9) and the cost is the rate of interest prevailing in that market, a rate of interest which is strongly influenced by the central bank.

As with other firms, we can distinguish between those costs that are fixed over some range of output and those that are variable. Also, quite conventionally, we can assume that the marginal cost of production is rising in the short run. Attracting more funds will normally mean offering greater inducements in the form of interest, or bonuses or other services, and so the unit cost of such funds will increase with their volume.

On the face of it, the outputs of financial institutions are 'loans' though these loans may take many different forms and may not always be easy to identify as such. In the case of banks and savings institutions the loans that they make to clients are obvious and show in their balance sheets as loans or 'advances' to customers. The loan nature of outputs from non-deposit institutions is not quite so obvious. Many of the funds received by insurance and pension companies are used to hold a diversified portfolio of securities purchased in financial markets. Where these securities are newly issued, the funds flow to the issuing firm and are, in effect, functioning as a loan. Many purchases, however, are purchases of existing securities from existing holders. In this case, financial institutions are in effect refinancing loans originally made by some other person or organization. We shall see in Section 1.4 that the existence of an active market for 'secondhand' securities, that is, for existing loans, is essential if new securities (new loans) are to be acceptable to lenders at a reasonable price.

However, to say that outputs are loans, in some form or other, is to tell less than half the story. Taken as a group, financial institutions offer a wide variety of services ranging from share dealing and share issues to tax and other forms of financial advice to the personal and corporate sectors. Indeed, in Part 5 we shall see that in some financial systems these so-called 'off balance sheet activities' have grown rapidly in recent years. Furthermore, in making funds available to borrowers, either directly or indirectly, financial institutions are making important changes to the nature of those funds. This transformation process itself may be said to be creating something and is often said to be the basis for regarding financial institutions as *financial intermediaries*. We turn to this crucially important transformation process in the next section.

Continuing our parallels with other types of firm, financial institutions derive revenue from their outputs. Most obviously, this revenue accrues from the interest that borrowers pay on the loans made by financial institutions. Where institutions are holding portfolios of securities their revenue comes from the dividend and interest payments on those securities. Where institutions offer off balance sheet services to customers, they charge fees. Like other firms, financial institutions will maximize profits when the difference between total revenue and total cost is at its greatest, that is, at the point where marginal cost equals marginal revenue.

This is not to say that financial institutions are necessarily profit *maximizers*. It is a characteristic of financial activity that it is subject to economies of scale for reasons we shall see in Section 1.3.2. Thus most financial systems tend to be dominated by large institutions. It is clear from their publicity, as well as their behaviour, that other objectives, such as size, growth and market share, are important to them.

1.3.2 Financial institutions as 'intermediaries'

Right at the beginning of this chapter we saw that, whatever specialist services an institution might provide, a major part of any financial institution's activity was to make loans to ultimate borrowers out of the funds which ultimate lenders made available to them. In doing this, we said that they were involved in a process known as 'intermediation' and that intermediation had important characteristics and consequences. What are these?

Rather obviously 'intermediation' means acting as a go-between between two parties. The parties will often be the ultimate lenders and borrowers but sometimes they will be other intermediaries. What are the characteristics of intermediation? The first thing to say is that intermediation involves a good deal more than simply introducing or bringing together two parties. One *could* imagine a firm offering a service whereby it maintained a register of potential lenders and potential borrowers and tried to match them up. This would work rather like a computer dating agency and rather like such agencies our firm would charge a commission for successful introduction. But this is not intermediation. If such activity has a name it is best described as broking. The process of intermediation requires that something be created by the transformation of inputs into outputs. At its simplest we might say that what intermediaries do is:

> to create assets for lenders and liabilities for borrowers which are more attractive to each than would be the case if the parties had to deal with each other directly.

Essentially what this means is that intermediaries transform funds which are made available to them normally for short periods into loans which are made available to ultimate borrowers for longer terms. This is sometimes summed up by saying that intermediaries 'borrow short and lend long'. What is being created in this process is liquidity and we can see this most clearly if we contrast the situation of direct lending with lending via an intermediary.

Take the case of someone wishing to borrow £30,000 to buy a house, intending to repay the loan, say, over 25 years. Without the help of an intermediary our borrower has to find someone willing to lend £30,000 for this same period and at a rate of interest which is mutually agreeable. The borrower might just possibly be successful. In that case the lender has an asset (the interest-bearing loan) and the borrower has a liability (the obligation to pay interest and eventually the obligation to repay the principal). In practice, however, even if the would-be borrower employed a broker, it seems unlikely that the search would be successful. Not many people wish to lend £30,000 to a comparative stranger and for a long period of time. Even if a potential lender could be found, the scale of risk involved (in lending to an unknown individual) and the illiquidity of the loan (the funds cannot be recovered at the lender's discretion for 25 years) would mean that the rate of interest demanded would be so high that the borrower would decline the offer.

Suppose now that some sort of savings institution were to emerge, and that it specializes in taking large numbers of small deposits, which it pools and lends as fewer larger loans and for long periods. It pays interest on the deposits and charges a higher rate of interest on the loans. Ultimate lenders and ultimate borrowers both benefit and indeed benefit by so much that they are prepared to lend and to borrow on such terms that allow the intermediary to make a profit. What are the benefits?

Firstly, provided that the institution keeps some proportion of the funds it receives in liquid form, and provided that depositors do not all wish to withdraw deposits at once, depositors can have instant access to their funds even though the vast majority of funds have been lent for a long period. The corresponding advantage to the borrower is the availability of long-term loans, even though, perhaps, no one wishes to lend for a long period. This is a process known as *maturity transformation*.

Secondly, a benefit for lenders is that the institution can *pool* lots of small deposits which taken in isolation would be unattractive to borrowers. These deposits can then earn a rate of interest from being lent which would not have been possible before. The corresponding benefit to borrowers is that they can borrow large sums even though lenders may not wish to lend large sums. Furthermore, by operating on a large scale, the savings institution can *reduce risk* for both parties. Partly it does this by employing staff,

paid out of the interest-spread between borrowing and lending rates, to assess the risk attaching to the loans it makes. Although each individual case is assessed on its merits, there are many similarities between cases, so the staff become specialists and highly competent by virtue of experience. Institutions also reduce risk by virtue of their ability to *diversify*. They can diversify by lending to a wide variety of people and organizations in such a way that an adverse event is likely to affect only a small proportion of loans. They can also diversify their sources of funds, so that a difficulty in raising funds from one source can be offset from elsewhere. Diversification is one of the characteristics of financial intermediaries that tends to benefit from economies of scale.

Lastly the institution reduces *search and trans-action costs* for both parties. Lenders know where the institution is. They make their deposits and walk away. Borrowers likewise know where the institution is. They telephone, write, or call in. Furthermore, although each transaction is in some sense unique, each can be fitted into a broad category – housing mortgage, personal loan, business overdraft, etc. This means that the terms on which funds are accepted and lent can be standardized. There is a set of rules for each type of deposit or other contribution and a set of rules for each type of loan. Lenders and borrowers accept these terms (or go elsewhere). This avoids the individual negotiation and drawing up of contracts, with attendant lawyers' fees and so on, that would be necessary if lenders and borrowers were to deal directly.

Clearly, this is quite a list of potential advantages. But it serves to emphasize what we said above, namely that *intermediaries create something*, they do not just pass (unmodified) funds between two parties. If we persist with the idea that something is created, the best general term to use is *liquidity*. This does not quite capture all of the advantages but from an economic point of view it captures everything that matters. What intermediaries are doing is making funds available (to lenders and borrowers) cheaply, readily and with a minimum of risk. We look now at why this matters and then, in the rest of this section, we look at some of the principles which underlie the behaviour of intermediaries and which allow them to create liquidity in this way. This is a complicated

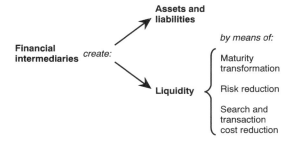

Figure 1.3 The intermediation process

Box 1.2 The creation of assets and liabilities

(a) Direct lending

Lender		Borrower	
Liability	Asset	Liability	Asset
	30,000		30,000
Total	30,000		30,000

(b) via an intermediary

Lender(s)		Intermediary		Borrower	
Liability	Asset	Liability	Asset	Liability	Asset
	5,000	30,000	30,000	30,000	
	6,000				
	10,000				
	9,000				
Total	30,000 (A)	30,000 (B)	30,000 (C)	30,000 (D)	

Total assets (= A + C) = 60,000
Total liabilities (= B + D) = 60,000

story and it may be helpful to sketch it first with the help of Figure 1.3.

We shall explore firstly the general consequences of financial intermediation. The first of these is the creation of financial assets and liabilities that would not otherwise exist. The second is the creation of liquidity. We shall indicate that the latter is probably more important from an economic point of view. It is also a complex process. We shall suggest that the creation of liquidity relies in turn on four processes: *maturity transformation*, *risk reduction*, the *reduction of search and transaction costs* and *monitoring*. Furthermore, we shall suggest that all four depend to a significant extent upon *economies of scale*.

The first consequence of financial intermediation is that in the presence of financial intermediaries there will be more financial assets and liabilities than there would be without. The growth of financial activity relative to other forms of economic activity therefore implies that financial assets are growing relative to real assets. Box 1.2 provides a simple illustration of this point.

In the direct lending case, our lender lends £30,000 to a borrower. As a result of the transaction, there is a financial asset of £30,000 (the loan seen from the lender's point of view) and a financial liability of £30,000 (the debt seen from the borrower's point of view). Strictly speaking, there has been no *creation* of anything. Prior to the loan the lender had a financial asset of £30,000, presumably in money form, so as far as the lender is concerned there is only a change in the composition of financial assets. Equally, there is no change in the total of borrowers' liabilities. Our borrower has incurred the liability of £30,000 in order presumably to buy a real asset, a

house perhaps. This asset has been transferred from a previous owner and the funds have been used to pay off the previous owner's debts.

Suppose now, that funds from several lenders equal to £30,000 are placed with an intermediary which then lends them out: additional assets and liabilities have been created. The (ultimate) lenders still have assets of £30,000 and the (ultimate) borrower has the liability of £30,000. To that extent, things are as they were in the direct lending case (except that we have multiple lenders). But in between the end users, the intermediary has also an asset (the loan) of £30,000 and liabilities (the deposits) of £30,000. Total financial assets and liabilities are now £60,000.

Whether the mere creation of additional financial assets and liabilities matters to the rest of the economy depends upon whether people's spending behaviour is affected by the total quantity of assets and liabilities. Remember that for every extra asset created there is an extra liability. There is no increase in *net* wealth. There is no straightforward answer to this question and we shall return to it again briefly in Section 1.5. What is much more likely to matter is the creation of liquidity which has accompanied this creation of assets and liabilities. Consider the position of the lenders to the intermediary. They have interest-earning assets which they can recover at short notice. Many economists take the view that people spend more (as a proportion of their income) when they know they have liquid assets they could draw on in an emergency. Certainly, our lenders in the second case seem to be in a more enviable financial position than the lender in the first, who could be in serious trouble if expenditure happened to exceed income. Furthermore, our lenders may also benefit from intermediation by having interest-earning assets which they would not have had at all otherwise, if for example there were no market for small loans. In the latter case, there would be less lending and borrowing in total. Perhaps the borrower in our example would have been unable to find funds. His real expenditure would not then have taken place, with possible repercussions on the rest of the economy.

We turn now to the second consequence of intermediation and to the question of how intermediaries are able to create liquidity, to 'borrow short and lend long'. A liquid asset is one that can be turned into money quickly, cheaply and for a known monetary value. Thus the achievement of a financial intermediary must be that lenders can recall their loan either (or both) more quickly or with a greater certainty of its capital value than would otherwise be the case. Notice that liquidity has three dimensions: 'time' – the speed with which an asset can be exchanged for money; 'risk' – the possibility that the asset may be realizable for value different from that which is expected; and 'cost' – the pecuniary and other sacrifices that have to be made in carrying out the exchange. At the same time, an intermediary has to offer liabilities to borrowers which are more attractive than direct lending and this almost always means offering loans which are larger and for longer periods than would otherwise be the case. On the face of it, borrowers' and lenders' wants conflict (as we saw in Section 1.2.1). How can they be reconciled and a profit drawn from their reconciliation?

In Figure 1.3, we have suggested that the reconciliation involves four processes: maturity transformation, risk reduction, search and transaction costs and monitoring. We look now at each of these in turn. We shall see that the processes overlap somewhat; nonetheless thinking in terms of four processes is still helpful.

Maturity transformation. Maturity transformation means that intermediaries accept funds of a given maturity, that is, funds which are liable for repayment to lenders at a given date or with a given degree of notice, and 'transform' them into loans of a longer maturity. Any deposit-taking institution will provide a dramatic illustration of this process. This is because they accept deposits of a very short maturity, some indeed repayable 'at sight' or on demand, and yet they simultaneously make loans which need not be repaid for several years. In the UK, building societies transform deposits into loans for periods up to 25 years.

The funds accepted by institutions appear as liabilities in their balance sheets while the loans into which they are transformed appear, with other items, on the asset side. Table 1.2 shows the consolidated balance sheet of the 'Big 3' German banks. Notice that liabilities are dominated by deposits, the bulk of which are repayable at notice of less than three months, while assets consist overwhelmingly of loans and advances, most of which will be for periods much longer than three months. These cannot be recalled without breaking the contract with borrowers. In practice, it may also be very difficult to demand repayment even of very short-term loans and overdrafts. Where these have been made to firms, a demand for repayment or a refusal to renew may simply lead to bankruptcy, in which the bank will have to compete with other creditors for repayment from any remaining assets. Notice, however, that while the majority of assets are therefore relatively illiquid, some remaining assets are very liquid. Banks can draw on their deposits at the central bank without notice and can sell bills and other securities for cash quite quickly. We shall see in a moment that retaining a small pool of highly liquid assets is part of the key to maturity transformation.

The ability of financial institutions to engage in maturity transformation depends fundamentally upon *size*. The advantages of scale come in two major forms. Firstly, with large numbers of depositors or other types of lender, intermediaries will have a steady inflow and outflow of funds each day. There will be fluctuations. On some days there will be net inflows and on some days net outflows. The larger the numbers the more stable these net

Table 1.2 German 'Big Banks'[1] balance sheet

Assets DM bn		%	Liabilities DM bn		%
Cash in hand and balances with central bank	9.6	1.4	Deposits of other credit institutions		
			– Sight	68.1	9.7
Lending to other credit institutions			– Time	154.9	22.1
– Advances	153.7	21.9			
– Securities	27.1	3.9	Deposits of non-banks		
			– Sight	97.3	13.9
Lending to non-banks			– Time (< 3 months)	67.5	9.6
– Loans and advances	374.5	53.3	– Time (> 3months)	58.1	8.3
– Bills discounted	14.4	2.0	– Savings deposits	88.9	12.7
– Securities	66.9	9.5			
Other assets	56.2	8.0	Bank savings bonds	9.6	13.7
			Capital	50.1	7.1
			Other liabilities	107.9	15.4
Total	702.4	100.0	Total	702.4	100.0

Note: [1] Commerzbank AG, Deutsche Bank AG, Dresdner Bank AG
Source: Deutsche Bundesbank, Monthly Report, March 1996 p.20*

flows will be. There will be variations in the flows in response to external shocks. There may be seasonal variations. There will certainly be variations too in response to other firms' behaviour. If competitors raise interest rates, net inflows will decline. But all these variations become more predictable as the number of lenders increases. The significance of this is that it is only *net* outflows against which intermediaries need to hold liquid assets as reserves. The reason that banks can hold so little cash in relation to all their other assets is that even at their maximum, net outflows on any particular day are extremely small in relation to the total stock of assets and, crucially, banks *know this with virtual certainty*.

Secondly, large size implies a large number of borrowers or a large quantity of funds which can be spread across a wide variety of assets. The larger the volume of assets, be they loans, securities or anything else, the greater the scope for arranging them in such a way that a small fraction is always on the point of maturing. This guarantees a steady stream of liquid assets. At best, assets can be arranged so that they mature so as to coincide with anticipated days of major net outflows. In the limiting case, a perfect match would mean that firms need hold no liquid assets.

Risk transformation. Financial intermediaries are able to reduce risk through a number of devices. The two principal ones are diversification and specialist management. The scale of operations is also relevant here. As a general rule, the opportunities for risk reduction increase with size.

It seems intuitively obvious that holding just one asset is more likely to produce unexpected outcomes than holding a collection or 'portfolio' of assets. This is the basis on which small savers are recommended to contribute to a managed fund, or to buy unit trusts. The managers of the funds can collect contributions from a large number of small savers and then distribute a comparatively large sum amongst many more assets than an individual saver could possibly afford to do, bearing in mind transaction costs. Precisely the same process is at work in a deposit-taking institution. The intermediary accepts a large number of small deposits, creates a large pool and then distributes that pool between a number of borrowers who, the intermediary can ensure, are borrowing to fund different, that is, diverse, types of activity. (The pool also enables the intermediary to adjust the size of loan to the needs of borrowers which will usually be much larger than the size of the average deposit.) Clearly, the larger the size of the institution the larger its pool of funds. Since the cost of setting up a loan, or buying securities, is more or less constant regardless of size, large loans and large security purchases have lower unit transaction costs than small ones. A large institution has the advantage therefore that it can diversify widely and cheaply even though it deals in large investments.

Precisely how and why diversification leads to a reduction in risk is a complex, technical question. For the moment, we can probably agree that the reason that common sense encourages us to diversify has something to do with the fact that assets do not all behave in the same way at the same time and that, therefore, if we hold enough different assets there will be occasions when the behaviour of some tends to offset the behaviour of others. The key certainly does lie in the fact that there is less than perfect correlation between movements in asset returns. What is harder to understand is that by combining assets in a portfolio, one can actually reduce the risk of the portfolio below the average of the individual risk of the assets contained within it. It is this that we look at in detail in Section 2.2, but Box 1.3 gives an extreme illustration of how 'diversifying' from just one to two assets reduces portfolio risk below the average for the two individual assets.

In addition to being able to reduce investors' risk by diversification, intermediaries also offer the risk reducing benefit of specialist expertise. It is extremely difficult and costly for individuals to research the status of would-be borrowers and their schemes. There are newspapers and magazines which claim to offer useful information about companies and their plans and sometimes they go so far as to offer 'tips' to would-be investors, but the quality of this information is much less than that which can be obtained by intermediaries recruiting and training 'analysts' who specialize in assessing the risk and likely performance of particular groups of potential borrowers. And here again, scale is important. As more information and experience is acquired it becomes easier to spot the essential characteristics of borrowers and their projects which make them into low, medium or high risks with high, medium or low potential returns.

Search and transaction costs. At one extreme, one can imagine the costs, pecuniary and otherwise, of direct lending where an individual lender has to search for, contact and arrange for an individually negotiated, legally binding contract to be drawn up.

Box 1.3 The gains from diversification

Imagine an investor faced with the opportunity to invest in either or both of two shares, *A* and *B*, the returns on which behave independently. Suppose that both are expected to yield a return of 20 per cent in 'good' times and 10 per cent in 'bad' times. Assume, furthermore, that there is a 50 per cent probability of each share striking good and bad conditions. Then it follows that investing wholly in *A* or wholly in *B* produces the expected return:

$$\hat{K} = 0.5\ (20\%) + 0.5\ (10\%) = 15\%$$

Notice that although the expected return averaged over a period of time will be 15 per cent per year, in any one year there will a 50 per cent chance of getting a high return and a 50 per cent chance of getting a low return. There is absolutely no chance whatsoever of getting the expected return! Risk, in the sense in which we have been using it, is infinite. Remember that this conclusion applies whether we hold *A* or *B*.

Now consider the possible outcomes if one half of the investor's funds are allocated to each of *A* and *B*. Since good and bad conditions can arise *independently* for each of *A* and *B*, it follows that four outcomes are possible, each of course with an equal probability of 25 per cent. The outcomes and the associated returns are:

Outcome	*A*	*B*	Return
1	Good	Good	20%
2	Good	Bad	15%
3	Bad	Good	15%
4	Bad	Bad	10%

Over the years the expected return will be:

$$\hat{K} = 0.25(20\%) + 0.25(15\%) + 0.25(15\%) + 0.25(10\%) = 15\%$$

The expected return is still 15 per cent, but in any one year receiving the expected return is now the most likely outcome!

More realistically, one can also imagine the costs faced by small savers trying to diversify their wealth across a range of securities. On each of these a minimum commission has to be paid and, being fixed, this therefore rises as a proportion of the value of the transaction as the transaction gets smaller. Looking at it another way, savers with small funds have to earn a bigger gross return to offset their higher transaction costs. A saver with less than £50,000 to invest and looking for diversification across a minimum of, say, 15 securities is likely to find the charges made by unit trusts and managed funds (typically 5 per cent of the initial investment and 1 per cent annual management charge) attractive. The lower costs available through an intermediary result, of course, from the ability to pool funds and to trade in large blocks of securities where the dealing commission is very small as a proportion of the value.

The same process is at work with deposit-taking institutions. One standard contract covers each class of deposit and each type of loan. The intermediaries' search costs are incorporated in the cost of prime site premises and in their advertising. The consequence of such spending is that lenders and borrowers know what services are available and where. Although prime sites and advertising are very expensive, once again the scale of operations almost certainly means that these search costs, absorbed by intermediaries, are less than the search costs that would be incurred by lenders and borrowers if they had to deal with each other directly.

We said at the beginning of this section that financial intermediaries clearly offered some benefit to borrowers and lenders since the latter were prepared to deal via the intermediary on terms which allowed the intermediary to make a profit (from a mixture of fees and the 'spread' between rates charged to borrowers and paid to lenders). Having seen what it is that intermediaries do (and how they do it) we are now in a position to see formally how benefits arise and why they are worth paying for.

We denote a lender by L and a borrower by B and we suppose that they have agreed to lend/borrow at a rate of interest, i, *in the absence of an intermediary*. Without an intermediary, however, both will be involved in search and transaction costs and these will eat into the return that the lender gets and will add to the costs for the borrower. If we denote the costs to the lender and borrower respectively as C_L and C_B and imagine that they are expressed as a percentage of the agreed loan then the *net* return to the lender, i_L, will be:

$$i - C_L = i_L \qquad (1.2)$$

and the *gross* cost to the borrower, i_B will be:

$$i + C_B = i_B \qquad (1.3)$$

Consequently, the difference between the actual cost to the borrower and the actual return to the lender, that is, having regard to their respective costs, is $(i_B - i_L)$ and is the sum of their combined search and transaction costs:

$$C_B + C_L \qquad (1.4)$$

Our argument in the last few paragraphs of course has been that financial intermediaries can reduce search and transaction costs. Let us then suppose that by dealing via an intermediary the costs for our borrower and lender would have been C_B' and C_L' respectively, where:

$$C_B' < C_B \text{ and } C_L' < C_L \qquad (1.5)$$

However, in order to supply the services that enable these cost reductions to take place, the intermediary makes a charge, ψ. This is assumed again to be expressed as a percentage of the loan. Indeed, it could take the form of charging a higher explicit interest rate to the borrower and paying a lower explicit rate to the lender. Clearly, in these circumstances there is an opportunity for profitable intermediation to be beneficial to both borrowers and lenders provided that:

$$(\psi + C_B' + C_L') < C_B + C_L \qquad (1.6)$$

Notice that the possibilities for profitable intermediation in (1.6) hinge solely upon intermediaries being able to reduce costs for lenders and borrowers cheaply. That is to say that the reduction in costs must be greater than the charge made by the intermediary:

$$(C_B + C_L) - (C_B' + C_L') > \psi \qquad (1.7)$$

We can see from our discussion above that this is a condition that should be widely met. We have tried throughout this section to argue that the costs faced by lenders and borrowers dealing directly are very considerable and that the savings available via intermediaries are substantial.

This illustration shows nothing of the other advantages of intermediation, those that arise from maturity transformation and risk reduction, for example. To incorporate these, we have to return to the agreed rate of interest, i. This, it will be recalled, was agreed between borrowers and lenders in the absence of an intermediary which was later introduced in order to reduce transaction and search costs, *ceteris paribus*. In practice, of course, we would expect the presence of intermediaries not just to reduce these costs but also to make lending and borrowing much more attractive in many respects. We could accommodate this in our illustration by allowing the agreed rate of interest, i, in (1.2) and (1.3) to tumble at the same time that costs were being reduced, in (1.5). This would not alter our illustration of profitable intermediation. It would simply mean that the agreed rate of interest assumed for the illustration would be much lower once intermediaries were introduced. The benefits from the cost-reducing aspects of intermediation would still depend upon the condition in (1.7), whatever the level of interest rates.

Monitoring. It is generally recognized that financial decisions between two parties are often characterized by asymmetric information. In particular, borrowers are likely to be much better informed about the uses to which they propose to put the funds than lenders can be. This asymmetry is another of the many disincentives to direct lending: the ultimate borrower knows how he is going to use the funds and can form a reasonable judgment of the likelihood of success and the likely rate of return on the project. The borrower may choose to share that information honestly and openly with the ultimate lender or may prefer to conceal it. But there is very little that the ultimate lender can do to check the accuracy of the information.

This asymmetry can often be alleviated by financial markets. As we shall see in Chapters 10 and 11, access to bond and equity markets usually requires that borrowers make specified information publicly available on a regular basis and there are severe penalties for firms that fail to do so or who produce information that seeks to mislead. Given that this information is available from all borrowers to all market participants, 'the market' can use its experience to develop its own 'rating' system, classifying certain types of firms and certain types of projects as more risky than others and pricing the loans accordingly.

However, market solutions to the asymmetry are not always available. Firstly, access to securities markets is expensive. The very requirements that make the information available impose costs on firms and small firms in particular will not feel it worthwhile to meet the administrative costs of a stock exchange listing. Furthermore, the issue costs associated with raising new funds by selling new shares, for example, are considerable and contain a large fixed cost element. Again, small to medium size firms will not find new security issues cost-efficient for the size of loan they require. Secondly, for persons and unincorporated businesses, markets are simply not appropriate.

The alternative solution is for intermediaries to take on the monitoring task. This involves the development of skills in discriminating between more and less risky projects and firms. One way in which this is done, of course, is to demand information as a condition of the loan; another is to develop a long-term association with successful clients so as to gain access to 'inside' information; yet another is to monitor carefully the *ex post* outcome of projects in which they have invested depositors' funds. These activities have a high fixed set-up cost but are subject to economies of scale with the result that while individuals are excluded from doing their own monitoring, the cost to each depositor when the service is provided by the bank is quite small.

Notwithstanding the various monitoring mechanisms available to banks, some degree of asymmetry is likely to remain. Banks can and do find themselves exposed to bad risk loans. The imperfect nature of the monitoring process gives rise to the conventional bank-type loan where the borrower is required to provide collateral for the loan and where the terms of the loan sometimes give the bank the power to make the borrower bankrupt.

1.4 Financial markets

In economics a market is any organizational device which brings together buyers and sellers. It does not need to be a physical location – though many towns and cities have 'market squares' and many of those host periodic markets. Some financial markets exist in specific locations. For example, trading on London's International Financial Futures Exchange (LIFFE) takes place using a system known as 'open outcry' where dealers are located in specific 'pits'. Trading takes place only during specified hours. By contrast, markets for foreign exchange by necessity 'bring together' buyers and sellers located in countries all over the world. The latest communication technology now permits financial institutions in the United States to deal in shares in Tokyo as readily as they can in New York. Until 1986, share dealing in the UK was concentrated on the trading floor of the London Stock Exchange. With the introduction of new technology, however, dealers quickly dispersed to their companies' offices.

1.4.1 Types of product

What is it that is traded in financial markets? The answer clearly is some sort of financial asset or liability. But briefer terms like 'financial instruments' or 'financial claims' are sometimes used.

Financial instruments come in a bewildering range of types. Table 1.3 lists just a small sample of instruments traded in financial markets. This is a very small sample from the range of financial instruments for which markets exist. Nonetheless, it is sufficient for us to discuss and illustrate different systems of market classification and thus to draw attention to similarities and differences between the markets for certain types of instrument.

First of all, one can distinguish between those markets for instruments tha can be traded directly between holders and potential holders and those that cannot. Markets for equities, bills and bonds are obvious examples of the former. However, we still talk of markets for pensions or life assurance and even, for that matter, of markets for bank deposits. Such instruments cannot be traded directly between third parties. Holders of unwanted pension or life

assurance benefits can dispose of them only by 'selling them back' to the issuers in exchange for money. The same is the case with bank or savings deposits. Nonetheless, for all these products there is a demand and there is a supply, and the terms on which the demand is satisfied will reflect supply and demand conditions.

Table 1.3 A sample of financial instruments

Bank deposits	Bond futures
Certificates of deposit	Currency futures
Treasury bills	Bond options
Central government bonds	Currency options
Local government bonds	Life assurance
Eurocurrencies	Pensions
Equities	Currency swaps

Alternatively one can distinguish markets for instruments that pay a fixed rate of interest from those for instruments where the rate of interest (or the rate of return) is variable. Government bonds probably provide the largest class of fixed interest assets. Most local government bonds and treasury bills are also fixed rate instruments. In France, Italy, Spain and Germany many housing mortgages carry a fixed rate of interest. In the UK, by contrast, most carry a variable rate. As a general rule, bank deposits pay variable interest (though occasionally time deposits pay a fixed rate), while equities, or company shares, pay dividends which are highly variable.

Another popular basis for distinguishing between markets is the *residual maturity* of the instruments traded in them. Some instruments – treasury and commercial bills, interbank loans, certificates of deposit – have a very short maturity when initially issued, generally less than three months, and thus have on average a much shorter residual maturity. Markets for these instruments are often called 'money markets' – markets for short-term money. This contrasts with 'capital markets' – markets for long-term capital. These include the market for company shares – instruments with a theoretically infinite life. They also include the market for government and corporate bonds which are commonly issued with initial maturities of 10–25 years, and the market for mortgages.

Finally, a distinction is often made between 'primary' and 'secondary' markets. This does not lead to a distinction based on the trading of different instruments but rather upon subsets of a given instrument. A primary market is a market for a newly issued instrument. (In a primary market an instrument can only be traded once.) The primary market for company shares, for example, consists of firms issuing new shares, the underwriters of the issue and those members of the general public willing to buy new issues. Notice that it is only in the primary market that firms actually raise (borrow) new funds. The corresponding secondary market is the market for existing instruments, in this example, for company shares that were first issued sometime in the past. No new funds are being raised. This does not, however, make secondary markets unimportant. Firstly, the existence of an active secondary market makes new issues more liquid than they would otherwise be. The fact that they can be easily sold on makes them more attractive to buyers and thus new issues can be sold at a higher price (and capital raised at lower cost) than would otherwise be the case. Secondly, new issues have to offer a combination of risk and return comparable with that available on issues being traded in the secondary market. The secondary market, in other words, is determining the cost of new capital. Thirdly, since the trading in secondary markets amounts to trading in claims on existing *real* assets, the secondary market provides a mechanism whereby the ownership and control of organizations can change hands. Many would argue that this is essential if 'good' management is to replace 'bad'.

As financial innovation proceeds, so new instruments emerge, and with them new markets. As a general rule, new instruments tend to fill the gaps between existing ones, often offering a combination of attractions currently available only in different instruments. This process is said to be taking us towards a 'complete' set of markets, a situation which economists tend to regard as desirable since it means that the facilities exist to satisfy the needs of every borrower and lender. As this happens, so it becomes more difficult to draw demarcations between markets, a problem of which regulators are only too well aware.

The behaviour of financial markets, like the behaviour of other markets, can be analysed using the apparatus of conventional economics. We demonstrate this in Chapter 5, at a general level, and in Part 4 of the book we look at a variety of markets in detail.

1.5 The financial system and the real economy

We have just seen that the function of a financial system is broadly to facilitate lending and borrowing. This enables people to arrange their expenditure over time in a way which is to some degree independent of their income. Lenders can store wealth for later consumption; borrowers can buy in advance of their income. As well as displacing expenditure through time, this is also displacing the use of resources between people. Lenders temporarily surrender a claim to goods and services while borrowers get the use of those goods and services. When we talk about 'the real economy', therefore, we mean that part of the economy which produces the real goods and services to which claims are being made as opposed to the financial part of the economy whose job is to enable the claims to be transferred on attractive terms. Clearly, the efficiency with which the real economy functions is of paramount importance since it ultimately determines the real standard of living. Countries which feel that their real economy is failing to perform as it should (and in rich economies this is usually judged by comparing the rate of growth of output with that of other rich economies) sometimes look to the financial system as one of the possible causes: is it too large, too small, inefficient, 'short-termist'? In this section, we consider three broad headings under which one can generalize about the relationship between financial activity and the real economy. These are: the level of aggregate demand, the composition of aggregate demand, and the allocation of resources.

1.5.1 The composition of aggregate demand

We are familiar now with the idea that one major function of a financial system is to make it easier for agents to borrow and to lend. In Section 1.3.2 we placed great emphasis on the possibility that without the help of intermediaries lenders and borrowers would be unable to negotiate acceptable terms, or at least that the rate of interest would be so high that there would be very little lending and borrowing. If we try now to formalize this a little we can say that one consequence of financial intermediation is that, *at any given rate of interest*, lenders will be more willing to lend and borrowers will be more willing to borrow than they would otherwise be. Much the same can be said about financial markets. Efficient markets with low transaction costs make it easy for holders of securities to buy and sell. Securities become more attractive to lenders than they would be if they had to buy and hold the security until it matured. Consequently firms, and others, can borrow more cheaply by issuing securities at lower rates of interest than would otherwise need to be the case. Figure 1.4a illustrates the effect using a familiar diagram. On the vertical axis, we have the rate of interest, i, and on the horizontal axis, the *flow* of funds lent and borrowed. The figure shows the supply of funds under conditions of a developed financial system, S, and the demand for them, again in a system which offers a range of choice of favourable conditions to borrowers. The flow of funds is shown by F^* at a rate of interest i^*. If lenders were not able to lend with security and for short periods, and if borrowers could only find one or two lenders after intensive and costly searching, the supply of funds would be much less, shown by S', and the demand for them also much less, shown by D'. In these circumstances the flow of lending and borrowing would be much less at F', and much more costly, at i'.

Figure 1.4b shows the effect upon real investment expenditure. Firms are assumed to undertake all those investment projects which yield an expected rate of return at least equal to the cost of funds (here, the rate of interest in Figure 1.4a). Marginal projects are assumed to have diminishing expected yields. Thus, for a given state of expectations regarding the rates of return on investment projects we say the flow of real investment spending is expected to be negatively related to the cost of funds and we can draw an explicit relationship, I in Figure 1.4b. Combining two diagrams, we can see that in the more favourable lending–borrowing conditions the cost of funds will be i^* and the flow of investment will be I^*. Without the advantages of a developed financial system, the cost of funds would have been i' and investment spending would be I' only.

In conclusion, then, we may say that the existence of a developed financial system offering a full range of instruments to match the needs of borrowers and lenders is likely to facilitate higher levels of investment, relative to consumption, spending than would otherwise occur. Indeed, in recent years it has become fashionable to argue that the *under*development of the financial system (the result of 'financial repression') in many poorer economies has led to their poor growth performance.

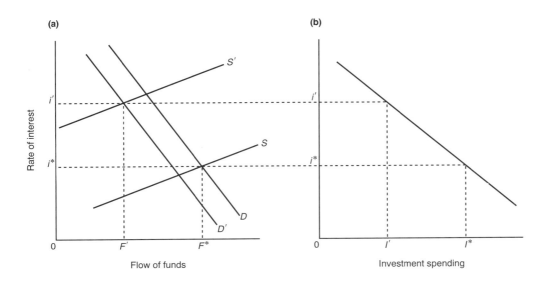

Figure 1.4 Financial intermediation encourages saving and investment.

1.5.2   The level of aggregate demand

In addition to affecting the *composition* of aggregate demand, there is the possibility that financial development may affect the *level* of aggregate demand and thus either the level of output, or the level of prices, or both. There are two channels through which such a connection may come about and both can be explored using the 'equation of exchange':

$$MV = PT \qquad (1.8)$$

where M stands for the stock of money, P for the average level of prices and T for the total volume of transactions in the economy. V is then a magnitude (usually referred to as 'velocity') which expresses the fact that the total *value* of expenditure, $P \times T$, is usually some multiple of the total quantity of money in existence. This, in turn, is possible because the *stock* of money circulates. The same Pound, peseta or Deutschmark can be used to make several purchases in the course of a year.

A common variation on Equation 1.8 is to replace T with Y, standing for the total volume of output of goods and services, or real GDP. PY then becomes spending on nominal income, or simply nominal GDP, rather than *total* spending which would include spending on secondhand assets, intermediate goods, and so on.

Suppose now that we put some restrictions on V. Suppose we say that it is likely to change only slowly and predictably[3]. Clearly if, for example, we took an extreme position and assumed V to be *constant*, then any change in M must be reflected by a change in PY, that is, in either the general price or the volume of goods and services produced. We shall ignore the complications of the split between the effect on P and Y for the time being. We can assume that it depends on how close the economy is to full employment.

For our purposes, what is important is that we have a connection between M and aggregate demand. In developed economies, money consists overwhelmingly of bank deposits, that is to say that it consists of the liabilities of banks. Clearly, therefore, any development in the financial system which causes an expansion of banks' balance sheets simultaneously increases the money stock and, *on the assumption that velocity is stable* (it does not have to be fixed), then we should expect an increase in aggregate demand, with whatever consequence may follow from that. This is the first, and perhaps the more obvious, of the two routes through which financial activity may affect the level of demand.

The second channel requires us to focus upon V. This we said is the ratio of PY to M ($V = PY/M$). What it is telling us is how much expenditure is being carried out, measured usually over a year, with a given level of money stock. If we think of this at the personal level, it reflects the total amount of spending that a household does over a year as a multiple of its average holding of money over the year. We said above that this obviously depends, *inter alia*, on how often the household receives its income. (If the chief income earner is paid monthly, a larger average money balance would be held than if s/he were paid weekly.) Conditions like this obviously change very slowly and, as we said above, the assumption has often been made that velocity changes very slowly and infrequently. But think again about our hypothetical family. In deciding on the average money balance to hold, the family obviously has to bear in mind their total expenditure, the timing of that expenditure and any possible variability in the timing of that spending. That is, part of their decision must involve a 'precautionary' motive. Consider now the decision they will make if money is the only liquid asset available to them. They have to hold sufficient money at all times not just to meet *planned* expenditure but also any *unplanned* spending in a given period. Contrast this with a situation where many liquid assets exist, assets which are not themselves money (are not acceptable in exchange) but which can be turned quickly and cheaply into money. In these circumstances, a shortage of money caused by the need for unplanned spending is much less serious. Money can be obtained quickly. If these 'near money' assets are attractive in themselves – for example, they may pay a better rate of interest – then

---

3 The traditional argument was that what determined the speed at which money could circulate was determined by 'institutional factors' – the intervals at which people were paid, the ease of switching between money and other assets – and that these changed very slowly.

our household will obviously be tempted to hold lower money balances, taking the risk that it may have occasionally to exchange some savings certificates for money. In these circumstances, then, it is prepared to hold less money in relation to spending. Let us now translate this into the aggregate ('less money is needed in order to finance the current level of aggregate demand') and then reverse it. We can now say that the existing money stock can finance a higher level of aggregate demand. *PY* can increase relative to *M* and velocity has increased.

Notice that the second channel does not concentrate upon banks. Any development in financial markets, intermediaries or products which creates attractive substitutes for money as a liquid store of wealth will enable people to economize on holdings of money, allow money to 'work harder' and cause velocity to rise. This is the version of the second channel of influence that most economists would recognize. It is just another way of stating the argument that we met earlier in connection with the consequences of intermediation. Intermediaries create liquidity and people's spending decisions will be influenced by their access to liquidity as well as by having money itself. This is a point of view which was famously advanced in the UK by the Radcliffe Committee in 1959 and would still be adopted by economists of a 'Keynesian' persuasion.

1.5.3 The financial system and resource allocation

In a perfect world, the funds that savers are prepared to make available should flow to their socially most beneficial use, and should do so in the cheapest and most efficient way. In principle, one could imagine a system that achieved this. Whether we were dealing with lending via markets or via intermediaries, savers' funds would need to flow to projects offering the highest returns for a given level of risk. The markets and intermediaries themselves would be subject to perfect competition and operating at minimum average cost. We should then need to be sure that the rate of return on the real capital employed represented society's valuation of the benefits flowing from its use. There must be no externalities, for example, and no monopoly returns.

For a given level of risk, there would be a uniform rate of return on projects and on the funds used to finance them and this would represent society's willingness to trade consumption now for consumption in the future. Most importantly, a project offering above average returns would be producing above average benefits. It would also have access to unlimited funds. With no monopoly conditions, such projects could be undertaken in larger numbers (adding more to aggregate benefits) until the returns on the project and on the funds equalled those available on other projects.

Introducing firms into the picture leads us to some other notable conclusions. Since, in theory, a firm is nothing but an administrative device for organizing real capital projects, the returns available to the owners of firms are simply the returns available from its capital projects. So long as the returns on the projects are greater than the returns required by the owners, more funds can be raised and the firm will expand (raising the general level of welfare all the time, remember) until the returns on capital just equal the cost of funds required by the owners. The owners, of course, are the shareholders. Their shares have a market value and if shareholders are happy that the firm's projects yield just the rate of return that they require, there will be no buying or selling and the share price will be in equilibrium. This is the price at which the firm has to issue new shares if it wishes to expand. The price reflects, again, the cost of funds. If the price were higher, funds would be cheaper; if the price were lower, funds would be dearer.

We have come a long way in a short distance, but what all this amounts to is a summary of the conditions that would have to prevail for us to be sure that funds were always going to those uses that produced the maximum benefit for society. It is not difficult to imagine circumstances in which this happy result will not be achieved.

Firstly, there are conditions relating to the operation of firms. The production of real goods and services is sometimes associated with externalities which means that the price people pay overestimates the real gain to society. Such goods and services are overproduced. Some industries are monopolistic. Their projects earn above average returns and it is not possible for such returns to be eliminated by additional production. Such goods and services are underproduced from a social point of view.

But there are in practice some defects in the operation of most financial systems as well. Financial activity is often *segmented*. That is to say that funds flow from particular sources to particular destinations. They are not free to flow to the most socially productive use. The reasons for this are sometimes informal or historical – households with surplus funds think first of accumulating interest-bearing deposits because securities have been seen as assets for the rich. Sometimes there are legal reasons – institutions that take small savings are obliged to channel a large proportion into government debt because it is seen as 'safe'. Sometimes the reasons are institutional – the minimum denominations of treasury and commercial bills are far too large for private savers, or minimum commissions are too large. The desire to break down such segmentation, and the argument behind it that this would make the system more efficient, has been a major driving force in policies of financial deregulation in recent years.

Another reason why an optimum allocation of funds may not occur lies in either the poverty or asymmetry of information. Acquiring information about the best returns available takes time and thus has a cost attached to it. Many people will think such costs not worth incurring. For many years, most European governments have been able to borrow from households more cheaply than from any other source and this may be as much the result of households' reluctance to search for better returns as it is the result of a desire for high security. This gives, in effect, a subsidy to public sector borrowing and investment.

Part of the return for holding some assets comes as a result of an appreciation of the asset's value – a capital gain. Clearly, such gains are expected as a 'natural' result of holding company shares over a long period and may be as important to investors as the periodic dividend payments. Provided the price goes up, investors make a gain. We may know that the market price should only reflect the productivity of the underlying assets but investors would be foolish, acting against their own self-interest, if they failed to buy (or to hold) shares whose prices they were sure would rise. Profitable investment is not only, therefore, a question of buying shares of firms

that are about to enjoy large profits; it is about buying the shares of firms that other people *think* are going to enjoy good times. You may even get rich by buying shares in firms that other people think that other people think are about to do well. Indeed, maybe the firm's profitability has nothing to do with it at all – you only need to be able to spot those shares that other people are about to buy (for whatever reason). This behaviour gives rise to what are sometimes known as 'fads' or speculative bubbles. Asset prices begin to rise, perhaps for good economic reasons. But once people think that the rise is going to continue there will be some who buy just because they believe the price is going to rise, not because they believe there is any fundamental reason why it should. And if enough buyers join in, the price *will* rise. At least, for a while. But we have to remember that while gambling on asset price movements may seem like harmless fun, or at least something that can only harm the gambler, a change in an asset's price is a change in the cost at which funds can be raised. A rise in the price of an asset makes raising capital cheaper; it encourages expansion; it makes it easier for the firm to take over ownership of its rivals. This is fine if there are sound underlying reasons – the firm may be more productive and better managed than its competitors. But it is a serious failing of the market if it happens for no reason other than a 'fad'.

We return to 'fads' in Section 5.5 while the general question of financial *market* efficiency is one to which we return in Chapter 25.

1.6 Summary

The primary function of a financial system is to reconcile the diverging interests of end users, lenders and borrowers. The system itself consists of a group of institutions and markets both of which help people to lend and to borrow. Financial institutions are often described as 'intermediaries' because of their particular ability to create the liquidity that lenders and borrowers want. This ability relies upon the transformation of maturity and risk and the reduction of costs. These processes are facilitated by the size of intermediaries.

The effects of a financial system are to make lending and borrowing cheaper and to increase liquidity. This in turn encourages investment and may also increase the overall level of spending in the economy. The efficiency with which the financial system channels funds from lenders to borrowers is also important for resource allocation.

Key concepts in this chapter

End users	Risk	Portfolio equilibrium
Ultimate borrowers	Return	Intermediation
Deficit units	Real investment	Maturity transformation
Surplus units	Financial surplus	Search costs
Ultimate lenders	Financial deficit	Transaction costs
Direct lending	Liquidity	Monitoring
Saving	Financial stocks	Velocity
Lending	Financial flows	Market segmentation
Hoarding	Portfolio choice	Market efficiency
Borrowing	Portfolio theory	

Questions and problems

1 Distinguish between surplus and deficit units.

2 Discuss the advantage to deficit and surplus units of using financial intermediaries and organized markets.

3 Suppose you wished to save for your retirement, in an economy with no financial system. What assets would you accumulate and why? What advantages would you have if you were able to contribute to a conventional pension fund?

4 With which financial institutions do you deal? Identify those with which you deal as a deficit unit and those with which you deal as a surplus unit. Which of them are deposit-taking institutions? Which of them are not?

5 Distinguish between broking and intermediation.

6 Why do people hold financial assets and liabilities simultaneously?

7 How are financial intermediaries able to engage in maturity transformation?

Further reading

A D Bain, *The Financial System* (Oxford: Blackwell, 2e 1992) Ch. 1

M Buckle and J Thompson, *The UK Financial System* (Manchester: Manchester U P) Chs 1 and 2

D Blake, *Financial Market Analysis* (London: McGraw-Hill, 1990) Ch.1

E Karakitsos, *Macroeconomics and Financial Markets* (Chichester: Wiley, 1996)

D S Kidwell, R L Peterson, D Blackwell, *Financial Institutions, Markets and Money* (London: Dryden Press, 6e, 1997)

J Madura, *Financial Markets and Institutions* (New York: West) Ch. 1

F Mishkin, *Financial Markets, Institutions and Money* (New York: Harper Collins, 1995) Ch. 2

E H Neave, *Financial Systems: Principles and Organization* (London: Routledge, 1997)

S Pressman, 'What do capital markets do, and what can we do about capital markets?', *Economies et Sociétés*, June 1996

S Valdez, *An Introduction to Western Financial Markets* (London: Macmillan, 1993) Ch.1

PART 2   Theory

Portfolio theory

2.1 Introduction

In this chapter we explain how lenders decide on the allocation of their surplus funds, or to put it another way, how they decide what assets to hold. The answer is that they will hold those assets that give them the rate of return they require, in view of the risk which attaches to the asset. So our question has now become 'how do lenders decide on the rate of return that they require on an asset?'. Stated briefly, our explanation is that this required rate of return on an asset consists of the risk-free rate of interest (set in the economy at large) plus a risk premium (reflecting characteristics of the individual asset). In this chapter we focus largely upon the risk premium. The setting of the risk-free rate of interest is explained in Chapter 3.

Notice that if we can answer this question we can also answer the question, for tradeable assets, of what

determines their *market price* since the equilibrium price must be that at which lenders think they are getting the right rate of return. Formal demonstrations of this appear in Section 5.3 where we bring together the risk premium and the risk-free rate in models of asset pricing, but it is not difficult to understand intuitively. If we take a simple asset which pays a fixed amount in perpetuity, then the rate of return is clearly the payment (D) divided by the price (P). Suppose all else remains the same (including the fixed payment) while asset holders decide that the return is no longer good enough, perhaps because more attractive assets appear. All they can do is sell. This drives down the price, increasing the payment as a fraction of the price (D/P increases), until a new, higher rate of return emerges which makes the asset attractive again. Thus, in explaining how investors decide upon the required rate of return, we are, in effect, explaining the demand side of a supply/demand framework of asset pricing.

2.2 Risk and return

In choosing what assets they wish to hold people are assumed to be *risk-averse, income maximizers* and thus to be seeking the maximum return for a given level of risk or, to put it another way, the minimum risk for a given level of return. The return on an asset is usually expressed as its average or *mean return* (μ) over a period of time. This will consist of any income (interest or dividend) that the asset earns plus any capital gain (or loss). Thus the return on an asset in period 1, K_1, is given by:

$$K_1 = \frac{D_1 + (P_1 - P_0)}{P_0} \qquad (2.1)$$

where P_0 is the price of the asset at the end of the previous period. The (arithmetic) mean return over n periods is:

$$\mu = \frac{\sum\limits_{t=1}^{t=n} K_t}{n} \qquad (2.2)$$

Risk is usually defined as *the probability that the actual return may differ from the expected return*. Notice that this view of risk embraces both the possibility that the actual return may exceed what we expect and the possibility that it may be less than we expect. *Actual risk* in this context is therefore symmetrical. However, people's *attitudes to risk* may be asymmetrical. They may be more concerned with the possibility of loss than with the possibility of gain. It is this asymmetric attitude that we are referring to in the phrase 'risk aversion'. 'Risk' may only mean an equal chance of winning and losing but people do not like it. Why should this be the case?

The generally accepted answer lies in the idea of the *diminishing marginal utility of wealth*. By this we mean that a given addition to wealth is valued less highly than the loss of an equivalent amount. Figure 2.1 illustrates the proposition. An individual is assumed to have a given amount of wealth, shown on

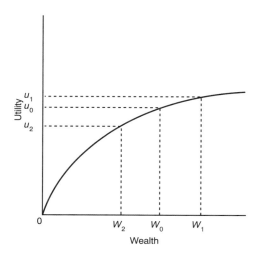

Figure 2.1 The diminishing marginal utility of wealth.

the horizontal axis by W_0. This yields a certain amount of utility, u_0, shown on the vertical axis. An increase in wealth from W_0 to W_1 increases utility from u_0 to u_1. A decrease in wealth *of an equal amount* is shown by the movement from W_0 to W_2.

Notice now that the reduction in utility is shown by the movement from u_0 to u_2 but that the distance $u_0 - u_2$ is greater than the distance $u_1 - u_0$. That is:

$$\frac{u_0 - u_2}{W_0 - W_2} > \frac{u_1 - u_0}{W_1 - W_0} \qquad (2.3)$$

If it is true that people are risk averse, they will be less willing to hold a risky asset than they will be to hold an asset with little or no risk. Indeed, as we said in Section 1.2.1, they will hold the more risky asset only if they receive a higher reward. But judging between assets on the basis of their risk requires that we be able to measure risk itself. As we shall see in Section 2.4, this can become quite complicated. But we can start with a simple idea. If we define risk as the probability that an individual outcome may differ from what was expected then it seems reasonable to suggest that we measure risk by examining the degree of variation in the return over a period. On our definition, an asset which has shown a wide dispersion of actual returns around the mean is riskier than one where returns have been tightly clustered around the mean value. In technical terms, the dispersion of values around a mean is expressed by the *variance*, σ^2. An alternative is the *standard deviation*, σ, the square root of the variance. The variance is found by:

$$\sigma^2 = \frac{\Sigma(K_t - \mu)^2}{n} \qquad (2.4)$$

Thus, we can now say that:

the key characteristics of any asset can be described by the mean value and the variance of its returns.

Notice that the former tells us what an investor can expect to earn from holding the asset over a period of time and the latter tells us the degree of risk associated with those returns.

Unfortunately, the mean and variance of an asset can only be known *ex post*, while investors' decisions must be forward looking. This means that they have to make decisions on the basis of what they *expect* to happen. This raises the very tricky question of just how people form expectations of future economic and financial events. The obvious starting point is that expectations are based in some way on what has happened in the past. However, 'in some way' leaves open a lot of possibilities. It seems reasonable perhaps to suggest that people are guided by what they have observed to happen in particular circumstances in the past, together with some assessment of the likely probability of those circumstances occurring again. On this basis, the expected return on an asset, which we write as $\hat{K}$, can be calculated as follows:

$$\hat{K} = \Sigma P_i K_i \tag{2.5}$$

where P_i is the probability of a particular state of affairs and K_i is the return expected in those circumstances. The corresponding calculation for the variance is then:

$$\sigma_2 = \Sigma P_i (K_i - \hat{K}_i)^2 \tag{2.6}$$

In Box 2.2, share A is expected to produce annual returns ranging from 8 to 18 per cent per annum depending on the state of the economy. The probability of the economy being in a state of 'boom', 'normality' or 'slump' in the next time period varies between 30 per cent, 50 per cent and 20 per cent respectively. The expected return on the share is 14 per cent and its variance is 12.0. Notice that its standard deviation, σ, is 3.46 per cent ($= \sqrt{12.0}$).

Box 2.2   Mean and variance

		Share A			
State	P_i	$K_i\%$	$P_i K_i$	$(K_i - \hat{K})$	$P_i(K_i - \hat{K})^2$
Boom	0.3	18.0	5.4	4.0	4.8
Avge	0.5	14.0	7.0	0.0	0.0
Slump	0.2	8.0	1.6	−6.0	7.2
		$\hat{K}_A = $ 14.0			$\sigma_A^2 = 12.0$

2.3   Diversification

It seems intuitively obvious that the degree of risk to which investors are exposed can be reduced by diversification. Indeed, this is one of the many benefits that intermediaries offer to lenders (see Section 1.3.2). We can show that this piece of common sense has a firm basis in fact. Furthermore we can also show that combining assets into a portfolio can usually reduce risk 'more cheaply', that is to say with a smaller sacrifice in return, than would be the case if we simply switched from one (single) risky asset to another less risky (single) one.

The most dramatic effect in risk reduction comes in the early stages of diversification, as we go from one to five to ten assets, say. In fact, after diversification to holding around 20 assets the degree of risk reduction that comes from further expansions of a portfolio is very small.

For simplicity, therefore, we shall illustrate the risk-reducing effect of diversification by expanding from a one-asset to a two-asset portfolio. Assume that we are faced with choosing between the share A in Box 2.2 and another share B which is expected to give a return varying between 12, 8 and 8 per cent per annum in the 'boom', 'normal' and 'slump' states. At this point, you should calculate the expected return and variance of share B in Exercise 2.1, before going on.

Exercise 2.1   Mean and variance

		Share B			
State	P_i	$K_i\%$	$P_i K_i$	$(K_i - \hat{K})$	$P_i(K_i - \hat{K})^2$
Boom	0.3	12.0			
Avge	0.5	8.0			
Slump	0.2	8.0			
		$\hat{K}_B = $			$\sigma_B^2 = $

Answers appear in the text below.

Obviously we could put all our funds into A or into B, or we could split our investment between the two. Consider firstly the effect upon returns. The general expression for portfolio return is:

$$\hat{K}_p = \Sigma w_i K_i \tag{2.7}$$

where w_i is the 'weight' or proportion of the portfolio allocated to each security and K_i is the return on each asset. (We have dropped the subscript t indicating a given time period in order to make the expressions easier to read.) We can apply the general expression in Equation 2.7 to our specific case. If, for example, we put one half of our funds into each of A and B (whose return in Exercise 2.1 is 9.2 per cent) then we have an expected return of:

$$\hat{K}_p = 0.5(14.0) + 0.5(9.2) = 11.6\,\%$$

Portfolio return is therefore quite simply the weighted average of its components.

When we consider the effect of diversification upon risk, however, the picture is more complex, but also more interesting. It is not a simple weighted average, though the proportions allocated to each asset do play a part. Using the standard deviation as the measure of risk the general expression for a two-asset portfolio is:

$$\sigma_p = \sqrt{X_A^2.\sigma_A^2 + X_B^2.\sigma_B^2 + 2X_A(X_B).cov K_A,K_B}$$

(2.8)

where X_A, X_B are the weights attaching to asset A and B in the portfolio. The first part of the expression:

$$X_A^2.\sigma_A^2 + X_B^2.\sigma_B^2$$

(2.9)

clearly is just a weighted average of the variances of each of the two assets (albeit weighted by the squares of the proportions held). The interesting part of Equation 2.8 is the second part:

$$2X_A(X_B).cov K_A,K_B$$

(2.10)

which features the covariance of returns between the two assets. The covariance can be written as:

$$cov K_A,K_B = \sigma_A.\sigma_B.\rho_{AB}$$

(2.11)

Notice that the covariance includes the standard deviation of each asset but it also includes a term, ρ_{AB}, which is the *correlation coefficient of returns* between A and B. While the variance of each asset, σ^2, measures the size of variability or dispersion of returns around the mean value, the correlation coefficient measures the degree to which the returns on any two assets, be they highly variable or not, actually *move together*.

This is clearly important if we are interested in risk and if we define risk in terms of variability. After all, we could imagine two assets each with a large variance which would therefore be very risky if held in isolation. But suppose that whenever the return on one went up, the return on the other went down. We

could then combine them in such a way that returns were constant because the variations would cancel out and the portfolio variance and standard deviation would be zero. We come back to this later in this section.

Let us see what happens in the present case. We have most of the information necessary for a solution to Equation 2.8. We shall assume that we split our investment equally between A and B and so X_A and X_B each have the value 0.5. The variances, σ_A^2 and σ_B^2, we have calculated above. What we do not yet have is a value for the covariance term, Equation 2.11. The covariance can be found as follows:

$$cov K_A,K_B = \Sigma P_i(K_A - \hat{K}_A)(K_B - \hat{K}_B)$$

(2.12)

where K_A and K_B are the returns on A and B in each state of the economy as shown in each of the tables above. (K_A and K_B are in effect short for $K_i(A)$ and $K_i(B)$.) In our case, therefore:

$$
\begin{aligned}
cov K_A,K_B &= \; 0.3(18-14)(12-9.2) \\
&\quad\; 0.5(14-14)(8-9.2) \\
&\quad\; 0.2(8-14)(8-9.2) \\
&= \; 3.36 + 0.0 + 1.44 \\
&= \; 4.8
\end{aligned}
$$

Putting everything together (including the variance of share B) we can now solve Equation 2.8 and find the standard deviation of our two-asset portfolio as follows:

$$\sigma_P = \sqrt{0.5^2(12) + 0.5^2(3.36) + 2(0.5)(0.5)4.8}$$

$$= \sqrt{3.0 + 0.84 + 2.4}$$

$$= \sqrt{6.24} = 2.50$$

Let us now summarize our three investment possibilities: putting all our funds into A, or all into B or dividing them equally between A and B in a portfolio, C.

	A	B	C
$\hat{K}$	14.00	9.20	11.60
σ	3.46	1.83	2.50

Investing entirely in A, we can expect a return of 14 per cent per annum if we are prepared to accept a standard deviation of returns of 3.46. If this seems too risky, one alternative is to invest entirely in B. This gives us a very large reduction in risk but we have to accept also a reduction in the expected return to 9.2 per cent. Looking at *C*, we can see that splitting our investment equally between *A* and *B* means, predictably, that we have to accept half of the reduction in returns but we can still get *more than half of the risk reduction effect* that we would have had from putting everything into *B*. A way of expressing this more formally is to say that in going from *A* to *B* we reduce risk at the rate of 0.34 for every unit reduction in return (1.63 / 4.8). In going from *A* to a split portfolio, *C*, however, we 'buy' the reduction at a rate of 0.40 for every one point reduction in return (0.96 / 2.4).

The reason for this reduction in risk per unit rate of return lies in the correlation coefficient of returns between the two assets. If we compare the way in which returns on share *A* and share *B* vary in different states of the economy, we can see firstly that they move together in the sense that they both go up when the economy moves from normal to boom but only the return on *A* goes down when we move from normal to slump. *B* is what might be called a good 'defensive' security. We can also see that the overall variability of *B* is less than that of *A*, which is what we discovered in calculating their variances. These differences mean that the returns are less than perfectly correlated – that is, the correlation coefficient is less than +1. We can calculate the correlation coefficient from the covariance by rearranging Equation 2.11.

$$\rho_{AB} = \frac{\text{cov}(R_A, R_B)}{\sigma_A . \sigma_B} \tag{2.13}$$

In this case, the correlation coefficient of returns is:

$$\rho_{AB} = 4.8 / (3.46 \times 1.83) = 0.76$$

Perfect correlation is indicated by a correlation coefficient of +1 while complete negative (offsetting) correlation is signified by a coefficient of –1. To see why the correlation coefficient is so important in reducing the risk of a portfolio below that of its component parts, consider the effect of these extreme values in the expression for a portfolio, Equation 2.8. Remember that we divided this complex expression into two parts: the first (Equation 2.9) was based on the variances of the portfolio's components, the second (Equation 2.10) featured the covariance of returns between the components. If the correlation

coefficient is negative then it follows that the covariance term (Equation 2.10) will be negative. The effect of the standard deviations of the individual securities contained in the covariance will then work to *reduce* the effect of the variances in the first part (Equation 2.8) of the portfolio risk formula and the negative effect will be at its greatest when the coefficient takes the extreme value of –1. On the other hand, for any value greater than zero, the effect of the correlation coefficient will be that the effect of the standard deviations in the covariance will be *added* to the effect of the variances in the first part of the portfolio risk formula. The covariance's contribution to risk will be greatest when the coefficient takes the value of +1. In these circumstances, there is no benefit from diversification and it follows then that the portfolio's risk must be equal to the weighted average of the standard deviation of its components. This is illustrated in Exercise 2.2.

Exercise 2.2

1 Calculate the covariance for our hypothetical portfolio, *C*, by substituting +1 for the correlation coefficient ρ_{AB} in Equation 2.11, leaving all other values unchanged. Then recalculate the standard deviation of the two-asset portfolio. Compare the risk attaching to this portfolio with the risk that you would incur by putting 50 per cent of your wealth into asset *A* and 50 per cent into asset *B*.

2 Recalculate the covariance and portfolio standard deviation again, setting $\rho_{AB} = -1$.

3 Leaving $\rho_{AB} = -1$, combine *A* and *B* in order to produce zero portfolio risk.

Answers appear in Box 2.3 overleaf.

The conclusion we have come to then, and it is fundamental to understanding the behaviour of individual investors and financial intermediaries, is that:

provided the returns on assets are less than perfectly correlated, the greater the degree of portfolio diversification, the lower will be the level of risk associated with a given return.

Box 2.3   Three answers

When $\rho_{AB} = +1$, and other values remain as they were, the standard deviation of our two-asset portfolio, C, = 2.64. This is because when returns are perfectly correlated, we know from Equation 2.11 that the covariance term in Equation 2.8 simplifies to $\sigma_A.\sigma_B$. Thus Equation 2.8 can be written:

$$\sigma_p = \sqrt{X_A^2.\sigma_A^2 + X_B^2.\sigma_B^2 + 2X_A(X_B)\sigma_A.\sigma_B}$$

This in turn simplifies to:

$$\sigma_p = X_A \sigma_A + X_B \sigma_B$$

which is simply a weighted average of the standard deviations of the returns on the individual assets.

When $\rho_{AB} = -1$, and other values remain as they were, the standard deviation of our two-asset portfolio, C, = 0.821. The reasoning parallels that

above, except that the simplification of the covariance term to $\sigma_A.\sigma_B$ is accompanied by a minus sign. Thus Equation 2.8 can be written:

$$\sigma_p = \sqrt{X_A^2.\sigma_A^2 + X_B^2.\sigma_B^2 - 2X_A(X_B)\sigma_A.\sigma_B}$$

This in turn simplifies to:

$$\sigma_p = X_A \sigma_A - X_B \sigma_B$$

We commented earlier in this chapter that if two assets were perfectly negatively correlated then it was possible to construct a zero risk portfolio. This requires merely that we choose appropriate proportions of each asset, that is, appropriate values for the X's. These values can be found as follows:

$$X_A = \sigma_B / (\sigma_A + \sigma_B), \quad X_B = \sigma_A / (\sigma_A + \sigma_B)$$

To make a zero risk portfolio from our two assets, A and B, requires $X_A \approx 0.35$ and $X_B \approx 0.65$.

2.4   'Market' and 'Specific' risk

Figure 2.2 illustrates this conclusion. As more securities are added to the portfolio, so the portfolio's standard deviation diminishes. Notice though that most of the risk reduction effect is achieved by the time the portfolio consists of 20 securities. Beyond that point, portfolio risk appears to settle at an irreducible threshold. Why should this be?

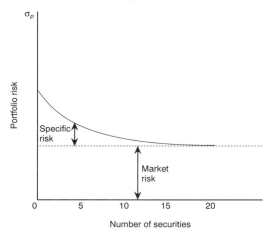

Figure 2.2 Benefits of diversification

The downward-sloping portion of the curve is explained by our discussion in the last section and hinges on the correlation coefficient of returns. For most assets, the correlation coefficient of returns with other assets is less than +1. Think carefully what this means. Something happens that causes the return on asset A, say, to rise. The returns on some other assets also rise but not to the same degree and returns on some assets are unaffected. It might even be that the returns on one or two assets move in the opposite direction. What this indicates is that each asset is affected to some extent by events which are unique to that asset. Combining assets in a portfolio means that the effect of a specific event on asset A, will be partially offset by the effect of some other event on asset B. As the number of assets increases, the scope for this offsetting also increases. Risk arising out of events unique to particular securities is called *specific*, *unique* or *unsystematic* risk. Examples of events giving rise to specific risk can be found in good and bad news about individual borrowers – news about individual firms or about the industry in which they operate.

The near-horizontal part of the curve is explained by the fact that in addition to unique events, assets are also exposed to common sources of risk. Most company shares will be adversely affected by a downturn in the economy. Risk arising out of economy-wide events is called *market* or *systematic* risk. Not all will be affected to the same degree: some securities will be very sensitive to market events, some less so. But diversifying from one to many assets, or even changing the composition of the portfolio entirely, cannot eliminate market risk. A rational, risk-averse, investor will do everything possible to diversify away specific risk, but market risk always remains.

Since it measures the dispersion of returns around the mean value from a security held in isolation, standard deviation (or variance) is an attempt to measure total risk. That is to say:

Total risk = market risk + specific risk = standard deviation

Since we have just seen that risk can be reduced by diversification and that rational investors will only hold an asset as part of a fully diversified portfolio, we might start to wonder whether the standard deviation, which we have so far accepted as a measure of risk, is always wholly appropriate. We shall see in Section 2.6 that we can distinguish for measurement purposes between market and specific risk and that the former is often more appropriate in investment decision making and thus in the pricing of assets.

2.5 'Efficient' and 'optimum' portfolios

The combination of risk and return offered by a portfolio can be plotted in a diagram showing the expected return on the vertical axis and the risk, in the form of standard deviation on the horizontal. In Figure 2.3, for example, we have plotted each of our single share portfolios, A and B, and the combined portfolio, C. C, we recall, is composed of equal amounts of A and B. We could, of course, calculate the risk/return combination for an infinite range of combinations of A and B. The solid curve drawn joining A and B traces all the possible risk/return combinations resulting from each possible mix of A and B. Notice that it is concave to the horizontal axis, indicating that combinations of A and B offer better combinations of risk/return than either A or B held individually. This is what we saw in Section 2.3.

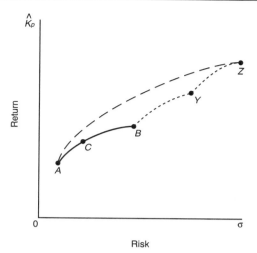

Figure 2.3 Efficient portfolios

However, A and B are not the only possible securities we could mix in a portfolio. We could construct a portfolio from varying proportions of share B and share Y, for example, or from combinations of Y and Z. The possible risk/return combinations of these *two-asset* portfolios are shown by the curves drawn with dotted lines. But why stop at combining just two assets? After all, we have just seen that the benefits of diversification increased with the number of assets that we combined together. Thus, if we were to combine three assets we would expect a better set of risk/return combinations than with two; if we combined four, the combinations would be better than with three, and so on. If we were to draw the risk/return combinations in Figure 2.3, therefore, we should expect the curve for a three-asset portfolio to lie above that for a two-asset one; the curve for a four-asset portfolio to lie above that for a three-asset one, and so on. In Figure 2.3, we shall assume that the 'envelope' curve, drawn with a dashed line, shows *all the possible risk/return combinations available* from combining *all* assets in *all* possible combinations. If we consider that we are dealing with ordinary company shares, then it shows what can be achieved by combining the total range of company shares in varying proportions. The number of possible combinations of course is astronomically large.

The envelope curve traces out the 'best' possible combinations of risk and return available to investors. This means that taking any point on the curve, it is just not possible to get a higher rate of return for the level of risk indicated, or to put it the other way round, it is not possible to get that rate of return for a lower level of risk. The combinations that lie on this curve are produced by what are called *efficient* portfolios, and the curve indicates the *efficient frontier*. We can see why in Figure 2.4. The curve is the envelope curve from Figure 2.3 showing all the possible risk/return combinations resulting from mixing the total stock of securities in varying proportions. Which particular combination an investor will choose will of course depend upon his or her particular risk/return preferences, about which we can say nothing. In Figure 2.4 we have drawn a set of indifference curves, *I1*, *I2* and *I3*, for a hypothetical investor. (Notice that they slope upward to the right and are convex to the horizontal axis. This is because risk is a 'bad', not an alternative good as we have in the more familiar use of indifference curves, and because the 'bad' becomes increasingly unattractive as we have more of it.) *I1* shows combinations of risk/return which are preferable to those on *I2* but the *I1* combinations are not available in this market. The best position that this investor can obtain is shown by the point of tangency between *I2* and the efficient frontier. This results from a portfolio which we have labelled *M*. What the investor will certainly not choose is either of the portfolios labelled *N1* and *N2*. *N1* offers less return for the same risk as *M* while *N2* offers more risk for the same return. Consequently, they lie on a lower indifference curve, *I3*. These are generated by *inefficient* portfolios, portfolios which lie inside the efficient frontier. The same will be true of any combination of risk/return lying inside the frontier – it will always be possible to get a higher return for given risk or a lower risk for given return by moving to a combination on the frontier. Inefficient portfolios are often said to be *dominated* portfolios because there is always another portfolio (lying on the frontier) which offers something better for no sacrifice. The rational investor will choose the point on the frontier that lies on the highest indifference curve.

If we pause to summarize for a moment, we can see that we have made some progress towards answering our question 'how do investors decide which assets to hold?'. We can say firstly that if they

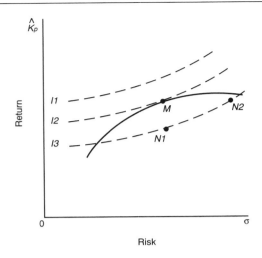

Figure 2.4 The choice of efficient portfolio.

are confronted with risky assets (which is usually the case) *they will hold those assets only in a diversified portfolio*. Furthermore, the *portfolio must be an 'efficient' one*. However, this is still rather vague. In a highly developed market for financial assets, the number of possible efficient portfolios could be enormous even though they form only a subset of all possible portfolios. From this subset, we have just seen, investors will choose that particular mix which just satisfies their preferences for risk and return but this could mean, at least in theory, that each investor holds a unique portfolio – corresponding to his or her unique tastes in risk and return. But we are now about to make two remarkable discoveries. The first is that there is *only one* particular mix of risky assets that rational investors will choose. This is called the *optimum portfolio*. The second is that this portfolio is the *whole market portfolio*, that is to say it consists of all the assets that are currently available in the market combined in just those proportions in which they exist in the market. We derive these surprising conclusions as follows.

Firstly, we introduce the possibility of risk-free lending. So far we have assumed that in order to get any positive return a lender has to accept some degree of risk. But this need not be the case. We shall see in the next chapter that a rate of interest is always paid to people who part with liquidity or lend their current ability to spend to someone else. This may only be a low rate of interest, since most lending does involve a risk and therefore attracts a risk premium. However, risk-free lending is possible. In most countries it is possible to buy treasury bills or other goverment guaranteed instruments whose risk is virtually zero. If we introduce risk-free lending then it follows immediately that we have another dimension to our choice. We could put all our resources in the risk-free asset. In Figure 2.5 this is shown by the point F. If we draw a line from F to a point of tangency, T, on the efficient frontier of risky portfolios we immediately create a new, more efficient frontier, at all points to the left of T. Why is this the case? Think first of all of what happens if we put all our wealth in either the portfolio represented by T, or in the portfolio represented by F.

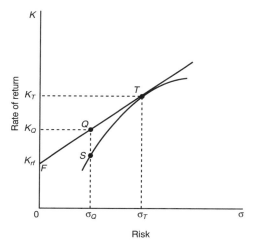

Figure 2.5 The optimum portfolio.

With 100 per cent of our wealth in portfolio T, we accept the combination of return and risk generated by that portfolio (K_T and σ_T in Figure 2.5). If, however, we put all our wealth in the risk-free asset, we should have the rate of return shown at F, that is the risk-free rate, K_{rf}, and zero risk. These are just

two possible portfolios. But there are many, many more which can be created by combining the specific risky-asset portfolio, T, with the risk-free asset, F. Suppose that we split our wealth equally between F and T.[1] What combination of risk/return would we achieve? The answer is shown by Q. Our return, K_Q, would lie halfway between the return on T, K_T, and the return on F, K_{rf}. This should come as no surprise since we have always said that the return on any portfolio was a simple weighted average of its components (Equation 2.7). What is a little more surprising, perhaps, is that by splitting the portfolio in equal proportions, we also get the level of port-folio risk, σ_Q, which lies halfway between F and T. This is surprising because in Section 2.3, where we emphasized the benefits of diversification, we stressed that risk was *not* likely to be a weighted average of the components of a portfolio. (Readers who find this puzzling should look again at the role of the correlation coefficient of returns towards the end of Section 2.3, before looking at Box 2.4, which explains the puzzle.)

Returning to Figure 2.5, if we are now persuaded that combining T and F in varying proportions

---

Box 2.4   Portfolio risk with a risk-free asset

Let T and F stand for the risky and the risk-free portfolios respectively. Let the proportion invested in the risky portfolio be $(1 - X_F)$. Then from Equations 2.8 and 2.11 we know that:

$$\sigma_p = \sqrt{(1 - X_F)^2 . \sigma_T^2 + X_F^2 . \sigma_F^2 + 2X_T(X_F) . \sigma_T . \sigma_F . \rho_{TF}}$$

But since $\sigma_F = 0$, by definition, and since ρ_{TF} also $= 0$, then:

$$X_T^2 . \sigma_F^2 = 0 \ and \ 2X_T(X_F) . \sigma_T . \sigma_F . \rho_{TF} = 0$$

Therefore:

$$\sigma_p = \sqrt{(1 - X_F)^2 . \sigma_T^2} \quad = \quad 1 - X_F . \sigma_T$$

σ_p is a linear function of the proportion of the portfolio invested in the risky portfolio.

---

[1] What we should think of when we say that we put varying proportions of our wealth into 'T' is that we buy miniature versions of T: small amounts of all the assets in T, but in the same proportions as they occur in the full-size T. Or we might think of our varying investment in 'T' as a purchase of small amounts of risky assets combined in such a way that they have the same risk/return characteristics as T. What is crucial is that our risky portfolio has the *same characteristics* as the portfolio T. Those characteristics can be reproduced in portfolios of any size.

generates a weighted average rate of return and a weighted average level of risk, then we can see that any combination of *T* and *F* puts us on the *straight line* between *T* and *F*. It should now be obvious, from our earlier discussion, that all possible portfolios lying along *TF* dominate those lying on the (curved) efficient frontier of risky assets which lies below *TF*. We can check this by comparing the risk/return characteristics of *Q* with those of *S*.

The second step in our argument that risk-free lending enables us to identify a unique, optimum, portfolio, therefore, is to appreciate that risk-free lending generates a new set of portfolios whose characteristics are superior to those of the (old) efficient set, generated solely by combining risky assets. Furthermore, the new efficient set is linear in the combinations of risk/return it offers.

The third step is to realize that identifying this new, superior, set itself identifies just one, *unique*, portfolio of risky assets that investors will choose. We can see this intuitively by looking again at Figure 2.5. Once we understand that efficient portfolios lie on the line *TF*, we can see that individual investors will construct portfolios to suit their own tastes by combining *only T* and *F*. If they are strongly risk averse, for example, most of their wealth will go into *F*; if they are willing to bear more risk they will put more wealth into *T*. They will choose a point, in other words, along *TF* to give them the required risk/return combination *by combining portfolio T with the risk-free asset F*. What they will not do is to choose any combination of risky assets other than *T*. Thus *so far as a choice of risky assets is concerned, T* is the only acceptable combination.

We can see how a unique portfolio is identified more formally, in Figure 2.6, which is Figure 2.5 with indifference curves added. Look at the leftmost indifference map. Here we have an investor who is more risk averse than the others. Without risk-free lending, her best available combination may be at *V*. But with risk-free lending, *V* becomes inefficient since a better combination is available at *V'* (*V'* dominates *V*). In order to get to *V'*, our investor needs to put some funds in the higher risk/return portfolio *T* and then bring down the overall level of risk by putting the rest in the risk-free asset. The proportion of the portfolio in the risk-free asset *F* is

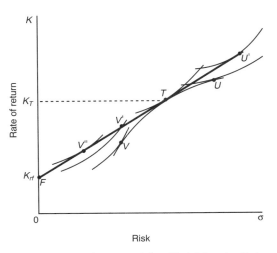

Figure 2.6 The optimum portfolio with risk-free lending.

shown by the distance *FV'* as a proportion of the total distance *FT*. The balance *V'T*, of course, shows the proportion invested in *T*. Her best combination is at *V''* which involves a ??? from risky to risk-free assets.

So much for our most risk-averse investor. Consider the central indifference map belonging to someone who is less risk averse. The highest indifference curve to which she can get access is the one tangential to the efficient frontier at *T*. She will choose to put the whole of her wealth into the risky asset portfolio *T*, since putting anything into the risk-free asset reduces the return in exchange for a reduction in risk which she does not want.

Now turn to our most adventurous investor, with the rightmost indifference map. Given only risky assets, his choice will be a portfolio composed in such a way as to yield the risk/return combination at *U*. But with risk-free lending comes the prospect of risk-free borrowing. Our adventurous investor can get a better risk/return combination by borrowing (at a rate which is less than the return on a risky portfolio) and using the loan to buy larger quantities of a less risky portfolio. In Figure 2.6 *U'* becomes available by borrowing at the risk-free rate and investing total wealth plus the borrowing in *T*.[2] The distance *TU'* as a proportion of *FT* indicates the amount of borrowing as a proportion of total wealth, a figure of 10 per cent, for example, meaning that 110 per cent of wealth is invested in *T*.

What this geometrical exercise has done is to identify *T* as the *only portfolio of risky assets that a rational investor will hold*. We have identified a unique or *optimum* portfolio. The question for the investor is no longer 'what combination of risky assets to hold' but 'what proportion of wealth to put into this particular portfolio and what proportion to lend at the risk-free rate?'

But we said earlier that we were going to identify not just a *unique* portfolio as the optimum portfolio, but also that we were going to show that this would correspond to the *whole market portfolio* of risky assets, currently available. How can we claim that? The answer to this is brief but quite startling. It relies heavily on the concept of equilibrium and the fact that all the risky assets in *T* can be traded. The argument is that the whole market portfolio of assets must be held by someone. Furthermore, since they can be, and are, actively traded, those who currently hold them are happy to hold them at their current prices and yields. But since *T* is the only combination of assets that rational investors will hold it follows that *T* and the whole market portfolio of risky assets must be one and the same.

2.6 The price of risk: the Capital Asset Pricing Model

The line $K_{rf}TU'$ in Figure 2.6 is often known as the *capital market line*, or *CML*, as it represents the market's view of the appropriate trade-off between risk and return. This is more easily seen if we redraw it without the indifference maps and re-label the optimum portfolio, *T*, as *M* to emphasize now that we recognize it as the whole market portfolio.

σ_m is the risk attaching to the market portfolio. From Figure 2.7 it is easy to see that the slope of the *CML* is given by:

$$\frac{(K_m - K_{rf})}{\sigma_m}$$ 2.14

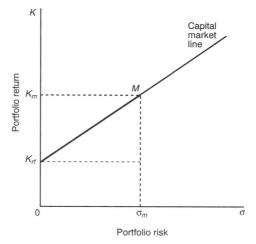

Figure 2.7 The capital market line.

Suppose for example that the risk-free rate were 10 per cent p.a. while the return and standard deviation on the whole market portfolio were 20 per cent and 8 per cent respectively. The market price for a unit of risk would then be $(20 - 10)/8 = 1.25$. Thus, for every unit increase in risk (a one-point increase in s.d.), investors would expect to receive an additional 1.25 percentage points over the risk-free rate. The return on any portfolio lying on the *CML* can then be calculated as:

$$K_p = K_{rf} + \frac{K_m - K_{rf}}{\sigma_m} . \sigma_p$$ 2.15

This should be read as saying that the return on a portfolio will be equal to the risk-free rate plus the unit price of risk times the number of units of risk attaching to the portfolio.

Alternatively, we may write $K_p = XK_m + (1-X)K_{rf}$, where *X* is the proportion of the investor's portfolio devoted to the market portfolio of risky assets and $(1 - X)$ is the proportion allocated to the risk-free assets. The standard deviation of the portfolio is simply $X\sigma_m$, since $\sigma_{rf} = 0$ by definition.

Equation 2.15 enables us to price any efficient

---

2 Borrowing at the risk-free rate is assumed for simplicity in Figure 2.5. It is not very realistic. Borrowers are likely to have to pay a higher rate of interest. This means that the extension of the line beyond *T* (*TU'*) should be flatter than *TF*, representing the fact that *borrowing* can only be done at a rate higher than K_{rf} and that *TU'* if extended backward would intersect the vertical axis at a point above K_{rf}. The difference between the points of intersection of *TF* and *TU'* on the vertical axis could be seen as the 'spread' or differential in interest rates paid to lenders and charged to borrowers.

portfolio. Our objective in this chapter, however, is to be able to price individual assets or, what we know amounts to the same thing, to be able to determine the rate of return required on an individual asset. Given that we now know how to find the market price of risk, we might think that the final step to finding the return on an individual asset is easy. Going back to Equation 2.15, we might say, for example, that an individual asset, A, should earn the risk-free rate plus a risk premium which is equal to the unit price of risk times the risk of the asset as represented by its standard deviation. (Formally, this would involve replacing σ_p with σ_A in Equation 2.15.) This might seem sensible, *but it would be quite wrong*.

The reason can be found in Sections 2.3 and 2.4 where we saw the benefits of diversification and we stressed that a rational investor would hold assets only as part of a fully diversified portfolio, a portfolio from which all individual or specific risk had been eliminated. But an asset's standard deviation measures *total* risk, that is to say the sum of market and specific risk. If that is the case, then using the asset's standard deviation would involve a considerable overestimate of the relevant risk. We can see this if we recall the hypothetical case where we take a very risky asset, A, (one with a large standard deviation) and combine it with another very risky asset, B, in circumstances where $\rho_{A,B} = -1$. This two-asset portfolio would have zero risk! The effect of adding asset B is to *reduce* risk. Its *relevant* contribution is negative, which is hardly what is expressed by a large standard deviation. If one were buying asset B in order to add it to a portfolio, it would clearly be foolish to take its individual standard deviation as a measure of its risk and then to insist on a high return to compensate for that apparently large risk.

If, as we said earlier, rational investors hold an asset only as part of a fully diversified portfolio, then the appropriate measure of risk is a measure of the risk attaching to that asset that cannot be diversified away. This is a measure of the asset's exposure to market risk. The extent of the asset's exposure to market risk depends upon, and can be found from, (1) the exposure to market risk of the whole market portfolio and (2) the covariance of the asset's returns with those of the whole market portfolio.

$$\beta_i = \frac{\text{cov}(K_i, K_m)}{\sigma_m^2} = \frac{\rho_{i,m}\sigma_i\sigma_m}{\sigma_m^2} = \frac{\rho_{i,m}\sigma_i}{\sigma_m} \quad 2.16$$

We can see in Equation 2.16 that the numerator expresses the covariance of the return on an asset with the return on the whole market portfolio, and that this in turn is expressed as a ratio of the variance of the market portfolio.

This measure of risk is usually referred to as a security's β-coefficient.[3] We can see why in Figure 2.8 which shows how one might make a visual comparison of the return on asset A with the return on the whole market portfolio. The comparison is given to us by the slope of the line. In a standard regression equation, this slope coefficient would commonly be labelled β.

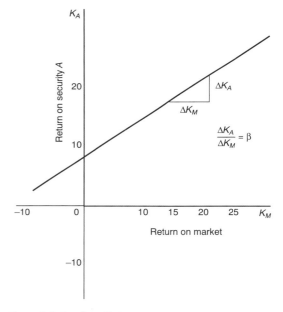

Figure 2.8 The β-coefficient.

We can now take the standard deviation of asset A, representing total risk, and disaggregate it in order to see the relative contributions of market and specific risk.

---

[3] The mathematical derivation of β is beyond the scope of a text like this. But it is widely available. Samuels *et al.* and Blake, both cited under Further Reading, provide a formal derivation.

Box 2.5   Total versus market risk

Imagine that we have the following information relating to an asset, i, and the market, m: $\sigma_i = 30\%$, $K_m = 25\%$, $K_{rf} = 10\%$, $\sigma_m = 20\%$. Suppose further that the correlation coefficient of returns between i and the market, $\rho_{i,m,} = 0.60$.

Firstly we can find the β-coefficient for i as follows:

$$\begin{aligned} \beta_i &= (\rho_{i,m}.\sigma_i) / \sigma_m \\ &= (0.6 \times 0.3) / 0.2 \\ &= 0.9 \end{aligned}$$

The risk attaching to i which is *relevant* to calculating its risk premium when included in a portfolio is 0.9. Notice that this is less than 1 and so its relevant or market risk is less than the average for the market as a whole. This is the case even though its *individual* or total risk, as measured by its standard deviation, is greater than that for the market as a whole, $\sigma_i > \sigma_m$.

Secondly, we can disaggregate total risk into its component parts:

$$\begin{aligned} \sigma_i &= \beta_i \, \sigma_m + \sigma_s \\ 0.3 &= (0.9)\,(0.2) + \sigma_s \\ \sigma_s &= 0.3 - 0.18 \\ &= 0.12 \end{aligned}$$

$$\sigma_A = \beta_A \, \sigma_m + \sigma_s \qquad (2.17)$$

Box 2.5 illustrates more formally how an asset with high individual risk when measured by its standard deviation may have a low risk when considered from the more relevant point of view of the risk it brings to a portfolio.

We have now established that the appropriate index of risk for an asset held as part of a fully diversified portfolio is β, a coefficient which expresses the risk of an individual asset relative to the riskiness of a whole market portfolio. Earlier in this section we said that we wished to know the appropriate measure of risk because this would help us to determine the required rate of return, $\bar{K}_A$. Following our approach to determining the required return on a *portfolio*, $\bar{K}_P$ in Equation 2.15, we might say that $\bar{K}_A$ would be equal to the risk-free rate of return, K_{rf} plus a risk premium derived from the price of 'average' risk adjusted for the relevant risk of the asset itself, where relevant risk is measured by its β–coefficient. We know, from Figure 2.7, how the market prices the level of risk associated with the whole market portfolio. It is the difference between the whole market return, K_m, and the risk-free rate, K_{rf}. If we now have a way of comparing the risk of asset A with the risk of a whole asset portfolio, then we have a way of calculating an appropriate risk premium for asset A. This is:

$$\beta_A(K_m - K_{rf}) \qquad (2.18)$$

which we can read as saying that:

the risk premium required on an asset, A, is equal to the whole market risk premium adjusted for the riskiness of asset A when compared with the whole market portfolio.

Clearly, if asset A n had the same risk characteristics as the whole portfolio it should also yield the same return. From Equation 2.15 we can see that this is:

$$\bar{K}_M = K_{rf} + [(K_m - K_{rf})/\sigma_m].\sigma_m$$

which simplifies to:

$$\bar{K}_M = K_{rf} + (K_m - K_{rf})$$

and therefore $\beta_A = 1$ in Equation 2.18. Generally, therefore, the return on A is:

$$\bar{K}_A = K_{rf} + \beta_A (K_m - K_{rf}) \qquad (2.19)$$

with:

$\beta_A = 1$ where A has the same risk characteristics as the whole market portfolio;

$\beta_A < 1$ where A is less risky than the whole market (what is sometimes called a *defensive* asset);

$\beta_A > 1$ where A is more risky than the whole market (what is sometimes called an *aggressive* asset).

Equation 2.19 is the equation for the *security market line* or *SML*, or what is sometimes called the *capital asset pricing model* or *CAPM*. It states that:

the required mean return on an asset is equal to the risk-free rate of return plus a weighted market risk premium, where the weight, β, depends upon the asset's risk characteristics when compared with the whole market.

This is drawn in Figure 2.9. It looks superficially similar to the *CML* (Figure 2.7) but the *CML*, remember, told us the additional return (above K_{rf}) required *from a fully-diversified portfolio, with varying degrees of risk*, σ_p. It is σ_p which appears on the horizontal axis. The *SML* shows the additional return (above K_{rf}) required on *an individual asset* whose

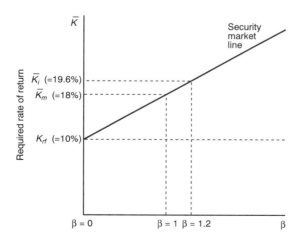

$\bar{K}$

Security market line

$\bar{K}_i$ (=19.6%)

$\bar{K}_m$ (=18%)

K_{rf} (=10%)

Required rate of return

β = 0   β = 1 β = 1.2   β

Figure 2.9 The security market line.

risk characteristics can be compared with those of a whole market portfolio. It is these characteristics, expressed by β, which are drawn on the horizontal axis. Expressed in terms of *pricing*, rather than *rates of return*, the message of the *CAPM* is that assets which are 'fairly priced' will yield a rate of return such that they plot on the *SML*.

Notice firstly that an asset with no relevant risk, β = 0, has a required rate of return equal to the risk-free rate while an asset with β = 1 has the same required return as the whole market portfolio. If we know the risk-free rate, the market risk premium and the asset's β-coefficient we can read off the required rate of return. For example, in Exercise 2.3 our hypothetical asset had a β-value of 1.2 while the risk-free rate was 10 per cent and the whole market rate was 18 per cent. In this case $\bar{K}_i = 10\% + 1.2(18\% - 10\%) = 19.6\%$.

To understand what might cause the required return to change, we need to be careful, as always, to distinguish between movements *along* and movements *of* the *SML*. Consider firstly movements along the curve. Since the curve plots the required rate as a function of β, movements along the curve will occur whenever anything happens to affect a share's β-coefficient. This means that its exposure to market risk has changed. An increase in exposure will move us up the *SML*, increasing the required rate of return; reductions in risk will move us down the *SML*.

The *SML* itself can change in two senses: its slope may change or it may be subject to a parallel shift. Its slope is given by $(K_m - K_{rf})/\beta$ and expresses the degree of risk aversion in the market. A change in slope will occur if, as we suggested in Exercise 2.3, there is a change in risk aversion. If for example there is an increase, then the market risk premium ($K_m - K_{rf}$) and the slope of the *SML* increase. The required rate of return on assets also increases since although their risk has not increased, risk itself is priced more highly.

The *SML* can also change its position by a parallel shift. This will happen when the risk-free rate changes, all else remaining as it was. There is no change in the degree of risk and no change in its price. But the risk-free rate to which the premium is added may go up or down. The required rate of return, of course, moves in the same direction.

Finally, notice that we can rewrite Equation 2.19

using the third version of ß in Equation 2.16:

$$K_A = K_{rf} + (K_m - K_{rf}).\frac{\rho_{A,m}\sigma_A}{\sigma_m} \qquad (2.20)$$

Rearranging Equation 2.20, enables us to make a more explicit comparison with the *CML* equation, 2.15:

$$K_A = K_{rf} + \frac{(K_m - K_{rf})}{\sigma_m}.\rho_{A,m}\sigma_A \qquad (2.21)$$

In the *CML*, the risk premium depends solely upon the standard deviation of the portfolio; in Equation 2.21 we can see that the risk premium for an asset depends similarly upon the standard deviation of the asset but also upon the way the asset behaves relative to the market, as shown by its correlation coefficient of returns. Once again, we can see why an asset with high total risk (large σ_A) can have low market risk when measured by β. It merely requires a small value for $\rho_{A,m}$.

2.7 Summary

Other things being given, the price paid for an asset determines its rate of return. If we can explain the return required on an asset, therefore, we can explain why the market prices an asset as it does. Our explanation of asset returns is that the required rate of return is equal to the risk-free rate of return plus a fraction or multiple of the premium required for 'average' or 'standard' risk.

The benchmark risk premium is the difference in return between a whole market portfolio of risky assets and the risk-free rate $(K_m - K_{rf})$. This represents the price required by the market for holding a fully diversified portfolio. That is to say it is the price required for holding the minimum level of risk for a given return, since all risk that can be avoided has been eliminated by diversification. It is the only risk that rational, risk-averse, investors will be prepared to hold.

An individual asset attracts a proportion of this whole market risk premium, determined by its β-coefficient. We use the β-coefficient, rather than the standard deviation of returns, as a more relevant measure of an asset's riskiness in this situation because, again, rational investors will hold an asset only as part of a fully-diversified portfolio. The β-coefficient is relevant because it measures the risk brought by an asset to a portfolio, taking account of its covariance of returns with the whole market as well as its standard deviation.

Key concepts used in this chapter

Risk	Total risk
Return	Market risk
Risk aversion	Specific risk
Standard deviation	Risk-free lending
Variance	Whole market portfolio
Mean	Whole market rate of return
Diversification	Capital market line
Covariance	Security market line
Correlation coefficient of returns	ß-coefficient
Efficient portfolio	Defensive security
Optimum portfolio	Aggressive security

Questions and problems

1 What is meant by risk in a financial context? Why are people assumed to be risk averse?

2 Why does the diversification of asset holdings generally lead to a reduction in risk?

3 Are there any limits to the benefits of diversification? If so, why?

4 Distinguish between market risk and specific risk.

5 Why does the return on assets reflect only their exposure to market risk?

6 If the riskiness of an asset can be described by its variance, why do we need the ß-coefficient?

7 Explain how you would expect each of the following events to affect the security market line and the required rate of return on a given share (imagine that each event occurs independently of the others):

(a) an increase in official short-term interest rates;

(b) a reduction in the degree of risk aversion in the market;

(c) an increase in the uncertainty of the share's future prospects.

Further reading

D Blake, *Financial Market Analysis* (London: McGraw-Hill, 1990) Ch. 13

K Cuthbertson, *Quantitative Financial Economics* (Chichester: Wiley, 1996) Chs 2 and 3

E J Elton and M J Gruber, *Modern Portfolio Theory and Investment Analysis* (Chichester: Wiley, 5e, 1995) Ch. 13

P G A Howells and K Bain. *Financial Markets and Institutions* (Harlow: Longman, 2e 1994) Ch. 1

F Mishkin, *Financial Markets, Institutions and Money* (New York: Harper Collins, 1995) Ch. 5

J M Samuels, F M Wilkes and R E Brayshaw, *Management of Company Finance* (London: Chapman and Hall 1990, 5e) Ch. 9

CHAPTER 3 The determination of short-term interest rates

Box 3.1

What you will learn in this chapter:

- The distinction between real and nominal interest rates
- The meaning of liquidity, risk and inflation premia
- The loanable funds and liquidity preference theories of interest and the assumptions behind them
- The Fisher effect and its role in linking nominal and real rates of interest
- The origin and limitations of central bank influence over interest rates

---

3.1 Introduction

No one interested in economics or finance would doubt the importance of interest rates. Consider just a few possible reasons:

- the rate of interest is a payment from borrowers to lenders;
- asset values move inversely with changes in interest rates;
- interest rates are part of the cost of firms' investments;
- interest rates affect the exchange rate;
- interest rates affect bank lending and monetary growth.

The first two in this list are particularly important in financial theory. For example, in the last chapter we established that lenders would require a reward which compensated them for the degree of risk that

they felt they were running by lending, and this was a reward which was paid *as a premium* on the 'risk-free' rate of interest. Later, in Chapter 5, we shall see that the prices of financial assets change in response, naturally enough, to changes in demand and supply. But we have already seen that the price that people are prepared to pay is determined by the rate of return that they require from an asset, and this is determined partly by the risk-free rate of interest.

In this chapter, therefore, we want to begin to explain how interest rates are determined. We start with the determination of the *short-term, risk-free, nominal rate of interest*. In the next chapter we go on to look at how a whole range of other interest rates, differentiated by term and by risk, are derived from the short-term, risk-free rate. One way of visualizing this two-stage process is to think that we are first going to examine the base or foundation level of interest rates, before going on to look at the superstructure built upon that base.

3.2 Interest rates defined and classified

The rate of interest is a payment from borrowers to lenders which compensates the latter for parting with funds for a period of time and at some risk. Put into real terms, it is often said that lenders are being encouraged to forego consumption now, in conditions of comparative certainty, in return for consumption later, in an uncertain future. This is a little misleading. In 'rewarding' savers for parting with funds, a rate of interest is, strictly speaking, rewarding savers for giving up the *ability to consume* if they should change their mind about saving. After all, there is a perfectly rational case to be made for people to save (forego *actual consumption*) at zero, or even negative, real interest rates since they will wish to provide for old age or other future periods of zero income.

Notice that the effect of interest rates is to influence behaviour which stretches over a period of time – lending *for a period*, foregoing the ability to consume *for a period*, investing in capital goods which yield a return *over a period*. The relevant concept of interest rate is thus, strictly speaking, the *expected* rate. However, we can only observe actual interest rates. Unless we state otherwise, we shall assume that expected and actual rates turn out to be the same.

Nominal interest rates are the rates of interest that are actually paid, in money form. They are the interest rates that we use in everyday discussion and which we see quoted in advertisements, in the media, and in official announcements. It is useful to think of nominal rates as consisting of four elements. Letting i stand for the nominal rate of interest, then:

$$i = r + \pi + l + \sigma \tag{3.1}$$

where r is the *real* short-term rate of interest, π is an *inflation* premium, l is a *liquidity* premium, and σ is a premium for risk.

The real rate of interest is the return that lenders require even if there is no risk and prices are constant. This is the 'pure' return for giving up the ability to spend, for even the shortest period of time. It is generally accepted that lenders prefer to lend for the shortest possible period. If this is the case, then long-term (real) interest rates will be higher than short-term ones and the difference might be described as a liquidity premium. If it is true that lenders require increasing inducements to part with liquidity for increasingly long periods then the inducements must be real (unless we assume that lenders suffer from 'money illusion'). Thus lenders will require compensation for any rise in prices that they expect to occur over the duration of the loan. Lastly, σ is a further premium required to compensate for whatever level of risk is perceived to attach to the loan. As we saw in the last chapter, the size of this premium in any specific case will depend upon the riskiness of the loan in question in relation to 'average risk' in the market and the price required

to compensate lenders for average risk. Of the four components making up the nominal rate, σ is not related to time.

Through Sections 3.3 to 3.5, we shall concentrate upon the determination of the risk-free, short-term nominal rate of interest. That is, we shall concentrate upon i, where i is composed of the two elements r and π. We shall use l and σ in the next chapter, to explain the structure of interest rates built upon the short-term risk-free rate.

3.3 'Market' theories of interest rate determination

Many economics textbooks present two apparently conflicting accounts of the determination of interest rates. (Some do it perhaps even without realizing it. The loanable funds theory (*LFT*) is the basis of interest rates in the microeconomic section while liquidity preference theory (*LPT*) is called on in the macroeconomic chapters.) *LFT* is associated with the 'classical' economists of the Nineteenth and early Twentieth centuries while *LPT* is a product of John Maynard Keynes' *General Theory of Employment, Interest and Money* (1936). The merits of the two approaches were the subject of a long and often bitter dispute between Keynes and his pupil (later colleague) D H Robertson.

3.3.1 Loanable funds theory

Briefly, *LFT* explained the level of interest rates as the outcome of decisions to invest and decisions to save. Decisions to invest resulted from the desire to enjoy the future output from capital assets while decisions to save resulted from a desire to accumulate wealth for the future through the rate of interest offered by investors. The essential point, from an economic point of view, was that the rate of interest was freely determined by the interaction of these two sets of decisions. At the going rate of interest, any decision to save (not spend) must be matched by a decision to spend on capital goods. If, for some reason, savers decided to save more, then the excess supply of saving would push interest rates down, and investment up, until a new equilibrium was reached at which saving and investment were equal. There could be no 'leakage' from the circular flow of income. In *LFT*, it is often said, the rate of interest is determined by the 'real' forces of *productivity* (of capital equipment, determining what borrowers could pay) and thrift (on the part of savers, determining their willingness to lend).

As we shall see in Section 3.3.2, this explanation of interest rates was attacked by Keynes in *The General Theory of Employment, Interest and Money* (1936). Before attacking it, he labelled the theory a product of 'classical' economists, though he also pointed out that it had never been very clearly stated. (It might be noted in passing that Keynes was never very clear as to whom exactly he included under the heading of 'classical' economists.) The label undoubtedly comes from the fact that the theory makes a number of assumptions that are common in the approach of Ricardo and Mill and, indeed, in the work of more recent economists who claim to have revived the classical tradition. The assumptions of loanable funds theory are:

- the economy is operating at full employment;
- prices are constant;
- there is a fixed supply of money;
- there is perfect information.

From a borrowing and lending point of view, the significance of these assumptions is as follows. With output fixed at full employment there are no fluctuations in income or employment and therefore no fluctuations in the supply of saving resulting from this source. There is no fluctuation either in the demand for money as a result of varying levels of transactions in the economy. With the money supply fixed, there is no alternative source of funds but savings out of current income. No new money is being created which might meet part of the demand for funds. If there is perfect information, there is no uncertainty. There will be no fluctuation in the demand for funds resulting, for example, from shifts in the demand for money as a safe haven for savings. There will be no fluctuation in 'hoards'. All savings will be made available in loanable form in order to benefit from the rate of interest. With no fluctuation in demand for hoards, the only source of demand for loanable funds comes from a desire to invest.

The effect of these assumptions is to ensure that the only supply of funds is saving, while the only demand comes from investment and the only influence on either is the rate of interest. We shall now look at *LFT* in more detail, remembering that *LFT* originally assumed constant prices. In these circumstances, the real and nominal rates of interest are identical. An explanation of the real rate is also an explanation of the nominal rate.

The real rate of interest

It is assumed that agents prefer consumption now to consumption in the future, that is to say that they have *positive time preference*. The real rate of interest is the rate of interest that lenders would need to compensate them for postponing consumption until some point in the future, given constant prices. The size of the inducement necessary to bring about the postponement is thus said to measure their *rate of time preference*. Individuals will differ in their rates of time preference, in the way that individual 'tastes' vary towards all activities, but as a general rule we might expect the rate of time preference to fall with increases in income. People with large incomes will find it easier, and more attractive, to postpone consumption now – in order to enjoy a more prosperous old age, for example – than people with incomes scarcely large enough to purchase day-to-day essentials. In the aggregate, therefore, we would expect high-income communities to have a lower rate of time preference and this is just another way of saying that, other things being equal, we would expect saving to increase (as a proportion of income) with increases in income.

As described in the last paragraph, therefore, the real rate of interest can thus be seen as an inducement to *savers*. On the other hand borrowers, or users of those funds, are normally assumed to want them for investment in assets which yield a future stream either of income or of services or of output.

Consider for a moment the purchase of real assets such as plant or machinery. Borrowers will purchase such assets if they have a positive *net present value*. That is to say that the assets will be attractive if they yield some net benefit in excess of their purchase price, running costs and the cost of borrowed funds. Formally:

$$NPV = -P + \sum_{t=1}^{n} \frac{CF_t}{(1+\overline{K})^t} \qquad (3.2)$$

where CF is the cash flow (net of any running costs) in each period t, and $\overline{K}$ is the required rate of return. The required rate of return on a project must obviously cover the cost of funds and this will mean matching the risk-free short-term rate of interest plus the various risk premia that lenders require. Any project that achieves this while leaving $NPV \geq 0$ will justify borrowing the funds to undertake it. Clearly, from Equation 3.2, the ability of a project to fulfil this condition for any value of $\overline{K}$ will depend upon its cashflows, that is to say upon its productivity. The greater the productivity of the asset, the higher the value at which $\overline{K}$ can be set without breaching the condition of a positive NPV. Thus, an investor's ability to pay any given price for funds will depend upon the productivity of the real assets. We shall see later, but especially in Chapter 9, that the return on financial assets should also, in theory, reflect the return on the underlying real assets. If we accept this for the time being, then we can see that the demand for funds, that is to say the price that borrowers will be prepared to pay, will depend upon the productivity of real assets.

According to this point of view, therefore, the equilibrium real rate of interest will be that rate at which the supply of funds from savers just matches the quantity demanded by investors. Figure 3.1 illustrates this situation. The supply curve of funds, S, is drawn upward-sloping because of its savings component reflecting the fact that the higher the rate of interest, the greater the number of people who will find that it exceeds their rate of time preference. The demand curve, D, is drawn downward-sloping, indicating that the lower the rate of interest the more projects can be found whose productivity generates a positive NPV. The equilibrium real interest rate is that at which the supply of funds is just equal to the demand, r_0.

Imagine now that the community's rate of time preference diminishes and the supply of lending increases at all rates of interest. This is shown by a downward shift of the supply curve to S'. There is now an excess supply of lending – the number of profitable projects at any rate being unchanged. In the circumstances, the interest rate falls to r_1, more

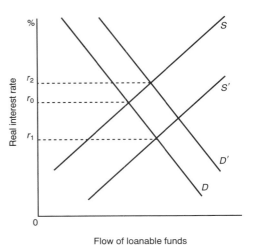

Figure 3.1 Loanable funds theory of the real rate of interest.

projects become profitable and the flow of lending and borrowing would be again in equilibrium.

Imagine now that, instead, there had been an increase in productivity. At r_0 there would be an excess of profitable projects. The demand curve shifts to D'. Competition for funds would push up the rate of interest. More potential lenders would find that the rate of interest exceeded their rate of time preference, more funds would be forthcoming and a new equilibrium would emerge at r_2.

The rate of inflation

We have just seen that the traditional explanation for a rate of interest payable to lenders by borrowers is that lenders are foregoing consumption for which they require compensation. Depending on their rate of time preference they may, for example, be willing to forego £100's-worth of current consumption provided that they are in a position to consume £105's-worth in one year's time. If this is the case, then the real rate of interest, r, is 5 per cent:

$$r = \frac{£105}{£100} - 1 = 0.05 = 5\% \qquad (3.3)$$

If prices are constant, a 5 per cent return on £100 requires a cashflow in one year's time of £105.

$$CF_{t+1} = £100 \times (1+r) \qquad (3.4)$$

With constant prices, a 5 per cent real return is achieved with a nominal rate of interest, i, of 5 per cent. The real and nominal rates are the same and we can write the required augmentation in terms of either the real or nominal rate of interest, that is:

$$(1 + i) = (1 + r) \tag{3.5}$$

Given the experience of inflationary episodes throughout Europe in the Twentieth century, the assumption of constant prices strikes us today as hopelessly unrealistic and might lead us to view loanable funds theory with scepticism. But it is not difficult to graft on to *LFT* an account of the determination of *nominal* interest rates under conditions of inflation. This explanation simply amounts to saying that nominal rates will differ from real rates by an amount necessary to compensate savers for rising prices and to ensure that borrowers do not benefit from them.

For example, suppose that prices are expected to rise by 8 per cent over the same period. (Notice again that it is the *expected* (or *ex ante*) rate of inflation that strictly matters.) Unless our lender suffers from money illusion, she will now require the future cashflow to be adjusted for the rise in the price level. The required cash flow in one year's time, CF_{t+1}, will be:

$$CF_{t+1} = £100 \times (1 + r) \times (1 + P^e) \tag{3.6}$$

where P^e is the expected rate of inflation. The required augmentation is now $(1 + r) \times (1 + P^e)$ and this must be reflected in the nominal interest rate. Thus when prices are rising:

$$(1 + i) = (1 + r) \times (1 + P^e) \tag{3.7}$$

and the formula for the nominal rate becomes:

$$i = (1 + r) \times (1 + P^e) - 1 \tag{3.8}$$

Notice that the expression $(1 + r) \times (1 + P^e)$ can be expanded as follows:

$$(1 + r) \times (1 + P^e) = 1 + r + P^e + (r)(P^e) \tag{3.9}$$

For modest rates of interest and inflation, the cross-product $(r)(P^e)$ is very small and can be ignored. In these circumstances, our outlay has to increase by:

$$1 + r + P^e \tag{3.10}$$

In our example, the cashflow required in one year's time can now be found:

$$CF_{t+1} = £100 \times (1 + r + P^e)$$
$$= £100 \times (1 + 0.05 + 0.08) = £113 \tag{3.11}$$

and the nominal rate of interest can be found (from Equation 3.3) by:

$$i = \frac{£113}{£100} - 1 = 0.13 = 13\% \tag{3.12}$$

At 'normal' rates of inflation and real interest rates, therefore, we can say that the required nominal rate of interest is approximately equal to the real rate plus the expected inflation rate:

$$i \approx r + P^e \tag{3.13}$$

Equation 3.13 is the equation for the short-term, risk-free, nominal rate of interest. If we replace P^e with π then Equation 3.14 is directly comparable with the first part of Equation 3.1.

$$i \approx r + \pi \tag{3.14}$$

Exercise 3.1   Real and nominal interest rates

Given the nominal rate of interest, i, and the expected rate of inflation, P^e, we can find the real rate, r, by rearranging Equation 3.8. Thus:

$$r = [(1 + i) / (1 + P^e)] - 1$$

But for low rates of interest and inflation we could rearrange the simpler expression, Equation 3.13:

$$r = i - P^e$$

1 Use each of these expressions to find the real rate of interest when nominal interest rates are 8% (= 0.08) and the expected rate of inflation is 4% (= 0.04).

2 Repeat the exercise setting the nominal rate to 20% and inflation to 15%.

3 Observe the difference between the two methods in each case.

Answers: see end of chapter.

The Fisher effect

By rearranging Equation 3.13, we can see that the real rate of interest is the difference between the nominal rate and the expected (*ex ante*) rate of inflation.

$$r \approx i - \dot{P}^e \qquad (3.15)$$

Furthermore, unless they suffer from money illusion, it is the real rate of interest which will matter to the decisions of lenders and borrowers. Unfortunately, we cannot observe the real rate directly since we cannot observe lenders' and borrowers' *expectations*. The only way around this problem, unless we engage in large-scale surveys of what agents expect, is to assume that what they expect generally turns out to be the case. If we do this, then it means that we can subtract the *actual* or realized rate of inflation (which, of course, we can observe after the event) from the nominal rate of interest which we can also observe. This gives us an *ex post* measure of real interest rates by rearranging Equation 3.14:

$$r \approx i - \pi \qquad (3.16)$$

Equation 3.13 (sometimes written as Equation 3.14) is often known as the *Fisher equation*, after Irving Fisher whose book, *Theories of Interest* (1930), provided the first systematic discussion of the relation between real and nominal rates. In fact, Fisher is often credited with the argument that the real rate of interest tends to be stable over long periods. This, after all, is plausible given the explanation of the real rate as the result of time preference and capital productivity. There is no reason to suppose that either of these would be subject to violent short-term fluctuations. The argument then went on to explain variations in the nominal rate as the result of changes in the expected rate of inflation. In actual fact, although Fisher does advance this suggestion as worthy of consideration, he himself recognized that the nominal rate of interest did not follow the rate of inflation very closely and much of the book is taken up with explanations of why such an obviously plausible theoretical idea was not strongly confirmed in practice. In spite of this, the proposition that the nominal rate of interest is made up of a stable real rate and a premium which closely follows the rate of inflation has become known as the *Fisher effect*.

Figure 3.2 shows the (*ex post*) real interest rate calculated by subtracting realized inflation from nominal short-term rates for four European countries since 1969. If we were to calculate the variances of real and nominal rates in each case, we might be able to show that real rates were more stable, but it is not so obvious that it can be seen clearly from the charts. In each country there have been significant fluctuations in real rates.

These fluctuations in the real rate do not necessarily disprove entirely the Fisher hypothesis that the nominal rate consists of a stable desired real rate plus a premium for expected inflation. It could be true that people's expectations of inflation are responsible for the nominal rate but that these expectations are frequently wrong. It is worth recalling, however, that in the world of loanable funds theory, from which the Fisher hypothesis developed, perfect information was assumed.

Because of its origin in the work of 'classical' economists in the Nineteenth century, *loanable funds theory* is often regarded as the 'traditional view' of interest rate determination. We can sum it up as follows:

- the short-term, risk-free real rate of interest is the sum paid by borrowers to lenders for the shortest posible period, in a world of constant prices and zero risk;
- the supply of funds is determined by people's willingness to save and this depends in turn upon their rate of time preference;
- the demand for funds depends upon the prospects for their profitable use and this depends in turn upon the productivity of the assets which such funds will be used to purchase;
- the short-term, risk-free, nominal rate of interest is composed of a real rate determined by time preference and productivity plus a premium which reflects the expected rate of inflation.

3.3.2 Liquidity preference theory

Keynes' attack upon loanable funds theory comes mainly in Chapters 13–17 of his *General Theory of Employment, Interest and Money* (1936).

Firstly, he argued, people's ability to save depended very much upon their level of income.

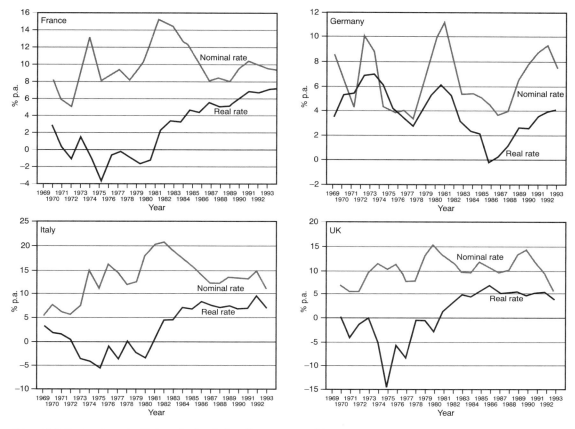

Figure 3.2 Real and nominal interest rates in four European countries.

Since he rejected the assumption of full employment it followed that *aggregate* income could fluctuate quite widely. In communities where income was well above subsistence level, it made sense to save even when interest was zero. (In Figure 3.1, therefore, the supply curve would intercept the horizontal axis and would need to be redrawn every time income changed.) The rate of interest played a secondary role by influencing how people decided to save. Interest was a reward for lending or parting with money and this was not necessarily the same thing as saving. After all, one could save (that is, not spend) by accumulating notes and coin and keeping them under the bed. (We first saw this in Section 1.1.) No interest would be payable then, even though saving would be taking place. If lots of people wished to hold idle money balances in this way, money would be scarce, and interest rates high even though saving would also

be at a high level. These are both points which we touched on in Section 3.2: *saving* may not depend upon interest rates, *lending* very likely does.

Because of his emphasis upon interest as the inducement to part with liquidity ('the ability to change one's mind' as we said in Section 3.2), Keynes chose to explain interest as the result of an interaction between the supply of money and the demand for money. We shall come back to the question of money supply and demand in Chapters 6 and 7, but to understand Keynes' argument and its implications, it is worth glancing at Figure 3.3.

The money supply is assumed to be fixed (by the actions of the central bank) and this is shown by the vertical curve, M_S. The demand curve, M_D, is drawn downward-sloping. One might explain the negative slope by reference to 'opportunity cost'. If we assume that money (= cash + bank sight deposits)

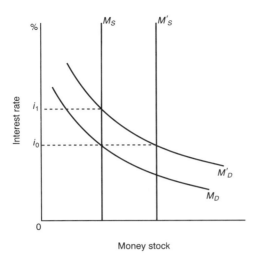

Figure 3.3 Money market equilibrium – the effect of demand shifts.

does not pay interest then at lower interest rates money's attractions as a perfectly liquid asset are greater than they would be when interest rates on alternative assets are high. Keynes' explanation, however, drew upon interesting psychological factors. When interest rates are low, people would expect the next movement to be upward. When interest rates rise, asset prices fall (Box 3.2 contains an illustration) and holders of assets suffer a capital loss. Thus, at low interest rates money avoids the risk of capital loss. The *position* of the curve depends upon people's need for money in exchange and this in turn depends upon the price level and the level of economic activity. Thus any change in nominal aggregate income causes the curve to shift.

One of the most important of Keynes' insights was to introduce expectations and uncertainty and thus to create a role for money as a safe haven in a treacherous world. We have seen that the downward slope of the curve arises from the increasing strength of *expectation*, when interest rates are low, that a capital loss may be just around the corner. But expectations of interest rate changes are not tied to absolute levels of actual rates. What may look like a low rate (set to rise) in one situation may look 'normal' in another. Thus at any actual rate, circumstances may change so as to cause expectations to change. The current rate, acceptable today, may look too low tomorrow. There will be a rush for money. At today's rate, the demand for money tomorrow may be much greater. Thus, introducing expectations in this way introduces the possibility that the demand curve may shift around. As a rule, anything that increases uncertainty tends to increase the attraction of money. The demand curve shifts

---

Box 3.2   Interest rates and asset prices

A fundamental principle of economics and finance is that the value of an asset lies in the stream of income or services or other benefits that it produces. In the case of financial assets, the benefit is usually an income stream or 'cashflow'. In order to arrive at a valuation the payments in this income stream have to be discounted – that is to say that the value of the more distant payments has to be adjusted downward to take account of the fact that we have to wait for them.

This is what we saw in Equation 3.2. It shows a cashflow as a series of payments identified as CF_t, where t indicates the time of their receipt. The value of the series is found by discounting each payment by $(1 + K)t$, where K is the rate of return that we require and t again denotes the period in which the payment is received. One can see immediately that a payment (CF) which lies a long way ahead (that is, has a high t value)

will be heavily discounted. This is because the corresponding denominator will have a high t value and will be raised to 'the power of t'.

But more importantly, notice what happens if we change the value of K. This also appears in the denominator. If we make it larger, the value of each CF is made smaller. Thus, when we sum the series of discounted CFs their value will be lower, the larger is the magnitude of K. All we need to remember now is that since K is the rate of return that we require, it must reflect the level of returns that are available elsewhere. That is, *it must reflect the going rate of interest*. If interest rates go up, K increases and the value of our asset goes down. If interest rates go down, K goes down and the value of our asset goes up.

There are numerical examples of changes in interest rates causing changes in asset prices in Sections 4.2 and 5.3.

upward (to M_D') and the rush to liquidity pushes up interest rates, from i_0 to i_1. If the money supply were to expand, to M_S' for example, the comparative shortage would be eliminated and the rate of interest would remain at i_0.

The significance of all this for Keynes' wider project was first of all that the rate of interest was no longer free to accommodate the flow of saving to the flow of investment. There could, for example, be leakages from the circular flow of income and spending leading to a fall in output and employment. Secondly, the possibility that the demand for money might be unstable meant that nominal interest rates (and therefore real interest rates) might fluctuate in response to psychological factors, causing instability in the real economy.

We can sum up the liquidity preference approach as follows:

- agents' actions determine *nominal* interest rates. Real rates will depend upon the behaviour of prices and the extent to which price changes are correctly anticipated;
- the nominal rate is determined by the demand for money relative to its supply;
- the demand for money depends upon the price level and upon the level of economic activity but it also depends upon the desire to hold money as a safe asset in an uncertain world;
- the degree of uncertainty that agents feel is highly variable, leading to fluctuations in the demand for money and hence in the nominal rate of interest;
- the supply of money is independent of the demand for it and is assumed to be fixed by the actions of the monetary authorities.

3.3.3 The determination of interest rates: an eclectic approach

Considered alone, neither the *LPT* nor *LFT* is entirely satisfactory. Loanable funds theory is appropriate for a perfectly static setting with output fixed at its full employment level, prices constant, a fixed money supply and perfect information. As we said, in those circumstances there would be no fluctuations in the demand for hoards, savers would lend all that they saved and the only demand for funds would be for investment. We could then say that the real rate of interest paid between borrowers and lenders would be determined by time preference (for savers) and the productivity of capital (for borrowers).

In economies as we know them, however, this is too simple. Interest is paid not just as an inducement to save but as an inducement to *lend money* and saving does not necessarily entail lending. Our savers would not earn interest, for example, if they simply accumulated notes and coin or some types of bank deposits. They have to be willing to *lend* the funds that become available from saving; and fluctuations in the demand for money (or 'hoards' in classical language) are perfectly reasonable in economies where output not only grows but fluctuates in its rate of growth and where uncertainty about the future makes occasional 'rushes to cash' entirely rational. Furthermore, in economies as we know them, saving is not the only potential source of funds. Banks are in business to lend and the normal result is a money supply where deposits are expanding as a result of this lending.

We need to take account of both complications and our suggestion is that we do this by thinking of 'new money' as an additional source of funds and of 'hoarding' as an additional demand. We begin with the former.

The supply of funds available to borrowers consists of both the funds that savers are prepared to lend *plus* any increase in the community's total stock of money. We shall see in Chapter 6 that the money supply expands when banks lend, since their lending creates deposits. Furthermore, this additional lending need not entail rising interest rates if employment is below its full employment level. Provided the central bank is prepared to provide banks with the necessary reserves at the going rate of interest, lending (and deposits) may expand for so long as banks can find willing (and creditworthy) borrowers. Whether we focus upon the bank loans or upon the bank deposits that they create, bank lending is an additional source of funds.

Our second complication, recall, is that savers may not wish to lend all that they save. In certain circumstances, they may wish to accumulate funds themselves, usually in the form of bank deposits. Adding to holdings of money is sometimes called additional 'hoarding' or adding to 'idle balances'.[1] Both the potential supply of new money and the possibility that more money may be demanded for hoards are additional influences on the supply and demand for funds which we must add to the traditional account which focuses only upon the actions of savers and investors.

Looking at the supply side, we can now say that the quantity of funds available to borrowers is:

saving − Δhoards + Δnew money

and the equilibrium condition will be that in which:

saving − Δhoards + Δnew money = investment

In practice, this condition is often rearranged to show sources of funds on one side and uses of funds on the other, thus:

saving + Δnew money = investment + Δhoards

Figure 3.4 is a modification of Figure 3.1 and shows the effect of incorporating these complications. The supply curve, *S*, is now labelled to make it clear that the potential supply of funds consists of both saving from income and also any addition to the money stock. It is drawn upward-sloping still because of the savings component which is assumed still to respond to interest rates. The demand curve, *D,* is drawn downward-sloping reflecting still the demand for funds for investment in real capital assets. More of these assets, as we said before, will have a positive *NPV* the lower is the rate of interest, but the curve also contains a demand for 'idle balances' which causes it to lie further to the right (and may cause it to be unstable).

In Figure 3.4 an increase in income, a decrease in time preference or an increase in the supply of new money each increases the availability of funds and causes the equilibrium rate of interest to fall, from i_0 to, say, i_1. Reversing the disturbance causes the curve to shift upward. On the demand side, an increase in productivity of capital assets or an increase in the demand for money causes the curve to shift outward and, starting from i_0, the equilibrium rate of interest will rise, say to i_2.

Notice that this account allows for a certain amount of flexibility in the relationship between real

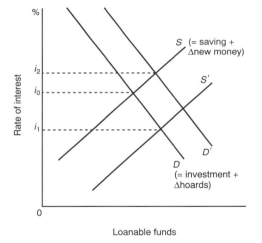

Figure 3.4 Loanable funds and liquidity preference theories combined.

S = saving + Δnew money; D = investment + Δhoards.

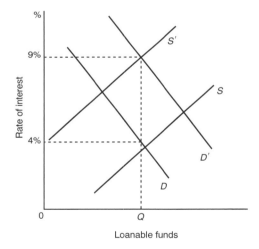

Figure 3.5 The effect of inflation in 'classical' theory.

S = saving + Δnew money; D = investment + Δhoards.

---

1 Take care not to think that the decision to accumulate bank deposits makes it possible for banks to lend more and thus to replace the lending that savers have decided not to do. The decision to accumulate deposits does not increase their quantity. If savers had decided to lend (by buying bonds, for example) the deposits would still have been in the banks and they would still have been matched by bank loans. But they would have been owned by borrowers and lending would have been equal to the bank loans *plus* the bond issue.

and nominal rates, at least in the short run. Imagine, for example, a monetary expansion which increases the supply of funds relative to the demand. In Figure 3.3 the supply curve shifts down and the nominal rate falls. More investment is undertaken and, without the classical assumption of full employment, output and employment will expand. With spare capacity, output may rise, again in the short run, with little, if any, effect on inflation. The new nominal rate now lies below the old nominal rate and, if inflation remains unaffected, the new *real* rate lies below the old real rate.

Under the classical assumptions of loanable funds theory this outcome would be impossible. Starting from full employment and constant prices, an expansion in the supply of new money would initiate an increase in spending and prices would rise, producing an increase in the rate of inflation from zero to, say, 5 per cent. Figure 3.5 shows what would happen from a classical perspective.

We begin with an equilibrium real rate of interest of 4 per cent which, given constant prices, is also the current nominal rate. A monetary expansion, however, causes inflation of 5 per cent and this is recognized accurately and equally by both borrowers and lenders. With inflation at 5 per cent, lenders demand 9 per cent for the current level of lending and the supply curve shifts upward. On the other hand, borrowers know that at 9 per cent they are paying a real rate of only 4 per cent. The demand curve also shifts upward. Notice two things. Firstly, that they both shift by the exact amount necessary to maintain the same levels of borrowing and lending. ('Real' behaviour is unchanged.) Secondly, the nominal rate is equal to the real rate plus an accurately anticipated inflation premium. In these circumstances, the Fisher hypothesis would be vindicated.

3.4   The role of central banks – 'administered' interest rates

The account that we have so far given of how short-term interest rates are determined stresses the role of private decision makers or what might be called 'market forces'. We have mentioned the monetary authorities, in the guise of the central bank, only once in saying that commercial banks can add to funds by creating money and that this need not involve a rise in interest rates if the central bank supplies the necessary reserves at a constant price.

However, to any student who keeps even a casual eye on current affairs this must seem odd. Scarcely a month goes by in any economy without the news-media reporting either that the monetary authorities have raised (or lowered) the level of official short-term rates or that financial markets are speculating that the authorities are about to do so. Box 3.3 shows a selection of typical recent headlines from newpapers doing just that.

If it is the case that short-term nominal interest rates are set by administrative decision then all the earlier discussion of this chapter is redundant. (If, on the other hand, interest rates are indeed set by market forces, then the currently fashionable argument that central banks should have more independence in their ability to set interest rates becomes pointless.) In this section, therefore, we devote our attention to the influence that central banks, acting on behalf of or independently from their governments, can exert over interest rates. We begin by looking at sources of influence and then go on to consider the constraints and limitations to this influence. But before we do, let us clearly distinguish the terms 'short *term*' and 'short *run*'. Throughout this chapter, our emphasis has been upon short-*term* interest rates. These, we know, are interest rates which apply to loans for short periods or short *terms*. In the rest of this section we shall suggest that these short-*term* rates may be influenced by central bank behaviour for short periods of time, that is to say in the short *run*. If this influence cannot be exerted over a long period of time, however, then we have to say that short-*term* rates are market-determined in the long *run*. This lesson will be useful in future. We often need to distinguish between the behaviour of short-*term* (or medium-*term* or long-*term*) instruments over a short period of time (the short-*run*) or a medium or long period (the medium *run* and long *run* respectively).

The ability of all central banks to exercise any influence over interest rates lies in their role as *lenders of last resort*. This in turn relies upon their role as monopoly suppliers of liquidity in the event of a general shortage of funds. In most European countries, central banks developed this role in the second half of the Nineteenth century or the early

Box 3.3: Central banks and interest rates

MARKETS REPORT
Fed raises US interest rates by 50 basis points
Financial Times, 2.2.95

'A surge in US business investment led to unexpectedly rapid economic growth in the first quarter, intensifying fears yesterday that the Federal Reserve would be forced to increase interest rates.'

(Financial Times, 3.5.96)

George repeats call for interest rate rise

By Graham Bowley and Robert Chote

Mr Eddie George, governor of the Bank of England, yesterday insisted that interest rates should rise again soon, rejecting the chancellor's argument that the strength of the pound makes it unnecessary.

His remarks, in a speech to bankers in Edinburgh, are likely to inflame the debate over interest rates between the Bank and Mr Kenneth Clark in the run-up to the election.

Financial Times 21.1.97

'At its meeting on December 14, 1995, the Central Bank Council of the Deutsche Bundesbank set the monetary target for 1996. The decision provided that the money stock M3 is to expand by 4% to 7% between the fourth quarter of 1995 and the fourth quarter of 1996. At the same time, the Central Bank Council decided to lower the discount and lombard rates by $\frac{1}{2}$ percentage point each to 3% and 5%, respectively, with effect from December 15, 1995, and to offer the next three securities repurchase transactions up to the beginning of January in the form of fixed-rate tenders at a rate of 3.75%.'

(Deutsche Bundesbank Monthly Report January 1996 p.19)

Warning that increase could worsen exporters' plight as sterling rises
Hold interest rate, CBI says
Financial Times, 22.1.97

years of the Twentieth. The need for a lender of last resort originated with the need to reassure depositors of the certain convertibility of their deposits into cash. In the early days of deposit banking when banks were numerous, small and local there was always the danger that a perfectly well-run and solvent bank could fail as a result of unexpected cash withdrawals or transfers to another bank. Indeed, in the earliest stages mere rumours of a cash shortage could be sufficient to bring about withdrawals and a failure which was quite unnecessary. Clearly the failure of one bank involves major hardship for its depositors but in the background loomed the nightmare that one failure might lead to more as depositors in sound banks panicked. Without a lender of last resort, the only solution would be for banks to hold very high levels of reserves (= cash + banks' deposits at the central bank). Since these reserves pay no interest, they act as a tax on banking activity and make bank intermediation more expensive and less efficient than it would otherwise be.

It is doubtful that many depositors these days give so much as a thought to the possibility that they will not be able to draw on their deposits whenever they feel like it. However, so long as full convertibility between deposits and cash is guaranteed, a lender of last resort is essential.[2] This requirement is reinforced where, as is generally the case, reserves pay no interest since banks then have an incentive to minimize holdings of such reserves. In some systems banks are required to observe a minimum *mandatory* reserve ratio, in which case they will be seeking to minimize holdings of additional, or what are sometimes called 'free' or 'excess', reserves. In cases where the minimum reserve ratio is a matter of choice (a *prudential* reserve ratio) there is no distinction between required and excess reserves.

The consequence of operating with minimum reserves is that banks can find themselves short of reserves at a particular moment for reasons that have little to do with prudence or foolishness. In the UK,

for example, the central government banks with the Bank of England, not with the commercial banks. A net payment of funds by the private sector to the central government, therefore, transfers deposits from commercial banks to the government's account at the Bank of England. This withdrawal (of liabilities) is matched on the asset side of the balance sheet by an equal transfer from commercial banks' reserves to the government's account at the Bank of England. Since reserves are only a very small proportion of deposits, this one-for-one reduction in deposits and reserves lowers the ratio dramatically.[3] Such private–public sector transfers are not easily predicted on a daily basis.

An individual bank in difficulty can, of course, remedy the position by borrowing in the interbank market. But in the event of a system-wide shortage of funds, the central bank becomes the monopoly supplier. The precise manner in which central banks operate to relieve shortages (or to mop up surpluses for that matter) varies between systems and reflects the differing histories and institutional arrangements in each system. Central bank relations with the commercial banking system is a theme in each of our later chapters on specific countries. However, it is worth noting that whatever the arrangements may be in detail, they fall into two broad categories. Either the central bank may *lend* funds for reserve purposes (often known as helping through the 'discount window') usually at a pre-announced rate of interest or it may *buy* short-dated non-reserve assets from banks at prices which may or may not be pre-announced.

The essential point here, however, is that the central bank is the monopoly supplier of funds and it can behave just like any other monopolist. It can either decide on the quantity of reserves to make available, and allow banks to bid between themselves for the available supply, or it can set the price and supply whatever quantity of reserves is required. In the former case, the quantity is fixed directly and the

---

[2] Not all would agree today. In the past few years there has been a revival of interest in 'free' banking in which market forces would force banks to behave in a way that would guarantee their stability. See the references to Dowd (1996), Benkston and Kaufman (1996) and Dow (1996) at the end of this chapter. The reference to Goodhart (1991) presents a fairly conventional case for the last resort role of central banks.

[3] For example, in a banking system running with a ratio of reserves to deposits of 1:10, a 5 per cent loss of deposits is matched by a 50 per cent loss of reserves and the reserve ratio falls from 1:10 to 1:19. We look at banks, reserve ratios and the money supply in more detail in Section 6.4

price follows; in the latter the price is fixed and the quantity demanded follows. Whichever it decides to do, its actions will determine short-term interest rates. This in turn sets a base to the level of interest rates since commercial banks will not engage in lending at rates which do not at least exceed the rate that they would have to pay for lender of last resort facilities. Deposit rates are then set at a discount to lending rates and arbitrage is assumed to keep bank and other short-term interest rates in line. Since banks are generally in the position of wanting to expand their loans and deposits, the central bank is generally in the position of having to supply additional reserves and can therefore set the price by one means or another. And it is movements in this price, whether it is known in different monetary systems as 'base rate', 'Lombard rate', 'repo rate', 'minimum lending rate', which are the subject of intense interest when commentators report that 'the Bank has raised (or lowered) interest rates'. [4]

On the face of it, we have here an account of interest rate determination which provides a much bigger contrast with our two 'market' theories than they do with each other. *If* the central bank is in a position to set short-term interest rates as a matter of administrative decision, then there is no need for elaborate theories about the level of interest rates.

As usual in economics, however, things are not quite so straightforward. Notice, firstly, that even if we accept the 'administrative' account unreservedly, we are only taking a view about the setting of *nominal* interest rates – the *real* rate will depend upon what happens to expectations about future inflation rates – and we only have an account of the setting of the shortest of short-term rates. (Most central banks would claim to set rates only in the overnight to seven-day range.) Nonetheless, we are still a long way from both loanable funds and liquidity preference. Can we establish firmly that either 'market' or 'administrative' accounts are superior? And if we cannot, then can we reconcile or combine them in some way? Since we observe central banks setting interest rates, telling us that they do so and telling us how they do it, it seems we have either to reject more market-based accounts or look

for reconciliation. This may not be so difficult as it seems, because if we consider the central bank's position in more detail we shall see that there are a number of constraints within which it must work and some of these are constraints posed by market forces.

Firstly, saying that central banks set interest rates (even very short-term nominal rates) does not mean that they are free to set these rates at whatever level they choose. Obviously, interest rates have to be set in order to achieve a number of objectives. We are familiar these days with the idea that objectives may pose conflicting demands on instruments. Since 1992, for example, Italy, France, Spain, and other countries including the UK have all had to face the dilemma of raising interest rates to protect weak currencies with the risk of ending a fragile recovery from recession.

Secondly, even where a single or overriding objective can be identified – these days it is usually a low rate of inflation – there may still be conflicting pressures on the interest rate instrument arising out of disagreement about which intermediate target to focus upon. For example, if inflation is the ultimate target, should the level of interest rates be chosen with a view to minimizing the rate of monetary growth, or to maintaining a high exchange rate?

Thirdly, when all these questions have been resolved, the setting of interest rates will often depend upon what is happening to interest rates elsewhere. For many European countries, the level of short-term interest rates is closely connected with rates available on Deutschmark assets. For 'open' economies like that of the UK, changes in German or US rates inevitably trigger questions about the next movement in sterling rates. This happens because capital is internationally very mobile. Thus, quite slight differences in the profits to be gained from holding Deutschmark rather than sterling assets, for example, cause savers to sell sterling assets and buy Deutschmark ones. Since assets are normally bought and sold in the currency of their denomination, this means that sellers of sterling assets (who now hold sterling) must now sell sterling itself in order to buy Deutschmarks. If this continues for only a short time, the price of sterling (in other currencies) begins to

---

4 See Table 9.4 for a list and explanation of official interest rates in a variety of countries.

fall. If, as is usual, governments have some desired exchange rate for the domestic currency, then domestic interest rates will have to rise.

Fourthly, and more directly relevant in the present context, it is virtually impossible for central banks to set interest rates that do not have the endorsement of financial markets. As we shall see in several later chapters, it is now possible for very large sums of money to be moved between financial centres at a moment's notice and at very low cost. It is very difficult, therefore, for the authorities to impose a level of short-term rates which is regarded as inappropriate by financial markets. Indeed, it is not difficult to find cases where central bank preferences and market preferences appear to have conflicted and where this happens it is usually market sentiment that ultimately triumphs. The experiences of Italy and the UK in being forced from the Exchange Rate Mechanism in September 1992 yield dramatic examples. One can say either that these incidents were demonstrations of the power of market sentiment when the countries concerned tried to maintain exchange rates (as opposed to interest rates) which markets thought unsustainable, or one can make the cases even more relevant by saying that the choice of exchange rate and interest rate were two sides of the same problem. *Given* their desire to maintain their ERM agreed exchange rates the Bank of England and the Bank of Italy pushed up interest rates to emergency levels. But markets took the view that these interest rates were still not high enough given the exchange rate objective. Faced with the choice of yet higher interest rates or leaving the ERM, the central banks chose the latter course.

Fifthly, if central bank decisions about interest rates can be clearly seen to be influenced by market forces in some rather dramatic situations, we need to look carefully at their decisions in more everyday contexts. After all, outward appearances will be the same (a central bank will make an official announcement, the media will treat it as 'news') whether the central bank is issuing an independent instruction which it expects everyone else to follow, or is confirming a situation which market practitioners have come to regard already as inevitable. Careful study of the financial press, for example, often reveals rises in short money rates, and may even show developing market sentiment that

interest rates must rise, in the few days immediately prior to an official announcement. Here, the central bank merely confirms what markets have already decided.

What all of this suggests is twofold. Firstly, central banks are certainly constrained in their ability to set interest rates and some of the most significant constraints are those imposed by markets' beliefs about what interest rates *ought* to be. Secondly, while central bank behaviour is clearly visible, it will always be reported as news, while market activity is more complex and obscure and receives less media attention. We therefore need to be cautious about interpreting the correlation between central bank interest rate statements and changes in interest rates as cause and effect.

3.5 A synthesis

The safest conclusion is that the setting of short-term nominal interest rates depends upon *both* market forces (which may be driven by some mixture of loanable funds and liquidity preference considerations of the kind we discussed in Section 3.3.3) *and* upon decisions by the monetary authorities. We might be able to make this vague conclusion a little more precise if we think of a 'short-run/long-run' distinction. We might want to say, for example, that for short periods the central bank has considerable power over the determination of short-term nominal rates (and if the economy is operating in a recession this may also yield an influence over real rates). Looking at Figure 3.6, for example, (which is based on our earlier Figure 3.4) we might envisage a situation where the flow of funds and the demand for them is initially consistent with an interest rate of i_0 and we might also assume that this is also the authorities' target rate. Imagine now that market sentiment anticipates a rise in interest rates (perhaps because of weakness in the exchange rate). There is an increase in liquidity preference and in Figure 3.6 the demand for funds shifts out to D', threatening to push interest rates up to i_1. If the central bank wishes to maintain interest rates at i_0, it can make it clear to banks that reserves will continue to be made available at the existing level of interest rates so that they can respond to the demand for funds without fear of a reserve shortage. Unlimited funds become available at the going rate and the supply curve effectively becomes horizontal as shown by the broken line, S'.

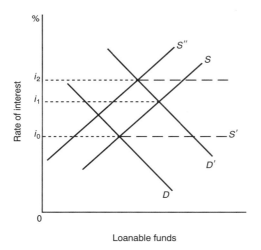

Figure 3.6 Interest rate determination – when the central bank has preferences.

In the longer term, however, which may only be as long as it takes for foreign exchange markets to realize what is happening, this policy may prove unsustainable. If continuous expansion of money and credit at the going level of interest rates is unacceptable in foreign exchange markets (perhaps because of its inflationary potential) then the pressure on the exchange rate will grow. The authorities are then faced with the familiar dilemma of conflict in objectives. Notice that the interest rate/exchange rate combination is unstable. Holding rates *given* at i_0 (and expanding money and credit) threatens a continually *declining* exchange rate. If preserving the exchange rate triumphs, the authorities may not just have to 'put' interest rates up to i_1 but may be forced to raise them further, say to i_2, by indicating that henceforth new reserves will be forthcoming only at a new, higher level of interest rates.

3.6   Summary

No one doubts that the behaviour of interest rates is important for both the real economy and for financial markets. The traditional account of interest rate determination focuses upon the 'real' factors of productivity and time preference. These forces set the *real* rate of interest and the nominal rate will simply be the real rate plus an inflation premium. This account treats the act of saving as equivalent to making available 'loanable funds'. Clearly, this need not be the case as Keynes pointed out. People may save without lending. Furthermore the ability to save rests also upon a level of income (which was variable) and not just an interest incentive. Keynes' liquidity preference theory focused upon the desire to hold money in relation to the supply that was available. We suggested that these accounts could be combined if one recognized that both the demand for liquid wealth and banks' creation of new money by lending affected the supply of loanable funds.

Both of these accounts, however, focus upon market forces. Neither is immediately reconcilable with what we frequently observe which is that 'the authorities' announce and appear to decide upon interest rate changes. On the other hand, we know that central banks are often constrained by market sentiment in what they can do about interest rates. Therefore a sensible way of looking at interest rate determination is to recognize the fundamental role played by market forces but then also to recognize the influence of central banks in the short run, provided their decisions do not stray too far from market sentiment.

This interplay between the authorities and market participants determines the short-term, nominal, risk-free, rate of interest. For a given rate of inflation, this fixes also the short-term, *real*, risk-free rate.

Key concepts used in this chapter

Nominal interest rate	Productivity	Liquidity preference theory
Real interest rate	Thrift	Lender of last resort
Inflation premium	*Ex post*	Short-term *v* short-run
Fisher effect	*Ex ante*	Long-term *v* long-run
Hoards	Loanable funds	
Rate of time preference	Loanable funds theory	

Questions and problems

1   Distinguish between nominal and real interest rates.

2   Using loanable funds theory, explain the likely effect on the supply of funds and the equilibrium interest rate of:
(a) an increased desire to save for old age;
(b) a reduction in taxes on income from savings.

3   Explain the Fisher hypothesis. What is the logic behind the idea that there should be a positive relationship between the rate of inflation and nominal interest rates?

4   What is meant by the terms *ex ante* and *ex post* as applied to real interest rates?

5   Use the loanable funds diagram to explain how you would expect an increase in inflationary expectations to affect:
(a) the supply and demand schedules;
(b) the nominal rate of interest;

(c) the *ex ante* real rate of interest.

6   Estimate the *ex post* real (short-term) interest rate over the past year. How does it compare with the nominal short-term rate?

7   Using liquidity preference theory, explain how you would expect the demand for money and the equilibrium rate of interest to be affected by:
(a) a growing anxiety that security prices might be about to fall;
(b) a growing belief that the central bank is about to tighten monetary policy?

8   Explain what central banks can do to prevent a rise in interest rates. What limits the central bank's ability to do this?

9   Using the financial press and/or official publications give a brief outline of the current policy on interest rates.

Further reading

A D Bain, *The Financial System* (Oxford: Blackwell, 2e 1992) Ch. 5

G J Benkston and G G Kaufman, 'The appropriate role of bank regulation', *Economic Journal*, 106 (436), 1996, 688–697

D Blake, *Financial Market Analysis* (London: McGraw-Hill, 1990) Ch. 2

S C Dow, 'Why the banking system should be regulated', *Economic Journal*, 106 (436), 1996, 698–707

K Dowd, 'The case for financial *laissez-faire*', *Economic Journal*, 106 (436), 1996, 679–687

C A E Goodhart, 'Are central banks necessary?', in *Unregulated Banking: Chaos or Order?* ed. F Capie and G E Wood (London: Macmillan, 1991)

P G A Howells, 'The determination of interest rates', *British Economy Survey*, Vol. 24(2), Section 4

P G A Howells and K Bain, *Financial Markets and Institutions* (London: Longman, 2e 1994) Ch. 7

J M Keynes, *The General Theory of Employment, Interest and Money* (London: Macmillan, 1936) Chs 13, 14

M Livingston, *Money and Capital Markets* (Oxford: Blackwell, 3e 1996)

D T Llewellyn, 'Money market operations of the Bank of England and the determination of interest rates', in *Current*

Issues in Monetary Economics (eds) T Bandopadhyay and S Ghatak (London: Harvester Wheatsheaf, 1990)

F Mishkin, *Financial Markets, Institutions and Money* (New York: Harper Collins, 1995) Chs 3 and 5

Answers to exercises

3.1 (1) 3.8% and 4%.

(2) 4.3% and 5%.

(3) the difference in the methods at low rates is 0.2%, while at the higher rates the difference is 0.7%.

The structure of interest rates

4.1 Introduction

In the last chapter we saw that any nominal interest rate, i, could be seen as the sum of four components:

$$i = r + \pi + l + \sigma \qquad (4.1)$$

where r is the real short-term rate of interest, π is an *inflation* premium, l is a *liquidity* premium, and σ is a premium for *risk*. We then concentrated upon the determination of the first two components in order to develop a theory of short-term nominal interest rates. But we know from everyday observation that any developed financial system is characterized by instruments offering a vast range of different interest rates (a range which expands again when we think about *rates of return*). This *range*, or *structure*, is the result of instruments offering facilities for borrowing and lending over different periods (or *terms*) and with differing degrees of *risk*.

We turn our attention in Section 4.2 to the way in which the term (l) of a loan may affect the rate of interest and in Section 4.3 we shall look at how it may also be affected by risk (σ). Together they give rise to a range of interest rate *differentials* or *spreads*. In Section 4.4 we shall look at two other factors which are often said to influence the structure of interest rates.

Remember, before we begin, that the rate of interest on any asset depends ultimately upon the supply and demand for that asset. The rate of interest on long-term loans therefore depends upon the willingness of lenders to lend long term compared with the desire of borrowers to borrow for long periods. Similarly, a premium on risky assets reflects the comparative unwillingness of holders to hold such assets. It is rather easy, when explaining differentials as the result of certain types of premia, to start to think of these premia as mark-ups which somehow have to be added 'naturally' or 'automatically'. There is nothing natural or inevitable about them. They are created by people's preferences. The market for loans considered as a whole contains a whole range of products which investors see as differentiated by risk and return. The market, in other words, is weakly segmented. The premia paid on loans of different types reflect agents' willingness to hold assets or incur liabilities with different characteristics.

4.2   The effect of term

As we can see from Equation 4.1, we expect both term and risk to be associated with positive *premia*. Indeed, we can turn the equation into a diagram, Figure 4.1.

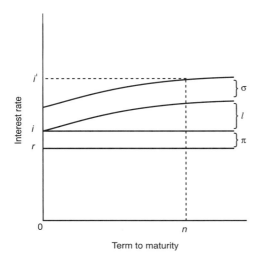

Figure 4.1 The composition of nominal interest rates.

In this diagram, we can see any nominal rate of interest as being made up of 'layers' corresponding to each of four components. r is the real, short-term, risk-free rate. i is the nominal rate, incorporating only an inflation premium. i' is the nominal rate on a risky loan with n years to maturity. Notice that we have drawn the figure with term to maturity on the horizontal axis and that the liquidity premium is shown to increase with the term. The same positive relationship would very likely appear between the risk premium and the degree of risk if we put risk on the horizontal axis.

Figure 4.1 suggests that for a given short-term rate of interest, long-term loans will cost more than short-term loans. The idea that a liquidity premium *positively* related to the term of a loan is 'normal' has a long pedigree and it can be explained in two ways.

The first, and simplest, explanation is the one we touched upon in Section 1.1. There we suggested that lenders generally prefer to lend for the shortest period while borrowers prefer to borrow for the longest possible period. We say 'generally' since preferences will vary between individual investors. Pension funds, for example, are more inclined to hold long-term assets because of their need to earn a guaranteed long-term income. However, if we assume, as seems reasonable, that *on balance* lenders prefer to lend short-term, then borrowers will have to pay lenders a premium for the use of longer-term funds in order to induce them away from their preferred position.

Lenders' preference for short-term loans, in this argument, arises out of uncertainty. Although lenders may *plan* to have funds available for lending for a long period, there is always the danger that they may need to have use of the funds earlier than they planned. Having funds tied up for a long period in those circumstances would then be costly, in either preventing the lender from carrying out urgent spending, or forcing her to borrow and pay interest, or leaving her unable to pay bills, which might in turn spell bankruptcy or at least major embarrassment. Short-term lending thus has a flexibility – the choice to use the funds once again for spending at short notice or to relend if convenient.

Borrowers' preference for long-term loans arises precisely because they wish to avoid the costs associated with having to renegotiate or replace loans when they mature. It helps if we bear in mind that in any economy there are agents who are debtors on a more or less permanent basis (firms, for example). They are not, as individuals might be, borrowing to cover a temporary shortage of funds. They know that when a loan falls due for repayment they will have to replace it and the uncertainty that they face is that the conditions (the rate of interest, for example) on which the loan can be replaced are worse than they were when the original first loan was taken out at the start of the investment project. Borrowers are therefore said to be prepared to pay more for long-term loans in order to avoid this *reinvestment* or *rollover* risk.

The liquidity premium is thus a premium required to tempt lenders from their short-term preference and it is a cost that borrowers are willing to pay in order to have guaranteed long-term use of funds. Notice that in Figure 4.1 the liquidity premium is shown increasing with the term of the loan *but at a diminishing rate*. Clearly, this suggests that lenders are prepared to discriminate sharply between lending for, say, one year and five years but are much less concerned about the difference between, say, a 20-year and a 25-year loan. One might rationalize this in a rather casual way by saying that the difference in length between a four- and five-year loan is 25 per cent while an additional 25 per cent on the term of a 20-year loan is an additional five years. More strictly, the reason for the diminishing rate of increase in the premium lies in the practice of discounting. The present value of any future income flow depends upon the rate at which we discount it and upon the length of time we have to wait for it. If i is an appropriate rate of discount then the discount term (by which we divide the income) is $(1+i)^t$, where t is the number of periods for which we have to wait. The effect of raising this denominator to the power t is to reduce the present value of future income payments quite quickly. Payments in 20 years' time are therefore very heavily discounted and lenders will thus be comparatively indifferent between lending for 20 or for 25 years.

It is not difficult to understand that lenders and borrowers may have different preferences regarding the length of loans and that this might explain the existence of positive liquidity premia. However, the idea that interest rates (and yields and rates of return when we come to them) vary positively with the term to maturity is much more general than its application to loans would suggest. This is because a second, probably more general, consideration is at work to produce such premia. Implicit in our discussion so far is the idea that once a loan is made for x years, it cannot be liquidated until x years have passed (except perhaps at some considerable penalty). This is of course generally true for what we might call *non-marketable loans*, loans of the kind typically made by banks or building societies or even by individuals between themselves. As we said in the introduction to this chapter, the fact that some loans are made for short periods and some for long makes them very highly differentiated products. However,

much lending, particularly where large amounts are concerned, is not of this kind. It involves the borrower issuing some form of instrument which is bought by lenders in a primary market. Such instruments, once issued, are tradeable in a secondary market. Company shares, corporate and government bonds and bills are obvious examples. In such cases, it makes little sense to say that buyers of newly issued 20-year corporate bonds require a liquidity premium to induce them to lend for 20 years, since they could sell the bonds at any time in a highly efficient market in order to retrieve the funds which they had initially lent. Buying a long-dated bond does not therefore mean that one is making a longer-term loan than if one had bought a short-dated bond and yet it is widely accepted in bond markets that, *other things being equal*,[1] longer-dated bonds will often carry a higher yield than shorter-dated ones.

The explanation lies in the behaviour of asset prices when market interest rates change. A firm (or government) which issues 20-year bonds in order to fund a deficit must obviously do so at a *price* and this must be acceptable to the market. Furthermore, the bonds must yield to their buyers a known series of payments which are desirable, at the price which has to be paid. These payments are often indicated by the 'coupon rate' which appears in the title of the bond. (A '10% Exchequer' bond, for example, carries a fixed payment of £10 to its holder every year.) If market interest rates change, the only way in which this fixed series of income payments to bondholders can adjust with them is if the market price of the bonds changes (falling when interest rates rise, for example). In Chapter 10, we shall give a formal proof that the sensitivity of asset prices to changes in interest rates is directly related to a concept known as 'duration', which itself depends upon the remaining life of the asset. Unfortunately, the mathematics are rather intimidating and, again, it is helpful to know more about the characteristics of bonds before attempting the proof. But we can *illustrate* the effect of term fairly easily. Imagine that we are dealing

---

[1] The 'other things' which are crucial are (a) expectations that future interest rates remain as they are now and (b) bonds are homogeneous with respect to default risk.

with a range of fixed-interest bonds which mature at a fixed point in the future. Then the formula for their value is:

$$P = \sum_{t=1}^{n} \frac{Ct}{(1+i)^t} + \frac{M}{(1+i)^n} \qquad (4.2)$$

This expression tells us that the bond's value consists of two elements. These are the sum of the coupon payments ($\sum C_t$) and the final payment of the maturity value (M). Notice that each element of cashflow has to be discounted. t is an index standing for the year (counting from now) in which the payment is made; n is the number of years to maturity. In every case we discount by $(1 + i)$ where i is the current market rate of interest for bonds of this duration and risk.

Imagine now that we are looking at two bonds which differ only in their term to maturity – one matures in two years; the other in five. This means that their redemption values, M, are equal and that their coupon payments C_t are also identical. Suppose that M is £100 and that we are dealing with 10 per cent bonds, so that C_t in each case is £10. The coupon payments are annual. Finally, let us assume that relevant market interest rates are 12 per cent.

The value of the two-year bond consists of the present value of two payments of £10, where the first is received in one years' time and the second in two years' time, plus the value of £100, also receivable in two years' time. From Equation 4.2 we know that each of these payments has to be discounted by the current rate of interest, that is by the term $(1 + 0.12)$. Using discount tables, we can see that the present value of £10 received in one years' time is £8.93. We can also see that £10 two years hence is worth £7.97 now, and that the present value of £100 in two years is £79.72. The total value of these payments, and the present value of this bond, is thus £8.93 + £7.97 + £79.72, or £96.62.

For the five-year bond we have a series of five payments, the first payable in one year and the last in five years. The value of this income stream, again discounted by the factor 1.12, is:

£8.93 + £7.97 + £7.12 + £6.36 + £5.67 = £36.05

The present value of £100 received in five years is £56.74, making the present value of the bond £92.79.

Now suppose that interest rates fall to 8 per cent. We should by now be familiar with the *direction* of

the effect which will be to increase the value of both bonds, but the question is by exactly how much in each case? The answer can be found by working through Exercise 4.1. This should be done before reading on.

Exercise 4.1   The effect of term on bond values

(a) Following the example in the text, find the present value of a 10 per cent bond, maturing for £100 in two years' time when the rate of interest is 8 per cent.

(b) Find the value of a five-year bond, with the same characteristics, when the rate of interest is 8 per cent.

(c) Compare their present values at this rate of interest.

(d) Now compare the present values calculated with interest rates at 8 per cent with the values calculated (in the text) when interest rates were 12 per cent. Which bond shows the largest price rise when interest rates fall?

When interest rates are 8 per cent, the present value of a 10 per cent bond maturing in two years is £103.56 (£9.26 + £8.57 + £85.73). The value of a five-year bond of identical characteristics in the same circumstances is £107.98 (£9.26 + £8.57 + £7.94 + £7.35 + £6.80 + £68.06). We can now compare the prices for these two bonds at the two different rates of interest. Table 4.1 summarizes the results.

Table 4.1 Term and value

Interest rate (i)	Term (n)	
	$n = 2$	$n = 5$
$i = 0.12$	96.62	92.79
$i = 0.08$	103.56	107.98

For a four-point change in interest rates, we can see that the price of a two-year bond changes by £6.94 (£103.56 – £96.62), equivalent to 7.2 per cent, while the price of a five-year bond changes by £15.19 (£107.98 – £92.79), equivalent to 16.4 per cent.

Thus, the fact that assets can be sold in secondary markets means that lenders can retrieve their funds (a long-term loan is not illiquid provided it is marketable) but what we have just demonstrated suggests that the risk that prices might be above or below what sellers require is greater for long-dated than short-dated loans. Hence, given certain other assumptions, we might expect a term-related premium to be paid, even on loans which are marketable, if they are loans made at a fixed rate of interest. The relationship between the yield on assets and their term to maturity, a subject known as the *term structure of interest rates*, is a major issue in financial economics, with a number of important applications. To discuss it in depth, we need to know more about the characteristics of assets, particularly bonds, and asset markets so we defer further discussion until Chapter 10. We accept, for now, that *positive* term premia are likely because of the preferences of lenders (for lending short in the case of non-marketable loans and for minimizing capital risk with marketable ones) and the preferences of borrowers (for borrowing long).

4.3 The effect of risk

We said in Section 3.2 that interest rates influence behaviour which involves commitments over a period of time. Loans are made for a period (even if they can be sold on in a secondary market, the original *intention* was a commitment for a period). Debts are entered into for a period of time. It will often be more difficult for a borrower than for a lender to get out of a loan contract since the funds may well have been invested in a long-term project with a long payback period. All of this means that lenders and borrowers are entering into contracts which involve some degree of *risk*.

As we already know from Section 2.2, 'risk' in financial terms refers to the possibility that outcomes may differ from what was expected and it is usually assumed that the degree of risk can be measured and expressed as a probability statement, calculated on the basis of past outcomes. The risk thought to attach to an individual loan or asset is thus obviously one element in the size of the risk premium. Remember (from Section 2.4) though that there is a second element. This is the 'price of risk'. By this we mean the price of 'average' or 'standard' risk and in Section 2.4 we saw that this is often taken to be represented by the difference in the rate of return on a portfolio of assets representative of the whole population of risky assets and the return on risk-free assets. We called this the 'market price of risk' and we noted that it would rise or fall with changes in the community's degree of risk aversion. The risk premium, σ, paid on a particular loan or asset will depend therefore upon the riskiness or the perceived riskiness of the loan itself relative to the representative portfolio multiplied by the market price of average or standard risk. A change in the risk premium, therefore, can be the result of changes in the characteristic of the asset (a change in its own riskiness) or the result of changes in the level of risk aversion in the community at large.

Risk can take many *forms*. For example, one can distinguish *default* risk (the borrower cannot repay the principal) from *capital risk* (the loan has a lower nominal value when it terminates – a possibility if one has to sell bonds in the open market rather than wait to maturity, for example) and from *income risk* (the possibility that the flow of interest, dividends or other payments are less than were expected).[2]

These forms of risk can have various sources. For example, it is common in the finance literature to distinguish between *business risk*, which means the risk which arises from the nature of the activity to which the borrower intends to apply the borrowed funds, and *financial risk*, the additional risk which arises from the overall pattern of financing that the borrower chooses.

We know also (from Section 2.4) that some risk attaching to individual assets (specific risk) can be diversified away by combining assets in a portfolio. When all the gains from diversification have been exploited, however, the fact remains that some loans will be riskier than others (by virtue of their differing

2 Notice that lenders making fixed interest but marketable loans (for example, bonds) are in effect avoiding income risk but only at the expense of accepting capital risk (the risk that they may have to sell before maturity at a price which is different from that which would be expected at maturity). This is the case that we discussed in the last section and one might say, therefore, that what we there called a 'term' premium could be seen as a 'risk' premium to compensate for the interest-sensitivity of bond prices.

exposure to market risk). It seems reasonable to suppose that savers willing to lend, let us say, £1 million at 10 per cent to a risk-free borrower would require a larger reward if they were to lend the same amount for a risky purpose. Thus lenders require a 'risk premium', a payment over and above the risk-free rate to induce them to lend a given amount. In a diagram, the supply curve of risky funds lies above the risk-free supply curve by the amount of this premium. The premium itself, of course, varies with the degree of risk and the market's attitude to risk.

Exercise 4.2   Interest rates – term and risk

1   Check the financial press to find the current yield on government bonds. Sketch roughly in a graph any relationship that you can see between the return and the term to maturity. (Hint: use *redemption yield*.)

2   Check the financial press for the return on corporate bonds. How does the return on corporate bonds compare with the return on government bonds? What explanation can you offer for any differential?

3   Let us suppose that we observe a premium in the rate of return on corporate bonds over the rate on government bonds and that over a period of time we see this premium increasing. What conclusions might we be tempted to draw?

Thus large corporations may be able to borrow by issuing corporate bonds which offer a rate which is only slighter greater than the rate paid by government on its bonds. On the other hand, we should expect that ordinary company shares will generally pay a better return (dividend payments plus capital growth) than corporate or government bonds. This is because dividends are variable and because the claims of ordinary shareholders, both to profits and to residual assets in the event of bankruptcy, rank well behind the claims of other creditors and of subscribers of fixed-interest capital.

4.4   Expectations and government borrowing

So far, we have said that different types of asset/liability will carry different rates of interest because they are essentially different products. They are differentiated by term and by risk. In this section, however, we shall see that even if we take a subset of instruments which look homogeneous, we may still see a range of interest rates payable on them. Our subset could be government bonds, or treasury bills, or, possibly, interbank deposits. In each of these categories, within any national market, the default risk is uniform (and very close to zero in most countries). European governments are not generally expected to default on their bond or bill obligations and, even if they were, there is no basis to suppose that default is more likely on long- rather than short-dated bonds or vice versa. Similarly, the market for interbank deposits is dominated by a few major banks of equal creditworthiness. Furthermore, within each category the instruments are homogeneous in the sense that they can be instantly traded, regardless of maturity. A three-month treasury bill does not require a longer commitment of funds than a one-month treasury bill. And yet it is usually the case that if we plot the interest rate (usually called the 'yield' in this context) against the term to maturity, we observe a pattern to which a smooth curve can usually be fairly closely fitted. This plot is known as a *time-yield curve*.[3]

The most commonly advanced explanation for a systematic relationship between yields and term, among assets which are homogeneous except with respect to term to maturity, is *expectations of future interest rates*. The argument is that if people expect short-term interest rates to be higher (lower) than they are now, *current* long-term rates will be above (below) current short rates; that is, expectations about *future* changes affect the *current* structure. Why the present should be influenced by events which have not yet incurred seems rather mysterious. But a moment's thought makes it at least intuitively

---

3 We shall look at time-yield curves, their construction and interpretation, in more detail in Chapter 10. We shall see, for example, that 'yield' (for bonds in particular) can be measured in a number of different ways. For the moment, readers who wish to scan the bond yield columns of a financial newspaper to form a mental picture or to do a freehand drawing of a current time-yield curve, should use the figures in the column showing 'redemption yield', or its equivalent.

obvious. Lenders willing to lend for a period longer than the minimum available clearly have a choice. They can either lend for the shortest possible period and then re-lend at the end of that period and re-lend again and so on, or they can agree to lend now for just one period corresponding to their investment horizon. Assume that the yield curve is stable. This must mean that lenders and borrowers are broadly happy with the current pattern of interest rates and therefore we have an equilibrium position. (If they were not, then there would be a general shift towards lending long, or vice versa, and the yield curve would be changing its shape.) If we have equilibrium, then it follows that lenders are currently indifferent about whether they lend for a series of short periods or one longer period. If we ask ourselves, 'in what circumstances would investors be indifferent between a series of short loans and one long loan?', the answer ought to strike us quickly that they will be indifferent when the returns they expect from both strategies are equal. In other words, the reward for the long strategy must be equal to what lenders think they will get from a series of short loans. The reward for the long strategy must equal the average of the series of short loans. This is where expected future rates enter the picture. Since we can only know the *current* short loan rate, we have to make an educated guess at likely *future* short rates. What we guess must be responsible for any observed difference between current short and long rates. That is, expected future short rates are implicit in any difference between current long and short rates.

Suppose for simplicity that a short loan is for one year and a long loan is for two years. Suppose, furthermore, that the current short rate (i_s) is 6 per cent while the current long rate (i_L) is 8 per cent. If this differential is stable then lenders are happy with the prospect of what they will earn by lending for one year and then renewing at the expected one-year rate compared with what they would get by lending now for two years. Formally, it must be the case that they expect:

$$(1 + i_s)\,(1 + \hat{i}_s) = (1 + i_L)^2$$

where $\hat{i}_s$ is the expected *future* short-term (one-year) rate.

Rearranging gives us:

$$(1 + \hat{i}_s) = (1 + i_L)^2 / (1 + i_s)$$

Substituting actual values gives:

$$(1 + \hat{i}_s) = (1.08)^2 / (1.06)$$
$$= 1.1664 / 1.06 \approx 1.10$$

If $(1 + \hat{i}_s) = 1.10$, then $\hat{i}_s = 1.10 - 1 = 0.10$ or 10%

In this example, therefore, we can see that if current short rates are 6 per cent and long rates are 8 per cent then this suggests that people expect short rates to rise to 10 per cent before the second period begins.

In this example, therefore, the yield curve slopes upward and long-dated bonds have a higher yield not because they involve a greater sacrifice of liquidity than short-dated bonds but because their current yield persuades those willing to lend for a longer period that they will do just as well from long-dated bonds as they will from holding a succession of short-dated ones, bearing in mind what is expected to happen to interest rates on short-dated bonds in future. Conversely, if the market expected short rates to fall in future, the yield curve would be downward-sloping. The argument then would be that investors would still be willing to hold (lower yielding) long-dated bonds because this would give them the same return as a succession of short-dated bonds, bearing in mind that short rates in future would be lower than they are now, and indeed lower than current long rates.

The relationship between yields on assets differentiated only by their term to maturity is known as the *term structure of interest rates* and we shall return to it in Chapter 10 when we study government bonds in more detail. The term structure (the shape of the yield curve) is an issue of great interest to economists precisely because it may be dominated by markets' perceptions of future interest rates. For example, if it does, and if those perceptions were generally correct, then we could use the yield curve and our calculations above to derive future *implied* short-term rates, that is, to calculate what future short-term rates were expected to be. The yield curve would be a useful forecasting tool. Furthermore, if we were to combine the yield curve with the Fisher hypothesis (see Section 3.3.1) then we could derive future implied interest rates and implied *inflation* rates.

To say that expectations of *future* short-term rates determine the relationship between *current* long and short rates is one thing, however; knowing what affects expectations is something else. And yet profitable investment in financial markets would be much easier if we did know how expectations were going to change. For example, we saw in Section 4.2 that bond prices would change inversely with changes in interest rates (and that long-dated bond prices would change by more than short-dated ones). Obviously, therefore, investors will wish to sell bonds if they expect interest rates to rise and to buy them if they expect a fall. Notice then that the expectation itself is sufficient to cause the changes in prices and yields that were expected! For an individual investor, the trick is to be first to anticipate any change in expectation.

One obvious source of influence on expectations will be all those events that markets think may herald a change in inflation. Faster credit growth, rapid falls in unemployment, a rise in imports relative to exports may all suggest that prices will rise more rapidly in future. If one assumes that higher inflation means higher interest rates, without necessarily believing in the full rigours of the Fisher hypothesis, then all these events suggest higher (rather than lower) future interest rates, and the yield curve will steepen.

Frequently anticipating changes in future rates of interest (and anticipating changes in expectations of changes) involves an appraisal of the authorities' monetary policy objectives and thus how policy instruments may be changed in response to events. This is easily understood in the light of our discussion about central banks' influence on short-term interest rates in Section 3.4. If the government is known to desire low inflation above all else, then all of the events that we mentioned in the last paragraph become connected with higher interest rates through a second channel: the authorities' response. For a real example, we may recall that in the early 1980s many governments pursued explicit money supply growth targets. Thus an overshoot, for example, in the figures immediately led to expectations that the authorities would raise short-term rates in order to reduce monetary growth in future. The consequence would be that the yield curve would steepen, showing an expectation of a regime of higher short-term rates in future. A rise in long-term rates means, of course, a fall in the price of longer-dated bonds and one can trace the markets' changing perceptions of what really mattered to the

authorities by tracing the changes in events to which bond prices are sensitive. In the early 1980s, as we just observed, the bond market was very sensitive to money growth figures. In the UK, this became less important in the mid-1980s, when money growth targets fell out of fashion and the market (and the yield curve) became very sensitive instead to quite small movements in the exchange rate, as the authorities were believed to have a policy of shadowing the Deutschmark.

One issue which has always had a significant effect upon the shape of the yield curve is the level of government borrowing. Financial markets in all countries pay close attention to the monthly government borrowing figures in relation to the anticipated outturn. As we have seen above, this may be for two seemingly conflicting reasons.

Firstly, higher than expected public sector borrowing may cause fears of a willingness on the part of the authorities to tolerate higher inflation than the market would like. In such cases, the markets are assuming that the increase in debt is likely to be financed by borrowing from the banking sector with a consequent increase in bank deposits and the money supply. Although the form of the link between the rate of growth of the money supply and the rate of inflation remains controversial both theoretically and empirically, there can be no doubt that there is a strong acceptance within financial markets of the proposition that money-financed government debt will cause inflation. As long as that remained true, an increase in government debt would generate inflationary expectations and creditors would demand higher interest rates in future to preserve the real rate of return on their funds. Given the time lags involved in monetary policy, however, we would not be talking here about an immediate increase in the inflation rate, but an increase more than a year hence. The yield curve would steepen from that point on.

On the other hand, if the authorities in question have a reputation established over a number of years of being tough on inflation, the markets may react to higher than expected public sector borrowing in a quite different way – assuming that the government would finance this increase in debt by borrowing from the non-bank public with the possibility that interest rates would need to rise immediately to bring this about. Even if it were possible for the government to borrow more from the non-bank public without interest rates having to rise, inflation-conscious authorities would very likely act to cause interest rates at the short end of the market to rise, precisely because it would be aware of the market fears of inflation mentioned in the previous paragraph. In such a case, an announcement of higher than expected borrowing would produce an expectation of an increase in short interest rates not accompanied by fears of longer-term inflation. The shape of the yield curve would clearly be different in this case from the previous one even though the markets would in both cases expect interest rates to rise at some point.

We have suggested that the assessment by the markets of the likely response of the authorities to higher government borrowing depends on the authorities' past anti-inflationary reputation. Much also depends on institutional arrangements. A strong belief has developed in recent years that central banks (such as the Bundesbank) which are constitutionally independent of government are likely to operate tougher monetary policies than those which are, in varying degrees, dominated by government. Thus, higher than expected government borrowing in Germany would very likely produce an expectation of an immediate increase in short-term interest rates, in contrast to the United Kingdom and Italy where such an announcement might produce fears of future inflation. These fears would be all the greater if there were an election in prospect because the markets would assume that the government would be unwilling to raise either taxes or interest rates for fear of losing votes.

There has recently been an interesting development in the German yield curve which can be traced to these market attitudes. It is generally expected that, despite strong German statements to the contrary, the European Central Bank, which is to operate monetary policy after the establishment of European Monetary Union (still scheduled to occur in 1999), will be less able to adopt a tough anti-inflationary stance than the Bundesbank currently does. For this reason, the markets are expecting an increase in German inflation after 1999 and German interest rates have increased sharply on financial instruments maturing after that date. This emphas-

izes the point that it is what is believed in financial markets which is crucial here. Whether any economic analysis underlying these beliefs is sound is of little relevance.

4.5   Summary

Any developed economy offers a wide range of financial instruments to lenders and borrowers. These offer a correspondingly wide range of rates of interest or other forms of return. The minimum return that will be available will be the risk-free, short-term nominal rate of interest. This will be available, obviously, on very short-term loans of zero risk. In practice, the rate on one-month treasury bills might be representative. Everything else will offer a rate of return in excess of this. On top of the short-term, risk-free rate there sits a structure of interest rates. This structure is determined by the willingness of lenders to hold assets which are not risk-free and short-term, relative to their supply. We generalize that two characteristics in particular affect demand. These are 'term' and 'risk' and they affect demand negatively. That is to say that as term and risk increase, lenders, on balance, become less willing to hold such assets and require 'premia' to induce them to do so. As we have said many times, lenders are assumed to be risk averse and to be attracted by liquidity.

But there many other influences on supply and demand for funds and if these operate in respect of particular classes of funds then they will contribute to the structure of interest differentials. One set of influences is the expectation that people hold about future movements in interest rates. Their investment decisions now will try to take account of future possible returns and those decisions will affect the current structure. Another influence, which has been topical in recent years, has been the public sector's demand for funds. If this demand were uniform across funds of all types, of course it would be irrelevant to the *structure* of rates. But, as we have seen, governments tend to borrow funds at longer maturities and this can, certainly in principle, affect relative returns.

Key concepts used in this chapter

Term premium	Implied future rates
Liquidity premium	Reinvestment risk
Risk premium	Non-marketable loans
Term structure	Default risk
Time yield curve	Capital risk
Interest-elasticity	Income risk
Interest spreads	

Questions and problems

1 Why might lenders demand a premium for lending long-term?

2 Does your answer to (1) explain why long-dated bonds often have higher yields than short-dated ones? If not, what alternative explanation can you offer?

3 Look at the financial press and find the current interest spread between 5-year and 10-year government bonds. Is there a positive term premium?

4 What conclusion might you draw about possible future interest rates if a positive term premium were to increase?

5 What name do we give to the pattern of yields available on bonds of different maturities?

6 Using the financial press, compare the redemption yield on one or more *corporate* bonds with that on *government* bonds with a similar term to maturity. How would you explain any differential?

7 What conclusions might you draw about future developments in the economy if corporate yields were to rise relative to yields on government bonds?

Further reading

A D Bain, *The Financial System* (Oxford: Blackwell, 2e 1992) Chs 5, 6

D Blake, *Financial Market Analysis* (London: McGraw-Hill, 1990) Ch. 2

R Glenn Hubbard, *Money, the Financial System and the Economy* (Reading MA: Addison Wesley, 2e 1997)

C A E Goodhart, *Money, Infomation and Uncertainty* (London: Macmillan, 2e 1989) Ch. XI

P G A Howells and K Bain, *Financial Markets and Institutions* (London: Longman, 2e 1994) Ch. 7

M Livingston, *Money and Capital Markets* (Oxford: Blackwell, 3e 1996)

F Mishkin, *Financial Markets, Institutions and Money* (New York: Harper Collins, 1995) Ch. 6

CHAPTER 5 The valuation of assets

Box 5.1

What you will learn in this chapter:

- How the risk-free rate of interest combines with a risk premium to determine the required rate of return on an asset
- Why it is that, in equilibrium, a tradeable asset will be priced so as to yield the required rate of return
- How to use the required rate of return to analyse asset price movements within a supply and demand framework
- The connection between the required rate of return and the 'fundamentals' of an asset's value
- Some of the implications of a market's failure to price assets according to their required rate of return

5.1   Introduction

In this chapter we want to bring together what we have learned so far from Parts 1 and 2 of this book, but especially from Chapters 2, 3 and 4. In Chapter 1 (Sections 1.4 and 1.5.3) we explained that other things being equal the price of assets moved inversely with their rate of return. Thus it follows that if we know the required rate of return, then (again all else being given) we know the price at which assets will be willingly held. In Chapter 2, therefore, we concentrated on the determination of the required rate of return. This, we said, would be equal to the risk-free rate of return and a risk premium calculated from the price of 'average' or whole market risk and the asset's individual risk characteristics relative to those of the market as a whole. An asset that is 'fairly

priced' will yield a return which places it on the security market line. The equation for asset A is:

$$\bar{K}_A = K_{rf} + \beta_A (K_m - K_{rf}) \qquad (5.1)$$

and we can interpret Equation 5.1, less formally, as saying that:

the required rate of return	=	the risk-free rate	+	the quantity of risk	×	the price of risk

In Chapter 3 we went on to explore the determination of the risk-free, short-term rate of interest. We said that this is the outcome of market forces, represented by the demand for and supply of loanable funds (where this included the money-creating activities of banks) modified, in some situations by the administrative decisions of central banks. In symbols, $K_{rf} = i = r + \pi$.

The 'fair' price of an asset will be such that:

$$K_A =$$

K_{rf} : The short term, risk-free rate of interest. The result of the interaction beween the supply of, and demand for, loanable funds, including banks' creation of money, and the intervention of central banks. In the terms of Chapter 3: $$K_{rf} = r + \pi$$

$$+$$

β_A: The share's β-coefficient, expressing its riskiness in relation to the riskiness of the whole market portfolio. From Section 2.5 we know that $$\beta_A = \frac{\mathrm{cov}\, K_A, K_m}{\sigma_m{}^2}$$

$$\times$$

$K_m - K_{rf}$: The premium required to induce investors to hold the level of risk associated with the whole market portfolio. This is the only fully-diversified portfolio that rational investors will hold (see Section 2.5).

Figure 5.1 The origin of the required rate of return.

We want now to see formally how it is that the required rate of return determines asset prices and how changes in the required rate cause asset prices to change. We can analyse the behaviour of asset prices using the conventional supply and demand apparatus. The theme of the rest of this chapter, therefore, is how we can incorporate changes in the required rate of return into a supply and demand framework. After some preliminary clarification (in Section 5.2) we shall do this (in Section 5.3) by looking at the markets for two 'stylized' assets, company shares and fixed-interest bonds. We say 'stylized' because we shall only describe these assets and their markets in the barest essentials – only as much as we need to understand the theory. The detail of these markets, and others, is discussed in Part 4 of this book.

Throughout Part 2 of this book we have been trying to provide an intelligible account of the orthodox theory of portfolio choice and asset valuation. In Section 5.4, therefore, we take a little space to raise some critical questions about the orthodox theory and to suggest that there are other, more controversial, ways of interpreting the processes that we have described so far.

Before we begin, though, we need to be absolutely clear what it is that we are trying to explain. Some preliminary clarification is therefore provided in the next section.

5.2 Supply and demand in asset markets

When we apply a supply and demand framework to the valuation of assets, there are two pairs of distinctions that it is useful to make. The first is the distinction between assets that are tradeable between third parties and those which can only be 'bought' and 'sold' between the original supplier and the original buyer. The second distinction is between stocks of assets and flows. We have met both of them before, in Sections 1.4.1 and 1.2.4 respectively. Most of us are likely to be more familiar with supply and demand as applied to flows – of newly created goods and services per period of time, for example. But we shall see that stock demand is at least as important in financial markets.

Tradeable assets

Let us assume to begin with that we are dealing with tradeable assets. These are securities like bonds, bills or company shares which, after issue, can be bought and resold many times. At any particular time, there exists a very large number of these assets. This is a *stock*. There may also be new issues taking place, in which case there is also a *flow* causing the stock to expand. In practice, the stock is likely to be very large relative to the flow and, frequently indeed, the flow will be zero. In equilibrium, this stock must be willingly held. This does not mean that there will be no trading. It simply means that another set of *flows*, the flows of orders to sell, match the flows of orders to buy at the prevailing market price. Clearly, in equilibrium, the price at which the stock is willingly held must be the same as the price at which trading is taking place. A fall (for example) in the price at which trades are taking place can only occur if the numbers wishing to sell at the earlier price increase relative to buyers and this means that more holders of the stock think it currently overvalued than think it currently undervalued. In trading, the price falls to a new equilibrium (sell orders match buy orders) only when once again the balance of those thinking it overvalued is matched by those who think it undervalued. Explaining the price of financial assets, therefore, amounts to explaining what it is that makes holders of the *stock* of assets willing to hold the stock at a given price. Furthermore, since changes in the stock (as a result of new issues, or cancellations for that matter) are small relative to the size of the stock and discontinuous, discussions of changes in price come down in practice to discussing changes in *demand* for the stock. The question becomes one of 'what makes investors change their view of the value of these assets?'. The appropriate diagrams are stock diagrams. The supply curve is vertical (and subject to small rightward movements as new issues take place). The demand curve is downward-sloping and it is shifts in the demand curve that occupy most of our attention when we discuss asset price changes.

This does not make flows irrelevant. Firstly, as we just said, flows of new issues cause the stock to expand. Continuous government borrowing on a sufficiently large scale could cause the stock of bonds to expand so rapidly that the price might fall, for example. Furthermore, we are sometimes interested in the details of the trading process itself. This happens when we come to discuss the role of 'market makers' in different trading systems. As we noted above, market makers are dealing in *flows* of orders to buy and sell and in making a margin or profit out of those orders. When we look specifically at the role of market makers we shall encounter more familiar supply and demand diagrams with flows on the horizontal axis and upward-sloping supply curves. Trading systems are among the institutional details which we postpone until Part 4 of this book.

Non-tradeable assets

Although, of course, we can still bring our conventional supply and demand apparatus to the analysis of markets for non-tradeable assets, the situation is rather different from the one we have just described. With tradeable assets, there exists a stock to be traded which exists even if the issuer of the assets decided to issue no more. With banks, savings institutions, insurance companies, pension funds and so on assets can be disposed of only by returning them to the originator and, in complete contrast with securities markets, the originator of the asset cannot stand aside from the demand. If there is an increase in the demand for IBM shares, for example, (because people think they are undervalued) this requires no immediate response from IBM. If there is an increase in the demand for insurance contracts from Allianz, by contrast, the firm can supply more. If demand continues at a high level, Allianz may revise the terms on which it issues the contracts, making them less favourable to investors but more profitable to itself, but it cannot stand aloof in the way that a company can from the market for its shares. This gives us a number of problems about the way in which we use our supply and demand apparatus.

Firstly, in most of these cases of non-tradeable assets there is no explicit price. There is an explicit yield, or rate of return, which *implies* a price but we normally draw supply and demand diagrams with respect to price. If we draw them with respect to yield, then the slopes must be reversed. As the yield on an asset rises, more investors will be willing to buy it, *cet. par.* By contrast, the higher the yield demanded by investors, the less willing issuers will

be to issue contracts. Secondly, there is the question of whether we are dealing with a stock or a flow. The correct answer to this is that we should deal with whichever seems to provide the most useful insights in a given situation. The apparatus is only a means to an end. In practice, the answer probably depends upon the time period in which we conduct the analysis. Of course institutions are opening new deposit accounts, new insurance, new pensions contracts and so on all the time. But accounts and contracts are being closed on a continuous basis too. The net flows may be very small or even zero in the short run. In this case we are dealing with a stock. The supply curve is vertical (and the demand curve slopes upward with yield on the vertical axis, remember). On the other hand, if the focus of attention is a longer period, we may prefer to discuss supply as a flow (with the supply curve sloping downward).

5.3 Asset valuation

Real assets are goods that provide a flow of output or services over a period of time. The output or service has a monetary value and so we can talk about assets as goods which yield a future stream of income. *Financial* assets are claims upon the real assets and upon their future income stream. The basic principle in the orthodox valuation of assets is that:

> the (present) value of an asset is equal to the sum of its future income stream (net of running costs), suitably discounted.

Notice that this gives rise, in theory, to an identity between the value of the underlying *real* assets (the sum of their discounted future income stream) and the value of the financial assets whose own income stream is simply the income generated by the real assets passed on to the current owners of those real assets. (We shall see in Chapter 11 that this identity may need to be modified in practice to take account of taxation.) Thus the value of a firm, for example, is equal to the future discounted income stream from the assets which make up the firm and this *should* (assuming no tax) be equal to the market value of the shares in issue.

The practical difficulties of asset valuation revolve around estimating the future income stream (which is at best uncertain), estimating the running costs, and choosing an appropriate rate of discount. These are very real difficulties. In practice, they are to some extent side-stepped by concentrating upon *relative* valuation. That means that most of the time practitioners in financial markets are looking to see whather an individual asset is over- or undervalued when compared with other assets for which it is a very close substitute. In these circumstances, it does not matter whether we view all assets as over- or undervalued because of an error that we make in estimating future income streams (for example), provided that the error is reproduced across all assets. We shall do the same and thus we focus here upon the third step, the discounting process. The next two sections are devoted to showing that the required rate of return provides the appropriate rate of discount.

5.3.1 Valuing company shares

Ordinary company shares provide their owners with a perpetual claim upon the earnings or profits of a firm. What is actually paid to shareholders is known as a *dividend* and is variable. This variability results firstly from the fact that earnings themselves are variable; secondly, from the fact that other people and agencies (bondholders and the tax authorities, for example) have a prior claim on those earnings and the size of this claim may vary; thirdly, the firm may decrease (increase) its 'payout ratio' if it wishes to increase (decrease) the size of its retained earnings, to finance real investment. This variability, combined with the fact that shareholders' claims on residual assets rank low in the event of bankruptcy, explains why company shares are generally regarded as having comparatively high total risk.

However, since the dividend payment is a claim on earnings and earnings are expected to increase over time (as a result of real productivity gains and inflation), dividends in a well-managed firm usually show an upward trend over a period of years. Clearly, if dividend payments are not to become infinitely large relative to a share's price (or alternatively if there is some 'normal', long-run relationship between dividend payments and prices) it follows

that a share's price will also follow an upward trend over a period of years. This capital appreciation may be a significant part of the total return on shares and thus a significant part of their attraction to investors.

The total return on company shares is thus made up of two elements, the *dividend yield* and the *rate of capital appreciation*. The dividend yield is simply the current dividend (D) divided by the market price (P) while the rate of capital appreciation is the capital gain made from holding the share while its price rises. Strictly speaking, it is the difference in price at the end of the period compared with the price at the beginning expressed as a percentage of the price at the beginning. If we denote this difference by g, then:

$$g = (P_1 - P_0) / P_0 \qquad (5.2)$$

and the total return can then be written as:

$$\overline{K} = D/P + g \qquad (5.3)$$

A very simple rearrangement of Equation 5.3 gives us an expression for price:

$$P = D/(\overline{K} - g) \qquad (5.4)$$

In equilibrium, therefore, given their dividend payments and growth prospects, the price of company shares depends upon the required rate of return. In Chapter 11 we shall see that Equation 5.4 is known as the Gordon constant growth model of share valuation. This is because we have implicitly assumed that g, the rate of capital appreciation, is constant. The treatment of the rate of capital appreciation is problematic and thus the Gordon model is just one of several we look at later, distinguished by the way in which they handle the growth issue. What they all share in common, however, is the presence of $\overline{K}$, the required rate of return in the denominator. Provided that this is the case then, with other things – dividend payments and growth – given, the price must *always* be determined by the required rate of return.

This is easily illustrated by substituting some plausible values in Equation 5.4. If, for example, a company, XYZ plc, were paying a dividend of 25p per share while the rate of capital appreciation were 15 per cent and the overall return required by shareholders were 22 per cent, then the share would be priced at:

= 25p / 0.22 – 0.15

= 357p

If now the required rate of return were to increase to 28 per cent, then the new price would be:

= 25p / 0.28 – 0.15

= 192p

A further example is provided in Exercise 5.1.

Box 5.1   Prices and rates of return

Assume that a share pays a single, annual dividend (D) and that the annual rate of capital appreciation is denoted by g, then we know that the annual rate of return, K, can be found from the expression:

$K = D/P + g$

Suppose that the rate of capital appreciation is 10% p.a. and the dividend payment is 30p.

(1) Find the current rate of return if the share's price is £3.75.
(2) Find the current rate of return if the share's price were £5.00.
(3) If the market thought a rate of return of 20% appropriate, what would happen to the share's price?

(Answers appear in Figure 5.2 below.)

Figure 5.2 shows how we can interpret these changes in rates of return and prices in a supply and demand framework. Notice firstly that the supply of shares in XYZ is a *stock*. If XYZ were in process of issuing new shares, the stock would be expanding but with no new issues the existing stock remains available for trading. This is shown by the vertical supply curve, S, in Figure 5.2. (The values in Figure 5.2 are the answers to the questions in Exercise 5.1.)

The demand curve for XYZ shares is shown by D. It slopes downward on the basis that the lower the price of XYZ shares, *ceteris paribus*, the higher their rate of return and thus the greater the demand for them. The initial equilibrium is shown by the intersection of the two curves and the equilibrium price is £3.75. (Notice that at this price, the rate of return is 18 per cent.) At this price (rate of return) sell orders match buy orders.

Let us imagine now, as in Exercise 5.1, that the required rate of return increases to 20 per cent. Shares in XYZ are less attractive at any given price than they previously were. At the original price of £3.75 sell orders exceed buy orders. This is shown by the downward shift in the demand curve from D to D''. At the original equilibrium price of £3.75 the shortfall in demand is shown by the distance ac. The new equilibrium price, the price at which the existing stock is willingly held, in the sense that sell orders match buy orders, is £3.00.

Finally, suppose that there is an increase in demand for the shares. The demand curve shifts to D'. At £3.75 there is excess demand, shown by ab, and buy orders exceed sell orders. The price rises. Let us suppose that it rises to a new equilibrium of £5.00. At £5.00, equation 5.3 tells us that the rate of return has fallen to 16 per cent.

In equilibrium, therefore, price settles at a level which equates the actual rate of return with the required rate of return. Notice that this equilibrium condition also implies that the firm's cost of capital is equal to the required rate of return. The cost of capital is the rate of return which a firm has to pay in order to raise additional funds. If the going rate of return on its existing shares is 16 per cent, then the cost of capital from a new share issue (ignoring transaction costs) is 16 per cent. In other words, the firms has to earn a 16 per cent return on its real capital which it then divides – paying some as

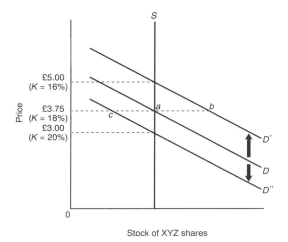

Figure 5.2 The demand for assets and their rate of return.

dividends and retaining the rest to ensure a rate of growth adequate to make a total return to shareholders of 16 per cent. In equilibrium, the going rate of return and cost of capital will equal the required rate of return. This is important, since we can now see that changes in the required rate of return not only lead to changes in price but also to changes in the cost of capital and thus, presumably, in the allocation of new funds which will always seek the best return for a given level of risk. In Section 5.4, we shall see that if assets are indeed priced (and the cost of capital is determined) by the required rate of return as we have suggested here, then an argument can be made that resource allocation is optimal. If asset prices and the cost of capital are not determined in the way described in this section, there are adverse implications for resource allocation. This possibility is explored in Section 5.5.

5.3.2 Valuing fixed interest bonds

Unlike company shares, fixed interest bonds provide their holders with a fixed income stream. In the UK, the income payments are known as *coupons*. Coupon payments can be expressed as a *coupon rate* by dividing by the par value of the bond. The coupon rate is often incorporated into the title of the bond alongside other information. For example, *Treasury 10% 2005* is a bond which pays £10 per annum to its holder and will mature (or be redeemed) in the year 2005. Notice that its *residual maturity* is the length of time from now to the redemption date. Its *original maturity* may have been very long (if it was issued many years ago) or it may have been quite short. We simply cannot tell. It is fortunate, therefore, that we are more interested in residual than original maturity. The income stream of such bonds amounts to a series of (known) coupon payments plus a terminal payment, which is also known and which is the redemption value of the bond. In these circumstances, the value of the bond is found by using the following expression (which we first met in Section 4.2):

$$P = \sum_{t=1}^{n} \frac{C_t}{(1+i)^t} + \frac{M}{(1+i)^n} \qquad (5.5)$$

However, some fixed interest bonds have no redemption or maturity date. These are sometimes called *perpetuals* or *consols*. The value of bonds with no redemption date can be found by setting $n_m = \infty$ in Equation 5.5.[1] With $n = \infty$, Equation 5.5 simplifies to:

$$P = C/i \qquad (5.6)$$

Irredeemable bonds are rather like company shares with zero growth and we can see this if we compare Equation 5.6 with Equation 5.3. If we eliminate g and we substitute C ('coupon') for D ('dividend') then Equation 5.6 is the same as Equation 5.3, except that Equation 5.6 has i rather than K in the denominator. But a few moments' reflection reveals that K and i are equivalents: they are both rates of return and, in equilibrium, when the asset is fairly priced, both i and K will equal the required rate of return for their respective assets. For example, by rearranging Equation 5.6 we can see that:

$$i = C/P \qquad (5.7)$$

and that i is thus the running yield calculated as the perpetual coupon payment divided by the price paid for the bond. The question remains, however, 'why, in equilibrium, are i (or K) also required rates of return?' This can be best answered by posing some other questions. 'Why should they not be the rates that investors *require*?' 'If the assets can be easily bought and sold, why should investors accept a price which means that they do not get the return that they require?' Surely, we must expect that if $K \neq \bar{K}$ the price will readily adjust until the two are brought into equality. In *equilibrium* the price will be that which delivers the required rate of return. Looking at Equation 5.6, we can now see clearly why the price of bonds (and other assets) varies with changes in market interest rates. It is because the asset must be priced in such a way that it provides the required rate of return and one obvious reason why the required

1 See the appendix to this chapter for some further bond pricing arithmetic.
2 The demonstration is more complicated for a redeemable bond, since 'yield' for redeemable bonds has several meanings. We shall

see in Chapter 10 that i in Equation 5.5 is known as the *redemption yield* (and that it is not easily calculated). We shall also see, crucially, that the redemption yield is the discount rate that makes the cashflows over the life of the bond equal to its price.

rate may change is that rates available on other assets in the market change.

As with company shares, therefore, the required rate of return is the appropriate rate at which to discount future income payments and thus, *ceteris paribus*, determines the equilibrium price of bonds. In the case of company shares, we used the capital asset pricing model to find the required rate of return. The *CAPM* says that the required rate is equal to the risk-free rate of interest plus a risk premium derived from comparing the riskiness of the asset with the riskiness of the whole market portfolio. We can also use the *CAPM* to find the required return on bonds. The theory behind the *CAPM* requires that we derive a β-coefficient for any risky asset by comparing the variance of returns on the asset with the variance of returns on the 'whole-market' portfolio. Interestingly, the extent to which bond prices fluctuate in response to changes in market conditions depends to a large extent upon their residual maturity. The price of bonds with a long residual maturity is more sensitive to changes in interest rates than is the price of short-dated bonds. We shall explore this more fully in Chapter 10, where we shall show that the concept of *duration* measures the interest-sensitivity of a bond's price with respect to changes in interest rates. We have already met the idea in Section 4.2 where we worked an exercise to show that the longer the maturity of an asset the more variable its price in response to a change in interest rates. For the moment, however, one can grasp the basic idea that price sensitivity varies positively with the term to maturity by remembering that bonds pay a series of *fixed* coupons. Thus when market interest rates are falling there is an advantage in receiving fixed payments, and the more fixed payments the greater the advantage. When interest rates are rising, fixed payments are less attractive and the more fixed payments there are, the greater the disadvantage. Thus, when interest rates change, the impact on price is greater for long-dated bonds. The effect of duration can be seen again in Exercise 5.2 which is an exercise in the pricing of two bonds with identical characteristics except that one has a residual maturity of four years while the other is irredeemable.

An irredeemable bond is simply a bond of infinitely long residual maturity. In Exercise 5.2 we see that a one-point rise in required rates of return

---

Exercise 5.2 Bond pricing

Assuming that the required rate of return is 8 per cent p.a., find the equilibrium price of:

1 a 6% bond maturing in four years time;
2 a perpetual 6% bond.

Calculate the new equilibrium prices if the required rate of return rises to 9 per cent p.a.

Note: (1) requires the use of discount tables.

(Answers appear in the text below.)

---

causes a fall in the equilibrium price of the irredeemable bond from:

£75 (= £6/0.08) to £66.66 (= £6/0.09)

while the price of the 'short-dated' bond falls from:

£93.37 (= £5.56 + £5.14 + £4.76 + £4.41 + £73.50)

to:

£90.27 (= £5.50 + £5.05 + £4.63 + £4.25 + £70.84)

The change in price of the irredeemable bond is £8.34 while the price change for the short-dated bond is only £3.10. The risk attaching to a bond, therefore, is contained in the interest-elasticity of its price and this in turn results largely from its duration.

We shall come back to the issue of duration and its relevance to bond prices in Chapter 10. For the moment, we only need to appreciate that, in equilibrium, bond prices, just like the prices of any assets, must adjust so as to provide their holders with the required rate of return and that this required rate of return will be equal to the risk-free rate (of appropriate maturity) plus a risk premium. For an individual bond, therefore, anything that changes the level of risk-free rates, or the general level of risk aversion in the market or the riskiness of the bond itself, will cause a change in the rate of return required and thus in the equilibrium price.

Figure 5.3 shows how we can interpret these changes in a bond's rate of return and its price in a supply and demand framework, just as we did with a company share. The supply of a bond available for trading is a *stock* and is shown by the vertical supply curve, *S*. The demand curve, *D*, is drawn downward-sloping to indicate that, *ceteris paribus*, the lower the

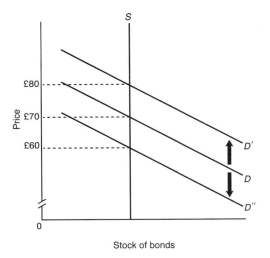

Figure 5.3 Bond prices and shifts in demand.

price the greater the quantity of a bond that investors will wish to hold because, as we know, the lower the price the higher the rate of return. In Figure 5.3, the initial equilibrium price is £70. Suppose now that market interest rates rise. Amongst the interest rates to rise will be the risk-free rate and this in turn raises the rate of return required on this bond. Investors are no longer willing to hold the stock of bonds while the rate of return is that rate generated by a price of £70. Sell orders exceed buy orders and the price falls. In Figure 5.3, the demand curve shifts downward to D' and the new equilibrium price – the price which yields an appropriate rate of return – is shown as £60. If, by contrast, market interest rates fell, the required rate on all bonds would fall. At £70

Exercise 5.3   Bond prices and yields

Assume that Figure 5.3 depicts the market for a 7% irredeemable bond.

1   What was the required rate of return at the original equilibrium price of £70?

2   To what level did the required rate rise to cause the equilibrium price to fall to £60?

3   To what level did the required rate fall to cause the equilibrium price to rise to £80?

(Answers appear in the text below.)

---

the bond in Figure 5.3 would yield a rate of return which exceeded that available elsewhere. This would encourage an excess of buy orders over sell orders which we would show by an upward shift in the demand curve to D''. The new equilibrium price is shown as £80. Exercise 5.3 requires the calculation of rates of return associated with each of these levels of demand.

The rate of return on a 7% irredeemable bond trading at £70 is 10 per cent. At £80 the rate of return falls to 8.75 per cent while at £60 the rate of return is 11.67 per cent.

Again, as with company shares, changes in the required rate of return are not only determining prices but also the cost of new funds. A firm whose 7% bonds currently trade at £70 can issue new bonds which (ignoring issue costs) bring in £100 for a commitment from the firm of £7 paid per year. If the bond's price falls to £60, new £100 bonds will not be bought unless the firm is willing to pay at least £11.67 for every £100 raised by the sale of those bonds.

5.4   The 'fundamentals' of asset valuation

The account that we have so far given of the determination of rates of return and of asset prices is a very orthodox or conventional one. In orthodox theory price adjusts in order that the asset provides the rate of return required by investors. When this condition is met, an asset is said to be *fairly valued* and its price equals its 'fair' or 'fundamental' value. This rate of return is derived from the risk-free rate of interest and a risk premium, and the latter in turn is equal to the quantity of undiversifiable risk attaching to the asset multiplied by the price of undiversifiable risk as set by the market for risky assets as a whole. Any change in these components changes the required rate of return and, *ceteris paribus*, the price of the asset. The reason that the price must adjust is that we assume that in the short run the income stream is unchanged. Thus, if we take shares as an example, we are assuming that dividend payments are fixed (by the performance of the company) and that the growth rate of dividends is also fixed (by the growth in productivity of the firm's assets).

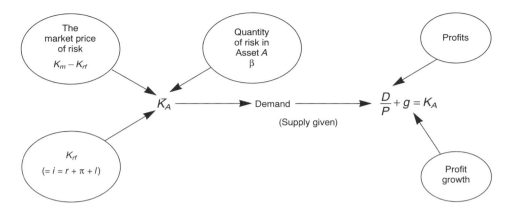

Figure 5.4 The capital asset *pricing* model.

Notice two features of this account. Firstly, *price is the dependent variable*. It is the price that adjusts in order to satisfy investors' requirements for a return. Secondly, the rate of return (and therefore the price) is the outcome of a *rational* process. That is to say that every element in the story can be explained by economic agents trying consistently to maximize the benefit from some *real* economic activity. Figure 5.4 brings together the whole picture as we have developed it in these first five chapters. It uses share prices as an example. We look at the schema first and then try to show how each of the elements can be presented as the outcome of a rational process.

Reading from left to right, the figure reminds us that the required rate of return is equal to the risk-free rate (K_{rf}) plus the quantity of risk (β) times the market risk premium $(K_m - K_{rf})$. This is the CAPM (from Section 2.6). The (nominal) risk-free rate of interest (i) is made up of a real rate of interest (r) (Section 3.3), an inflation premium (π) (Section 3.3) and a term premium (l) (Section 4.2). This is the outcome of the interaction of the supply of and demand for loanable funds in conditions of zero risk, occasionally modified by central bank policy decisions. It is primarily the result of lenders trying to maximize their return from surrendering a current claim to consumption and borrowers trying to maximize the return from the projects in which they invest borrowed funds.

The risk premium on a whole market portfolio $(K_m - K_{rf})$ is the return required over and above the risk-free rate by investors endeavouring to maximize

return while minimizing risk. The market risk premium is what they demand for a portfolio from which all diversifiable risk has been eliminated (Section 2.5).

In equilibrium, the required rate must be matched by the actual rate of return and for company shares this means the sum of the dividend yield (D/P) and the earnings growth rate (g). The dividend available to shareholders depends upon the profit made by the firm and this depends upon the productivity of the underlying assets which constitute the real capital of the firm and the price which consumers are prepared to pay for the output from that capital equipment. In a perfect world, the price that the community is prepared to pay represents the addition to total welfare provided by the marginal unit of output. Provided that price is just equal to this marginal benefit, then total welfare is being maximized by the output from these assets and shareholders are earning a just reward for their contribution to satisfying these needs. The growth in dividends depends upon the rate of growth of productivity of the underlying assets, a rate which depends upon the firm's management's ability to follow a sound policy of reinvestment and to manage the assets. In the short run, all of these are given, except price.

Price is thus the dependent variable which adjusts in order to meet the requirements of a 'rational' process. Because the rationality lies in the behaviour of agents engaged in *real* economic activity, we tend to describe these determinants of a share's price as its *fundamentals*. If P is determined by $\overline{K}$ (given D and *g*) we say that price is determined by the underlying fundamentals.

5.5   An alternative interpretation

Before leaving this section of the book, however, it is worth pausing to reflect on the overall picture that we have drawn and to consider how well it, or its implications, reflects the reality which we think we see.

The first point to make perhaps is that where tradeable financial assets are concerned, the dominant discourse concerns *prices* and not rates of return. It is true that newspapers report and commentators discuss deposit accounts and insurance and pension policies in terms of rate of return. But where an asset is tradeable almost all comment relates to its recent, latest and next-most-likely price movement. Rates of return are just not part of the conversation. This may not be significant. It may be that everyone discussing asset prices automatically carries the corresponding rate of return in his or her head and talks only of 'price' because it is more convenient than 'rate of return'. On the other hand, it may be that the financial community talks in price terms because price is genuinely more interesting, and not simply the reciprocal of a rate of return. This is not a silly idea; one can see why it could happen. For example, if we go back to our share valuation formula, Equation 5.3, we can see that a price change is part of the rate of return. In the long run, dividends increase (*g* is positive). If dividend yields are not to rise to infinity, (that is *D/P* is stationary), then *P* must also rise. And we all know that investors are in practice very interested in the capital appreciation of shares which may well be a larger part of the total rate of return than the dividend yield.

But we know that prices change because of changes in demand, whatever may be the ultimate cause of the demand shift. A shift in demand causes a change in price just as effectively if it is the outcome of a (false) rumour about a change in interest rates as it does when it is the outcome of an actual change. And once we separate the desire to buy or sell from actual events and link it to *expectations* of events we open the door to the possibility that demand may shift in response to a very wide range of forces, ranging from those that might be more or less rational in origin to those that have no logical connection with asset values.

Let us think about some possibilities, beginning with events which are strictly rational (in the sense we are using here) and then moving towards the more fantastic (but not impossible). An *actual* change in the risk-free rate of interest causes a change in asset prices because it changes the demand for the asset by changing the present value of its future income stream by changing the rate at which we discount that future income stream. Holding the asset when the interest rate changes thus leads to a capital gain (a positive contribution to the overall rate of return) or a capital loss (a negative one). It makes sense, therefore, for investors to try to anticipate changes in interest rates. In these circumstances, demand will shift, and prices will change when agents *expect* a change in interest rates. An *expected* event causes an *actual* event. For an individual investor, however, making a capital gain or avoiding a capital loss does not require a belief or expectation that interest rates will change in the very near future. It requires only a belief (or expectation) that other investors believe or expect that interest rates are going to change and that they are going to buy or sell on the strength of that expectation. Indeed, it is not necessary even to believe that other investors believe that interest rates are going to change but only that other investors are going to buy (or sell) *for whatever reason*. This gives rise to two features of investor behaviour, one of which is certainly observable, while we cannot be sure about the second. The first is the sensitivity of demand (and price) to actual events which might help to predict interest rate changes. This often involves forming an implicit government policy reaction function. For example, if investors know that the government is particularly concerned about the rate of growth of credit and the build-up of inflationary pressures, the announcement of a big rise in bank lending causes asset prices to fall because investors make the connection between an undesirable credit surge and the likelihood of a rise in official interest rates to try to stop it. In small open economies, changes in the balance of trade often cause asset price changes through the same (interest rate anticipation) mechanism.

The other feature of investor behaviour which follows from wanting to participate in capital gains and avoid capital losses is the apparent 'herd' behaviour which leads a rising asset price (for example) to go on rising even after any fundamental reason for an increase has ended. A situation where this happens is known as a *bubble*. Sometimes, as with the Big Bull Market in the United States, 1928–29, the buying behaviour affects the whole market. The 1987 crash might be an example of herd selling. It is not possible to be absolutely sure whether investor behaviour corresponds to that of a bubble merely by observation. It is always possible to argue that the market's aversion to risk is diminishing or that investors genuinely think that future growth in productivity is going to be much higher than in the past (a lower *k*, higher *g*, remember). Or, alternatively, that they genuinely think that the fundamentals are getting very rapidly worse. It is, though, hard to believe that fundamentals or even people's perception of the fundamentals of asset values could change so much and so rapidly during the great booms and crashes of asset prices. It is very tempting to think that investors are looking after their own short-term self-interest by sticking with the herd.[3] As John Maynard Keynes once famously remarked '...it is not sensible to pay 25 for an investment of which you believe the prospective yield to justify a value of 30, if you also believe that the market will value it at 20 three months hence' (Keynes, 1936 p.155). Indeed, if you were a fund manager who insisted on dealing in assets on the basis of their fundamentals when everyone else was buying in a bubble and making large profits, your clients could accuse you of negligence.

If it *is* true that investors in tradeable assets are sometimes buying and selling on the basis of what they expect the price to do in the very near future, rather than on the rate of return offered by the asset, then Figure 5.4 gives a misleading picture. Causalities are reversed. Investors are aiming at a target price for the asset and the rate of the return becomes the dependent variable. In the world we have just described, buying and selling drives the price, as it always does, to an equilibrium where sell orders match buy orders, but the rate of return, instead of determining this price, is itself determined by it.

Which of the two pictures we have just described is the more accurate is an important issue. The rational determination of prices by the required rate of return is essential if resources are to be allocated efficiently as we described in Section 1.5.3. We said there that the return to investors was just enough to compensate them for surrendering their ability to purchase real resources plus whatever degree of risk was involved in so doing. The rate of return that they required was the cost of capital. The fact that consumers were ultimately prepared to pay a price for the goods produced by the real capital assets financed by investors indicated that their welfare gain from the goods produced just matched the sacrifice of the providers of finance. No *net* benefits could result to society by changing either the volume of investment or its composition.

This happy situation is not the outcome if people buy assets just because the price is rising (or sell just because the price is falling). In these circumstances the return to investors could settle anywhere and, where it settles, the cost of capital also settles. For example, take the case where a company's share price rises on the rumour of some new product development and, even when the rumour subsides, the price goes on rising because investors are impressed by its recent capital appreciation. Perhaps its price before the rumour was £2 and the dividend payment was 8p per share. The dividend yield was 4 per cent and this was the cost (in terms of dividend per pound raised) of raising new capital by issuing new shares. Suppose that after a few weeks' buying the price settles at £3. If the firm now decides to raise new capital by issuing new shares then the cost (in dividend per pound raised) is now 8/300 or 2.66 per cent. In the circumstances, the firm may be encouraged to expand, though there is no indication

---

[3] Another point to remember is that once we recognize the importance of 'perceptions' we should also recognize that people's perceptions are influenced by emotions. Good news in the present may make us more optimistic about future events *which have no rational connections with the good news*. In the first half of 1994, for example, the Italian bond market showed little clear trend, but it rose sharply after the Italian football team won the World Cup. (We are grateful to Simon Maggs for drawing our attention to this incident.)

that the benefits to society from the output that it produces have increased. Furthermore, the firm's enhanced share price makes it easier for it to make a bid for other firms (by issuing some of its own shares to shareholders of the target firm). There are resource allocation arguments in favour of takeovers. For example, a poorly performing firm, if correctly valued, will have a low share price and will be a target for more efficient firms who will bring their more efficient management to the poorly performing firm. But where a firm is valued as the result of a bubble, its price is no longer an indication of superior performance. We cannot then expect that benefits will follow if it takes over a firm which is priced more cheaply – but correctly.

5.6   Summary

The present value of an asset is equal to the sum of the future stream of income payments that it provides, each payment suitably discounted. The rate of discount is also the rate of return on an asset and so the appropriate rate of discount is the *required* rate of return. In equilibrium, the asset's price will equal its present value and its actual rate of return will equal the required rate of return.

The required rate of return is given by the risk-free rate plus the quantity of undiversifiable risk multiplied by the market price of risk. An asset whose price is determined according to these principles is said to be priced according to its fundamentals since the determinants of its price all reflect the rational decisions of agents engaged in real economic activity. If assets are priced according to these principles, a case can be made that capital is being allocated in an optimal way.

However, there are occasions when asset prices behave in a way that suggests that other forces are at work. It is hard, sometimes, to believe that the fundamentals of an asset's value change so fast or so much that they can account for dramatic changes in asset prices. In these circumstances it is tempting to think that price takes on a momentum of its own. Instead of the required rate of return determining the price, the price is driven by some herd-like behaviour on the part of investors with the result that the rate of return becomes the dependent variable and may settle anywhere, with no rational foundation. In these circumstances, we cannot be sure that capital is being allocated efficiently.

Key concepts used in this chapter

Tradeable assets	Coupon rate	Actual rate of return
Non-tradeable assets	Original maturity	Required rate of return
Present value	Residual maturity	Actual price
Dividend	Redeemable bonds	Equilibrium price
Dividend yield	Irredeemable bonds	Fundamentals
Capital appreciation	Perpetuals	Bubbles
Coupon	Consols	

1 Imagine that the central bank raises short-term interest rates. Discuss and explain the effect on:
   (a) the rate of return required by investors in bonds;
   (b) the price of ordinary company shares.

2 Suppose that investors expect inflation to increase in future. *Explain* the likely effect on bond prices. (You may wish to refer to Figure 4.1.)

3 How would a fall in interest rates affect the required rate of return on securities? Using a supply and demand diagram, show the effect of this fall upon the equilibrium price of a security.

4 You are advising a friend who holds company shares whose return plots below the security market line (see Chapter 2). Would you advise her to hold or to sell? Explain your answer.

5 Imagine a security whose price has been unchanged for several days. What does this stable price imply about the buying and selling of that security?

6 Suppose that you decide to take a round-the-world cruise and that you will pay for this by (a) selling bonds and (b) withdrawing your savings deposits from a bank. What effect does (a) have

on the total quantity of bonds in existence? What effect does (b) have on the quantity of savings deposits? Explain any difference.

7 Explain the basic principle underlying the valuation of any asset.

8 How would you expect the price of (a) a short-dated bond and (b) a long-dated bond to be affected by a given increase in market interest rates? How would you account for any difference?

9 What do we mean when we say that an asset is priced acording to its 'fundamentals'? In what sense might it be argued that securities priced according to fundamentals are priced according to rational principles?

10 From the financial press, collect some recent reports of security market behaviour. Do those reports suggest to you that price changes are driven by changes in desired rates of return or by expectations of future price changes?

11 Suppose that you hold shares in a company whose future profitability you think is likely to decline, but you see that these shares are still being recommended for purchase in the financial press. What would you do?

Further reading

D Blake, *Financial Market Analysis* (London: McGraw-Hill, 1990) Ch. 13
E J Elton and M J Gruber, *Modern Portfolio Theory and Investment Analysis* (Chichester: John Wiley, 5e, 1995) Chs 18, 20
P G A Howells and K Bain, *Financial Markets and Institutions* (London: Longman, 2e 1994) Ch. 6.
F Mishkin, *Financial Markets, Institutions and Money* (New York: Harper Collins, 1995) Ch. 4
S Pressman, 'What do capital markets do, and what can we do about capital markets?', *Economies et Sociétés*, June 1996

When n_m is small, Equation 5.5 is fairly easily solved. However, when n_m is large, calculating the present value of a stream of coupon payments can be tedious. Thus, it is worth remembering that the present value of a stream of income payments can alternatively be written as:

$$\frac{C\left(1 - \dfrac{1}{(1 + i)^{n_m}}\right)}{i}$$

Substituting this into Equation 5.5, we can then find the price more easily as:

$$P = \frac{C\left(1 - \dfrac{1}{(1 + i)^{n_m}}\right)}{i} + \frac{M}{(1 + i)^{n_m}} \qquad (A5.1)$$

Note also that if $n_m = \infty$, the value of $\dfrac{1}{(1 + i)^{n_m}} = 0$ and $\dfrac{M}{(1 + i)^{n_m}} = 0.$

Hence the value of a perpetual bond is:

$$\frac{C(1 - 0)}{i} + 0 = \frac{C}{i} \qquad (A5.2)$$

Money and banking

Banks and the supply of money

6.1 Introduction

In the next two chapters we turn our attention to banks and the supply of and demand for money. There are four reasons for this.

Firstly, banks themselves form one particular subset of financial intermediaries. In most developed countries they also make up a *large* subset of financial intermediaries and so they are worth studying for this reason alone.

Secondly, the liabilities of banks are the principal components of any country's money supply and so the behaviour of banks is intimately connected with changes in the supply of money. We pointed out in Section 1.5.1 that one general effect of any increase in financial intermediation is the creation of liquidity, but if the increased activity involves primarily banks,

then the increase in liquidity takes the specific form of 'money'.

Thirdly, many economists take the view that changes in the money supply have important effects upon the economy, especially if the changes are large or sudden. *Exactly* what these effects may be, and whether they have an impact in the short run or in the long run and whether the effects are temporary or permanent, are matters of controversy. But the fact remains that whatever version of this view one accepts, bank behaviour may have effects upon the economy which is rather different from that of other intermediaries.

Fourthly, even if one doubts the importance of money in the economy, anyone interested in finance has to recognize that governments and central banks certainly behave as if it matters. Thus they tend to adopt policies which set at least broad limits to the desirable rate of monetary growth and then take such action as they can to keep monetary growth within those limits. This leads them invariably to make changes to short-term interest rates (as we saw in Section 3.4) – raising them to reduce monetary growth, for example.

For all these reasons, therefore, the behaviour of banks is an important issue. In this chapter, we concentrate upon questions which are related to the theme of money *supply*. This leads us to consider what money is, how the components of the money supply change over time, how money is created and finally what the authorities can do to control its creation.

In Chapter 7, we shall focus upon questions which are related to the theme of money *demand*. This leads us to consider how people decide how much of their wealth to hold in monetary form and how their behaviour is affected by a mismatch between the quantity of money available and the quantity they wish to hold. It is here that the controversy about the effects of changes in money supply have their origin. People may respond in ways that have little lasting effect upon the economy, or their attempts to adjust to monetary shocks may be very important. This behaviour is summed up in what is known as the 'transmission mechanism'. In Chapter 8 we shall look at what governments have thought about the importance of money at various times and how these views have been reflected in policy.

6.2   The definition of money

6.2.1   Some general principles

One traditional way of defining money is to look at what it does, or what we require it to do, and then to see what in practice we use for that purpose. We shall do that in a moment but first let us begin by clarifying some important terms which sometimes cause confusion in discussions of what money is.

We begin with *real wealth*. Wealth (alternatively called *capital*) is a *stock* of assets, including human capital, which can be used to produce a *flow* of goods and services over a period of time. Thus we are all familiar with the idea that we use some of our human capital (in the form of labour) each year in order to produce a flow of new goods (books, computer programs, mobile phones and so on) or services (such as lectures or taxi rides) each year. In any year, we shall consume, that is, use up, a large proportion of the income we produce. The rest is saved. We shall also use up a proportion of wealth in the production of that income. Clearly, wealth consumed or used up in the production of income must be replaced each year or the production process must eventually grind to a halt.[1] Saving is an addition to wealth. If saving is sufficient to replace the wealth

consumed then we say that *net investment* is zero. If saving exceeds the consumption of wealth then we have positive net investment. Our real wealth increases and opens up the possibility that more of it may be devoted to production in future. The real economy expands. All of these concepts, wealth, capital, income and saving, are expressed so far in *real terms*. That is to say we are talking about *volumes* of goods, services and skills. These volumes determine what we can *really* consume, save, invest and so on. It is these volumes that *really* matter to our welfare. Whatever price or value we place upon these volumes makes no difference to their quantity and no difference to our real welfare.

In everyday language, however, we think and talk about income, saving, wealth and so on in *money terms*. We shall see just why that is in the next paragraph. But it is important to be absolutely clear that 'money' is merely some token in which we choose to reckon these magnitudes and use to carry out exchanges. Classical economists used to describe money as a 'veil' – meaning something which partially hid what was really going on, but which had no effect upon it. In Section 7.3 we shall see that it might be going too far to say that the quantity of money available has no effect at all on real behaviour but it is crucial at this stage to realize that 'money' is something that exists quite independently of the real goods and services, income, wealth and so on which it is being used to measure or exchange. Consider now why 'money' is so intimately connected with the measurement and exchange of goods and services that there is sometimes a danger of confusion.

Firstly, when it comes to measuring the *total* volume of production, income, saving, wealth and so on we require some common standard in which to express them. In other words, we need a *unit of account*, and that is provided by 'money'. Thus we may talk of this year's national income as £600bn and we may forecast that over the next year it will grow to £620bn.

Furthermore, while it may be true that the production of real goods and services determines our

---

[1] (Real) income was famously defined by Hicks (1946) as all that output that could be consumed while leaving us as well off at the end of the period as the beginning. This is restating what we have said, with different priorities. Looking at total output, Hicks insists on deducting sufficient saving to *ensure* that wealth is unchanged. What is left is income which can be consumed or some further saving may be carried out, adding to future wealth.

real income and the amount that we can save and add to real wealth, we do not individually consume what we produce. Typically, we sell our labour to employers who organize production and pay us wages and salaries in the form of 'money' which they in turn receive from buyers of the goods and services or by borrowing. What this tells us is that modern economies are 'exchange' rather than 'barter' economies. This brings us to another function of money which is its use as a *medium of exchange*. The movement from barter to the use of money brings with it a large saving of resources. These gains, which come under the general heading of seigniorage,[2] include a large reduction in the information costs involved in comparing relative prices of goods and services throughout the economy.[3]

The movement from barter to exchange, using money, brings also a greater flexibility from being able to separate income and consumption decisions in time. In a barter economy, a decision to save would mean setting aside something that one had produced in the hope that it might be useful at some time in the future or, alternatively, exchanging it now for some other good again in the hope that it might turn out to be what one needed. With money, one can decide to save now, in the knowledge that those savings will definitely be needed at some time in the future but without knowing exactly when, or in exactly what form or for what purpose. When the time comes, the savings, in money form, can be converted into whatever is required. Because saving (adding to wealth) is being carried out by holding 'money', money is said here to be functioning as a *store of wealth*.

Finally, in a monetary exchange economy, it is often advantageous to carry out exchanges and payments at different times. Clearly, it is not much benefit to households to arrange a daily delivery of milk or newspapers to their home if they are required to go to the dairy or newsagent every day to pay for the milk or newspapers. One of the many benefits of a monetary economy is the availability of credit. But

credit will only be possible if there is some form in which debts and credits can be recorded to everyone's satisfaction and if there is some acceptable form in which the debts can be finally extinguished. We know, of course, that debts are recorded in money form (money's role as a unit of account again) and it is accepted that they will eventually be settled using 'money'. This is money acting as a *standard of deferred payment*.

These – the *unit of account, medium of exchange, store of wealth* and *standard of deferred payment* – are the roles that money is traditionally said to perform. The major ones, by which we mean that they may be a means whereby money may have some effect upon the rest of the economy and about which there is certainly some controversy, are the *medium of exchange* and *store of wealth* functions. The next question is: 'does identifying these functions enable us to identify "money"?'

So far as the unit of account, medium of exchange and standard of deferred payment roles are concerned, it seems very clear that 'money' must be something which is universally acceptable. What it is that makes one asset in particular universally acceptable is an interesting question which has fascinated economists over the years. One can lay down certain physical essentials – it must be cheap to produce, highly divisible and convenient to carry – but an asset could have all these qualities and still not function as money. One can appeal to official regulations. Most countries define certain assets as *legal tender*, meaning that people *must* accept them in exchange. In the UK, for example, notes and coin are defined as legal tender, at least for transactions of specified type. But most transactions (by value) are carried out in most economies by a much wider range of assets. The dominant medium of exchange in most economies is bank deposits. One might argue that these are made acceptable by the understanding that they are fully convertible on demand into legal tender and that legal tender itself is ultimately guaranteed by the State. It seems hard to imagine, however, that if the idea of legal tender were to be

2 *Seigniorage* may be defined as the gains which accrue to the issuer of a currency because the issuer (a government, for example) obtains real resources in return for non-interest-bearing, non-repayable debt.

3 Information costs involved in a non-monetary system can be reduced by the development of more sophisticated forms of barter. Nonetheless, costs within a barter system remain very high.

abandoned bank deposits would cease to function as the main medium of exchange.

Money's ability to function as a store of value does not rely so heavily upon its general acceptability but requires another characteristic which may also be important in making it acceptable. This is stability in its value. To be persuaded to use money as a store of value, people must be persuaded that its future purchasing power will be little different from what it is now. At the very least, people will wish to be assured that there is not a general tendency for its purchasing power to diminish. This requirement may not be absolute. Since money yields numerous benefits, it will not lose its attractiveness, even as a store of value, until the rate of depreciation reaches such a pace that it outweighs the benefits. Such rates have, of course, been reached at various time and places. The Weimar Republic and Hungary in the 1920s, some Latin American states in the 1970s and perhaps Russia in 1994–5 yield examples of what happens when confidence in the currency finally collapses because of doubts about its future purchasing power. Those that can do so move their savings out of the country (adopting dollars or Deutschmarks as alternative stores of value) and exchange takes place using alternative commodities.[4] It is to avoid situations like this, and the disruption to trade that follows, that governments and central banks place such emphasis upon minimizing inflationary pressures. In conditions of hyper-inflation, no amount of legislation about 'legal tender' will make the official currency acceptable.

The important lesson that we must draw from this 'acceptability' criterion is that it does not provide a timeless definition of 'money'. What is widely acceptable now was not generally acceptable even a hundred years ago. Indeed, there was a time when people were reluctant to accept government issues of notes and coins of low intrinsic value. Defining token money as 'legal tender' was initially introduced by monarchs and governments which wished to enjoy the seigniorage benefits of issuing token money of low intrinsic value but found that their subjects were reluctant to move away from gold and silver coins.

More importantly for us, however, is that the acceptability criterion means that 'money' continues to change. This in turn poses problems for authorities wishing to control the amount of money in circulation – especially if they try to do it by 'direct' or non-price methods of control. In most economies, the general public, banks and other financial institutions have become very adept at developing money substitutes. In the next section we shall see that there have been major changes in official definitions of money in recent years and that these have been necessary because of changes in private sector behaviour.

6.2.2 Official definitions

In this section we look at the assets which various monetary authorities choose to recognize as components of their money stock. What is apparent for each country is that money can be defined 'narrowly' or 'broadly'. The normal practice is to attach numbers to these official magnitudes using the lowest numbers to refer to the narrowest magnitudes. In the next four tables we describe the national definitions of money currently in use in Germany, France, Italy and the USA.[5] We also give the recent magnitudes of the various components of the monetary definitions so that the approximate proportions can be seen. In an ideal world, the definitions would be consistent across countries, and we shall see in a moment that there are indeed some similarities. But there are some significant differences of detail and these illustrate very clearly what we saw in the last section, namely, that which assets function as money depends upon their acceptability in that role. This in turn depends upon the particular history and monetary institutions of each country. The fact that the broad money definition in Germany excludes building society deposits, while in the UK they are included, is a reflection of the different way in which people treat these deposits.

The narrowest definition of money is that which makes up the *monetary base* or *high powered money*.

---

[4] Quite often cigarettes, since they meet the criteria of divisibility and low carrying costs.

[5] Except where indicated, the descriptions and the magnitudes are all taken from the IMF's monthly publication, *International Financial Statistics*.

This consists of notes and coin (or 'currency' or 'cash' as it is sometimes called). Most monetary aggregates include assets held only outside banks (that is, by the 'non-bank private sector' or simply 'nonbanks' as we describe them in the tables below). But the monetary base is unique in including cash held both by nonbanks and in the vaults of the commercial banking system. It also includes commercial bank deposits at the central bank. The name 'high powered money' is derived from the base:multiplier model of money supply determination (see Section 6.4). In this model, the monetary base forms a stock of highly liquid potential 'reserves' on the basis of which commercial banks can create broad money as a multiple of the monetary base.[6] Since the multiple is often very large, this model predicts a large change in broad money from a small change in the base – changes in the base thus appear very powerful.

In Germany, there is also Central Bank Money or *CBM*. Central bank money can best be understood as a weighted average of the components of *M3*. Thus, it is a 'synthetic' or derived aggregate and has much in common with 'divisia' aggregates (see below). *CBM* is the sum of all of the components (by value) that enter into *M3*. But instead of aggregating them at face or nominal value, the components are given diminishing weights as their liquidity diminishes. Thus notes and coin (or 'currency') are included at face value (that is, with a weight of 0) while demand (or 'sight') deposits are multiplied by a weight of 0.167 and time deposits by a weight of 0.081. These weights (except for currency) are equivalent to the reserve ratios which banks are required to hold against each of the components.

The next monetary aggregate in most systems is *narrow money*, sometimes called *M1*. This consists of notes and coin, but this time only the notes and coin held by nonbanks[7] together with nonbanks' holdings of bank *sight deposits*. These are deposits which can be used (to make payment or to exchange for cash) on demand. They are sometimes referred to

as demand or checking deposits. Until recently, it used to be a characteristic of sight deposits that they did not pay interest. The benefits to depositors lay in the fact that banks did not charge for the money transmission services to which these accounts gave access. In some monetary systems, however, a distinction can now be made between sight deposits that do pay interest and those that do not. In such systems, this generates a subset of narrow money known as *non-interest-bearing narrow money*.

In many monetary systems there is also an *M2* aggregate. As a rule, this is a broader or more inclusive measure of money than *M1*, though not so broad as *M3*. Exactly what is included in aggregates broader than *M1* is, as we noted above, very much a reflection of the particular characteristics of a

Table 6.1 Money definitions in Germany

Name	Components	Size[1]
Monetary base	Currency in circulation and with banks + commercial banks' deposits with the central bank	314
CBM (Central Bank Money)	The components of M3 (see below) weighted by their reserve requirements and aggregated	265[2]
M1	Currency outside banks + domestic nonbanks' sight deposits (including government deposits outside the Bundesbank)	734
M2	M1 + domestic nonbanks' time deposits + funds borrowed for less than four years	1207
M3	M2 + domestic nonbanks' savings deposits at statutory notice	1876
Extended M3	M3 + domestic nonbanks' deposits with domestic banks' foreign branches and foreign subsidiaries and bearer bonds with maturities of < two years in the hands of domestic nonbanks	2240[2]

Notes: [1] DM bn., seasonally adjusted, end-95Q4.
[2] Deutsche Bundesbank, *Monthly Report*, April 1996

6 In *International Financial Statistics*, what we have called the monetary base is titled 'reserves'.
7 The repeated use of the phrase 'non-bank private sector' or "nonbanks' as an alternative to 'the general public' serves to emphasize an important point, namely, that with the exception of

the monetary base, money exists only when it is held outside banks. There is no quantity of monetary assets somewhere in store, waiting to come into circulation. Whatever else money is, it is what people are willing to hold. We return to this when we discuss the demand for money in Chapter 7.

country's monetary system. In Germany and France the addition to *M1* is essentially similar – some form of savings deposits, while in the USA the difference between *M1* and *M2* includes some savings deposits but also Eurodollar deposits held with overseas branches of US banks and even some outstanding repurchase agreements. This reflects the fact first of all that such assets are significant in quantity in the USA and also a belief by the Federal Reserve that in the USA people treat them with a degree of 'moneyness' that means they should be included. The same need not apply in other countries. There is one exception to the definition of *M2* as lying on a direct line from *M1* to *M3*. In the UK, *M2* is used to refer to an aggregate which tries to measure 'retail deposits'. These are deposits held by households, mainly for transactions purposes. Unlike *M1*, therefore, they include building society deposits. Since *M3* did not contain building society deposits this was a leap beyond *M3*. But UK *M2* also excludes large sight deposits held by firms with banks and in that sense was narrower than *M1*.

The next definition, used in all systems, is that which captures the components of *broad money*. This incorporates time deposits, deposits for which, strictly

Table 6.2 Money definitions in France

Name	Components	Size[1]
Monetary base	Currency in circulation and with banks + commercial banks' deposits with the central bank	293
M1	Nonbanks' holdings of currency + domestic nonbanks' sight deposits with banks	1527
M2	*M1* + nonbanks' interest-bearing sight deposits with banks and savings banks	2866
M3	*M2* + nonbanks' deposits in foreign currency + selected money market securities (CDs, bills issued by financial institutions and by the Caisse Nationale des Télécommunications)	5173
M4	*M3* + Treasury money market instruments and corporate commercial paper	

Notes: [1] Fr.fr. bn, not seasonally adjusted, end-95Q1
Source: IMF, *International Financial Statistics*, Jan. 1997.

Table 6.3 Money definitions in Italy

Name	Components	Size[1]
Monetary base	Currency in circulation and with banks + commercial banks' deposits with the central bank	189
M1	Nonbanks' holdings of currency and sight deposits with banks	597
M2	*M1* + plus nonbanks' holdings of bank certificates of deposit + nonbanks' holdings of bank savings deposits and postal savings deposits	1006
M3	*M2* + nonbanks' holdings of bankers' acceptances + nonbanks' holdings of Treasury Bills	n/a[2]

Notes: [1] Trillion Lira, not seasonally adjusted, end-94Q4.
[2] Data not available since 1/92
Source: IMF, *International Financial Statistics*, Jan. 1997

speaking, notice of withdrawal is required. Needless to say, time deposits pay interest. Unlike sight deposits, within any system time deposits come with many different terms attached. They vary with respect to the period to maturity, from one week to one year, for example. They vary in the interest rates they pay – typically higher rates for longer maturities – and they vary in their penalties for early withdrawal. Since the late 1960s, some time deposits have provided their owners with a *certificate of deposit*, stating the amount and the terms of the deposit. This 'CD' in turn has been tradeable in organized markets, giving the underlying deposit something of the liquidity characteristics of a sight deposit. These variations mean that although all countries publish official measures of broad money, the components show variations between countries. *M3* in France, for example, includes selected money market instruments, assets which (with the exception of CDs) are not included in UK definitions until we get beyond *M4*. In Italy, CDs are included in *M2*.

So far, we have measured the quantity of money by simply aggregating all its components at their nominal value. While this may be an obvious (and straightforward) approach it suffers from both a theoretical and a practical weakness. At the theoretical level, simple aggregation implies that we are dealing with homogeneous assets. We seem to be

Table 6.4 Money definitions in the USA

Name	Components	Size[1]
Monetary base	Currency in circulation and with banks + commercial banks' deposits with the central bank	435
M1	Nonbanks' holdings of currency and bank sight deposits	1139
M2	*M1* + overnight repurchase agreements issued by all depository institutions + overnight Eurodollar deposits held by US residents in foreign branches of US banks worldwide + 'small' time deposits (<$100,000) + money market deposit accounts	3693
M3	*M2* + large time deposits and term repurchase agreements + term Euro-dollars held by US residents in foreign branches of US banks worldwide + balances in 'institution only' money market mutual funds	4453
L	*M3* + nonbanks' holdings of bankers' acceptances, commercial paper and short-term Treasury securities	5459

Notes: [1]US$ bn.
Source: IMF, *International Financial Statistics*, Jan. 1997

saying, for example, that *from a monetary point of view*, £1 bn of CDs is the same as £1 bn of notes and coin. The mere fact that CDs pay interest while notes and coin do not, however, indicates some degree of differentiation since otherwise no one would hold notes and coin. At the practical level, economists are usually interested in the closeness of the relationship between a monetary aggregate and income. This is likely to increase with the extent to which the aggregate is dominated by assets used for trans-actions. However, as we have seen, it is difficult to know exactly where to draw the line between whole classes of assets for this purpose. Notes and coin and sight deposits are all perfectly liquid and are obvious transactions media but we know that time deposits can be switched to sight deposits quickly and cheaply and that other, apparently less liquid, assets have sufficient liquidity that they could still be relevant to transactions, albeit to a lesser degree. The Divisia approach involves weighting each of the component assets according to the extent to which they provide transactions services. If this could be done accur-

ately, then the resulting index should measure the quantity of money available in the economy for transactions purposes and should be more closely linked to expenditure and income.

The weights given to each asset are often said to represent the 'user cost' of the asset. To measure the user cost, we must first choose a benchmark asset which provides *no* transactions services. For example, the Bank of England publishes a Divisia index going back to 1977 based upon the components of *M4* and using the rate on three-month local authority deposits (the 3mLA rate) as the benchmark. We then subtract the rate of interest on the component asset from the rate on the benchmark asset (the 3mLA rate). Notes and coin are given a weight of one representing the difference between the 3mLA rate and zero. Each other asset, a_i, is then given a lesser weight, w_i, equal to the difference between the benchmark rate and its own rate, i_i, as a fraction of the benchmark notes and coin differential. In symbols:

$$w_i = (3\text{mLA rate} - i_i)/(3\text{mLA rate} - 0)$$

The index, D, is then the sum of the nominal value of each asset adjusted for its appropriate weight:

$$D = \sum a_i.w_i$$

If it is the transactions services of money in which we are primarily interested, then Divisia clearly possesses several attractions.

Before we leave this discussion of the definition of money, we look briefly at the UK aggregates and their recent history. This will provide further illustration of the points that we made above, namely, that what is acceptable as money varies with time and between countries with different institutional arrangements. But it also shows something further. In recent years, governments have often thought it important to control the growth of money, in order to confine it within a 'target' range. (We look at the techniques of control in Section 6.5 and at the theory behind it in Section 7.4.) Inevitably, such a policy requires the choice of one or more aggregates for control and the choice should be made ideally in the light of theory. For example, if it is thought that the growth rate of money matters because of its role as a medium of exchange, it makes sense to target a monetary aggregate like *M1*, where the components are mainly used for transactions purposes. Table 6.5 shows how the status of various aggregates has changed over the years in the UK.

One might ask why there have been so many changes, with new aggregates being developed while old ones are discontinued and while others change from being 'targeted' to merely 'monitored'. We can offer three reasons. We have already stressed that which assets fulfil different parts of money's functions varies over time. *M1* in the UK, for example, does not include building society deposits, and might once have been a suitable 'transactions' aggregate when building society deposits were used overwhelmingly as a savings medium. But when building societies started to provide money transmission services during the 1980s, *M1* seemed no longer appropriate and a new, *M2*, aggregate was developed (see above). By 1989 it was impossible to avoid the conclusion that building society deposits

were indistinguishable from bank deposits and so *M3* was replaced as the official definition of money by *M4*. Secondly, in some regimes aggregates seem to be subject to 'Goodhart's Law' which states that any past relationship between a monetary aggregate and some other variable will break down the moment that the aggregate becomes the subject of attempted control by the authorities. Thirdly, of course, there are occasional shifts in the theory behind monetary policy. If, instead of focusing upon a transactions medium, we begin to think that it is the general level of 'liquidity' in the economy that influences people's spending plans then policy should shift towards targeting a broader aggregate. Ultimately what Table 6.5 shows is just how difficult it is (or at least has been for the UK) to define 'money' in an unambiguous and lasting way.

Table 6.5 UK monetary aggregates

Name	Components	First published	Discontinued	Targeted
M0 (wide monetary base)	Notes and coin outside the Bank of England + banks' operational deposits	June 1981		1984– [1]
NIBM1 (non-interest-bearing M1)	Notes and coin in circulation + NBPS[2] holdings of non-interest bearing sight bank deposits	June 1975	May 1991	
M1	NIBM1 + NBPS holdings of interest-bearing sight bank deposits	Dec. 1970	July 1989	1982–4
M2	NIBM1 + NBPS holdings of interest-bearing retail deposits with banks and building societies + NBPS holdings of National Savings ordinary accounts	Sept. 1982[3]		
M3 (£M3 until May 1987)	M1 + NBPS holdings of bank time deposits + NBPS holdings of CDs with banks	March 1977[4]	July 1989	1976–86
M3c (M3 until May 1987)	M3 + NBPS holdings of foreign currency bank deposits	Dec. 1970[4]	July 1989	
PSL1	M3 − NBPS bank time deposits with original maturity > 2 years + NBPS holdings of bank bills, treasury bills, local authority deposits and certificates of tax deposit	Sept. 1979	May 1987	
PSL2	PSL1 + NBPS building society deposits (excluding term shares) + short-term National Savings instruments	Sept. 1979	May 1987	1982–4

Table 6.5 continued

Name	Components	First published	Discontinued	Targeted
M4	M3 + NBPS building society shares, deposits and CDs – building society holdings of bank deposits, CDs and notes and coin	May 1987		
M4c	M4 + NBNBSPS[5] bank and building society foreign currency deposits	May 1987	May 1991	
M5	M4 + NBNBSPS holdings of bank bills, treasury bills, local authority deposits and certificates of tax deposit + short-term National Savings instruments – building society holdings of bank deposits, CDs and notes and coin	May 1987	May 1991	
'Liquid assets outside M4'	M5 + NBNBSPS holdings of bank and building society foreign currency deposits + further liquid assets of NBNBSPS and overseas sectors (see text)	May 1991		
DCE (Domestic credit expansion)	*Change* in bank lending to the non-bank private and public sectors	Dec. 1972	March 1986	1967–9 1976–9
'Divisia'		August 1993		

Notes: [1] 'monitored'
  [2] NBPS = non-bank private sector
  [3] Not to be confused with an earlier M2 aggregate (Dec. 1970 - Dec. 1971) which was roughly midway between M1 and M3.
  [4] £M3 and M3 included public sector £ bank deposits until March 1984
  [5] 'Non-bank, non-bank building society private sector', sometimes known as 'M4 private sector' (M4PS)

6.3 Banks' balance sheets

In the last section we noted that bank deposits feature in all measures of 'money'. Indeed, in all of the *M1–M3* measures, for example, bank deposits are the dominant component. Thus it follows that changes in the stock of money entail changes in bank deposits and vice versa. Since bank deposits dominate the liability side of banks' balance sheets, and since balance sheets must also balance, it follows that changes in the money supply require changes in banks' assets as well. In order to explain how changes in the money stock occur, therefore, we need to be familiar with the structure of banks' balance sheets.[8] Table 6.6 shows the balance sheet of a commercial bank, simplified to the essentials we require, and employing some symbols with which we need to be familiar.

---

[8] For the UK, we shall assume that building societies are included within the general category of 'banks'. This is not quite accurate since building societies hold their own reserves with banks rather than with the Bank of England. It makes little difference to our analysis, however. A detailed explanation of the relationship between building societies, banks and the Bank of England is contained in Howells (1993).

Table 6.6 A commercial bank's balance sheet

Assets		Liabilities	
Notes and coin	C_b	Capital and shareholders' funds	S_f
Deposits at the central bank	D_b	Customer deposits	D_p
Loans to the money markets	L_m		
Investments	I_b		
Loans to the public sector	BL_g		
Loans to the general public	BL_p		

How can we relate this balance sheet to our discussion in the last section? Firstly, we saw earlier that the monetary base comprised notes and coin in circulation and with banks as well as banks' deposits at the central bank. Clearly, the last two components are assets to banks and they are shown in the top left corner of Table 6.6 as C_b and D_b respectively. The first component, notes and coin in circulation with nonbanks, we can denote C_p (standing for 'cash with the public'). Thus we can now write:

$$\text{Monetary base} = C_b + D_b + C_p \qquad (6.1)$$

Recall that we said that banks' holdings of the monetary base, $C_b + D_b$, functioned as highly liquid reserve assets. We could thus write:

$$\text{Monetary base} = R + C_p \qquad (6.2)$$

where R now stands for bank 'reserves'. Notice that the rest of the asset side is made up of loans to nonbanks in some form or another. L_m represents loans made for very short periods (often overnight or 'at call') to the money markets or other financial institutions; I_b represents investments in the form of securities, typically short-dated government bonds or treasury bills. BL_g and BL_p represent loans to the government (or 'public sector') and to the nonbank private sector, respectively. We saw in Section 4.2 that longer-term loans generally pay a higher rate of interest than shorter ones. Thus, looking at the structure of assets we can draw two conclusions. Firstly, yields are likely to increase as we read down

the list (C_b of course pays no interest, nor in most systems do D_b); secondly, banks will wish to maximize their holdings of investments and loans and minimize their holdings of reserves.

Turning to bank liabilities, D_p – deposits of the non-bank public – form the major component of most definitions of money. As we saw in the last section, D_p will consist of sight deposits, time deposits and CDs. On the same principle that we just restated, sight deposits will pay little or no interest, while time deposits and CDs will pay interest which increases with the term for which the deposits are made.

Like any other firm, a bank makes profits equal to the difference between revenues and costs. Revenues will consist of interest from the assets listed above together with fees and commissions charged for the services that they offer to customers. Costs will consist of interest paid to depositors, wages and salaries, premises and capital. Focusing on the balance sheet, profits will flow from the difference between the interest received from assets and the interest paid on liabilities. In these circumstances, an obvious question to ask is why do banks hold non-interest-bearing reserves ($C_b + D_b$), when other assets would produce a positive return?

The answer comes in two parts. Firstly, as we saw in Section 1.3.2, banks engage in 'maturity transformation'. This means that their liabilities are of shorter maturity than their assets and can thus be withdrawn more readily than banks can realize their assets.[9] Secondly, banks are central to the payments mechanism which means that withdrawals (and receipts) of deposits are continuous. On some occasions, withdrawals and receipts will cancel and *net* withdrawals will be zero. However, as a general rule they will not and some days will see net receipts and others will see net withdrawals. Box 6.2 summarizes the ways in which net withdrawals may take place.

The public's confidence requires that deposits be convertible into cash on demand and thus banks have to maintain sufficient cash, or central bank balances which they can exchange for cash. Because of their role in ensuring convertibility, the level of bank reserves is usually expressed as a ratio to their

---

9 Indeed, this 'playing the yield curve' is precisely why they earn more on assets than they pay on liabilities.

Box 6.2   Sources of net withdrawals from banks

We need to distinguish between withdrawals from individual banks and withdrawals from the banking system as a whole.

Withdrawals from individual banks

- Customers of bank A make net payments to customers of other banks.

- Customers of bank A make net drawings of notes and coin from bank A.

- Customers of bank A make net payments to the public sector.

Withdrawals from the system as a whole

- Bank customers make net drawings of notes and coin from banks.

- Bank customers make net payments to the public sector.

deposits. This is known as the *reserve ratio*. In some monetary systems, this ratio is set down by regulation (a *mandatory ratio*) and in others it is left to banks' own judgement (a *prudential ratio*) though there is usually an obligation on banks to inform the central bank of any intended change. In some systems, the ratio differs for different types of deposit, naturally being highest for sight deposits and decreasing against deposits with increasing terms to maturity. Table 6.7 summarizes the reserve ratio arrangements for a number of countries.

So far we have considered a static position. We have a given quantity of money, the largest part of

Table 6.7   Reserve requirement ratios (% of reservable liabilities)

	France	Germany	UK	USA[1]
Demand deposits	1.0	5.0	–	12.00
Time deposits	0.5[2]	2.0[3]	–	3.00

Notes:
[1] The first $3.2m of reservable liabilities exempt;
[2] < 1 yr to maturity, 0% > 1 yr to maturity;
[3] Plus savings deposits.

Source: Adapted from Batten *et al.* (1990) and *Euromoney*, country surveys (various issues)

which comprises bank deposits, while the rest is made up of the notes and coin from the monetary base which are not held as banks' reserves. Letting M_s stand for some unspecified definition of money, therefore, we have:

$$M_s = D_p + C_p \qquad (6.3)$$

We want now turn our attention to *changes* in the money supply and how banks' balance sheets are involved in such changes. The essential point to remember in working through the following illustrations is that balance sheets always balance and therefore any change that we make on one side must be matched by an equal change (with the same sign) on the opposite side or by an equal change (with opposite sign) on the same side.

In Table 6.8, we illustrate the process of loan (and deposit) creation using two banks, though to economize on space we have reduced the list of both banks' assets from what we saw in Table 6.6. In particular, we want to demonstrate three general principles. The first concerns the relationship between loans and deposits. In Table 6.8 bank A agrees to make additional credit facilities available to a customer. But stop to consider that there is a difference between a bank agreeing to a customer's demand for extra credit facilities and the extra loan *coming into existence*. The latter can only happen when the borrower writes a cheque on which the bank has to make payment. The loan comes into existence when the bank makes the payment. The importance of this distinction is that it shows that a loan cannot come into existence until someone is paid. That means that *for every loan created, someone must receive an addition to his or her deposit*. Loans and deposits must increase together. The loan comes into existence when the client draws a cheque. In bank A then, BL_p is shown with a (+) and we must look for some corresponding and simultaneous increase in D_p. In a multi-bank system, it is quite likely that a customer will make payment to someone who banks elsewhere. In our example, the borrower from bank A makes payments to a client of bank B. Thus in bank B, we show D_p with a (+). Notice that we are now violating our fundamental rule that balance sheets must balance. Assets appear to exceed liabilities for Bank A, while the position is reversed for bank B. Clearly this cannot be correct.

To complete the picture, we have to focus upon 'reserves'. We said earlier in this section that banks need to hold a safe minimum level of reserves in order to meet customer withdrawals. Sometimes they will be withdrawals of cash; sometimes, as here, they will be transfers of deposits to other banks; sometimes, if the government banks with the central bank, they will be transfers to the government's accounts at the central bank. In our illustration, the payment by the customer of bank A to the customer of bank B is matched by a transfer of bank A's deposits at the central bank to bank B's account at the central bank. Thus for bank A, D_b acquires a (–) while D_b for bank B acquires a (+). This adjustment restores the balance.

The second principle is that of portfolio equilibrium (which we first met in Chapter 2). Consider what has happened to the *composition* of these balance sheets, since the creation of the loan. Loans and deposits have increased, relative to all other assets and liabilities. Bank A has a balance sheet unchanged in size but it now has replaced low (or zero) earning assets with higher earning customer loans. Notice also that its reserve ratio has therefore fallen and further adjustments will very likely be necessary. Bank B has a *larger* balance sheet now. It also has a *higher* reserve ratio than it previously had. This is because its reserves have increased by the same absolute amount as its deposits; that is, they have increased in the ratio 1:1 while the initial ratio was less than 1:1. If we assume that the initial balance sheet position was one of equilibrium – that is to say that the bank was happy with the distribution of its assets and liabilities having regard to their relative risks and returns – it is unlikely that this new position is also one of equilibrium. We should expect to see that there will be some further readjustment.

The third principle involves the reserve ratio. In our illustration, loans and deposits have increased equally, *all other assets and liabilities unchanged*. One aspect of the balance sheet composition that must have changed, therefore, is the ratio of reserves to deposits. $D_b + C_b$ are now smaller relative to D_p (and of course to L_p) in bank A than they were before. If we follow Equation 6.2 above and call banks' holdings of cash and central bank deposits 'reserves', we can write the reserve ratio as R/D_p. It is this that has diminished (because D_b has dimin-

Table 6.8 Loans increase in a multi-bank system (I)

Bank A			
Assets		Liabilities	
Notes and coin	C_b	Capital and shareholders' funds	S_f
Deposits at the central bank	$D_b (-)$	Customer deposits	D_p
Loans to the public sector	BL_g		
Loans to the general public	$BL_p (+)$		

Bank B			
Assets		Liabilities	
Notes and coin	C_b	Capital and shareholders' funds	S_f
Deposits at the central bank	$D_b (+)$	Customer deposits	$D_p (+)$
Loans to the public sector	BL_g		
Loans to the general public	BL_p		

ished while D_p is unchanged). Whatever a bank may think about the composition of the rest of its balance sheet, this is one relationship about which it can hardly be indifferent. Clearly, if there is a mandatory ratio, the bank is under an obligation to see that this ratio is maintained. Even if the ratio is prudential, a bank has a target ratio based on its own experience of what is a safe level of reserves, given the deposits and withdrawals that its customers make. If this new loan threatens to take the ratio below its desired level, the bank has to think about how to obtain additional reserves. For bank B's reserve ratio to be restored to its original value, by contrast, bank B would have to *increase* its deposits by some multiple of the extra reserves it received.

In the example above, notice that the extra lending was carried out entirely by one bank while the extra deposits appear entirely in a different bank. In practice, in a multi-bank system, we should expect all banks to be making similar decisions. If economic conditions lead customers to ask for more credit, this is not likely to affect one bank any more than another. Thus what we have shown in Table 6.8 is a

Table 6.9 Loans increase in a multi-bank system (II)

Bank A			
Assets		**Liabilities**	
Notes and coin	C_b	Capital and shareholders' funds	S_f
Deposits at the central bank	$D_b(-)[+]$	Customer deposits	$D_p[+]$
Loans to the public sector	BL_g		
Loans to the general public	$BL_p(+)$		

Bank B			
Assets		**Liabilities**	
Notes and coin	C_b	Capital and shareholders' funds	S_f
Deposits at the central bank	$D_b(+)[-]$	Customer deposits	$D_p(+)$
Loans to the public sector	BL_g		
Loans to the general public	$BL_p[+]$		

Table 6.10 The central bank's balance sheet

Assets		*Liabilities*	
Loans to commercial banks	CBL_b	Commercial banks' deposits	D_b
Loans to government	CBL_g	Government deposits	D_g
Foreign exchange reserves	F	Notes and coin in circulation	C_p
Holdings of government debt	B_g		

very incomplete story. In Table 6.9 we show a more realistic picture. Beginning with the position as we left it in Table 6.8, bank B now also makes additional loans to its customers (these later adjustments are shown in square brackets). Thus in bank B, $BL_p[+]$. These will be paid to customers of bank A ($D_p[+]$), with corresponding transfers of central bank deposits from bank B ($D_b[-]$) to bank A ($D_b[+]$). Notice carefully the final position. Both banks have made loans and both banks have clients holding more deposits. In the course of the process, there have been transfers of central bank deposits ('reserves') between the two banks which cancel. Once again our fundamental principles hold. Balance sheets balance; an increase in lending means an increase in money; a change in lending (and deposits), *ceteris paribus*, means a change in the reserve ratio and in the ratio of capital and shareholders' funds to assets and liabilities. Exercise 6.1 provides an opportunity to work through a three-bank example of the relationships we have just described.

Before leaving this examination of bank balance sheets and their importance in money supply changes,

we need to go one further step and integrate the central bank's balance sheet. This is shown in Table 6.10. Central bank assets, like those of commercial banks, are loans in some form or other. CBL_g indicates central bank loans to government while B_g stands for central bank holding of government bonds. Other assets include foreign exchange reserves, F. Liabilities, again like those of commercial banks, are overwhelmingly customers' deposits but customers are the commercial banking system, D_b, and government, D_g. Notes and coin in circulation are also liabilities of the central bank. (We have ignored capital and shareholders' funds.) None of the changes that we have examined so far has had any impact on the aggregate figures in the central bank's balance sheet. In our multi-bank example there were transfers of banks' deposits, D_b, between two banks. This means that the central bank moves such deposits from one bank to another in its own accounts, but this has no effect upon the total. There are, however, some transactions which will affect the aggregates in the central bank's balance sheets.

The most common are those transactions involving the public's exchange of bank deposits for cash and vice versa; and those that involve flows between the public and private sectors. Let us take the case where the public increases its holdings of notes and coin (C_p) surrendering deposits (D_p) as it does seasonally, at Christmas, for example. In commercial banks' balance sheets we have $D_p(-)$ matched initially by $C_b(-)$. It is unlikely that banks will wish to be short of cash for very long, however, and they will quickly draw more notes and coin from the central bank. This second step sees C_b restored, while the reduction in bank assets is transferred to $D_b(-)$. These transactions have their counterpart in the central bank's balance sheet where banks' exchange of central bank

---

Exercise 6.1   Loans create deposits

Imagine a system with just three commercial banks, A, B and C, whose balance sheets are shown below.

Bank A		Bank B		Bank C	
A	L	A	L	A	L
$C_b = 10$	$D_p = 1000$	$C_b = 10$	$D_p = 1000$	$C_b = 10$	$D_p = 1000$
$D_b = 40$		$D_b = 40$		$D_b = 40$	
$BL_p = 950$		$BL_p = 950$		$BL_p = 950$	

where D_p are customers' deposits, C_b is cash (notes and coin) held by banks, D_b are banks' deposits at the central bank and BL_p are loans to the non-bank public. Bank reserves, R, consist of $C_b + D_b$ and a bank's reserve ratio is thus R/D_p. Assume that nonbanks hold 500 in notes and coin (C_p).

1 What is the size of the money stock, $C_p + D_p$?
2 Calculate the reserve ratio, R/D_p, for each bank and for the system as a whole.

Suppose now that Bank A increases its loans (BL_p) by 10 and that its customers use this lending to pay 5 to clients of Bank B and 5 to clients of Bank C.

3 Show the new balance sheet position for each bank.
4 By how much has the money supply increased?
5 Calculate the new reserve ratio for each individual bank and the aggregate reserve ratio.

Suppose now that Bank B also increases its lending by 10 and that its customers use this lending to pay 5 to clients of Banks A and C, and that Bank C increases its lending by 10 and that its customers use this lending to pay 5 to clients of Banks A and B.

6 What is the size of the money stock now?
7 What is the reserve ratio for each bank?
8 What is the aggregate reserve ratio?
9 What quantity of bank deposits are customers of each bank now holding?

Suppose that customers of each bank now decide to increase their holdings of notes and coin(C_p) by 5.

10 What effect does this have on the total money supply?
11 What effect does this have on the composition of the money supply?
12 What effect does this have on the aggregate reserve ratio?

---

deposits for cash is shown by $D_b(-)$ at the central bank. But so far as the central bank's balance sheet is concerned, this is offset by $C_p(+)$ and the balance sheet still balances, and is unchanged in size.

Suppose now that the general public makes net payments to the government. (The government is running a budget surplus.) At commercial banks, we have the sequence $D_p(-)$ and $D_b(-)$. At the central bank we have $D_b(-)$ matched by $D_g(+)$, as government deposits increase. The money supply has decreased (by the reduction in D_p) and banks have become less liquid: R/D_p has fallen. At the central bank, there may be further adjustments if the $D_g(+)$ is reduced in order to pay off some of the borrowing from the central bank, CBL_g.

Suppose by way of contrast that the government runs a budget deficit. It may borrow from the central bank. In this case, as the government spends the loan:

$CBL_g(+)$, $D_p(+)$ (as the general public receives the payments from government). These new customer deposits are matched in commercial bank balance sheets by $D_b(+)$ and this same $D_b(+)$ appears in the central bank's balance sheet as the counterpart to the initial $CBL_g(+)$. Bear in mind also that $D_b(+) = D_p(+)$ and thus banks' reserve ratio, R/D_p, increases and banks are more liquid.

The flows of funds that we have just seen may be described as 'spontaneous'. They have arisen from the imbalance between government expenditure and tax revenue. But it is always open to governments and central banks to buy or sell government debt, regardless of their financing needs. Such sales/purchases will cause induced flows. By buying government bonds from the non-bank public, the central bank initiates the sequence $B_g(+)$, $D_p(+)$ as the public receives payment, and this is matched in commercial bank balance sheets and at the central bank by $D_b(+)$. The money supply is increased and banks are more liquid. Conversely, a sale of government debt to the non-bank public results in the sequence $B_g(-)$, $D_p(-)$ and $D_b(-)$. The money supply is reduced and the banks are less liquid.

In the next section we shall see that there are further flows which cause changes in loans, deposits and the money supply. We list them all in Box 6.3.

6.4 Models of money supply determination

We have seen that most measures of money are dominated by bank deposits. In the last section we saw that changes in the quantity of money must involve changes in banks' balance sheets. Furthermore, since balance sheets must always balance, a change initiated at one point must be matched or compensated for by a change at some other point. Our accounting conventions tell us, for example, that *if* banks make new loans, there will be new deposits while *if* people exchange their deposits for government debt, customer deposits diminish along with banks' deposits at the central bank. But simply observing these interactions can tell us nothing about causality. We know what is involved when the money supply changes but we do not know what, *as a rule*, initiates those changes. When it comes to explaining why changes in the money supply occur, we need something further.

It is usual to analyse money supply changes using one of two models. These we shall call the *base-multiplier* model and the *flow of funds* model. When we examine them in a moment we shall see that they also consist of a set of accounting identities and therefore they do not in themselves tell us anything about causality. However, the purpose of any model is to provide a helpful simplification and summary of a complex reality. Its role is to give us useful insights into real behaviour. It follows therefore that when we have two models, as we have here, then this must mean that there are two rival views of how the world 'really works'. Each model, in other words, implies a world which it describes best. We shall take the base-multiplier model first, and we shall see straightaway

that it is constructed in such a way that it fits one very distinctive view of the money creation process.

The base-multiplier model

We begin with a summary of the model's key characteristics. (This will help us later to make direct comparisons with the flow of funds model.)

- The model focuses upon stocks.
- The stocks in question are the stock of monetary base and the stock of deposits at commercial banks.
- The monetary base is under the direct control of the monetary 'authorities' (some combination of the government and the central bank).
- The authorities' decisions are therefore central to any change in the quantity of money.

Because the model assumes that it is the authorities' decisions which cause changes in the money supply, the model is often said to assume that the money supply is *exogenously* determined. 'Exogenously determined' means determined by variables outside the economy itself.

Central to the base-multiplier model is the fractional relationship between reserves and deposits which we noted in the last section.

We begin with three definitions which we have already met:

$$\text{monetary base} = C_b + D_b + C_p \qquad (6.1)$$

or, alternatively, where $C_b + D_b$ = bank reserves, R, then:

$$\text{monetary base} = R + C_p \qquad (6.2)$$

$$\text{money supply} = D_p + C_p \qquad (6.3)$$

Letting B stand for the monetary base, the next step is to express the whole of the money supply as a multiple of the whole of potential reserves M_s/B, as in Equation 6.4.

$$\frac{M_s}{B} = \frac{C_p + D_p}{R + C_b} \qquad (6.4)$$

Dividing through the right-hand side of the equation by D_p gives us:

$$\frac{M_s}{B} = \frac{(C_p/D_p) + (D_p/D_p)}{(R/D_p) + (C_p/D_p)} \qquad (6.5)$$

The ratio C_p/D_p is the ratio of cash to bank deposits held by the non-bank public, the public's 'cash ratio', and the ratio R/D_p is the banks' reserve ratio which we met earlier. Letting α and β stand respectively for these ratios we can express Equation 6.5 more succinctly as follows:

$$\frac{M_s}{B} = \frac{\alpha + 1}{\beta + \alpha} \tag{6.6}$$

and:

$$M_s = B.\left(\frac{\alpha + 1}{\beta + \alpha}\right) \tag{6.7}$$

The quantity of money is thus equal to the monetary base multiplied by the term in brackets, the bank deposit multiplier or m. Exercise 6.2 provides an illustration of the process.

In differences:

$$\Delta M_s = m.\Delta B \tag{6.8}$$

and in rates of change:

$$\dot{M}_s = m.\dot{B} \tag{6.9}$$

Clearly it is possible to express any magnitude as a ratio of another and to rearrange their components as a series of identities. The fact that the money supply is so frequently presented as a multiple of the monetary base, where the value of the multiplier depends upon the two ratios α and β, suggests strongly that some useful behavioural insights should be available as a result. What are they?

Let us assume first of all that the values of α and β are given, then the multiplier, m, is correspondingly fixed and the money supply bears a fixed relation to the quantity of base. But this is only one, rather modest, insight. The more ambitious insight which it purports to offer is that by controlling the quantity of the base the monetary authorities can control the quantity of money. This line of argument stems from the components of the base. These are notes and coin $(C_p + C_b)$ plus banks' deposits with the central bank (D_b). All are liabilities of the central bank (see Table 6.10) and can, *in principle* at least, be varied by the authorities themselves. This is the key to the base-multiplier model's connection with exogeneity. The model is dominated by precisely those variables over which the authorities would have control in a world of exogenous money and says nothing about the variables (the demand for bank lending) which one would wish to focus on in the case of endogeneity.

The example usually given of the authorities' ability to adjust their own liabilities for monetary purposes is that of 'open market operations' where the central bank buys (sells) government debt in the open market. A purchase (sale) of debt increases

---

Exercise 6.2   The base-multiplier process

Imagine the same system that we saw in Exercise 6.1, with the same banks and the same balance sheets.

Bank A		Bank B		Bank C	
A	L	A	L	A	L
$C_b = 10$	$D_p = 1000$	$C_b = 10$	$D_p = 1000$	$C_b = 10$	$D_p = 1000$
$D_b = 40$		$D_b = 40$		$D_b = 40$	
$BL_p = 950$		$BL_p = 950$		$BL_p = 950$	

In this exercise, nonbanks hold a total of 300 in notes and coin (C_p).

1   Calculate the size of the banks' reserve ratio.
2   Calculate the size of the public's cash ratio.
3   Using Equation 6.6, calculate the size of the multiplier.
4   Recalculate the size of the multiplier if the banks' reserve ratio rises to 0.07.
5   Calculate the value of the multiplier if the public's cash ratio now falls to 0.08.
6   Using the multiplier's *original* value in (3), calculate the change in the money supply that would result from an open market purchase of bonds from the non-bank public of 200.
7   Find the new values for D_p and C_p.

(decreases) the quantity of bank deposits, D_p, held by the non-bank public. At the same time, an equal and matching quantity of funds is credited (debited) to commercial banks' accounts with the central bank, D_b. At this stage, we might call it the first round, there has been an increase (decrease) in the money supply and in banks' reserves (and the base) exactly equal to the open market transaction. This is the same sequence that we described at the end of the last section and Exercise 6.2 provides an illustration of the process.

In the base-multiplier model the money supply depends upon the size of the base, B, and the multiplier which itself depends upon the magnitudes α and β. A given relationship between B and M_s requires given values for α and β. So far, we have assumed that this is the case but we need now to consider that assumption carefully.

The decision to hold notes and coin in relation to deposits (by the non-bank public) and the decision to hold reserves (by banks) are complex portfolio decisions which must be open to continuous reappraisal. Furthermore, this decision is likely to be subject to feedback from some of the variables which changes in money supply might also affect. The obvious case is the vector of interest rates.

In the case of α, the public's cash ratio, demand is likely to be affected by the rate of interest on bank deposits, r_m, and technical considerations relating to the ease and convenience of replenishing cash holdings from cash dispensers and the efficiency of the money (that is, deposit) transmission mechanism operated by banks, T. Thus we may write:

$$\alpha \equiv C_p/D_p = f\ (r_m, T) \qquad (6.10)$$
$$-\ ?$$

where the symbols below the variables indicate the sign of the partial derivative.

Banks' decisions to hold reserves will depend firstly upon the cost of holding reserves, that is to say on the rate of interest earned on reserve assets, r_r, relative to the rate paid on all other assets, r_o. In many systems, the UK included, r_r is zero. The quantity of reserves held will depend also upon the cost of being short, that is, upon the rediscount rate charged for lender of last resort facilities, r_d. Reserve holdings will also depend upon any mandatory reserve requirement, RR, and, lastly, upon the variability of inward and outward flows to which banks are subject, σ. Hence:

$$\beta \equiv R/D_p = f\ (r_r, r_o, r_d, RR, \sigma) \qquad (6.11)$$
$$+\ -\ +\ +\ +$$

Consider now what happens to the multiplier if α and β do change. Look again at Equation 6.6 and remember that α and β both take values less than 1, indeed they will usually be very small fractions. Thus it is apparent that a reduction in either the public's cash ratio or banks' reserve ratio, or both, will cause a rise in the value of m, and an increase in M_s relative to B.

$$M_s = f\ (B, \alpha, \beta) \qquad (6.12)$$
$$+\ -\ -$$

Substituting Equations 6.10 and 6.11 into Equation 6.12, we can see that α, β and the money supply itself will be affected by quite a number of factors.

$$M_s = f\ (B, r_m, T, r_r, r_o, r_d, RR, \sigma) \qquad (6.13)$$
$$+\ +\ ?\ -\ +\ -\ -\ -$$

Notice firstly the reversal of signs on most of the variables (their effect on the multiplier and thus on the money supply is the opposite of their effect upon the ratios α and β). Notice also the importance of interest rates and interest rate relativities.

We noted earlier that one of the most important insights apparently offered by the base-multiplier model was into the exogeneity of the money supply. This was based upon two propositions: firstly, that the monetary base consisted of central bank liabilities and thus was under the central bank's control and secondly that the multiplier was, if not fixed, at least stable. From Equation 6.14, however, we can identify a number of variables over which the authorities should have some influence and could therefore use to control the money supply:

$$M_s = f\ (B, r_b, RR, r_d, r_r) \qquad (6.14)$$
$$+\ +\ -\ -\ -$$

where r_b is the rate of interest on government bonds, one of the rates subsumed until now in r_o. A change in B is a change in the multiplicand; changes in r_d, RR, r_b, and r_r cause a change in the size of the multiplier itself.

The base-multiplier model, with constant values for α and β, underlies the familiar M_s curve, drawn vertically in interest-money space. The money supply is independent of the rate of interest and the curve shifts with changes in the base. *Indeed, the curve will be vertical and it will shift also with changes in the size of the multiplier, provided that changes in the multiplier take place independently of changes in the interest rate on the vertical axis.*

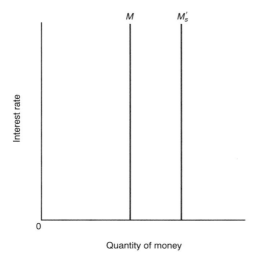

Figure 6.1 Completely exogenous money.

Figure 6.1 shows a stock of money, M_s, determined by a given stock of monetary base, B, and a given multiplier value, m. M'_s, shows a money stock which has expanded by virtue of either an increase in the base or in the value of the multiplier. In the former case:

$$\Delta M_s = \Delta B \times m \qquad (6.15)$$

while in the latter:

$$\Delta M_s = B \times \Delta m \qquad (6.16)$$

But in Equation 6.11 we saw that banks' reserve ratios, β, are likely to be negatively related to r_b, the rate of interest on bonds. If this is true, then Equations 6.13 and 6.14 tell us that the money supply will be positively related to such changes. (The argument, remember, was that as the rate on other assets, such as bonds, in their portfolios rose, banks would economize on non-interest-bearing reserves in order to hold more bonds.) This is significant for our diagram, since the rate of interest on the vertical axis is likely to be the bond rate. The usual reason for

drawing Figure 6.1 is to discuss money market equilibrium – the interaction between the supply of money and the demand for it. We draw the demand curve downward-sloping, because we assume that the demand is inversely related to the opportunity cost of holding money, and this is often represented by r_b, the bond rate. Even if we choose something else, provided it is the opportunity cost of holding money it must be the return on some non-money asset which is still likely to feature in banks' balance sheets and so our argument will still apply: the higher the rate of interest in Figure 6.1, the smaller will be β and the larger will be the money supply, M_s. In these circumstances, the money supply curve should be drawn with a positive slope, as in Figure 6.2.

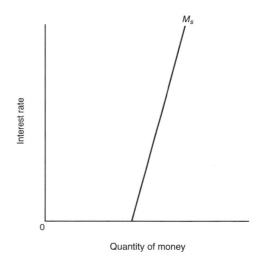

Figure 6.2 Exogenous money with some interest elasticity.

The flow of funds model

By contrast with the base-multiplier model:

- the flow of funds model focuses upon flows;
- the flows in question are flows of new lending;
- the demand for new loans is generally positive;
- 'control' of the money supply means controlling its *growth* rate.

The demand for new lending is assumed as a rule to be positive because the demand for loans, at any given rate of interest, is determined by the level of economic activity and the level of prices. Since both of these tend to increase over time, there is a tendency for firms and households to increase their borrowing from banks over time. The demand for loans is *endogenous* – it is determined by other variables within the economic system. Control of the money supply in this model requires either that the authorities control the demand for loans or that they control banks' ability to respond to the demand. Clearly, *so far as the model is concerned*, either is possible. Monetary control could depend upon the central bank controlling the quantity of reserves available to banks, in the way that we saw above. However, the tendency is to use the flow of funds model to analyse money supply changes in monetary regimes where the central bank acts on the demand for loans, usually by changing short-term interest rates. The central bank sets its rediscount or official dealing rate at what it feels is an appropriate level for the demand for lending (and monetary growth) that it wishes to see, and then accepts the need to supply the reserves required by banks in the light of the demand for loans (and deposits). In these circumstances, *given* the level of interest rates, the money supply itself becomes endogenous.

Our definitions and symbols are the same as those we have used throughout this chapter. The first step is to remember (from Section 6.3) that banks' deposit liabilities are matched by loans of some form. Then it follows that *changes* in one must be matched by changes in the other. Thus:

$$\Delta D_p \equiv \Delta BL_p + \Delta BL_g \qquad (6.17)$$

but since the money stock consists also of notes and coin, we may write changes in the money stock as:

$$\Delta M_s \equiv \Delta C_p + \Delta BL_p + \Delta BL_g \qquad (6.18)$$

Consider now the origin of ΔBL_g. The starting point is the total of government or public sector borrowing, the *PSBR*. This can be financed by selling government debt to the non-bank private sector, ΔG_p. It can also be financed by selling foreign exchange for the domestic currency which provides an 'external' source of finance, Δext, or, as a last resort, it can be financed residually, by borrowing from the banking system, ΔBL_g. Since the take-up of newly issued notes and coin, ΔC_p, also provides finance to the government, though in most countries incidentally rather than deliberately, we can write the government financing identity as:

$$PSBR \equiv \Delta G_p + \Delta C_p + \Delta ext + \Delta BL_g \qquad (6.19)$$

(Notice that the PSBR appears without the Δ sign. It is already a *flow*, whose *stock* counterpart is (roughly speaking) the National Debt.)

We can now combine Equations 6.18 and 6.19 to show that changes in M_s depend upon the size of the PSBR and its *non-bank* methods of finance, since they together determine ΔBL_g.

$$\Delta M_s \equiv \Delta C_p + \Delta BL_p + PSBR - \Delta G_p - \Delta C_p - \Delta ext \qquad (6.20)$$

The two references to ΔC_p obviously cancel and the outflow of foreign currency in exchange for sterling is an addition to the money supply. Thus making these adjustments to Equation 6.20, we have what is commonly described as the key flow-of-funds identity. In Equation 6.21 we have also reordered the terms to match the most common presentation.

$$\Delta M_s \equiv PSBR - \Delta G_p + \Delta ext + \Delta BL_p \qquad (6.21)$$

Unlike the base-multiplier model, the flow of funds approach focuses attention upon the demand for credit, by both the public and the private sectors. Given the many different ways in which both the public and private sectors can borrow, it follows that there are quite a number of loan-related flows which could have some impact upon the money supply. We saw some earlier in Section 6.3. Box 6.3 provides a complete list.

Box 6.3   Flows that change the stock of money

- Central bank loans to government (ΔCBL_g)
- Central bank sales or purchases of government debt (ΔB_g) from:
  - the government
  - banks
  - non-bank private sector
- Changes in central bank holdings of foreign currency (ΔF) as a result of transactions with government or foreign exchange market intervention
- Bank loans to the nonbank private sector (ΔBL_p)
- Bank loans to the public sector (ΔBL_g)
- Bank purchases/sales of government debt (ΔB_g) from the non-bank private sector
- Bank purchases of government debt (ΔB_g) directly from government to finance a government deficit.

We saw earlier that the base-multiplier approach to the money supply process *implied* certain ways in which the authorities should act in order to control the money supply. So too does the flow of funds model, though naturally it directs our attention to the importance of controlling the demand for bank loans. This brings us quite quickly to a major role for interest rates in influencing the growth of money. This is clearly seen if we take each of the variables in turn.

The PSBR is the balance of government revenue from tax (and charges) and expenditure. It is thus the outcome of fiscal policy instrument settings and the level of economic activity. As such, and in economies where a large part of government spending is cyclically determined and non-discretionary, it is not an obvious candidate for use as an instrument for monetary control. Governments, and their electors, have preferences about public services and about taxation which have their own implications for the PSBR. Furthermore, under the Maastricht 1991 convergence criteria, the PSBR is limited to 3 per cent of GDP and so the only choice that will be available to governments will be to reduce the PSBR below this level in order to reduce the rate of monetary growth. At the moment, most countries will find it difficult to meet this criterion by 1999 and so the prospect of manipulating the PSBR for monetary control purposes is a very distant prospect.

Look now at the second component of Equation 6.21 which tells us that *ceteris paribus* the larger the quantity of government debt sales, G_p, to the NBPS, the lower the rate of monetary expansion. Furthermore, *ceteris paribus*, one would expect that larger debt sales would require higher interest rates. An active policy of using debt sales for monetary control purposes requires governments to accept whatever level of interest rates may be necessary to sell the debt. Ideally, this would require government debt to be sold entirely by auction. This is a position towards which the UK has moved slowly over the past 15 years, but most governments have preferred to maintain some control over medium- and long-term interest rates by selling debt only when they think that markets will accept it at current yields and prices.

In Equation 6.21 monetary growth will increase with increases in the sale of domestic currency in exchange for foreign currency. The limitations to the use of foreign exchange transactions as a monetary policy instrument are obvious. Net purchases of domestic currency, aimed at reducing monetary growth, will force the exchange rate up, under a floating exchange rate regime, causing a fall in import prices. This, and the rise in export prices, will weaken the balance of payments which slower monetary growth is often meant to strengthen. Under a fixed exchange rate regime, the device is simply not available.

Clearly, the use of PSBR, debt sales and foreign exchange transactions for monetary control are subject to formidable constraints. This means that monetary control within this model is forced to focus upon the regulation of lending to the non-bank private sector. As we shall see in a moment, this emphasis is further strengthened by the private sector's domination of bank lending flows in most monetary systems. The model, as we said above, is agnostic with respect to the nature of that control. It could be that the central bank maintains rigid control of bank reserve assets in the same way as that envisaged in the monetary base model. This would prevent banks from *supplying* loans. Most monetary regimes have, at various times, used some form of direct control aimed either at the growth of deposits or at the growth of lending. However, the tendency over the past 20 years has been to move increasingly towards 'market methods'. 'Market methods' means 'price' and that in turn means interest rates. In most regimes now, it is changes in short-term interest rates that are used to influence the *demand* for bank lending. The next section reviews briefly a number of possible ways in which the authorities can influence monetary growth.

6.5 Controlling the money supply

In Section 6.3, we established that changes in the money supply are bound to involve changes in the stock of bank deposits and that the balance sheet identity means that changes in bank deposits must be matched or compensated for by changes elsewhere in the balance sheet. Remember also the principle of portfolio equilibrium. A change in any component of the balance sheet is likely to have further repercussions as banks adjust their portfolios in the light of prevailing risks and returns. In theory, therefore, an intervention at any point in the balance sheet could have some effect upon the money supply. However, the first and fundamental choice that the authorities face is whether to act by 'direct' or quantity controls, or by price. All these possibilities add up to a formidable choice. We summarize them below.

1. Price effects on bank deposits

A rise in official interest rates (see Section 3.3.3) causes all short-term rates to rise in sympathy. However, if deposit rates can be held down, the return on non-money assets rises *relative* to money and agents will be less willing to hold money. Since money can only exist if it is held by nonbanks, this increase in the cost of holding money reduces the money supply (or its rate of growth if we think in terms of flows). The most famous example of this technique was 'Regulation Q' in the USA which limited interest that could be paid on deposits. In the UK, and in other countries, the interest paid on *sight* deposits was limited until the past few years by the commercial decision of banks. So long as deposit rates are restricted or at least 'sticky', the authorities can exert some control over the money stock by varying interest rates.

2. Quantity effects on bank deposits

Regulations on the rate of growth of deposits were a feature of the 'supplementary special deposit scheme' or 'corset' during the 1970s. It was effective in the short term but banks and their clients eventually devised techniques such as the 'bill-leak' which allowed borrowers to borrow (but from nonbanks) and enabled banks to charge commissions (to replace their interest charges). The result of this 'disintermediation' was that borrowing and spending carried on pretty much as though the regulations were not there, although the money supply (and bank lending) statistics gave the impression of control. This episode illustrates the weakness of all direct controls, namely that they encourage innovative behaviour which undermines the regulations.

3. Price effects on bankers' deposits at the central bank

This could mean varying the interest rate paid on banks' deposits at the central bank. A rise in rates (r_r) would encourage banks to hold more reserves, ß would increase and the multiplier and money supply would fall. Not used.

Alternatively, it could refer to changes in the rediscount or lender of last resort rate (r_d). An increase raises the cost to banks of being short of reserves and having to borrow from the central bank. This would encourage banks to be more cautious, increasing β and reducing the multiplier and the money supply. Changes in r_d are a major technique of monetary control but more likely through the mechanism described in (7) below.

4. Quantity effects on bankers' deposits

Changing the quantity of reserves available to banks is often presented as the major method of monetary control. As we saw at the end of Section 6.3, the authorities can buy (sell) government bonds which increases (decreases) D_p as well as D_b. The change in the latter causes a change in the ratio of reserves to deposits (R/D_p) and restoring this ratio to its original value requires multiple changes in D_p (see Box 6.3). The authorities' use of 'open market operations', as described here, is often presented in textbooks as *the* obvious technique of monetary control. It has many disadvantages, however, which mean that it is very rarely used in practice. These disadvantages are set out in Box 6.4.

5. Price effects on banks' holdings of government securities

Imagine that the authorities increase the rate of interest offered on government bonds and that banks increase their holdings. For commercial banks, I_b rises while D_b falls. At the central bank of course $D_b(-)$, while $D_g(+)$. *Provided that the government does not spend the funds it receives from banks* (shown by $D_g(+)$), there is no immediate change in the money supply but since banks' reserve ratio (R/D_p) has fallen, banks will need to reduce their lending and deposits as a secondary effect. The technique is not used in practice, though a rise in

Box 6.4 Monetary base control rejected

Virtually every monetary economist believes that the CB [central bank] can control the monetary base... Almost all those who have worked in a CB believe that this view is totally mistaken.
(Goodhart, 1994 p.1424)

The base-multiplier model of money supply determination is presented in almost every macroeconomics textbook as the only explanation of money supply determination. Furthermore, it is *implied* in all those texts which, lacking a formal model, still present the money supply as a curve drawn vertically in interest-money space. And yet, as Goodhart says, no central bank uses open market operations with a view to changing the size of the base in order to achieve a multiple change in deposits. Even in 1981, at the 'high tide of monetarism' when monetary targets were universally adopted, the Bank of England considered explicitly moving to a system of MBC and just as explicitly rejected it. Why the model continues to dominate in textbooks when the real world consistently rejects it is an issue we do not have time to discuss, but we can offer a number of reasons for the rejection.

- Firstly, MBC is a quantity control. In a pure system of MBC, supply would be fixed (some positive interest-elasticity notwithstanding) and fluctuations in demand would have to be absorbed entirely by price. If the authorities were trying to target the base over very short periods, the fluctuations in short-term interest rates could be extreme. The authorities are always reluctant to create situations in which interest rates may be very volatile. Targeting the base, averaged over a longer period, would ease this problem by allowing some day-to-day flexibility in quantities but so long as quantities are targeted rather than price, price must fluctuate.

- Secondly, while the base consists of liabilities of the central bank and one might expect the central bank to be fully in control of its own liabilities, this is not always the case. Firstly, the central bank has to know in advance what will happen to its liabilities in the course of ordinary transactions. F will change as the Bank engages in foreign exchange transactions, CBL_b will fluctuate as a result of the Bank's lender of last resort role and CBL_g and B_g will fluctuate if the central bank has to provide

residual finance to governments when debt sales to the non-bank public fail to match the PSBR. Most central banks make daily predictions about these flows and inform banks and money markets of their plans. It is quite common for the financial press to report the predictions and outcomes. The errors are very large.

- Thirdly, even if the central bank knew what effect its ordinary transactions were going to have on the base this does not mean that it could take the appropriate measures. Knowledge that the base was going to expand more rapidly than desired does not mean that the Bank can suddenly organize a bond issue in order to offset it. Again, this problem becomes more acute the shorter the targeting period. But even if the aim were to achieve an average rate of growth on a quarterly basis, frequent sales of government debt could be very disruptive to financial markets. To ensure the sale of the correct *quantity* governments would have to adopt a pure auction form of sale and thus would have to accept the market clearing price. Once again we are back to volatile interest rates, this time at the longer end of the spectrum.

- Fourthly, in some systems there would need to be major structural changes. For example, it is doubtful whether MBC is compatible with an overdraft system of borrowing where banks agree maximum credit limits with their clients who then use whatever fraction of the limit they need. In the aggregate, this is often of the order of 50–60 per cent. A tightening of monetary policy would inevitably mean that firms would want to use more of their overdrafts; and banks (unable to get reserves) would then face the choice of either allowing the loans and breaching the reserve ratio requirement or defaulting on their promises to borrowers. MBC would also require governments to bank with the commercial banking system rather than the central bank so that payments between the public and private sectors would not cause continuous and large fluctuations in D_b.

- Fifthly, there is an asymmetry in the operation of MBC caused by the fact that most bank assets are non-marketable. This means that an open market purchase of debt will increase D_p, D_b and β as predicted and banks, being more liquid, can try to increase their lending. But a sale, causing a reduction in D_p, D_g and β, requires banks to reduce loans. But loans are not, as a rule, marketable. They can only be reduced by insisting on repayment (or refusing to renew). This is likely to prove very disruptive to trade, resulting in bankruptcies.

- Sixthly, if reserves pay no interest then reserve requirements act as a tax on bank intermediation since they increase its cost. This occurs because the remaining, earning, assets have to earn a higher return to compensate for the zero return on reserves. This increases the spread between deposit and lending rates, which many would regard as the appropriate way of calculating the cost of intermediation.

As with any tax, the supply curve is shifted to the left. Less intermediation is 'bought' and 'sold' at a higher price.

- Finally, MBC raises doubts over the central bank's lender of last resort role. As we have seen, bank deposits are convertible into cash on demand (albeit with interest penalties in some cases). However, the flows that we have discussed in this section could mean that perfectly well-run and solvent banks might find themselves short of reserves. Would the central bank still offer the convertibility guarantee if such a shortage arose, as it well might, in a period of tight MBC?

interest rates on government bonds is likely to be a side effect of any rise in official interest rates intended to reduce the money supply (or rate of growth).

6. Quantity effects on banks' holdings of government securities

An alternative to price inducements to increase or decrease holdings of government debt is regulation. *Requiring* banks to hold more or less government debt has broadly similar effects upon the money supply and on bank liquidity to those resulting from price. However, if the return on government securities is below the rate required to justify the holdings in the absence of regulation, then the regulation acts as a tax on banking and a subsidy on government debt. One could then take the standard view that the effect of the tax will be a lower level of bank intermediation than would otherwise be the case, and a smaller money stock. There have been occasional examples of balance sheet regulations which influence bank holdings of government debt – the UK regulations embodied in *Competition and Credit Control* (1971–81) provide an example – but they are generally rejected now along with most direct controls.

Since 1993, banks in the Group of 10 have had to observe rules on capital adequacy laid down by the 'Basle Committee'. This requires banks to observe a specified ratio of capital to 'risk-adjusted assets'. Government debt has a low risk weighting and banks

may sometimes decide to hold more government debt in order to lower the value of their risk-adjusted assets, but these regulations are aimed at improving and maintaining the solvency of banks and not at monetary control. The regulation of banking and other financial activity is discussed further in Chapter 24.

7. Price effects on bank advances to the non-bank private sector

Through its lender of last resort role a central bank can raise (lower) the level of short-term interest rates. Other things being equal, this moves the non-bank private sector up (down) its demand curve for bank credit. Assuming some negative interest-elasticity, bank advances fall (rise). At first glance, the process could scarcely be simpler. However, there are some problems.

Firstly, we are here discussing stocks but in the real world the authorities are concerned with *flows*. In a world where nominal magnitudes are generally increasing it is the rate of increase that the authorities seek to influence. Experience suggests that the demand for new bank lending is not very interest-elastic while the flow of such lending is subject to a wide variety of other influences. With a low interest-elasticity, the behaviour of the curve itself becomes critical. In a recession, for example, it seems plausible that 'distress borrowing' will, for a period at least, push the curve to the right. If the recession is itself related to the present conduct of monetary policy then we have a malevolent circle in which a rise in interest rates pushes us up an (inelastic) curve, which simultaneously moves outward.

Secondly, while this mechanism appears not to involve the demand for money, a rise in rates will make bank deposits *more* attractive. We saw in (1) above that if deposit rates were sticky (or could be held down) then any rise in interest rates would make holding money less attractive. This would reinforce the negative effect of a rise in interest rates on lending. However, in many European countries now, even sight deposits bear market-related interest rates. This means that a rise in official rates pushes up money's own rate as well and this secondary mechanism is lost. Nonetheless, changes in short-term interest rates are currently the favoured mechanism of monetary control.

8. Quantity effects on bank advances to the non-bank private sector

If price effects on bank advances have been the cornerstone of recent monetary control, quantity effects were their predecessors. Quantity controls usually consisted of target rates of growth of bank credit being laid down by the central bank, with penalties if they were exceeded. The obvious advantage of quantity over price controls is that they avoided fluctuations in interest rates. In particular, a tight monetary policy could be operated without high interest rates. However, any direct control must involve non-price rationing and, with it, the risk of inefficiency and inequity. Furthermore, the control is likely to be evaded as the passage of time pushes the cost of complying towards the cost involved in circumvention. In the present climate which favours free markets, the disadvantages of direct control are felt to outweigh any advantage.

9. The size of the PSBR

Other things being equal, the larger the PSBR the greater will be the amount that the government has to borrow from banks and, *ceteris paribus*, the greater the flow of new loans and deposits. This is demonstrated in Equation 6.21. Adjusting the PSBR for monetary control purposes is impractical, however, for reasons which we saw in Section 6.4.

Most EU governments are more concerned with reducing their PSBR in order to meet the Maastricht criteria. These conditions have monetary implications, but rather more for interest rates than for money supply.

10. Price effects on government debt sales to the NBPS

We have seen that selling government debt to nonbanks reduces the money supply. The sequence is $D_p(-)$ matched by $D_b(-)$ for commercial banks. At the central bank, $D_p(-)$ is offset initially by $D_g(+)$. This may be followed by $D_g(-)$ matched by $L_g(-)$. Banks' reserve ratio is also reduced and banks may need to make multiple reductions in loans and deposits (as described in Box 6.4). This is the process that is often described as 'open market operations'.

Selling government debt to the general public at interest rates higher than those currently prevailing is often a feature of a tight money policy, but it is intended more to limit the quantity of new money created by bank lending to government rather than to achieve a particular quantity change in reserves. The relevant framework is Equation 6.21 rather than Equation 6.15.

Anything that makes government debt, of any sort, more attractive to the non-bank public will have these effects. New savings products, with attractive terms and conditions, have often been developed in phases of tight monetary policy.

11. Quantity effects on government debt sales to the NBPS

Monetary authorities do not normally impose requirements that the general public should lend to the government. Forced loans have had a bad press since numerous monarchs throughout Europe were variously deposed and/or executed for adopting such a policy.

12. Price effects on the external impact on deposit growth

The objective here is to cause transactions involving foreign exchange which will cause the domestic money supply to grow more slowly. In the flow of funds identity Equation 6.21 is represented by Δext. Remember that Δext is shown as contributing positively to a change in the money supply. If we take Germany as an example, then this will happen when overseas citizens buy goods or assets in Germany. Either the overseas buyers make payments to sellers in Deutschmarks (in which case Deutschmarks previously held outside Germany and thus excluded from the official measures of money are now included) or overseas buyers buy Deutschmarks from the Bundesbank which takes foreign currency in exchange. The effect is the same as if the central bank had bought government debt from nonbanks, paying them with domestic currency.

In order to reduce monetary growth, the mechanism needs to be reversed. In other words a capital *outflow* needs to be induced. And herein lies the major difficulty with the manipulation of external flows for monetary control purposes. The main objective of a tight money policy is likely to be a reduction in the rate of inflation, usually to a rate which is similar to those of major trading partners. In other words, the purpose of tight money is to ensure that the country's balance of payments either improves or does not deteriorate. And yet tight money, engineered via external flows, requires that the balance of payments gets worse.

13. Quantity effects on the external impact on deposit growth

Quantitative measures mean exchange controls. Restricting outflows makes the money supply higher than it would otherwise have been while restricting inflows has the opposite effect. Germany has used control on inflows to reduce the rate of monetary growth and one might view the relaxation of exchange controls in the UK in 1979 (in the hope of encouraging outflows) as a sort of negative inflow control. The advantage of exchange controls is that appropriate flows can, in theory, be created without disturbing the balance of payments. However, the first phase of the planned movement to a monetary union (initiated in July 1990) included the removal of all exchange controls between European countries. This has been largely completed and it is difficult to see, even if progress towards unification slows to a halt, that this policy will be reversed.

6.6　Summary

There are numerous theoretical and practical difficulties involved in defining money. The former stem from a circular argument: we cannot say what assets function as money unless we know what it is that money does, but we cannot be sure what role is being played by money itself unless we know which assets we should be studying. The latter stem from the fact that whatever functions as money is defined by custom, and customs change.

In spite of these difficulties the monetary authorities in any country have to take a stand and define money in some practical way. The uncertainty is reflected in the fact that money in most countries is defined both 'narrowly' and 'broadly'. At the moment, all commonly used measures of money are dominated by bank deposits. It follows therefore that anything that causes a change in the size and composition of bank balance sheets is likely to cause a change in the quantity of money and conversely that any change in the quantity of money must be reflected in changes in banks' balance sheets.

There are two ways of modelling the money creation process. One, the base-multiplier approach, focuses upon stocks and makes discretionary decisions by the authorities central to changes in the quantity of money. The other, the flow of funds approach, focuses upon flows and sees expansion as the norm. In this model, the authorities occupy a subordinate role in which they do what they can to influence the demand for new loans and thus the rate at which the money supply expands.

The base-multiplier model points to control of the monetary base, or bank reserves, as the obvious means of controlling the money supply; the flow of funds model points to action to control bank lending. At present, 'market' methods of influence are preferred and that essentially means using interest rates.

Key concepts used in this chapter

Real income	Legal tender	Time deposits	Market methods of
Real wealth	Monetary base	Certificate of deposit	control
Money income	High powered money	Divisia	Price effects
Unit of account	Bank reserves	Reserve ratio	Direct controls
Medium of exchange	Narrow money	Mandatory ratio	Quantity effects
Store of wealth	Broad money	Prudential ratio	Disintermediation
Standard of deferred	Sight deposits	Base-multiplier model	
payment	Demand deposits	Flow of funds model	

Questions and problems

1 Distinguish between 'broad' and 'narrow' measures of money.

2 Why do countries usually have several official measures of money?

3 For your own economy, find recent figures for GDP (at current prices) and for a measure of narrow money and a measure of broad money. Calculate narrow money velocity and broad money velocity.

4 Why do official measures of money change over time?

5 Using the base-multiplier framework, explain why the money supply curve is likely to be positively sloped, rather than vertical.

6 Using the base-multiplier framework, explain the effect on the money supply of (a) an increase in the size of the base and (b) an increase in the central bank's official dealing rate (r_d).

7 Using a flow of funds framework, explain the effect upon the creation of new deposits of:

(a) an increase in the *PSBR*, *ceteris paribus*;

(b) a reduction in the central bank's official dealing rate, *ceteris paribus*.

8 Summarize the arguments against quantity controls on bank deposits and bank lending.

Further reading

M J Artis and M K Lewis, 'Money Demand and Supply', in T Bandyopdhyay and S Ghatak (eds), *Current Issues in Monetary Economics* (Hemel Hempstead: Prentice-Hall, 1990)

A D Bain, *The Financial System* (Oxford: Blackwell, 2e 1992) Ch. 12

Bank of England Quarterly Bulletin (1988), 'Bank of England Operations in the Sterling Money Market', October

D S Batten, M P Blackwell, I S Kim, S E Nocera and Y Nozecki, '*The Conduct of Monetary Policy in the Major Industrial Countries: Instruments and Operating Procedures*', IMF, Washington DC, July 1990.

Deutsche Bundesbank, Monthly Report

Euromoney (monthly)

C A E Goodhart (1994) 'What should central banks do? What should be their macroeconomic objectives and operations?',

Econ Journal, 1994 (Nov) 1424–36

S Heffernan, *Modern Banking in Theory and Practice* (Chichester: Wiley, 1996)

J R Hicks, *Value and Capital* (Oxford: Clarendon Press, 1946)

P G A Howells, 'Institutional Changes and the Money Supply', *British Economy Survey*, 22(2), (1993) 13–17

P G A Howells, 'Banks, Building Societies and the Money Supply', *British Economy Survey*, 23(1), (1993) 13–18

D T Llewellyn, 'Money Market Operations of the Bank of England and the Determination of Interest Rates' in T Bandyopdhyay and S Ghatak (eds), *Current Issues in Monetary Economics* (Hemel Hempstead: Prentice-Hall, 1990)

A Mullineux, *Financial Innovation, Banking and Monetary Aggregates* (Aldershot: Edward Elgar, 1996)

The demand for money

7.1 Introduction

Having considered the money supply process, we begin this chapter by looking at the economic significance of changes in the supply of money – in particular, the relationship between the supply of money and nominal income (that is, GDP at market prices). Changes in the level of nominal income may, in turn, affect the price level and/or the level of real income and it is these that are of interest to voters and policy makers. This series of linkages between the money supply, prices and real income (and hence employment) is frequently referred to as the *transmission mechanism of monetary policy*. The conventional approach is to consider these through the interaction between the supply of money and the demand for money – the quantity of money that economic agents *wish* to hold at a given time. This requires us to look, in turn, at the factors that influence the demand for money. Our final step in the chapter will be to bring material concerning the supply of and demand for money together to consider the principal issues facing monetary policy.

7.2 The demand for money – an introduction

We have seen that people, in the aggregate, hold a stock of wealth from which they derive income which they may, in turn, consume or save (adding to their stock of wealth). The decision as to how to hold their wealth (that is, which types of asset they choose to hold) will influence the amount of income they derive from their wealth and hence their ability to consume. The decision will involve some trade-off between the expected rate of return on different types of assets, the risk associated with holding those assests and the fluctuations in return on them. This risk may relate to a possible loss in the nominal value of an asset or to a loss in real value through inflation. It follows that we may compare different assets (for example, financial versus real assets; equities versus bonds) and ask how much of each people are likely to hold in their portfolios under different circumstances. Money is one possible component of wealth and hence in asking about the demand for money we are asking why people choose to hold some of their wealth in the form of money, which pays a zero or low rate of interest, rather than in the form of other assets which bear a higher rate of return. We also wish to consider the circumstances under which the proportion of wealth held in the form of money will change.

We begin with the simple proposition, based on the role of money as a *medium of exchange*, that people need to hold part of their wealth in the form of money at times when they wish to purchase goods and services or settle bills for previous purchases. This suggests that the amount of money people choose to hold on average over a period must be related to the average amount of expenditure people wish to undertake during that period and to the nature of the receipts and payments system. For instance, someone who knew that he had to settle a credit card bill for a known amount on the fifteenth of the month, or wished to purchase directly a particular good at a known price on that day, would be able to convert other assets into money in sufficient time to make the payments. How long he would need to hold the known amount of money would depend on how quickly other assets could be converted into money and on such things as the manner in which that was done, the acceptability of cheques and the opening hours of banks. There would be no sense in anyone holding more money than strictly needed because higher rates of return could be obtained on other assets. Thus, income received in the form of money on the first of the month would be converted into other assets and only converted back into money in sufficient time to make the payments on the fifteenth.

If we were to assume that the institutional arrangements mentioned above changed only slowly over time, changes in the amount of money required in the aggregate would depend entirely on the determinants of planned expenditure. For households, this would depend on the form of the consumption function that we adopted, but we might say that the demand for money was determined essentially by the level of current or permanent income and/or the level of wealth. Although we shall see in Section 7.4 that this is a considerable simplification, it provides us with a sufficient basis for considering the impact of changes in the supply of money on nominal income. It also allows us to write a simple money demand equation:

$$M_D = kP.Y \qquad (7.1)$$

where M_D is the demand for money, P is the price level, Y is aggregate real output and hence $P.Y$ is the current level of nominal income. k is a constant

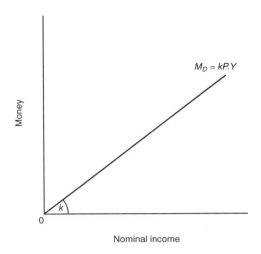

Figure 7.1 The demand for money and nominal income.

expressing the relationship between nominal income and the demand for money. Figure 7.1 shows this information in the form of a demand for money curve.

We have noted above several factors of relevance to this diagram. Firstly, although we have mentioned the possibility of using other measurements of income, we have settled in the diagram and equation for current nominal income. This is usually done because statistics are readily available for current income. Secondly, we have noted that changes in the receipts and payments system will influence the relationship between expenditure and the demand for money. These will cause k to change and the curve to shift over time. One might, for example, expect the financial system to become more sophisticated over time and to allow people to economize on the use of money. This would cause k to fall and the money demand curve to rotate to the right. Thirdly, it is apparent that other factors which influenced the relationship between income and consumption expenditure (the consumption function) would influence the relationship between income and the demand for money. Thus, the curve may move because of changes in, amongst other things, the level of wealth, the distribution of income or the age composition of the population. k is therefore not likely to be constant but may change only relatively slowly over time.

7.3   The transmission mechanism of monetary policy

The usual analysis of monetary policy assumes that the supply of money is exogenous. Thus, if the supply of money is different from the demand for it, the money market is only able to move to equilibrium if the demand for money adjusts to make it equal to the existing money stock. This will happen if those variables that influence the demand for money change. If the aggregate supply of money is greater than the existing demand for it, individual economic agents will be holding excess money balances and will seek to reduce their holdings of money. However, if the money stock is fixed exogenously[1], the actions of individuals cannot reduce the aggregate supply of money. It follows that we are interested in how the attempts of individuals to reduce their holdings of money might change economic variables in such a way as to make them willing to hold more money.

How might this work? A single economic agent will seek to exchange any excess money balances for another type of asset – one that is a close substitute for money itself. The most likely close substitutes for money will be highly liquid assets which can quickly and with little risk of loss be converted into money – assets such as other short-term financial assets which may be sold in organized markets and whose price is largely determined by the money value of the asset at maturity (bills, bonds maturing in the near future). As the demand for these assets rises, their prices increase and the yield on them falls, making them less attractive. This could have two effects: (a) it could cause the demand for money itself to increase since the interest rate being received for forgoing an element of liquidity will have fallen; (b) it will make less liquid financial assets relatively more attractive and cause part of the impact of the excess money balances to shift to them. We can thus imagine the increased demand for non-money financial assets moving along a chain organized in terms of degrees

of liquidity. Clearly, however, if effect (a) is strong, effect (b) will be weak. Thus, one thing we need to know is the strength of the relationship between the rate of interest on other assets and the demand for money. Should the demand for money be highly interest-elastic, excess money balances would disappear quickly and there would be relatively little impact on anything else in the economy. Starting from a position of equilibrium in the money market, an exogenous increase in the supply of money would cause a small fall in interest rates and this would be sufficient to persuade economic agents to hold the larger quantity of money now in existence.

Suppose, however, that the demand for money is not interest-elastic: effect (a) is weak and effect (b) is strong. This is likely to mean that an exogenous increase in the supply of money will have a considerable impact on the interest rates on non-money assets. As interest rates fall, we would expect investment expenditure (on new capital equipment, new buildings, stocks of intermediate goods held by firms) to increase. We would also expect increased demand in the housing market and a rise in expenditure on consumer durables since interest payments represent a significant part of the cost of them to the average household. As incomes and expenditure rise, people will need to hold more money to carry out their expenditure plans. The demand for money rises and we return to equilibrium. In this second case, then, we might have a strong relationship between the supply of money and nominal income, causing an increase in prices and/or an increase in output and employment.

From the point of view of monetary policy, there is an extra issue. For the authorities to be able to hope to determine the rate of inflation through control of the rate of growth of the money supply, it is not sufficient that there be a *strong* relationship between the supply of money and the price level. The relationship needs also to be *predictable*. This will be the case if the demand for money is stably and predictably related to interest rates and real income.

Many complications can be introduced into this

---

[1] An exogenous money supply is one where the central bank determines the money supply using techniques such as monetary base control. The mechanics of this process were examined in Section 6.4.

basic story. One textbook idea is that there are no close substitutes for money – defining money as the only asset that can be used in final settlement of debt makes it unique. If no asset is an adequate substitute for money, the idea of the effect of an increase in the supply of money moving along a chain of assets in terms of degrees of liquidity disappears. People holding excess money balances might use them to acquire any other type of asset, real or financial. If they acquire real assets, there may be a link between the money supply and nominal income which is not dependent on the impact of an increased supply of money on interest rates. In practice, however, liquidity is bound to be an important consideration in the choice among assets, especially for households and firms which need to make regular payments on outstanding debt. In any case, although logically satisfying, this approach provides a definition of money which is empirically extremely difficult to pin down, especially if one is trying to establish a relationship between money and nominal income rather than between money and total transactions of all kinds (including expenditure on secondhand goods and financial assets).

Of much greater concern is the objection to the assumption of an exogenous money supply. Let us assume instead an exogenous level of consumer confidence. Suppose that consumer confidence rises, leading people to be prepared to go into greater debt in order to trade up in the housing or motor vehicle markets or purchase new consumer durables. To the extent that banks are willing and able to meet this increased demand for loans, expenditure, income, bank deposits and the money supply all increase. The same event (the increased confidence) generates increases in both the demand for money (to carry out the increased expenditure) and the supply of money. It is true that the central bank may be able to make it difficult for banks to meet the increased demand for loans, but only at the expense of higher interest rates (see Section 9.4). It is also possible to object to the notion of exogenous consumer confidence but to do so is to contradict what has become the dominant explanation of cyclical variations in aggregate consumer spending. We shall return to issues such as this at the end of this chapter after we have looked more closely at the demand for money.

7.4 The demand for money – a more complete approach

There are two basic problems in the analysis of the demand for money. Firstly, the demand for money cannot be measured directly. We can (once we have agreed upon a definition) measure the money stock. We cannot, however, know whether people wish to be holding that quantity of money under the existing circumstances. This is of great importance since any impact from the money markets on the rest of the economy will come about only when demand is not equal to supply – when demand is less than supply and people attempt to increase their money balances by selling other assets; or when demand is greater than supply and they seek to use their excess money balances to acquire other assets. The simplest approach to this problem is to assume that people are always in equilibrium or, at least, move very quickly to a new equilibrium position following a shock in the form of an unexpected increase or decrease in the money stock. Alas, empirical studies do not appear to bear this out.

The second basic problem concerns the level at which to conduct the analysis. In relation to the supply of money, we are dealing with the money stock for the economy as a whole. However, because the demand for anything is subjective and varies from person to person, the natural way for an economist to consider demand is at the household or microeconomic level. Thus, we ask what proportion of its wealth a household will hold in the form of money under different circumstances. Nonetheless, since we wish to deal with the interaction between supply and demand, we ultimately wish to come to conclusions about the *aggregate* demand for money for the economy. It is common practice to assume that the demands of all households could, in theory, be added together to arrive at this total, although it is also usual to admit the existence of serious aggregation problems. This last is an understatement. It is just not possible to arrive at an aggregate demand for money by adding up household demands. Thus there is inevitably a gap between theoretical and empirical studies of the demand for money – all demand for money functions which are tested are macroeconomic relationships between the aggregate demand for money and other economic variables. These empirical analyses of the aggregate demand for money have come to dominate the subject. The nature of the econometrics used in those studies has become more important than any underlying theoretical analysis. Nonetheless, we cannot understand the general nature of empirical money demand functions without some consideration of theory.

7.4.1   The theory of the demand for money

We have seen that our interest in the demand for money from the point of view of the transmission mechanism resolves itself into three questions – the extent to which the demand for money changes (a) as interest rates change and (b) as real income changes; and the stability of the relationship between the demand for money and interest rates and real income.

We have suggested in Section 7.2 that the demand for money should be determined essentially by some measure of income or wealth. There are three problems with this story. Firstly, the conversion of money into other assets and back again is not costless. It may involve brokerage fees (in the purchase of bonds or equities, for example); it will certainly take time and there may also be travel and information costs. Some costs will be related to the size of the amount being transferred; others will be fixed costs. These costs must be set against the extra income which would be earned from holding assets other than money, that is, against the interest rate differential between other assets and money. Given that some of the costs are fixed, this may mean that it would not be worthwhile for people to convert small amounts of money into other assets and back again for limited periods of time. People with low incomes may simply hold their wealth in the form of money. In the aggregate, the introduction of *transfer costs* into the analysis has two effects:

- It affects the relationship between income and the demand for money since the decision as to whether or not to convert money into other assets and back will depend on the size and the form (fixed or variable) of the transfer costs; in terms of Equation 7.1 and Figure 7.1, it causes k to change and the money demand curve to rotate.

- It introduces a relationship between the demand for money and the differential between the interest rate payable on other assets and that payable on money.

This latter relationship plainly will be negative since, given the level of transfer costs, the greater the interest differential is, the more worthwhile it will be to hold other assets rather than money. There is an obvious simplification here, however. We have distinguished two rates of interest – that on money itself and that on 'other assets'; but since money may be switched into a variety of assets, each with a different rate of return, we are bound to have a problem in choosing an average or 'representative' asset to compare with money. Indeed, the average rate of return on money itself will depend on the definition of money we are using! Let us leave this to one side for the moment and concentrate on another issue – the stability of the relationship between interest rates and the demand for money. We could treat the inclusion of interest rates into the analysis in terms of Figure 7.1. It could have two influences on that diagram:

(a) changing the value of k and causing the curve to rotate;

(b) moving the whole curve so that it has a positive intercept on the vertical axis, since we are suggesting that changes in interest rates could influence the demand for money quite independently of changes in the level of income and expenditure.

However, the relationship between the interest rate and the demand for money is of sufficient importance to warrant being considered separately. Thus, we may write:

$$M_D = \tilde{M} - l.i \qquad (7.2)$$

where $\tilde{M}$ is the level the demand for money would reach, *ceteris paribus*, at zero interest rate; i is the interest rate on a representative asset and l expresses the *ceteris paribus* relationship between the representative interest rate and the demand for money. In Figure 7.2, we show the relationship between the demand for money and interest rates.

Since we can calculate the impact which a change in interest rates will have on the interest income we

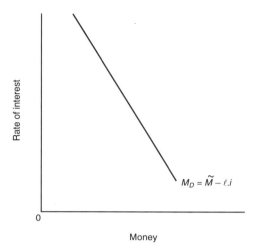

Figure 7.2 The demand for money and the rate of interest.

Exercise 7.1   Influences on the demand for money curve

1   Consider how the demand for money curve in Figure 7.1 (the curve relating the demand for money to *income*) will change as a result of the following:

   (a) an increase in the proportion of retired people in the population, thus reducing the economy's propensity to save;
   (b) an increase in wealth;
   (c) an increase in the rate of interest.

2   Consider how the demand for money curve in Figure 7.2 (the curve relating the demand for money to *the rate of interest*) will change as a result of the following:

   (a) an increase, *ceteris paribus*, in the rate of interest on *money*;
   (b) a fall in income;
   (c) an increase in wealth;
   (d) an increase in the costs of moving from money to other assets and back.

---

receive from any given mixture of non-money and money assets, we should have no problem in constructing such a demand schedule for money with interest rates as the independent variable.

We begin by assuming that transfer costs, incomes and expenditures are given and known. We also assume that the interest rate on money itself does not change. Then, as shown in Figure 7.2, the demand curve for money will slope down to the right. The curve will shift when incomes or transfer costs change. Also, since we have used a single measure of the rate of interest (on other assets) on the vertical axis, the curve will shift when the interest rate on money itself changes, thus changing the relative interest rate between money and other financial assets. On the basis of our argument so far, the demand for money curve should otherwise be stable. Exercise 7.1 deals with the direction in which the curve will shift with changes in the underlying variables.

The second problem with our initial story is that people do not often know exactly how much money they will need to settle debts or make purchases; nor, in many cases, will they know exactly when the payment will need to be made. Given that there is likely to be some cost associated with failing to make the correct payment on time (extra interest on credit card bills, penalty interest on overdrawn bank accounts, inconvenience, loss of customers...), people

will normally choose to hold more money and to hold it for longer periods than they strictly need to meet their monetary obligations. One way of modifying our story would be to follow the approach of Keynes in *The General Theory* and distinguish among *motives* for holding money. Thus, we would distinguish so far between the *transactions demand* for money (the basic relationship between income and the demand for money, on the assumption that both the size and the timing of the payments we needed to make in money were known) and the *precautionary demand* for money which would allow for the uncertainty associated with the amount and timing of monetary payments.

The advantage of this approach is that it allows us to think separately of the factors that might influence any additional amount of money demanded over and above the minimum amount required for transactions purposes. Keynes himself stressed the link between the additional precautionary amount held and the total required for transactions purposes. Thus, the standard treatment of the precautionary demand was to see it as being stably related to the transactions demand and hence to income. Transactions and precautionary balances were amalgamated to form *active money balances*. However, just as with

---

Box 7.2   The demand for money curve and the precautionary demand

Consider Figure 7.1

Including a precautionary demand for money would increase the amount of money demanded for each level of income. If the precautionary demand was genuinely just an extension of the transactions demand, k would increase but the form of the equation would not change and the demand curve would rotate to the left.

Consider Figure 7.2

Incorporating a precautionary demand for money could be considered as just another reason for the demand for money to be higher at each level of the interest rate. The demand for money curve would shift out to the right.

It would be logical, however, to assume that people balance the utility gained from holding additional money balances to protect themselves against uncertain patterns of expenditure with the cost of holding these balances (the rate of interest foregone). Then, incorporating a pre-cautionary motive into Figure 7.2 would shift the curve further away from the original curve at lower rates of interest than at higher rates. The slope of the demand for money curve would change. One could also incorporate floors and ceilings of money holdings into the diagram, but not very satisfactorily.

Answers to Exercise 7.1

1 (a) Consumption rises as a proportion of income; higher money balances are required to meet the additional expenditure. The curve rotates left.
   (b) As wealth increases, consumption increases as a proportion of income and the curve rotates left.
   (c) As interest rates increase, there are two possible effects.
       (i) Expenditure possibly falls as a proportion of income, although this is not certain. (ii) The opportunity cost of holding money increases and people seek to economize on money balances. The curve is very likely to rotate right, reflecting the slope we have assumed in Figure 7.2

2 (a) The interest differential between money and other assets falls, lowering the opportunity cost of holding money. At any given interest rate on other assets, people will be more willing to hold money. The curve shifts to the right.
   (b) As income falls, the demand for money falls at all interest rates and the curve shifts to the left.
   (c) As wealth increases, the demand for money increases at all interest rates and the curve shifts right.
   (d) Increases in the costs of moving into and out of other financial assets reduce the opportunity cost of holding money and the curve shifts right.

---

transactions balances, precautionary balances will be related to the rate of interest since the costs of finding oneself with less money than needed for transactions purposes may also be weighed against the extra interest payments available from holding assets other than money. Box 7.2 discusses how the precautionary demand for money may be included in the demand for money diagram as well as providing the answers to Exercise 7.1.

A more organized assessment of the precautionary demand for money is possible through an expression of the uncertainties surrounding the transactions motive in terms of probabilities. Clearly the difficulty of assessing how much money would be needed would increase as the variability of incomes

(and hence expenditures) increased. Thus, the risk that any given level of money holding would prove insufficient would be greater, the greater was the variability of incomes. Other things being equal, people would hold higher precautionary balances the more variable income levels were. This introduces the idea that the demand for money is not related simply to income levels but to the variance of incomes. This stochastic approach to the demand for money led to the development of models which suggested that the money balances held by an individual would lie between a floor and a ceiling. While one can continue to identify an equilibrium or return point (based upon the assumptions made about the nature of transfer costs) to which money balances eventually return, actual holdings only return to that point when they reach either the floor or the ceiling. As money balances fall below the return point, there is now only a probability that the amount held will be too low. It is only when that probability becomes sufficiently high (when the floor was reached) to offset the income gain from holding less money that any action would be taken. Again, money balances will be allowed to rise until a point (the ceiling) when the probability that the extra balances will be needed has become sufficiently small to be outweighed by the additional income available from switching into other assets.

Putting our argument together, we can see that the demand for money should depend on the differential between the interest rates on non-money assets and money in comparison with the transfer costs of switching between these two groups of assets *and* the risk arising from the lack of certainty regarding the amount of money balances actually needed for transactions purposes. Since we have assumed that we can express this risk in terms of probabilities, it should follow that its existence should not upset the stability of the relationship between interest rates and the demand for money. This relationship will change if people's attitude to risk changes (if they become more or less risk averse). An assumption about the existing attitude to risk is thus another factor underlying the demand for money curve. Changes in attitude to risk will cause the curve to shift in exactly the same way as would changes in income, transfer costs or the rate of interest on money but there is no reason to believe that it is likely to happen at all often.

Despite the fact that the distinction of a precautionary motive allowed careful analyses of precautionary balances, the motives approach has always worried economists. This is because the distinction of a number of motives gives the feeling that one should be able to calculate the amount of money held for each motive and then simply add them up to produce a total demand for money for any household. However, as we have seen, this is not the case with the transactions and precautionary demands since both are influenced by the interest rate differential between money and non-money assets. Thus, a decrease in the interest rate on non-money assets would, *ceteris paribus*, produce an increase in the money balances held but those extra balances

would be transactions balances if they turned out to be needed for transactions purposes but precautionary balances if they were not so needed. In other words, the same balances could satisfy both motives.

The third inadequacy in our basic demand for money story is that it does not take into account the fact that the capital value of non-money assets may change while they are being held whereas the nominal value of money itself must remain unchanged over time. One may choose to hold a non-money asset because of the higher interest rate payable on it but this would not be profitable if the capital value of the non-money asset fell before one needed to convert it back into money for transactions purposes. It follows that the decision as to how much money should be held must also take into account the risk that the value of non-money assets will change in the near future. Other things being equal, people will hold more money than is needed for transactions purposes if they feel that the money value of non-money assets will fall in the near future. On the other hand, to turn around a common warning issued to investors, the value of assets may rise as well as fall. Anyone who thought that the value of non-money assets was likely to rise would seek to economize on the holding of money balances in order to increase the capital gains available to the holders of non-money assets. It is this motive for varying the money balances people hold that Keynes called the *speculative demand*.

Any analysis of the speculative demand, then, requires us to develop a theory of the formation of people's expectations regarding the direction of price changes of non-money assets. This introduces a complication since one of the major influences on the price of non-money financial assets is the interest rate in the economy. Indeed, if one takes, as Keynes did, as the representative non-money asset a non-maturing bond which produces a regular income fixed in money terms, changes in the general rate of interest in the economy will be the only influence on its price (see Section 5.3.2). Thus, what we need is a theory of the formation of expectations about future interest rates.

In itself this is no problem. Consider, however, the position if the existing rate of interest is one influence on people's expectations regarding likely future changes in that rate. We have so far argued that an increase in the interest rate on non-money assets will, *ceteris paribus*, cause the demand for money to fall. Suppose, however, that this increase engenders in people a belief that a further change in interest rates will soon follow. They might believe that the interest rate is now higher than is sustainable and believe that it will soon fall again or they may feel that the rise signals the beginning of a cycle of interest rate rises and that it may soon be moving up again. Either way, the change in interest rates will have influenced people's expectations regarding the prospect of capital gains or losses from holding non-money assets and thus will have influenced the speculative demand for money. Yet another possibility is that people believe that the interest rate will remain at its new level or, at least, that they have no reason for believing that movement in one direction is any more likely than movement in the other.

If they believed that interest rates would soon fall again, they would believe that holding non-money assets would produce a capital gain in the future and thus would want to hold *less* money than would be suggested from our earlier two motives. That is, the impact of the initial interest rate rise on the demand for money would be more strongly negative than would otherwise be the case (the demand for money would be more interest-elastic). The reverse belief about the future direction of interest rates would cause people to hold more money than previously suggested – the increase in interest rates would have two counteracting effects: the demand for money falling for transactions and precautionary motives but increasing on account of the speculative motive. A belief that the interest rate was likely to remain unchanged following the initial rise would, of course, cut the link between the existing interest rate and expectations regarding future movements in it.

Much depends in this analysis on the nature of the uncertainty regarding future interest rate changes. If we believed that the world was sufficiently predictable for us to be able to calculate probabilities about the future direction of interest rate changes and hence about future non-money asset prices, we could incorporate these into our analysis. We would make an assumption about the probable direction of change and this would become yet another element underlying the demand curve for money. Unless the behaviour of the economy (or of the people running

it) changed significantly over a period of time, we would have no reason to revise our probability calculations and there would be no reason for the demand for money curve to shift. We would still believe that the relationship between interest rate and the demand for money was a relatively stable one.

Suppose, however, that we did not have sufficient knowledge of the economy and its functioning to have any clear idea of what might happen next – that we had no adequate basis for assigning probabilities to possible future changes in interest rates. We would still need some basis for our decisions and so we would search for some rough and ready rule of thumb: a belief, for example, that some particular level of interest rates was the 'normal' level and that any movement away from it would produce a belief in a return to it. Such rules of thumb may be subject to sudden and not easily explicable change. Thus, we may, for no apparent reason, alter our belief about the 'normal rate'. In this case, *even if there were no change in the existing interest rate*, we might believe that it was about to change. This would produce a change in the demand for money and the demand for money curve would be subject to sudden shifts. The relationship between the demand for money and the rate of interest would, in such a case, be unstable. The demand curve, as shown in Figure 7.2, would move unpredictably and may do so because of changes in the supply of money itself. The effects of this are shown in Figure 7.3 in Box 7.3.

It is clear from this discussion that speculative money balances cannot simply be added to (or subtracted from) the demand for money which might arise from the other two motives. If people hold larger money balances than would appear to be strictly necessary, this could be for either precautionary or speculative motives and, since both may be influenced by the existing interest rate, it is not possible to separate the two. The same sum of money may act to protect them against the risk of changes in both the amount of money they need for transactions purposes and the price of non-money assets.

Nonetheless, the above consideration of reasons for holding money can suggest the factors we need to look at in constructing a money demand function which might help us to predict the aggregate demand for money in the economy as a whole. Before we move on to this, however, we need to deal with

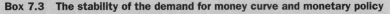

Box 7.3   The stability of the demand for money curve and monetary policy

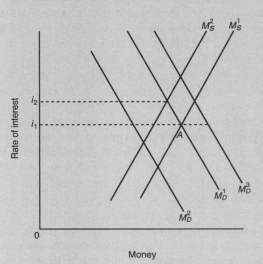

We begin with a positively sloped money supply curve, M_s^1, (see Section 6.4 for a discussion of the slope of the money supply curve) and a negatively sloped demand for money curve, M_D^1, which we assume to be stable. The equilibrium interest rate is i_1 (at A). Assume next that the government wishes to push interest rates up in the hope of influencing the level of expenditure and the rate of inflation in the economy. We may assume an exogenous money supply and move the money supply curve to M_s^2, raising interest rates to i_2 or we may assume that the central bank is able to push the interest rate rate up directly to i_2, causing the money supply curve to shift – the difference is of no significance to us here. What is important, however, is whether the demand for money curve is stable. If it is, we remain at i_2 and the government will have achieved the first part of its objective. Suppose, however, that people respond to the increase in interest rates by believing that the interest rate will soon fall again. This leads them to believe that the prices of non-money assets will soon rise and so they reduce their money balances to buy non-money assets. The demand for money moves back to M_D^2 and government policy will have been less effective than had been hoped. Alternatively, return to our initial equilibrium position (A) and assume that the government has no plans to change policy. However, people fear that the rate of interest might rise. This might cause them to increase their demand for money (either because the speculative demand rises or because they increase their borrowing and advance spending plans) and the demand for money curve moves right. What happened next would depend on whether the money supply was exogenous or endogenous and on the impact that any change in the rate of interest would have on expenditure and income (remember that changes in income will cause the demand for money curve to shift). We cannot hope to analyse all such changes here but the important point is that any instability in the demand for money curve will make monetary policy difficult, if not impossible.

another issue which we have so far neglected – the effect of changes in prices. We suggested above that money retained its value over time. Plainly, this is not true of its real value. An increase in the general price level reduces the real quantity of goods and services which may be purchased with the existing stock of money. This raises three issues.

Firstly, if the basic reason for holding money at all is to allow the purchase of goods and services, it is reasonable to suppose that as prices rise, people will need to hold more money to purchase the same quantity of goods. In other words, *ceteris paribus*, the demand for money in real terms will stay more or less the same as the price level changes. This can be handled in one of two ways – by incorporating the price level as one of the variables influencing the demand for money (with the price elasticity of demand assumed to be fairly close to unity) or by converting the dependent variable into the demand for real money balances by dividing the nominal demand for money by a general price index.

The second issue is more difficult and concerns not the price level itself but the rate at which the price level is changing (the rate of inflation). It is also related to an issue we raised earlier regarding the choice of interest rates. We need to return to the problem that there exists a range of non-money assets into which we could in theory switch any excess money balances and these different assets would have different rates of return. The obvious response is to say, as we did earlier, that it is the differential between the interest rate on money and that on its closest substitute which is of relevance to us. On the other hand, acceptance of the argument that money is a unique asset would imply that all other assets would be equally poor substitutes for it. This leads to the idea of incorporating into the demand for money function the rates of return on a range of alternative assets. It is usual to select three types – bonds, equities and real assets. That leads to the question of the rate of return on real assets. In comparison with money, the rate of return on real assets is the rate of inflation since it provides a measure of the rate at which money loses value. There is, then, a theoretical reason for including the rate of inflation as one of the independent variables we might use to explain the demand for money.

Thirdly, the importance of money as *the* liquid asset *par excellence* is based on the notion that money can be held without risk. Modest and predictable inflation does not call that idea into question to the extent that agents can protect themselves against inflation. This is no longer the case if rates of inflation are volatile and difficult to predict since the future real value of all financial assets including money itself becomes uncertain. However difficult it is to forecast future rates of inflation, economic agents must attempt to do so in order to make a rational decision regarding the holding of assets.

7.4.2 The aggregate demand for money function

We have mentioned above that our practical aim in considering the demand for money is to discover whether the *aggregate* demand for money is stably and predictably related to real income and the rate of interest. Consequently, aggregate demand for money studies have centred on tests to try to discover whether or not this is the case. This usually takes the form of regression analysis in which the aggregate demand for money is expressed as a function of a number of independent variables. A logical starting point of such an analysis would be to derive the independent variables we wanted to include in the demand for money function from the theory of the demand for money. If we were to do this we might, on the basis of our discussion above, come up with a list something like the following:

- The interest rate on representative non-money assets, possibly including the rate of inflation;
- The interest rate on money;
- The transfer costs of switching between money and non-money assets;
- The level of income;
- The variance of income;
- The expected change in the rate of interest;
- An index of prices.

There are several practical problems associated with this list. Firstly, there would be little point in including the interest rate on more than one non-money financial asset since interest rates on financial assets tend to move together. Furthermore, we saw in Section 3.3 that nominal interest rates may be strongly correlated with the rate of inflation. Thus to include *both* an interest rate on a financial asset *and* the rate of inflation would disturb the relationship between either one of them and the demand for money. However, omitting variables which would contribute to the explanation of the demand for money results in the equation being mis-specified. One result of this may be that testing of the equation may seem to reveal an instability in the demand for money which would be removed if the equation could be properly specified. Thirdly, transfer costs are difficult to measure since they vary from one individual to another and from one company to another depending on the circumstances. Since it is usually assumed that transfer costs are likely to change slowly over time, they are thus usually left out of aggregate demand for money equations.

Fourthly, there are no objective *ex post* measures of the expected variables included in the list above. The best that can be done is to estimate expected future values of variables on the basis of forecasts using currently available information (making a judgement in doing so as to the best available forecasting model). These estimates can then be entered into the demand for money equation on the assumption of rational expectations – that agents do, indeed, make use of the best available forecasting models. A more usual approach is to replace the expectational variable with an available proxy or to represent it econometrically in some other way (for example, by a dummy variable or a trend term).

Fifthly, wealth and income present problems. The justification for the inclusion of wealth is such that ideally a broad, all-inclusive definition is required. But the broader the definition of wealth, the more difficult it is to obtain a satisfactory measure for it. In any case, since income can be viewed as a return on the holding of wealth (human and non-human), the inclusion of both a broad definition of wealth and income presents problems. Many alternatives have been tried including narrower definitions of wealth, the use of permanent income and measures of consumption expenditure. All present difficulties.

Sixthly, as we mentioned in Section 7.2, we have no direct measure for the demand for money. All that we can do is to use the supply of money. If we were to make no other adjustments to the equation, this would be tantamount to assuming that the money market was always in equilibrium. Even if we accept this, we are left with the question of which measure of the supply of money we should use. This is complicated by the variety of definitions of money in use in different countries, as we saw in Section 6.2. Theories are of very little help here although concentration on the transactions demand for money leads in the direction of narrow definitions of money. In practice, econometricians are happy to accept the definition of money that yields the most accurate predictions and not worry about the theoretical justification for it. Problems have arisen in recent years from changing definitions of monetary aggregates and financial innovations which change both the roles of financial institutions (and thus the extent to which their liabilities may act as money) and attitudes towards the various types of financial assets.

Finally, there is a problem with the time period covered by the studies. Supporters of the notion of a stable demand for money only claim stability in the long run. However, if the demand for money is unstable in the short run, we need to be able to explain why, and do it in such a way that this instability is compatible with long-run stability. Further, long-run studies (which typically use annual observations or temporally averaged data) face problems because of the many changes in definitions of the variables which occur over time

and because some elements which we suggested above could be assumed constant, such as transfer costs and payments systems, and thus omitted from the equation, clearly will change over long periods of time. In any case, the distinction between long-run and short-run studies is purely arbitrary. There is no theoretical definition of the long run in macroeconomics other than that it is the period necessary for the economy to return to equilibrium – a definition which is useless for empirical work.

The net result of these problems is that the standard regression equation used in demand for money testing is quite a long way removed from the theoretical arguments we have considered above. A standard aggregate money demand equation, linearized by taking logs, is:

$$ln\ m_t = ln\ \beta_0 + \beta_1\ ln\ Y_t + \beta_2\ ln\ i_t + v_t \qquad (7.3)$$

where m is the real value of the money supply (the money supply divided by a price index); Y a measure of aggregate real income; i an interest rate on a representative financial asset; and v a random variable. A common required addition is the lagged dependent variable (the real value of the supply of money): $\beta_3\ ln\ m_{t-1}$. This simply accepts that there are bound to be time lags in adjustment and thus it is a reflection of the idea that a movement to a new equilibrium following a change in one of the independent variables will not be instantaneous. In the early days of testing it was assumed that these time lags would be quite short and thus that the role of the lagged dependent variable would not be very great. The other principal hopes of the testers of functions such as this were that:

(i)   the signs would be as indicated by the theory (most obviously a negative relationship between i_t and m_t;

(ii) the constants would indeed turn out to be constant;

(iii) the independent variables (Y_t and i_t) would between them predict a high proportion of the demand for money; and

(iv) v_t would prove to be random, indicating that it did not incorporate a missing variable with a systematic relationship with the demand for money.

7.4.3   Testing the demand for money – the outcome

Studies in both the USA and the UK up until the early 1970s appeared to produce satisfactory results. The demand for money was found to be interest-elastic but elasticities were relatively low. The majority of studies produced income elasticities close to unity. The demand for money appeared to be correctly specified in real terms. Time lags between interest rate and income changes and the demand for money seemed from long-run studies to be relatively short, although this was called into doubt in short-run studies. Crucially, demand for money functions appeared to be reasonably stable.

However, in the early 1970s the demand for money function began to show signs of instability in both the UK and the USA. In the USA between 1973 and 1975, real money balances steadily declined, falling by about 7 per cent, whereas demand for money equations estimated with data for the 1950s and 1960s had predicted a mild decline in 1974 followed by a recovery in 1975. Thus, existing demand for money equations were seriously *over-predicting* the demand for money, whereas in the UK equations from the 1950s and 1960s *underestimated* the demand for money. Equations also broke down in several other OECD countries. The problem showed up in ways other than the failure of equations to predict accurately. For example, extending the data used for estimating equations to include the 1970s produced changes in the coefficient on the lagged dependent variable which suggested unreasonably long adjustment processes. Things began to wrong again in both the USA and the UK in the early 1980s when income velocity began to fall sharply and demand for money functions estimated on pre-1982 data seriously underestimated the demand for narrow money in the mid-1980s. Box 7.4 discusses changes in broad money velocity in six countries between 1970 and 1991.

Several explanations of these problems have been proposed, most of which have sought to preserve belief in the view that the demand for money is stable, in the long run. Firstly, and least disruptively, it has been argued that the demand for money remained stable even in the 1970s and 1980s but that the equations derived from the pre-1970s studies failed to identify the stability because of faulty specification of the equation or the dynamics in the model. The fault thus lay with the econometrics and the problem could be overcome by altering lag structures or the functional form of the equation, especially by including important variables that had been omitted from the equation. Some recent papers have, for example, argued for the inclusion of a term representing relative prices of consumer durables, non-durables and services in addition to the general index of prices.

Secondly, it was argued that there had been changes affecting the arguments of the function, resulting in unpredictable shifts in the demand for money function and/or in the slope of the function. To retain belief in the long-run stability of the function, it was then necessary to argue that such changes were limited to a particular, dramatic period of time and that once the system had adjusted, long-run relationships would re-emerge. The problems in the early 1970s were attributed to a variety of causes including the change from an international fixed exchange rate system to floating exchange rates (or the changes in exchange rate expectations which became much greater under floating exchange rates) and, in the UK, to changes in the approach to the control of the money supply. The difficulties in the 1980s, however, were overwhelmingly attributed to financial innovation and other types of institutional change although uncertainty resulting from the large swings in inflation rates over the period has also been mentioned.

Institutional change is not new. Particular changes may affect the demand for money in different ways and thus to some extent their impacts may cancel out over time. Further, there is little to worry about if the changes occur steadily over time since their effects will be predictable. Problems will only arise if changes are sudden and frequent or are induced by levels of, or changes in, other variables within the demand for money function. Financial innovations, for instance, may occur in waves, causing discrete short-term jumps in demand for money functions. Again, a period of prolonged high interest rates may encourage the development of financial innovations, allowing money balances held for transactions purposes to be reduced. Thus, there is the possibility of a ratchet effect – when interest rates are high, it pays to spend time and effort on the development of

Box 7.4   Changes in velocity

'Velocity' is the term given to the ratio of GDP at market prices to the stock of money. Strictly speaking, this is 'income velocity'; a less common measure of velocity is 'transactions velocity' which involves dividing total spending (including spending on intermediate and secondhand goods and on financial assets) by the money stock. Clearly, transactions velocity will always be much larger than income velocity. Our interest in velocity lies in the fact that if there is a stable relationship between the quantity of money and total spending then it *may* be the case that controlling the quantity of money gives us

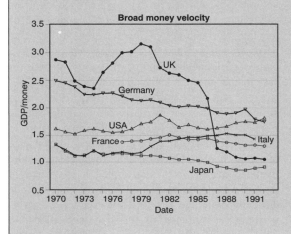

some control over total spending. Notice that this requires that 'money causes spending' but a stable velocity does not guarantee this: velocity will be stable if 'spending causes money' in which case controlling money has no effect on spending. Stable velocity is only a necessary condition for a policy of controlling monetary growth.

Both our definitions of velocity recognize that we can divide by whatever measure of money we think appropriate. If we divide by *M1*, we will have a measure of narrow money velocity; dividing by *M3* or *M4* gives us broad money velocity. The chart above shows the behaviour of broad money velocity in several countries, mainly from 1970 to 1992. It shows quite clearly that velocity is not constant! In some countries it rises over the period and in others it falls. Remember though that what matters is *stability*. Provided they can predict the path of velocity, governments can still operate a policy of monetary control (by adjusting the growth rate to allow for changing velocity). It is unpredictable and dramatic changes in velocity that make it impossible to set money growth targets. The chart shows why Germany has maintained an interest in monetary targets in recent years while other countries, and the UK in particular, have abandoned them.

financial innovations such as the introduction of different types of bank accounts or the introduction of automated teller machines. Having been introduced, these innovations are not reversed when interest rates fall again because the costs involved are mainly set-up costs (for example, computing hardware and software). Thus such financial innovation is likely to have both: (a) caused the constant to have fallen and (b) caused the interest-elasticity of the demand for narrow money to increase (as shifts between demand deposits and high interest-bearing deposits have become much easier).

Attempts to reflect the effects of financial innovation in empirical work have been of several kinds. For example, it was argued that the problems of the 1970s could be overcome simply by including long-term interest rates in the function and redefining money, overcoming the problems arising from the growth of

interest-bearing demand deposits by excluding them from the definition of money. A more usual approach was to incorporate additional variables into the money demand equation. For instance, instead of narrowing the definition of money it was possible to seek to cope with the increased payment of interest rates on demand deposits by adding money's own rate of interest to the equation. Among other variables included have been the change in the number of bank branches per head of population, the ratio of currency to total money stock and of non-bank to bank financial assets and past peak levels of interest rates. Such attempts to adjust equations to reflect institutional change have often not produced satisfactory results. However, this may reflect the difficulty of capturing in equations the many ways in which institutional change may influence agents' actions rather than indicating that financial innovation has not been the principal cause of the apparent instability. A particular problem is that, to the extent that they are induced rather than autonomous, the factors causing financial innovations may be taken into account elsewhere in the equation. Econometricians have largely sought to use cointegration techniques to identify long-run stability amidst the short-run fluctuations.

Thirdly, blame was placed upon the assumption of equilibrium and new approaches to disequilibrium were developed. Associated with these has been the development of the buffer stock approach to the demand for money – a formalization of the old idea that the existence of money allows the separation in time of sales and purchases (the store of value function of money). A distinction is drawn between 'demanding' money as a means of payment and being willing to 'accept' it temporarily because of the costs associated with adjusting stocks of less liquid assets. This work has built upon the precautionary demand for money models discussed earlier which see individuals as being willing to allow their money holdings to fluctuate between a floor and a ceiling.

In short, economists have responded to the apparent instability in the demand for money in the 1970s and 1980s with a great deal of verve and imagination. In recent years, hardly an issue of an economics journal has appeared without an article claiming evidence for another reason why the demand for money function is truly stable. Nonetheless, we should at least mention the existence of a small number of economists who saw the problems with the function as evidence for the proposition which they had always supported that such a function either could not sensibly be defined at all or was bound to be unstable. One view of this kind derives from the endogenous money hypothesis mentioned above (see Section 6.4). This holds that in order to carry out spending plans, agents obtain bank loans. The act of spending these loans creates money in the form of additional bank deposits. As long as banks freely meet the demand for loans, the supply of money can be seen to be adjusting to the demand for it. Spending plans drive the whole process. Since investment plans, in particular, are influenced by waves of optimism and pessimism there is no reason to believe that the demand for money will be stably related to real income. In its extreme form, the endogenous money hypothesis holds that there is no demand for money function independent of the supply of money. People are willing to hold whatever money is created through the banking system.

7.5   The implications for monetary policy

A common summary view is that there is some evidence of stability in the long-run demand for money relationship but that short-run adjustment lags are variable, making it difficult to estimate a stable short-run demand for money function for targeted variables. Thus, even if the long-run function is stable, governments are unlikely to know the lags between changes in the money stock, prices and real income. Further, where they use interest rates as the instrument of monetary policy, as most governments do, structural lags between money stock changes and variations in final objectives may make the money stock of little value as an *intermediate objective*.

Several alternatives have been advanced. In recent years, many academics have supported a commitment to a nominal GNP target on the part of the monetary authorities (see, for example, Frankel with Chinn, 1995). This assumes a close long-run relationship between nominal GNP and the rate of inflation. It is possible to go even further and abandon intermediate goals altogether, targeting the rate of inflation directly. This practice has been followed by the governments of Canada and New Zealand. The Governor of the Bank of England, Eddie George, has also described British policy in this way. It would be more accurate, though, to describe British policy, following its failed attempt between 1976 and 1985 to treat the money stock as an intermediate objective, as eclectic, with monetary policy decisions being based upon a range of indicators including money stock and monetary base figures, the rate of inflation, the level of unemployment, the exchange rate and asset prices. The main objections to the use of the rate of inflation as a final objective without using an intermediate objective is that the rate of inflation may be influenced, especially in the short run, by too many variables including some which are outside the control of monetary authorities.

Amongst all of this uncertainty, the Bundesbank has remained steadfast in its support for the setting of money supply targets supported by the control of

Box 7.5   The pragmatism of German monetary policy

The Bundesbank has maintained its support for
the setting of money supply targets supported by
the control of money market liquidity through
minimum reserves. This can be justified by
Germany's record of low inflation over many
years and by academic studies which have
shown that the demand for money function has
remained much more stable than in other
countries, although some doubts have recently
begun to emerge.

The measure of the money supply that is
recommended by the Bundesbank as providing a
reliable early warning system to policy makers in
Europe in general is *M3* (see Table 6.1). It is clear,
however, that routine *M3* figures do not provide
an especially clear guide to the Bundesbank's
policy decisions. One example of this can be seen
in the period between 1991 and early 1994. In
early 1994, it was reported that 'special factors'
had interfered with *M3* figures. The annualized
growth rate of M3 for 1993 was 8.1 per cent. This
was more than 1.5 points above the top of the

target range then being used, but worse was to
come. It rose sharply to 20.6 per cent in January
1994. This was said to be due to two factors:

(i) liquidity kept in short-term deposits in
expectation of rising long-term interest rates;
and
(ii) heavy borrowing by house buyers concerned
to pre-empt any interest rate rises.

In addition, there was a reversal of a rush of
funds overseas to avoid a new withholding tax
which had taken place in 1993. In fact, the
Bundesbank had begun cutting interest rates in
September 1992 when *M3* was *above* the target
range and rising. It then continued with small
interest rate cuts through 1993. It seems clear that
the Bundesbank takes the inflation rate into
account as well as money supply figures. The
Bundesbank also freely admits the extent to
which its monetary policy actions are
constrained by international forces.

money market liquidity through minimum reserves.
It also continues to support the adoption of a policy
of this kind by the European Central Bank after the
establishment of European Monetary Union (an issue
discussed in Chapter 22). Nonetheless, as is indicated
in Box 7.5, the Bundesbank has been pragmatic in
the operation of its monetary policy.

There has also been academic support for the
targeting of the exchange rate, a policy followed to a
large extent by many members of the European
Monetary System, although the loosening of the
system after 1993 returned to them a good deal of
freedom to choose domestic intermediate objectives.

7.6   Summary

The demand for money in an economy provides an
important link between monetary policy and changes
in the level of nominal income and hence the rate of
inflation (this link is known as the transmission
mechanism of monetary policy). Thus, it is necessary
to enquire into the nature of the demand for money.
Although we are interested principally in the aggregate

demand for money, the normal approach is to begin by
asking why individuals might choose to hold money
when they could receive a higher rate of return on their
wealth by holding other assets. It is clear that people
hold money because they need it to carry out their
expenditure plans. Those plans are likely to be strongly
influenced by income and thus income will be a major
determinant of the demand for money. However, other
factors are also likely to influence the demand for
money. The rate of interest is crucial among these
since changes in the supply of money influence
interest rates. If interest rates, in turn, have a strong
effect on the demand for money, the supply of and
demand for money in the economy are interrelated and
this will cause problems for the monetary authorities.
It is possible indeed that the demand for money
function is unstable, making the operation of monetary
policy extremely difficult. Although theory provides a
contribution to this debate, ultimately it is only
possible to arrive at an answer regarding the stability
of the demand for money through empirical testing.

However, it is not possible to arrive at the
economy-wide demand for money through the
aggregation of household demand for money functions. Thus, empirical testing takes place only at the

macroeconomic level. There are many practical difficulties associated with this testing and the results over the past 25 years have been inconclusive. The demand for money function appeared to become unstable in the 1970s and 1980s and much work has gone into trying to reverse and/or explain that conclusion. The continued uncertainty surrounding the demand for money function causes the issue of the effectiveness of monetary policy to remain controversial.

Key concepts used in this chapter

Transmission mechanism	Speculative demand	Interest elasticity
Medium of exchange	Intermediate objectives	Financial innovation
Transactions demand	Active money balances	Buffer stocks
Precautionary demand	Velocity of money	

Questions and problems

1 Explain why the question of the stability of the demand for money is an important issue.

2 Why is it not possible to add up transactions, precautionary and speculative balances to obtain an overall demand for money?

3 Why is it not possible to add up the demand for money of individual households to obtain an aggregate demand for money for the economy?

4 Explain the various arguments suggesting that there is a relationship between the interest rate and the demand for money.

5 Collect figures for broad money velocity in Germany, the USA, France, the UK, Japan and Italy for the years after 1991 and extend the graph shown in Box 7.4. Have any significant changes occurred since 1991?

6 Collect figures for broad money velocity for the Netherlands, Austria, Spain, Portugal, Ireland and Greece between 1970 and the present and show the information in a graph. How have changes in velocity in those countries compared with changes in the countries reported in Box 7.4?

7 List the difficulties associated with the empirical testing of demand for money functions.

8 Discuss how useful all of the work done on the demand for money has, in fact, been. Should our response to the difficulties be: (i) let us give up testing the demand for money now, the exercise is pointless; or (ii) we need more research into this important topic?

9 Collect figures for the broad money stock, the rate of inflation and the rate of interest in Germany and in any two other European countries. Does monetary policy in these countries appear to have been influenced more by the changes in the money stock or the changes in the rate of inflation?

Further reading

M J Artis and M K Lewis, *Money in Britain: Monetary Policy, Innovation and Europe* (Hemel Hempstead: Philip Allen, 1991), Ch. 4

P Atkinson and J-C Chouraqui, 'The formulation of monetary policy: a reassessment in the light of recent experience', *Monetary Policy and Financial Systems No. 1*, OECD Working Paper No 32 (Paris: OECD, 1987)

I Biefang-Frisancho-Mariscal, H-M Trautwein, P Howells, P Arestis and H Hagemann, 'Financial innovation and the demand for money in the UK and in West Germany',

Weltwirtschaftliches Archiv, June, 1987, 302–25

J A Frankel with M Chinn, 'The stabilising properties of a nominal GNP rule', *Journal of Money, Credit and Banking*, 27(2), 1995, 318–334

C A E Goodhart, 'The conduct of monetary policy', *Economic Journal*, 99/396, June, 1989, 293–346

D E W Laidler, *The Demand for Money* (New York: HarperCollins, 1993, 4e)

H Visser, *Modern Monetary Theory* (Aldershot: Edward Elgar, 1991), Ch. 6

CHAPTER 8 Monetary policy

Box 8.1

What you will learn in this chapter:

- That how the effects of monetary policy are divided between output and prices is a controversial issue
- The importance of the role of 'expectations' in models which try to explain whether monetary impulses can have lasting effects upon output and unemployment, only temporary effects or, generally, no effects at all
- Why, even if expectations are formed according to the 'policy impotence' model, monetary policy seems still to have some effect upon output and unemployment
- The basis for the argument that elected governments have an incentive to conduct monetary policy with an inflationary bias
- How the transfer of monetary policy to an independent central bank might eliminate this bias

8.1 Introduction

In Chapter 7 we saw that economists are very interested in the factors determining the demand for money. This is because if we know what determines the willingness to hold money, we can form some idea of how agents will respond if and when the quantity of money changes. The demand for money is thus essential to the *transmission mechanism* linking monetary 'shocks' to aggregate demand. However, monetary policy is concerned with a further question. This is: *given* that a monetary shock has some effect upon aggregate demand, how is the effect of that demand shock divided between prices and output?

In this chapter we shall see that views about the appropriate conduct of monetary policy have changed quite dramatically in the past 30 years with respect to both the issues we have just raised. However, since we had some extensive discussion of the transmission mechanism in the last chapter we shall concentrate here upon views about the effect of demand shocks caused by monetary disturbances. We shall see that policy has moved through four distinct phases. In chronological order they may be summarized as:

- Agreement that monetary shocks cause limited demand shocks and these demand shocks have lasting effects upon output and employment and in some circumstances the rate of inflation;
- A widespread view that monetary shocks cause considerable demand shocks but these demand shocks have only a temporary effect upon output and employment but lasting effects upon inflation;
- A controversial period in which it is argued by some that monetary shocks cause demand shocks but these demand shocks have only a temporary effect on output and employment in very limited circumstances. Otherwise, the effect falls entirely upon the rate of inflation;
- The most recent period in which, again controversially, it is argued that although monetary policy has little ability to influence anything but the rate of inflation there are incentives for governments to spring 'monetary surprises' to try to influence output and

employment. Monetary policy thus has an inflationary bias which can be eliminated only by transferring its conduct to some agency that has no such incentives.

We shall look at each of these phases in turn and at the theory underlying them. We have named the phases after key concepts associated with each; their significance will become apparent in the discussion. Firstly, in Section 8.2 we look at the first phase, which we have labelled 'the simple Phillips curve'. In Section 8.3 we look at the second phase where we shall see that the role of 'expectations' becomes crucial. In Section 8.4 we turn our attention to the most recent and controversial developments which we call the period of 'the policy irrelevance theorem'. The final, and most controversial, phase is dominated by the arguments for 'central bank independence'. These arguments are explored in Section 8.5 and we have followed this (in Section 8.6) with a brief look at the arrangements for the independence of the Bank of England, announced as this book went to press. Section 8.7 summarizes.

8.2   The simple Phillips curve

For 25 years after World War II, most governments conducted macroeconomic policy upon the basis that their instrument settings would have an effect upon aggregate demand and that changes in aggregate demand would have 'real' effects, that is upon output and employment, provided that there was spare capacity in the economy. Furthermore, as a general rule, it was felt that fiscal policy – changes in government spending and taxation – probably had more powerful and predictable demand effects than monetary policy. In the UK at least this view of the transmission mechanism was summed up by the Radcliffe Committee which rejected the importance of the money stock but laid greater emphasis upon the vaguely defined concept of 'general liquidity'. As for central bank adjustments to short-term interest rates, their effect was largely symbolic. They might have some effect also upon the availability of 'liquidity' but this could be better achieved by direct controls on liquidity (Radcliffe, 1959).

More relevant for our purpose, however, is the belief, prevalent at the time, that changes in aggregate demand could have real effects provided that the economy was operating at less than full employment. Little thought was given to what precisely was meant by 'full employment' or to the question of how unemployed resources could persist in an economy where limited resources faced insatiable wants and where markets were free to respond to relative price signals. In the early part of the period, say from 1945 to 1960, the connection between demand and employment was probably based upon a few stylized facts: unemployment was high in the 1930s when demand was low; it was non-existent during the war years when demand for everything outstripped supply; and it did seem to be the case through the 1950s that small increases in unemployment could be reversed by expansionary demand management.

After 1958, the idea that governments could effectively 'choose' the level of employment and output, up to some critical full employment level, enjoyed what appeared to be overwhelming *empirical* support from the work of A W Phillips (1958). The 'Phillips curve' plotted the relationship between the recorded level of unemployment (U) and the rate of change of money wages (W) (as a proxy for inflation since data was not available for the earlier years) from 1861 to 1957. Figure 8.1 shows a curve fitted to this data.

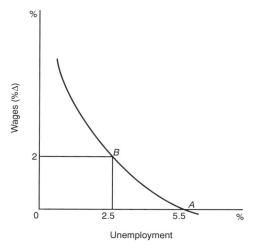

Figure 8.1 The simple Phillips curve.

The implication seemed clear. The historical evidence suggested firstly that the economy could be run at various levels of unemployment and, consequently, output. Secondly, it suggested that varying the level of unemployment could be done without any positive inflation until the level of unemployment fell to 5.5 per cent. The third implication, and this is crucial in the light of later developments in this field, was that governments could choose to run the economy at even lower levels of unemployment if they so wished, but in exchange they would have to accept some positive rate of inflation. On the evidence, they could, for example, choose point B in Figure 8.1, achieving an unemployment level of 2.5 per cent provided that they were prepared to accept the inflation rate of 2 per cent. Thus was born the idea of a *stable* trade-off between unemployment and inflation. We firstly illustrate this trade-off and then see that it raises some awkward questions.

Let us assume first of all that we can take the rate of change of money wages as a proxy for the rate of inflation. The Phillips curve then suggests that the rate of inflation is a function of the level of unemployment, which we might write:

$$\dot{P} = b_1.1/U \qquad (8.1)$$

As unemployment falls the rate of inflation increases. The sensitivity of the relationship is determined by the coefficient b_1, the curve in Figure 8.1 becoming steeper, for example, with larger values of b_1.

Suppose now a situation where the value of U is such that $\dot{P} = 0$ (5.5 per cent, at point A in Figure 8.1). In this setting, markets, including the labour market, are in equilibrium. Workers receive a money wage which they recognize as having a *real* value which induces them to supply the amount of labour that produces 5.5 per cent recorded unemployment. Equally, employers are prepared to pay the current money wage, knowing its real value and knowing that, given the current level of productivity, demand for their products and so on they can earn normal profits.

Now imagine that the government introduces a demand shock, with a view to reducing the level of unemployment to 2.5 per cent, and is willing to accept 2 per cent inflation as the trade-off. As U falls, demand pressure increases. Firms produce more in response to the increased demand and hire more workers, paying them a higher money wage to induce

extra work. Suppose that they are offered an increase in money wages of 2 per cent. More labour is forthcoming (U falls) because employment has become more attractive since real wages appear to have increased by 2 per cent. In Figure 8.1 we move up the Phillips curve from point A to point B, and all appears to be well.

However, it is commonplace in economics to assume that people are rational, utility maximizers and that they are well informed. The first two assumptions carry with them the corollary that agents respond to changes in *real* magnitudes. In our example, unemployment falls (output expands) because workers expect to be better off in *real* terms by the increase in money wages. But if the rate of inflation (at point B) is now 2 per cent, then the contracts which have just been signed no longer deliver a real increase in wages of 2 per cent. In fact, once the inflation rate has fully adjusted to the new pressure of demand, there will be no change in real values at all. The negotiated 2 per cent will only be enough to keep pace with inflation. And if we hold to our assumption that rational agents are only influenced by real changes, we must now expect that workers will revise their plans to supply labour when they find that there is no real wage increase. If the planned *real* wage increase is to materialize under these new inflationary conditions, then the wage contract has to increase nominal wages by an amount sufficient to deliver the intended *real* change *plus* an amount sufficient to compensate for inflation. In this case, if $P = 2$ per cent, a real increase of 2 per cent requires a money or nominal increase of 4 per cent. The point of this illustration is that it shows that the assumption of rational, well-informed agents leads us to expect that people take the rate of inflation into account in setting prices, since what they are concerned with is *real* values. If they do not behave in this way, then we have to imagine that they are not rational (something that economists are always reluctant to do!) or that they are not well informed enough to realize what is happening and that they mistake changes in nominal or money values for changes in real ones. This may be more plausible, and it is known as *money illusion*.

We can now see why, if agents take inflation into account, the stable trade-off between inflation and unemployment shown in the 'simple' Phillips curve in Figure 8.1 is threatened. At point *B* prices are now rising by 2 per cent per annum. The 2 per cent increase in money wages no longer gives an equivalent increase in real wages. Indeed, the real wage is unchanged. If we maintain our assumptions about rational, well-informed agents, we must expect that their behaviour will revert to that which prevailed at the old real costs and rewards. Unemployment (and output) return to their original level. All that has changed is that prices are now rising by 2 per cent per annum. Knowing this, rational agents will take 2 per cent inflation into account in setting future contracts and there is a likelihood that 2 per cent thus becomes established as the new rate of inflation. If this happens then in Figure 8.2 we are at point *C*.

8.3   The 'expectations augmented' Phillips curve

In Figure 8.2, we move from point *B* to point *C* because agents come to realize what is happening to the rate of inflation. The time it takes for them to realize this and to take it into account in their behaviour obviously depends upon how they 'learn' about the rate of inflation. If they learn slowly, then point *B* might be an available option to governments for a significant period of time, the transition to *C*

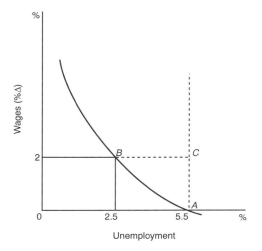

Figure 8.2 Expectations-augmented Phillips curve.

happening only slowly. On the other hand, if the learning takes place quickly, point *B* will be short-lived. We shall see in the next section that it might even be possible for agents to *anticipate* what is going to happen to inflation. In this case, point *B* never materializes and we go directly from *A* to *C*. If we rule out the latter case for the moment and accept that learning takes time, then what we saw at the end of the last section leads us to the conclusion that the Phillips curve may be downward-sloping in the short run but that in the long run it is vertical. The length of the short run depends upon how quickly people learn what is happening to the price level and upon how quickly contracts can be revised.

What we have described as 'learning' is usually described in the monetary policy literature as *expectations formation*. The idea that expectations should play an important role in economic and financial decision making is no surprise to us. In Section 2.2, for example, we noted that decisions to buy assets must be based on the return people *expect* and yet the only firm information that they have concerns past returns. In Section 3.3.1, we drew a distinction between the nominal and real rate of interest, a distinction which depended upon the *expected* rate of inflation. In Section 3.3.2 we saw that Keynes thought the demand for money (and thus the current rate of interest) depended upon how agents thought interest rates were going to change. In Section 4.4 we were interested in agents' expectations of the behaviour of *future* short-term interest rates and listed factors – expected inflation, the rate of credit expansion, the level of government borrowing – that might influence these expectations. In Section 5.5 we saw that asset prices might be affected by what agents thought would happen to asset prices in future. Notice, however, that although we have frequently stressed the importance of expectations and we have sometimes listed factors which seem relevant to a particular set of expectations, we have said nothing about the manner in which that information is used in order to *form* expectations.

There are essentially three approaches which economists take to 'expectations'. The first is to treat expectations as exogenous. This means that expectations are formed by influences largely outside the economic system. This would be legitimate if we felt that the state of expectation depended upon such 'psychological' factors that no amount of studying human behaviour could ever lead us to general conclusions about a connection between 'economic' events and expectations. This is a position that Keynes sometimes took, in talking about the 'animal spirits' of entrepreneurs, for example. At other times, however, he often wrote as though uncertainty about the future caused agents to rely very heavily upon past experience or 'convention' as he often called it.

The idea that past experience should play a large part in forming people's expectations seems eminently reasonable and forms the basis of a second approach to expectations formation known as *adaptive* or *backward-looking expectations*. In this case, people expect events to continue as they did in the past, where the recent past is more important than the distant past. We might, for example, expect inflation next year to be equal to some weighted average of the past five years, where the weight given to this year's rate is quite large, with the weights given to earlier years declining quite sharply.

Yet another idea suggests that agents form their expectations taking past experience into account but doing so in a way that enables them to construct a 'model' of the economy. This model then gives them some guidance about the likely *future* effect of *current* events. In a sense, therefore, such expectations are *forward looking* but are more frequently called *rational* expectations because this is the way in which we would expect rational economic agents to form expectations. Rational agents should make the best use of all available information and not just the past behaviour of the variable in which they are interested. The theory of rational expectations has had a major impact in economics and finance in recent years. We shall meet it again in Chapter 12, when we look at foreign exchange markets. It is also a major theme of Chapter 25 where we discuss the 'efficiency' of financial markets.

For the moment, we need to understand that the possibility of a Phillips curve-type unemployment–inflation trade-off depends upon the speed with which people learn about what is happening to inflation; and the speed of this learning depends upon how expectations are formed. It is easy to see why the trade-off should depend upon speed of learning. Assume that learning takes some time so that the

transition from *B* to *C* is slow. This is because agents failed to take the *future* rate of inflation into account accurately and quickly. If, in our example, workers had *known* that inflation was going to be 2 per cent, they would have asked for 4 per cent. If employers had refused, then workers would not have accepted more employment. We would have gone directly from *A* to *C*. The simple Phillips curve disregarded expectations and thus created the impression of a *stable* trade-off between unemployment and inflation. In the next section we shall examine an argument that correct expectations are formed so quickly that there is *never* a trade-off. In this section we look briefly at an intermediate position which shows more precisely what is necessary for monetary shocks to have at least a short-run effect on employment and output.

The simple Phillips curve of Section 8.2 takes no account of expectations. This is clear in Equation 8.1 where the rate of inflation depends solely upon demand pressure, captured by the term $1/U$. This is easily modified to incorporate a role for expectations.

$$\dot{P}_t = b_1.1/U_t + b_2.0\dot{P}_t^e \qquad (8.2)$$

(We add the time subscripts, t, since time is about to become critical.) Current period inflation now depends upon the *current* level of demand pressure (as before) but also upon current expectations of inflation. The term b_2 captures the extent to which inflation expectations, howsoever they are formed, are incorporated into current price setting behaviour and thus the rate of inflation. If $b_2 = 0$, then we have the simple Phillips curve case where expectations play no part. $b_2 = 0$ therefore indicates total money illusion, while $b_2 = 1$ indicates complete absence of money illusion. We shall assume that $b_2 = 1$, unless otherwise stated. Notice that this does *not* mean that the inflation rate is correctly and instantly anticipated. It only means that whatever expectations people have are fully incorporated. As we shall see in a moment, the expectations themselves could be persistently wrong.

The question then is how are inflation expectations formed? The early attacks upon the simple Phillips curve used the assumption that *current expectations* of inflation are based upon *past actual* rates (Friedman, 1968). Current expectations are a weighted average of past actual rates, with the weight on each past rate declining as it becomes more remote. In the terms of our discussion above, these criticisms were based upon an adaptive or backward-looking approach to expectations. The significance of backward-looking expectations formation can be illustrated if we simply assume that expectations are based solely on the most recent past period. If this is the case, then:

$$\dot{P}^e_t = \dot{P}_{t-1} \tag{8.3}$$

Substituting into Equation 8.2 we then have the rate of inflation given by:

$$\dot{P}_t = b_1 1/U_t + b_2 \dot{P}_{t-1} \tag{8.4}$$

Current inflation is thus the outcome of current demand pressure plus last period's inflation rate. There are two very important implications of Equation 8.4.

The first implication is that monetary policy can only influence the inflation rate if it succeeds in changing demand pressure and thus the level of output and employment. To see this, assume that unemployment takes a value such that $b_1.1/U_t = 0$. Current inflation will equal last period's inflation. Current inflation can change only if demand pressure, and U, change. In the short run at least the Phillips curve must have a negative slope and monetary policy has at least a short-run effect upon the real economy.

The second implication is that if demand pressure is such that $b_1.1/U_t > 0$, then maintaining that level of pressure must result in *accelerating* inflation. This is just a formal presentation of the criticism of the simple Phillips curve that we saw at the end of the last section. If the government persists with an attempt to maintain unemployment at a level that creates inflationary pressure, the short-run Phillips curve will shift *continuously* upward. Exercise 8.1 provides a numerical illustration.

If there are levels of U such that $b_1.1/U_t > 0$ and inflation *accelerates*, there must be some value of U at which $b_1.1/U_t = 0$. At this level of U, there is no demand pressure, and inflation is constant. (Inflation in each period is equal to that of the previous one.) This level of unemployment is known variously as the *non-accelerating inflation rate of unemployment* (happily shortened to *NAIRU*) or the *natural rate of unemployment*, 'natural' because this is the level of unemployment that the economy will settle at if governments do not attempt to raise aggregate demand to inflationary levels. In a sense, therefore, this 'natural rate' might be regarded as 'full employment', though it need not, of course, correspond to a situation where the recorded level of unemployment equals zero. When demand pressure begins to cause inflation there will still be positive unemployment made up of people moving between jobs or lacking the necessary skills or being in the wrong place. And if the official unemployment count depends upon the number of people claiming welfare benefits, as it does in the UK, then changes in the rules governing eligibility for those benefits will cause changes in the recorded number of unemployed associated with zero inflation. The 'natural rate' is unlikely to be a constant number.

Exercise 8.1 Adaptive expectations and the rate of inflation

Suppose that the current rate of inflation is determined as specified in Equation 8.3. Calculate the rate of inflation:

(a) this year
(b) next year
(c) in two year's time

if $b_1 = 0.1$, b2 = 1.0, $U_t = 5\%$ (= 0.05), last year's inflation rate was 2%. Assume that unemployment is *unchanged throughout the three-year period*.

Answers: see end of chapter

8.4 The policy irrelevance theorem

If expectations are backward-looking or adaptive, monetary policy will still affect output and employment in the short run, but in the long run, when eventually expectations catch up with reality, it can only affect the rate of inflation. However, while it may be perfectly sensible to suggest that people form their expectations on the basis of the recent past, it may be too simple to suggest that this is the only source of information they use.

Let us suppose that knowledge of the past enables agents to build up an accurate picture about how the economy works. Suppose, moreover, that their 'model' is one in which changes in the rate of monetary expansion cause changes in the rate of inflation after a period of time.[1] If they know this, then their expectations of future inflation will be based upon the government's current monetary policy. Expected inflation is no longer equal to past inflation, but is a function of what people believe current policy will produce. If this is the case, and assuming that agents are working with a quantity theory model, the second (expectations) term in Equation 8.4 needs to be modified to one that features the current rate of monetary growth, $\dot{M}$, relative to the natural rate of growth of output, $\dot{Y}^*$.

$$\dot{P}_t = b_1.1/U_t + b_2.(\dot{M}_t - \dot{Y}_t^*) \qquad (8.5)$$

Notice that in making this modification, we have made expectations *forward-looking*. What people expect inflation to be is based upon what they think the effects of current policy *will be*.

In the terms that we used above, agents are now forming *rational expectations*, 'rational' because agents, acting in their own self-interest, are making the best use of all available information in making any judgement. Failure to do this will result in them making mistakes (see Chapter 25)[2], and if they make mistakes that they could avoid, then either they are not acting rationally or they are not concerned to maximize their own welfare. Neither of these possibilities is allowed in orthodox economics.

The suggestion that agents form their expectations 'rationally' is credited initially to Muth (1961) though the best known application of it in an economic policy context was by Lucas (1973). Since then, the 'rational expectations hypothesis' (REH) has played a large part in the development of macroeconomics and has come to be associated with what is known as the 'New Classical Macroeconomics', so-called because it combines the rational expectations proposition with the assump-

tion of market-clearing in order to produce much the same predictions about the macroeconomy that 'Classical' (pre-Keynesian) economists produced.

At this juncture we need only appreciate the crucial point that in saying that people do not make avoidable errors in forecasting inflation, the REH is saying that agents, on balance, make correct forecasts. We can see why, if we consider the ways in which the forecast can differ from the actual outturn. In Equation 8.6 P^e_t is the expectation of next period's inflation formed in period t. P_{t+1} is the rate of inflation that actually materializes in the next period, $t+1$, while μ is an error term. Thus:

$$\dot{P}_{t+1} = \dot{P}^e_t + \mu_{t+1} \qquad (8.6)$$

It is central to the REH that in a series of repeated forecasts the error term, μ, should have a mean of zero and be uncorrelated with previous values of itself and uncorrelated with the actual inflation rate. These conditions ensure that there is no information contained in μ that could be used to improve future forecasts. If $\mu \neq 0$, we would have forecasts that consistently over- (or under-) forecast the outturn. Future forecasts could be improved by making an appropriate allowance. Equally, correlations between the error term and earlier errors, or actual outturns, would suggest a pattern in the forecast errors which we could uncover and use to improve future forecasts.

Returning to the Phillips curve, we can see that the implications of the REH approach are quite startling. We noted in the last section that it was the speed with which agents realized what was happening to inflation that determined how long it took the economy to move through the sequence A–B–C (in Figure 8.2) and thus determined for how long monetary shocks could have any effect upon output and employment. If it is correct, the REH approach is saying that, when agents notice a monetary shock is taking place, their expectations of inflation will

---

1 This amounts to saying that they have a 'quantity theory' view of the world. Velocity is stable, so that there is a reliable connection between money and spending. Meanwhile, output can grow only at its 'natural rate'.

2 In Chapter 25 we revert to the practice of using ^ over a variable to indicate an expected value. That is common practice in many finance texts; unfortunately, the same convention does not apply to economics texts where it is more usual to denote an expected

value with the superscript *e*. We have used both because we think it will help students who may be reading our exposition of a particular issue simultaneously with treatments in other books. We hope that trying to be consistent with other texts is more helpful than being consistent through all of our chapters. Readers who do find our practice confusing should keep one finger in the glossary where we make the meaning of each *e* and ^ variable clear.

adjust *immediately*. We go straight from A to C and monetary policy is impotent as regards 'real' variables. Exercise 8.2 illustrates the different responses we should expect between agents who form expectations adaptively (as in the last section) and those who form them according to the REH.

Notice, though, that this does not mean that monetary policy *never* has any real effects. We used the phrase 'when agents notice a monetary shock is taking place…'. Clearly they cannot incorporate a monetary expansion into their model in order to make the correct inflation prediction if they do not know it is happening or for some reason cannot recognize it for what it is. Monetary 'surprises', therefore, can have short-term real effects, but we need always to remember that agents can learn also about surprises. A government is unlikely to introduce a surprise without reason. Once that reason becomes understood, a surprise is no longer possible and policy will be impotent once again.

The suggestion that monetary policy is completely irrelevant to real variables unless it is carried out in such a way as to 'surprise' well-informed agents was bound to be controversial. Moreover, it also appeared to be a testable hypothesis and these two characteristics ensured what Goodhart (1989, Ch. 13) described as a 'cottage industry' of testing. He reports 63 tests of the impotence hypothesis for seven different countries. Only 17 of these appeared to confirm the hypothesis that only unanticipated monetary shocks had real effects. The majority suggested that monetary policy had real effects whether it was anticipated or not.[3]

Although monetary policy impotence is a large claim, it may be less striking than one of the *implications* of the hypothesis. This is that the persistent and major deviations of real variables – output, employment, capital formation and so on – from trend, which we have seen in recent years, is due to people being 'surprised' by movements in the general level of prices. To appreciate this implication we return to Equation 8.2. Since variations in the level of unemployment occur with divergences in actual output (Y_t) from equilibrium output, (Y_t^*), we

---

Exercise 8.2   Adaptive and rational explanations

Imagine that the rate of inflation was 2 per cent last year while the rate of growth of output has been running at about 3 per cent for the past few years. Suppose also that the government announces a target rate of monetary expansion for the next year of 7 per cent with the aim of expanding demand and lowering the level of unemployment.

1   What would be your best forecast of the rate of inflation over the next year if you formed your expectations adaptively?

2   What would your forecast be if you formed them in a forward-looking manner?

3   In the circumstances described, how would you react to the offer of a 4 per cent increase in money wages if you formed your expectations adaptively?

4   How would you react if your expectations were forward-looking?

Answers: see end of chapter

---

can rewrite Equation 8.2 as:

$$P_t = b_1.(Y_t - Y_t^*) + b_2.P_t^e \qquad (8.7)$$

Continuing with the assumption of no money illusion, $(b_2 = 0)$, then:

$$b_1.(Y_t - Y_t^*) = P_t - P_t^e \quad \text{and}$$

$$Y_t - Y_t^* = 1/b_1(P_t - P_t^e) \qquad (8.8)$$

The difference between actual and equilibrium output is a function of the difference between expected and actual inflation, the forecasting error. But under rational expectations we know that the forecasting error should be purely stochastic with mean zero and no auto-correlation. However, the UK, like the USA and most European economies, has experienced major booms and recessions over the years. During the 1950s, the pattern was referred to as 'stop–go' and was certainly thought of at the time as being associated with demand management policies. More recently, in 1980–3 and again in

---

[3] A problem with all tests of hypotheses about expectations-determined events is that rejections are hard to interpret. They may indicate a rejection of the genuine hypothesis ('expectations *do not* play the expected role') or they may indicate that expectations are actually crucial, but are usually wrong. The problem is that any such test is a simultaneous test of joint hypotheses.

1990–3 the UK experienced two periods of major recession when output was below potential. In 1987–89 output was above potential. On this evidence therefore, if we persist with an REH-type analysis, we have to say that agents make frequent and large forecasting errors. They seem not to be well informed about movements in the price level. Furthermore, since the deviations persist (and often have the appearance of cyclical behaviour) the forecast errors show incontrovertible signs of autocorrelation.

Given both the quantity and quality of information that is available about current changes and likely future movements in the price level, it is difficult to believe that agents make frequent, large and persistent (that is, autocorrelated) errors in the way the theory suggests. Price level data and leading indicator data is available monthly. It is amongst the more reliable information that is regularly published. It is also reported in a high profile way. Furthermore, anyone lacking the necessary information to make a judgement can obtain it quickly and very cheaply. At the same time, the major post-war fluctuations (in the UK economy) coincide, with one exception, with policy responses to pressures on the exchange rate.[4]

If it seems unlikely that mistaken assessments about the general price level are responsible for monetary policy's impact on real variables, what is the explanation? The possible answers are many and varied and most go (again) beyond the scope of this book. But one issue worthy of careful attention is the nature of markets, *in practice*. Much economic theory works on the assumption that market prices are perfectly (that is, continuously) flexible. It is assumed that they work *as if* prices were being continuously adjusted by a mythical auctioneer who gathers all bids so that no trades take place at disequilibrium prices. Consequently, markets always clear. The appeal of this assumption lies, like the REH itself, with the idea that economic agents are fundamentally rational, self-interested individuals and that trading at disequilibrium prices, prices that generate quantities that agents do not want, is inconsistent with such rationality.

But this overlooks a reality which is that such flexibility is conspicuous by its rarity. In Part 4 of this book, we shall see that it is a characteristic of only a subset even of financial markets. In dealer or 'quote-driven' markets, for example, dealers quote a two-way price *for a period of time* until sufficient information has accumulated, through inventory changes, to suggest that a change is essential. Many markets for goods and services exist where adjustments take the form of quantities in the first instance. Labour markets are both quantity and price inflexible over long periods. The reasons for these inflexibilities are many and are increasingly well understood. They have to do primarily with costs, information and uncertainty. It takes time to adjust prices, and price adjustments involve real resources. At the least, there is no reason to assume that traders will adjust prices until the cost of sticking with a misaligned price exceeds the cost of changing it. In the presence of uncertainty (about the permanence of an apparent demand shift, for example) and incomplete information (about the quality of goods and services from rival traders, for example) a rational, self-interested response may be to continue as before until the picture clarifies.

> … in the real world many markets do *not* clear perfectly and instantaneously, even though market agents behave rationally and efficiently with regards to the formation of expectations under conditions of imperfect and costly acquisition of information. In short, an assumption of rational, efficient market agents does not also validate an assumption of perfectly clearing markets.
>
> (Goodhart, 1989 p.23).

Consider now the implications of having *some* fix-price firms in an economy. We begin at the end of a week's trading, in full equilibrium, where everyone knew the pattern of relative prices as well as the general price level: expectations were fulfilled. Expectations are then formed about next week's trading. Now let us introduce a monetary expansion. Initially, there is an excess of real balances and an increase in spending. Recognizing this monetary shock, flex price firms raise their prices immediately. The increase in spending is partially damped as real balances are reduced by the price rises and,

---

[4] The exception is the 1973–6 'oil shock', though even here part of the recession may be attributed to policy responses to the oil price rise.

additionally, the pattern of demand is switched toward the fix-price producers. So long as there are some fix-price producers, however, the adjustment in the general price level must be incomplete and some increase in real balances (and expenditure) must remain. Output and employment in fix-price firms, and in the economy as a whole, increase. The monetary expansion has real effects.[5]

8.5 Governments, inflationary incentives and independent central banks

Many of the same people who have argued that monetary policy is ineffective in real terms have also held that elected governments which act also as the monetary authority of their economies have a strong incentive to practise expansionary monetary policy in the hope of producing real effects. Several possible reasons have been advanced for this apparently short-sighted behaviour.

All of these reasons start from the position that governments, and the politicians who comprise them, act (as market agents are assumed to do) entirely from self-interest. Two possible directions may be taken from here. Firstly, the government may be considered as a unit that seeks to gain advantage for itself at the expense of the citizens of its own country. One way in which it can gain is by creating inflationary surprises. This can occur because any expansion of the money supply provides a once-and-for-all gain for the issuer of money equal to the difference between the face value of the money and its cost of production. This gain (known as *seigniorage*) may take a number of forms. For example, by inducing an inflation the government succeeds in reducing the real value of the national debt. In effect, an expansionary monetary policy acts as a tax on the savings of the citizens. If we follow through the logic of the expectations-augmented Phillips curve discussed above, we see that each time the government seeks to create an inflationary surprise it succeeds only in ratcheting up the rate of inflation in the economy while achieving no long-run increases in employment or output. This suggests

that as long as the costs of higher inflation rates for an economy are greater than any short-term gains associated with higher employment or output, monetary policy should always be designed to keep inflation low. In the strong version of the theory which proposes that monetary policy has no impact on real variables *even in the short run*, the argument for tight monetary policy appears to be irrefutable.

The problem with this argument is that it is difficult to see why governments should act to gain at the expense of their citizens. One obvious approach to this is to see governments as sets of individual politicians who are seeking only to retain power. They thus choose those policies which they believe will ensure their re-election (they seek to maximize votes). Thus, they have an incentive to increase government expenditure in order to win the votes of electors wishing for greater spending on health, education, defence or other government programmes. However, a fear that increased tax rates and higher interest rates might lose votes provides the government with an incentive to run large budget deficits financed by increases in the money supply. This would be particularly effective politically if voters suffered from money illusion and believed that the monetary expansion would cause unemployment to fall. Of course, in line with the theory outlined above, this could, at best, only work in the short run – but it might be sufficient to win the ensuing election.

After the election, unemployment would again rise and the economy would be burdened by a higher rate of inflation. To reduce this inflation, the government might then have to cut demand sharply, inducing a recession with further increases in unemployment. This would make the government very unpopular between elections but could put it in a position to expand the economy again in time to win the next election. Such a process is referred to as the political business (or electoral) cycle – an unnecessary cycle with real costs for the economy which is generated by the need for governments to face elections. This would not lead to ever-increasing inflation but would involve real costs for the economy as inflation would fall following each election only at the expense of

5 This passage draws heavily upon Laidler (1988).

high, albeit short-term, unemployment. The economy would face a regular and unnecessary stop–go cycle which would create uncertainty and interfere with its longer-term growth prospects.

According to the theory, governments could bring about a reduction of inflation without creating a recession only if market agents believed that the monetary authorities were genuinely committed to low inflation – that is, if the statements by monetary authorities that they intended to bring about low inflation were held by market agents to have *credibility*. The difficulty is that market agents, aware of the expansionary incentives faced by governments, will not believe government statements. The past behaviour of the monetary authorities will have given the government an inflationary *reputation*. Under these circumstances, government policies are held to be *time inconsistent*. When the economy is experiencing high inflation, the optimum policy for the government is to reduce the rate of growth of the money supply in order to reduce inflation. However, once the inflation rate has fallen, a new optimum policy emerges – that of expanding the economy in an attempt to reduce unemployment and hence win votes.

We have seen, however, that market agents may be assumed to learn quickly that governments will be attempting to gain at their expense by creating inflationary surprises. It is difficult to understand under these circumstances why voters should also not learn in the same way. If they were to do so, governments would no longer gain votes through monetary expansions prior to elections and would hence lose the incentive to behave in this way. Nonetheless, economists continue to assume that the need to be elected creates incentives for governments to follow inflationary monetary policies, either creating political business cycles or constantly ratcheting up the inflation rate.

In either case, it appears to follow that consistent and tight monetary policies can only be guaranteed if monetary policy decisions are not made by elected governments but are placed in the hands of politically independent central banks (controlled by unelected experts).[6] We have seen problems with the

structure of this argument – that the policy ineffectiveness proposition can be criticized from a theoretical perspective *and* does not appear to have strong empirical backing. In addition, attempts to find evidence for the existence of political business cycles have not, on balance, been successful. Studies that have claimed to show that such cycles have existed are outnumbered by those that can find no evidence of electoral cycles.

Supporters of politically independent central banks have therefore sought to add strength to their argument through a different kind of empirical study. This has looked at the degree of *central bank independence* and attempted to find correlations between this and the rates of inflation in the respective countries. These studies (see, for example, Alesina and Summers (1993)) have, by and large, claimed to find such correlations within developed economies as well as failing to find correlations between the independence of central banks and rates of economic growth. The implication is that countries with politically independent central banks can maintain lower rates of inflation with no loss in terms of economic growth.

There are, however, several difficulties with these studies. Firstly, the 'independence' of central banks is not easily measured. Many characteristics may contribute to the degree of independence of a particular central bank from its government (Box 8.2 considers such characteristics). These characteristics must be weighted in order to produce some composite index of independence. Such a process may inevitably be subjective and different researchers might rank central banks differently in terms of independence. Although it is accepted that the Bundesbank must rank highly on any index of independence, there is sufficient doubt about other central banks to raise doubts about the apparent correlations between independence and inflation rates.

Secondly, the existence of this correlation provides no guarantee of a causal relationship from central bank independence to low inflation rates. It is at least equally plausible that some third factor has been responsible for both the independence of the central bank and the low rate of inflation or, indeed, that any

---

6 Arguments for and against central bank independence are summarized in Box 22.2.

apparent correlation is entirely accidental. For example, it has been argued that low rates of inflation in Germany have been due principally to a strong anti-inflationary attitude among German people as a result of particularly unpleasant (and politically and socially damaging) episodes of inflation. This has meant that there has, until very recently, been little or no disagreement among the major political parties over the need to keep inflation rates low. Under such circumstances it was easy for the government to hand power over monetary policy to an independent central bank and there have been relatively few disagreements between the Bundesbank and the government over monetary policy.[7] Thus, it may well have been the case that German governments would have followed much the same monetary policy as that chosen by the Bundesbank.

Nonetheless, there has during the 1990s been a widespread acceptance among economists and politicians of the desirability of politically independent central banks. Although the movement towards making central banks independent embraced non-European economies such as New Zealand and

Australia, the key to the changes can be found in the requirement in the Maastricht Treaty on European Union that the European Central Bank (after Economic and Monetary Union) must be independent of all governments and of the European Commission and that all EMU member-country central banks must also be independent.[8] This has been largely responsible for the increased independence granted to the central banks of France, Spain and Italy. This requirement of Economic and Monetary Union can be seen as needed to persuade the German people and authorities to participate in EMU since the Bundesbank has come to be accepted within Germany as a symbol of the determination to maintain low rates of inflation and to preserve the value of the Deutschmark. This has meant that the only way Germany might be persuaded to cede power from the Bundesbank to the European Central Bank would be if the ECB is made in the image of the Bundesbank.

Another major reason for the practical movement towards central bank independence in many countries has been the acceptance, in a world of highly mobile capital, of the dominance of financial markets. It has become widely accepted that a country's long-term interest rates might fall if only governments could convince the financial markets of the genuineness of their expressed determination to keep inflation low. One way of trying to achieve this has been to hand control of monetary policy over to the central bank on the grounds that financial markets will have more trust in the anti-inflationary credentials of the central bank than in those of the elected government.

If this in fact occurs, we have a classic example of self-fulfilling beliefs. We have suggested that the theoretical arguments in favour of taking the control of monetary policy out of the hands of elected governments are not strong and that the empirical evidence is also rather weak. It remains that, so long as these views are accepted in financial markets, it will be in the interests of governments to accept them also. Strength is added to this proposition by the view

---

[7] Notable exceptions to this included disagreement over the rate at which Ostmarks were converted to Deutschmarks at the time of German unification, and over a government plan to revalue its holdings of gold in early June 1997 in order to meet more easily the

conditions for membership of EMU. The government emerged victorious in the first disagreement; the Bundersbank won out in the second.

[8] This issue is dealt with in Section 22.3

that governments are not, in practice, giving up very much since the increased mobility of international capital has made it increasingly difficult to operate national monetary policies markedly different from those being followed in other countries.

8.6   The independence of the Bank of England

It is of interest to apply the above discussion to the issue of the independence of the Bank of England. The first major action of the newly elected Labour government in the UK was to announce, on 6 May 1997, that the Bank of England was to be granted operational independence from the UK Treasury and that interest rates would in future be set by the Bank rather than by the government following consultation with the Bank, as had previously been the case. On the surface, this appeared a somewhat unlikely act since it had been accepted that governments more to the political left would be less willing to give up power over monetary policy to a non-elected body.

We have seen above, however, that so long as the markets believe that the independence of the central bank provides a stronger guarantee of a low-inflation policy, governments may see the granting of independence to the central bank as a route to lower long-term interest rates. Such an argument might be more appealing to left-leaning governments which might be suspected by financial markets of continuing to harbour expansionary aims. The move might also be seen as necessary to give the UK government the possibility of joining Economic and Monetary Union should it wish to do so. It remained that the Chancellor's action in making the Bank of England operationally independent angered a number of traditional Labour Party supporters. In the light of this and of the points raised in Box 8.2, it is worth considering exactly what additional powers were granted to the Bank of England and what was removed from its control.

Let us consider, firstly, the interest rate decision itself. Under the new regime, interest rates in the UK are determined by the new Monetary Policy Committee of the Bank of England. This committee has nine members – five from the Bank of England and four nominated by the Chancellor. This meets the

independence requirement that Bank members are in the majority. This is less strong than it seems, however, since the government retains control over the appointment of the future Governor and Deputy Governors of the Bank of England. In addition, government-nominated members of the Monetary Committee will have relatively short terms of office (five years) and be subject to re-appointment. The five-year term contrasts with the 14-year term of office of members of the Board of the US Federal Reserve. It is generally argued that short terms of office coupled with the possibility of re-appointment allows the possibility of some degree of government influence over existing central bank board members since they may seek to please the government in order to ensure their own re-appointment.

More important, however, is the meaning of the term 'operational independence'. The Chancellor has retained the power to set the inflation target for the economy, leaving to the Bank what might be seen as the relatively technical job of setting interest rates in order to achieve that target. Thus, the Chancellor has preserved the ability of the government to choose a relatively expansionary policy. In practice, the Chancellor could not immediately raise the inflation target, allowing an easing of monetary policy, even if he wanted to do so. Such an action would have caused the market to lose immediately its belief that the granting of greater powers to the Bank gave a guarantee of continued low inflation. In this case, any hoped-for gains in terms of a lower risk premium in UK interest rates would not have materialized. Thus, the Chancellor simply carried forward the inflation target set by the previous government. Nonetheless, the Chancellor gave himself some degree of control over the monetary policy stance to be pursued by the Bank.

Two other issues are of some importance. Until 6 May, the Bank of England, unlike the Bundesbank and the Federal Reserve, had three major functions. It was the country's monetary authority (under the control of the Treasury); it was the banker to the British government and as such had the responsibility of financing the UK national debt; and it acted as the supervisory authority over the country's banking system[9].

In the past, a conflict had often been seen to exist between the first two of these roles. Thus, the need to sell a large amount of government debt may have led the Bank to prefer relatively stable interest rates (to remove uncertainty about future bond prices) at a time when monetary policy appeared to require sharp changes in interest rates. It has been argued that a potential conflict also exists between the roles of monetary authority and banking system supervisor. The point here is that the banking supervisory authority will wish to maintain trust in the banking system by preventing, as far as is possible, the collapse of banking institutions. If there are a number of banks known to be in weak financial positions, the supervisor might be reluctant to tighten monetary policy for fear that this will force the weaker banks to default. The result might be that a central bank with both supervisory and monetary roles would operate, on average, a looser monetary policy than it would if it did not have supervisory responsibility.

In the UK's case, on 6 May, the responsibility of the Bank of England for selling government debt was removed and handed over to the Treasury. Later in May, it was announced that the Bank would also lose its supervisory responsibilities. The actions of the British government could be seen to have set the Bank free to determine UK interest rates and to remove all possibilities of conflict of interest, allowing a concentration on monetary policy alone. On the other hand, as we have seen, other aspects of the government's granting of independence to the Bank of England leaves it still subject to government influence to a greater extent than is the case with the Bundesbank.

8.7   Summary

The conduct of monetary policy in most countries has changed markedly in the course of the past 30 years or so. Until the mid-1970s, monetary policy, along with fiscal policy, was frequently used as one element in a programme of demand management which aimed to smooth out fluctuations in real variables like output and employment. The belief that governments had a choice between high levels of output and employment on the one hand and low inflation on the other was symbolized by the original Phillips curve.

From the mid-1970s onwards, however, the idea that real variables could be influenced for any long period lost conviction. Eventually, as part of the rational expectations revolution, it came to be argued that no real effects were possible at all. However, while monetary theory took this very pessimistic turn, governments continued to operate monetary policy as though sometimes they could boost or restrain demand with beneficial results. This led to the accusation that democratic governments were bound to operate monetary policy with an inflationary bias and that this ultimately eroded a government's credibility whenever it did wish to reduce inflation. The way to avoid this, it was argued, was to 'precommit' monetary policy to low inflation and the popular way of doing this in recent years has been to hand the operation of monetary policy to an independent central bank.

Key concepts used in this chapter

Transmission mechanism	Natural rate of unemployment
The simple Phillips curve	Policy irrelevance theorem
Real wages	Forward-looking expectations
Nominal wages	Adaptive expectations
Money illusion	Fix-price markets
Expectations formation	Flex-price markets
Expectations augmented Phillips curve	Credibility
Backward-looking expectations	Reputation
Adaptive expectations	Time inconsistency
NAIRU	Central bank independence

---

9 A function performed in Germany by the Aufsichtsamt, the Federal Banking Supervisory Office.

Questions and problems

1 Explain what is meant by the transmission mechanism.

2 Using the simple Phillips curve, show how governments might use an expansionary monetary policy in order to lower the rate of inflation. Why is there a 'trade-off'?

3 Distinguish between real and nominal wages. If you expect the rate of inflation to be 5 per cent over the next year, what change in nominal wages would you require in order (a) to maintain real wages unchanged; (b) to increase real wages by 3 per cent?

4 If the rate of inflation has been running at 3 per cent per annum for the past few years, what increase in nominal wages would you require in order to enjoy a 2 per cent increase in real wages? Explain the assumptions which you have to make in order to answer this question.

5 Why does the way in which expectations are formed influence the impact of monetary policy?

6 Explain what is meant by a monetary 'surprise' and why this may affect the economy in a way that differs from monetary events that are anticipated. Make clear any assumptions that you need to make.

7 Why is it argued that governments might seek to create inflationary surprises?

8 Explain the ideas behind the notion of the political business cycle. Do they seem to reflect the realities of political behaviour?

9 Look at Box 8.2 and consider the relevance of each of the points listed to the issue of the political independence of a central bank.

Further reading

A Alesina and L Summers, 'Central Bank Independence and Macroeconomic Performance: Some Comparative Evidence', *Journal of Money, Credit and Banking,* 25 (2) (1993), 151–62

M Friedman, 'The Role of Monetary Policy', *American Economic Review,* 58 (1968), 1–17

C A E Goodhart, *Money, Information and Uncertainty* (London: Macmillan, 2e 1989) Chs 1 and 13

A Griffiths and S Wall, *Applied Economics* (London: Longman 5e, 1993) Ch. 19

D Laidler, 'Some Macroeconomic Implications of Price Stickiness', *Manchester School,* 56 (1988)

R Lucas, 'Some International Evidence on Output-Inflation trade-offs', *American Economic Review,* 63 (1973), 326–34

J Muth, 'Rational Expectations and the Theory of Price Movements', *Econometrica,* 29 (1961), 313–335

A W Phillips, 'The Relation between Unemployment and the Rate of Change of Money Wages in the United Kingdom, 1861–1957', *Economica,* 25 (1958), 283–301

Committee on the Working of the Monetary System: Report, Cmnd. 827 (London: HMSO, 1959). The 'Radcliffe' Committee

D K Whynes, 'The Political Business Cycle' in D Greenaway (ed.), *Current Issues in Macroeconomics,* (London: Macmillan 1989)

Answers to exercises

Exercise 8.1

(a) 2% + 2% = 4%
(b) 2% + 4% = 6%
(c) 2% + 6% = 8%

Exercise 8.2

1 2%
2 4%
3 I would expect a *real* wage increase of 2%
4 I would expect no change in *real* wages

Markets

Money markets

9.1 Introduction

Financial markets can be classified in many different ways. One very simple and very common classification distinguishes between *money* markets and *capital* markets. The distinction is based upon the length of the loan when it is first made (that is, on the 'initial maturity'). In money markets, funds are borrowed and lent for a maximum of one year. However, many loans are for less than one year when they are initially made (many are 'overnight'). This, combined with the fact that many existing one-year loans were made some time ago, means that the average maturity of outstanding debt in money markets is much shorter. Within this two-part classification there are further possibilities. We can distinguish (money) markets for several different instruments; or we can distinguish by the way in which they are traded; or we can distinguish by the identity of the borrower. Table 9.1 provides a list of

money markets distinguished largely by instrument. The table begins with those markets where the borrowing/lending is carried out through the issue of securities which can be bought and sold in a secondary market. These are the discount market itself, and the markets for commercial paper (CP) and certificates of deposit (CDs). We then subdivide the discount market by borrower, noting that it trades bills issued by three distinct classes of borrower. By contrast, the interbank market is a 'market' for deposits that cannot be traded. Money market deposits have much the same characteristics. Repurchase agreements involve a sale of securities with an agreement to buy them back in the near future for a price that determines the cost of the funds obtained. One consequence that follows from this variety of short-term instruments is that they are priced (or 'quoted') in two different ways. Some are quoted on a *yield* basis, while others are quoted on a *discount* basis. We note this distinction in the table (by *y* and *d* respectively) and explain it in the next section. Finally, we need to bear in mind that most of these markets exist for instruments issued in the domestic currency, and also, increasingly, for instruments denominated in a currency other than that of the country in which they are traded. Such instruments are identified by the prefix 'Euro-', though this is strictly a misnomer since the currency can be *any* currency (US or Hong Kong dollars, or Yen, for example). Hence, most financial centres trading CDs and commercial paper will also trade Euro-CDs (ECDs) and ECP.

Although Table 9.1 shows an apparently wide variety of instruments available to short-term lenders and borrowers, the fact that they are all short-term instruments makes them very close substitutes for one another. This in turn means that price movements (for money market securities) and movements in rates of return (for all money market instruments) are very highly correlated. It also means that differentials between the returns on different instruments are usually very small. This is reinforced by the fact that money markets are usually dominated by large traders – banks, savings institutions, government and corporate treasury departments – to whom small differences in yield can still mean large differences in profit or loss. One consequence of this is the need for a convenient form for expressing fractions of yields or interest rates. This is done by quoting *basis points* (or bps) where one basis point equals 1/100 of 1 per cent. Basis points have become an internationally recognized standard. Of course, it follows equally that some method is needed for quoting small changes in price. Alas, these methods are not universal. In the UK and USA the smallest unit of price change is 1/32 while in continental Europe the unit is 0.01.[1] For some reason, both units have come to be known as *ticks* in everyday use. But saying in London that UK treasury bills are 'up three ticks' suggests a larger price change than a similar remark about schatzwechsel in Frankfurt.

Distinguishing financial markets into markets for 'short-' and 'long-term' loans is common practice, and useful since instruments within each category are close substitutes for each other. But, while some institutions have a particular need to lend or borrow short-term while others specialize in long-

term lending or borrowing, most lenders and borrowers use both groups of markets at some time. For example, remember what we said in Section 4.4.1 about the effect of interest rate expectations on lenders' decisions. Imagine a lender who normally prefers to lend for a short period (in the money markets). If he thinks that short-term rates are likely to fall in the very near future, he might prefer on this occasion to lock into current rates for a longer period (via the capital markets). Equally, firms who think that interest rates will be lower in future might decide to borrow short on a temporary basis in spite of their normal preference for long-term borrowing.

As a source of short-term finance, the money markets are, naturally, important to a wide range of institutions. They are important also for another reason which takes us back to Chapter 3 'The *level* of interest rates' and Chapter 6 'Bank lending and the money supply'. This is that central banks exercise their influence over short-term interest rates, via the money markets (either the discount market or interbank market in practice). Money markets are the focus for this official activity for a combination of reasons. Firstly, as we all know, banks offer a guarantee to their clients that their deposits can be converted on demand into cash and therefore banks need to hold the necessary liquid reserves. Secondly, because these reserves (generally) pay no interest, banks hold the minimum quantity; their demand for reserves is highly interest-inelastic. Thirdly, since banks must make settlement on a day-to-day basis, shortages of reserves must be relieved by immediate (that is, *very* short-term) funds. Finally, in a system-wide shortage of funds the central bank becomes the sole supplier. We shall see how this works, in a little more detail, in Section 9.4.

In the next section, we explain the characteristics of each of the instruments being traded in the money markets. In Section 9.3 we look at the use and characteristics of the markets themselves in each of several European centres; in Section 9.5 we note the rapid growth of Eurocurrency markets and the causes and consequences of this growth. Section 9.6 summarizes.

Table 9.1 Money markets

The discount market	
Treasury bills	*d*
Local authority/utility bills	*d*
Commercial bills	*d*
The market for commercial paper	*d*
The certificate of deposit market	*y*
The interbank market	*y*
Money market deposits	*y*
Repurchase agreements	*y*

d quoted on a *discount* basis; *y* quoted on a *yield* basis

---

[1] We have used decimals rather than fractions in all illustrations and exercises

9.2 Money market instruments: characteristics and yields

9.2.1 The discount market

This is a market in which short-term securities are issued and traded. Bills are usually issued with initial maturities of from one to three months, six months, and, less usually, twelve months. For this reason, it would be inconvenient and expensive to set up the arrangements for paying interest in the normal way, for securities which would attract at most one interest payment, and so the practice is to issue the bills at a discount to their *par* or maturity value. Thus a three month bill with a par value of £250,000 might be issued for £240,000, a discount of £10,000. Clearly it is essential that the amount by which the bill is discounted should be convertible into a *rate* in order to allow comparison with the return on other financial instruments. The simplest way to do this is to calculate the return as a *rate of discount, d*. The formula for the rate of discount is:

$$d = \frac{M - P}{M \cdot n_{sm}} \tag{9.1}$$

where P is the price, M is the par or redemption or maturity value and n_{sm} is the period to redemption (that is, from settlement of purchase to maturity) *expressed as a fraction of a year*. In the UK, a year is reckoned as 365 days while in the US markets and in continental Europe it is taken to be 360 days. In our example, therefore, the discount of £10,000 is equivalent to a *rate* of discount of:

$$d = (250,000 - 240,000) / (250,000 \times 0.25) = 16\%$$

Notice that as the bill approaches maturity, the value of n_{sm}, and thus the value of the denominator, falls. If nothing else changed, therefore, the return on the bill would increase as it approached maturity. To prevent this from happening, it is the bill's price that rises as it approaches maturity.

By rearranging Equation 9.1, it is quite easy to find the price at which a bill must be sold in order to yield a given rate of discount. Suppose, for example, that we wish to lend for two months at a rate of 10 per cent. Then:

$$P = M - d(M.n_{sm}) \tag{9.2}$$

and thus:

$$P = 250,000 - 0.1(250,000 \times 0.166) = 245,835$$

Equation 9.1 enables us to compare the return on all securities where the return is calculated on a discount basis. But these are not directly equivalent to returns calculated on the more familiar yield (or 'add-on' in the USA) basis. This is because on a discount basis the gain (£10,000) is being expressed as a proportion of the maturity value of the security – the sum received *on redemption*, whereas a conventional rate of interest is calculated by expressing the gain as a fraction of the *outlay*. In our first example, we can see that if we substitute £240,000 (the outlay) in the denominator, the discount of £10,000 converts to a rate of interest of 16.6 per cent. If we let i stand for the interest rate (or 'add-on' rate or *equivalent yield*), then this can be found as follows:

$$i = \frac{M - P}{P.n_{sm}} \tag{9.3}$$

and it is a simple task to compare Equations 9.1 and 9.3 in order to see that the maturity value in the denominator of Equation 9.1 is replaced by the smaller (discounted) market price in Equation 9.3. *Given* either the yield or the rate of discount we can convert between the two as follows:

$$d = \frac{i}{1 + i.n_{sm}} \tag{9.4}$$

$$i = \frac{d}{1 - d.n_{sm}} \tag{9.5}$$

It is important to remember that a given rate of discount offers a better return than an equivalent yield of the same numerical value.

Bills are often distinguished by their origin. They are issued by central government, local authorities and financial and non-financial institutions. We say more about these distinctions in the next section.

Exercise 9.1

A one month bill for £100,000 is issued at a discount of £1,000

Find:

1 the *rate* of discount
2 the equivalent yield
3 the price at which it will trade with two weeks remaining to maturity, market interest rates unchanged.

Answers: see end of chapter

9.2.2   The commercial paper market

Commercial paper (CP) is the other market in which funds are priced on a discount basis. In effect, a firm issues a promise to pay the holder of the paper at some specified future time. In most countries, access to the market is regulated, usually by specifying that firms must have a stock exchange listing and meet some minimum capital requirement. As a rule, the promise to repay is unsecured by any specific assets and this has led many firms issuing commercial paper to seek a credit rating from one of the major bond rating agencies. The difference between the yield on the highest rated paper and unrated ('junk') paper varies between 100 bp (that is, 1 per cent) and 150 bp. Most paper is issued with an initial maturity between 7 and 45 days. Because of the short duration, there is little by way of a secondary market for commercial paper. The issue is usually handled by a specialist commercial paper dealer, often a subsidiary of a bank, and the dealer will usually offer to repurchase CP from investors.

Yields are calculated in exactly the same way as the (discount) yield on a bill (see Equation 9.1). In Europe, the CP market is a product of the past ten years or so (only 1991 in Germany), though in the USA it began in 1970 where it is now very large, accounting for over 80 per cent of the world total of commercial paper in issue. Amongst the European countries, France has the largest domestic CP market. In the UK the market has remained comparatively underdeveloped, partly because bank lending, as an alternative source of finance, has been comparatively free of restrictions for many years and

also because firms prefer the traditional discount market which is very highly developed in the UK and has the attraction that the Bank of England stands as a ready buyer of many bills. (See Section 9.4).

9.2.3   The certificate of deposit market

A certificate of deposit is a statement to the effect that a lender has deposited a specified quantity of funds for a specified period with a specified bank at a specified rate of interest. It is, in other words, a receipt for a time deposit. As with other money market instruments, denominations are comparatively large (a minimum of £50,000 in the UK, $100,000 in the USA). The significance of having such a receipt lies in the fact that in most countries there exists an active secondary market in which they can be traded, making them into *negotiable* CDs (NCDs). Thus we have a situation with the traditional advantages of a time deposit (the borrower gets a large loan for a fixed period, the lender receives a premium rate of interest as compensation for the loss of liquidity), but one with the added advantage that the lender can, if needs be, have instant access to funds by selling the CD. Because of this liquidity, the borrower pays and the lender accepts a slightly lower rate of interest than would be the case on a corresponding time deposit with no certificate. Just like bills or commercial paper, a CD has a maturity value (equal to the sum deposited plus the interest payment initially agreed upon). However, unlike bills and CP, CDs are priced on a *yield basis*. The interest paid on the CD is often linked to the rate paid on money market deposits (see *interbank deposits* below). Thus, if a three-month interbank deposit paid interest of 10.25 per cent, the equivalent CD might be priced on the basis of LIBID less 0.25 per cent, that is, 10 per cent. In the circumstances, the 10 per cent payable on maturity is equivalent to the *coupon rate* (c) on a conventional bond and the maturity value in three months' time will consist of the initial deposit (D) *plus* interest payment. In this case, therefore:

$$M = D \times (1 + c.n_{im}) \tag{9.6}$$

where n_{im} is the number of days from *issue* to *maturity* as a fraction of a year. The market price of the CD is then given by discounting the maturity value by the current yield adjusted for the period to maturity. Thus:

$$P = \frac{M}{1 + i.n_{sm}} \qquad (9.7)$$

If, as we have assumed here, the coupon rate reflects the yield currently available on comparable three-month instruments at the time of issue, then,

$$M = 100,000 \times (1 + 0.1 \times 0.25) = 102,500$$

and $P = 100,000$, the issue price.

However, if market rates of return on comparable instruments change, this will be reflected in a change in the price of CDs. Imagine, as an example, that after one month the yield, i, on two-month negotiable instruments falls to 8.5 per cent. Then, using Equation 9.7, we can see that the price of our CD will be:

$$102,500 / (1 + [0.085 \times 0.166]) = 101,156$$

(Check that the market price at two months to maturity would have been £100,826, if the yield had remained at 10 per cent.) Given the pricing equation (Equation 9.7), it follows that if we know the price at which a CD of given coupon and given maturity is trading, we can find its current yield. This is done by expressing the gain, the difference between purchase price and maturity, as a percentage of the purchase price and adjusting that percentage to an annualized rate:

$$i = \left(\frac{M}{P} - 1 \right) \cdot \frac{1}{n_{sm}} \qquad (9.8)$$

Readers should satisfy themselves that Equation 9.8 is equivalent to Equation 9.3.

The first negotiable CD market began in New York in 1961, the sterling CD market opening in London in 1968. Since then markets for negotiable CDs have grown rapidly in all European centres with the exception of Germany. The problem for German banks until recently has been the comparatively high reserve requirement on time deposits. As we noted in connection with quantitative controls on bank balance sheets (Section 6.5), a non-interest-bearing reserve requirement acts as a tax on banking activity. If, for example, a bank issues a DM 500,000 CD on which the reserve requirement is 5 per cent, then it can on-lend only 95 per cent of the deposit, that is, DM 475,000. Suppose now that interest rates (and thus the coupon rate on the CD) are 10 per cent. The reserve requirement has the effect of raising the cost of the deposit to the bank by 52 basis points (10%/0.95 = 10.52). This puts domestic CDs at a disadvantage with Euro-CDs and with other domestic instruments where reserves are lower. Indeed, the exceptionally rapid growth of the Eurodollar-CD market is partly explained by tough reserve requirements on domestic dollar CDs in the USA. The Bundesbank lowered reserve requirements in February 1993 but it remains to be seen whether this will encourage an expansion of the DM-CD market.

Exercise 9.2

1 Find the value of a 5% negotiable six-month CD for £200,000
2 What would its price be if interest rates were 6 per cent when 146 days remained to maturity?
3 What would its current yield be if its market price were £195,000 with 146 days remaining?

Answers: see end of chapter

9.2.4 The interbank market

Unlike the other money markets, the interbank market is a market for (non-negotiable) deposits. The deposits can be disposed of only by withdrawing them from the borrower. The initial maturity of the deposits can range from overnight to one year, though the shorter maturities are the more popular. The deposits are the assets of banks with surplus funds and the liabilities of banks who bid for them in order to fund their lending commitments. Thus, the deposits provide an attractive means whereby individual banks can adjust their cash position, being neither too liquid (foregoing profitable lending) or short of liquidity (with the possibility in the extreme case of being unable to honour customers' cheques). The use of the market by banks making continuous adjustments to their liquidity positions largely accounts for the high level of activity at the short end of the maturity spectrum.

The interest rate paid on interbank deposits represents the marginal cost of one important source of funds for banks. A decision to lend may require the lending bank either to withdraw deposits which it earlier made in the market or to attract funds from other banks. Clearly, the loan must offer a return which covers the (opportunity or explicit) cost of funds and thus will be priced on the basis of interbank rate, *plus* a mark-up reflecting the risk thought to attach to the loan. In the UK, the interbank rate is known as LIBOR, London Interbank Offer Rate, and is widely used as a benchmark rate for setting loan and deposit rates by the addition or subtraction of appropriate margins. Equivalent rates can be found in all financial centres (PIBOR in Paris, FIBOR in Frankfurt, for example).

9.2.5 Money market deposits

Money market deposits are large, fixed-term, bank deposits made by non-banks. These are usually large corporations but may be municipalities or other public bodies. In the UK, it is also the custom for local authorities to *borrow* by accepting large fixed-term deposits. These are usually for seven days, though sometimes longer. All such deposits pay interest at rates linked to interbank rate.

9.2.6 Repurchase agreements

A repurchase agreement is an agreement to buy securities from a seller on the understanding that they will be repurchased at some specified price and time in the future. In this deal, the seller is the equivalent of the borrower and the buyer is the lender. The repurchase price is higher than the initial sale price, and the difference in price constitutes the return to the seller. Deals are quoted on a yield basis, using Equation 9.3 (or 9.8). Thus if the Bundesbank agrees to a repurchase deal with a German bank, involving treasury bills, it may buy them for DM1 m, agreeing to resell in three months for DM1.008 m. If so, the yield can be found as follows:

$$i = (1.008 - 1.0) / (1.0 \times 0.25) = 8\%$$

In this example, the sale price of DM1 m is likely to be slightly less than the market value of the bills at the time of purchase. This margin offers some protection to the lender in case the borrower goes bankrupt or defaults for some other reason. The size of the risk, and thus this margin, depends in large part upon the status of the borrower, but it also depends upon the precise nature of the contract. Some repo deals are genuine sales. In these circumstances, the lender owns the securities and can sell them in case of default. In some repo contracts, however, what is created is more strictly a collateralized loan with securities acting as collateral while remaining in the legal ownership of the borrower. In the case of default, the lender has only a general claim on the lender and so the margin is likely to be greater.

> **Exercise 9.3**
>
> Moneylenders plc arranges a purchase of securities for £5,900,000 with an agreement to resell them in 70 days for £6,000,000.
>
> 1 What is the repo rate earned by Moneylenders plc?
> 2 For what price would they have to be resold in order to provide a return of 10 per cent?
>
> *Answers:* see end of chapter

9.2.7 Reading the Financial Times

Commentary and data on money market behaviour are carried on the *Financial Times* 'Currencies and Money' page. Much of the material in which we are interested here, therefore, in intermixed with information about exchange rates. (We discuss this page's foreign exchange content in Chapter 12.)

Box 9.2 reproduces the two tables that are most relevant to the present discussion. The 'London Money Rates' table shows interest rates available on each of the instruments described above, for different periods to maturity as appropriate. If we look at the one-month column, for example, we see that a bank could lend in the interbank market at an (equivalent annual) rate of $5\frac{7}{8}$ per cent and could borrow at $6\frac{1}{8}$ per cent. In the next row, we see that sterling CDs could be sold at prices which gave an equivalent annual return of 6 + 1/32 per cent (the cost of 'borrowing') and could be bought for a price equivalent to 5 + 11/32 per cent (the rate on lending). (Check that this differential in interest rates implies the correct differential in trading prices; that is, for holders of CDs, the selling price is below the buying price). Notice that the mid-point in the CD range is slightly lower than the mid-point for interbank rates: we predicted this in our discussion above on the grounds that the secondary market in which CDs can be traded makes them more liquid than a time deposit of the same maturity.

In the next row, we have the annualized discount rates on one-month Treasury Bills. Notice that the mid-point of the buy/sell range is slightly lower again, reflecting the high liquidity that comes from a very active secondary market and also the extra security that comes from the Treasury Bill being a government instrument and thus immune from default risk. However, we must not exaggerate the differential between Treasury Bills and CDs. Remember (from above) that the return on a bill is an annualized rate of discount calculated on the redemption or par value. This is not directly comparable with rates calculated on a more conventional (yield) basis, as CD and interbank rates are. The equivalent yield on these bills is slightly higher than the (discount) rate quoted in the table.

The commentary provided on the 'Currencies and Money' page provides any interpretation of these figures that may be necessary. Frequently, this will amount to little. The column will report any significant flows of funds between the government and commercial banks which affect banks' liquidity position and could set up forces for a change in interest rates unless it were offset by central bank intervention in the money markets. These interventions would also be detailed in the column. The commentary will be particularly detailed, however, when the Bank of England engages in money market operations in order to bring about a change in interest rates. These official money market operations are described in detail in Section 9.4 below.

Box 9.2 Reporting the money markets

These two tables are taken from the *Financial Times* 'Currencies and Money' page, 31 October 1996

WORLD INTEREST RATES

MONEY RATES

October 30	Over night	One month	Three mths	Six mths	One year	Lomb. inter.	Dis. rate	Repo rate
Belgium	3 1/16	3 1/8	3 1/8	3 1/8	3 7/32	6.00	2.50	–
week ago	3 1/32	3 1/8	3 1/16	3 1/16	3 3/16	6.00	2.50	–
France	3 5/16	3 5/16	3 3/8	3 15/32	3 9/16	3.35	–	4.75
week ago	3 11/32	3 5/16	3 13/32	3 1/2	3 19/32	3.35	–	4.75
Germany	3 11/16	3 1/8	3 1/8	3 1/8	3 1/4	4.50	2.50	3.00
week ago	2 15/16	3 1/8	3 3/32	3 1/16	3 5/32	4.50	2.50	3.00
Ireland	5 1/2	5 5/8	5 5/8	5 11/16	5 11/16	–	–	6.25
week ago	5 9/16	5 5/8	5 11/16	5 11/16	5 11/16	–	–	6.25
Italy	8 1/16	7 13/16	7 11/16	7 7/16	7 3/16	9.00	7.50	8.38
week ago	8 3/16	7 13/16	7 13/16	7 19/32	7 5/32	9.00	7.50	8.38
Netherlands	2 29/32	2 31/32	3	3 3/32	3 7/32	–	3.00	3.30
week ago	2 13/16	2 31/32	2 15/16	3	3 3/32	–	3.00	3.30
Switzerland	1 9/16	1 11/16	1 25/32	1 13/16	1 29/32	–	1.00	–
week ago	1 1/4	1 11/16	1 19/32	1 5/8	1 5/8	–	1.00	–
US	5 3/16	5 9/32	5 7/16	5 15/32	5 5/8	–	5.00	–
week ago	5 7/16	5 8/32	5 3/8	5 15/32	5 3/4	–	5.00	–
Japan	1/2	3/8	13/32	7/16	17/32	–	0.50	–
week ago	7/16	3/8	13/32	13/32	17/32	–	0.50	–
■ $ LIBOR FT London								
Interbank Fixing	–	5 3/8	5 1/2	5 9/16	5 23/32	–	–	–
week ago	–	5 3/8	5 17/32	5 5/8	5 27/32	–	–	–
US Dollar CDs	–	5.08	5.07	5.12	5.24	–	–	–
week ago	–	5.08	5.10	5.19	5.41	–	–	–
ECU Linked Ds	–	4 3/32	4 3/32	4 3/32	4 1/8	–	–	–
week ago	–	4 3/32	4 3/32	4 1/8	4 5/32	–	–	–
SDR Linked Ds	–	3 5/32	3 7/32	3 5/16	3 15/32	–	–	–
week ago	–	3 5/32	3 7/32	3 5/16	3 15/32	–	–	–

$ LIBOR Interbank fixing rates are offered rates for $10m quoted to the market by four reference banks at 11am each working day. The banks are: Bankers Trust, Bank of Tokyo Mitsubishi, Barclays and National Westminster.
Mid rates are shown for the domestic Money Rates, US$ CDs, ECU & SDR Linked Deposits (Ds).

UK INTEREST RATES

LONDON MONEY RATES

Oct 30	Over-night	7 days notice	One month	Three months	Six months	One year
Interbank Sterling	6 3/4 - 4	6 - 5 3/4	6 1/8 - 5 7/8	6 1/4 - 6	6 3/8 - 6 1/8	6 11/16 - 6 7/16
Sterling CDs	-	-	6 1/32 - 5 31/32	6 1/8 - 6 1/16	6 1/4 - 6 3/16	6 1/2 - 6 7/16
Treasury Bills	-	-	5 15/16 - 5 7/8	5 15/16 - 5 7/8	-	-
Bank Bills	-	-	5 15/16 - 5 7/8	6 - 5 15/16	6 1/8 - 6 1/16	-
Local authority deps.	6 5/8 - 6	6 - 5 3/4	6 1/16 - 6	6 1/8 - 6 1/16	6 5/16 - 6 3/16	6 9/16 - 6 7/16
Discount Market deps	6 3/4 - 5 3/4	6 1/16 - 5 15/16	-	-	-	-

UK clearing bank base lending rate 6 per cent from October 30, 1996

	Up to 1 month	1-3 month	3-6 months	6-9 months	9-12 months
Certs of Tax dep. (£100,000)	2 1/2	5 1/2	5	5	4 3/4

Certs of Tax dep. under £100,000 is 2 1/2pc. Deposits withdrawn for cash 1 1/4pc.
Ave. tender rate of discount on Oct 25, 5.6282pc. ECGD fixed rate Stlg. Export Finance. Make up day Oct 31, 1996. Agreed rate for period Nov 26, 1996 to Dec 24, 1996, Scheme III 7.25pc. Reference rate for period Oct 1, 1996 to Oct 31, 1996, Schemes IV & V 6.001pc. Finance House Base Rate 6pc from Oct 1, 1996

The 'World interest rates' table shows current short-term rates available in a variety of countries. The upper part of the table gives rates available on deposits ranging from overnight to one year in maturity and for each of these rates currently available shows underneath the rate that was available one week ago, so that investors can see the direction in which short-term rates have been moving. The last three columns, at the right-hand end, show the current (and one week ago) levels of official short-term rates set by central banks in their dealings with money markets. These official rates are explained in Table 9.4 below.

The interest rates shown in the upper part of the table are the rates available on deposits made in the domestic currency. The lower part of the table shows the rates available (now and one week ago) on a variety of short-term instruments denominated in units of international significance. It shows the rate that banks in London are prepared to pay for US$ deposits in London and the rates available on CDs denominated in US$. It also shows rates available on deposits linked to European currency units (ECUs) and to the IMF's special drawing rights (SDRs).

9.3 Characteristics and use of the money markets

The bills that are traded in the discount market usually come from one of three sources.[2] The major, and historically the most important, source is the central government treasury. Such bills are known as *Treasury Bills* in the UK and USA (usually shortened to T-bills in the latter); 'bons du trésor' in France and 'schatzwechsel' in Germany. Although treasury bills circulate quite widely after issue, at least between financial institutions, they are usually sold initially to designated institutions. These are banks and discount houses in the UK; anyone with a central bank account in France; any institution registered also for the purchase of government bonds in Germany and to 'primary dealers' in the USA. Their initial issue usually involves a sale by auction (weekly in the UK, France and USA but with no set timetable in

Germany). Auctions can take one of two forms: the *bid-price* auction where successful bidders pay the price that they bid, and *striking-price* auctions where bids are ranked by descending value and all successful bidders pay the (uniform) price of the lowest bid necessary to clear the market. As a general rule, the 'bid-price' auction is the more common. (In the UK, the striking-price method is sometimes used for the auction of bonds, when the process is known as a *tender*. In the UK, therefore, 'auction' tends to mean 'bid-price auction'.) Amongst money market instruments, treasury bills tend to offer the lowest yield, since they are default-free and also because most central banks are prepared to discount treasury bills on demand for cash which is important to deposit-taking financial institutions who in turn guarantee to supply cash on demand to their depositors. We shall see in Section 9.4 that treasury bills and 'eligible' commercial bills (see below) feature largely in central bank operations to set short-term interest rates.

In much of continental Europe, but not in the UK, there are also large markets for local authority (municipalité, département, länder) bills and bills issued by public corporations such as SNCF, Deutsche Bundesbahn and Deutsche Bundespost.

The third major source of bills is large corporations. *A commercial bill* is a promise by one firm to pay another a fixed amount at some specified time in the near future. As with treasury bills, the initial maturities range usually from one to six months. The promise is given in respect of some good or service which has been purchased and the par or maturity value of the bill includes a sum over and above the value of the goods, which is the interest payable to the seller for having to wait for payment. The seller 'draws' a bill on the buyer of the goods who 'accepts' the obligation to pay at a specified time and place. The point about a market for these bills, however, is that once issued they can be traded. The supplier, in our example, need not wait until the bill matures in order to receive payment. The bill can be sold whenever funds are required. Assume for simplicity that short-term interest rates are unchanged since the bill was first drawn up. The

---

[2] For a detailed discussion of the mechanics of bill issue, acceptance and discounting see Valdez (1993) Ch. 5

price obtained will stand at a discount to the maturity value and the size of the discount will depend upon factors with which we are now familiar. It will depend upon the period to maturity (since this determines the *rate* of discount). It will also depend upon the market's assessment of risk, which in this case means the risk that the issuer of the bill will default. If short-term interest rates *do* change then the discount will get bigger (as rates rise) or smaller (as rates fall).

The fact that the discount rate on commercial bills depends upon the risk of default means that discount rates on commercial bills are generally higher than rates on government or public authority bills. It also gives rise to an important distinction between classes of bills. Some bills may be drawn on banks who have agreed to accept them on behalf of the buyer of the goods. Since the status of such banks is generally well known, their acceptance of bills usually leads to such bills (*bank* bills) carrying a lower rate of discount than they would if they had been accepted by the buyer of the goods. Furthermore, acceptance by certain specified banks, of the highest standing, renders the bill *eligible* for discount with the central bank. This in turn means that the central bank guarantees to discount these bills for cash in the event of a system-wide shortage of liquidity. This immediately gives these bills a special status since they have almost the characteristics of deposits with the central bank while at the same time they provide a positive rate of return. All deposit-taking institutions hold some eligible (commercial) bills and treasury bills as second-line reserves.

In the UK, the commercial bill market received a considerable boost starting in 1974 as a result of what became known as the 'bill-leak'. At several intervals during the 1970s the Bank of England tried to limit bank lending (and monetary growth) by penalizing banks which allowed their interest-bearing deposits to grow beyond set limits (see Section 6.5). As a result, frustrated firms took to raising short-term funds by issuing bills to which banks gave their acceptance. Thus firms, for the most part, got the funds they required while banks were able to replace lost interest income with fee income from supporting the bill issues. For UK banks this was one of the earliest introductions to 'off balance sheet' activity, an issue to which we

return in connection with regulation of financial institutions in Chapter 23.

In the next section we shall see that central banks conduct 'open market' operations, of various sorts, in many of the instruments traded in the money markets in order to influence short-term interest rates. It is only with treasury bills, however, that central banks are involved in the 'primary' or new issue market. With all other instruments central banks are operating in the secondary market – the market for instruments already issued by the private sector. Since it is a characteristic of all money market instruments that their minimum denominations are very large (Ffr1 m for bons de trésor, £0.1 m for UK commercial paper, $10,000 for US t-bills, for example), it is easy to understand that money markets are markets for 'wholesale funds'. The borrowing and lending involves government and large, financial and non-financial corporations. Access to money markets for the personal sector has to be indirect, through some intermediary that is prepared to pool small investors' funds, purchase money market instruments and then pass on money market interest rates (*less* a deduction for expenses) to investors. In the United States, where access to interest-bearing deposits was further restricted by 'Regulation Q' until 1980, the demands of small investors gave rise to the 'money market mutual fund'. Between 1973 and 1980 US MMMFs' assets grew from nothing to over $200 bn. The impact on banks was considerable, as the personal sector withdrew deposits in order to get the market interest rates offered by MMMFs, and led to the ending of regulation Q in 1980. From 1982, banks were allowed to offer deposit accounts to 'retail' customers which offered both money market rates and limited checking or payment facilities.

Similar developments occurred in the UK in the late 1970s, though here it was the minimum size of money market instruments rather than regulation that excluded the personal sector from the market. These minimum thresholds led some merchant banks to offer 'high interest cheque accounts' to selected customers. Once again, the principle was to pool retail deposits and use them to buy large denomination CDs, bills or money market deposits. As with US MMMFs, UK banks found that they needed to impose restrictions on such accounts in order to pay the highest possible rates while keeping the operating costs of such accounts to a minimum. In 1980, for example, a typical account required a minimum deposit of £2,500 (equivalent to £6,000 in 1996 – quite high for the personal sector) and set a minimum value for each cheque transaction of £100 (in order to limit the number of transactions for which the account would be suitable).

9.4   Official intervention in the money markets

In Section 6.5 we examined a number of techniques that the monetary authorities in any country could use in order to influence the rate of growth of bank lending and money supply. The list was long, but we could divide the techniques into 'direct' or quantity controls and 'indirect' or 'market-based' controls. We noted in that section that most countries had at some time experimented with some forms of direct control but that in recent years the trend had been towards market-based methods. Indeed, according to a recent IMF survey (Batten *et al.*, 1990), while there may be some differences in *intermediate targets*, there is little difference in monetary policy *operating techniques* between the major economies. Essentially, 'market-based' simply means setting the level of short-term interest rates and allowing the market to determine both the quantity and the distribution of money and credit. Clearly, setting the level of short-term interest rates must involve some form of official intervention in the money markets. The main theme of this section is the form that this intervention takes. That is, we are mainly concerned with operating techniques. But we begin with a brief discussion of the intermediate targets of monetary policy.

'Intermediate targets' are the immediate or nearest targets of policy. They contrast with the *ultimate targets* or *objectives* of policy and they are used primarily in some sort of feedback mechanism or reaction function to tell the authorities whether their *monetary policy instruments* have been correctly set.

As a rule, the ultimate targets or objectives of monetary policy include some combination of inflation and output. However, the connection between monetary policy instruments and prices and output are neither direct nor instantaneous. Thus, by the time the rate of inflation itself tells the authorities that their instrument settings are wrong it is too late to change them. Changing them in response to inflation *now* may simply mean they are wrong again by the time they begin to work. In most countries, therefore, the authorities prefer to be guided by some intermediate target which responds more directly to instrument changes but is also connected in a fairly predictable way with the future inflation rate. During the 1970s and 1980s, the intermediate target in most countries was the rate of growth of some monetary aggregate(s) and policy instruments were adjusted to keep this growth within a target range. However, during the 1980s it became obvious in many countries (Germany perhaps is the exception) that the connection between monetary aggregates and the ultimate targets of inflation and output was becoming progressively weaker. As a result, many governments switched towards regarding the level of interest rates themselves, or the exchange rate, as intermediate targets.[3] The desire to maintain stable exchange rates within the EMS, and the Plaza agreement in 1985 on the need for monetary policy coordination between the G7, reinforced the need for attention to exchange rates.

Table 9.2 summarizes the intermediate targets of monetary policy for France, Germany, Italy, the UK and USA since 1980, indicating such revisions as have taken place. The table shows that the growth rate of monetary aggregates has been an intermediate target in all these countries at some time. The precise definition of each aggregate can be found in Section 6.2. For each country, the targets are listed in descending order of priority. What the table also shows is that, since the mid-1980s, a money supply target has been predominant only in Germany.

Whatever the intermediate target, however, the operating techniques in all these countries are re-

Table 9.2 Intermediate targets of monetary policy since 1980

France	Germany	Italy	UK	USA
1980+	*1980+*	*1980+*	*1980+*	*1980+*
M2 growth rate. Exchange rate.	CBM growth rate (M3 growth rate from 1988). Some attention to yield curve since 1990.	M2 growth rate Exchange rate	M3 growth rate Exchange rate rate	Non-borrowed reserves growth
1987+ Exchange rate. M2 growth rate.		*1986+* Exchange rate. M2 growth rate.	*1986+* Exchange rate. Asset prices. M0 growth rate. Inflation rate (since 1992)	*1982+* Federal Funds Rate. 'Broad credit' growth Exchange rate.

markably similar: the central bank uses open market operations in order to exploit its position as the monopoly supplier of bank reserves.

In practice, 'operating on bank reserves' is consistent with the central bank behaving in a number of different ways which can be characterized along a spectrum. At one end of this spectrum, the central bank can set the rate of interest which it wishes to see form the basis for all other short-term rates. In order to maintain this rate, the central bank will have to supply whatever quantity of reserves banks require.

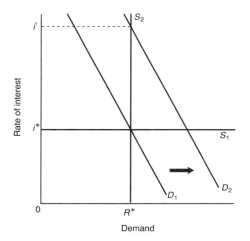

Figure 9.1 Interest versus reserve targeting.

In effect, in this situation, the supply of reserves is perfectly elastic at the target interest rate. In Figure 9.1, demand for reserves increases from D_1 to D_2. In order to maintain the target interest rate at i^*, reserves are supplied in whatever quantity is necessary along S_1. Alternatively, the CB can set a quantity target for reserves, engaging in open market operations so as to provide only the target quantity. In this case it must accept whatever level of short-term rate is necessary to clear the market. In Figure 9.1 the target quantity of reserves is shown by S^*. In these circumstances, the increase in demand takes us along S_2 to an interest rate i'.[4]

Economic theory suggests that the choice between these extremes should depend upon the nature of the origin of the shock to the demand curve. If, for example, the increase in demand for reserves results from an aggregate demand shock which threatens to push demand beyond its trend growth rate, then accommodating the demand for reserves at the going rate of interest enables banks to respond to demands for money and credit which may lead to higher inflation. If, by contrast, the shock stems from an increase in demand for money resulting from financial innovations which cause agents to wish to hold more money in their wealth portfolios, then holding to a rigid reserve quantity target will cause interest rates to rise with a generally deflationary effect upon the real economy. The emerging

---

4 This discussion, and Figure 9.1, both involve an element of simplification. Both describe a static situation whereas, in practice, the demand curve is continually shifting to the right. A *quantity* target is not therefore a target set at an absolute level (R^*) in the figure, but a target rate of growth. In Figure 9.1, this would appear as limiting the rate at which the supply curve, S^1, was allowed to move to the right. With a quantity target the rightward shift of the supply curve would often be less than the rightward shift of demand, and interest rates would rise. An interest target would require that the supply curve were allowed to shift rightward at the *same rate* as the demand curve.

consensus amongst central banks during the 1980s was that shocks to the demand for reserves were increasingly the outcome of changes in portfolio preferences. Thus, the tendency was increasingly towards interest rate targeting and reserve accommodation. Behind this, however, was an increasing awareness of the *practical* difficulties involved in operating quantitative controls over the monetary base. These were outlined earlier, in Box 6.4.

In practice, therefore, central banks choose to set the price rather than the quantity of reserves and thus make the setting of short-term interest rates their chosen policy instrument. This they do by making reserves available, at the target price.[5] Changes in officially determined rates are then transmitted by arbitrage (or sometimes simply by conventionally determined mark-ups) to a broad spectrum of short-term rates. Changes in short-term rates then affect the price of bank loans and thus the quantity demanded, as well as affecting the return on a wide variety of assets. If the change in these returns is a change *relative* to the rate of return on money, then there is an impact also on the quantity of money demanded.[6] Equally, changes in short-term rates in one country change the rate of return on short-term assets in that country relative to others and cause changes in exchange rates via capital flows.

Essentially, central banks can influence interest rates by exploiting their position as lenders of last resort or monopoly suppliers of liquidity in a general shortage. Since the tendency is for most economies to expand over time (and for nominal values to increase where inflation is positive) there is almost always a positive demand for net new bank lending (and net new deposits) at current interest rate settings. This generates the parallel tendency for banks to require recurrent increases in reserves (which as we saw in Section 6.3 are liabilities of the central bank). This is further reinforced in the countries listed in Table 9.2 by the fact that central

banks meet some of this demand by lending reserves on a short-term basis. The fact that this assistance is continuously maturing means that banks have a continuing need for new assistance which central banks can supply at rates of their own choosing (though subject of course to the (mainly international) constraints which we touched on in Section 3.4). The facilities through which the central bank can provide assistance are virtually the same in all countries. Firstly the central bank can engage in one or other form of *open market operations*. This simply means entering the money markets itself as a buyer (or seller). Alternatively, it can lend directly to banks (*'through the discount window'* as it is sometimes called). The past 15 years or so have seen a considerable convergence in money market intervention techniques (for reasons we explain below). The most obvious is a decline in the amount of discount window lending and greater emphasis upon open market operations, particularly, in recent years, repurchase agreements. Lending via the discount window still takes place in the USA (at 'discount rate') and in Germany (at 'Lombard' rate) but direct lending is now a marginal source of funds in all developed systems.

'Open market operations' simply means the authorities' buying and selling of securities in markets open to all participants. For example, let us suppose that a central bank wishes to raise interest rates, using open market operations. In such a case, it may offer to buy treasury or eligible commercial bills at a lower price than it did on the last occasion of assistance. This increase in the official discount rate is usually sufficient to signal to all market participants that all short-term rates should change by a similar amount. Alternatively, it may enter the repo market as a buyer, but again offering to buy at a price that represents an increase in the cost of funds to borrowers. If it wishes rates to remain as they are, which is of course the more common case, it simply

---

[5] We need to be careful to distinguish (minor) day-to-day changes in the demand for reserves which result, for example, from payments between the treasury and the private sector. These are always routinely accommodated since it would be impossibly disruptive to have day-to-day interest rates fluctuating, perhaps quite dramatically, around a stationary mean. The shocks we have discussed here are shocks which are sufficiently major, and sustained, as to require a discretionary policy response.

[6] This is a condition which it has always been difficult to achieve when targeting broad money aggregates which contain a high proportion of interest-bearing deposits whose returns move with other short-term rates. Where financial innovation has led to the payment of interest on sight deposits this condition is hard to achieve even for narrow money aggregates.

offers to deal at current prices and yields. Box 9.3 contains a report of the Bundesbank signalling a cut in interest rates by offering cheaper repurchase facilities. Until the 1960s most central banks confined their dealings to short-term government securities (treasury bills *plus* bonds approaching maturity). However, most central banks now deal also in certificates of deposit and commercial paper as well as the bills and repos that we used for illustration.

Box 9.3   The Bundesbank cuts interest rates

Surprise over size of reduction aimed at boosting German economic recovery

Bundesbank cuts repo rate to 3%

Bundesbank rate cut is welcomed in France but not by holders of D-Marks

Source: FT Extel

By Andrew Fisher in Frankfurt, David Owen in Paris and Richard Adams in London

The Bundesbank yesterday cut one of its key interest rates more sharply than expected in an apparent bid to reinforce the German economic recovery and help support the shaky French franc.

The German central bank lowered its securities repurchase (repo) rate, through which it influences the money market, from 3.3 per cent to a new low of 3 per cent, citing slower growth in the money supply as the main reason for the move.

European share and bond prices moved ahead on the news and the dollar strengthened against the D-mark.

In London, news of the Bundesbank's decision was greeted with shouts of surprise on trading floors.

The Bank of France quickly followed, cutting its intervention rate by 0.2 of a percentage point to 3.35 per cent.

Last month, President Jacques Chirac criticised the management of France's banking system and said French and German interest rates were "clearly too high". His remarks are widely believed to have contributed to this month's depreciation of the franc.

Yesterday, the French currency and the Paris stock market responded favourably to the reductions. The franc rose strongly against the D-mark, to FFr3.409 at close of trading in London, from FFr3.421 on Wednesday.

The benchmark CAC-40 index closed ahead 0.86 per cent at 2,017.87, recouping virtually all the ground lost the previous day.

September PIBOR contracts, which show the level of French interest rate expectations, rose to 96.07, up 31 basis points on the day. At this level dealers expect French interest rates to be about 3.93 per cent next month.

A repo rate cut had been expected after the Bundesbank took no action at its last council meeting in July, but most economists and traders had expected a cut to around 3.2 per cent. Several economists thought further repo cuts and even a lower discount rate – currently 2.5 per cent – were now possible.

The article above is taken from the *Financial Times*, Friday August 23 1996, and reports the decision by the Bundesbank to reduce its official dealing rate from 3.3% to 3%. There are three points of general interest illustrated here. The first is that the reduction in interest rates raised share and bond prices. We saw earlier in this chapter that if interest rates fall the price of money market instruments increases. Since these instruments are to some extent substitutes for shares and bonds, we must expect them to move in the same direction. Secondly, we should note that the article stresses the unexpected nature of the reduction. If it had been expected, it would already have been incorporated in prices and would have had little or no effect when announced. Thirdly, notice how quickly an event in German markets has an impact across the world. The US$ and the Ffr strengthen against the DM; the Bank of France cuts its official dealing rate; share prices rise throughout Europe.

Table 9.3: Instruments used in central bank operations

	France	Germany	Italy	UK	USA
Outright purchase	GS[1]	GS	GS	GS, CP	GS
Outright sale	GS	GS	GS	GS, CP	GS
Repurchase	GS, CP[1]	GS	GS	GS, CP	GS
Matched sale and purchase	GS, CP	–	–	–	GS

Note: [1] GS = government securities (including treasury bills); CP = commercial paper (including commercial bills).
Source: Batten *et al.* and *Euromoney* country surveys (various issues).

The fundamental source of its power, as we said in Sections 3.4 and 6.5, is that the central bank is the monopoly supplier of liquidity in the event of a system-wide shortage. Furthermore, the facilities for exploiting this power are very similar in money markets throughout the world. By comparison, the differences between operating techniques are fairly trivial. Table 9.3 shows the instruments through which selected central banks conduct their open market operations and the similarities are obvious.

Table 9.4 shows the interest rates that the same selected central banks try to influence via these

operations. Careful inspection of the final column shows that it is essentially the same range of short-term rates that central banks seek to influence.

We noted above that there has been a convergence of operating procedures in recent years towards open market operations. Both the reasons for this, and the institutional changes necessary to bring it about, vary from country to country. In the USA and the UK the changes were small. In Italy and France the necessary changes were considerable but for Germany rather less. The general principle underlying the shift has been the move towards less

Table 9.4 Official and key money market interest rates

Rate	Description	
France	*Taux des pensions sur appels d'offres*[1]	Rate on repo agreements offered at the discretion of the Banque de France. Sets lower bound to rates.
	Rate on 5- to 10-day repurchase agreements	Rate set by Banque de France for 5-,10-day repos available as emergency funding at the discretion of financial institutions. Typically above short-term market rates and sets upper bound.
Germany	Discount rate	Rate charged by Bundesbank for rediscounting eligible paper. Typically sets lower bound to rates.
	Lombard rate	Rate charged by Bundesbank for collateralized short-term loans to institutions. Typically sets upper bound to rates.
	Repurchase rate	Rate set by Bundesbank on its periodic repo agreements.
Italy	Discount rate	Rate charged by Banca d'Italia for discounting eligible paper. Sets lower bound.
	Rate on fixed-term advances	Rate charged by Banca d'Italia for fixed-term advances to banks. Sets upper bound.
United Kingdom	Bank of England dealing rates	The rates at which the Bank of England rediscounts bills of various maturities.[2]
United States	Discount rate	Rate charged by the Federal Reserve on short-term lending to depository institutions.
	Federal funds rate	Rate charged in the interbank market for lending between depository institutions.

Source: Batten *et al.* and *Euromoney* country surveys (various issues).
Note: [1] Translated as 'rate on tender for repurchase agreements'.
       [2] Until February 1997; the rate on government bond and bill repo agreements thereafter.

direct regulation of markets. When market participants are free to operate with few constraints, direct controls are fairly easily circumvented. Where this is not possible, the controls impose a cost on the service which drives clients elsewhere, a freedom again which comes with deregulation. Recent developments in France provide a useful illustration, though a very similar picture could be drawn based on the UK in the late 1960s.

Before 1985, the French financial system was highly segmented, with each segment regulated by a different authority and largely by administrative decree. This was because with borrowers and lenders confined to their own specified segment, there was no mechanism (arbitrage or competition, for example) whereby the effect of central bank money market operations could be transmitted generally through the rest of the system and also because, before 1985, there were anyway no money market securities through which the Banque de France could conduct open market operations. This, in turn, meant that monetary policy had to be implemented separately in each segment and this required the development of quantitative rules and guidelines for the quantity and distribution of credit for each segment.

There were several reasons for change. Firstly, as we noted earlier, where these controls are effective they impose a cost. As financial markets elsewhere were liberalized, it became both easier and cheaper for French corporations to raise funds outside France. This would clearly become a bigger problem as national barriers to monetary and financial activity were removed in the cause of further European integration. Furthermore, and this was a perfect repetition of the UK experience in the 1960s, direct regulation encourages firms to set up at the margin of the regulations. The target of any regulation has to be defined with precision. Once defined, it is an invitation to those who wish to circumvent it to develop an activity which falls just outside. The result then is that the regulations (and their bureaucracy) either have continually to expand or become ineffective. Finally, when the EMS was established in 1979 and the French authorities committed themselves to stabilizing the franc within it, they required a mechanism capable of reacting quickly enough and with sufficiently broad effects to

fluctuations in the external value of the franc. The only mechanism that would operate in a sufficiently widespread and non-discriminatory way was the level of short-term interest, provided, of course, that interest rates in one segment were free to influence interest rates in another. Substantial structural changes to French financial markets were undertaken in 1985 and the move towards a monetary policy based on money market intervention began.

The move from discount window lending to open market operations represents a further step along the same road towards market liberalization. Lending via the discount window requires the authorities to advertise or 'post' a rate of interest at which it will provide assistance. The authorities are therefore clearly setting short-term rates. There is, firstly, a technical question about whether they are in a position to make the correct judgement about the rate necessary in a particular situation. They may, for example, judge that economic conditions require a rise in interest rates of 50 bps, but raising their lending rate by 0.5 per cent will not *necessarily* cause market rates to rise by the same amount if they have underestimated the degree of liquidity in the market. But in some countries there has been a 'political' problem too. Announcing an official discount rate makes the authorities visibly responsible for the setting of interest rates. In systems like the UK, France and Italy where the central bank is accountable to elected governments, there is sometimes a reluctance to change rates (particularly to raise them) when economic circumstances require. Open market operations give the authorities freedom to exploit the markets' own perception of the shortage/surplus of funds and, less convincingly, to claim that interest rate changes are the result of market forces.

A good example of this is provided by Bank of England money market operating procedures since 1981. The Bank of England no longer announces a 'Bank Rate' or 'Minimum Lending Rate' as it once did. It now makes a twice daily forecast of the money markets' liquidity position (having regard to the factors listed in Box 9.4). Based on this forecast it would then state that it is willing to purchase, rediscount or engage in a repo of bills, dealing only with a subset of banking institutions known as discount houses. The term 'discount' stems from their traditional function of discounting (government and commercial) bills, holding these as assets on one side of their balance sheets and financing them by taking deposits from the rest of the banking system, at very short notice or even 'at call'. This provides a second line of highly liquid reserve assets for the banking system as a whole and it is these deposits that banks withdraw in times of shortage, passing the shortage to the discount houses who then approach the Bank of England with offers to sell bills. The Bank does not specify the price/discount rate at which it will deal, nor the residual maturity, which is usually very short (< 14 days). This leaves discount houses to set the initial price/rate of discount, which might in some degree reflect their sense of urgency about the position as they see it. The Bank may then accept or reject the price/discount rate, forcing new offers at what it thinks is an appropriate rate. If this rate differs from that on previous deals in corresponding bills, this is taken to indicate a change in the desired level of short-term rates. Since the Bank's official dealing rate is setting the price of a key source of marginal funds for banks, its immediate effect falls upon interbank rates which change immediately. Since, as we have seen, many other rates are set by reference to LIBOR, these change automatically. Those that are not linked 'administratively' change rapidly as possible arbitrage opportunities emerge.

In dealing with the discount houses rather than directly with banks themselves, the Bank of England's money market operations introduce an extra layer into the procedures for relieving surpluses and shortages of liquidity. In December 1996, the Bank announced two significant changes to its operations. The first was to widen the range of institutions with which it was prepared to deal directly to include also banks (in general), building societies and securities houses. The second was to widen the range of instruments in which it would deal. Instead of confining its transactions to treasury and 'eligible' commercial bills, the Bank would also enter into repo agreements in short-dated govern-

ment bonds. In widening the range of institutions and concentrating upon repo deals (rather than outright purchases) in bills and bonds, the Bank's proposals move UK money market operations towards the practices of other European countries. Perhaps most significantly, the new arrangements bring the Bank of England's operations into line with those envisaged for the European central bank in a European Monetary Union. These procedures have operated since March 1997 .

9.5 The Eurocurrency markets

In the introduction to this chapter we noted that most of the instruments we were going to analyse as part of money market transactions existed in both a domestic currency form and a 'Euro-' currency form. A Eurocurrency instrument is in fact any instrument denominated in a currency which differs from that of the country in which it is traded. Thus it follows that 'Euro-' instruments can be found all over the world and have no obvious connection whatever with Europe. The 'Euro-' prefix is just a reminder that the practice of trading instruments denominated in foreign currencies began with the US$ being traded in Europe. Since dollar deposits first began to be held in European banks in the late 1960s, the Eurocurrency markets have grown very rapidly, the stock of Eurocurrency assets being estimated by 1995 at over $6,000 bn. In the 1980s alone they expanded over threefold. The Euro*currency* markets predate the markets for Euro*bonds* (which we discuss in the next chapter). We look firstly at the factors behind the growth of Eurocurrency instruments[7] and then at some of the possible consequences.

Under the Bretton Woods system of fixed exchange rates established after World War II, the US$ functioned as an intervention currency, an international means of payment and store of value. The worldwide demand for dollars was met by a combination of US balance of payments deficits and

---

[7] Readers may care to note the similarities between the forces driving the growth of Euro*currency* activity and those behind the growth of the Euro*bond* markets. The latter are listed in Box 10.7. The role played by regulation is particularly striking in the two cases.

Box 9.4   Money market flows

The following flows will cause changes in money market liquidity. The headings used are the terms employed in *Financial Times* money markets reports for the UK. The explanations, however, are written in general terms, applicable to any money market. In each case, the event is described in such a way that it produces a *reduction* in liquidity to which the central bank will have to respond by supplying additional funds in whatever quantity and at whatever price it thinks appropriate.

• *Exchequer transactions*

– net payments to the exchequer

  If the government banks with the central bank (as it does in the UK), then net payments to government by the private sector will lead to a transfer of funds from banks' balances at the central bank into government accounts.

– net official sales of gilts

  The net purchase of government bonds by the private sector is just one way in which net payments may be made to government with the money market consequences described above.

– net receipts of sterling on the Exchange Equalization Account

  If the central bank intervenes to support the domestic currency, it sells foreign currency in exchange and thus drains the market of the domestic currency.

• *Change in the note issue*

When the public makes net withdrawals of banknotes, retail banks replenish their holdings of notes from the central bank which debits their balances accordingly.

• *Bills maturing in official hands/sales of treasury bills*

When bills (or other instruments) held by the central bank mature, payments flow to the central bank from those who issued the bills. The purchase of treasury bills (or other government debt) by money market institutions also causes a flow of funds from the market to the central bank.

• *Unwinding of previous assistance*

Previous assistance given by the central bank to the market, a repo deal for example, will be for a fixed period. At the end of that period market institutions will have to repay the loan or repurchase the bills and this requires a flow of funds from the market to the central bank.

• *Bankers' balances below target*

If the previous day's clearing has left banks' balances at the central bank below their desired level, banks will withdraw funds lent in the money market.

---

dollar borrowings from US banks, the resulting deposits being held until the early 1960s, mainly with US banks. In the mid-1960s, however, the US authorities began to impose controls on currency outflows which limited access to these (US-stored) deposits for overseas owners. This combined with two further, long-running, disadvantages. The first was 'Regulation Q' which limited interest payments on deposits. The second, mainly relevant to Eastern bloc countries, was the risk that dollar deposits might be impounded for political reasons. The result was that non-US owners of dollar deposits began to place them with European banks and, later, with European subsidiaries of US banks.

Since reserve, deposit insurance, capital and other regulatory requirements are usually imposed with respect to banks' holdings of deposits in the domestic currency and act as a tax on deposit business, a further contributory factor to the long-term growth of Eurocurrency business was the ability of Eurobanks to offer their services at more competitive rates than domestic institutions. 'Eurobanks' is actually something of a misnomer. Most are departments or subsidiaries of major banks with a clear national identity. Most countries are involved, although the largest shares lie with banks whose headquarters are in Japan or the USA.

When we come to look at the consequences of Eurocurrency development, it should be said immediately that there is nothing fundamentally different between a bank that specializes in Eurocurrency business and a bank that concentrates on domestic deposits and lending, from an economic point of view. Both help channel funds between surplus and deficit units and, in so far as they create assets and liabilities which are more attractive to end users than would be the case if the latter dealt directly with each other, they help to mobilize funds which might otherwise have lain idle. However, there are two possible consequences of Eurobanking activity which have attracted considerable attention.

The first is the effect upon world money supply and liquidity. If, as we said above, Eurobanks are able to mobilize funds which would otherwise lie idle (through the usual processes of maturity and risk transformation) then private sector liquidity is increased. Furthermore, if we introduce into the banking system a further layer of institutions whose liabilities are money, as is plainly the case with any Eurocurrency, then we introduce the possibility of further multiple deposit creation against a limited quantity of reserves. Most Eurobanks hold reserves with major US banks or with major banks operating in the domestic monetary system. Imagine, for example, that a US resident moves dollars from a domestic bank to a Eurodollar bank. In the domestic bank, there is a rearrangement of ownership of deposits (from a nonbank to the Eurobank). In the Eurobank, there is an increase in customer deposits matched, of course, by an increase in reserves. However, the bank's liquidity has increased (on the assumption that its reserve:deposit ratio is less than one). If its response is then to increase its advances and if those advances are redeposited, then a further expansion of the Eurobank's balance sheet is possible. Numerically at least, the significance clearly depends upon two ratios, r, the reserve ratio and d, the redeposit ratio. The multiplier will take the value:

$$\frac{1}{1 - d\,(1 - r)} \qquad (9.9)$$

Estimates of the size of the Eurodollar multiplier range widely from the very high figure of 18.4[8] down

to 1.15[9]. Part of the explanation for the wide range of estimates lies in the difficulty of identifying reserves held against Eurodollars in Eurobanks which are branches of domestic US banks. The reserves held by the parent bank do not distinguish between the types of deposit against which they are held.

A second consequence, or group of consequences, arises from the increasing difficulty of operating an independent domestic monetary policy. Clearly, any attempt to control domestic monetary expansion can be partially thwarted at least by frustrated UK borrowers taking out Eurodollar (for example) loans and exchanging the proceeds for spot sterling. Such would be a predictable response whether the monetary restrictions came in the form of higher interest rates or some form of MBC. Furthermore, high UK interest rates, which would be part of a restrictive monetary policy, may attract an inflow of Eurocurrencies which could then be exchanged for sterling at a guaranteed price (under fixed exchange rates), increasing both the money supply and UK banks' cash reserves. In principle such an inflow can be sterilized by sales of securities but there is the obvious danger that security sales themselves widen the gap between domestic and Eurocurrency interest rates, leading to an increased inflow. With floating exchange rates it is the exchange rate itself that has to adjust.

9.6 Summary

Money markets enable lenders and borrowers to trade short-term funds. Some markets consist of negotiable securities which can be bought and sold between third parties while others are deposits which can be extinguished only by withdrawal. Since it would make no sense to arrange for interest payments on very short securities, these are usually issued at a discount to their par or maturity values. This means that comparisons between the yields on different money market instruments are not directly comparable. Rates of discount have to be converted to equivalent yields.

---

[8] Makin, 1972
[9] McKinnon, 1977. Lewis and Davis, 1987, give a figure of 1.25.

The markets are used overwhelmingly by large corporations and by government. The minimum denominations of instruments are very large and trading and trades take place at very 'fine' margins, measured in basis points. However, the personal sector can get access to money market rates of return via a number of indirect routes which require the creation of mutual funds by an intermediary.

From an economic policy point of view, the most important feature of the money markets is that central banks play a dominant role which they can exploit when they wish to change the level of short-term interest rates.

Key concepts used in this chapter

Money markets	Spreads	Money market mutual fund
Capital markets	Rate of discount	Policy instrument
Yield basis	Equivalent yield	Intermediate target
Discount basis	Striking price	Ultimate target
Basis points	Bid price	Open market operations

Questions and problems

1 Distinguish between 'money' and 'capital' markets. In what circumstances might (a) lenders and (b) borrowers abandon their usual preferences?

2 Why are the interest rate spreads between money market instruments generally very small?

3 Why does the yield on a discount security exceed the discount rate?

4 Which of the following offers the highest return:

   A three-month bill with a discount rate of 8 per cent?

   A three-month NCD with an interest rate of 8.25 per cent?

   A six-month bill with a discount rate of 8 per cent?

   A six-month NCD with an interest rate of 8.25 per cent?

5 The yield on 30-day commercial paper is 7 per cent. What is its discount rate?

6 Who are the main participants in money markets?

7 How can the personal sector get access to money market rates of return?

8 Explain briefly how the monetary authorities might intervene in the money markets in order to influence the growth of money and credit.

9 Discuss the proposition that the monetary authorities can control either short-term interest rates or the quantity of bank reserves, but not both.

10 How does economic theory suggest that the authorities should choose between an interest rate target and a reserves quantity target?

Further reading

A D Bain, *The Financial System* (Oxford: Blackwell, 2e 1992) Ch. 12

Bank of England Quarterly Bulletin (1987), 'The Instruments of Monetary Policy', August

Bank of England Quarterly Bulletin (1988), 'Bank of England Operations in the Sterling Money Market', October

Bank of England Quarterly Bulletin (every issue) 'Financial Market Developments'

Bank of England Quarterly Bulletin (1995) 'Changes in UK Gilt-edged and Money Markets', February

Bank of England Quarterly Bulletin (1997) 'The Bank of England's Operations in the Sterling Money Markets', February, p. 12

D S Batten, M P Blackwell, I S Kim, S E Nocera and Y Nozecki, 'The Conduct of Monetary Policy in the Major Industrial Countries: Instruments and Operating Procedures', IMF, Washington DC, July 1990.

D Blake, *Financial Market Analysis* (London: McGraw-Hill, 1990) Ch. 4

M Buckle and J Thompson, *The UK Financial System* (Manchester: Manchester U P) Chs 10 and 12

Euromoney

M Livingston, *Money and Financial Markets* (Oxford: Blackwell, 3e 1996) Ch. 16

M K Lewis and K T Davis, *Domestic and International Banking* (Hemel Hempstead: Philip Allan, 1987)

D T Llewellyn, 'Money Market Operations of the Bank of England and the Determination of Interest Rates' in T Bandyopdhyay and S Ghatak (eds), *Current Issues in Monetary Economics* (Hemel Hempstead: Prentice-Hall, 1990)

J Madura, *Financial Markets and Institutions* (New York: West, 2e 1992) Ch. 5

J Makin 'Demand and supply functions for stocks of eurodollars: an empirical study', *Review of Economics and Statistics*, 4 (1972)

R I McKinnon 'The eurocurrency market' *Essays in International Finance* (Princeton N J: Princeton University Press, 1977)

M Stigum, *The Money Market* (Homewood Ill: Dow Jones Books, 1990)

M Stigum and J Mann, *Money Market Calculations* (Homewood Ill: Dow Jones, 1981)

P Temperton, 'The London Money Market' in D Cobham (ed.), *Markets and Dealers* (Harlow: Longman, 1992)

R Vaitilingam, *The Financial Times Guide to Using the Financial Pages* (London: Pitman, 3e 1996)

S Valdez, *An Introduction to Western Financial Markets* (London: Macmillan, 1993) Chs 5 and 6

Answers to exercises

Exercise 9.1		Exercise 9.2		Exercise 9.3	
1	12.05%	1	£205,000	1	8.83%
2	12.17%	2	£200,195	2	£6,013,150
3	£99,542	3	12.3%		

Bond markets

10.1 Introduction

By contrast with bills, and the other money market instruments that we met in the last chapter, the issue of bonds provides a long-term source of funds. Even the shortest-dated bonds have an initial maturity of more than one year, though most, as we shall see, have much longer lives when they are initially issued. Traditionally, bonds offer a fixed rate of interest and bondholders usually have a claim on the issuer which comes before other creditors (such as shareholders, for example) in the case of the issuer's bankruptcy. Bonds issued by governments and large corporations who are unlikely to default are therefore regarded as relatively safe investments.

However, most bonds also have a fixed nominal value. This has meant that their real value has often been sharply eroded by inflation. Indeed, we shall see later that bond markets are very sensitive to any

event which appears to foreshadow higher inflation, prices fluctuating sharply and inversely with changes in inflation expectations. This means that bond-holders are exposed to capital risk if they do not intend to hold the bonds to redemption. The high and variable rates of interest and inflation of the 1970s and 1980s led many bond markets to experiment with innovations such as index-linked and variable rate bonds.

The biggest innovation of all in recent years, however, has been the massive growth in the Eurobond market. As we saw with the money markets, instruments can be issued in the currency of the country in which they are traded ('domestic' instruments) or, increasingly, they can be issued in the currency of another country. Yen-denominated bonds issued in London, for example, or HK$-denominated bonds issued in Frankfurt are all known as Eurobonds.

In this chapter we begin by looking in more detail at the types and characteristics of bonds available. In Section 10.3 we then look at the different meanings that can be attached to the term 'yield' as it applies to bonds and at the mathematics of bond yield calculation. This naturally requires us to consider the pricing of bonds, to which we had an introduction in Sections 5.3 and 5.4. Section 10.4 looks at the types of risk to which bondholders are exposed and at the work of the risk-rating agencies. Section 10.5 examines the term structure of interest rates while Section 10.6 looks at the users of bond markets, borrowers and lenders, and at some of the institutional features of bond markets and trading. One of the major developments of recent years has been the rapid growth of Eurobond markets.

Although Eurobonds share many of the characteristics of domestic bonds, and are priced and traded in similar ways, we have chosen to deal with this particular development, in order to emphasize its dramatic expansion, in a separate section, 10.7. Section 10.8 summarizes.

10.2   Bonds: types and characteristics

As we said at the outset, bonds are traditionally fixed interest, long-term securities. 'Long-term' means at least a year, though many are issued with an initial maturity of 20 years or more. For purposes of reporting prices and yields, bonds are often classified by time to maturity but what matters, of course, is the length of time to maturity *from now*, that is, what matters is *residual maturity*.

The classification commonly used is:

> < 5 years' residual maturity: 'shorts'
> 5–15 years' residual maturity: 'mediums'
> > 15 years' residual maturity: 'longs'

In the UK there are six issues of 'undated' government bonds dating from the 1914–18 war.

All bonds are issued with a *par value*. This is the price at which they will be redeemed at maturity. This is not necessarily the price at which they are issued – they may be issued at a discount or premium to their par value. In the UK, the par value is £100, in the USA $1000, in Germany DM1000. Conventional bonds pay a fixed amount to their holders at set intervals throughout their life. This amount is set in absolute terms and is known as a *coupon*, for reasons we shall see in a moment. It is a simple task to convert the coupon to a *coupon rate*, by dividing by the par value. Thus a UK bond that paid a £5 coupon per year, or a German bond that paid DM50 per year, would both have coupon rates of 5 per cent, and would be referred to as '5 per cent bonds'. Notice that if an investor does happen to buy the bond when its price is equal to its par value and holds it to redemption, then the yield to the investor is also 5 per cent. The investor invests £100 (or DM1000) and receives £5 (or DM50) per year until his or her outlay is returned. The characteristics we have so far listed

are usually all included in the name or title of a bond. Thus, for example, we may see:

Electricité de France $8\frac{3}{4}$% 2022

or

Treasury 10% 2001

The title of the former bond indicates that it will pay £8.75 per annum until the year 2022, when it will be redeemed at its par value, while the latter will pay £10 per annum until 2001, when it too will be redeemed. Box 10.6, later in this chapter, features a table from the *Financial Times*, listing UK government bonds identified by coupon and redemption date.

As a general rule, the ownership of domestic bonds is 'registered'. That is to say that the issuer of the bonds maintains a register of current owners and pays them the coupon when it falls due. (In the UK, US and Italy, most coupons are paid in two equal, six-monthly instalments, though a minority are paid annually or quarterly. In France, Germany and the Netherlands annual payments are the norm.) However, some domestic bonds and most Eurobonds are *bearer bonds*. That is to say that there is no register: possession of the bond itself is proof of ownership. Owners of bearer bonds claim their interest payments by detaching the appropriate coupon supplied attached to the bond and sending it to the issuer at the appropriate time. The universal use of the term 'coupon' for the interest payment dates from the time when all bonds were bearer bonds. Occasionally, one comes across *zero coupon bonds*. These are bonds which pay no interest but must then be issued at a discount to their redemption value in order to provide a return to investors in the form of capital appreciation. Thus, zero coupon bonds are simply long-dated versions of the bills we analysed in Chapter 9. In the USA some bond dealers 'strip' the coupon payments from bonds and deal in the coupon payments and the (now discounted) bonds separately. The advantage of zero coupon/ discount characteristics lies largely in the differential tax treatment of income and capital gains in some countries. Bonds with the traditional characteristics that we have just described are sometimes known as *straight*, or *plain vanilla* or *bullet bonds*, to distinguish them from the more recently developed variants which we come to shortly.

Bonds are issued by governments and by large financial and non-financial firms. Where public corporations, such as SNCF or Deutsche Bundesbahn, issue bonds these generally share the characteristics of, and are classified with, government bonds. As a rule, (private) corporate bonds show a greater degree of variation in their characteristics than do bonds issued by the public sector. We return to this in a moment.

As with money market instruments, the terminology used in different countries is not always helpful, terms for 'bills' and 'bonds' tending sometimes to merge at the margins.

The terminology of bonds issued by private sector institutions can also pose a problem. The most general term, covering all types of bonds issued by private firms, is *corporate bonds*. Within this category, however, are a number of subdivisions. These arise mainly from differences in the claim on a firm's assets which the bond gives to bondholders, rather than in the financial characteristics of the bond (though the claim on assets naturally affects the risk and therefore the yield attaching to the bond).

Debentures are a subset of bonds which are secured on the assets of a firm. They may be secured by a *fixed charge* on specific assets or a *floating*

Table 10.1 Government bond terminology

France	Obligations Assimilable de Trésor (OATS)[1]
Germany	Bundesschatzanweisungen (2–4 years initial maturity)[2]
	Bundesobligationen (5 years initial maturity)
	Bundesanleihen (10–30 years initial maturity)
Italy	Buoni del Tesoro Poliennali (2–10 years initial maturity, fixed-rate)
	Certificati Credito del Tesoro (2–10 years initial maturity, variable rate)
	Certificati del Tesoro con Opzione (6 years initial maturity with 3-year redemption option)
UK	Government bonds or 'gilt edge' ('gilts')
US	Treasury notes (1–7 years initial maturity)
	Treasury bonds (> 7 years initial maturity)

Notes:
[1] Note that the French government also issues 2- and 5-year bonds which it calls 'Bons de Trésor à Interêt Annuel' or 'BTANs'. 'Bons de Trésor' is also the term used for 'bills' – see Chapter 9.
[2] All known colloquially as 'Bunds'.

charge on the firm's assets in general. Fixed-charge debenture holders rank above floating-charge debenture holders but it is the floating-charge debenture holders (in the UK) who have the power to ask for a firm to be declared insolvent.

Corporate bonds with no charge over a company's assets are known as *unsecured loan stocks* while those bonds guaranteed by a third party, most usually the parent company or group to which the issuer belongs, are known as *guaranteed loan stocks*. When it comes to risk, guaranteed loan stocks would normally be ranked better (that is, lower risk) than unsecured loan stocks, but behind floating-charge debentures which in turn rank behind fixed-charge debentures. Again, all of these bonds can offer the traditional characteristics of vanilla or bullet bonds, or they may involve one or more of the additional characteristics listed below.

Some corporate bonds are *convertibles*. In addition to the normal characteristics of a bond, they carry the option to convert at some point in the future either to other types of bond issued by the firm, or more usually to its equity. Other corporate bonds with options attached to them are *callable* or *puttable bonds*, meaning that their redemption date can be decided later at the discretion of the issuer (callable) or the holder (puttable). Some corporate bonds (and some government bonds too) are *double-dated*. That is, their redemption can take place (at the issuer's discretion) at any time between two dates, which are usually included in its title.

As a result of the high and variable inflation rates of the 1970s and 1980s some corporate and government bonds are *index-linked*. This means that their par value is uprated periodically in line with a price index and that the coupon payment is also increased by the amount of the recent change in the index. The same conditions gave rise to bonds that pay a coupon which is adjusted in line with some other, usually short-term, interest rate. For some reason, such bonds issued by the public sector are known as *variable rate bonds* while their corporate counterparts are known as *floating rate notes*.

Preference shares have characteristics which place them between bonds and equities. We discuss them in Chapter 11, when we discuss company shares.

Eurobonds, as we know, are bonds issued in a currency which is not the currency of the country of issue. The Eurobond market has been the most innovative of all bond markets and we look at it later in Section 10.7. Eurobonds should not be confused with *foreign bonds* – bonds denominated in domestic currency but issued in that country by non-residents. In London, for example, foreign firms may issue *bulldog bonds*, denominated in sterling, while UK firms may issue *yankee bonds*, denominated in dollars, in the USA.

10.3 Bond yields

We already know enough about financial assets to appreciate that the yield on a bond is going to be determined to a large extent by the price that we pay for it and the periodic 'coupon' payment that we receive from the issuer of the bond. While this is true, there are some other considerations which we have to take into account. For each of the additional factors that we take into account, we have a rather different meaning of the term 'yield'. Worse than this, not only do we have different definitions of yield, but 'price' itself has two meanings when we discuss bonds. We look at price first.

Recall that the interest payment on a bond is called the coupon and that it is paid either annually or semi-annually. Imagine a bond with semi-annual coupon payments. One might buy it, for example, just after a coupon payment, and thus wait nearly six months' for the next; or one might buy it with only two months to go to the next coupon payment. If we were to pay the same price for the bond in both cases, then clearly the yield would be lower in the former case (where we get the coupon after six months waiting) and higher in the latter (where we get the same income after only a short wait). Everyone would wish to hold the latter bond and there would be no market for the former. In practice, of course, the market prices the long-wait bond below the short-wait one, with two consequences. Firstly, the yields are made equivalent by the different prices offsetting the different waiting periods; secondly, the market price of bonds varies cyclically with the length of wait to the next coupon payment. If everything else is unchanged over the year, a bond's price will follow the pattern shown in Figure 10.1.

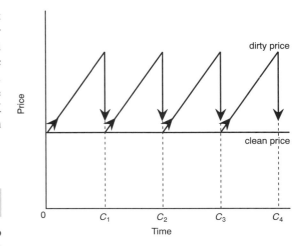

Figure 10.1 Clean and dirty bond prices.

The increase in the *dirty* price between each coupon payment date, C_1 and C_2 for example, represents *accrued interest*. Accrued interest is that fraction of the coupon payment which has been 'earned' since the last payment date.

$$AI = \frac{C}{2}\left(\frac{n_{lc}}{182}\right) \qquad (10.1)$$

In Equation 10.1, A_i stands for accrued interest and n_{lc} is the number days since the last coupon payment. The market price, incorporating accrued interest, is also commonly known as the dirty price, meaning that the price, which one usually explains by reference to other, more interesting, variables, is, additionally, contaminated by the position of the bond between its coupon payment dates.

Naturally enough, the *dirty* price can be contrasted with the bond's *clean price*, where the effect of accrued interest is ignored. In most countries, the price actually quoted for bonds – in the financial press and on trading exchanges – is the clean price. However, when the bond is traded it is understood that a buyer (for example) will pay to a seller the clean price, plus an amount of accrued interest which is the seller's share of the coupon payment which will later be paid to the new owner.

One might well wonder why this complication is necessary. There are essentially two reasons, one analytical and the other distinctly practical. The first, we have touched on. Bond prices fluctuate for a number of reasons. We shall see in a moment that the main cause is changes in market interest rates, but inflationary expectations and risk also play a part. Changes in these variables cause large changes in bond prices and they are irregular and hard to predict. Thus, these are the interesting variables for bond analysts and they act upon the clean price. The fact that the market price also vary continuously as a linear function of the period to the next coupon payment is a mere mathematical necessity. It is of very little interest and thus, as we said above, it 'contaminates' the interesting picture. The practical reason for the distinction lies with taxation. In many tax systems, income is taxed differently from capital gains. A rise in market price resulting solely from the accrual of interest is in effect the result of the coupon or income payment and should be taxed as income. By contrast, an increase in the bond's clean price for other reasons is a change in its capital value and should be taxed as capital gain.

Before we leave the issue of price, there is one further complication. We said a moment ago that the market or dirty price included accrued interest which represented the seller's share of the coupon payment which would be paid in full to the buyer, even though the buyer may not have held the bond for very long. A moment's thought should suggest that it is not administratively practical, in the case of registered (as opposed to bearer) bonds, to make coupon payments to the buyers of bonds who buy the bonds only a few days before the coupon payment date. It takes time for the registrar's office to record a change of ownership and to organize payment to hundreds of thousands of bondholders. There is thus a 'cut-off' date for sales, after which the next coupon payment will go to the previous, rather than the new, owner. After the cut-off date the bond is said to trade *ex dividend*, meaning without the benefit of the coupon payment. This means, of course, that the new owner will have to hold the bond for *more than* six months before receiving a coupon. During this period, instead of the dirty price being made up of the clean price *plus* accrued interest, the market price will actually lie *below* the clean price.

Figure 10.2 shows the situation. If nothing else changes, the clean price is constant throughout the year. The market price, however, fluctuates as we saw

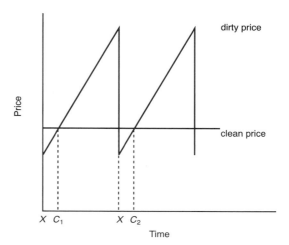

Figure 10.2 The effect of ex-dividend dates.

in Figure 10.1. The clean and dirty prices are equal on the coupon date, C. After the coupon payment date, the dirty price accumulates accrued interest. During this period the buyer will get the whole of the next coupon payment and is therefore compensating the seller by passing a share of it to him or her. The accrual of interest (and the increase in the dirty price) continues to the ex dividend date, X, after which the next coupon payment goes to the seller. In these circumstances, the compensation must flow from seller to buyer. This happens when the dirty price drops overnight and buyers can buy at a price below the clean price until the next coupon payment date. The formula for accrued interest now becomes:

$$AI = \frac{C}{2}\left(\frac{n_{xt} - n_{xc}}{182}\right) \tag{10.2}$$

where C is the coupon payment, n_{xt} is the time in days since the last *ex-dividend* date and n_{xc} is the time in days from the last ex dividend date to the next coupon payment.

Notice that the numerator of Equation 10.2 may be either positive or negative, depending on the date on which the calculation is done. In the illustration in Box 10.2, the numerator is positive and so there is a fractional *addition* of interest (0.56 of £4) to the clean price. The seller is being compensated for not receiving the coupon even though he had held the bond 56 per cent of the coupon period. But it is quite

---

Box 10.2   Bond prices and accrued interest

Imagine a plain 8 per cent £100 bond which pays its coupon in equal half-yearly instalments on 1 June and 1 December each year. Suppose further, only for simplicity, that it has a long residual maturity and that long-term interest rates are 8 per cent. Its clean price will be £100 and this will also be the dirty or market price on 1 June and 1 December, when there is no accrued interest to take into account. Now let us assume additionally that the bond goes 'ex dividend' 30 days before the coupon payment date. If it is now 10 September, we can calculate the accrued interest using Equation 10.2.

Firstly, the relevant coupon payment will be:

$$C/2 = £8/2 = £4$$

The number of days between the ex dividend date and the coupon payment date is 30 days (by assumption) and so:

$$n_{xc} = 30$$

The number of days between now and the last ex dividend date is 132 (= 2 May–10 September) and so:

$$n_{xt} = 132$$

Substituting these values into Equation 9.2 gives:

$$AI = 4 \{(132 - 30) / 182\} = 4 (0.56) = 2.24 \text{ or } £2.24p$$

On 10 September, therefore, the market or dirty price of this bond will be £102.24p.

Exercise

Find the market price of this bond on 12 November, assuming nothing else has changed. (The answer is in the text).

---

possible for this fraction to be negative. If we were thinking to buy the same bond on 11 November, for example, we should find that the fraction is $- 0.1$ $((11 - 30) / 182)$. In this case, the clean price would be reduced by £0.40p ($- 0.1 \times £4$). This is because the coupon payment of £4 will go to the seller and the buyer needs compensation for holding the bond but not receiving the next coupon.

It is obviously important for traders to know whether the quoted price is the clean or dirty price, but we shall see now that the distinction is important also because some measures of yield are calculated using the clean price while some use the dirty price.

We begin our examination of bond yields by beginning with the more straightforward measures, and moving later to more sophisticated ones. The examination is not exhaustive, however. We confine our attention to 'plain' or 'vanilla' bonds and even then we have omitted some of the least-used yield concepts. Readers who have occasion to calculate 'yields to call' or 'yields to put' or yields on index-linked bonds, are referred to the more comprehensive treatments in Blake (1990), Livingston (1996) and Elton and Gruber (1995).

Box 10.3   Why bond prices change – *in the short run*

The stock of bonds is given and prices fluctuate because of shifts in demand (in Figure 5.3 the supply curve is fixed). The demand curve for bonds shifts when bondholders revise their view of the value of holding bonds. If the revision applies to bonds in general, then the bond market as a whole rises or falls (and, remember, yields fall or rise). If the revision applies to one particular bond, or more likely a group of bonds with a particular maturity, then there is a change within the structure of bond prices and yields. Since, for most bonds, the income stream (the coupon payments) is given, changes in investors' valuation must come from changes in i – the rate of discount or the required rate of return. This means that bond prices change because there is a change in the level of risk-free interest rates or in the risk premia which bondholders attach to those risk-free rates. Thus we would expect the bond market, *as a whole*, to fall when central

(Box 10.3 *continued*)

banks announce a rise in official dealing rates and to rise when interest rates are reduced. The price of bonds issued by particular firms, or sometimes by particular governments, may fall, for example, if bondholders think they see an increase in the risk of default. If a risk-rating agency changes a bond's risk classification, there will certainly be a change in price.

If bond prices only changed with *actual* changes in interest rates or with actual changes in risk, explaining those price changes would be easy. But we often see the bond market rising or falling when nothing else appears to change at all. We must always remember that with trade-able securities it is only possible for investors to make a capital gain (or avoid a capital loss) if they can *anticipate* what is going to happen to prices. This leads bond investors to be searching continually for indicators of what is *going to happen next* to interest rates or to risk premia. And prices will change, because investors will buy and sell, if there is only a change in what people think is going to happen next, even if they are wrong! And once we start to think about what causes changes in people's expectations of interest rates, we create a virtually endless list of possible events. Consider, for example, how bond prices might respond to the following:

(a) an unexpected announcement of an increase in official interest rates
(b) an unexpected increase in the rate of inflation
(c) an announcement of rapid credit growth in an economy enjoying a boom
(d) an announcement of increased retail sales in an economy in the depths of recession
(e) a government statement that it intended to halve the rate of inflation by the time of the next election
(f) the publication of better than expected export figures

Suggestions:

(a) prices fall; (b) assuming that the government's policy is to minimize inflation, prices fall in anticipation of a rise in interest rates; (c) as for (b); (d) since the economy is in recession, there is no simple connection with inflation or interest rates and prices may not be affected; (e) depends on whether investors believe their government, but prices probably fall; (f) probably leads to stronger currency and may allow government to reduce interest rates – prices probably rise.

Notice how frequently the mechanism connecting events to price changes involves inflation and interest rates, that investors often need to make a judgement about government policy and reaction, and that this often involves looking at the wider state of the economy.

Box 10.3a   Why bond prices change – *in the long run*

Over time, the stock of bonds increases (in Figure 5.3, the supply curve shifts to the right). This happens, firstly, because on balance firms expand and new firms are created, and, secondly, because governments frequently run budget deficits which are financed largely by the issue of new bonds. For a given demand schedule, the rightward drift of a supply curve would lead us to expect a decline in prices (and a rise in yields). But we know that this does not happen. Bond yields certainly rise over periods of time, but they also fall over other periods. There is no continuous upward trend, even though there is a continuous increase in the stock of bonds.

Our supply and demand framework tells us immediately that if the supply curve shifts continuously to the right without a continuous fall in prices (rise in yields), then it must be that something is pushing the demand curve to the

right, and it is not difficult to see what that something is. We saw in Section 1.2 that the buyers of financial assets are agents who are running a financial surplus and that this surplus must result in a net acquisition of financial assets. Furthermore, this net acquisition of financial assets is a flow of spending which constitutes an addition to their stock of wealth. Over time, therefore, there is a more or less steady demand for extra financial assets to add to the stock of wealth. In our diagram, the demand curve for bonds moves to the right over time because new lending occurs every year. The extent to which the demand curve shifts per period of time depends upon the size of the financial surplus in that period and the major influence on that is the level of income out of which people can save. When the economy is expanding rapidly, the additional saving, the additional financial surplus and the additional demand for *new* bonds will be large.

We can now see that the long-run trend in bond prices (and yields) will depend upon the relative rates of shift of the supply and demand curves. This in turn depends upon the demand for new borrowing (acting on the supply curve) relative to the demand for new bonds to add to wealth (acting on the demand curve). There is no *inevitable* trend. If, for example, governments run large deficits for a number of years, the demand for the new bonds at the current rate of interest may not expand sufficiently quickly. If that is the case, then prices will tend to decline (and yields will rise). This is a development which is often predicted by politicians who wish to reduce the level of government spending and the size of the deficit. But it could easily happen that annual deficits are not large enough to match the rising demand. If that happens, persistent budget deficits will be accompanied by falling yields and rising prices.

10.3.1   Running yield

Imagine the simple case where one buys a bond, holding it for a period and then selling it for the price that one paid. In this case, the return on the bond consists of the periodic coupon payments and the *rate* of return relates this income stream to the price that was paid for it. This is shown in Equation 10.3, where C is the coupon payment, P is the *clean* price and cy stands for what is known as the *running* or *interest* or *current yield*.

$$cy = \frac{C}{P} \tag{10.3}$$

It might seem strange to use the clean price in this calculation, since we usually think of the yield as the return that we receive in relation to actual outlay which in this case would be represented by the dirty or market price. The explanation for this practice can be derived from Figure 10.2. Figure 10.2 shows that the market price of a bond must vary systematically as a (linear) function of the number of days to the next coupon payment date. Since C is constant, it therefore follows (from Equation 10.3) that the systematic fluctuation in P would produce a systematic and opposite fluctuation in current yield. Indeed, we could, if we wished, draw a figure for the behaviour of running yield over time. It would be the reverse of Figure 10.2 with running yield declining systematically from one ex dividend date, jumping back to its initial level on the next ex dividend date.

Box 10.5, later in this chapter, contains a *Financial Times* listing of UK government bonds and shows the interest yield in the first column of figures.

10.3.2   Simple yield to maturity

Useful though the concept of running yield may be, it has the severe limitation that it takes no account of any capital gains or losses that investors will experience if they buy the bond when its market price differs from its par value, with the intention of holding it to redemption. Suppose, for example, that instead of long-term interest rates being 8 per cent, in our earlier illustration, they are 10 per cent. Then it follows that our long-dated 8 per cent bond will not have a clean price of £100 on its coupon date, since there will be no buyers for an existing asset that pays 8 per cent when newly issued assets pay 10 per cent. In fact, to make it attractive, its price must stand at a discount to par. If it is a very long-dated bond, its clean price is likely to be about £80 (since the £8 coupon paid on an outlay of £80 is equivalent to 10 per cent). Someone buying this bond and holding it to redemption will enjoy a running yield of 10 per cent but will also benefit from a capital gain of £20 when the bond matures. We thus need some means of converting this capital gain into an equivalent annual return which can be added to the current yield. One way of achieving this is to calculate the *simple yield to maturity or smy*. The method is shown in Equation 10.4.

$$smy = \frac{C}{P} + \frac{100 - P}{n_m \times P} \tag{10.4}$$

C and P are the coupon and the *clean* price, as above, while n_m is the number of years to maturity. We can see, therefore, that the simple yield to maturity begins by taking the running yield, calculated as in Equation

10.3, C/P. It then adds to this the capital gain (that is, the difference between the redemption value and the clean price), expressed as a percentage of the outlay spread over the number of years of the investment.

10.3.3   Redemption yield

The simple yield to maturity is certainly a more useful expression of yield for investors who intend to hold a bond until redemption. But both the current yield and the simple yield to maturity suffer from the shortcoming that they ignore the fact that the coupon payments made over the life of a bond can be reinvested at the going rate of interest and thus understate the overall return that is available to bondholders. *Redemption yield* or *ry* takes account of the coupon payments and the fact that they can be reinvested, as well as any capital gain or loss that might occur between purchase and redemption. Unfortunately, its calculation ceases to be a straightforward matter. The redemption yield is the return that equates the discounted values of the bond's cash flows back to its *dirty* price. In other words, *ry* is the internal rate of return. Finding the redemption yield involves solving for *ry* in the rather forbidding expression, Equation 10.5.

$$P_d = \left(\frac{1}{(1 + \frac{1}{2}ry)^{n_{tc}/182}}\right) \times$$

$$\left(\sum_{t=0}^{Q-1}\frac{C/2}{(1 + \frac{1}{2}ry)^t} + \frac{M}{(1 + \frac{1}{2}ry)^{Q-1}}\right) \quad (10.5)$$

In Equation 10.5, n_{tc} is the number of days between the current date and the next coupon payment; *ry* is the yield to maturity; *Q* is the number of coupon payments before redemption and P_d is the dirty price, that is, the clean price plus accrued interest. Equation 10.5 might usefully be compared with Equation 5.5, the earlier expression that we saw for the valuation of a bond with a fixed period to maturity. In Equation 10.5,

the expression between large brackets to the right of the '×', corresponds to Equation 5.5, except that it has been modified to take account of the semi-annual payment of coupons. In Equation 5.5 we used *i* to discount the future cash payments on our (annual coupon) bond back to its current price; in Equation 10.5 we use *ry*. Thus *i* and *ry* in the two expressions are equivalent. However, we used a second simplification in Equation 5.5. We ignored the relationship between the date of valuation, 'today', and the coupon payment date. By implication, in Equation 5.5 we were assuming that we were valuing the bond on its coupon payment date. In Equation 10.5, the expression to the right of '×' uses *ry* to discount the future cash flows back to the next coupon payment date but, recognizing that the next coupon payment date may not be today but could be any fraction of a half-year away, we discount that value back to the present, wherever that may be in relation to the next coupon payment date, by using the expression to the left of '×'.

The value of *ry* cannot easily be found. It has to be done by iteration, using repeated values for *ry* until the value for the right-hand side of Equation 10.5 converges on the bond's dirty price. For a computer (or calculator with appropriate programmable functions) it is the work of a moment. Without such technology it can be done by using two approximations. From Equation 5.6 it might be recalled that (by setting $n_m = \infty$) the valuation of a perpetual bond simplified to:

$$P = C/i \quad (10.6)$$

The same would follow in Equation 10.5 if we set $Q = \infty$.[1] Naturally enough, if we set n_m (or Q) very large, but less than infinity, then Equation 10.6 would be approximately true.[2] Recalling that *i* and *ry* are equivalent, then it becomes a fairly simple matter, for very long-dated bonds at least, to choose a value for *ry* in Equation 10.6 which generates a price reasonably close to the current dirty price. By then choosing a second value for *ry*, so as to generate a

---

[1] In Equations 5.5 and 10.6, *i* is the internal rate of return and the redemption yield on a perpetual bond since *i* is the rate of interest that discounts the cash flows of a perpetual bond back to its present value. If Equation 10.6 is rearranged to find *i*, that is, $i = C/P$, it can be seen that the rearrangement is equivalent to the

equation for current yield, Equation 10.3. Thus, for a perpetual bond, current yield and redemption yield are identical.
[2] In practice, the approximation is satisfactory for bonds with residual maturity in excess of 15 years.

Box 10.4   Interpolating redemption yield

Suppose that we wish to find the redemption yield for an 8% bond with just over 20 years to redemption. The bond is currently trading at £95 and there are 40 days to the next coupon payment.

Using equation 10.6, we can make a first, rough, estimate:

$$ry = 8/95 = 8.42\%$$

Substituting 0.0842 in Equation 10.5 and solving for the price gives us £99.03. Since the bond is actually trading at £95, then our estimate of the redemption yield is clearly too low.

For a second trial, suppose that we take an estimate of 9.0%. Substituting this into Equation 10.5 gives a price of £93.98. This price lies below the actual market price, but the two prices taken together give us a basis for a more accurate estimate of redemption yield.

Firstly, we can see that the correct redemption yield lies nearer to 9.0% than it does to 8.42%. In fact, if we round our estimated prices to £99 and £94 for simplicity, we can see that the real price of £95 lies 4/5 of the way along the £99–£94 range. This might suggest that the redemption yield that we require lies 4/5 of the way along the interest rate spectrum of 8.42%–9.0%. 4/5 of this difference is 0.46. If we add this to 8.42% and solve Equation 10.5 once more using a redemption yield of 8.8%, we shall find that the estimated price does indeed match the actual price of £95.

This last step is an example of linear interpolation. If we let the subscripts 1, 2 and a stand for the first estimate, the second estimate and the actual values respectively, then we can summarize this last step formally:

$$ry_a = ry_1 + ((ry_2 - ry_1) \times P_1 - P_a / P_1 - P_2)$$

---

second price which 'brackets' the actual price, we can interpolate the precise redemption yield which makes the prospective cash flows equal to the dirty price. Box 10.4 provides an illustration.

For 'short'-dated bonds (less than 15 years), this approximation does not produce satisfactory results,

but experience suggests that the following works reasonably well:

$$Approximate\ ry = \cfrac{C + \cfrac{M - P}{n_m}}{\cfrac{M + P}{2}}$$

Exercise 10.1   The interpolation of redemption yields on short-dated bonds

Find an approximate yield to maturity for a 5% bond with just over three years to maturity, when there are 50 days left to the next coupon payment and there are six coupons remaining. The bond is currently trading at £92. From this approximation, find the exact yield to maturity.

Hints:

1 From the expression above:

   (approximate) $ry_1 = (5 + (100-92/3)) / (100 + 92)/2 = 7.986 \approx 8.0\%$

2 Substitute 8.0%, and the characteristics of the bond, into Equation 10.5 and calculate a trial price, P_1.

3 Use another trial value (ry_2) which is bound to produce a second trial price (P_2) for this bond

such that the actual price (P_a) lies between P_1 and P_2.

4 Use the interpolation formula from the illustration in Box 10.4 to find the exact redemption yield.

5 Substitute the interpolated value for ry into Equation 10.5 and check that it does give the correct market price.

Answer:

Taking ry_1 as 8.0% gives a P_1 of £94.76; taking ry_2 as 10.0% gives a P_2 of £90.39. Using the interpolation formula tells us that the redemption yield for an actual price of £92 is 9.263%.

where n_m is the number of years of residual maturity. After the initial estimate, the method follows that for long-dated bonds.

Box 10.5, later in this chapter, contains a *Financial Times* listing of UK government bonds and shows the redemption yield in the second column of figures.

10.3.4   Holding period yield

In many circumstances redemption yield will be a more relevant measure of yield than either current yield or the simple yield to maturity. However, it makes two assumptions which will make it inappropriate in certain circumstances. Firstly, and obviously, it assumes that investors hold the bond to redemption. Less obviously, while it takes into account the effect of compound interest on the coupons when they are reinvested (unlike the simple yield to maturity), it assumes that the coupons can be reinvested at the constant redemption yield. The first assumption is obviously inappropriate to investors who intend to sell before redemption. For them, it is not the par value that matters but the price of the bond at the time they wish to sell. The second assumption will often be inappropriate for many bondholders, especially in a period of fluctuating interest rates. Ignoring accrued interest (that is, assuming that the bond is bought on a coupon payment date), the holding period yield (*hy*) is the rate that satisfies the expression:

$$P_d(1 + \tfrac{1}{2}rh)^{2n_m} = (C/2)(1 + \tfrac{1}{2}i_1)^{2n_m-1} +$$

$$(C/2)(1 + \tfrac{1}{2}i_2)^{2n_m-2} + \dots + (C/2) + P_1$$

$$(10.7)$$

where i_1, i_2 and so on are the rates of interest at which the first coupon, second coupon and so on can be reinvested, while P_1 is the price for which the bond is eventually sold. Solving for *hy* is done as follows:

$$hy = \left(\left[\frac{(C/2)(1 + \tfrac{1}{2}i_1)^{2n_m-1} + \dots + (C/2) + P_1}{P_d}\right] - 1\right) \times 2$$

$$(10.8)$$

In many respects, bonds appear to be very low-risk investments. Compared with shares, for example, the income stream is fixed. Bonds issued by most governments are default-free. Furthermore, in the case of corporate bonds, bondholders have a comparatively strong claim on any remaining assets in the event of the firm's bankruptcy.

This does not make them risk-free, however. In this section, we shall consider three types of risk to which bonds are subject:

1 Default risk
2 Reinvestment risk
3 Capital risk.

10.4.1   Default risk

Bonds, particularly government bonds, may be relatively secure instruments but this does not mean that their issuers *never* default. Corporations do go bankrupt and even governments can have problems. The Bank of Credit and Commerce International failed in 1991; Baring's bank failed in 1995; Eurotunnel unilaterally suspended interest payments on part of its debt in October 1995. In August 1982 the Mexican government announced that repayment of principal would be deferred and in 1991 there were doubts about the Italian government's ability to meet all its debt obligations exactly as specified. All such events mean that bond investors have to take default (or *credit*) risk seriously.

As always, investors face considerable costs in acquiring the information necessary for the assessment of the risk they face. This creates the opportunity for *credit rating agencies* to exploit economies of scale and specialist expertise in order to provide assessments of risk. This service is purchased by issuers of bonds who find that a reputable credit rating enables them to borrow on better terms than would be the case if investors had no guidance. The best known agencies are Moody's and Standard and Poor's (both based in the USA) and IBCA, a UK-based organization which merged with the French firm Euronotation in 1992.

Box 10.5 reports a Croatian Eurobond issue

receiving a credit rating in January 1997. Notice firstly that the report confirms that getting a rating is expected to be beneficial. But notice also that the rating given to Croatian Eurobonds was 'BBB–'. The picture on the right shows the ratings used by the three agencies and this shows that 'BBB–' (or its equivalent) is a long way below the best. In fact, bonds rated from AAA to BBB (inclusive) are sometimes referred to as 'investment grade' bonds since it is only these bonds that professional invest-ment managers are normally prepared to hold. Croatian bonds barely qualify, therefore. On the other hand, it is only when we get down to grade D that we are dealing with bonds which are either in default, or are likely to be in default. It follows from this that the difference in yield required by the market as we move from one grade to another looks comparatively small, usually less than 30 basis points. (But we must always remember, as we saw in Chapter 9, that these small differentials are being paid on very large sums and so quite fine differences have the ability to move large sums of money.) Bonds rated below BBB are known as 'speculative' or even 'junk' bonds. (Note that 'junk', in this context, does not mean 'worthless'.)

The rating agencies are, naturally enough, mainly concerned with the ability of the bond issuer to meet his or her obligations. But in addition to this concern with 'ability to pay', the agencies also take into account the nature and terms of the obligation in the bond and, just in case things go wrong, the protection and claim that bondholders have. The case of Eurotunnel illustrates what is at issue here. Like many large corporations, Eurotunnel has issued more than one type of bond. The differences between these bonds often involve differences in the rights of the bondholders. The suspension of interest in 1995 applied only to the 'subordinate' debt. Holders of this subordinate debt had relatively little power and a low priority claim in the event of the firm's liquidation. Consequently, this debt was rated more speculatively by S and P and carried a higher yield than 'primary debt'.

10.4.2   Reinvestment and capital risk

Since, for conventional bonds, coupon payments are fixed for the life of the bond and since the par or maturity value is also fixed, it follows that pur-chasing a bond and holding it to redemption provides a known, fixed, rate of return. The redemption yield is fixed. However, we have already seen that the holding period return remains uncertain. This uncertainty arises (a) because we cannot be sure of the yield we can get on the coupon payments when we reinvest them and (b) our circumstances *may* change such that we have to sell the bonds before maturity, and we cannot then be certain of the price we shall get. Both of these uncertainties derive from a common source: a change in interest rates.

Naturally enough, bond yields must reflect these risks, by incorporating a premium which reflects both the degree of risk and the strength of the market's aversion. We have already met the idea that some bond prices are more sensitive to interest rate changes in Section 5.3.2. It is now time to look carefully at why this is the case and also to explore ways of measuring the degree of interest rate sensitivity. For the latter, we shall examine the concept of *duration*. Two other, less common, measures are *convexity* and *dispersion*. Details of these can be found in Blake (1990, Ch. 5) and Livingston (1996, Ch. 10).

Imagine a bond which makes annual coupon payments. Then:

$$Duration =$$

$$\frac{\dfrac{1C}{(1+ry)^1} + \dfrac{2C}{(1+ry)^2} + \ldots + \dfrac{n_m(C+M)}{(1+ry)^{n_m}}}{P_d} \tag{10.9}$$

If we now recall (from the appendix to Chapter 5) that we can dispense with the summation by using the alternative expression for the present value of an annuity:

$$P = \frac{C\left(1 - \dfrac{1}{(1+ry)^{n_m}}\right)}{ry} = C/ry(1 - [1+ry]^{-n_m}) \tag{10.10}$$

then:

$$Duration =$$

$$\frac{\left[\dfrac{C(1+ry)}{ry}\right]\left[\dfrac{1-(1+ry)^{-n_m}}{ry}\right] + \left[\dfrac{n_m(M - C/ry)}{(1+ry)^{n_m}}\right]}{P_d} \tag{10.11}$$

Box 10.5   Bond credit ratings

Credit rating boost for Croat eurobond debut

By Kevin Done, East Europe Correspondent

Croatia's hopes of a successful debut in the international bond market grew yesterday after it received investment grade ratings from two leading international rating agencies.

The former Yugoslav republic, which is preparing to launch its first foreign currency eurobond next month, was awarded a BBB-rating, the lowest investment grade, by both Standard & Poor's of the US and IBCA, the European agency.

Moody's, the other leading US agency, is expected to release its first assessment early next week.

Croatia is rated at the same level as Hungary and Slovakia. It is also rated the same as Poland and Latvia by S&P and, outside east Europe, it is on a par with Greece and Tunisia.

Mr Bozo Prka, Croatian finance minister, said yesterday that the country would seek to raise $250m in its debut foreign currency eurobond. It would have a maturity of five years, which was "unimaginable until very recently," he said.

The issue will be arranged by a syndicate of 15 international banks led by Merrill Lynch of the US and Union Bank of Switzerland. The price will be determined following a 20-day roadshow to institutional investors in Asia, the US and Europe beginning in the Far East this weekend.

Croatia, like other countries in eastern Europe, is hoping to take advantage of the increasingly keen appetite among investors for emerging market risk. Earlier this week both Latvia and Moldova received their first international ratings, with Latvia assessed BBB investment grade by S&P and Moldova Ba2 (BB) speculative grade by Moody's.

Credit ratings reflect the perceived risk of default by a borrower on its debt. A strong rating, implying reduced risk to investors, usually means lower funding costs for the borrower.

IBCA said that the BBB-rating for Croatia reflected both the impressive way the economy had been stabilised, with the lowest rate of inflation of the transition economies and substantial export earning capacity and potential. External debt was still modest compared with both gross domestic product and foreign exchange receipts.

The agency said it believed the risks of Croatia becoming embroiled in another war were now small with frontiers mutually recognised by Croatia, Bosnia and Yugoslavia. The rapid Croatian military build-up meant there was now a balance of power in the region.

Tensions in Bosnia could "taint Croatia by association", however, and harm both tourist earnings, the "potential jewel" in foreign currency earnings and foreign direct investment.

East Europe credit ratings *
Long-term foreign currency

IBCA	S&P	Moody's
AAA	AAA	Aaa
AA+	AA +	Aa1
AA	AA	Aa2
AA–	AA–	Aa3
A+	A+	A1
A	A	A2
	Slovenia	
	Czech Rep	
	A–	A3
A–		Slovenia
Slovenia		
Czech Rep		
BBB+	BBB +	Baa1
		Czech Rep
BBB	BBB	Baa2
Poland	Latvia	
BBB–	BBB–	Baa3
Croatia	Croatia	Slovakia
Slovakia	Slovakia	Poland
Hungary	Hungary	Hungary
	Poland	
	Investment grades	
	Speculative grades	
BB+	BB +	Ba1
Russia		
BB	BB	Ba2
Lithuania		Russia
		Lithuania
		Moldova
BB–	BB–	Ba3
Romania	Russia	Romania
Kazakhstan	Romania	Kazakhstan
	Kazakhstan	
B+	B+	B1
B	B	B2
B–	B–	B3

It also warned that progress in structural reform had been "patchy" with particularly slow progress in privatisation. IBCA forecasts growth of 5.5 per cent in GDP this year following an estimated 6.5 per cent in 1996, with inflation remaining around 3.5 per cent a year.

Source: Financial Times, 18 January 1997   **Sources:* IBCA, Standard & Poor's, Moody's

For purposes of illustration, imagine a bond with a £5 coupon paid annually, redeemable in three years' time, and a par value of £100. If the redemption yield is 8 per cent, then (from Equations 5.5 or Appendix 5.1) its current price must be £92.268.

Substituting these values into Equation 10.11 gives:

$$[(67.5) \times (2.577) + (89.306)] / 92.268 = 2.853$$

Notice what happens to duration if the coupon had been £6, redemption yield and period to maturity remaining constant. Firstly, we would of course expect the price of the bond to be higher. Using Equation 5.5 again, $P = £94.36$. Solving Equation 10.11 again using the new coupon and new price but leaving the redemption yield and maturity as before gives:

$$[(81.0) \times (2.577) + (59.537)] / £94.846 = 2.829$$

We find that the higher coupon gives us a lower value for duration.

Consider now what happens if we change the redemption yield. Suppose that we leave everything as it is ($C = 6$; $n_m = 3$), but increase the redemption yield to 12 per cent. Firstly, the market price falls to £85.589. More interestingly, duration is reduced to 2.819.

From these illustrations, we can draw three conclusions about duration, maturity, coupon and redemption yield, at least as they apply to *coupon-bearing, redeemable* bonds:

Duration and maturity. For a given coupon, duration increases with maturity. Thus, other things being equal, long-dated bonds are more sensitive to interest rate changes, and therefore riskier, than short-dated bonds.

Duration and coupon. For a given maturity, duration diminishes as the coupon increases.

Duration and redemption yield. For a given maturity, duration diminishes as redemption yield increases.

From this it follows that the riskiest bonds, that is, those whose prices are most sensitive with respect to interest rate changes, are those with long maturities and low coupons. Furthermore, the riskiness of all bonds is greater when interest rates are low.

These propositions apply to coupon-bearing bonds with a fixed period to maturity. Note that zero coupon (pure discount) bonds and perpetual bonds are special cases which behave rather differently. Firstly, for a zero coupon bond we set $C = 0$ in Equation 10.11. The duration is thus equal to maturity (n_m) and zero coupon bonds have the greatest duration and price volatility for bonds with that maturity. Secondly, for an irredeemable bond, in Equation 10.11 we set $n_m = \infty$. For perpetual bonds then *duration* = $(1/ry) + 1$.

Duration is defined as the weighted average maturity of a bond. The logic behind the idea of 'weighted average maturity' is that for bonds which pay regular coupons, the total cash flow from that bond is spread over a period (from now to the date of maturity). Depending upon the characteristics of the bond, this cash flow could be heavily weighted towards the immediate future or towards the more distant future. Since changes in the discount rate always have a larger effect upon distant payments than upon short ones, a bond where the weight of payments is soon should be less interest-sensitive than a bond where the weight of payments lies further away. Duration, therefore, is trying to capture the average time that it takes to receive the cashflow. The weights are the relative discounted cashflow in each period and the weighted average is simply the sum of those weights.

This is easier to see if we go back to Equation 10.9 and consider an example which compares duration for two bonds, each paying a 5 per cent annual coupon, trading at par, with $ry = 5$ per cent, but bond A maturing in two years and bond B maturing in three years' time. For bond A:

$$D = (4.776 + 190.476) / 100 = 1.953$$

While for bond B:

$$D = (4.776 + 9.070 + 272.114) / 100 = 2.859$$

Notice that for both bonds duration is less than the period to maturity. This must be the case since some cashflow in both cases comes from interim coupon payments. In the case of bond A, one may say that the interim coupon payments contribute 0.0478 of the duration value of 1.953, while the final coupon *plus* maturity payment contributes 1.9057. As proportions, these represent 2.44 per cent and 97.56 per cent respectively. For bond B, duration is 2.859, to which interim coupon payments contribute 0.138, while the redemption payment contributes 2.721. As proportions, these represent 4.83 per cent and 95.17 per cent respectively. With the longer dated bond a larger weight attaches to the interim coupon payments.

We can now show formally that duration is a measure of interest rate risk. Assuming still that coupon payments are annual, then the present value of a bond is given (see Equation 5.5) by:

$$P_d = \sum_{t=1}^{n} \frac{C}{(1+ry)^t} + \frac{M}{(1+ry)^{n_m}} \qquad (10.12)$$

Differentiating with respect to $(1 + ry)$

$$\frac{\Delta P_d}{\Delta(1+ry)} = -C\sum_{t=1}^{n} \frac{t}{(1+ry)^{t+1}} - M\frac{n_m}{(1+ry)^{n_m+1}} \qquad (10.13)$$

If we now multiply both sides by $(1 + ry)/P_d$ we have:

$$\frac{\Delta P_d / P_d}{\Delta(1+ry)/(1+ry)} =$$

$$\frac{C}{P_d}\sum_{t=1}^{n_m} \frac{t}{(1+ry)^t} - \frac{M}{P_d}\frac{n_m}{(1=ry)^t} = -D \qquad (10.14)$$

The leftmost expression in Equation 10.14 is the elasticity of the bond price with respect to $(1 + ry)$. The larger the value of duration, the larger the (negative) elasticity.

10.5   The term structure of interest rates

The *term structure of interest rates* refers to the pattern of interest rates available on assets differentiated *solely* by their term to maturity, and a plot of these rates against the period to maturity is known as a *time yield curve*. An example is provided in Figure 10.3.

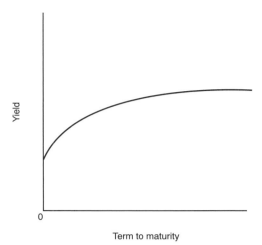

Figure 10.3 A time yield curve.

The central issue of term structure discussions is the effect that the period to maturity has upon yields, when all other possible explanations for yield variation have been removed. In order to study the term structure, therefore, we need a large population of assets which are homogeneous, particularly with respect to default risk, but exist in a wide range of maturities. Not many asset groups can meet these requirements. The most obvious candidates in most countries are government bonds. They are all issued by the same (and therefore constant risk) issuer, and they exist in a wide variety of maturities. Some term structure investigations use treasury bills for the same reason, though the range of maturities is limited to < 1 year, of course. Occasionally interbank deposits are used, though the maturities are even more restricted. Because the 'term structure' so often means the term structure of yields on government bonds, and also because one theory (the 'term premium' theory) of the term structure draws upon technicalities which we have just been discussing, this is the obvious place in which to examine it more closely.

Before we begin, however, we need to be clear that one can plot a yield curve for every meaning of the term 'yield' which we identified in the last section. Fortunately, in practice, discussions of the yield curve are almost always discussions of the curve which plots redemption yields against period to maturity. Unless we state otherwise, 'yield' means 'redemption yield' throughout this section .

Box 10.6 Bond yields and maturity

The table reproduced below is taken from the London *Financial Times* for 26 October 1996 and shows the behaviour of UK government bond prices and yields on Friday 25 October. The table illustrates a number of points which we have already discussed in this chapter. Notice:

- The title of each bond includes the coupon rate and redemption date
- The bonds are listed in increasing order of residual maturity
- The first column of figures shows the interest or running yield
- The second column of figures shows the redemption yield
- The third column of figures shows the current price in pounds and '32nds'
- The next column shows the price change during Friday's trading
- The final columns show the highest and lowest price in the previous 52 weeks.

UK GILTS PRICES

Notes	Yield Int	Yield Red	Price £	+ or –	1996 High	1996 Low
Shorts" (Lives up to Five Years)						
Conversion 10pc 1996	9.98	5.73	$100\frac{1}{4}$	......	$103\frac{1}{4}$	$100\frac{1}{4}$
Treas 13$\frac{1}{4}$pc 1997‡‡	13.03	5.82	$101\frac{23}{32}$	......	$107\frac{5}{32}$	$100\frac{1}{2}$
Exch 10$\frac{1}{2}$pc 1997	10.35	5.84	$101\frac{13}{32}$	......	$107\frac{5}{16}$	$100\frac{7}{16}$
Treas Cnv 7pc 1997‡‡	6.95	5.97	$100\frac{3}{4}$	$+\frac{1}{32}$	$101\frac{15}{32}$	$100\frac{11}{16}$
Treas 8$\frac{3}{4}$pc 1997‡‡	8.56	6.00	$102\frac{3}{16}$	......	$107\frac{23}{32}$	$102\frac{3}{16}$
Exch 15pc 1997	13.82	6.05	$108\frac{1}{2}$xd	$-\frac{1}{16}$	$114\frac{27}{32}$	$102\frac{21}{32}$
Exch 9$\frac{3}{4}$pc 1998	9.37	6.21	$104\frac{1}{32}$	$+\frac{1}{32}$	$106\frac{7}{8}$	$103\frac{31}{32}$
Treas 7$\frac{1}{4}$pc 1998‡‡	7.16	6.26	$101\frac{5}{16}$	$+\frac{1}{32}$	$109\frac{19}{32}$	$100\frac{5}{8}$
Treas 6$\frac{3}{4}$pc 1995–98‡‡	6.75	6.76	100xd	......	$104\frac{1}{8}$	$99\frac{9}{16}$
Treas 15$\frac{1}{2}$pc '98‡‡	13.35	6.44	$116\frac{3}{32}$	$+\frac{3}{32}$	$122\frac{9}{16}$	$115\frac{7}{8}$
Exch 12pc 1998	10.88	6.55	$110\frac{9}{32}$	$+\frac{1}{32}$	$114\frac{9}{16}$	$110\frac{5}{32}$
Treas 9$\frac{1}{2}$pc 1999‡‡	8.97	6.55	$105\frac{15}{16}$	$+\frac{1}{8}$	$108\frac{9}{16}$	$105\frac{9}{16}$
Treas Fltg Rate 1999	–	–	$99\frac{31}{32}$	......	$100\frac{5}{32}$	$99\frac{7}{8}$
Exch 12$\frac{1}{4}$pc 1999	10.90	6.59	$112\frac{13}{32}$	$+\frac{3}{16}$	$116\frac{21}{32}$	$110\frac{19}{32}$
Treas 10$\frac{1}{2}$pc 1999	9.64	6.64	$108\frac{15}{16}$	$+\frac{3}{16}$	$112\frac{3}{16}$	$108\frac{21}{32}$
Treas 6pc 1999 ‡‡	6.09	6.58	$98\frac{15}{32}$	$+\frac{5}{32}$	$99\frac{1}{4}$	96
Conversion 10$\frac{1}{4}$pc 1999	9.36	6.74	$109\frac{1}{2}$	$+\frac{3}{16}$	$112\frac{17}{32}$	$108\frac{13}{32}$
Conv 9pc 2000‡‡	8.45	6.78	$106\frac{17}{32}$	$+\frac{7}{32}$	$108\frac{27}{32}$	$104\frac{15}{16}$
Treas 13pc 2000	10.86	6.89	$119\frac{11}{16}$	$+\frac{5}{16}$	$124\frac{15}{32}$	$119\frac{3}{32}$
Treas 14pc 1998–1	12.59	6.36	$111\frac{5}{32}$	$+\frac{1}{32}$	$116\frac{23}{32}$	$110\frac{3}{4}$
Treas 8pc 2000‡‡	7.70	6.88	$103\frac{15}{16}$	$+\frac{9}{32}$	$105\frac{7}{8}$	$101\frac{3}{32}$
Treas Fltg Rate 2001	5.70	–	$99\frac{27}{32}$	......	$99\frac{7}{8}$	$99\frac{3}{4}$
Treas 10pc 2001	9.01	6.98	111	$+\frac{9}{32}$	114	$100\frac{23}{32}$
Five to Fifteen Years						
Treas 7pc 2001 ‡‡	7.01	7.02	$99\frac{13}{16}$	$+\frac{5}{16}$	$101\frac{3}{32}$	$96\frac{1}{2}$
Treas 9$\frac{3}{4}$pc 2002	8.71	7.18	$111\frac{31}{32}$	$+\frac{13}{32}$	$114\frac{5}{8}$	$108\frac{7}{8}$
Treas 8pc 2003‡‡	7.68	7.19	$104\frac{5}{32}$	$+\frac{7}{16}$	$105\frac{23}{32}$	$99\frac{31}{32}$
Treas 10pc 2003	8.73	7.26	$114\frac{17}{32}$	$+\frac{1}{2}$	$117\frac{5}{32}$	39
Treas 11$\frac{1}{2}$pc 2001–4	9.88	7.08	$116\frac{3}{8}$	$+\frac{9}{32}$	$121\frac{5}{8}$	$114\frac{9}{16}$
Funding 3$\frac{1}{2}$pc 1999–4	4.19	6.24	$83\frac{7}{16}$	$+\frac{1}{2}$	$84\frac{21}{32}$	$78\frac{3}{4}$
Conversion 9$\frac{1}{2}$pc 2004	8.46	7.40	$112\frac{11}{32}$xd	$+\frac{1}{2}$	$114\frac{9}{16}$	$107\frac{15}{16}$
Treas 6$\frac{3}{4}$pc 2004‡‡	7.03	7.37	$96\frac{1}{16}$	$+\frac{15}{32}$	$97\frac{7}{32}$	$91\frac{5}{16}$
Conv 9 $\frac{1}{2}$ pc 2005	8.44	7.46	$112\frac{9}{16}$	$+\frac{21}{32}$	$114\frac{23}{32}$	$108\frac{1}{32}$
Treas 12$\frac{1}{2}$pc 2003–5	9.76	7.32	$128\frac{3}{32}$	$+\frac{17}{32}$	$131\frac{3}{8}$	$123\frac{15}{16}$

Notes	Yield Int	Yield Red	Price £	+ or –	1996 High	1996 Low
Treas 8 $\frac{1}{2}$pc 2005‡‡	7.97	7.46	$106\frac{5}{8}$	$+\frac{5}{8}$	$108\frac{21}{32}$	$101\frac{7}{8}$
Treas 7$\frac{1}{2}$pc 2006‡‡	7.51	7.51	$99\frac{27}{32}$	$+\frac{21}{32}$	$101\frac{23}{32}$	$94\frac{13}{16}$
Treas 7$\frac{3}{4}$pc 2006‡‡	7.65	7.54	$101\frac{5}{16}$	$+\frac{19}{32}$	$103\frac{1}{4}$	$96\frac{5}{16}$
Treas 8pc 2002–6‡‡	7.83	7.36	$102\frac{3}{16}$	$-\frac{5}{32}$	$104\frac{11}{32}$	$97\frac{7}{8}$
Treas 11$\frac{3}{4}$pc 2003–7	9.65	7.31	$121\frac{13}{16}$	$+\frac{15}{32}$	$125\frac{3}{32}$	$118\frac{15}{32}$
Treas 8$\frac{1}{2}$pc 2007 ‡‡	7.98	7.57	$106\frac{9}{16}$	$+\frac{21}{32}$	$108\frac{27}{32}$	$101\frac{9}{32}$
Treas 9pc 2008 ‡‡	8.14	7.62	$110\frac{17}{32}$	$+\frac{21}{32}$	$112\frac{13}{16}$	$103\frac{11}{32}$
Treas 8pc 2009	7.81	7.68	$102\frac{3}{8}$	$+\frac{11}{32}$	$104\frac{1}{2}$	$96\frac{31}{32}$
Treas 6 1/4pc 2010‡‡	7.19	7.78	$86\frac{7}{8}$	$+\frac{9}{16}$	$88\frac{5}{16}$	$81\frac{3}{4}$
Conv 9pc Ln 2011 ‡‡	8.14	7.77	$110\frac{1}{2}$	$+\frac{5}{8}$	$112\frac{13}{16}$	$104\frac{5}{8}$
Over Fifteen Years						
Treas 9pc 2012‡‡	8.14	7.80	$110\frac{19}{32}$	$+\frac{23}{32}$	$113\frac{3}{16}$	$104\frac{23}{32}$
Treas 5$\frac{1}{2}$pc 2008–12‡‡	6.81	7.58	$80\frac{13}{16}$	$+\frac{17}{32}$	$82\frac{3}{4}$	$75\frac{7}{8}$
Treas 8pc 2013‡‡	7.88	7.82	$101\frac{1}{2}$	$+\frac{3}{4}$	$103\frac{13}{16}$	$9\frac{5}{16}$
Treas 7$\frac{3}{4}$pc 2012–15‡‡	7.84	7.83	$98\frac{29}{32}$	$+\frac{25}{32}$	$101\frac{13}{32}$	$93\frac{13}{32}$
Treas 8pc 2015‡‡	7.87	7.82	$101\frac{19}{32}$	$+\frac{3}{4}$	$103\frac{7}{8}$	$95\frac{11}{16}$
Treas 8$\frac{3}{4}$pc 2017‡‡	8.05	7.87	$108\frac{11}{16}$	$+\frac{13}{16}$	$111\frac{1}{4}$	$102\frac{1}{2}$
Exch 12pc 2013–17	8.67	7.86	$138\frac{3}{8}$	$+\frac{15}{16}$	$141\frac{3}{8}$	$130\frac{13}{16}$
Treas 8pc 2021‡‡	7.87	7.83	$101\frac{5}{8}$	$+\frac{25}{32}$	$103\frac{3}{8}$	$95\frac{13}{32}$
Undated						
Consols 4pc	8.07	–	$49\frac{19}{32}$	$+\frac{11}{32}$	$50\frac{31}{32}$	$46\frac{3}{8}$
War Loan 3$\frac{1}{2}$pc‡‡	7.94	–	$44\frac{3}{32}$	$+\frac{5}{16}$	$45\frac{1}{2}$	$41\frac{3}{16}$
Conv 3$\frac{1}{2}$pc '61 Aft.	5.77	–	$60\frac{21}{32}$	$+\frac{3}{16}$	$62\frac{1}{4}$	$58\frac{5}{16}$
Treas 3pc '66 Aft.	8.22	–	$36\frac{15}{32}$	......	$38\frac{1}{16}$	$34\frac{9}{16}$
Consols 2$\frac{1}{2}$pc	7.91	–	$31\frac{5}{8}$	$+\frac{11}{32}$	$33\frac{1}{8}$	$29\frac{5}{8}$
Treas. 2$\frac{1}{2}$pc	8.01	–	$31\frac{7}{32}$	$+\frac{13}{32}$	$32\frac{3}{16}$	$29\frac{1}{8}$

Notes	Yield (1)	Yield (2)	Price £	+ or –	1996 High	1996 Low
Index–Linked (b)						
4$\frac{5}{8}$pc '98‡‡ (135.6)	0.36	2.20	$114\frac{3}{16}$xd	$+\frac{1}{32}$	$114\frac{3}{8}$	$111\frac{3}{16}$
2$\frac{1}{2}$pc '01 (78.3)	2.53	3.12	$185\frac{11}{16}$	$+\frac{9}{32}$	$185\frac{25}{32}$	$176\frac{1}{4}$
2$\frac{1}{2}$pc '03 (78.8)	2.80	3.24	$181\frac{23}{32}$	$+\frac{3}{8}$	$181\frac{3}{4}$	$171\frac{27}{32}$
4$\frac{3}{8}$pc '04‡‡ (135.6)	2.89	3.28	$118\frac{11}{16}$	$+\frac{5}{16}$	$118\frac{23}{32}$	$112\frac{31}{32}$
2pc '06 (69.5)	3.06	3.36	$191\frac{1}{32}$	$+\frac{5}{8}$	$191\frac{1}{8}$	$179\frac{13}{32}$
2$\frac{1}{2}$pc '09 (78.8)	3.19	3.43	$171\frac{29}{32}$	$+\frac{11}{16}$	172	$161\frac{1}{32}$
2$\frac{1}{2}$pc '11 (74.6)	3.26	3.48	$177\frac{23}{32}$	$+\frac{3}{4}$	$177\frac{29}{32}$	$166\frac{7}{16}$
2$\frac{1}{2}$pc '13 (89.2)	3.33	3.52	$146\frac{3}{32}$	$+\frac{11}{16}$	$146\frac{13}{32}$	$136\frac{7}{16}$
2$\frac{1}{2}$pc '16 (81.6)	3.39	3.57	$155\frac{15}{32}$	$+\frac{23}{32}$	$155\frac{23}{32}$	$145\frac{1}{16}$
2$\frac{1}{2}$pc '20 (83.0)	3.45	3.60	149	$+\frac{23}{32}$	$149\frac{7}{16}$	$138\frac{15}{16}$
2$\frac{1}{2}$pc '24‡‡ (97.7)	3.45	3.59	$123\frac{15}{16}$	$+\frac{21}{32}$	$124\frac{13}{32}$	$115\frac{3}{16}$
4$\frac{1}{8}$pc '30‡‡ (135.1)	3.45	3.59	122	$+\frac{21}{32}$	$122\frac{15}{32}$	$113\frac{21}{32}$

Prospective real redemption rate on projected inflation of (1) 10% and (2) 5%. (b) Figures in parentheses show RPI base for indexing (ie 8 months prior to issue) and have been adjusted to reflect rebasing of RPI to 100 in February 1987. Conversion factor 3.945. RPI for February 1996: 150.9 and for September 1996: 153.8.

Other Fixed Interest

Notes	Yield Int	Yield Red	Price £	+ or –	1996 High	1996 Low
Asian Dev 10$\frac{1}{4}$pc 2009	8.68	7.90	$118\frac{3}{32}$	......	120	$111\frac{31}{32}$
B'ham 11$\frac{1}{2}$pc 2012	9.09	8.45	$126\frac{1}{2}$xd	......	128	$119\frac{1}{2}$
Ireland Cap 8$\frac{1}{2}$pc '10	8.04	–	$105\frac{3}{4}$	......	$105\frac{3}{4}$	$105\frac{3}{4}$
9pc Cap 1996	8.65	–	104	......	104	104
13pc '97–2	11.72	–	$110\frac{7}{8}$	......	$110\frac{7}{8}$	$110\frac{7}{8}$
Leeds 13$\frac{1}{2}$pc 2006	10.11	–	$133\frac{1}{2}$	......	$136\frac{1}{2}$	129
Liverpool 3$\frac{1}{2}$pc Irred.	8.97	–	39	......	41	$37\frac{1}{2}$
LCC 3pc '20 Aft.	8.82	–	34	......	36	$32\frac{1}{2}$
Manchester 11$\frac{1}{2}$pc 2007	9.31	8.20	$123\frac{1}{2}$xd	......	$124\frac{1}{2}$	117
Met. Wtr. 3pc 'B'	3.75	6.95	80	......	80	$73\frac{1}{2}$
N'wide Anglia 3$\frac{7}{8}$pc 2021	–	4.24	143	......	$143\frac{1}{2}$	133
4$\frac{1}{4}$pc IL 2024	–	4.36	$137\frac{7}{8}$	......	$139\frac{7}{16}$	$130\frac{1}{2}$
Utd Mex States 16$\frac{1}{2}$pc 2008	12.22	–	135	......	$136\frac{1}{2}$	122

● 'Tap' stock. # Tax-free to non-residents on application. E Auction basis. xd Ex dividend. Closing mid-prices are shown in pounds per £100 nominal of stock. Prospective real Index-Linked redemption yields are calculated by HSBC Greenwell from Bank of England closing prices.

We said at the beginning of this section that the 'term structure' is often studied by looking at yields on government bonds, and that the yields in question are usually redemption yields. Examine carefully the second column of figures in the table. At the very shortest end of the maturity spectrum, the redemption yield is 5.73%. Moving up the maturity spectrum, yields reach 7.00% for bonds with five years to maturity. They continue to rise through the medium range reaching 7.77% for bonds maturing in 2011. Thereafter, yields level off at about 7.80%. Clearly, on 25th October, the yield curve for UK government bonds was upward sloping.

We examine three theories which try to explain the relationship between term to maturity and yield: the *expectations*, the *term premium* and the *preferred habitat/market segmentation* theories. They are presented in this order which roughly corresponds to their importance in the specialist literature. It is useful to note at the outset that the theories are not mutually exclusive. The yield curve *could* be determined by expected future interest rates, with a term premium reflecting the general level of risk aversion and 'local' premia or discounts reflecting the abundance or shortage of bonds in a particular part of the maturity spectrum.

10.5.1 Expectations theory

The idea that the term structure could be explained by reference to market expectations of future interest rates dates at least from Irving Fisher (1896, 1930) and was discussed extensively by Hicks (1939).[3]

The term structure of interest rates presents investors with a variety of interest rates on assets differentiated solely by their term to maturity. At the very least an investor looking to invest for L-years has a choice between holding a 'long' bond to maturity in L-years at a 'long-term' rate of interest, i_L[4], which is currently known, and holding a succession of short-dated bonds, only the first of whose rates of interest, i_1, is currently known, reinvesting the proceeds at the end of each period in another short-dated bond whose rate of interest, $\hat{i}_2$, is not known now, but can only be anticipated.

Let us assume that an investor wishes to invest for two years ($L = 2$) and that the investor is risk neutral. Furthermore, let us suppose that s/he knows the current one-year rate of interest (i_1), the current two-year rate of interest (i_L) and holds a confident expectation about the one year rate ($\hat{i}_2$) that will prevail in one year's time. Then it follows that s/he will be indifferent between these two investment strategies when:

$$(1 + i_1)(1 + \hat{i}_2) = (1 + i_L)^2 \qquad (10.15)$$

Furthermore, knowing i_1 and i_L, we can solve for the expected, or *implied*, future spot rate, $\hat{i}_2$, as follows:

$$\hat{i}_2 = \frac{(1 + i_L)^2}{(1 + i_1)} - 1 \qquad (10.16)$$

In recent years, some authorities have taken to referring to the implied future spot rate as a *forward* rate.

Turning now to the relationship $i_L - i_1$, the relationship between long and short rates, it follows from Equation 10.16 that if $i_L > i_1$, then $\hat{i}_2$ is also greater than i_1, that is to say that the investor expects future one-year rates to be above current one-year rates. Rearranging Equation 10.16 tells us indeed that with $i_L > i_1$, then $\hat{i}_2$ must also be greater even than i_L.

$$i_1 = \frac{(1 + i_L)^2}{(1 + \hat{i}_2)} - 1 \qquad (10.17)$$

The common sense of this of course is that an investor willing to buy a one-year bond now at a rate of interest below the going two-year rate must expect at the end of the first year to be able to replace the first one-year bond with a second which pays a (one-year) rate of interest which is higher than the current two-year rate by the amount necessary to produce an average return over the two years just equal to $(1 + i_L)$. As Shiller (1990) helpfully points out this is analogous with the marginal cost/average cost relationship. When the yield curve is rising, forward rates must be higher than spot rates of the same maturity and vice versa when the yield curve slopes downward. This is shown in Figure 10.4.

Turning from the individual investor to the market for one- and two-year bonds as a whole, equilibrium, indicated by stable bond prices, will exist when all investors are indifferent between holding two one-year bonds and one two-year bond, that is to .say when the market as a whole takes i_L to be an average of the known one-year rate, i_1, and the *expected* future one-year rate $\hat{i}_2$. Were this not to be the case,

---

[3] More recent extensions and modifications of the theory appear in Malkiel (1966) and Roll (1970).

[4] Remember that yields throughout the following discussion of term structure are assumed to be nominal redemption yields (yields to maturity). The long-term rate should therefore strictly be written ry_L.

However when we talk about nominal long-term redemption yields, we are talking, most of the time, about what is for many purposes the long-term nominal interest rate, i_L. Through the remainder of this section we have used the symbol i_L for reasons of brevity, and clarity in the mathematical expressions.

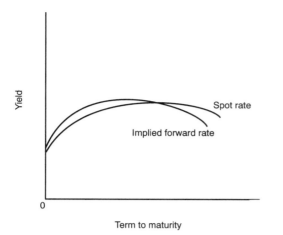

Figure 10.4 The spot rate–implied forward rate relationship.

suppose for example that i_L were greater than the average of the two short rates, then arbitrage between long and short bonds would push up the price of long bonds until i_L was reduced to the average of the short rates. Notice that the argument depends upon complete substitutability between long and short bonds. We return to this in the next section.

The principles which underlie the choice between one- and two-year bonds can of course be generalized to cover bonds of all maturities. In our example, we took i_L to be the rate on two-year bonds. Thus reordering Equation 10.15 we have:

$$(1 + i_L)^2 = (1 + i_1)(1 + \hat{i}_2) \qquad (10.18)$$

and thus:

$$i_L = \sqrt{(1 + i_1)(1 + \hat{i}_2)} - 1 \qquad (10.19)$$

Equation 10.19 is very closely approximated by the linear expression:

$$i_L = \frac{i_1 + \hat{i}_2}{L} \ or \ \left(\frac{1}{L}\right)(i_1 + \hat{i}_2) \qquad (10.20)$$

where L defines the period to maturity of the bond on which i_L is paid. Thus with i_L paid on a two-year bond, the value of i_L (from Equation 10.20), is:

$$\left(\frac{1}{2}\right)(i_1 + \hat{i}_2) \qquad (10.21)$$

that is to say, a simple average of the two one-year rates. More generally, however, we may say that:

$$i_L = \frac{i_1.K + \hat{i}_2.(L - K)}{L} \qquad (10.22)$$

where K is the period of time on which i_1 is paid and $(L - K)$ is the remaining period to maturity on which $\hat{i}_2$ is expected to be paid. According to the expectations theory, therefore, any 'long-term' rate of interest, i_L, is said to be a *weighted* average of expected future short-term rates, where K and $L - K$ (in Equation 10.22) are the weights.

Plotting the (actual) yields on offer at any particular time (in effect plotting the value of i_L from $L = 1$ to $L = \infty$, since undated bonds or 'consols' are available) produces what is called the 'time yield curve'. Figure 10.5 shows just three possible shapes for this curve, corresponding (1) to the situation where future short rates are expected to rise ($i_L > i_1$ in our example); (2) to the situation where future short rates are expected to remain unchanged ($i_L = i_1$); (3) to the situation where future short rates are expected to fall ($i_L < i_1$).

The diagram needs careful interpretation, particularly with regard to the horizontal axis. It is important to remember that the time/yield curve shows the rate of interest available *now* on assets of varying periods to maturity. *It must not be read as telling us those interest rates that will prevail at a particular time from now. If* the expectations hypothesis holds, then the yield curve implies forward rates but it does not show them. What it shows are today's rates.[5]

Since, according to the expectations theory, the shape of the curve depends entirely upon the market's expectation of the future level of interest rates, the curve obviously could take any shape. It could approximate any of the three cases in Figure 10.5, but it could also be humped, if investors thought interest rates would first rise and then fall; or it could have a trough, indicating the expectation of a fall followed by a rise. Several humps, troughs or even mixtures of both are possible. The ability of the expectations theory to explain any particular shape is

---

[5] Theoretically, the rates reported in a time/yield curve are those which prevail *simultaneously*. In empirical work, therefore, the rates should be those that existed at a single moment. It is not, strictly speaking, appropriate to construct a time/yield curve from data recorded even at different times of the same day. Theoretical purity is not always possible in empirical work, of course, and this requirement explains the tendency for researchers to use rates recorded at the end of a day's trading.

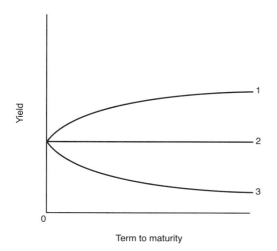

Figure 10.5 Three time yield curves.

limited only by our ability to supply sufficiently ingenious rationalizations for investors' interest rate expectations. It follows equally that no conceivable shape to the curve could lead us to a firm conclusion about the validity of the expectations theory. However, it is worth noting that the theory draws some informal support from the observed tendency for the time/yield curve to slope downwards when interest rates are historically high, and to slope upwards when rates are near the bottom of their range. This would be consistent with the idea that investors perceive a band of 'normal' interest rates to which they expect future rates to return whenever current rates are at or outside the limits of the band.

One of the most interesting developments in the recent study of the term structure is the possibility of extracting information about future interest and inflation rates from the shape of the yield curve. The argument is that *if* the expectations theory is accepted, and we then add the assumption that those expectations are generally correct, then the shape of the curve should be an accurate predictor of future nominal interest rates. (Indeed, this would be true even if the term structure also contained a term

premium, provided such a premium were stable.) Taken in general, the findings from empirical tests have not supported the hypothesis. Mankiw and Miron (1986 p.216) offer one fairly representative judgement. 'Contrary to the expectations theory, the slope of the yield curve appears to exhibit no predictive power at any time since 1915'.[6] However, in spite of the failure to find widespread evidence in its support, the expectations hypothesis has continued to attract attention. This is undoubtedly due to its attraction, when combined with the 'Fisher hypothesis', as a predictor of inflation in a period when inflation has emerged as a major policy issue and when conventional indicators of the policy stance have failed. We saw in the last chapter that monetary policy in several countries in the 1980s was initially based upon the pursuit of monetary growth 'rules' or 'targets', on the argument that a stable velocity of circulation together with a 'natural rate' of productivity growth would produce a close connection between monetary growth and inflation. Given these rules or targets, policy could then be easily judged for 'slackness' or 'tightness' depending on whether the targets were achieved or under- or overshot. We are not concerned here with the pretty dismal record of failing to hit the targets. More relevant is the fact that in both the USA and the UK a dramatic collapse in velocity destroyed the money–inflation link. The targets, even had they been achieved, no longer indicated anything of significance.

Combining the expectations theory of the term structure with the Fisher hypothesis seemed to offer an ingenious alternative way of interpreting the state of policy. The Fisher hypothesis is that nominal interest rates are composed of a (fairly stable) real rate plus an inflation premium. Thus *if* (after Fisher) expected nominal interest rates *are* composed of a stable *ex ante* real rate plus an inflation premium, and *if* the shape of the yield curve *is* determined wholly by rational expectations of future short rates, then in telling us about future nominal interest rates the yield curve would be telling us about the market's

---

6 Their explanation is interesting. The failure of the market to anticipate future interest rates accurately coincides with the setting up of the Federal Reserve Board and its subsequent interventions in the money market to set interest rates according to its policy preferences. (This activity was examined in the last chapter.) If this is true, it amounts to saying that, left to itself (for example, before 1915) the market is quite efficient in the judgement it makes about future interest rates, but it simply cannot outguess the next move of central banks committed to using interest rates at their own discretion.

expectation of future inflation and therefore about (the market's interpretation of) the current tightness or laxity of monetary policy. Unfortunately, tests of its predictive ability, both of future short-term interest rates and of the rate of inflation, have not generally suggested that it is particularly effective.

It is not altogether essential, however, for the term structure to be an accurate predictor of future inflation or interest rates for it to have some role in the formulation and evaluation of policy. Provided, for example, that one thought the shape of the curve was generally correct in pointing to the *direction* of change in future rates, then it could still function as a guide, especially if there were little else. This seems to have been the case in the USA and in Germany (and to a lesser extent in the UK) during the period of falling interest rates in 1992–3. The authorities made a succession of small cuts in official discount rates while watching the yield curve for any sign of steepening. Provided all rates came down broadly in step, the policy was 'justified'. But when a cut in short rates caused the curve to steepen this was taken as evidence that the probability of a higher inflation in future had increased and the cuts stopped.

10.5.2 The term premium theory

If the expectations theory is attractive because it is consistent with one frequently observed feature of the curve's behaviour, the term premium theory is attractive for the same reason. But the feature this time is the curve's historical tendency to slope upward except when interest rates are at very high levels, indicating that, as a general rule, higher yields are available on bonds with longer maturities. Clearly, this is a problem for the expectations theory. If the curve does, as a rule, slope upward when current interest rates are in their 'normal' range, the expectations account would lead us to believe that investors expect future interest rates, as a rule, to be higher than today's. It does not seem very likely that investors expect interest rates to rise persistently over time.

The question for the term premium theory therefore is what characteristic might longer-dated bonds possess which makes them *systematically* unattractive, so that investors must be paid some premium to induce them to hold longer bonds? One

obvious, but wrong, suggestion might be that investors require a 'liquidity premium' to induce them to 'lock up' their funds for a long period. Hicks, following Keynes in the *General Theory*, advanced the idea that investors required a premium to induce them to hold longer-dated bonds. Hicks, however, was careful to refer to a 'risk premium'. The problem lies in what one understands by 'liquidity'. Strictly, as we have had occasion to point out elsewhere in this book, liquidity refers to the ease with which an asset can be converted into money, *with capital certainty*. Most assets can be converted into money quickly, and even cheaply, if the rate of exchange sufficiently favours the buyer. A long-dated bond is no less liquid than a short-dated one, in the limited sense of investors being able to sell the bond for cash. There is, in most developed countries and certainly in the UK, a highly developed secondary market for government securities (as we shall see in the next section). The possibility that holders of long-dated bonds require a 'liquidity premium' has nothing to do with any difficulty in disposing of long bonds. We must not confuse a bond's term to maturity with the period for which investors must hold it. Terms like 'risk premium' or 'term premium' are less likely to cause this confusion than 'liquidity premium'.

What else might it be about a long-dated bond that requires the payment of a term premium? The answer lies in Equations 10.12 and 10.14. The first shows that the market price fluctuates with interest rates while the second shows that the interest-elasticity increases with duration. A future change in interest rates thus causes a capital gain or loss for bond-holders who may wish to sell before maturity. Uncertainty about future interest rates has introduced risk. In itself, however, the recognition of risk does not add anything to our understanding of the term structure that is not already supplied by the expectations theory. The expectations theory recognizes that people do not know what future interest rates will be. The yield curve takes the shape dictated by the weight of expectation in the market as to what future rates will most probably be. Only if the expectations theory included an additional supposition (which it does not) that investors generally made upwardly biased estimates of future interest rates would we have any reason to expect a generally upward-sloping curve. If we take the more reasonable view that there is no reason why market participants should consistently under- or over-estimate the future level of rates, there must be an actuarially even chance of under- or over-estimation and thus, on average, expectations should turn out to be correct. Thus, the specific recognition of risk notwithstanding, there is still no reason to expect a general tendency for the curve to slope upward.

Suppose, however, that investors had an asymmetrical attitude to the actuarial symmetry of winning and losing.[7] Suppose that they attach more *significance* to the possibility of loss than to the possibility of gain. One obvious and frequently suggested justification for this possibility is that wealth is subject to diminishing marginal utility – a given increase yields less satisfaction than the loss of satisfaction which follows from a decrease of equal magnitude. In these circumstances, investors are said to be *capital risk averse* and the market is dominated by *capital risk aversion*. While risk itself may not take us far in explaining the upward-sloping tendency, *capital risk aversion* most certainly does. Imagine investors faced with the choice between a default-free, demand deposit and a (default-free and so on) security giving the same return but having (obviously) a longer term to maturity than the demand deposit. Suppose also that investors hold confident expectations that interest rates will remain as they are and that they rate the possibility that interest rates may (unexpectedly) rise *equally with the possibility that rates may fall*. Actuarially, investors expect the same return from both investments but clearly, if risk aversion is present, they will choose the deposit unless some interest premium or other form of inducement is offered to persuade them to hold the (risky) security.

In the presence of capital risk aversion we can see why a premium might be demanded for a term security when compared with a zero-term deposit. Furthermore, knowing that the interest-elasticity of bond prices varies with duration, we can now see why longer-term securities are seen as more risky than mediums, and mediums as more risky than shorts and thus why the term premium should increase with the term to maturity.

According to the term premium theory, any long-term rate of interest, i_L thus contains a risk- premium, θ_L, which is dependent upon the degree of capital risk aversion in the bond market and the residual maturity of the bond on which it is paid. In Equation 10.23, for example, the risk premium, θ_L, on a bond with (L) periods to maturity is proportional to (L) with the proportion, p, indicating the market's degree of capital risk aversion.

$$\theta_L = p(L) \tag{10.23}$$

As with the expectations theory, mere observation of yield curves does not allow us to endorse or reject the risk premium theory. Any of the curves in Figure 10.5, and indeed any other curve we may care to imagine, *may* contain evidence of a term-related risk premium. Indeed, as we said at the opening of this section, the term premium theory is not inconsistent with a role for expectations. In Figure 10.5 curve (1) is clearly consistent with a positive term premium. *If* we knew that investors expected the current rate, i_1, to continue unchanged ($i_1 = \hat{i}_2$) then curve (1) would be determined *solely* by the term premium and its slope would be given by p in Equation 10.23. In Equation 10.24, $i_1 = \hat{i}_2$, but $i^* = \theta^* + \hat{i}_2$

$$i^* = (1 + i_1)(1 + \hat{i}_2) + \theta_L - 1 \tag{10.24}$$

However, it is also possible that the market expects future rates to rise ($i_1 < \hat{i}_2$) but by only a small amount, the rest of the positive slope being made up by p. But a term premium is also consistent with curve (2) – investors expect future rates to fall slightly but this is exactly offset by capital risk aversion; it is even consistent with (3) – the market expects future rates to fall sharply but this is partially offset by risk aversion. And if risk aversion can modify any of the curves in Figure 10.5, it follows that it could modify

---

7 In fact, an equal chance of interest rates rising or falling by the same amount does not produce a strict actuarial symmetry. The result is biased in favour of *capital gain*. This arises because in the pricing formula we divide by the gross interest rate $(1 + i)$. Suppose that the bond in Equation 5.5 has an annual coupon of £6 $(C = 6)$ and pays £100 $(M = 100)$ in four years $(n_m = 4)$. If interest rates are 10 per cent $(i = 0.1)$ then the market value is currently £87.08. If interest rates fall to 9 per cent, the formula prices the bond at £90.11, a capital *gain* of £3.03. A one point *rise* in interest rates, by contrast, causes the price to fall to £84.19, a capital *loss* of only £2.89.

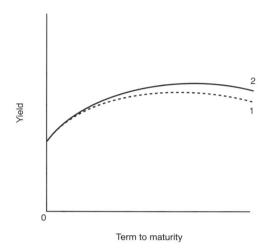

Figure 10.6 Adding a positive term premium.

any shape of curve dependent upon any set of expectations about the future level of interest rates.

Figure 10.6 shows a yield curve (1) determined solely by expectations (where investors think interest rates are already high but expect them to rise still further before falling in the long term), and a yield curve (2) where the same interest rate expectations apply, but the shape of the curve is modified by capital risk aversion.

As an explanation of the alleged upward bias in the term structure, the risk premium theory relies upon *capital* risk aversion in the bond market. Capital risk is not the only form of risk to which investors may be averse, however. For some investors, most likely institutions, fluctuations in *income* may be more important. Institutions such as life assurance companies, for example, have long-term liabilities in the form of the returns to investors guaranteed by virtue of the policy when it is issued or sold. These returns have to be earned from assets purchased with contributions which the company receives long after the contract was written. Clearly, at the time of purchase asset prices (yields) could be high (low). One way to limit the risk is to buy long-dated bonds when yields are high and hold them to redemption. Income risk aversion thus pulls in the opposite direction from capital risk aversion. In these circumstances, there is a systematic bias towards long-dated bonds. *Ceteris paribus* one would expect

long-dated bonds to have a higher price (lower yield) than short-dated bonds, and the yield curve would tend to slope downwards.

There is no *theoretical* reason for capital risk aversion to dominate and thus for the term premium to be positive. Its sign, as well as its size, is an empirical matter.

10.5.3   Preferred habitat theory

Notice that risk aversion and the term premium theory require us to drop the implicit assumption of the pure expectations theory that the bonds are homogeneous except with respect to their term to maturity. Differences in period to maturity create different risk characteristics to which investors may be sensitive. Preferred habitat, and its more extreme version, market segmentation, theory takes heterogeneity so seriously as to argue that investors have distinct preferences for parts of the maturity spectrum.

For example, pension funds as well as life assurance companies are significant holders of long-dated bonds, while banks and building societies hold mainly shorts. This preference, ultimately related to the pattern of their liabilities, encourages a concentration of skill and expertise in the observation and analysis of 'segments' of the market in order to take advantage of arbitrage opportunities. Moving outside these segments may involve significant costs. The observation that balance sheet and operational pressures may cause investors to focus upon a particular part of the maturity spectrum led Culbertson (1957) to suggest a 'Market Segmentation' theory of the term structure and Modigliani and Sutch later (1966) to their 'Preferred Habitat Theory'.

On both views, the shape of the yield curve will be influenced by the demand for and supply of bonds within each particular segment. Suppose, for example, that government took the decision to fund successive PSBRs by issuing debt in the 7–10-year maturity range, everything else remaining unchanged. Eventually, we should expect to see the price of 7–10-year bonds fall relative to the price of longer and shorter debt, and yields would rise. *Cet. par.* the yield curve would display a 'hump' in this maturity range. However, if we were to assume complete substitutability throughout the full maturity spectrum, as the expectations theory implicitly does, such a hump would never materialize. As prices began to fall (yields rise), investors from adjacent parts of the spectrum would switch out of (slightly) longer and shorter bonds to take advantage of the emerging higher yields. This in itself would limit the rise in 7–10-year yields but it would also lower the price (and raise the yields) of bonds in the adjacent parts of the spectrum. With complete substitutability, ripples of adjustment would spread along the whole curve, with the result that the whole curve would shift upward while retaining its original shape.

If, however, investors occupied a preferred habitat they would be reluctant to move from their chosen part of the spectrum. Resistance would not be total. We would expect some premium over yields in adjacent spectrums at which a movement would be triggered. (Indeed, our earlier argument that a premium may have to be paid to induce capital (income) risk averters to hold long (short) dated bonds could be seen as special cases of preferred habitats.) The size of this premium will depend upon the strength of preference. In these circumstances, the continued issue of bonds in one part of the spectrum will cause a 'hump' to emerge while concentrated redemptions would cause a 'trough'. The significance of the preferred habitat theory is that it presents the maturity spectrum as the sum of many segments each inhabited by investors whose preferences are derived from many influences (not just their attitudes to capital and income risk) and thus admits the possibility of a yield curve with any number of inflexions.

With complete segmentation, resistance to movement from the preferred habitat would be total and the 'humps' and 'troughs' correspondingly larger.

Once again, such behaviour can be combined with other influences. A market dominated by capital risk averters might expect short rates to fall progressively over the next 15 years, but the yield curve could show a trough in the 12–14 year range if, in a segmented market, such bonds were in particularly short supply.

10.6   Characteristics of the bond markets

Fixed interest securities are issued in all countries by a wide range of institutions wishing to raise funds for longer than one year. The list includes central governments, local or regional administrations, other public bodies and corporations[8] and private firms. Table 10.2 shows the value of bonds issued in selected markets, distinguishing by broad category of issuer. It shows, in particular, the size of the US bond market, relative to its European counterparts.[9]

Table 10.2 tells us nothing about how these stocks have come about. Governments, as a rule, run budget deficits, which guarantees a continuous flow of new issues from the public sector. Such a persistent flow of new issues, we noted earlier, causes the stock (supply) to expand continuously. But there is also a net flow of new issues from firms, as existing firms expand and new firms are created. One factor which has been particularly relevant to the new issue of corporate bonds in recent years has been the behaviour of interest rates. During the 1970s high and volatile interest rates seem to have discouraged firms from entering into long-term fixed-interest commitments and temporarily the new issue of corporate bonds slowed to a trickle in most European markets. (These were the same conditions that forced

Table 10.2 Bond issues (ECUmn, year to end July 1996)

	Corporate bonds	Public sector	Foreign	Total
New York[1]	499,870	677,820	34,834	1,212,524
Paris	1,245	795	503	2,543
Germany	19,863	1,517	976	22,386
Italy	660	194	6	860
London	4,145	183	3,442	7,770
Tokyo[2]	369,938	559,208	12,057	941,204

Sources: European exchanges – Federation of European Stock Exchanges, *European Stock Exchange Statistics*, July 1996; New York and Tokyo – OECD *Financial Statistics*, February 1997 Pt 1, sect. 2, converted at the current exchange rate.
Notes: [1]Calendar 1995.
[2]Calendar 1996

---

8 Except in the UK where public sector bond issues are centralized in the government's public sector borrowing requirement (PSBR).

9 The Yen bond market is also very large, much closer to the US than to European equivalents.

several governments to experiment with index-linking and variable rate bonds in order to fund their deficits.)

The issue of new bonds is one obvious way of comparing the size of markets: it enables us to compare the scale of new funds being raised by this method. However, it may give us very little guide as to the level of activity in the market. To measure the scale of activity in these markets we need to look at *turnover*, the total value of bonds, old as well as new, bought and sold per period. Table 10.3 shows the turnover in bond markets. It is noticeable that the value of turnover is much greater than the value of funds raised through new issues for all countries and exchanges, though the difference is less dramatic for New York.

Table 10.3 Bond turnover (ECU bn, year to end July 1996)

	Corporate bonds	Public sector	Foreign	Total
New York[1]	n.a.	n.a.	n.a.	5,988
Paris	112	5,365	25	5,502
Italy	5	2,646	<1	2,651
London	10	678	19	707
Germany	53	954	41	1,048
Tokyo[2]	n.a.	n.a.	n.a.	28,129

Sources: European exchanges – Federation of European Stock Exchanges, *European Stock Exchange Statistics*, July 1996; New York and Tokyo – OECD *Financial Statistics*, February 1997 Pt 1, sect. 2, converted at the current exchange rate.
Notes: [1]Calendar 1995.
[2]Calendar 1996

10.6.1 Primary markets

In most financial centres, the methods for making *new* issues of corporate bonds are the same as for the issue of new ordinary company shares. In the UK, for example, corporate bonds may be the subject of a 'public offer for sale' either at a fixed price or by auction. Alternatively, they may be issued by a 'placing'. In this case the institution responsible for

issuing the bonds places them directly with investors with whom it already has contacts. The institution responsible for handling the issue will be a merchant bank or a securities dealer.

The methods for making new issues of government bonds, however, are often different. This is because the sale and redemption of government bonds is an important instrument of monetary policy and the central bank needs to be certain that its wishes can be made quickly effective in the market for government bonds. In the UK, the Bank of England is responsible for the terms on which new bonds are issued and for the timing of such issues. The traditional method, still used, is the sale by tender in which the Bank of England offers a specified quantity of stock for sale on a particular day at a minimum price and invites bids. If the offer is undersubscribed, all bids are accepted; if it is oversubscribed, the highest bids are accepted but at a common price – usually the minimum bid price necessary to clear the sale.[10] If the offer is undersubscribed, the Bank retains the unsold stock and releases it onto the market subsequently, when conditions permit. Stock issued in such a way is known as *tap stock*.

The second method of issue involves the auction of stock, in which no minimum price is set. The stock is sold to the highest bidders at the price they bid.[11] This is a method which was first used in 1987 and represents a distinct stage in the evolution of debt management policy. From the point of view of the money supply and credit aggregates, sales by auction have the advantage that the issuer can set the volume, knowing that it will be fully subscribed, since the price will adjust to ensure that this is so. Thus, the desire to sell a given volume of stock consistent with targets for the money supply can generally be met. With a sale by tender the price is set, with the result that the volume of sales becomes uncertain. The two methods simply illustrate the age-old principle that one can control the price or the quantity, but not both.

The third method of issue is for the Bank of England to 'buy' the stock itself and to release it to the market as conditions permit: the 'tap' method of issue.

---

10 This is an example of the striking-price auction we first met in Section 9.3.

11 An example of the 'bid-price' auction of Section 9.3.

In Germany, government bonds are generally 'plain' or bullet bonds, and there have inevitably been large issues following the reunification of Germany in 1990. Long-term government bonds ('Bunds' – see Table 10.1) are issued in three ways. A tranche of any new issue is offered initially at a fixed price to a 'Federal Loans Syndicate' of designated financial institutions. The remainder are then subsequently sold at auction to anyone who cares to bid, while the Bundesbank retains a small proportion for future monetary policy operations. Medium-term bonds ('Bobls') are sold to a network of financial institutions as market conditions permit, rather in the way of the Bank of England tap method. The short-term Bundesschatzanweisungen are sold by auction. Auctions of German bonds are bid-price auctions, conducted at regular intervals.

In France, the standard method of issue is by competitive bid-price auction to designated 'primary dealers' ('Spécialistes en Valeurs du Trésor') according to a regular timetable.

As the figures in Tables 10.2 and 10.3 show, the Italian bond market is dominated by government bonds, reflecting Italy's long history of public sector deficits. Even more than other systems therefore, the Italian bond market has to be able to cope with large and frequent government bond issues in an orderly way. Dealers in bonds are divided into three groups ('dealers', 'primary dealers' and 'specialists in government bonds') according to the scale of their commitment to make markets in government bonds and to take up new issues. New issues are offered to the latter two groups who are invited to bid in a marginal ('strike-price') auction. In return these dealers have preferential access to the Bank of Italy and are members of the 'MTS', a computerized market for the wholesale trading of government bonds. This market accounts for about 95 per cent of trading in government bonds compared with the Milan stock exchange where retail trading accounts for the remainder of trading in government bonds. (Figures in Tables 10.2 and 10.3 are the sum of the two markets.)

10.6.2 Secondary markets

When it comes to trading *existing* bonds, markets can be classified in a number of ways depending upon

Dealer ('quote-driven')
London Stock Exchange
NASDAQ

Matching ('order-driven' or 'auction')
Hong Kong
Zurich
Paris
Madrid
Frankfurt
Milan
Toronto

Mixed
London Stock Exchange
Tokyo
Amsterdam
New York

Figure 10.7 Security market trading systems.

the way in which the trading is carried out. Figure 10.7 provides a schematic typology, with a selection of bond and equity markets allocated to the type of market which they most closely resemble. Unfortunately for us, the picture is confused by the use of multiple terms with the same meaning.

As the figure shows, the most basic distinction is between *matching* and *dealer* markets. For reasons we shall see in a moment, matching markets are sometimes described as 'order-driven' or 'auctioneer' markets while dealer markets are sometimes called 'quote-driven' markets. In matching/order-driven/ auctioneer markets there is a further distinction between *continuous* and *call* (or 'batch') markets. (Dealer/quote driven markets are always continuous).

In matching markets, trades take place when dealers can match orders to buy and orders to sell. Hence they are responding to 'orders' and in trying to find a price that will match the maximum number of buy and sell orders they are acting very much like traditional 'auctioneers'. The matching process may be continuous or it may take place at specified times. As Figure 10.7 shows, the majority of bond (and equity) markets are matching markets and the majority of these work on both a continuous and a call basis. There is a call auction at the beginning of the day in which all orders accumulated since the last close of trading are executed, followed by continuous trading throughout the day. Buyers and sellers can normally specify with their order whether they wish it to be exercised immediately or at the next call.

Notice that the system does not depend upon auctioneers holding their own inventories. There is no need since they only 'buy' from a seller when they simultaneously 'sell' to a buyer.

By contrast, in a dealer market, the dealer 'makes' a market by holding his own inventories of stocks and announces (continuously) a price at which he is prepared to buy and sell (rather like a dealer in secondhand cars or antiques). The picture here is one in which those who wish to buy or sell know in advance what price is available and they are responding to that price. This is why a dealer market is described as a *quote-driven* market.

What consequences follow from these different structures? As a rule, call (or batch) markets are cheaper to operate than continuous markets. The obvious drawback, however, is that prices are established only at discrete intervals and price changes can be sharper when the trades are called than they would be in continuous markets. On the other hand, although pricing is continuous and large volume deals can be done at low unit costs, continuous markets and dealer markets especially are expensive to operate. As we said above, major financial markets tend to be of the continuous kind. In the light of our previous point it is worth noting that a continuing criticism of the London Stock Exchange since its major reforms in 1986 has been its inability to provide a cheap service for small to medium sized trades, and that this contrasts sharply with a steep decline in the unit cost of large trades.

The costs of buying and selling securities are twofold. Firstly dealers may charge a commission. This is usually calculated as some percentage of the value of the transaction of the deal, subject to some minimum and maximum figure. (It is these minimum and maximum thresholds that lead to low unit costs for large deals and discriminate against small investors.) In addition, investors will normally face a 'bid' price, at which the dealer will buy, which is below the price at which the dealer will sell or 'offer' securities. One measure of the quality of a market, as we shall see in a moment, is the narrowness of the bid–offer spread around the equilibrium price.

There are other consequences too – in the speed with which prices change and the causes of price changes. To understand these differences we need firstly to distinguish between *information traders* and *noise* or *liquidity traders*. Information traders are investors who buy and sell securities in order to profit from what they think is their superior information about the securities (or their superior interpretation of information). Noise or liquidity traders are those who trade for any other reason. As a rough approximation we might regard information traders as the 'professionals'. They are the investors who make the best use of available information about the security's fundamental value. Information traders use information to price bonds according to the principles set out earlier in this chapter and they value equities according to the dividend discount models in the next chapter. If we jump to Chapter 25, it is information traders who make financial markets informationally efficient. By contrast, noise traders buy and sell in response to their own view about where the security's price is going next, *whatever the basis of that hunch may be*. We should not dismiss them as 'amateurs' or suggest that they are necessarily foolish. 'Noise trader' is a category that would include the technical analysts or 'chartists' described in Section 11.3.

The reason we make the distinction here is that information traders have a crucial role in dealer markets. Recall that in a dealer market, the dealer stands ready to buy and sell at a quoted price. Information traders give dealers a strong incentive to set the correct price (correct in the sense of reflecting all relevant information). If dealers did not do this, information traders would have an advantage which they would be able to exploit at the dealers' expense, given the commitments that dealers have to make and stand by. Suppose, for example, that a trader believes, in the light of carefully studied information, that a security trading for $4.90 is worth $5. Let us assume that he buys it from a dealer, its price subsequently rises to $5, and he sells it back to the dealer. His 10 cent profit is made at the dealer's expense. It is because dealers must hold inventories of stocks and deal on demand that they must continuously make the best prices. Thus prices will change quickly and *they will change in response to information rather than trades*. In dealer markets, prices may change even when no dealing takes place.

By contrast, prices in auctioneer markets change *only* in response to trading. Information is relevant to market prices only in so far as it causes people to wish to buy and sell, and only then when it causes a liquidity imbalance, an excess of buy orders over sell orders or vice versa.

In most financial centres, secondary trading in corporate bonds is carried out by the same dealers in securities that make markets in ordinary company shares. (We say more about these in Section 11.5.) As a general rule, however, the stock of corporate bonds and the trading in them is very much smaller than that of equities. (Bond markets are large overall because of the accumulation of government bonds.) One consequence is that the bid–offer spread is often much larger than it is on the equities traded by the same firms and certainly much larger than the spreads on government bonds being traded in the same market.

As with new issues, and for the same reason, secondary trading in government bonds is usually subject to arrangements which are rather different from those applying to corporate bonds. Markets in government stock are frequently made by the same firms that deal in equities and bonds but they will be subject to separate and additional regulation by the central bank. In the UK, for example, although any securities dealer can in theory make a market in government stock, since the 'Big Bang' reforms of 1986, the market for government stock has been dominated by the 'gilt-edge market makers' (or GEMMs). They hold government stocks and deal on their own behalf but also act as clients for brokers.[12] The reason for this domination is that, being 'recognized' by the Bank of England, they enjoy certain advantages. These are: (1) borrowing facilities at the Bank of England; (2) access to inter-dealer brokers;[13] (3) a direct dealing relationship with the Bank of England; (4) a facility for making 'late' bids at auctions.

In return for all this, there are considerable obligations. Firstly, while a GEMM may very likely be part of a securities dealer making markets in all types of stock, it must be separately established with its own capital. (In December 1996 the Bank of England announced plans to lift this requirement.) Secondly, GEMMs may not deal in equity shares and while they may deal in other fixed-interest securities these must not be convertible into equities. Thirdly, they accept to make 'continuous and effective two-way prices' at which they are committed to deal up to a specified bargain size. Fourthly, the size of transactions and the risk exposure that a GEMM can accept are subject to regular review and discussion with the Bank of England. (The December 1996 announcement envisaged an easing of the capital adequacy requirements in future.)

Since GEMMs are members of the London Stock Exchange, all of these obligations and regulations are additional to the conditions laid down for membership. Indeed, when we say that in the UK 'most securities are traded on the London Stock Exchange' it is only the fact that GEMMs are members and subject to its rules that gives this statement any sense today. Before 1986, when all securities dealing took place in one physical location, it was literally true. Brokers would make their way to one jobber for the ordinary shares of British Petroleum and then to another jobber for 'Treasury 10% 2002', as their clients required. But like (virtually) all securities dealing in London since 1986, the gilt-edge 'market' is screen-based and the dealers, rigidly demarcated from other dealers in other securities as we have just seen, are located in offices dispersed through the City of London.

As we explain in Section 11.5, one of the objectives of the Big Bang reforms was to increase the size and capital resources of market-making firms in the London Stock Exchange in order to make its services more competitive with those of other financial centres. One way of assessing the changes in the quality of a market is to look at transactions costs. Before 1986, commissions on average size deals, of £0.5–1m, ranged between £100 and £250. Since Big Bang, such commissions

---

[12] An illustration of the 'dual-capacity' role which became common in London after 1986. See Section 11.5.2.

[13] Inter-dealer brokers (IDBs) are intermediaries who buy and sell stock from and to GEMMs in conditions of anonymity. This enables a GEMM which has purchased (for example) a long line of one particular stock to sell parts of it on to other GEMMs without their knowing that it has this large holding and deliberately lowering their bid prices. In so far as the IDB system makes it easier for GEMMs to trade large blocks of stock without dramatic effects on prices, IDBs contribute the market's 'depth' – a term which is explained in Section 11.5.2.

have disappeared and, furthermore, bid–offer spreads have also narrowed from about 0.125 per cent to 0.0625 per cent for short-dated stocks and from 0.25 per cent to 0.125 per cent for long-dated stocks.[14]

10.6.3 Reading the Financial Times

One of the most comprehensive bond market information services readily available to the general public is provided by the *Financial Times*, in its UK and European editions.

In the UK edition, most of the relevant information is provided on the page headed 'International Capital Markets'. This provides two written reports on recent events. One is for 'Government Bonds', which comments on the previous day's activities in government bonds in the main centres in which they are traded. The other is for 'International Bonds' which comments in the same way on the previous day's developments in the markets in various countries, for corporate bonds. The same page also incorporates a number of tables. The table showing prices, yields and price changes for UK government bonds was reproduced above in Box 10.6. A second major table shows price and yield data for international bonds – both corporate and government. Another table, headed 'Bond Futures and Options', provides data on bond futures and options denominated in each of the major currencies, together with information on where these contracts are traded. (We look at this in more detail in Chapters 12 and 13).

The remaining data, which we reproduce in Box 10.7, is of two kinds. The first relates to the UK bond market, mainly in the form of a series of indices. The upper two-thirds of this table, for example, concentrates on UK government bonds. All indices containing *FT-Actuaries* in their title (and there are several of them as we shall see in Chapter 11) are produced jointly by the *Financial Times* and the Institute of Actuaries (in London) and the Faculty of Actuaries (in Scotland). Broadly speaking, the Actuaries are responsible for the design of the index (deciding what to include and

what to omit, for example) while the *FT* collects the daily price information and computes the index value. The first column is an index of prices for bonds of various maturities, distinguishing between 'straights' and 'index-linked' and the *percentage* change in that index since the previous day. The index represents the movement in price of a portfolio constructed of equal proportions of all UK government stocks and the base year is 1975. It is continually adjusted for new issues and redemptions and for movements of individual stocks from one maturity band to another. To the right of the price data is a series of columns showing the average gross redemption yields for bonds in each maturity band. The yield is shown for the previous day, for the day before that and for the corresponding day one year earlier. Rather than quoting one average redemption yield for each maturity, the table gives an average for 'low coupon', 'medium coupon' and 'high coupon' stocks, where low, medium and high are defined in the footnotes. The yield on index-linked stocks requires investors to make assumptions about the future rate of inflation. Index-linked yields are therefore always published twice: one set on the assumption of 5 per cent inflation, the other on the assumption of 10 per cent. Again, the information here enables changes over the past 24 hours and over the past year to be seen.

The lower part of the table shows, firstly, the movement over the last five days of the FT's own fixed interest indices: one for UK government securities and one for fixed interest securities as a whole. The figures also show the level of each index one year ago and the highs and lows for the current year. In each case, the index is composed of only a sample of relevant securities. The footnotes to the table show the base years (1926 and 1928).

Lastly, in the bottom right hand corner, we see the movement over the last five days in an index for the volume of trading in UK gilt edged stock. The top line shows the simple index level for each day; the bottom line shows the level each day of the index averaged over the preceding five days.

There is also a table which provides summary

---

14 That is, from 4 to 2 'ticks' and from 8 to 4 'ticks' respectively.

Box 10.7   Bond data from the *Financial Times*

FTSE Actuaries Govt. Securities   UK Indices

Price Indices UK Gilts	Wed Oct 30	Day's change %	Tue Oct 29	Accrued interest	xd adj. ytd		··· Low coupon yield ··· Oct 30 Oct 29 Yr. ago	· Medium coupon yield · Oct 30 Oct 29 Yr. ago	··· High coupon yield ··· Oct 30 Oct 29 Yr. ago
1 Up to 5 years (21)	121.45	−0.28	121.78	2.71	8.04	5 yrs	7.20 7.06 7.45	7.11 7.46	7.29 7.17 7.55
2 5-15 years (19)	149.49	−0.31	149.95	2.82	9.09	15 yrs	7.81 7.82 8.03	7.81 8.07	7.83 7.84 8.16
3 Over 15 years (8)	166.78	0.27	166.33	3.76	9.83	20 yrs	7.91 7.92 8.08 7.88	7.90 8.12	7.91 7.93 8.20
4 Irredeemables (6)	192.02	0.19	191.65	4.64	8.83	Irred.†	7.97 7.99 8.21		
5 All stocks (54)	143.96	−0.18	144.23	2.99	8.92				

Index-linked							····· Inflation 5% ····· Oct 30 Oct 29 Yr. ago		····· Inflation 10% ····· Oct 30 Oct 29 Yr. ago
6 Up to 5 years (2)	202.76	−0.17	203.11	0.46	5.28	Up to 5 yrs	3.13 3.08 3.23		2.47 2.42 2.10
7 Over 5 years (10)	194.23	−0.48	195.16	1.41	4.17	Over 5 yrs	3.57 3.54 3.68		3.37 3.33 3.48
8 All stocks (12)	194.08	−0.44	194.94	1.30	4.21				

Average gross redemption yields are shown above. Coupon Bands: Low: 0%-7¾%; Medium: 8%-10¾%; High: 11% and over. † Flat yield. ytd Year to date.

FT Fixed Interest Indices

	Oct 30	Oct 29	Oct 28	Oct 25	Oct 24	Yr ago	High*	Low*
Govt. Secs. (UK)	93.88	93.90	94.14	94.27	93.83	93.69	96.34	91.59
Fixed interest	115.46	115.31	115.56	115.50	115.40	112.07	116.45	110.74

Gilt Edged Activity Indices

	Oct 29	Oct 28	Oct 25	Oct 24	Oct 23
Gilt Edged bargains	85.3	122.5	97.6	101.1	88.7
5-day average	99.0	106.9	98.9	109.5	120.9

© FTSE International Ltd 1996. All rights reserved. * for 1996. Government Securities high since compilation: 127.4 (09/01/35), low 49.18 (03/01/75). Fixed Interest high since compilation: 133.87 (21/01/94), low 50.53 (03/01/75). Basis 100: Government Securities 15/10/26 and Fixed Interest 1928. SE activity indices rebased 1974.

BENCHMARK GOVERNMENT BONDS

		Coupon	Red Date	Price	Day's change	Yield	Week ago	Month ago
Australia		6.750	11/06	95.6270	+0.410	7.37	7.53	7.97
Austria		5.875	07/06	98.4400	−0.010	6.09	6.08	6.11
Belgium		7.000	05/06	106.1200	−0.010	6.13	6.10	6.37
Canada *		7.000	12/06	103.9500	+0.120	6.46	6.43	7.13
Denmark		8.000	03/06	107.5000	−0.100	6.88	6.85	7.10
France	BTAN	5.500	10/01	102.2925	–	4.98	4.95	5.29
	OAT	6.500	10/06	103.7000	−0.060	6.00	5.98	6.18
Germany Bund		6.250	04/06	101.6100	−0.070	6.02	6.01	6.15
Ireland		8.000	08/06	107.4500	−0.100	6.93	6.90	7.18
Italy		9.500	02/06	108.5800	+0.230	8.16†	8.10	8.84
Japan	No 140	6.600	06/01	122.4122	+0.410	1.50	1.59	1.77
	No 182	3.000	09/05	103.3170	+0.820	2.55	2.69	2.85
Netherlands		8.500	06/06	118.3300	−0.050	5.94	5.93	6.03
Portugal		9.500	02/06	112.1900	−0.510	7.62	7.59	8.05
Spain		8.800	04/06	105.8300	−0.300	7.88	7.81	8.11
Sweden		6.000	02/05	92.0422	−0.410	7.30	7.23	7.62
UK Gilts		8.000	12/00	103–06	−17/32	7.08	6.91	7.05
		7.500	12/06	99–11	−8/32	7.59	7.55	7.78
		9.000	10/08	110–01	−6/32	7.70	7.68	7.91
US Treasury *		6.500	10/06	100–20	+5/32	6.41	6.58	6.71
		6.750	08/26	100–18	+8/32	6.70	6.86	6.93
ECU (French Govt)		7.000	04/06	104.0700	−0.540	6.41	6.35	6.52

London closing. *New York closing   Yields: Local market standard.
† Gross (including withholding tax at 12.5 per cent payable by nonresidents)
Prices: US, UK in 32nds, others in decimal   Source: MMS International

Bond data taken from the 'International Capital Markets' page of the *Financial Times*, 31 October 1996.

---

information about the behaviour of 'Benchmark Government Bonds' in each major financial centre. Benchmark bonds are bonds, usually of five or ten years to maturity, chosen from each major bond market. They are selected for their similar characteristics, which enables comparisons to be made between the behaviour of yields in the different countries. As usual, the table shows us the latest price changes and enables us to see how yields have moved over various, recent, periods of time.

10.7   Eurobonds

In addition to issuing bonds in their domestic market, large borrowers may make use of international bond markets. There are two types of international bonds. The first are known as Eurobonds. These (like all Euro- instruments) are bonds issued in markets other than that of the currency of denomination. A Eurodollar bond, for example, must be issued in a non-US market. The second type are known as

Table 10.4 Eurobond Issues, 1995

By currency of denomination			By country of origin		
Currency	US$mn	% of total	Country	US$mn	% of total
DM	72,691	19.6	Germany	57,240	15.4
FFr	12,733	3.4	France	19,799	5.3
Yen	64,540	17.4	Japan	33,216	8.9
Lira	11,715	3.2	Italy	16,151	4.3
£	21,614	5.8	UK	22,817	6.2
US$	144,408	38.9	US	68,506	18.5
ECU	7,069	1.9			
Other	36,551	9.8	Other	153,592	41.4
Total	371,321	100.0	Total	371,321	100.0

Source: ONS, *Financial Statistics*, April 1996, Pt 1, § 1, Table BE1a

foreign bonds. These are bonds denominated in the same currency as the market in which they are issued, but issued by a non-resident. (These are the foreign bonds listed in Tables 10.2 and 10.3.) The first Eurobond was issued in 1963, but growth of the market was subdued until the 1980s. Table 10.4 gives details of the issue of Eurobonds in 1995. It shows the distribution of issues by country, and the distribution by currency. The importance of Eurobonds denominated in US$ and the importance of US Eurobond issues are both immediately obvious.

There are many reasons behind the growth of Euromarkets. Like other financial instruments, the attractiveness of Eurobonds to issuers and to holders depends in the short run upon yield relativities. Davis (1992) offers a detailed analysis of short-run variations in Eurobond issues which features these relativities *inter alia*. The longer-run trend, however, is the result of several longer-term factors. The oldest of these goes back to the late 1950s and 1960s and lies in the reluctance of East European countries to hold dollar-denominated assets in the USA for fear that they might be frozen if relations deteriorated sharply enough in the depths of the Cold War. A further reason was the succession of large US current account deficits during the 1970s which led to an accumulation of dollar holdings in Europe. However, most of the explanation lies in various fiscal and other regulations in domestic markets which encouraged borrowers and lenders to find ways of trading which were subject to lighter control. This does not mean that there are no restrictions on

Eurobond dealing. The International Securities Markets Association (ISMA) has drawn up rules and procedures but we shall see that the heavier regulation of domestic markets provides several incentives to issue Eurobonds. The role of regulation in the process of financial innovation is a major contemporary issue and we take it up in Chapters 23 and 24. To make it easy in those chapters to refer back to the development of the Eurobond market as an illustration, we have highlighted the regulatory stimuli responsible for its growth in Box 10.8.

The main influences on the currency of denomination are the demands of international trade together with a desire for denomination in 'strong' currencies. In Table 10.4, therefore, the predominant role of dollar Eurobonds followed by denominations in Japanese Yen and Deutschmarks is hardly surprising.

Just as the development of the whole Eurobond market can be seen as an innovative response to regulations governing other long-term financial instruments, there have been notable innovations within the market. The dominant type of Eurobond remains the 'straight' fixed rate ('straight' or 'bullet') bond (whose price will be determined in the way that we saw earlier in this chapter). As a proportion of total issues, 'straights' have usually accounted for between 60 and 80 per cent. However, the 1980s saw the development of the *floating rate note* (FRN) and a family of equity-related bonds. At various times in the 1980s FRN accounted for nearly 40 per cent of total Eurobond issues while equity-related Eurobonds reached a peak of 30 per cent of issues in 1989. Years

> **Box 10.8   Regulation stimulates Eurobond markets**
>
> There are numerous regulations applying to domestic markets which have encouraged lenders and borrowers to find alternative locations for trading. Amongst those relevant to the Eurobond market are as follows:
>
> - 'Regulation Q' in the USA limited the interest that could be paid on time deposits. This encouraged US residents to keep dollars outside the USA and thus led to the growth of Eurodollar deposits. With time, holders of deposits looked for other dollar assets into which they could diversify without returning the dollars to US regulation.
>
> - Under legislation introduced in 1963, US corporations were restricted in the amount of capital they could raise domestically in order to fund their overseas operations.
>
> - In most countries, interest on bonds is paid net
>
> of tax to domestic holders and witholding tax is deducted on interest paid to overseas bondholders. Eurobonds pay tax gross.
>
> - In most countries, issuers of domestic bonds are required to maintain a register of owners. The cost of maintaining the register is a disadvantage to the issuer and being identified as the owner of bonds is a disadvantage to some bondholders.
>
> - Domestic bond markets usually impose stringent accounting and other disclosure conditions on bond issuers in order that their bonds may be listed (and therefore traded) on recognized securities exchanges. Again this imposes costs but it also slows down the issuing process, exposing the firm to the risk of changes in financial conditions between the decision to issue and raising the funds.

of high equity-related issue have tended to be years of low FRN issue and vice versa, leaving the dominant position of straights untouched. FRNs are bonds whose coupons are set by adding a mark-up to some variable benchmark interest rate, often LIBOR or the interbank rate in some other centre. Coupons are paid at six-monthly intervals and are re-set each time in the light of changes in the benchmark rate. Equity-related bonds are bonds which give their holders some future access to the issuer's equity stock. *Convertible Eurobonds*, like convertible domestic bonds, give the holder the right to convert into the equity stock of the issuer at some specified time in the future and on terms which are set out at the time of issue of the bond. Alternatively, bonds may have *equity warrants* attached. Warrants give the bondholder the option to convert to equity on specified terms but, unlike convertibles, the warrants are securities in their own right and can be detached and sold separately.

The main issuers of Eurobonds are sovereign governments, banks (including building societies in the UK) and large corporations. In 1993, for example, 25 per cent of all FFr Eurobond issues were made by Crédit Local de France, SNCF, Crédit National and the European Investment Bank, while two major issuers of DM Eurobonds were the UK

and Italian governments, wishing to rebuild their DM reserves. The main holders are banks and large managed funds (life assurance, pension funds and unit and investment trusts in the UK).

The method of issue in the primary market has evolved markedly over time. At the moment (1996) the usual method is for an issuer of bonds (the borrower) to approach a *lead manager* for the issuer, usually an investment bank. The lead manager recruits additional banks to form a *syndicate*, within which some banks will be identified as underwriters and sellers. The function of the underwriters is to guarantee to buy the stock at a set minimum price if it cannot be sold above this price by the sellers. The lead manager then buys the whole issue on terms previously agreed with the borrower and then distributes the bonds throughout the syndicate for onward sale to the public. In this arrangement, known as the *bought deal*, the risk (of failing to sell to the public at the anticipated price) lies with the lead manager and the underwriters. Since 1990 it has been common practice to superimpose upon this arrangement an agreement between members of the syndicate not to discount bonds when selling to the public until the issue has been completely disposed of. This is known as the *fixed price re-offer technique*.

The secondary market for Eurobonds centres on *reporting dealers*. These are usually a subdivision of a merchant bank or of a general securities dealer. Each reporting dealer makes a market in a subset of Eurobonds. The dealers are members of the ISMA (see above) and must submit every day a list of the bonds in which they are prepared to deal and the prices and quantities. The ISMA circulates this information publicly. Prices, however, are 'indicative' and not 'firm' as they would be for market makers in most domestic bonds. Reporting dealers can also deal amongst themselves using the facilities offered by inter-dealer brokers (see Section 10.6 above).

Although most European authorities insist that domestic issuers of Eurobonds use lead underwriters in their home country (so it can be said for example that SNCF issues Eurobonds 'out of Paris') London has become and remains the centre for the bulk of new issues. It also accommodates most secondary market trading. In recent years, and partly because of London's success in attracting such a large share of this rapidly growing activity, the question of what makes a financial centre attractive has begun to receive considerable attention (Grilli, 1989; Davis, 1990; Cobham, 1992).

In the case of London and the Euromarkets in general, the following factors appear to be of particular relevance. Firstly, dating from its long-established tradition as a financial centre, London has been able to offer a supply of well-trained labour and a supply of suitable premises concentrated within a relatively compact area. There is also a regulatory regime which is seen as being sympathetic to financial activity in its willingness to consult and in its determination to minimize turnover taxes and barriers to competition. Personal and corporate rates of taxation are now low by international standards. These regulatory benefits are reinforced by a stable political system which is unlikely to produce sudden, radical change. Furthermore, the absence of exchange controls since 1979 has made London an attractive location for a wide range of international activity in recent years. More generally, English language and law are both widely used in international financial business. Fortuitous, but important, is London's position in a time zone which allows trading to run consecutively with the trading in the other two main international financial centres, Tokyo and New York.

10.8 Summary

'Bonds' are securities which enable borrowers to raise funds for long periods but leave lenders with the convenience of being able to sell their loan if they need to retrieve their funds. As a general rule, bonds pay a fixed rate of interest and have a fixed period to maturity. These are the 'plain' bonds on which we concentrated in this chapter. The price of bonds depends upon the coupon which they pay, upon the current level of market interest rates and the residual period of the bond's life. The prices of bonds with a long residual maturity are generally more interest-sensitive than the prices of short-dated bonds. As with all assets, the yield on bonds varies inversely with their price. There are several measures of bond yields.

If we plot the yield on bonds against the residual period to maturity, we often observe a pattern. This distribution of yields is known as the term structure of interest rates and the plot is known as a time/yield curve. There are several theories of what determines this pattern of yields. The expectations theory is particularly interesting since it says that current long-term rates are the average of expected future rates. It is an interesting theory since, if it is true, *and* if expectations are generally correct, then we can derive implied future short-term interest rates and the derivations will generally be correct.

Once issued, bonds are traded in a secondary market for which there exist a variety of trading arrangements. As a general rule, trading in bonds is carried out by firms which also deal in company shares and other securities, though dealers in government bonds are often subject to regulations which are additional to those of the stock market in which they work. The market for government bonds is generally much larger than the corporate bond market. Most European markets have recently embarked on a series of reforms similar to those that occurred in London in 1986. One significant difference, however, is that European centres have opted for 'continuous auctioneer' ('order-driven') rather than 'continuous dealer' ('quote-driven') markets.

Key concepts used in this chapter

Eurobonds
Foreign bonds
Original maturity
Residual maturity
Par value
Coupon
Coupon rate
Bearer bonds
Zero coupon bonds
Straight bonds
Debentures
Convertible bonds
Index-linked bonds

Floating rate notes
Bulldog bonds
Accrued interest
Dirty price
Clean price
Market price
Ex dividend
Current, running or
    interest yield
Simple yield to
    maturity
Redemption yield
Holding period yield

Default risk
Reinvestment risk
Capital risk
Credit rating
Junk bonds
Duration
Term structure of
    interest rates
Time yield curve
Term premium
Capital risk aversion
Income risk aversion
Preferred habitat

Expectations theory of
    the term structure
Market segmentation
Floating rate notes
Equity warrants
Convertible Eurobonds
Syndicate
Lead manager
Bought deal
Reporting dealer

Questions and problems

1 Distinguish between clean and dirty bond prices and explain how each is calculated.

2 A bond with four years to maturity and a coupon of 7 per cent has a current market price of £102.50. What is: (a) the current yield; (b) the simple yield to maturity; (c) the redemption yield?

3 A 12 per cent bond will be redeemed at par on 1 March 2002. If the yield to maturity on 2 March 1997 is 8 per cent, what is the price of the bond?

4 Other things being equal, the prices of long-dated bonds are more sensitive to changes in interest rates than are the prices of short-dated bonds. Why is this the case?

5 Outline the possible effects upon bond prices of each of the following events and explain your reasoning. (Assume that each occurs in isolation from the others.)
   (a) The current account shows an unexpectedly large deficit;
   (b) In the midst of a recession, the central bank announces a small cut in interest rates;
   (c) Three months before an election, with the economy growing strongly, the government announces a cut in income tax;

   (d) An increase in the central government borrowing requirement which was widely expected;
   (e) The price of oil falls unexpectedly;
   (f) The Bundesbank announces an increase in money supply which exceeds the target range.

6 If the current (redemption) yield on bonds with one year to maturity is 6 per cent, while the yield on bonds maturing in three years is 8 per cent, what does this imply about one-year yields in three years' time?

7 What assumptions have you had to make in Question 6 in order to obtain a forecast of the future spot rate?

8 In what circumstances might the shape of the yield curve tell you something about (a) the future level of interest rates and (b) the future rate of inflation?

9 Why might the yield curve incorporate a *positive* term premium.

10 Who are the main participants in bond markets?

11 Why is it possible for governments to run repeated budget deficits without causing bond yields to rise continuously?

Further reading

A: General

Bank of England Quarterly Bulletin, 'Bond Prices and Market Expectations of Inflation', 35 (1995), 160–5

Bank of England Quarterly Bulletin, 'The Gilt-edged Market: The Bank of England's relationship with the gilt-edged market makers and inter-dealer brokers', 37 (1997) 199–201

Bank of England Quarterly Bulletin (1995) 'Changes in UK Gilt-edged and Money Markets', February

D Blake, *Financial Market Analysis* (London: McGraw-Hill, 1990) Ch. 5

M Buckle and J Thompson, *The UK Financial System* (Manchester: Manchester U P, 1995) Ch. 9

D Cobham (ed.) *Markets and Dealers: The Economics of the London Financial Markets* (London: Longman, 1992)

J Culbertson, 'The Term Structure of Interest Rates', *Quarterly Journal of Economics*, 71 (4) (1957)

K Cuthbertson, *Quantitative Financial Economics* (London: Wiley, 1996)

E P Davis, 'International Financial Centres – an Industrial Analysis', *Bank of England Discussion Paper*, 51 (1990)

E P Davis, 'The Eurobond Market', in D Cobham (ed.), *Markets and Dealers: The Economics of the London Financial Markets* (London: Longman, 1992)

E J Elton and M J Gruber, *Modern Portfolio Theory and Investment Analysis* (Chichester: John Wiley, 5e, 1995) Chs 20, 21

Euromoney

I Fisher, *The Theory of Interest* (New York: Macmillan, 1930)

V Grilli, 'Europe 1992: Issues and Prospects for the Financial Markets', *Economic Policy*, (1989) 4, 388–421

R Harington, 'The Sterling Bond Market', in D Cobham (ed.), *Markets and Dealers: The Economics of the London Financial Markets* (London: Longman, 1992)

J R Hicks, *Value and Capital*, (Oxford: Clarendon Press, 1939)

M Kohn, *Financial Institutions and Markets* (New York: McGraw-Hill, 1994) Ch. 19

M Livingston, *Money and Financial Markets* (Oxford: Blackwell, 3e 1996) Ch. 10

F R Macauley, *Some theoretical problems suggested by movements in interest rates, bond yields and stock prices in the US since 1856* (New York: NBER, 1938)

B. Malhiel, *The Term Structure of Interest Rates* (Princeton: Princeton Univ. Press, 1966)

J Madura, *Financial Markets and Institutions* (New York: West) Ch. 6

N G Mankin and J A Niron, 'The Changing Behaviour of the Term Structure of Interest Rates', *Quarterly Journal of Economics*, 101 (1986)

F S Mishkin, *The Economics of Money, Banking and Financial Markets* (New York: Scott Foresman, 2e 1989) Ch.4

F Modigliani and R Sutch, 'Innovations in Interest Rate Policy', *American Economic Review* (1966)

M Pagano and A Roell, 'Trading Systems in European Stock Exchanges: Current Performance and Policy Options', *Economic Policy*, (1990) 10, 65–115

M Pagano and A Roell, 'Auction and Dealership Markets: What is the Difference?', *European Economic Review*, (1992)

L S Ritter and W L Silber, *Principles of Money, Banking and Financial Markets*, (New York: Basic Books, 7e, 1992) Ch. 29

R Roll, *The Behaviour of Interest Rates*, (New York: Basic Books, 1970)

S Valdez, *An Introduction to Western Financial Markets* (London: Macmillan, 1993) Ch. 6

R Vaitilingam, *The Financial Times Guide to Using the Financial Pages* (London: Pitman, 3e 1996)

B: Sources of data

Bank of England Quarterly Bulletin (every issue), 'Financial Market Developments'

Euromoney (monthly) and *Euromoney Country Surveys* (annual) (London: Euromoney Publications)

Federation of European Stock Exchanges, *Stock Exchange Fact Sheet* (monthly)

OECD, *Financial Market Trends* (triannual) (OECD: Paris)

OECD, *Financial Statistics*, part 1, § 1 and 2 (monthly) (OECD: Paris)

Stock Exchange Quarterly (London: London Stock Exchange)

Stock Exchange Quality of Markets Fact Sheet (quarterly) (London: London Stock Exchange)

Equity markets

Box 11.1

What you will learn in this chapter:

- The types and characteristics of ordinary company shares
- A variety of approaches to evaluating the market price of shares
- Why share prices behave as they do
- The characteristics of equity trading arrangements, their main participants and recent developments
- How to read, interpret and analyse equity market reports

11.1   Introduction

For many people, the phrase 'financial markets' means equity markets. This is curious because we shall see that in many financial centres the amount of trading in equities, measured by value, falls a long way short of trading in bonds and a long way short of trading in foreign exchange. And yet general news broadcasts on radio and television invariably quote the latest movement in some index of equity prices, when they would not consider for a moment broadcasting information on bond yields or money market interest rates, both of which have considerable relevance to everyone.

There are several reasons for the disproportionate amount of popular attention focused on equities.

Firstly, it is equity markets that have provided the most spectacular fluctuations in the history of financial markets. There are many examples of spectacular crashes (preceded by major booms of course) including: the South Sea Bubble of 1720; the Mississippi Bubble of 1719–20; the Wall Street Crash of September 1929 and the Crash of October 1987.[1] Secondly, it may simply be that there is more 'news' behind company shares. Most bond markets are dominated by government bonds and their prices are driven, as we have seen, by whole market events such as changes in interest rate expectations. The price of individual corporate bonds can be affected by company-specific events, but the impact will always be limited because of the fixed coupon payment and the preferential claim that a bondholder has on a firm's assets. It is ordinary company shares that hold out the prospect of truly large gains and losses. Company share prices are continually affected by company-specific events and these can be quite colourful, ranging from the company chairman who describes his own products as rubbish, or drowns at sea with the workers' pension funds, to the discovery by a research team of a treatment for AIDS. Since ordinary shareholders have a residual claim on profits and profits can range from the negative to the infinite, the potential for losses and gains is correspondingly large. Thirdly, since shareholders are the legal owners of firms, the buying and selling of shares involves the transfer of ownership. Sometimes that transfer itself is news,

---

[1] A useful survey and discussion of these events is contained in Garber (1990). A much more detailed but highly readable account of the 1929 crash is in Galbraith (1961) while the *Bank of England* *Quarterly Bulletin*, February 1988, contains an article which describes and offers some explanation of the events of 1987.

especially if one firm is making an unwelcome bid to take over another, since mergers and takeovers may involve 'rationalizations' and redundancies. These in turn can affect employees of the two firms and perhaps even a regional economy if a large plant is closed.

A fourth possible reason is that many European governments are now following the policy begun 15 years ago in the UK of privatizing hitherto state-owned firms. To take just a few famous examples, since 1993, the German government has privatized Lufthansa and Deutsche Telekom, France has privatized Banque National de Paris and Elf Aquitaine. In Italy, Credito Italiano and Banca Commerciale Italiana are now in private hands. The two main reasons behind these privatizations are firstly that state-owned firms providing goods and services which are already provided by the private sector are less efficient, and secondly that firms in private ownership are probably more likely to take advantage of cross-border merger and amalgamation opportunities that will arise as the European market becomes more integrated. However, there may be another reason. We shall see below (Section 11.5) that all continental stock markets have been very concerned about losing business to London since the reforms that took place there in 1986. One certain effect of these privatizations will be to increase sharply the size of domestic markets in securities. For example, the French privatization programme, relaunched in 1993, is planned to raise FFr280 bn which is the equivalent of 10 per cent of the value of equities quoted on the Paris Bourse in 1993. Furthermore, like the UK Thatcher governments in the 1980s, the French government has linked privatization to attempts to popularize individual direct shareholding. 1992 saw the introduction of the 'Plan d'Epargne en Actions' which, like personal equity plans in the UK, enabled 'small' investors to invest in shares without becoming liable to capital gains and income tax; in 1993 'Balladur bonds' were introduced to enable savers to buy a fixed interest rate instrument which would be convertible later (in 1997) into the shares of privatized firms. These incentives were also linked to the development of the domestic stock market through the argument that small investors would always prefer to trade in their 'home' exchange. The scope for encouraging indi-

vidual direct investment is considerable: direct investment in equities is limited to about 5 per cent of households in France and Germany, compared with 20 per cent in the UK (and USA). It follows from this that in continental Europe, the ownership of company shares is even more concentrated in the hands of financial institutions than it is in the UK. In particular, it is banks that are major shareholders, which is a further contrast with the UK where banks hold only short-dated fixed interest securities and shares are held largely by pension funds, long-term insurance companies and mutual funds. We return to these differences between financial systems in Part 5 of the book, noting for now that the privatization programmes have raised the profile of equity markets in the popular imagination.

Table 11.1 shows the scale of privatization receipts in 1995.

Table 11.1 Privatization receipts, 1995 (US$ mn)

France	Germany	Italy	Japan	UK	USA
5,715	518	7,191	–	4,747	250

Source: OECD, *Financial Market Trends*, Spring 1996, p.17

In this chapter, the next section outlines the characteristics of ordinary company shares. Section 11.3 explains a number of approaches to valuing shares, concentrating upon dividend discount models but touching briefly on other methods, including technical analysis. In the course of these discussions it will become apparent that the events that can cause people to change their view of the appropriate value of company shares are many and varied, compared with those that affect bonds, for example. For this reason, we include a section (11.4) which shows how a selection of typical events can be connected with changes in share prices – individually and in the aggregate, in the short and the long run – using the formal models that we have examined in Section 11.3. Section 11.5 discusses the characteristics of equity markets in Europe and elsewhere, including data on capitalization and turnover. It continues the discussion about trading structures that we began in Chapter 10 and includes a section on interpreting and analysing the equity market data in the *Financial Times*. Section 11.6 summarizes.

11.2 Company shares: types, characteristics and returns

A joint stock firm, often referred to rather loosely as a 'corporation', is one that can raise capital by the issue of bonds and shares to the general public. At the time of its incorporation, such a firm must specify the quantity (and type) of shares that it proposes to issue. In the UK, these specifications are contained in a firm's *memorandum* and *articles of association*. These documents will specify, for example, the total of *authorized* shares. Authorized shares may be issued, that is, they have been sold to shareholders, or they may be authorized but as yet *unissued*. The two main classes of shares are *equity* (*or ordinary*) shares and *preferred* shares. In the USA, equities are more frequently referred to as *common stock*. The holders of ordinary shares are legally the owners of the firm. This means that they have voting privileges which allow them to appoint and dismiss members of the board of directors; in most countries company legislation also specifies those decisions about which directors have to consult shareholders and obtain their permission. Because they are the owners of the firm, ordinary shareholders receive a share in the profits of a firm after all prior claims have been met. The prior claims include payments to creditors, including interest to bondholders, and all taxes. With the shareholders' permission, the directors will also retain a proportion of profits (the *retention ratio*)[2] in order to finance new investment projects. The shareholder's share of profit is paid in the form of a *dividend* per share. We can now readily see why equities are generally thought to be riskier assets than bonds. With straight bonds, at least, the income (coupon) stream is fixed. With ordinary shares the dividend per share may vary for one or more of several reasons: the trading success of the firm may rise or fall; interest rate or tax changes may take a larger or smaller slice of profits; changes in the retention ratio will cause dividends to rise or fall, even when post-interest, post-tax profit is unchanged. When issued, ordinary shares have a *par* value, though this is of little interest unless the firm

becomes insolvent. The issue price is usually well above the par value and, once issued, it is the market price in which investors are interested.

In addition to receiving a dividend, ordinary shareholders would normally expect to benefit over time from an increase in the capital value of their shares. Each share represents a claim on the *nominal* profits of the firm. These, and thus dividends, will rise over time and if the share price were to remain constant the yield would rise continuously towards infinity. Since the return on shares must bear some relationship to the returns on other assets, it follows that share prices must rise over time if the yield is to remain stable.

Preferred shares pay a fixed dividend (and in that sense are like a bond). Preferred shareholders rank behind bondholders, however. Thus, in periods of low earnings bondholders may be paid when preferred shareholders (and ordinary shareholders also of course) get nothing. Furthermore, unlike bondholders, preferred shareholders have no power to declare the firm insolvent. Predictably, there are many variations on the preference theme. With *cumulative preferred shares*, unpaid dividends are cumulated and become payable when earnings permit. *Convertible preferred shares* carry rights to convert to ordinary shares on specified terms and at specified times. And there are other variations.

The fact that the income stream from ordinary shares is uncertain naturally makes share valuation more difficult (than, say, bond valuation). The difficulties are further increased because it is difficult to establish precisely the degree of risk for any individual share and thus it is difficult to calculate an appropriate rate of discount.

The dominant approach to valuing company shares is known as *fundamental analysis*. This is the approach that we took in Section 5.4. An alternative, which attracts occasional attention, is known as *technical analysis*. In the next section, 11.3, we shall look in some detail at the pricing or valuation of ordinary company shares, concentrating mainly on the former methods, though saying a little also about the latter. Because the behaviour of share prices is subject to so many, and often unpredictable,

---

2 We shall later refer to the *payout ratio*. The payout ration is 1 *minus* the retention ratio.

influences, we devote Section, 11.4 to what causes changes in share prices, rather than summarizing the relevant variables in two boxes as we did for bonds.

11.3 Equity pricing

11.3.1 Dividend models

In Chapter 5 we had an introduction to equity pricing which consisted of discounting a share's dividend payments. This approach gives rise to a series of what are called *dividend models* of share valuation and it grows out of the conventional approach to asset valuation which we are now familiar with. This approach says that the present value of an asset consists of the sum of its future earnings, each discounted at an appropriate rate which recognizes the time we have to wait and the risk or uncertainty attaching to the earnings.

Recall from above that company shares have no redemption date or redemption value. In that sense, equities are like perpetual or irredeemable bonds. If we assume that dividend payments go on forever at a constant level, then:

$$PV = \frac{D_1}{(1+K)} + \frac{D_2}{(1+K)^2} + \frac{D_3}{(1+K)_3} + \ldots$$
(11.1)

or, more compactly:

$$PV = \sum_{t=1}^{t=\infty} \frac{D_t}{(1+K)^t}$$
(11.2)

where D stands for the dividend payment and K for the discount rate. If D is given and the payments go on forever, Equation 11.2 simplifies to :

$$PV = \frac{D}{K}$$
(11.3)

which is the same formula that we used for valuing a perpetual bond in Section 5.3.2, except that D, the dividend, replaces C, the coupon, and K replaces i, the rate of interest.

In the last chapter we discounted the coupons of perpetual bonds by the current long-term interest rate

and by simple rearrangement of terms we could show that the long-term interest rate by which we were discounting was also the rate of return that perpetual bondholders would receive if they bought bonds at a price which was equal to the present value arrived at as a result of that discounting. Doing the same here gives us:

$$K = \frac{D}{P}$$
(11.4)

The discount rate thus *is* the rate of return. Furthermore, *in equilibrium*, it must be the case that the rate of return that investors receive must be the *required* rate of return. (If you are doubtful, ask yourself 'why should investors accept anything else?' If the actual return is not equal to the required rate, investors are free to sell (or buy), causing prices and yields to change until they get the return they require)[3]. So now we may say that, in equilibrium, the rate at which future earnings are discounted is the investors' required rate of return.

There is one further equivalence which we need to note. In Equation 11.4, K is also the cost of capital for a firm which is financed solely by the issue of shares with a constant dividend payment. K is the return that investors require and this is the return that they actually receive because the firm pays the current level of dividend. If it wishes to raise new capital by issuing new shares at this price, then the firm must accept the future commitment to pay this level of dividends. Imagine for a moment that the firm cut its dividend, trying to reduce the cost of its new capital. If $\bar{K}$ is the *required* rate of return investors will accept the new issue of shares only when the price falls to a level that preserves the value of $\bar{K}$. Let us repeat: if $\bar{K}$ is the rate of return required by investors, then this is the cost that the firm has to pay for new capital.

As we have seen, the required rate of return for equities is represented by $\bar{K}$ and this is the same $\bar{K}$ which we saw derived, in Chapter 3, with the help of the capital pricing model. For an asset, A, recall:

$$\bar{K}_A = K_{rf} + \beta_A(K_m - K_{rf})$$

where K_{rf} is the risk-free rate of interest, $K_m - K_{rf}$ is the whole market risk premium and β_A is an index of the riskiness of asset A when compared with the

---

3 The ideas being discussed here were first treated, in a very basic way, in Sections 5.3.1 and 5.3.2.

market as a whole. Thus, in Equation 11.3, we discount the perpetual, and constant, dividend stream by a rate $\overline{K}$ which takes into account the current level of risk-free rates, the market's pricing of average or benchmark risk as represented by the whole market portfolio, and the riskiness of the asset itself.

However, while equities may be like perpetual bonds in having no redemption date or value, the assumption of constant dividend payments is clearly quite unrealistic. We noted above that equities are riskier than bonds precisely because their dividend payments can fluctuate for a variety of reasons. Furthermore, with the passage of time one would expect dividends on average to grow. This is because new investment enlarges the firm's productive capital, leading to larger output, and also because dividends are paid out of money profits and inflation will cause money values to increase, even when there is no change in volume. We could make the model rather more realistic, therefore, by allowing dividends to grow.

The simplest assumption that we can make about growth is that growth occurs at a constant rate, g. Thus:

$$PV = \frac{D_1}{(1+\overline{K})} + \frac{(1+g)D_1}{(1+\overline{K})^2} + \frac{(1+g)^2 D_1}{(1+\overline{K})^3} +$$

$$\frac{(1+g)^3 D_1}{(1+\overline{K})^4} + \dots \qquad (11.5)$$

Simplifying Equation 11.5 and assuming that the market prices the share at its present value, then:

$$P_0 = PV = \frac{D_1}{(\overline{K}-g)} \qquad (11.6)$$

where P_0 is the current price. Equation 11.6 is known as the *constant growth model*, or *Gordon growth model* after Gordon (1962).

Notice that we can rearrange Equation 11.6 in order to show that the required rate of return, $\overline{K}$, is the sum of the dividend yield and the rate of growth of dividends.

$$\overline{K} = \frac{D_1}{P_0} + g \qquad (11.7)$$

Notice also that g is the rate of capital appreciation, so that Equation 11.7 is equivalent to writing the total return on a share as its current yield plus its capital growth. The equivalence between the growth of dividends and the rate of capital appreciation can be seen when we consider that if:

$$P_0 = \frac{D_1}{(\overline{K}-g)} \qquad (11.8)$$

then the price in the next period must be:

$$P_1 = \frac{D_2}{(\overline{K}-g)} \text{ where } D_2 = D_1(1+g) \qquad (11.9)$$

Thus:

$$P_1 = \frac{D_1}{(\overline{K}-g)}(1+g) \qquad (11.10)$$

Substituting Equation 11.8 into Equation 11.10:

$$P_1 = P_0(1+g) \qquad (11.11)$$

The change in price between one period and the next takes place at the rate $(1+g)$. That g is the percentage capital gain is then easily shown by rearranging Equation 11.11:

Exercise 11.1 Share valuation – dividend models

Wyndham Wines plc is a company whose dividends have been growing at a steady 15 per cent for the past few years. *Last* year it paid a dividend of 30p. Its shares are calculated to have a β-coefficient of 1.4, while the risk-free rate of interest is 6 per cent and the market risk premium is 10 per cent.

Using Equation 11.6, calculate a 'fair price' for Wyndham Wines' shares.

Suppose now that the central bank raises the official interest rates by 1 per cent, the market risk premium and the share's β-coefficient being unchanged. What

effect will this have on the price of Wyndham Wines' shares?

Suppose now that in the course of the year Wyndham Wines announces the disposal of a soft-drinks subsidiary in Spain. This part of the business has always had highly variable earnings and analysts calculate that selling it off should reduce Wyndham Wines' β-coefficient to 1.3. Calculate a new fair price.

Answers are in Box 11.2.

Box 11.2   Some solutions

The fair price is given by Equation 11.6:

$$P_0 = D_1 / (K - g)$$

If we take the data given in Exercise 11.1 for purposes of illustration, we can calculate an initial fair price of Wyndham Wines shares as follows:

$$D_1 = D_0 (1 + g) = 30p (1 + 0.15) = 34.5p$$

$$\overline{K} = K_{rf} + \beta(K_m - K_{rf}) = 6\% + 1.4(10\%) = 20\%$$

$$g = 15\%$$

Thus:

$$P_0 = 34.5 / (0.2 - 0.15) = 690p \text{ or } £6.90$$

If the central bank raises official interest rates from 6% to 7% and all else is unchanged, then we have to recalculate $\overline{K}$.

$$\overline{K} = 7\% + 1.4(10\%) = 21\%$$

Substituting 21% in the denominator,
$$P_0 = 34.5 / (0.21 - 0.15) = 575p \text{ or } £5.75$$

If Wyndham Wines reduces its β-coefficient by disposing of a problem subsidiary, then, with all else unchanged, $\overline{K} = 7\% + 1.3(10\%) = 20\%$. Thus:

$$P_0 = 34.5 \div (0.2 - 0.15) = 690p \text{ or } £6.90$$

The price returns to its original level.

$$P_1 = P_0 + gP_0 \tag{11.12}$$

and thus:

$$g = \frac{P_1 - P_0}{P_0} \tag{11.13}$$

In Equation 11.6 $\overline{K}$ must be greater than g in order to yield a finite result. In practice, this condition is likely to hold if we remember that $\overline{K}$ is the cost of capital to firms. Imagine for a moment that the situation were reversed, that is, $g > \overline{K}$. The growth rate would exceed the cost of capital. This would be extraordinarily fortunate for any firm and the firm would expand as rapidly as it could. Its demand for capital would push up $\overline{K}$ and this would be further reinforced as other firms were attracted into the market. As a result of this expansion, demand would eventually be satisfied and g would fall. The rise in $\overline{K}$ and the fall in g would eventually reverse the inequality. $\overline{K} < g$ is not a sustainable condition.

Consider now the origins of g. Assume, for a moment, constant prices. The growth of the firm's earnings depends upon how much it adds to its capital stock, that is, its net investment, and the productivity of that additional investment. Let E_t stand for the firm's earnings, v_t for net investment and ϕ for the payout ratio – the fraction of earnings paid out as dividends. (All variables are in per-share form.) Then:

$$v_t = (1 - \phi) E_t \tag{11.14}$$

Assume that the investment generates a return of ω per year, then earnings will increase by ωv_t per year. Thus:

$$E_{t+1} = E_t + \omega v_t = E_t[1 + \omega(1 - \phi)] \tag{11.15}$$

And since:

$$E_t[1 + \omega(1 - \phi)] = E_t(1 + g) \tag{11.16}$$

by definition, then:

Exercise 11.2   Share prices and yields

In Exercise 11.1 we saw that the required rate of return on Wyndham Wines plc's shares was 20 per cent p.a.

1   Using the information given in Exercise 11.1, identify separately the dividend yield component and the capital gain component.

2   Suppose that there is a reduction in the market

price of risk so that the market risk premium falls to 9 per cent, risk-free rates remaining at 6 per cent and the β-coefficient remaining at 1.4. What happens to (a) the total return on Wyndham Wines' shares and (b) the dividend yield?

Answers at end of this chapter

$$g = \omega(1 - \phi) \qquad (11.17)$$

If we now substitute Equation 11.17 into Equation 11.6 we are on the verge of some interesting discoveries.

$$P_0 = \frac{D_1}{\overline{K} - \omega(1 - \phi)} \qquad (11.18)$$

Remember that ϕ is the payout ratio (or 1 *minus* the retention ratio), the fraction of earnings paid out as a dividend. We can now rewrite the numerator of (11.6):

$$P_0 = \frac{\phi E_1}{\overline{K} - \omega(1 - \phi)} \qquad (11.19)$$

Notice that changing the payout ratio changes both the numerator and the denominator, and *in the same direction*. A reduction in the payout ratio reduces the

dividend payment, but it also increases the growth rate. This is what, intuitively, one would expect. If the firm pays out less as dividends, retaining more of its earnings in order to invest more, one might expect that shareholders will lose dividend income but one might also expect some compensation in the form of faster capital gain. Indeed, we can show that if a firm is in the long-run equilibrium position where the return on new capital investment is just equal to its cost of capital that is,$(\overline{K} = g)$, and we also assume:

- Taxation which does not discriminate between capital gains and income
- Zero transactions costs in buying and selling equities

then the compensation when the payout ratio changes is complete. The reduction (for example) in dividend

---

Box 11.3   Dividend payouts and the value of shares

If we assume that a firm uses all retained earnings to finance new investment and that there is no other source of investment funds, then Equations 11.6 and 11.19 are equivalent. Imagine now a firm whose earnings or profits are the equivalent of 50p per share and it has a policy of paying out half of its earnings as dividends, retaining the rest for investment projects which produce a real return of 20 per cent p.a. In equilibrium, the return on capital projects will equal the required rate of return and so this too is 20 per cent p.a.. Assume, finally, that its earnings growth rate has been steady at 10 per cent p.a. for the last few years. Then, from Equation 11.19 we can see that:

$$P_0 = 0.5(50p) / [0.2 - 0.2(1 - 0.5)]$$
$$= 25p / [0.2 - 0.1]$$
$$= 25p / 0.1 = 250p = £2.50$$

Suppose now that the firm takes the decision to invest more of its earnings and raises the retention ratio to 60 per cent. If all else is unchanged, then:

$$P_0 = 0.4(50p) / [0.2 - 0.2(1 - 0.4)]$$
$$= 20p / [0.2 - 0.12]$$
$$= 20p / 0.08 = 250p = £2.50$$

In these circumstances, the dividend policy pursued by the firm has no effect upon the value of its shares (and no effect upon the cost of capital which remains at 20 per cent). But remember the assumptions that we made:

- The cost of capital must be just equal to the return on capital;
- Income and capital gains must be treated equally by the tax system;
- There must be no transaction costs in the buying and selling of shares.

The last two conditions are important to shareholders. If, for example, capital gains are taxed at a lower rate than income, then shareholders will prefer a lower payout ratio in order to earn more of their return through capital gain. Furthermore, because they keep more of their 20 per cent return after tax, they will be willing to accept a pre-tax rate of return of less than 20 per cent and the cost of capital to the firm will consequently be lower.

As another example, retired shareholders may prefer income to capital gain and thus would demand a higher return (impose a higher cost of capital) if a firm operated a low payout ratio. But if there are no transactions costs, they should have no objection to low payouts and large capital gains because they will be able to create an income by selling some shares every so often, without diminishing the value of their shareholding. This is one of several practices available to shareholders which have become known as the 'home-made alternative'.

Thus the assumptions are important. Dividend policy will *not* be irrelevant if they do not hold.

yield will be just matched by the increase in capital gain, leaving the cost of capital and the return to shareholders unchanged. This is known as the Miller–Modigliani (1961) *dividend irrelevance hypothesis*. Box 11.3 provides a numerical illustration.

Because the Gordon model assumes a constant rate of growth of dividends throughout the whole period of the company's life, it is often referred to as a *one-period* model. Clearly, the assumption that firms grow at a constant rate throughout their life is unrealistic. More typically, we might expect that a firm would grow at a rapid rate in the early years (this could be the period when g is temporarily greater than $\overline{K}$). During this first period, earnings growth may still be constant, but at a high rate. After this initial period, earnings grow more slowly. In this second period, earnings growth may well be constant again, but at a lower rate. In practice, many analysts would take this long-run steady-state growth rate to be equal to the growth rate of nominal *GDP*, since the growth rate of the economy as a whole consists of nothing more than the sum of the growth rates of its productive units. A simple *two-period* model can therefore be constructed in which the current price is calculated by discounting a series of earnings expected to grow at a constant rate, g_1, for a period of

N years, and then at a new constant rate of g_2 indefinitely after N.[4]

In the simplest two-period model, the transition from an unusual to a permanent growth rate is assumed to occur instantly, in one sudden step. This too is rather unrealistic. It is more probable that the end of a high growth period (for example) is indicated by a decline in the growth rate *over a period*, until it settles at the permanent level. This gives rise to a *three-period model*, in which there is a high growth phase, a transition phase and a permanent growth phase. Figure 11.1 shows the behaviour of earnings growth in a simple two-period model (the solid line) and compares it with the behaviour of earnings growth in a three-period model (the dashed line).[5]

11.3.2   Price earnings ratios

In the last section we defined ϕ, the payout ratio, as 1 *minus* the retention ratio. If we let λ be the retention ratio, then we can rewrite Equation 11.17 as:

$$g = \omega\lambda \qquad (11.20)$$

Substituting into Equation 11.7 gives:

$$\overline{K} = \frac{D_1}{P_0} + \omega\lambda \qquad (11.21)$$

Recall, from the last section, that ω, the return on the firm's investment projects, could be less than, equal to, or greater than its cost of capital. Thus $\omega = a\overline{K}$, where $a = <1$, 1 or >1. As we also said in the last section, we might normally expect firms to invest in all those projects up to the point where the productivity of capital just matches the cost of capital (that is, $a = 1$). Recall furthermore that dividends are equal to the fraction of earnings paid out ($D = \lambda y = (1 - \phi)y$). This being so, then:

$$\overline{K} = \frac{(1 - \lambda)E}{P} + \overline{K}\lambda \qquad (11.22)$$

A simple rearrangement of Equation 11.22 then yields:

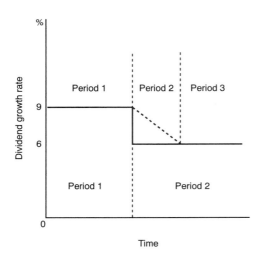

4 See Elton and Gruber (1995) Ch. 18 for details.
5 The mathematics are explained in Elton and Gruber (1995) Ch. 18.

Figure 11.1 Dividend growth in 2 and 3 period models.

$$\bar{K} = \frac{(1-\lambda)E}{(1-\lambda)P} = \frac{E}{P} \qquad (11.23)$$

E/P is the firm's *earnings–price ratio*. In the UK, it is more common to talk about the inverse, P/E, the *price–earnings ratio*. Notice that since $E/P = \bar{K}$, $E/P < 1$, while $P/E > 1$ and so the price–earnings *ratio* is in fact a *multiple*.

Equation 11.23 gives us a means of evaluating a share's price. Simple rearrangement tells us that:

$$P = \frac{E}{\bar{K}} \qquad (11.24)$$

Provided that a firm is investing in projects which are earning just the firm's cost of capital, then if the market price of the share is such that it exceeds $E/\bar{K}$, this is an indication that it is overpriced and a signal to sell. If, however, the market price is below $E/\bar{K}$, it is underpriced and this is a signal to buy.

Notice now what happens if we drop the assumption that the firm is investing in projects whose return just matches its cost of capital, $\omega = \bar{K}$. It was this condition that gave us the relationship in Equation 11.23. If, however, $\bar{K} \neq \omega$, (that is, $a \neq 1$), then the denominator of Equation 11.23 becomes $(1 - a\lambda)$. Inspection of Equation 11.23 shows quite readily that (given values for E and P) the larger is a, the return on investment projects relative to the cost of capital, the higher the value of K, the actual rate of return.

We can now see that if $\omega > \bar{K}$ ($a > 1$), then $K > \bar{K}$ and if $\omega < \bar{K}$ ($a < 1$), then $K < \bar{K}$, where K is the actual rate of return. For a firm where the former condition holds (a rapid growth phase):

$$K = \frac{(1-\lambda)E}{(1-a\lambda)P} > \bar{K} \qquad (11.25)$$

But in equilibrium the actual rate of return must match the return required by shareholders. If $K > \bar{K}$ the prospect of this excess rate of return will encourage net purchases of the stock with the consequence that its price will increase until the actual return is brought into equality with the required return. In other words, a share with high growth prospects will have a lower earnings–price

ratio than one with normal growth prospects. In the UK, of course, this relationship is expressed with reference to the price–earnings multiple. A high growth share has a *high P/E* ratio. Box 11.4 provides an illustration.

It is a short and simple step now to see how the information contained within a firm's P/E ratio can be combined with knowledge of the required rate of return to evaluate the price of a share for a company with *any* type of growth prospects, with a view to buy/sell recommendations. We have merely to find the value of P in Equation 11.25 that makes $K = \bar{K}$. Equation 11.26 shows us how:

$$P = \frac{(1-\lambda)E}{(1-a\lambda)\bar{K}} \qquad (11.26)$$

Box 11.5 provides an illustration.

As a means of evaluating the price of a share, however, one might raise two questions about the use of P/E ratios in this way. Firstly, one might ask, how is it *fundamentally* different from the dividend discount model? We are still, as in the dividend discount model, checking the market price to see whether or not it provides the required rate of return where the required rate of return is still being established by reference to the capital asset pricing model. Furthermore, one might ask, if it is not fundamentally different, does it perhaps have some advantage in convenience? The answer to that is 'not obviously'. In the dividend discount model, we discounted the dividends actually declared by the firm, after allowing for their rate of growth. In Box 11.5, we substituted earnings for dividends but then we needed to know the retention ratio and the rate of return on the firm's investment projects relative to its cost of capital. There is no obvious economy of information or ease of calculation in doing that.[6]

When it comes to the use of P/E ratios in practice, therefore, we should not be surprised if their application is rather different from our illustration above. When we first met the practice of asset valuation (in Section 5.3) we noted that analysts are often interested in *relative* valuation. That is to say

---

[6] Furthermore, there are considerable drawbacks to working with earnings since a firm's published earnings can vary considerably according to the accounting methods being used. This is not an

issue we can pursue here but it is widely discussed in textbooks of corporate finance. There is a very good illustration of the problem in Blake (1990).

Box 11.4   High growth means high *P/E*

Sarum Sausages plc has earnings per share of 50p. It regularly retains one-half of its earnings for investment in new plant and equipment. It is financed entirely by the issue of ordinary shares and its cost of capital is 15 per cent p.a. In the past, the return on new plant has been just enough to match the cost of capital. Equation 11.24 allows us to calculate the fair price of its shares as:

50p/0.15 = 333.33p

However, this year it plans to introduce a new product – wild boar sausages – and calculates that it will be able to earn a return of 20 per cent on the equipment required for the new production line.

The first question we might ask is what will happen to the actual return on Sarum's shares, if everything else, including their price, remains as it is. Substituting the appropriate values in Equation 11.25 gives:

$$K = (1 - 0.5) \times 50 \ / \ (1 - 1.33(0.5)) \times 333.33$$

$$= 25 \ / \ (1 - 0.665) \times 333.33$$

$$= 25 \ / \ 111.665 = 0.2239 = 22.39\%$$

Clearly, therefore, at their current price Sarum's shares would yield a return well in excess of that currently required by shareholders. Naturally enough, the shares will be seen as much more desirable than they previously were. The demand for the shares increases and prices rise. If the required rate of return remains at 15 per cent we can use Equation 11.26 to calculate the new equilibrium price:

$$P = (1 - 0.5) \times 50 \ / \ (1 - 1.33(0.5)) \times 0.15$$

$$= 25 \ / \ (1 - 0.665) \times 0.15$$

$$= 25 \ / \ 0.0502 = 497.5p$$

Look now at the *P/E* ratio in the normal growth phase and the high growth phase. In normal conditions, the *P/E* was 333.33/50 or 6.666. When it became apparent, however, that Sarum faced a particularly rapid period of earnings growth the *P/E* ratio jumped to 497/50 = 9.94.

---

they are more concerned with the question of whether an asset yields a return which is greater than other assets with similar characteristics (or, equivalently, of whether its price is lower). It is for purposes of relative valuation that the *P/E* ratio is more commonly used. We look now at how that is done.

The price–earnings ratio tells us the price that an investor has to pay in order to buy a claim on a flow of earnings (which might be paid out as dividends or retained for re-investment and capital growth). Other things being equal, an investor would prefer to pay the lowest price per £ of earnings. Thus, a firm with a *P/E* ratio below the norm for the sector in which it operates might be considered 'cheap'. Notice, however, that this is only an indication that the share is *relatively* cheap. There is nothing in *this* use of *P/E* ratios to justify the *absolute* level of prices of shares in this sector. Notice also that the share will be relatively cheap if we have indeed compared it with other shares where 'other things are *genuinely* equal!'. A low *P/E* ratio may not indicate underpricing; it may simply indicate that something about the firm

gives its earnings a higher degree of risk and makes it less attractive relative to its earnings. Conversely, a firm with a high *P/E* ratio may not be overpriced. It may be that there are characteristics of the firm that suggest that it has very good growth prospects. Its currently high price, relative to earnings, means that shareholders receive a low dividend yield (D_1/P_0) but this is compensated by a high capital growth rate, *g*. We must be careful to compare like with like.

Because analysts commonly use *P/E* ratios in their assessment of share value, the *P/E* ratio is one of the essential pieces of information that the *Financial Times* publishes daily. Box 11.6 shows an extract from the information published by the *FT* on 5 November 1996.

As Box 11.6 shows, *P/E* ratios can vary quite substantially, even within one sector, but it is important only to compare *P/E* ratios for companies which are strictly comparable. At one end of the P/E range, Gibbs Mew has a *P/E* of 10.3. Gibbs Mew was a small, provincial brewery for whom brewing and beer sales (as opposed to food and entertainment)

Box 11.5 Share pricing by *P/E* ratio

Consider again the situation facing Sarum Sausages in Box 11.4. From Equation 11.20 we know that its new investment should cause earnings growth over the year of $\omega\lambda$, the return on its investment multiplied by the retention ratio. The growth rate in this case, therefore, will be $0.2 \times 0.5 = 0.1$ or 10 per cent. In the next period, therefore, Sarum's earnings should be 55p per share.

Using Equation 11.25 again we can calculate the equilibrium price in the next period, assuming that shareholders still impose a cost of capital of 15 per cent and that the possibility of installing new plant which earns 20 per cent remains.

$$P = (0.5 \times 55) / ((1 - (1.333 \times 0.5)) \times 0.15)$$

$$= 27.5 / (0.335 \times 0.15)$$

$$= 27.5 / 0.0502 = 547\text{p}$$

At a price below £5.47, shares in Sarum Sausages plc are cheap and would be an obvious 'buy' recommendation. At any price above £5.47 the shares are expensive and investors would be recommended to sell before the market re-prices them correctly.

constitute the major part of the business. At the other end of the spectrum, we see Pizza Express and Ramsden's with *P/Es* around 40. These are both fast food outlets which had grown very rapidly in recent years. (There is further discussion of the data in Box 11.6 in Section 11.5 below.)

Used in this way, to try to identify anomalies in relative pricing, we can now see that there are major differences between the dividend discounting approach to share valuation and the *P/E* approach. Firstly, as we said above, comparing *P/E* ratios is an exercise in *relative* evaluation. We cannot ever say that a share is 'fairly priced'. Judged by absolute standards, having regard to risk and the market price of risk, for example, a whole sector of shares may be grossly overvalued, but we still have to say about a company whose *P/E* ratio lies below the sector norm for no apparent reason that it is *undervalued*. The reason for this lies in the second contrast between the two methods. Used in the way we have just described, *P/E* ratios tell us nothing explicit about the quantity of risk or about the price of risk. All the influences on a share's price, except earnings themselves, are bundled up in a collective way in the ratio. Finally, it is worth noting that, in order to be

Box 11.6 *Financial Times* share price data

The table to the right shows the information published by the *Financial Times* on shares in the 'Breweries, Pubs and Restaurants' sector. The name of the company is followed by one or more symbols whose meaning has to be checked in the notes to the whole table. They mainly indicate further information which is available.

The table next shows the price and the change in the price between the opening and closing of trading on 4th November 1996. The next two columns show the highest and lowest price reached in the preceding year. The market capitalisation ('MktCap£m') shows the value of the company at the current share price. Gross yield ('YldGr's) is the (pre-tax) dividend per share divided by the share price. The final column gives the price–earnings ratio.

BREWERIES, PUBS & REST

	Notes	Price	+ or −	52 week high	52 week low	Mkt Cap£m	Yld Gr's	P/E
Aberdeen Steak H.	✠	70	....	90	36	8.40	–	10.5
Bass	†	785½	–1	846½	667	6,928	3.7	16.9
Belhaven Brewery	♣	189½	....	202	189½	38.2	–	14.5
Break for the Border	웃	52½xd	....	76	40	13.0	3.9	16.4
Burtonwood	웃†	178	–2	205	161	37.0	4.0	15.9
Century Inns	웃♣	163½	....	168	115	64.7	–	11.6
City Centre	웃♣	135	....	135½	91	261.9	2.1	25.4
Compass	웃†	610	+2	621	434	1,935	1.6	29.1
Eldridge,Pope A.	웃✠†	245	....	266	172	51.5	2.4	22.6
Enterprise Inns	웃gW	224	....	*237½	135¾	105.7	3.6	16.3
Fuller A.	웃♣	452½	....	540	408	62.0	2.5	15.5
Gibbs Mew	웃♣	307	–1	340	298	42.7	4.1	10.3
Greenalls	웃♣†	571	+3½	636	505	1,685	3.2	15.5
Greene King	웃♣g	650½	....	*671	567¾	393.6	3.0	16.3
Grosvenor Inns	웃♣	199	–1	285	190	28.3	3.6	21.1
Groupe Chez Gerard	웃♣	245xd	....	259	191	45.8	1.4	Φ
Holt (J)	웃†	2775xd	....	3475	2775	80.5	2.6	14.9
Inn Business	♣Z	70½	+1½	72	45	33.5	1.0	33.3
Luminar	L	350½	–4	364½	253	52.6	2.1	19.6
Mansfield	웃	299	....	355	298	193.5	2.5	14.6
Marston Thomp	웃	294	–½	353½	275	265.2	3.1	12.0
Morland	웃♣†	586	....	673	516	161.2	2.6	17.7
My Kinda Town	웃♣	166½xd	....	186½	116	42.0	2.3	Φ
Paramount	웃	6¾	....	7¼	4½	8.01	4.1	10.8
Pembertons Grp	✠	18½	+¼	21	8½	5.12	–	Φ
PizzaExpress	웃♣	503½xa	....	536½	206	305.1	0.7	38.8
Ramsden's (H)	♣	382½	....	438	245	33.7	1.6	41.0
Regent Inns	♣	272½xd	....	*273½	121½	230.0	1.0	31.7
Scottish & New	웃	643	+6½	700	582	3,960	3.8	22.2
Tom Cobleigh	웃♣L	240	....	265	173	95.6	1.4	30.0
Vaux	웃†	248	....	313	246	350.7	5.2	12.8
Wetherspoon (JD)	웃♣	1212½xd	....	1215	635	468.0	0.9	30.9
Whitbread	웃	740½	+7	759	631	3,598	3.7	16.0
Wolv & Dudley	웃†	612	–1½	693	519	410.7	3.2	13.9
Yates Brothers	웃♣	391½	+½	407	273	154.6	1.1	28.7
Young A.		632½	....	650	425	18.3	3.0	25.0
N/V		542½	....	580	367	30.9	3.5	21.4

useful, the *P/E* ratio approach has to assume that equity markets are to some degree inefficient, at least for short periods. That is to say that the approach relies upon being able to find shares which are mispriced relative to others. There is simply no point in examining *P/E* ratios if we begin from the assumption that the market is so efficient that share prices are always 'correct' share prices. We return to this major issue in Chapter 25.

11.3.3   Asset values

It is not uncommon, when reading commentaries on share prices, to meet the statement that 'the current share price is at a premium (or discount) to the firm's asset value'. What the former means is that the present price of the share gives the firm a value which is greater than one would arrive at by valuing its component assets individually and then summing the component values. The implication of the statement, of course, is that the share price is 'too high', should be lower, will probably fall shortly when the market recognizes the anomaly, and should be sold (or at least not bought). Notice immediately that this is again a statement about *relative* value, though this time the comparison is with the underlying assets of the same firm rather than with another firm. As it stands, it says nothing about the underlying assets being correctly valued in any absolute sense. One could defend asset valuation as a source of absolute values, *if* one could argue that the underlying asset values were absolutely correct. If that were so, then a statement that the share price (for example) is at a premium to asset value tells us *both* that it is too high relative to asset values but also that it is absolutely too high, since the underlying assets are correctly valued in an absolute sense. The question this poses, however, is how do we arrive at an absolute valuation for the underlying assets? The answer to that is that we can only get it by the standard practice of discounting the future earnings of those assets by some appropriate, risk-adjusted, discount rate. And if we do that, then we are essentially back to a discounted dividend model of valuation. Thus, if asset valuation is to mean anything strictly different from the approach we outlined in Section 11.2.1, then we have to treat it as

another approach to relative valuation which might be useful in certain circumstances.

Why might one want to use it? One clue is given to us when we examine why the value of the firm, represented by its share price, might differ from the value of its component assets. This often happens because the component assets are valued on the basis of the going market price for similar assets. Thus, one might consider what price could be got for the firm's premises, sold simply as commercial premises. To this one would add the market price of any equipment, sold separately from the site. In addition, there would be market prices for its vehicles, office furniture, stocks of raw materials, finished goods and so on. It is not difficult now to see why share value and asset value (defined in this way) might differ. It is usually the case that the assets, when sold off separately, have to compete with a large number of very similar secondhand assets. However, when combined together in the hands of a skilled management which is able to produce a unique good or service for which there is high demand, the value of the assets when *constituting the firm* could be considerably higher. This is another way of saying that the valuation of the component assets is incomplete. There is something else which adds value when they are combined as this particular firm. The obvious omission is the management or 'human capital' and the reason that it is left out of the valuation is that there is no recognized market for human capital (since the abolition of slavery). The problem is recognized as particularly acute in certain industries. Firms specializing in marketing and other media-related activity provide frequent examples. Their tangible, marketable assets often consist of little more than premises, office furniture and the usual computing and communications equipment. None of this is highly specialized and once placed on the market it competes with a large volume of similar equipment. The bulk of the 'value' of such firms lies in the management and employees. It is their creative skill that enables the firm to generate large earnings relative to its asset value.

On the face of it, therefore, asset valuation does not look generally very useful as a means of determining a share's (and firm's) value. However, we can say that evaluating a share's price by looking at the value of the underlying assets is particularly useful whenever the question of selling the underlying assets arises. Such a situation is almost invariably associated with mergers and takeovers for two reasons.

Firstly, the share price relative to asset value may enable us to identify 'bargains'. If, for example, a firm's share price values it at a discount to its assets, this is saying that the firm can be bought at a price which is less than that which could be realized by selling its assets on the secondhand market. This makes the firm an obvious target for takeover, since the bidding (or predator) firm knows that once it has possession it faces a choice of profitable strategies. It might decide to keep the target firm in operation, using its own management to improve its performance. If this looks unattractive, it can simply close the firm and sell the assets for a higher price than the price it paid.

Secondly, the takeover of a thriving firm may be encouraged if the predator firm thinks that it can sell part of the target business for a profit. In this case, selling some of the target firm's assets is being used to finance the takeover. Doing this successfully depends upon being able to identify some assets in the target firm which are contributing less than their market value to the price of the share. This seems to be possible where the target firm is large and consists of several quite distinct operations. In this situation, the firm's accounts will often make it possible to identify the contribution to total earnings (or dividends) that each division makes. This enables analysts (and predators!) to say whether the earnings of the assets in their present use gives them a value which is greater or less than their value on the open market. In the late 1980s there were a number of takeovers which resulted in the subsequent sale of some or all of the assets taken over. The practice was common enough to acquire its own name, 'asset stripping'.

Where the price of a share values the firm at a discount to its asset value, this is a signal to buy since the undervaluation is not likely to persist for the reasons we have just seen. [7]

11.3.4 Technical analysis

An entirely different approach to the valuation of equities is known as *technical analysis*, or *chartism* to give its popular name. The core of technical analysis uses visual representations of past price movements to identify patterns which, it is believed, repeat themselves. Typically, the past price movement of a security will be plotted using a line or point and figure chart. The analyst then focuses upon the most recent price movement in order to identify a pattern. These patterns go under a variety of colourful names, such as 'head and shoulders', 'wedges', 'flags' and so on. Once such a pattern has been identified, the behaviour of the share in the more distant past can be searched for signs of a similar pattern and, most importantly, the behaviour of the price at the end of that pattern. Sometimes, there will be no comparable pattern in the share's history. Then the analyst will look for the same pattern in similar shares in order to see what happened next in their case. (See also Box 12.6.)

Clearly, we have come a long way from explaining a share's price by reference to its fundamentals. Nothing explains the price in technical analysis except the past movement in the share's price. This is interesting, and makes technical analysis highly controversial in the eyes of many. This is because technical analysis conflicts with the efficient markets hypothesis (which we discuss in Chapter 25). The weakest form of the EMH suggests that all the information that can be obtained from *past* movements in a share's price is already incorporated in the share's *current* price. Thus, if a 'head and shoulders' pattern means that the price is pausing before a major fall, and it is known that this is what a head and shoulders pattern means, then shareholders will sell instantly and the price will fall so quickly that no one can take advantage of the information. According to the weak form EMH, the only thing that can change a share's price is 'news' and news, by definition, is unpredictable. If this is the case, then the ability of technical analysts to predict price movements successfully must be the result of

---

[7] Identifying and recommending shares that value the firm at less than its asset value has often been one strategy followed by newspaper share tipsters.

luck. It will not be sustained; their predictions will eventually go through a correspondingly bad patch and *in the long run* technical analysis will not enable analysts to earn above average returns.

Nonetheless, technical analysis remains very popular. It also contributes to the liquidity of the market since it increases the diversity of views about a share's price. If technical analysis leads some investors to have views about a share's next movement that differ from those of other investors, this simply helps to ensure that there will always be some people willing to buy when others are willing to sell.

11.4 Share price movements

We begin by distinguishing between the behaviour of share prices in the aggregate (what might be called 'equity market movements') and the behaviour of individual share prices. We then distinguish between the short run and the long run.

11.4.1 Whole market – short run

As with bonds, in the short run the supply of equities is fixed. In a market diagram, the supply curve is vertical.[8] The demand curve slopes downward, indicating that when prices are lower (and yields higher) *relative to other assets*, there will be a greater willingness to hold equities. With a given stock, changes in prices (and yields) are the result of demand shifts. Prices will change when investors' perception of the value or fair price of shares in general changes. If something happens to cause investors to put a lower value on shares, for example, the demand curve shifts downward until shares in general seem attractive again at the new price and yield. To explain changes in the *general* level of prices we have to look at general or 'whole market' events.

Look again at Equation 11.6. We know that share prices will change if there are changes to D_1, g or $\bar{K}$.

Investor perceptions of future dividends in general will obviously be responsive to changes in the outlook for the economy as a whole. The movement from boom to recession, for example, or the prospect of a tighter fiscal policy will lead to a 'downgrading' of dividend forecasts. A reduction in the numerator, of course, reduces the value of shares. Similar events might also lead to a downward revision of g, the rate at which future earnings and dividends are expected to grow. Remember also that firms' payout ratios are irrelevant to shareholders only if the tax system is neutral between income and capital gains and transaction costs are zero. Imagine that a newly elected left-wing government reveals plans for higher tax rates on 'unearned' income, perhaps arguing that this will encourage firms to retain earnings (reduce their payout ratios) and increase their investment. As we saw in Box 11.3, shareholders might be quite indifferent to this, if their lower dividends are replaced by larger capital gains, *provided that they can make a costless sale* of a few shares every time they require income. If they cannot, then this tax change will push share prices down, since shareholders will insist on higher pre-tax yields to compensate for the higher tax on dividends.

For many firms, a fall in the exchange rate will lead to an upward revision of g, since imports from competitors will be dearer and the firm's own exports will become cheaper in foreign markets. As a general rule, therefore, a depreciation in the exchange rate helps equity markets, notwithstanding the fact that governments may try to prevent the depreciation, or at least to slow it down, by raising interest rates. An interesting exception to this rule in Europe is the Italian equities market, which almost invariably moves positively with the exchange rate (*Euromoney* (Italy), 1996). A depreciation causes share prices to fall because there are relatively few large exporting firms quoted on the Italian exchanges and so the market has only to take account of the implications for inflation and interest rates. Both are likely to increase and this will depress prices, as we see in the next paragraph.

The largest source of market-wide influences, however, is always likely to be found in interest rates

---

[8] Readers who want to refresh their memory of this should go back to the discussion surrounding Figure 5.2.

or expectations of interest rate movements. Recall that $\overline{K}$ in Equation 11.6 is the sum of a risk-free rate and a risk premium derived from the market's current pricing of risk in general ($K_m - K_{rf}$) and the firm's relative risk characteristics, β. A change in β, of course, reflects a change in the characteristics of the firm itself and is therefore not relevant in this context. However, a change in official interest rates causes a change in K_{rf} and, other things being equal, must cause a change in $\overline{K}$. (Precisely this case is discussed in Case Study number 1.) Notice that a general change in $\overline{K}$ would follow also if there were a change in the market's risk aversion. If, for example, investors generally took the view that equities as a class of assets were becoming more risky, then the market risk premium ($K_m - K_{rf}$) would widen, increasing $\overline{K}$ for all equities and leading to lower prices.

11.4.2 Individual shares – short run

Individual shares will, of course, be affected by all those events that affect the prices of shares in general. However, there will in addition be firm-specific events which have their impact on D_1, g and $\overline{K}$. The first two may obviously be boosted by news of new product developments or by the granting of new patents giving a firm protection to exploit a particular product for a specified period. Conversely, a firm's share price is likely to react badly when a profitable patent comes to an end or a rival develops a competing or superior product. Through most of 1996, the shares in 'privatized utilities' in the UK were depressed because of plans by the Labour Party to impose a windfall tax if they formed the next government. The argument behind the windfall tax was that these ex-nationalized firms had been sold to the private sector at too low a price (at a cost to the general taxpayer in other words) and that since then shareholders had made unreasonable gains. Throughout Europe and the United States, firms are subject to legislation to deter restrictive practices and the development of monopolies which might work against the public interest. News that a firm is to be investigated by the anti-monopoly authorities is often sufficient to cause a fall in its share price – not just because it may have to end some monopoly practice which has been profitable in the past (driving down

D_1 and g), but simply because the inquiry itself is expected to divert a large amount of management time and effort which would have gone into running the firm into preparing answers to the regulator's questions. Another development that often gives rise to the most spectacular short-term price rises is news of a takeover bid, especially if that takeover bid is resisted. The market regards the bid as evidence either that the bidding firm can operate the assets of the target firm more efficiently (raising future levels of D and perhaps g as well) or simply that the target company is underpriced. (This raises serious questions about the efficiency with which the market values firms, an issue we discuss in Chapter 25.) Even if shareholders doubt that the firm will be more profitable in the long run, a contested bid almost invariably results in the bidding firm having to make one or more higher offers. Naturally, if it raises the price at which it is prepared to buy the shares, their price goes up.

It is possible also for firm-specific events to have their impact on $\overline{K}$. Recall that the firm-specific component of $\overline{K}$ is β, an index of the firm's riskiness relative to a whole market portfolio. Many large corporations consist of a widely diversified range of subsidiaries, often the result of past takeovers and mergers. It is not unusual for some subsidiaries to perform better than others, nor is it unusual for subsidiaries to have different risk characteristics. (These differences were often the reason for combining them in the first place!) Where this is the case, then the β-coefficient of the whole corporation, β_c is just the value-weighted average of the β's of the individual subsidiaries. Formally:

$$\beta_c = \sum w_s \cdot \beta_s$$

where w_s is the value of each subsidiary expressed as a fraction of total firm value, and β_s is the β-coefficient of each subsidiary. We can now see that the acquisition (or disposal) of any subsidiary whose individual ß differs from the corporation average, β_c, must cause a change in β_c. Thus, even if interest rates remain unchanged and there is no change in the market's pricing of risk, the riskiness of the firm itself can change, causing a rise (or fall) in the required rate of return $\overline{K}$.

In Box 11.7, we have reproduced the table called 'Highlights of the Week' which is published every

Box 11.7   Changes in share prices

The table below is taken from the *Financial Times*, 9 November 1996. It shows thirteen major price changes for individual stocks and the changes in two popular share indices. The first column of figures shows the price at Friday's close. This is followed by the total price change over the week and then the highest price and the lowest price in the previous 52 weeks. For our purposes, it is the last column which is most interesting since it tries to suggest some reason for each of the price changes.

For the two indices which try to represent share price movements 'in general' we must expect some market-wide event. We are told that the market in general declined because of 'inflation concerns'. In our formal models, this worry about inflation enters as a worry about future increases in interest rates. These would raise K (and might also reduce g). The other events are all specific to individual shares and illustrate well the range of events which can have an impact on individual share prices.

■ Highlights of the week

	Price y'day	Change on week	52 week High	52 week Low	
FTSE 100 Index	3910.8	−37.7	4073.1	3523.4	**Inflation concerns**
FTSE 250 Index	4395.6	−33.6	4568.6	3887.7	**Inflation concerns**
Airtours	670	−12$\frac{1}{2}$	714	308	**MMC investigation**
British Airways	576$\frac{1}{2}$	+19$\frac{1}{2}$	615	453	**Hope over US/UK trade talks**
BT	361$\frac{1}{2}$	+10$\frac{1}{2}$	385	326$\frac{1}{2}$	**MCI merger deal**
Compass Group	597$\frac{1}{2}$	+10$\frac{1}{2}$	621	434	**SBC Warburg placing**
East Midlands Elect	593$\frac{1}{2}$	+49	744	479	**Takeover signal**
Fairway Group	81$\frac{1}{2}$	−28	117$\frac{1}{2}$	80$\frac{1}{2}$	**Profits warning**
JKX Oil & Gas	119	−9$\frac{1}{2}$	191	105$\frac{1}{2}$	**Fund manager reduces stake**
Lloyd Thompson	174	+4$\frac{1}{2}$	194	135$\frac{1}{2}$	**Share buy-back**
Mackie Int	145	−71$\frac{1}{2}$	387$\frac{1}{4}$	109	**Profit warning**
Northern Elect	605$\frac{1}{2}$	−25$\frac{1}{2}$	724	484	**Bid referral worries**
PowerGen	546$\frac{1}{2}$	+27$\frac{1}{2}$	625	462	**UBS "buy" recommendation**
Rolls-Royce	246$\frac{1}{2}$	−5	270	156	**MAM sells stake**
Roxboro Group	123	−97	316	123	**Profit warning**

Saturday in the UK *Financial Times* and shows the change in two major share price indices over the week together with the major changes in individual share prices. The final column offers some very brief explanation for each change. It provides a useful illustration of the variety of events that can affect individual share prices.

Exercise 11.3   Share price changes

Look at the list of events said to cause changes in share prices in the table of Box 11.7. For each individual share, try, so far as possible, to explain how the event fits into our formal models of share price behaviour.

Suggestions are provided in the appendix to this chapter.

Before leaving this discussion of short-term changes in share prices, remember that price movements only need events to be *expected*. If people *expect* an announcement of lower profits, they will sell as quickly as possible. They will certainly sell before the announcement itself, and the selling will drive prices down. And the selling will drive prices down even if the expectation turns out to be wrong. If the expectation is wrong, share prices may recover again after the announcement but that does not alter the fact that expectation caused the first movement. On the other hand, if the expectation turns out to be correct, there will be no further movement in prices at the time of the announcement. That is why, in Case Study number 1, the *Financial Times* report of the rise in UK interest rates places so much stress upon the unexpected nature of the event. Asset prices fell because the rise in interest rates was 'news'. If it had been expected, it would already have been incorporated in the price and would have had little, if any, effect. In Section 5.5 we included a quotation from John Maynard Keynes which suggested an even more extreme role for expectations. According to Keynes, one did not even have to expect a piece of genuine economic news in order to make buying or selling the rational thing to do. One only had to expect that other people expected some news and were going to buy or sell. Indeed, one might forget about news altogether and simply concentrate on what one thinks other people are going to do. If this is true then prices are not moved by events ('level 1') or even *expectations of events* ('level 2') but by *expectations of other people's expectations* ('level 3'). In Keynes's words:

> We have reached the third degree where we devote our intelligences to anticipating what average opinion expects the average opinion to be. And there are some, I believe, who practise the fourth, fifth and higher degrees.
>
> (Keynes, 1936 p.156)

11.4.3 Whole market – long-run

In the long run, the aggregate stock of company shares will expand. The supply curve will shift to the right. This happens because new firms are established and existing firms convert to joint-stock or 'corporate' status. Naturally, some firms will fail, while some firms will find it advantageous to buy in some of their existing shares. Nonetheless, one would expect a net increase in the aggregate stock of shares over time.

The speed at which this happens will depend to some extent on the state of the economy. When the economy is booming, firms have more need for new capital for expansion. Furthermore, it is likely that share prices themselves will be high in a boom because investors expect good profits and a high rate

of growth of dividends. In Section 5.3.1 we went to some trouble to establish that the required rate of return on shares, $\bar{K}$, was the equivalent of the firm's cost of capital. High share prices, therefore, are equivalent to a low cost of capital.[9] When the cost of capital is low, firms will be encouraged to expand.

The net flow of new issues is likely to be particularly marked if the cost of equity capital is low relative to other sources of funds. This too can happen in a boom where a rise in the rate of inflation looks likely. Higher inflation rates may lead to higher interest rates and thus a reduction in the present value of all assets, but for equities higher inflation will mean a more rapid growth in nominal profits and, *ceteris paribus*, a higher rate of growth of dividends. There is no such compensation for bondholders whose returns are fixed in nominal terms. Thus, in the later stages of a boom, when investors become concerned about inflation, it is not unusual for bond yields to rise relative to equity yields and thus for shares to become, relatively, a cheaper source of capital than bonds.

In the long run, then, we would expect a net increase in the stock of company shares, though the rate of expansion may fluctuate. In a market diagram, the continued rightward shift of the supply curve, other things unchanged, suggests a downward movement in prices, and a continuous shift to the right suggests a continuous downward price trend. This, clearly, is wrong. Share prices do sometimes fall dramatically and they do sometimes experience periods of long gentle decline but they do not suffer from a continuous decline. Equally, seen from the yield side, yields do not rise continuously with time. In the long run, real yields (that is, allowing for inflation) are commonly assumed to be 'stationary'.[10] From this, we are driven to the conclusion that, in the long run, the demand curve also shifts to the right, that is, the demand for shares also increases. And it is easy to see why this should be the case, especially if we recall the discussion in Sections 1.2.3 and 1.2.4. There is a *net* demand for financial assets every time a unit or sector saves in

---

9 An informal way to understand this is to remember that in return for a given dividend payment the issue of one extra share raises more capital if its price is high than it does when its price is low.

10 'Stationarity' in a formal, statistical, sense means that a time series has a constant mean, variance and covariance. In others words, it does not matter from where we draw a sample of observations in the series, we get the same values. Clearly, this condition cannot hold if the data is subject to a time-related trend.

excess of its real investment. If we take households, for example, a sector which normally runs a financial surplus, households make a *net* acquisition of financial assets every year. A *net* acquisition means an acquisition in excess of disposals. Thus, each year there is a demand by households to add to their stock of wealth, and company shares, directly or indirectly via a managed mutual fund, will be part of the additional wealth that they wish to acquire.

As with shifts in supply, there will be fluctuations in the rate of shift. In a boom, with low unemployment and high incomes, the scope for aggregate saving will be greater and out of this greater saving there will be a more rapid acquisition of financial assets. The behaviour of demand for shares over time will also depend upon the attractiveness of shares as an investment relative to other assets. In the UK, for example, it was a frequent complaint from industry that there were too many incentives for households to accumulate housing wealth. These incentives included tax relief on mortgage interest payments and capital gains tax exemption on the sale of homes. Successive governments in the 1980s and 1990s began reducing the real value of the interest tax relief on house purchase and created tax incentives for investment in company shares using what became known as 'Personal Equity Plans'. Differences in the rate of growth of demand for and supply of company shares over time will lead to occasional trends in prices and yields, but these are trends which are quite quickly reversed.

11.4.4   Individual shares – long run

Individual shares will, of course, be subject to the same long-run influences that apply to the equity market as a whole. Individual shares suffer from discriminatory tax regimes and benefit from market-side inducements to buy shares. Beyond these influences it is difficult to isolate long-run effects on *individual* shares because any long-run tendency is usually a signal for something to change. If, for example, a firm's share price establishes a long-term downward trend because of declining earnings, and this performance is unique to that particular firm within a profitable sector, then the declining price is a sign of management failure and the firm will quickly become a takeover target. By contrast, an *individual* firm which is a runaway success will quickly find other firms diversifying into its area of activity and the growth in profits will eventually slow.

It is easier to identify trends for whole sectors or categories of firms. The fortunes of whole sectors tend to be associated with structural changes in the economy, or with long-term technological change. Thus, after 1921, dividends on the shares in coal mining and railway companies steadily declined, and with them went the value of the shares. In both cases, the problem was one of the long-run development of rival products and technologies. By contrast, in the 1990s a new and fashionable sector has emerged, under the general heading of 'biotechnology'. These were firms set up to exploit recent technological breakthroughs in the manipulation of the genetic code in DNA. The ultimate prize was seen as the development of effective drugs for cancer, AIDS, arthritis and other afflictions which had so far resisted all conventional treatments. Many companies enjoyed the sight of their newly issued shares increasing rapidly in price even before they had produced any products for sale. This may be a sector set for long-run growth.

11.5   Equity market characteristics

Equities are issued in all countries by firms wishing to raise long-term capital. Table 11.2 shows the value (in £bn) of equities outstanding in selected markets at the end of 1994, together with new issues during that year.

The total *stock* of equities is no indication of the scale of trading activity in the markets. Table 11.3 shows total equity turnover in selected markets.

11.5.1   Primary markets

As with bonds, the bulk of trading in equities involves the buying and selling of existing stock. However, a major consequence of this secondary market activity is that it supports a primary market in which investors are more willing to buy new issues, and provide new funds, knowing that they can

Table 11.2 Value of equities outstanding and new issues (£ bn)

	Stock (end 1994)			New issues (during 1994)		
	Domestic	Foreign	Total	Domestic	Foreign	Total
New York	2712.9	138.5	2851.4	49.1	6.5	55.6
Paris	288.5	n.a.	288.5	6.2	n.a.	6.2
Germany	304.2	n.a.	304.2	n.a.	n.a.	n.a.
Italy	115.6	n.a.	115.6	8.1	n.a.	8.1
London	774.6	1982.8	2757.4	20.4	10.6	31.0
Tokyo	2294.2	n.a.	2294.2	8.5	n.a.	8.5

Source: *Stock Exchange Quarterly*, Spring 1995, Tables F1 (stocks), F4 (new issues).

subsequently sell the stocks quickly and cheaply if they so wish.

In most financial centres, the methods for making *new* issues of new ordinary company shares involve either a sale to the general public – *a public offer for sale* – or a placing. In each case a financial institution, usually a merchant bank or a securities trader, *underwrites* the issue. Underwriting involves the purchase of the stock on agreed terms from the issuer with the promise to distribute it subsequently to shareholders using one of the methods just described. The advantage to the issuing firm is that it knows both the quantity of funds that the issue will raise and the cost of those funds. Indeed, these will be agreed with the underwriter sufficiently far in advance that they will form part of the basis on which the firm decides whether or not to go ahead with the issue. Clearly, the underwriter is accepting a degree of risk in providing this service. Firstly, there is the risk that the issue may be overpriced with the result that the underwriter cannot then subsequently dispose of the whole issue at that price or better. Secondly, there is the risk that although the price initially agreed was correct, the market falls between the time that the underwriter takes up the new issue and distributes it to share-

Table 11.3 Equity turnover (£ bn, 1994)

	Domestic	Foreign	Total
New York	1477.4	158.8	1636.2
Paris	126.7	2.5	129.2
Italy	95.5	0.1	95.6
London	303.0	359.3	662.3
Germany	399.4	11.6	411.0
Tokyo	559.2	0.5	559.7

Source: *Stock Exchange Quarterly*, Spring 1995, Table F3

holders. Again, the underwriter is left with unsold stock. Because of the risk involved, it is common for large issues to be underwritten by a *syndicate*, a group of merchant banks or securities dealers.

New issues will take place when either a firm decides to raise funds by adding to the number of shares already in issue, or when a firm decides to raise funds by 'going public' for the first time. The former case is often described as a *rights issue* since existing shareholders are given a guaranteed opportunity to buy shares in the new issue, provided that they exercise the right within a specified period. The purpose of this is to protect existing shareholders from the enforced dilution of their holding in the firm. 'Rights' give the shareholder the opportunity to maintain his or her percentage of the ownership of the firm.

With rights issues, it is possible also to compare the price of new shares at the time of issue with those already being traded. It is usual to observe a discount. This is difficult to explain by reference to economic theory. Since the new shares, after issue, have exactly the same characteristics, benefits and risks as existing shares (indeed are indistinguishable from pre-existing shares) it is hard to see why they should have a different value. The explanation that is often advanced is that the discount represents a price that underwriters are prepared to pay to preserve their reputation. A new issue which is undersubscribed is often the source of comment in the financial press and might be thought to suggest poor judgement on the part of the underwriter(s). This might make it harder for them to attract underwriting business in future. If this is true, it is worth considering carefully who is really paying the price of protecting this reputation. If we assume that the need to sell at a discount to existing prices is built into the negotiations between the firm and the underwriter, then part at least of the discount at least is being met by the firm. In accepting that the shares will ultimately be issued at a discount, it is accepting a smaller volume of funds and thus a higher cost of capital than may be necessary.

11.5.2 Secondary markets

As we saw in Chapter 10, various trading structures are possible in securities markets. At the moment (1996) the London Stock Exchange (or International Stock Exchange as it briefly called itself from 1987 to 1991) is mainly a 'quote-driven, continuous' market, although 'order driven' trading in the shares included in the FTSE-100 index began in October 1997. Prior to 1986, quotes were made by jobbers who held inventories of stock and acted on their own behalf as principals. Under the pre-1986 rules, they could deal only with brokers, who acted as investors' agents. The same rules limited broking and jobbing firms to partnerships with unlimited liability and also permitted firms to work to a scale of fixed minimum commissions. During the 1960s and 1970s a number of pressures built up for change (Cobham, 1992). The event that finally forced a reappraisal of these arrangements was the removal of exchange controls in the autumn of 1979. Even before this, a certain amount of trading in UK securities was being carried out in other centres, mainly in New York where deregulation, economies of scale and new technology meant much lower commissions. The ending of exchange controls opened the flood gates. UK fund managers diversified rapidly into overseas securities, dealing with overseas market makers. It was clear not just that minimum commissions made London uncompetitive but that the Stock Exchange member firms were simply too small to take on the large increased holdings of international stocks that investors now required and to exploit the economies of scale that the new trading and information technology offered. In the course of 1985 Stock Exchange members came to accept: (a) opening up membership of the Exchange to corporations with limited liability; (b) the ending of minimum commissions; and (c) the replacement of the broker-jobber roles by single capacity market makers. This opened the way for large financial institutions to become members and to invest heavily in the new screen-based technology.

Since 1986, it is these single capacity market makers who provide the quotes for the London market. The Stock Exchange regulations require market makers to quote continuous two-way prices at which they are prepared to deal in return for which they can display their quotes on the SEAQ (Stock Exchange Automated Quotations system) screens and have access to stock borrowing facilities and the TALISMAN electronic settlement system.

One obvious consequence of Big Bang was the arrival of many new firms and an injection of large amounts of capital into the London Stock Exchange. The obvious question is whether or not it has improved the functioning of the market. This is a question for which the relevant data is published in the Stock Exchange's quarterly *Quality of Markets Review*. Quality is assessed according to four criteria:

- *Liquidity:* Measured by 'turnover' (the value of transactions) and 'velocity' (the value of transactions as a proportion of the stock of securities). Velocity increased sharply with Big Bang but fell away after the 1987 Crash and remains (1997) at pre-Big Bang levels.

- *Depth:* Measured by the degree of competition and the ability to sell large quantities without affecting price. Trends in the former can be established by monitoring the number of market makers for each type of stock and in the latter by examining the difference between the bid/offer price for different bargain sizes. Before Big Bang there were 13 jobbers making markets in UK equities. After the reforms, this rose to 33 but has since fallen to 29. As a percentage, the spread between the lowest offer price and the highest bid price for the largest quoted bargain sizes is very little more than the spread at its smallest although all spreads widened after the Crash. Bargain sizes with the narrowest spreads are now much larger than they were before Big Bang.

- *Visibility:* Refers to the amount of information that is available to market participants. The Big Bang reforms are generally regarded as increasing visibility since both bid and offer prices are quoted (rather than just mid-price. Furthermore, all quoted prices are instantly available on screen together with information about the volume of trades in major stocks.

- *Transaction costs:* The immediate effect of Big Bang (when the number of market makers was at its greatest) was to reduce commission levels on all bargains. However, since 1988 commission levels on smaller deals (<£20,000) have risen and are now higher than they were before the reforms. For larger deals, however, commissions have fallen and for deals over £100,000 they have fallen sharply.

In most respects, therefore, the reforms of the London market have achieved what was hoped for them. The market is larger and more competitive. Larger deals can be done with smaller commissions and with smaller impact on prices than hitherto. The quality of information available to market participants is also better. The one area of concern remains the costs of trading for small investors. While these remain high, investment via managed funds which can exploit their economies of scale in transactions costs will continue to be attractive and the drift away from direct ownership of shares by individuals will continue.

Many of the major upheavals of the London market have since been reproduced in other European markets, partly because of the competition that the reformed London market posed.[11] Tables 11.2 and 11.3 both show the very large part that trading in foreign equities plays in the London Stock Exchange. This is business which has developed rapidly since the 1986 reforms and many of the foreign equities being traded in London are those of firms based in other European countries. If we summarize the core of the London reforms as having four elements – continuous electronic trading, dual capacity, liberalization of commissions and freedom of entry – then by 1990 the Paris Bourse had adopted them all, Frankfurt was planning to move to a similar system by 1995 and Madrid and Milan were committed to reform on lines identical to the Paris model. In detail, the Paris arrangements differ from

those of London insofar as the market makers (Sociétés de Bourse) operate a computerized auctioneer system of trading. They do not normally quote continuous two-way prices but execute deals when buy and sell orders cross. In the typology of Figure 10.7, Paris (and the other European markets following the same pathway) are 'continuous auction' rather than 'continuous dealer' markets.

In a continuous auction market, buyers and sellers submit orders to the market maker specifying respectively an upper and lower limit at which they are prepared to trade. Buy orders are then matched to sell orders, so far as possible, by computer and a price is struck and declared. Any offers which cannot be executed at that price are kept until the price moves within their limit or the instruction to buy or sell is withdrawn.[12] Compared with the quote-driven or dealer system it is immediately apparent that the order-driven system apportions the risk rather differently. In a dealer system, the dealer holds inventories of stocks on his own behalf, to which he adds the sell stocks that he receives and from which he executes buy orders. Clearly the price of this inventory will fluctuate with changes in the market price of stocks. Meanwhile, the buyer/seller has the advantage of knowing with certainty the price at which his or her order will be executed. In an auction system, the market maker holds no significant inventories and accepts no stocks except in so far as he matches them instantly with a buyer. The counterparties to the transaction, however, cannot know in advance the exact price at which their order will be carried out. The risk to the latter is moderated by the setting of price limits and by the fact that auction markets, just like dealer markets, display continuous and detailed trading information on screen which enables potential buyers and sellers to see the price at which the last trade was carried out and any trend that might be developing.

It is difficult with such a short period for comparison to draw general conclusions about the quality of market provided by the London and European models since only Paris and London have any established record. The papers by Pagano and

---

[11] For a detailed discussion of the reforms in French and German securities markets after 1986 see Story (1995) especially pp. 24–53.

[12] A detailed description of the system is provided in Valdez (1993) Ch. 9.

Roell (1990, 1992) attempt some preliminary suggestions. An interesting finding is that for average size deals in the 16 stocks traded on both SEAQ (in London) and CAC (in Paris), the *fourchette*, effectively the bid–ask spread, in Paris, is smaller than the *touch*, in London. Even more interesting was their observation that the touch on these stocks in London doubled when the CAC was closed. However, the average size of deal in Paris was smaller than in London and there were very few large trades. Thus, in terms of our indicators above, there is some evidence that transaction costs are lower on deals in Paris but also that the market lacks depth and visibility when compared with London. The lower transaction costs observed in continental auction systems explain the decision to adopt trading of FTSE-100 shares in London from October 1997.

With motives similar to those which drove the Paris reforms, the German government announced far-reaching plans for the equities market in 1992. The proposals to create *Finanzplatz Deutschland* (the 'German financial marketplace') include: bringing the country's eight stock exchanges together into one major market in Frankfurt;[13] abolishing the stock exchange turnover tax; creating a centralized regulatory body; encouraging the creation of a futures and options exchange; the introduction of money market mutual funds; and the computerization of stock trading. We noted at the beginning of this chapter that personal ownership of shares is limited in Germany. This is just one aspect of the lack of an 'equity culture'. The stock market plays a very small role in the financing of firms. There are fewer than 700 listed companies and liquidity is very limited in all but the few largest firms. Bank finance plays a much more important role and even where firms are listed, the shares are very often held by a few institutions, mainly banks themselves. Even insurance companies, large holders of equities in the UK and USA, hold over 80 per cent of their portfolios in government bonds. We shall take a more detailed comparative look at financial systems in Part 5 of the book.

For firms, the listing of their shares on an organized stock exchange carries many advantages. Principal amongst these is that very large amounts of capital can be raised at a reasonable cost because the ownership and risk is widely dispersed amongst investors who can reliquish their commitment quickly and easily. However, 'listing' invariably carries considerable costs and obligations. Costs come in the form of payments to the exchange itself and also in the form of 'disclosure requirements'. Firms with a stock exchange listing are required to make certain categories of financial information continuously available to the general public and to publicize any major changes that occur to their circumstances. These obligations are intended to reduce the information advantage which firms have over their shareholders and thus provide some degree of protection for the latter. Because of these costs, small and medium-sized firms are often deterred from applying for a listing on a major stock exchange and this has led most countries to develop second (or even third) tier markets, with lower charges and less demanding obligations. For example, in the UK until recently small firms were able to join the Unlisted Securities Market (USM) which opened in 1980. The desire by the European Union to standardize stock exchange listing requirements (see *Bank of England Quarterly Bulletin*, May 1990) led to the conditions for USM membership becoming so similar to those of the main markets that the two were merged in 1996. The requirement for a market with low entry and compliance costs remained, however, and this has been provided since 1996 by AIM, the alternative investment market.

11.5.3   Reading the Financial Times

Up-to-date information on activity in equity markets is carried in all serious newspapers that report business news. It is also available increasingly these days on television screen text services such as Ceefax or Teletext. For professional investors, very detailed

---

13 Germany is a federal state and the tendency for each of the Länder to have its own financial institutions and regulators is a legacy of the decentralization of the financial system forced upon Germany by the Allies in the period of post-war reconstruction (D.

Marsh, *The Bundesbank* Ch. 6 (London: Heinemann 1992)). In practice, there are three major securities markets: Frankfurt, Düsseldorf and Munich. The figures from all eight exchanges are aggregated in Tables 11.2 and 11.3.

and sophisticated 'real-time' data is available by telecommunication from commercial suppliers. One of the most comprehensive services of information readily available to the general public, however, is provided by the *Financial Times*, in its UK and European and US editions.

Data on share prices, changes, yields and *P/E* ratios is listed on two pages headed 'London Share Service'. Shares are grouped according to the principal activity of their firms. Look again at Box 11.6 which contains data for the 'Breweries, Pubs and Restaurants' sector. The purpose of the groupings is, obviously, to make it easy for investors to find the company in which they are interested (companies are listed alphabetically within each sector) but it also has the important effect of making it easier for investors to compare data across similar types of firm. When we discussed *P/E* ratios (and the data in Box 11.6), recall, we stressed how important it is to compare like with like. As we would expect, the data for individual shares includes the price at the previous day's close, the change during the day, the highest and lowest price within the last 52 weeks, the market value of the firm (number of shares in issue × price), the dividend yield (before tax) and the *P/E* ratio.

Commentary on equity price behaviour is spread over two pages. The second of the two is headed 'London Stock Exchange' and focuses upon events in the UK market on the previous day. The purpose of the commentary is to explain any overall trend in the market and to guide investors to the main individual share price movements and to give a brief explanation of them. The page also has additional data. One column lists the shares which (the previous day) reached either their highest or lowest price for the past 52 weeks, 'New 52 Week Highs and Lows'. Another lists the trading volumes in major stocks. This provides interesting confirmation of what we said in Section 5.2 when we first discussed financial markets, namely that large trading volume does not mean large price changes. Prices change when there is a change in the balance of investors who think the current valuation is too high or too low. There will always be a dispersion of opinion and so there will always be buying and selling, but if there is an equal balance the price need not change. On Wednesday 30 October 1996, Bank of Scotland shares provided one of the largest volumes traded but the price was

unchanged; on less than half that volume, the Zeneca share price fell by one per cent.

Most of the data, however, is 'summary' data. This includes 'Best (and Worst) performing sectors' but mainly it is index data of some form. Because there are so many different shares listed, the only manageable way to describe and to measure the behaviour of the market as a whole, and especially over a long period of time, is to use an index number. One obvious and important use for such an index is to tell us the rate of return on a broad portfolio of stocks which could be used to approximate K_m, the whole market return, in the capital asset pricing model. The *Financial Times* publishes nine broad-based share price indices, which it has developed with the help of the Faculty and Institute of Actuaries. (We saw in the last chapter that the latter decide on the design and the components of the index, while the *FT* collects the data and calculates the index value.) The most commonly quoted index is probably the *Financial Times Stock Exchange 100 (FTSE 100* or 'Footsie' for short). This is a 'real-time' index, meaning that it reflects changes in the price of its constituents as they actually happen. It was introduced in February 1984 (the others began in 1962) when a new futures contract based on UK equity prices was launched and needed a continuous record of market price movements. The components of the index are the 100 largest UK firms judged by their market capitalization. It is thus a weighted average, unlike the US 'Dow industrial average' which is, as its name implies, simply the average of (the largest) 30 industrial firms. Membership changes, obviously, as firms merge, or get taken over, and as relative market values change. There is a certain amount of status involved in membership of the *FTSE 100* but more important from a practical point of view is that there appears to be a 'membership effect'. When a firm joins the index, its share price tends to rise (and to fall, when it leaves). This is because the performance of many investment funds is judged against the index and therefore fund managers feel it appropriate to hold a significant stake in each of the index's constituents in their fund. The other *FTSE* indices are larger. The *FTSE All-Share* contains 898 stocks. Other indices contain 250 or 350 shares or include only small companies (the *FTSE SmallCap*). Being much larger, movements in these indices are calculated less frequently, usually on a daily basis. The statistical calculation of these indices is explained by the *Financial Times* itself (Greenhorn, 1985) and the details of the constituent firms (in each index) and their weighting within the index are published quarterly in the *FT*. The 'London Stock Exchange' page also has a table containing index data for 37 industrial groups. For every index, the data provided includes the current value of the index, the previous day's change, and the index value for each of the three previous days and a year ago. In addition, the figures include the average gross dividend yield for the stocks in the index as well as 'net cover' (the number of times by which earnings exceed dividend payments)[14] and the *P/E* ratio. We

are reminded again of the importance and frequency of relative valuation since these are intended to be useful benchmarks against which to judge the characteristics of individual shares.

The other page of commentary is headed 'World Stock Markets' and is divided into sections reporting on 'Americas', 'Europe' and 'Asia Pacific'. Once again, the intention is to give some explanation of the latest movement in each market as a whole, but the range of markets to be covered means that activity in individual shares is reported only when dramatic. (News about individual firms is more likely to be found in the 'Companies and Finance: Europe' pages, elsewhere in the paper.) The European market news published on 31 October 1996 is shown in Box 11.8.

Box 11.8   European markets report

It is very clear (though hardly surprising) from the *Financial Times*' report of European markets that individual equities are affected by very similar events to those which we saw driving UK share prices in Box 11.7. Takeover rumours, reports of good (and bad) trading periods, the possibility of beneficial tax changes all feature.

The more striking and more interesting lesson to be drawn from the reports, however, is the extent to which equity markets are subject to common trends. The report begins with interest rate worries in the UK and USA and thereafter every opening paragraph for every western European market begins with the news that share prices generally fell. This is one consequence of what has become known as the 'globalization' of financial markets. What it means is investors can increasingly make their choice of financial assets from markets across the world. The reasons for this are essentially twofold.

The first is that developments in technology in the past 15 years have made it possible for large financial institutions to develop subsidiaries in almost every major market and yet to maintain instant communication between individual subsidiaries and between the subsidiaries and the parent company. Thus investors in the USA using the services of Merrill Lynch, say, in New York know that they can place an order for securities being traded almost anywhere in the world since the order will simply be forwarded to

the most appropriate of Merrill Lynch's 500+ offices. Naturally enough, major investors expect their agents to be continually alert for the best bargains wherever they happen to be. If interest rates rise in New York, some funds will move instantly from European financial centres to take advantage of the higher rates. European currencies will weaken against the dollar and fears will grow in Europe that European interest rates will also have to rise.

The second reason is the trend towards deregulation of financial markets that has also been apparent in the past 10 to 15 years. This usually begins with governments removing regulations which discriminate between domestic institutions and markets, so as to encourage competition in domestic financial services. But in the UK, USA and the European Union this has led on to participation in markets being opened to foreign firms. The case of the UK's 'Big Bang' in 1986 (discussed earlier in this section) provides a classic case in point. The European Union itself is committed to a common European Financial Market and is working at the moment to harmonize (and generally reduce) regulations governing financial activity. This is discussed in Chapter 20. One obvious consequence of this globalization is that events in one centre, very often a major centre like New York, are instantly transmitted to other markets.

---

14 For example, 'net cover' of 2 means that earnings were twice the level of dividends. Thus, taking the reciprocal of net cover is one way of estimating the payout ratio (see Section 11.3.1).

(Box 11.8 *continued*)

Bourses decline after UK rate rise

EUROPE

Bourses were showing some resilience at the beginning of the day, but they lost heart after the UK interest rate rise and a Goldman Sachs prediction that the US Federal Reserve would raise rates by 125 basis points over the next 12 to 18 months.

The dollar, too, was losing further ground, and Wall Street compounded matters as it looked at US September home starts - both treasuries and the Dow lost early gains by the American mid-morning.

FRANKFURT was reminded, all too soon, of Tuesday's forecast from six German economics institutes that the next Bundesbank interest rate move could be upwards. The Dax index ended 10.78 lower at 2,664.72 after an intraday high of 2,692.11, turnover rising from DM7.4bn to DM8.3bn.

Individual shares reflected the shifting mood of the bourse. Deutsche Bank climbed more than a percentage point after it said that Mr Rolf Breuer, an investment banker and a member of the group's management board, would succeed Mr Hilmar Kopper as chief executive. However, the shares ended just 5 pfg high at DM70.40.

Volkswagen made a high for the day of DM602.50, favouring positive group progress reports rather than the news that a Frankfurt court had rejected the VW defamation suit against General Motors and Adam Opel. However, it, too, subsided to close DM4.50 higher at DM598.

AMSTERDAM reversed early gains to close with the AEX index 4.66 lower at 577.09. Financial groups came under fire after the British rate move, with ING down Fl1.40 at FL52.20 and ABN Amro FL1.20 lower at Fl95.80.

BolsWessanen hit Fl31.10, and closed FL1 higher at FL29.60 in high volume of 3.09m shares, although it denied early UK speculation that Grand Metropolitan might be planning a take-over bid for the Dutch food and drinks group. In retailing, De Boer's planned merger with its unlisted rival, Unigro, took the supermarket group up Fl12.50 to FL106.80.

ZURICH became increasingly cautious and profit-taking pulled the SMI index back from a high of 3,752.3 to close 8.9 weaker at 3,723.1.

Against the trend, Swissair held on to a SFr1 advance at Sfr987 on hopes that Sabena, the Belgian carrier in which Swissair has a 49.5 per cent stake, was close to an accord with unions.

Tag Heuer closed SFr12.5 lower at SFr206.5, compared with the SFr245 a share offer price on September 27, as investors continued to demonstrate their doubts about the issue.

PARIS put a lot of work into consumer stocks as the CAC-40 index, higher for most of the day, finally succumbed, to close 0.98 down at 2,124.76 in turnover of FFr4.8bn.

Luxury goods group LVMH jumped FFr38, or 3.4 per cent, to FFr1,153 on its FFr12.6bn acquisition of the US-based duty free goods chain DFS. LVMH emphasised the strengths of DFS in the Asia-Pacific region and emerging countries. Dior rose FFr22, or 3.5 per cent, to FFr659 in sympathy.

Pernod, the drinks group, rose FFr2.40 to FFr277 after the French social affairs minister, Mr Jacques Barrot, agreed to cut proposed tax rises on spirits in the 1997 budget to 4.97 per cent from 17.1 per cent.

However, Peugeot was the biggest loser on the day, falling FFr24, or 4.3 per cent, to FFr535 on worries about the medium-term outlook for carmakers now that the government's new car buying incentive has ended.

MILAN was weak, although continuing demand for Eni, the energy giant, and a late recovery in bond futures helped limit the damage. The Comit index lost 1.83 to 605.13, which the realtime Mibtel index finished 94 lower at 9,588.

Eni picked up L27 to L7,261 in turnover of around L200bn, or about 30 per cent of the market's total trade.

Mr Carlo De Benedetti's financial holding company Cofide continued to attract demand and jumped 4.2 per cent. The shares were L26.3 higher at L645.3 in volume that picked up to 4.7m shares from a recent daily average of 1.4m shares. Olivetti, the troubled high-technology group, gave up another L11.3 to L441.

Fiat lost L95 to L3,966, although analysts noted that the fall came in thin trade and without any large sell orders.

Stet, the telecommunications holding company, fell L136 to L5,032 on disappointment that its privatisation might be delayed until after next March, although the treasury insisted that the sell-off would go ahead during 1997.

The banking sector also fared poorly, with Mediobanca down L194 at L7,840 and Creditor Italiano L50 weaker at L1,540.

MADRID pushed Telefonica down Pta70, or 2.6 per cent, to Pta2,580 after Tuesday's Goldman Sachs downgrade, noting in passing that the stock had risen by 8.8 per cent in the previous 12 sessions. The general index fell 3.14 to 375.89 and turnover was high at Pta63.7bn.

WARSAW rebounded sharply after a 10-session fall, the Wig index closing 406.9, or 3.2 per cent, higher at 13,280.2. **BUDAPEST** similarly saw the Bux index claw back 75.16, or 2.1 per cent, at 3,592.55, having lost 5.7 per cent since mid-October. But **PRAGUE** stated gloomy with the RPIX index down 28, or 2.7 per cent, to 1,023 in record turnover.

FTSE Actuaries Shares Indices

Oct 30   **The European Series**

Hourly changes	Open	10.30	11.00	12.00	13.00	14.00	15.00	Close
FTSE Eurotrack 100	1758.16	1758.98	1758.78	1759.76	1757.30	1756.38	1755.60	1754.97
FTSE Eurotrack 200	1818.74	1820.47	1819.58	1819.38	1816.81	1817.28	1814.08	1811.04

	Oct 29	Oct 28	Oct 25	Oct 24	Oct 23
FTSE Eurotrack 100	1758.14	1775.01	1766.58	1772.46	1777.80
FTSE Eurotrack 200	1812.44	1832.23	1821.67	1820.24	1829.37

Base value 1000 (26/10/90); High/day: 100 - 1761.07; 200 - 1820.73 Low/day: 100 - 1753.53 200 - 1811.04 † Partial.

Written and edited by William Cochrane and Michael Morgan

As with London, other markets also express general movements in asset prices by the use of indices. The French CAC (*Cotation Assistée en Continu*) index began in 1987 when the Paris Bourse reforms began. Like the FTSE 100 it is recalculated continuously while the market is open. It is also a weighted average index, the weights being derived from the comparative capitalization of the 40 shares included in it. As with most share price indices, the *n* shares which comprise the index are the *n* largest shares (by capitalization) in the market, but the CAC-40 takes the largest firms from each sector, rather than the 40 largest in the market as a whole. The SBF-250 index, based on a weighted average of the 250 largest firms, has been published since 1993. This is recalculated only twice a day, but has the interesting characteristic that it contains dividend payments as well. In effect, it is charting the progress of a portfolio of the largest 250 shares, not just as measured by the capital value of the shares but by the change in capital values plus the dividends received by a shareholder of such a portfolio.

The German DAX (Deutscher Aktienindex) is another index which calculates a total return by adding dividend payments to the change in capital value of a weighted average of the top 30 shares. Germany has a number of regional markets which, though smaller than Frankfurt, are more significant than regional exchanges in France or the UK. The DAX incorporates price changes from all the country's exchanges. It is a real-time index, unlike the Commerzbank index which is calculated only once a day and is based upon a weighted average of the top 60 shares quoted on the Düsseldorf exchange.

11.6 Summary

'Equities' are ordinary company shares. Their holders are the legal owners of the firm and their shares bring them benefits in the form of dividend payments, which are a claim on the firm's profits, and capital appreciation, as the firm's earnings increase. The 'fundamental' analysis of shares involves the discounting of future dividend earnings though analysts sometimes use P/E ratios and asset values. 'Technical' analysis, by contrast, studies the past behaviour of share prices. Like all prices, the prices of shares change when there is a shift in demand, or supply, or both. With shares, such shifts occur when investors change their view of the appropriate value for the share, whether this view comes from dividend discounting, asset values or past price movements. There are many events that cause investors' valuations to change. More importantly, we need to remember that the price of any financial asset will change merely because investors expect an event to happen, whether it actually does so or not.

Once issued, shares are traded in secondary markets where a variety of trading arrangements are possible. Since 'Big Bang' the London Stock Exchange has been organized as a continuous dealer market although major shares are now traded on a continuous auction basis. Continental equity markets have been caught up in the reform trend in order to compete with London and have acquired similar characteristics. However, European markets have generally opted for continuous auction rather than continuous dealer trading structures.

Key concepts used in this chapter

Articles of association	Payout ratio	Placing
Ordinary shares	Dividend irrelevance hypothesis	Underwriter
Common stock	Constant growth model	Syndicate
Equities	One-period model	Liquidity of markets
Shares in issue	Two-period model	Depth of markets
Authorized shares	Price-earnings ratio	Visibility
Preferred shares	Asset values	Technical analysis
Dividend	Rights issue	
Retention ratio	Offer for sale	

Questions and problems

1 Wilton Wayfarers plc is a chain of travel agents whose earnings have grown steadily at 12 per cent p.a. for several years and are expected to do so for the foreseeable future. Calculate the equilibrium price for their shares if the three-month treasury bill rate is 6 per cent, the shares have a ß-coefficient of 1.2 and the return on the *FTSE-100* portfolio is currently 18 per cent.

2 What new price would you predict for these shares if the Bank of England raised the treasury bill rate to 7 per cent, *ceteris paribus*?

3 What is rate of return to shareholders in (2) above?

4 Why is this rate of return also the firm's cost of capital?

5 Explain what is meant by the *retention ratio*.

6 Explain why an increase in the retention ratio may have no effect on the value of a firm's shares. Specify carefully the assumptions that you need to make for this to be true and work a numerical example to illustrate it.

7 Explain what is meant by a *P/E* ratio and discuss how it may be used to value the shares of a firm.

8 In Box 11.6, Compass plc has a *P/E* ratio of 29.1 while Bass plc has a ratio of only 16.9. Does this mean that Compass is overpriced? Explain your answer.

9 After careful consideration, Wilton Wayfarers plc decides to drop African adventure holidays from its range of package tours since political uncertainties have made earnings from these tours extremely variable. It decides to put more effort into marketing European weekend breaks, for which there has always been a steady demand. Use the capital asset pricing model to analyse the likely effect upon the required rate of return on Wilton's shares and use a supply and demand diagram to show how this change will affect the share's price.

10 From a recent Saturday issue of the *Financial Times*, take the 'Highlights of the Week' table and write a brief *theoretical* rationale for the change in price of some of the shares reported.

11 Explain what is meant by a 'quote-driven continuous market' for securities. What advantages does it have over other types of trading arrangement?

Further reading

A: General

Bank of England Quarterly Bulletin, 'New Equity Issues in the United Kingdom', May 1990, 243–52

D Blake, *Financial Market Analysis* (London: McGraw-Hill, 1990) Ch. 6

M Buckle and J Thompson, *The UK Financial System* (Manchester: Manchester U P, 1995) Ch. 8

D Cobham, 'The Equity Market' in D Cobham (ed.) *Markets and Dealers: The Economics of the London Financial Markets* (London: Longman, 1992)

D Cobham and S Bonetti, 'Financial Markets and the City of London', in D Cobham (ed.) *Markets and Dealers* (London: Longman, 1992)

K Cuthbertson, *Quantitative Financial Economics* (London: Wiley, 1996)

E J Elton and M J Gruber, *Modern Portfolio Theory and Investment Analysis* (Chichester: John Wiley, 5e, 1995) Chs 18, 19

J K Galbraith, *The Great Crash*, 1929 (London: Penguin, 1961).

A Greenhorn (ed.), *A Guide to Financial Times Statistics* (London: Financial Times Business Information, 1985)

P M Garber, 'Famous First Bubbles', *Journal of Economic Perspectives*, 4(2), (1990) 35–54

M J Gordon, *The Investment, Financing and Valuation of the Corporation* (Irwin: Homewood Ill, 1962)

M Kohn, *Financial Institutions and Markets* (New York: McGraw-Hill, 1994) Ch. 19

M Livingston, *Money and Financial Markets* (Oxford: Blackwell, 3e 1996) Ch. 19

M H Miller and F Modigliani, 'Dividend Policy, Growth and the Valuation of Shares', *Journal of Business*, (1961) 163–96

M Pagano and A Roell, 'Trading Systems in European Stock Exchanges: Current Performance and Policy Options', *Economic Policy*, (1990) 10, 65–115

M Pagano and A Roell, 'Auction and Dealership Markets:
What is the Difference?', *European Economic Review*,
(1992)

L S Ritter and W L Silber, *Principles of Money, Banking and
Financial Markets* (New York: Basic Books, 7e, 1992)
Ch. 29

T Schoen, *The French Stock Exchange* (Chichester: Wiley,
1995)

J Story, 'The Politics and Markets of German Financial
Services' *Institute for German Studies Discussion Paper,*
No.IGS95/3 (Birmingham: University of Birmingham,
1995)

J M W Tadion, *Deciphering the Market* (Chichester: Wiley,
1996)

S Valdez, *An Introduction to Western Financial Markets*
(London: Macmillan, 1993) Ch. 9

R Vaitilingam, *The Financial Times Guide to Using the
Financial Pages* (London: Pitman, 3e 1996)

B: Sources of data
Euromoney (monthly) and *Euromoney Country Surveys*
(annual) (London: Euromoney Publications)
Federation of European Stock Exchanges Fact Sheet (monthly)
(Brussels: Federation of European Stock Exchanges)
OECD, *Financial Market Trends* (triannual) (OECD: Paris)
OECD, *Financial Statistics*, part 1, § 1 and 2 (monthly)
(OECD: Paris)
Stock Exchange Quarterly (London: London Stock Exchange)
Stock Exchange Quality of Markets Fact Sheet (quarterly)
(London: London Stock Exchange)

Answers to exercises

Exercise 11.2

1 Dividend yield = D_1/P = 34.5 / 690p = 5%
Capital gain = g = 15%

2 (a) K = 6% + 1.4(9%) = 18.6%
(b) Dividend yield = $K - g$ = 18.6% − 15% = 3.6%

Appendix to Chapter 11

In this appendix we suggest ways in which the market news reported in Box 11.7 could be interpreted in the light of the theoretical discussion in Section 11.3. Thus, they can be read as answers to Exercise 11.3. However, they should be read only as possibilities. In most cases, the links between the event and the price change can be theorized in various ways.

The first company in the list, Airtours, is the owner of several chains of travel agents and a leading supplier of 'package' holidays in the UK. The *FT* reports that its share price fell by $12\frac{1}{2}$p because of an announcement that it was to face an investigation by the UK Monopoly and Mergers Commission into the possibility that its position as major retailer enabled it to discriminate against smaller suppliers. The immediate effect will be to divert management time and expertise to preparing a case for the MMC. If the MMC finds an abuse of market power has taken place, it is likely to impose conditions that will reduce Airtours' profitability in future. Both effects are likely to diminish D and g for a period.

British Airways shares are reported to have benefited from discussions between the USA and UK trade authorities over the opening up of domestic US air routes to overseas carriers. British Airways has a reputation as an efficient and profitable airline and the expectation is that earnings and dividends will be increased if BA were to get more access to the US market.

Earlier in the week British Telecom had announced an agreed merger with a major US telecommunications provider. This had become possible because the US authorities had begun a programme of deregulation of telecommunications in the USA. The market's judgement was that BT would be able to use its extensive experience of operating in a deregulated market to earn higher profits from MCI's assets. The implication is obviously that earnings (and dividends) will benefit, but there may also be some benefit in risk reduction to BT as well. The world telecommunications market is dominated by a few large firms and it may be one in which economies of scale are very important. Being large may help to guarantee the future stability of earnings.

The merchant bank SBC Warburg issued new shares on behalf of the Compass Group during the week. The immediate effect of this increase in the supply of Compass Group shares was to push down the price slightly. A fall in price in response to an increase in supply may be exactly what one would expect. However, we need to fit it into our framework. The easiest way to do that is to suppose that the market felt that earnings in the immediate future would not increase by enough to enable dividends *per share* to grow as much as in the past.

East Midlands Electricity looked likely to become a target for a takeover bid, and the market anticipated that the final price is likely to be near to £5.93. This might in turn be an indication that the predator company thinks it can improve the profitability of East Midlands assets such that D or g will increase to justify this price. Or it may simply be a classic example of the argument that if someone else values East Midlands Electricity at 49p more, then we need to buy it because its price is going up. (See Section 5.5).

Fairway Group have let it be known that profits are likely to be lower than hitherto expected. It is the surprise that lowers the price. If the market has correctly anticipated the eventual profits then the price is not likely to change again when the profits are finally announced, even though the reduction may be quite large. This is a warning that earnings are going to be lower and either D will be lower or there will be less investment and lower g in future.

A major (pension, life assurance or unit trust) manager has sold enough shares in JKX Oil and Gas for the market to notice. Since fund managers are assumed to be well informed, the market has taken the view that some aspect of D, g or K has been perceived too optimistically in the past.

Lloyd Thomson has reduced the number of shares in issue by buying some of them back. The immediate effect is that existing earnings have to meet dividend payments on fewer shares. Either the dividend payments should be larger or the firm should increase its investment (and future growth rate).

Mackie International has indicated that profits are likely to be lower than expected with the same effects as for Fairway Group above.

Northern Electricity has recently been the subject of a takeover bid and its shares have risen as a result (see the case of East Midlands Electricity above). But there is now some feeling that the bid may be referred to the Monopolies and Mergers Commission and either stopped or made subject to some regulation. Either would mean that the initial price rise was not justified and the share price has slipped back.

PowerGen has been recommended for purchase by the Union Bank of Switzerland. Once again, it is assumed that a reputable broker is making a recommendation to its clients based on information which may be better than that available to everyone else. Maybe the next dividend payment will be larger or future growth will be higher than was previously expected. Maybe UBS have spotted some change in PowerGen's activities that suggest a lowering of its β-coefficient is appropriate.

A major investor in Rolls-Royce has sold its shares. 'Why?' is the obvious question. On the basis that MAM may know something (about D, g or K), other investors decide that Rolls-Royce is only worth holding at £2.46$\frac{1}{2}$p.

Roxboro Group is giving the same warning as Fairway and Mackie above, with the same result.

Foreign exchange markets

12.1 Introduction

The foreign exchange (forex) market allows payments to be made across national boundaries by establishing the prices of national currencies in terms of other currencies. The product (foreign exchange) consists of national currencies, each of which has an exchange rate with every other currency. Exchange rates should, in theory, be determined in markets by the forces of demand and supply, although in practice the exchange of the currencies of most developing countries is so heavily controlled by governments that the official rates of exchange have little to do with market forces.

Market participants can be split into five groups:

- *End users* of foreign exchange: firms, individuals and governments who need foreign currency in order to acquire goods and services from abroad or to move capital as part of their regular economic activities;
- *Market makers:* large international banks who hold stocks of currencies to allow the market to operate continuously and who make their profits through the spread between buying and selling rates of exchange;
- *Speculators:* banks, firms and individuals who attempt to profit from outguessing the market;
- *Arbitrageurs:* banks that make profits from buying in one market at the same time as selling in another, taking advantage of small inconsistencies which develop between markets;
- *Central banks* who, on behalf of their governments, enter the market to attempt to influence the international value of their currency – perhaps to protect a fixed rate of exchange, or to manage to varying degrees an allegedly market-determined rate.

It is clear from this list that it is possible to play multiple roles in the market. For instance, international banks may act in up to four capacities, while firms and governments may be end users on occasions, speculators on others.

In Section 5.4 we met the notion that the price of an asset can be explained by the rational behaviour of end users of the asset trying consistently to maximize the benefit from some real economic activity. In such a case, we said, the price may be said to be determined by its underlying *fundamentals*. Applying this to the foreign exchange market, we can identify the fundamentals of an exchange rate as economic factors which are important influences on the current and capital accounts of the balance of payments. These include relative productivity, relative rates of inflation and interest rate differentials across countries. Changes in these basic influences on demand and supply cause exchange rate adjustments. According to this view, an exchange rate is always either at an equilibrium rate or moving towards a new equilibrium position. Unfortunately, it is hard to discern in the everyday behaviour of the markets any tendency towards anything we might define as equilibrium.

It is difficult even to define an equilibrium position. One common idea is that the equilibrium exchange rate is the rate that produces balance in the balance of payments but since countries trade with many partners, and balance of payments equilibrium does not require balance with each trading partner, this does not give us a clear idea of the desirable exchange rate between the domestic currency and any one foreign currency. There may also be grounds for desiring the set of exchange rates that produce balance in the balance of trade rather than in the overall balance of payments. An influential alternative view of equilibrium stresses the role of the exchange rate in maintaining *purchasing power parity* (discussed below in Section 12.4.3) among countries.

12.1.1 The growth in the size and complexity of the market

The increasing interdependence of countries in recent years has led to a dramatic growth in the proportion of financial transactions with an international aspect. As exports and imports have grown as a percentage of the GDP of all developed countries, so too has the proportion of firms which earns foreign exchange and/or requires foreign currencies to purchase raw materials or intermediate goods. Because exchange rates may change rapidly, such firms are exposed to *foreign exchange risk* – the risk that losses may arise from rises or falls in the value of a currency in terms of the firm's domestic currency. Firms have sought to protect themselves from this risk and/or to seek profits through speculation. The desire to protect against risk has led to the development of markets designed to provide insurance (forward, futures and options markets) and the exploitation of techniques such as interest rate and currency *swaps* which involve the simultaneous exchange of spot and forward contracts. The growth in the size of the market between 1989 and 1995 can be seen in Table 12.1.

The depreciation of the dollar against most major currencies was more pronounced in the three years to

Table 12.1 Global forex market turnover (daily average, in US$ bn)

	April 1989		April 1992		% change	April 1995		% change
	Amount	Share	Amount	Share	1989–92	Amount	Share	1992–5
Total reported turnover	907		1293		33	1867		44
Adjustment for double counting	−373		−508			−707		
Estimated gaps in reporting	56		35			70		
Estimated global turnover	590		820		39	1230		48
Spot transactions	350	59	400	49	14	535	43	34
Outright forwards and forex swaps	240	41	420	51	75	695	57	65

Data for 1989 and percentage change 1989–92 based on 21 reporting countries
Data for 1992 and 1995 based on 26 reporting countries
Source: Bank for International Settlements

April 1995 than in the preceding three-year period and this contributed to raising the dollar value of non-dollar transactions. When re-calculated at constant dollar exchange rates, the expansion in global turnover between 1992 and 1995 was fairly comparable with that between 1989 and 1995 – around 30 per cent. As is shown in Table 12.2, the London market remains clearly the biggest market. Other important foreign exchange markets in order of size are: New York, Tokyo, Singapore, Hong Kong, Zurich and Frankfurt.

Although people associate the demand for foreign exchange with the needs of international trade, these have accounted for only a small proportion of the explosion in the number of foreign exchange transactions. A much higher proportion has derived from the great increase in international capital mobility which has characterized the past 30 years. Both large multinational firms and governments have sought to tap international capital markets to widen their access to funds and/or to lower the costs of borrowing. To meet these demands, international banks have grown hugely in size, new markets have opened up and expanded (most notably the Euromarkets, discussed in Chapters 9 and 10), and

Table 12.3 Use of selected currencies on one side of a transaction as a percentage of global gross forex market turnover

Currency	April 1989	April 1992	April 1995
US$	90	82	83
DM	27	40	37
¥	27	23	24
£	15	14	10
FFr	2	4	8
SFr	10	9	7
Can $	1	3	3
ECU	1	3	2
Aus $	2	2	3
Other EMS	9	13	13
Other reporting countries	3	3	2
Other currencies	19	8	8
All currencies	200	200	200

Data for 1989 based on 21 reporting countries. Data for 1992 and 1995 based on 26 reporting countries. Data for 1989 and for Finland in 1992 include futures and options. Data for 1989 for DM exclude domestic forex trading involving DM in Germany. Data for 1989 cover local currency trade only except for US$, DM, ¥, £, SFr and ECU.

Source: Bank for International Settlements

Table 12.2 Total reported forex market turnover adjusted for local double-counting by country (%age share)

Country	April 1989	April 1992	April 1995
UK	26	27	30
USA	16	16	16
Japan	15	11	10
Singapore	8	7	7
Hong Kong	7	6	6
Switzerland	8	6	5
Germany	–	5	5
France	3	3	4
Australia	4	3	3
Denmark	2	2	2
Canada	2	2	2
Belgium	1	1	2
Netherlands	2	2	2
Italy	1	1	1
Other	7	8	5

Data for 1989 based on 21 reporting countries. Data for 1992 and 1995 based on 26 reporting countries.

Source: Bank for International Settlements

again new instruments have been developed. In 1995, 60 per cent of the turnover on the London foreign exchange market derived from forward transactions. Of these, over 90 per cent were swap transactions. Again, some 90 per cent of all transactions were in the interbank market, rather than involving end users. The importance of specific currencies also changes over time: trades involving sterling fell from 14 per cent to 10 per cent between 1992 and 1995. As is shown in Table 12.3, the US dollar remains the most used currency, still being involved in more than twice as many transactions as the Deutschmark.

The combination of increasing international interdependence and uncertainty has given governments a greater interest than ever in movements in the international value of their currencies. The increased volatility of exchange rates, as the world has lurched between systems of fixed and floating exchange rates, with varying degrees of government intervention, has led to much attention being paid to attempts to forecast changes in them. To understand why exchange rates fluctuate as much as they do, we need to look closely at the nature of exchange rates and the functioning of foreign exchange markets.

12.2 The reporting of foreign exchange rates in the *Financial Times*

Every Monday, the *Financial Times* publishes a table of world currencies which covers approximately 200 countries and some 150 different currencies[1], ranging from the Afghanistan Afghani to the Zimbabwe dollar, including such well-known currencies as the Pataca, the Colon and the New Dong. As well as each currency being used by residents within their own country, there is certain to be some international demand for it to allow the purchase by foreigners of domestic goods and services (every country has some foreign tourists, journalists and diplomats). The international demand for most currencies, however, is small. Foreign citizens and firms are unwilling to accept many currencies in settlement of debt and governments do not hold them in their foreign exchange reserves or use them to intervene in currency markets. This may be because of foreign exchange risk or *sovereign* or *political* risk – the fear that government regulations may prevent or restrict the conversion of a currency into other currencies. Currencies which are not fully convertible are not part of international liquidity (the world money supply). Only the currencies of a few industrial countries are willingly held by other governments and are part of the international trading system. A small number of these currencies (key currencies) are freely used in transactions not involving the issuing countries and are used by central banks to intervene in foreign exchange markets (intervention currencies). Nonetheless, there remains the potential for a set of market-determined exchange rates for each currency. Even where such a

market does not exist officially, there are black markets, expressing demand and supply conditions.

Such demand and supply conditions can be shown in a standard diagram. However, care needs to be taken in the definition of the rate and in the labelling of the axes of exchange rate diagrams. Because an exchange rate is a relative price, it can be expressed in either direction – if the pound goes up against the dollar, the dollar goes down against the pound. If we are interested in the exchange rate of the Deutschmark it is logical to think of it as our medium of exchange, or numéraire, and to express the price of all other currencies in terms of DMs. This should lead us to ask:

How much in DMs does it cost to buy $1, Fl1 (Netherlands guilder), ¥100, £1 (British pound or sterling) or L100 (Italian lire)…?[2]

The answer to this question takes the form:

DM1.686 = $1; DM0.891 = Fl1; DM1.358 = ¥100; DM2.733 = £1; DM0.101 = L100.[3]

We are quoting the price of the foreign currency in each case (the domestic currency is being quoted against the foreign currency). This is known as the *direct quotation* (denoted by E_S) of the exchange rate and is the form used in most countries. Figure 12.1 shows the expression of market conditions in this form.

Note that on the vertical axis we have the price of the foreign currency ($) in terms of the home currency (DM) – the price of US$1 in Deutschmarks. On the horizontal axis, we have the quantity of the foreign currency (dollars) supplied and demanded. Note further that if there is an increase in demand for dollars (the demand curve shifts up from D_1D_1 to D_2D_2), the exchange rate rises (from E_S^1 to E_S^2). That is, it now costs more DM to buy $1 than before – the value of the DM has fallen. Thus, an increase in the exchange rate of a currency expressed in direct

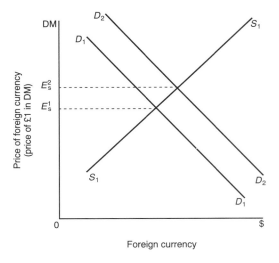

Figure 12.1 Supply and demand using direct quotations.   *Figure 12.2* Supply and demand using indirect quotations.

quotation indicates that the value of the currency has fallen.

For British students in particular, there is a complication because the UK uses the *indirect quotation* (denoted by S_S) of the exchange rate in which the price of the domestic currency is expressed. This asks how much foreign currency exchanges for one unit of the domestic currency (foreign currencies are quoted against the domestic currency):

What is the price of £1 in US dollars, deutschmarks, yen, Spanish pesetas (Pta)… ?

The answers are in the form:

£1 = US$1.621; £1 = DM2.733[4]; £1 = ¥201.328; £1 = Pta231.39.

This method conflicts with the normal idea of a price but it does have one advantage. The relevant diagram has the price of the domestic currency (sterling) in foreign currency (US dollars) on the vertical axis and the quantity of the domestic currency demanded and supplied on the horizontal axis. Now, an increase in demand for dollars will be shown as an increase in the supply of sterling in order to acquire the extra dollars. The supply curve for sterling moves down

(from S_1S_1 to S_2S_2) and the exchange rate falls (from S_S^1 to S_S^2) – meaning here that the value of sterling also falls (see Figure 12.2). Thus, we can talk either of a fall in the value of the domestic currency or of a fall in its exchange rate.

Box 12.2 provides additional information on the expression of exchange rates in the *Financial Times* and Exercise 12.1 gives you some practice in the manipulation of rates.

Exercise 12.1

You are given the following indirect quotations of the dollar against the French franc, the Belgian franc and the peseta.

$1 = FFr5.6895 – 5.6905
$1 = BFr34.7580 – 34.8080
$1 = Pta142.730 – 142.760

1 Calculate the mid-points and the direct quotation of each of these rates.

2 Calculate the exchange cross rates between:
    (a) the French franc and the Belgian franc;
    (b) the French franc and the peseta;
    (c) the peseta and the Belgian franc.

4 Note that the direct quotation of the DM in terms of sterling is the same as the indirect quotation of sterling in terms of DM.

Box 12.2   The expression of exchange rates in the *Financial Times*

The *Financial Times* generally follows the British practice and provides the *indirect quotation* – the amount of a foreign currency (for example DM) that can be bought with one unit of the home currency at the close of the London market on the last day of trading before the publication of the newspaper. The *Financial Times* gives these figures for both the pound and the dollar in their columns headed *Pound Spot Forward against the pound* and *Dollar Spot Forward against the Dollar* (see Table 12.4). It gives the *closing mid-point* ($1 = DM1.6862) and the *bid–offer* spread (859–865). These last figures are the last three decimal places of the bid and offer rates respectively, giving a closing exchange rate of:

$1 = DM1.6859–1.6865
       (bid) (offer)

The **bid** rate is the rate at which market-makers stand ready to **buy** the currency in question (in this case the home currency, dollars). Thus, we are told that market makers were prepared at the close of the market to buy dollars at a rate of DM1.6859 = $1. The **offer** (or **asked**) rate is the price at which the market maker is ready to sell the home currency ($). That is, for every dollar market makers required DM1.6865. The difference between the two (the bid–offer spread) covers the market makers' costs and provides their profits and thus its size will reflect the degree of risk associated with holding the currency in question ($). Since $/DM contracts are the most heavily traded contracts on the London market (making up 22 per cent of all business in 1995), the market is very deep and

there is little chance of sudden, large movements in the exchange rate. Consequently, the bid–offer spread represents only a tiny percentage of the value of the currency. Spreads are often quoted in terms of *points* or *pips* where a point is 0.0001 and a pip is 0.00001. Thus, in our rates quoted above, the bid–offer spreads are:

DM1.6859–1.6865 = 0.0006 = 6 points or 60 pips.

The **closing mid-point** is the average of the bid and offer rates and provides a single figure for the exchange rate ($1 = DM1.6862). If the dollar were to weaken, these figures would fall – it would cost fewer DM to buy $1.

Direct quotation

Given an indirect quotation, the direct quotation can be calculated as its reciprocal. Thus, if we divide $1 by the indirect quotation given above (DM1.6859-1.6865), we get: $0.5932–0.5929 = DM1.

The direct quotation refers to the value of the foreign currency (DM) and thus the bid rate is now the rate at which the market maker will be prepared to buy DM (and sell dollars). In order to make a profit, market makers must buy at a lower rate than they sell. Thus, the correct form of the direct quotation of the $ will be:

$0.5929–0.5932 = DM1
bid   offer

If the dollar were to weaken, these figures would rise – it would cost a higher proportion of a dollar to buy one DM.

12.2.1   Spot and forward rates of exchange

As we have seen, about 40 per cent of foreign exchange transactions are *spot* transactions – purchases/sales of foreign currency for immediate delivery, which means that the transaction must be completed within two working days of the contract being made (the date of the actual payment of funds is called the value date). Forward rates of exchange relate to contracts entered into now for promised delivery in the future. The most common periods for forward contracts are one-month and three-months,

although much longer periods are possible especially for heavily traded currencies.

Table 12.4 shows the *Financial Times* table headed *Dollar Spot Forward against the dollar*. The closing mid-point and the bid–offer spread columns are discussed in Box 12.2. Extra information regarding spot exchange rates is given in the columns headed *Change on day* and *Day's mid*. Both of these columns relate to mid-points of exchange rates. The *Change on day* column indicates whether the dollar has risen or fallen in value since the close on the previous day. Thus we see that the change against the

Table 12.4

DOLLAR SPOT FORWARD AGAINST THE DOLLAR													
Feb 14		Closing mid-point	Change on day	Bid/offer spread	**Day's mid** high	low	**One month** Rate	%PA	**Three months** Rate	%PA	**One year** Rate	%PA	J.P Morgan index
Europe													
Austria	(Sch)	11.8667	−0.0058	642 - 691	11.9015	11.8310	11.852	1.5	11.8067	2.0	11.6117	2.1	103.4
Belgium	(BFr)	34.7830	−0.037	580 - 080	34.9050	34.6950	34.723	2.1	34.5955	2.2	34.0555	2.1	103.5
Denmark	(DKr)	6.4262	−0.0028	252 - 272	6.4480	6.4100	6.4173	1.7	6.3989	1.7	6.3172	1.7	105.3
Finland	(FM)	4.9991	+0.0116	953 - 028	5.0075	4.9673	4.9903	2.1	4.9716	2.2	4.8891	2.2	83.5
France	(FFr)	5.6900	−0.0065	895 - 905	5.7102	5.6720	5.6817	1.8	5.6637	1.9	5.588	1.8	105.9
Germany	(DM)	1.6862	−0.0009	859 - 865	1.6917	1.6808	1.6833	2.1	1.6773	2.1	1.6525	2.0	104.8
Greece	(Dr)	263.720	+0.32	670 - 770	264.300	262.820	265.275	−7.1	267.845	−6.3	278.87	−5.7	66.6
Ireland	(I£)	1.5831	+0.0026	821 - 840	1.5865	1.5735	1.5826	0.3	1.5823	0.2	1.5794	0.2	-
Italy	(L)	1662.00	+1.85	190 - 210	1668.12	1655.68	1664.73	−2.0	1667.89	−1.4	1668.78	−0.4	76.7
Luxembourg	(LFr)	34.7830	−0.037	580 - 080	34.9050	34.6950	34.723	2.1	34.5955	2.2	34.0555	2.1	103.5
Netherlands	(Fl)	1.8923	−0.0002	920 - 925	1.8985	1.8870	1.8885	2.4	1.8805	2.5	1.845	2.5	103.3
Norway	(NKr)	6.6899	+0.0269	889 - 909	6.7289	6.6092	6.6861	0.7	6.6805	0.6	6.6549	0.5	102.9
Portugal	(Es)	169.610	−0.09	560 - 660	170.400	169.130	169.815	−1.5	170.11	−1.2	170.885	−0.8	94.9
Spain	(Pta)	142.745	−0.15	730 - 760	143.300	142.400	142.843	−0.8	142.855	−0.3	142.075	0.5	77.6
Sweden	(SKr)	7.3626	−0.0461	588 - 663	7.4264	7.3546	7.3598	0.5	7.3499	0.7	7.3026	0.8	86.0
Switzerland	(SFr)	1.4625	+0.0098	620 - 630	1.4645	1.4548	1.4587	3.2	1.4508	3.2	1.418	3.0	102.9
UK	(£)	1.6210	−0.0011	205 - 215	1.6245	1.6160	1.62	0.7	1.6179	0.8	1.6077	0.8	97.6
Ecu	–	1.1525	−0.0007	520 - 530	1.1562	1.1493	1.1539	−1.4	1.157	−1.5	1.1736	−1.8	-
SDR†	–	0.72423		-	-	-	-	-	-	-	-	-	-
Americas													
Argentina	(Peso)	0.9993	−0.0006	993 - 993	0.9993	0.9993	-	-	-	-	-	-	-
Brazil	(R$)	1.0492	+0.0006	491 - 492	1.0493	1.0487	-	-	-	-	-	-	-
Canada	(C$)	1.3501	−0.0025	498 - 503	1.3519	1.3492	1.3478	2.1	1.3427	2.2	1.3152	2.6	86.4
Mexico	(New Peso)	7.7805	−0.013	780 - 830	7.7850	7.7750	7.8985	−18.2	8.165	−19.8	9.0255	−16.0	-
USA	($)	-		-	-	-	-	-	-	-	-	-	104.5
Pacific/Middle East/Africa													
Australia	(A$)	1.3056	+0.0029	051 - 060	1.3082	1.3050	1.3071	−1.4	1.309	−1.0	1.3145	−0.7	98.0
Hong Kong	(HK$)	7.7495	+0.0005	490 - 500	7.7500	7.7485	7.7494	0.0	7.75	0.0	7.761	−0.1	-
India	(Rs)	35.9170	−0.02	870 - 470	35.9800	35.8700	36.132	−7.2	36.592	−7.5	-		-
Israel	(Shk)	3.3425	−0.0001	394 - 456	3.3459	3.3387	-	-	-	-	-	-	-
Japan	(Y)	124.200	−0.46	150 - 250	124.820	123.780	123.725	4.6	122.72	4.8	118.52	4.6	122.3
Malaysia	(M$)	2.4840	−0.0013	835 - 845	2.4885	2.4832	2.4869	−1.4	2.4922	−1.3	2.5135	−1.2	-
New Zealand	(NZ$)	1.4394	+0.0017	388 - 399	1.4419	1.4368	1.4449	−4.6	1.4492	−2.7	1.4807	−2.9	-
Philippines	(Peso)	26.3450	−0.003	200 - 700	26.3700	26.3200	-	-	-	-	-	-	-
Saudi Arabia	(SR)	3.7505	-	503 - 506	3.7507	3.7502	3.7508	−0.1	3.7512	−0.1	3.7531	−0.1	-
Singapore	(S$)	1.4180	−0.0007	175 - 185	1.4185	1.4169	1.4158	1.8	1.4112	1.9	1.39	2.0	-
South Africa	(R)	4.4165	+0.003	150 - 180	4.4280	4.3960	4.4572	−11.1	4.5322	−10.5	4.847	−9.7	-
South Korea	(Won)	875.150	+9.15	100 - 200	875.200	875.000	-	-	-	-	-	-	-
Taiwan	(T$)	27.5400	-	200 - 600	27.5770	27.5100	27.5401	0.0	27.5403	0.0	-		-
Thailand	(Bt)	26.0950	+0.07	700 - 200	26.1700	26.0300	26.185	−4.1	26.3525	−3.9	26.99	−3.4	-

† SDR rate per $ for Feb 13. Bid/offer spreads in the Dollar Spot table show only the last three decimal places. Forward rates are not directly quoted to the market but are implied by current interest rates. UK, Ireland & ECU are quoted in US currency. J.P. Morgan nominal indices Feb 13: Base average 1990=100.

DM was −0.0009, indicating that the mid-point of the dollar against the DM had fallen from DM1.6871 to DM1.6862 since the previous evening. In a table in which the exchange rates are directly quoted, a negative sign here would indicate that the domestic currency had strengthened.

The day's mid provides figures for the highest and lowest values of the dollar during the day's trading. Thus we learn that on 14 February 1997, the dollar fluctuated between DM1.6917 (high) and DM1.6808 (low) before settling at the closing rate of DM1.6862. The extent of the range over which the currency traded during the day gives an idea of the volatility of the exchange rate. It is also often of some interest to see whether a currency finishes the day close to its high or its low for the day. In our case, the dollar finished up almost exactly in the middle of its trading range for the day. One possible pattern of trading is that the dollar rose in early trading (from DM1.6871 to DM1.6917) before falling to DM1.6808 and then coming back off its floor to the closing rate of DM1.6862 – only down by 9 points (90 pips) on the day.

Although the London foreign exchange market closes officially at 5 p.m., foreign exchange trading does not stop at that time. The market does not have a physical location. Trading takes place via computer link, telephone and telex among the major participants and thus can continue after 5 p.m. In addition, trading takes place on foreign exchange markets in other countries. The value of currencies goes on changing across the world in a number of major markets whose trading hours overlap. The three principal forex markets are London, New York and Tokyo but these markets do not cover the whole 24 hours and significant markets have developed elsewhere, notably in Los Angeles, Hong Kong, Singapore, Bahrain, Zurich, Frankfurt and Paris. When the London market opens the next day rates will have changed, perhaps considerably, from those quoted as the closing London rates in the *Financial Times*. It is for this reason that the newspaper also provides a small column headed *Pound in New York* which provides information on what has happened to the value of the pound against the dollar in the New York market after the London market has closed. It is also worth noting that the exchange rates quoted on the Currencies and Money page of the *Financial Times* are rather different from the exchange rates available to tourists and other small users of foreign currencies. This issue is dealt with in Box 12.3.

Most of the remaining information in Table 12.4 relates to the forward market in foreign exchange. Information is provided on the rate of exchange for forward contracts involving the delivery of a foreign currency in one month, three months and one year's time. Consider the *One month* column. The one-month rate for the DM against the $ is given as DM1.6833, below the spot rate of DM1.6862 – the exchange rate for dollars one month in advance was lower than the spot rate by DM0.0029. In other words, against the dollar the DM was trading at a *premium* of DM0.0029. In direct quotation (spot: $0.5930 = DM1; forward: $0.5941), we would say that the dollar was trading at a *discount* of $0.0011 against the DM. But since the table is quoting foreign currencies against the dollar, the following column, which gives the annual rate of premium or discount, is shown as positive – the DM was trading one month forward at a premium of 2.1 per cent per annum against the dollar. This is obtained by multiplying the one-month premium (DM0.0029) by 12 to convert it into an annual figure, dividing by the spot exchange rate (DM1.6862), and multiplying by 100 to produce a percentage rate:

$$\frac{(0.0029)12}{1.6862} \times 100 = 2.1\% \tag{12.1}$$

The Greek drachma (Dr) one month forward was trading at an annual discount of 7.1 per cent – the one-month forward rate was $1 = Dr265.275, rather higher than the spot rate of $1 = Dr263.720. We shall look at why some currencies trade at a forward premium and others at a forward discount in Section 12.3.1. Another point which we shall explain in Section 12.3.1 can be observed by comparing the one-month, three-month and one-year premiums or discounts in the cases of Germany and Greece. We see that the percentage per annum premium is

---

Box 12.3   Official versus tourist rates of exchange

There are two obvious differences between official and tourist exchange rates. Firstly, tourist rates are worse for both buyers from and sellers to the foreign exchange office – there is a much bigger spread between bid and offer rates. Secondly, foreign exchange offices often make commission charges as well as benefiting from the wider bid/offer spread. How can one explain this?

Remember that the spread (+ commission charges) covers costs and provides profits for dealers. Tourist transactions are on average small and administrative costs are likely to be high relative to turnover. This is particularly likely since exchange offices are usually centrally located in high property rental areas and, for the convenience of customers, keep generous hours and hold a wide range of currencies, some of which may have quite large risk associated with them. Part of the large spreads and charges can, then, be explained by the costs of providing the service.

In addition, however, there is certainly an element of what the market will bear. The principal forex markets are characterized by large numbers of operators and a high degree of knowledge of available rates. The considerable degree of competition forces profit margins down to very low levels, although market makers still do very well in absolute terms because of the size of the transactions.

There is a much lower level of consumer knowledge in tourist forex markets and a much smaller degree of competition among suppliers. By and large, tourists take the rate that they are offered, grumble about it though they may.

virtually unchanged for the DM against the dollar (2.1% for one month and three months forward and 2.0% for one year forward). For the drachma, however, the percentage discount falls considerably – from 7.1% for one month to 6.3% for three months and 5.7% for one year.

From the information provided in Table 12.4, it is possible to calculate through the $, the exchange rate between any pair of the 38 currencies listed. That is, it is possible to calculate the *exchange cross rate*, defined as an exchange rate calculated from two other rates, for instance the exchange rate of the DM against the Swedish krona (SKr) derived from the US$–SKr and the US$–DM rates. Table 12.4 tells us that:

$US1 = SKr7.3588–7.3663
        bid   offer

– the market maker stands ready to buy dollars at SKr7.3588 and to sell them at SKr7.3663. We also see that:

$US1 = DM1.6859–1.6865
        bid   offer

To obtain the indirect quote of the DM against the SKr we must divide the SKr rates against the $ by the DM rates against the $, but we need to be careful about the figures we use. The relevant cross transaction is to sell SKrs for dollars and use dollars to buy DM. Thus, we divide the bid rate for SKr against the dollar (7.3588) by the offer rate of DM against the dollar (1.6865), giving DM1 = SKr4.3634. To find

the offer rate of DM against the SKr we need the other pair of rates, dividing the offer rate of SKr against the $ (7.3663) by the bid rate of DM against the $ (1.6859), giving DM1 = SKr4.3694. Thus, the market maker pays SKr4.3634 for each DM but sells DM at SKr4.3694. The mid-point is SKr4.3664. The equivalent figures for the direct quote are:

DM2.2887–2.2918 = SKr10
  bid   offer

That is, the market maker pays DM2.2887 for each SKr10 and sells for DM2.2918.

To make life easier, the *Financial Times* publishes a table of exchange cross rates involving 17 currencies. This makes use of the mid-points of exchange rates, rather than providing separate bid and offer rates. The exchange cross-rates table published on 15 February 1997 is reproduced here as Table 12.5.

By taking a currency in the left-hand column and reading across the table, we find the exchange rates of 16 other currencies against that currency (the indirect quotation). We have, for example:

DM1 = BFr20.63; DM1 = FFr3.375; DM1 = Es100.6; DM1 = £0.366, DM1 = ¥73.66
and so on.

To find the exchange rate of the currency against other currencies (the direct quotation), find the currency across the top of the table and read down. In this way, we find from the Swiss franc (SFr) column that:

Table 12.5

CROSS RATES AND DERIVATIVES
EXCHANGE CROSS RATES

Feb 14		BFr	DKr	FFr	DM	I£	L	Fl	NKr	Es	Pta	SKr	SFr	£	C$	$	Y	Ecu
Belgium	(BFr)	100	18.48	16.36	4.847	1.816	4778	5.440	19.23	487.6	410.6	21.16	4.205	1.774	3.883	2.875	357.0	2.496
Denmark	(DKr)	54.11	10	8.852	2.623	0.983	2585	2.943	10.40	263.8	222.2	11.45	2.275	0.960	2.101	1.556	193.2	1.350
France	(FFr)	61.12	11.30	10	2.963	1.110	2921	3.325	11.75	298.0	251.0	12.93	2.570	1.084	2.373	1.757	218.2	1.525
Germany	(DM)	20.63	3.813	3.375	1	0.375	985.7	1.122	3.966	100.6	84.71	4.365	0.868	0.366	0.801	0.593	73.66	0.515
Ireland	(I£)	55.06	10.18	9.008	2.669	1	2631	2.995	10.59	268.5	226.1	11.65	2.315	0.977	2.138	1.583	196.6	1.374
Italy	(L)	2.093	0.387	0.342	0.101	0.038	100.	0.114	0.402	10.20	8.593	0.443	0.088	0.037	0.081	0.060	7.472	0.052
Netherlands	(Fl)	18.38	3.397	3.007	0.891	0.334	878.4	1	3.534	89.63	75.48	3.890	0.773	0.326	0.714	0.529	65.63	0.459
Norway	(NKr)	52.01	9.613	8.509	2.521	0.945	2485	2.829	10	253.6	213.6	11.01	2.187	0.923	2.019	1.495	185.7	1.298
Portugal	(Es)	20.51	3.790	3.355	0.994	0.372	980.0	1.116	3.943	100.	84.21	4.340	0.862	0.364	0.796	0.590	73.23	0.512
Spain	(Pta)	24.35	4.501	3.984	1.181	0.442	1164	1.325	4.683	118.7	100.	5.153	1.024	0.432	0.946	0.700	86.95	0.608
Sweden	(SKr)	47.26	8.734	7.732	2.291	0.858	2258	2.571	9.086	230.4	194.0	10	1.987	0.838	1.835	1.359	168.7	1.179
Switzerland	(SFr)	23.78	4.395	3.890	1.153	0.432	1136	1.294	4.572	115.9	97.64	5.032	1	0.422	0.923	0.684	84.90	0.593
UK	(£)	56.38	10.42	9.224	2.733	1.024	2694	3.067	10.84	274.9	231.5	11.93	2.371	1	2.189	1.621	201.3	1.407
Canada	(C$)	25.76	4.760	4.214	1.249	0.468	1231	1.401	4.952	125.6	105.8	5.450	1.083	0.457	1	0.741	91.96	0.643
US	($)	34.78	6.428	5.690	1.686	0.632	1662	1.892	6.687	169.6	142.8	7.360	1.463	0.617	1.350	1	124.2	0.868
Japan	(Y)	28.01	5.176	4.582	1.358	0.509	1338	1.524	5.385	136.6	115.0	5.926	1.178	0.497	1.087	0.805	100.	0.699
Ecu		40.07	7.406	6.556	1.942	0.728	1915	2.180	7.704	195.4	164.5	8.479	1.685	0.711	1.556	1.152	143.1	1

Danish Kroner, French Franc, Norwegian Kroner, and Swedish Kronor per 10; Belgian Franc, Yen, Escudo, Lira and Peseta per 100.

SFr4.205 = BFr100; SFr2.2570 = FFr10;
SFr0.868 = DM1; SFr1.024 = Pta100
and so on.

The table also allows us to find quickly the amount of a currency quoted in indirect quotations – by glancing at the diagonal running from left to right.

12.2.2 Exchange rate indices and currency baskets

It may be useful to know what is happening to the value of a currency in general as well as to specific exchange rates. Since the punt might, for example, rise against the $ but fall against the DM and the yen, exchange rate indices are prepared showing the average performance of a currency against a basket of other currencies. Because the punt's relationship with some currencies is much more important than with others from the point of view of Ireland's overall trading position, an exchange rate index (the *effective exchange rate*) shows changes in the value of a currency against a *weighted average* of the values of a number of other currencies. Weights are based on the importance in trade of different currencies, taking into account competition in third markets. Thus, an exchange rate index for the punt would give a much higher weight to the pound than, for instance, to the Portuguese escudo (Es).

Effective exchange rate indices are provided for the pound and the dollar in the *Financial Times*. In the *Pound Spot forward against the pound* table, the Bank of England Index for sterling is shown in the final column while the equivalent column for the dollar gives the J P Morgan index for the dollar. Consider the J P Morgan index in Table 12.4. The figure beside each currency, other than the dollar itself, shows what has happened to that currency relative to the dollar since 1990 (the base of the index is the average for 1990). We see that the Austrian schilling (Sch) had risen against the dollar by 3.4 per cent since 1990 while the Japanese yen had risen by 22.3 per cent. Among those currencies that had fallen in value against the dollar were the Finnish markka (FM) (16.5 per cent), the Spanish peseta (22.4 per cent) and the Greek drachma (33.4 per cent). Currencies beside which there are blanks (such as the Indian Rupee and the New Zealand dollar) are

insufficiently important to US trade to be included in the index. The figure beside the dollar itself, 104.5, is the trade-weighted average of the figures for the individual currencies.

The spot exchange rate we have dealt with so far is also known as the *nominal exchange rate*. A firm may become uncompetitive in foreign markets either because the value of its domestic currency has risen (causing the prices of its products expressed in foreign currencies to rise) or because the prices in domestic currency of its products have risen. Consequently, to judge the competitive position of a country's firms against those of another country, we must adjust the nominal exchange rate to reflect the differences between the inflation rates in the two countries. This gives us the *real exchange rate* between two currencies. The formula for calculating the real exchange rate depends on whether the nominal rate is quoted in indirect or direct terms. Assume an exchange rate of £1 = L2694.1 (the indirect quotation of the pound sterling against the Italian lira). Assume further that the UK's expected inflation rate over the next year is 2 per cent per annum as against 4 per cent for Italy. We might then calculate the real exchange rate of sterling as:

$$S_R = S_S + (\dot{P}_D^e - \dot{P}_{Fe})S_S \qquad (12.2)$$

where S_R and S_S are respectively the real and nominal exchange rates, both in indirect quotation, and $\dot{P}_D^e$ and $\dot{P}_F^e$ are the domestic (UK) and foreign (Italian) expected inflation rates respectively. Thus, the real exchange rate of sterling is:

$$£1 = 2694.1 + (1.02 - 1.04)2694.1 = L2640.2$$

The real exchange rate being below the nominal exchange rate indicates that British goods will in the future be more competitive (because of the lower expected inflation rate) than is suggested by the nominal rate. Expressing the exchange rate in direct form, we have £0.03712 = L100 and the real exchange rate formula becomes:

$$E_R = E_S + (\dot{P}_F^e - \dot{P}_D^e)E_S \qquad (12.3)$$

where E_R and E_S are respectively the real and nominal exchange rates, both in direct quotation. This gives:

$$L100 = £0.03712 + (1.04 - 1.02)0.03712 = £0.03786.$$

Now, the higher future competitiveness of UK goods is indicated by the real exchange rate being *above* the nominal rate.

Currency baskets have uses other than providing the basis for the calculation of exchange rate indices. Two important baskets in current use in the world economy are the Special Drawing Right (SDR) and the Ecu (European Currency Unit). The SDR is a weighted average of five currencies (the US dollar, the yen, the Deutschmark, the French franc and the pound sterling). Its value is given against the dollar in Table 12.4 – $1 = SDR0.72423. All IMF accounting is in SDRs; and SDRs were issued to countries in the 1970s and early 1980s to form part of the international reserves of IMF members.

The Ecu is the unit of account of the EU. It is also used for the expression of central rates of exchange in the exchange rate mechanism of the European Monetary System. The Ecu is a weighted average of the currencies of the member countries of the EU (whether they are in the exchange rate mechanism of the EMS or not). Weights depend on each country's GDP and its importance in international trade and are changed from time to time, most recently in 1995 with the entry of Austria, Sweden and Finland into the EU. An oddity of the *Financial Times* dollar table is that, although it generally gives the indirect quotation of the dollar, in the cases of the pound (£), the punt (I£) and the Ecu, the direct quotation is given. Thus, we see in Table 12.4 that $1.1525 exchanged for one Ecu. On the same basis as the rest of Table 12.4, this is $1 = Ecu0.8677.

12.3   The efficient market hypothesis

We look in detail at the efficient market hypothesis (EMH) in Chapter 25 but we introduce it here in an informal way to help us to explain some of the relationships underlying trading in foreign exchange markets. In the context of financial markets, the degree of efficiency refers to two issues:

(a) whether markets adjust to new conditions through changes in prices (flex-price markets) or changes in quantities (fix-price markets), with markets remaining out of a genuine market-clearing equilibrium for a considerable period of time; and

(b) the speed with which flex-price markets move to new equilibrium positions.

A fully efficient market is a perfect market in which adjustment to a new equilibrium occurs instantaneously as soon as conditions that bear upon the market price change. Such a market must have a large number of independent profit-maximizing participants, none of whom are powerful enough to influence prices. All information relevant to the market price must become immediately available to all participants. It follows that only normal profits can be earned. Super-normal profits require the possession of some degree of monopoly power and/or of some privileged access to information – both of these we have ruled out by definition. Equally it follows that past changes in market prices have no influence on future prices. We begin in equilibrium. Future price changes derive solely from new information ('news') and this may equally be suggesting a fall or a rise in the price. In other words, new events influencing the market are random and prices are said to take a random walk. A corollary of the EMH is that no one can outguess the market and so there is no scope for speculation. Anyone who 'bets against' the market, and this includes the central banks of developed countries, certainly loses and, since we are assuming rational economic behaviour, no one acts in this way.

But what information is relevant? The implication of the EMH is that everyone has access to the best model – in our case of the determination of exchange rates – and derives from this model an understanding of the relevance of news. There is no particular view as to the nature of this model other than that it is the best one available, in the sense that it provides a better explanation of exchange rates than do all other existing models. The best model might be a model embodying the market fundamentals referred to in Section 12.1 above. However, it might also contain other economic news and/or news about political events or institutional changes. As we shall see in Section 12.6, where we discuss the views of chartists, the best available model might not include market fundamentals at all.

If foreign exchange markets were *fully* efficient,

spot and forward exchange rates would adjust immediately to any new information received and the existing forward rates would be a good predictor of future spot rates of exchange. This is because someone needing foreign currency in three months' time could either buy it now three months forward at the existing forward rate or could wait and buy it in three months' time at the spot rate of exchange then ruling. In a perfectly informed market, the cost of these two actions must be equal. If they were not equal, a profitable arbitrage opportunity would exist and the actions of arbitrageurs would (as we shall see below) bring the two rates into equality. In practice, the forward rate is not a perfect predictor of the future spot rate. As well as transaction costs, information is neither perfect nor free. Thus, there are costs and benefits associated with acquiring additional information and at some point, the costs of doing so outweigh the gains from being able to make an even better forecast of the future spot rate of exchange. Further, some uncertainty attaches to the future spot rate of exchange and so we would expect the forward rate to differ from the future spot rate to allow for a *risk premium.*

It is possible to accept this, but to adopt a weaker version of EMH, for example that forward rates better predict future spot rates than do other theories of exchange rate determination. This does not require the belief that everyone in the market acts rationally on the basis of correct information since the actions of speculators must be taken into account. Speculators might bet on the relationship between, say, the three-month forward rate and the actual spot exchange rate in three months' time. If the forward rate doesn't on average equal the future spot rate, speculators are missing profit opportunities. For example, if the forward price of the DM is typically less than the spot rate when the forward contract matures, one could regularly buy the DM forward, re-sell it spot and make a net profit. It follows that all one needs to assume is that speculators are abundant and well informed and dominate the forward market. In this case, speculation is said to be *stabilizing* – it pushes the exchange rate back towards its equilibrium rate – and performs the same role as arbitrage does in a case where no risk is involved.

Any reading of actual market reports quickly makes it clear how difficult it is, in practice, to interpret news and to decide what information is relevant to the determination of the exchange rate. It is common, for instance, for a market to adjust to 'news' but then to go through a process of reinterpretation, sometimes drawing different inferences from it, other times discarding it altogether as irrelevant. Again, different sets of economic indicators often provide apparently conflicting information about the state of different aspects of the economy and hence of exchange rate fundamentals. There is always a degree of uncertainty as to what is genuine news and what is not. Some examples of these difficulties are provided in Box 12.4.

It is hardly surprising that there are difficulties in interpreting news since perfect models of the determinants of prices in any market do not exist. Particular problems with the impact of news arise when market participants are using different models or are switching from one model to another. Information which is irrelevant to market price and which succeeds in confusing market participants is called noise, since it interferes with 'price signals'. One relatively small modification of market efficiency involves the acknowledgement of noise and of short-run disequilibrium in the market but the continued belief in long-run equilibrium. However, in financial markets in which there are many participants and information is rapidly transmitted with the use of modern technology, the period of disequilibrium is often held to be very short. We have seen that the period may be shortened further by the operation of arbitrageurs and speculators. Let us consider next the role of arbitrage in the relationship between forward and future spot rates of exchange. To do this, we must develop a number of important relationships among interest rates, exchange rates and rates of inflation.

12.3.1 Interest rate parity

We saw in Section 12.2.1 that forward foreign exchange rates are quoted as being at either a premium or discount to the spot exchange rate. To begin to examine why some currencies are at a forward discount and others at a forward premium, consider the position of three investors A, B and C, each of whom has FFr one million to invest in a

---

Box 12.4 The market interpretation of news

The following examples are taken from the Foreign Exchange and Money Markets column of the *Financial Times*, 15 February, 1997.

'The market was surprised by a 0.3 per cent fall in the January US producer price index, which gave the US Treasuries markets more reason to rejoice. The PPI figure took the wind out of the dollar's sails in Europe, as the market downgraded the chances of the Federal Reserve tightening interest rates.

'Earlier in the day the dollar hit its highest level for four years against the yen, and neared the psychologically important level of ¥125, before sliding back in late trading, possibly because of fears over the possibility of co-ordinated central bank moves to curb its rise by entering the market.'

Comment

Early in the day the dollar had risen against the yen. It had then declined for three reasons:

(a) It had almost reached a psychologically important level – such levels tend to form barriers to further movements of exchange rates in the same direction. That is, the prospect of the dollar breaking through the ¥125 barrier seemed somewhat unlikely and caused some people to sell the dollar in anticipation that it would fall away from ¥125.

(b) There was a fear that the central banks of the major countries were worried about the increasing strength of the dollar (and the weakness of the yen) and would enter the market together, selling dollars for yen and forcing down the value of the dollar. This also led to some selling of the dollar in anticipation of the central banks' action.

(c) The fall in the PPI, which indicated a lower level of future inflation in the USA, had not been expected by the market. Rather, it had thought that the Federal Reserve would be worried by the threat of inflation and might increase US interest rates. They had bought dollars in anticipation of this in the hope of making a speculative profit when the interest rate rose. Following the release of the PPI figures, the chances of an increase in interest rates seemed much less strong.

The last of these reasons also affected the value of the dollar against European currencies. The prospect of an interest rate rise had, as well, been acting to push down the price of government bonds (US Treasuries). Thus, the reduction of the threat of future inflation and of a consequent interest rate rise caused bond prices to rise.

---

secure form for three months. *A* buys French government securities at existing French interest rates. *B* sells the francs for Italian lire and uses them to buy Italian government securities which bear a higher interest rate than French securities. Suppose, however, that over the three months, the value of the lira falls relative to that of the franc. Then, when B comes to reconvert the lire into francs, he may have incurred a loss – the higher interest rate on Italian securities may have been more than offset by the decline in the value of the Italian currency. An operation of this kind is known as *uncovered interest rate arbitrage* – it is *interest rate arbitrage* because it seeks to take advantage of interest rate differentials; it is uncovered because the investor is not protected against exchange-rate risk.

C takes advantage of the existence of the forward exchange market to obtain cover against this risk. Thus, at the same time that she buys Italian government securities, *C* sells three months forward the amount of lire which she will receive in three months' time. In this way, she locks in the existing forward exchange rate. Then, when the Italian securities mature, *C* simply fulfils the forward contract and finishes up back in francs. She has engaged in *covered interest arbitrage*, having taken no risk in the process. Clearly, the actions of *A* and *C* are directly comparable and, in a well-informed market, the rates of return available to *A* and *C* quickly move to equality. *A*'s rate of return is the interest rate on three-month French government securities. *C*'s rate of return consists of two elements:

(i) the interest rate on three-month Italian government securities;

(ii) the forward exchange premium or discount involved in selling lire forward.

Assume next that, at the beginning of the three-month period, the franc and the lira were trading with no forward premium or discount (spot and forward rates were exactly the same) but that Italian interest rates were higher than French interest rates for comparable securities. Clearly, then, C's investment strategy would be better than A's and large numbers of investors would follow C. In other words, they would:

(a) sell French securities (forcing their price down and pushing the yield on them up);
(b) buy lire spot (forcing up the spot exchange rate of the lira – increasing the number of francs needed to buy 100 lire);
(c) buy Italian securities (forcing their price up and yields on them down); and
(d) cover their exchange rate risk by selling lire three months forward (forcing down the three-month forward exchange rate of lire).

This process would continue until the rates of return available on the strategies of A and C came into equality (with some small allowance for the transactions costs involved), establishing covered interest parity. What is the final outcome? French interest rates start below Italian rates, but French interest rates rise while Italian rates fall. Thus, the interest rate differential between the two countries is reduced. The spot exchange rate of the lira rises while the forward rate falls, opening up a difference between the two (forward, the lira trades at a discount). The arbitrage opportunity remains until the interest rate differential between the two currencies equals the forward discount on the lira (again, allowing for transactions costs). This establishes a general rule:

The currency of the country in which interest rates are higher trades at a forward discount; the currency of the country with the lower interest rates trades at a forward premium.

We can go further. If there are no opportunities for profitable arbitrage (there is *covered interest parity*) and there are no transaction costs, then the differential between the two interest rates (known as the *interest agio*) should equal the forward discount on the currency of the high-interest-rate country (the exchange agio). We can express the exchange agio in our France/Italy case in terms of the direct quotation of the franc (the domestic currency) against the lira (the foreign currency).

$$\frac{i_D - i_F}{1 + i_F} = \frac{E_F - E_S}{E_S} = \frac{E_F}{E_S} - 1 \qquad (12.4)$$

where i_D and i_F are the interest rates in the domestic (French) and foreign (Italian) currencies respectively; E_S and E_F are the spot and forward rates of exchange (expressed in direct quotation). It follows then that:

$$E_F = \frac{1 + (i_D - i_F)}{1 + i_F} E_S \qquad (12.5)$$

Consider an example. In the *Financial Times* of 15 February 1997, the one-year interest rate on the Italian lira was quoted as 6.75 per cent (0.0675); that on French francs as 3.28 per cent (0.0328). Thus, the difference between the two rates was 3.47 per cent (0.0347) or, in the terminology we used in Chapter 9, 347 basis points. The spot rate of exchange of the franc in direct quotation was FFr0.3424 = L100. We should then have had:

$$E_F = [1 + \frac{(0.0328 - 0.0675)}{1.0675}] \times 0.3424 = 0.33127$$
$$(12.6)$$

That is, the one-year forward rate of the lira should have been FFr 0.3313 = 100 lira, with the franc at a one-year forward premium of = FFr0.0111 per L100.

To express exchange rates in indirect quotation and still have our signs correct, we must change the formula to:

$$\frac{i_D - i_F}{1 + i_F} = \frac{S_S - S_F}{S_F} \qquad (12.7)$$

and:

$$SF = \left[\frac{1}{(1 + \frac{i_D - i_F}{1 + i_F})} \right] S_S \qquad (12.8)$$

The indirect quotation of the franc against the lira on the day in question was FFr10 = L2920.9. The forward discount should have been L101.5 and the forward exchange rate FFr10 = L3019.0. For ease of expression, we have been dealing here with a 12-month period. To calculate the expected three-month or one-month forward rate we must divide the annual interest-rate differential by four or 12. Thus, the one-month interest rates on the franc and the lira at the close of the markets on 14 February 1997 were

3.25 and 7.44 respectively. The interest rate differential was 4.19[5] (or 419 basis points) but these were *per annum* rates. Our formula gives us an annual forward discount for the lira of L118.5. To obtain the forward discount for one month we divide this by 12, giving a one-month forward discount of L9.9 and a one-month forward exchange rate of FFr10 = L2930.8.

Because of transaction costs, we would not have expected our estimate to be perfectly correct, but a glance at the real figures shows that we have more than transaction costs to worry about. Our interest rate differentials above were 4.19 per cent on one-month money and 3.47 per cent on one-year money. Comparing our calculations with the actual forward exchange rates on the day in question we have:

one month:
Actual FFr0.3413 = L100 or FFr10 = L2930
    (lira discount 3.7 per cent p.a.)
Estimate FFr0.3412 = L100 or FFr10 = L2930.8
    (lira discount 4.1 per cent p.a.)

one year:
Actual FFr0.3349 = L100 or FFr10 = L2986.4
    (lira discount 2.2 per cent p.a.)
Estimate FFr0.3313 = L100 or FFr10 = L3019.0
    (lira discount 3.4 per cent p.a.)

Plainly, the differences between our estimates and the actual rates are too large to be accounted for by transactions costs alone, especially for the one-year forward calculations. The direction of the differences are also striking. The interest rate parity theorem depends on the assumption that securities in one country bear the same degree of default risk but this cannot be assumed in practice. Of particular relevance to our example is the fact that Italian government securities were, up until recently, seen to be more risky than were the securities of most western European governments because of the high Italian budget deficit and public debt as a percentage of the country's GDP. Thus, the credit rating attributed to Italian government securities by the international credit-rating agencies was relatively low and Italian interest rates needed to be higher on

otherwise equivalent securities to persuade investors to hold them (Italian interest rates included a risk premium). This remains one reason for the fact that Italian interest rates are generally higher than French rates. However, should this not have caused the forward discount on the lira to be *greater* than that suggested by the interest rate parity theorem? A glance at the figures above shows that this was not the case in February 1997 – the lira was at a smaller forward discount than the interest rate parity theorem would have led us to expect.

A clue to the explanation is provided by the quite sharp decline in Italian interest rates over longer periods, producing a quite sharp fall in the differential between French and Italian interest rates (4.125 per cent for one-month money; 3.47 per cent for one-year money). The market, it seems, was making a judgement that the lira might strengthen in the future, possibly because of an expected decline in Italian inflation rates or increased confidence in the ability of the Italian government to tackle the problem of its budget deficit or, as we shall see in Chapter 22, because of a judgement that Italian membership of EMU in 1999 seemed now more likely. At the end of Section 12.2.1, we drew your attention to a similar case involving the Greek drachma – noting the sharp fall in the forward discount on the drachma as the time period increased from one month to one year. Such special cases do not, however, destroy the general applicability of the interest rate parity theorem which usually holds much more closely than in the case of the Italian lira examined here.

12.3.2 Differences in interest rates among countries – the Fisher effect

We have established a relationship between spot and forward exchange rates. Several other questions follow, some of which we have already begun to consider.

(a) Why do interest rates differ among countries?
(b) What determines the existing spot rates of exchange?

---

[5] Note for future reference the quite large difference in the differential for one-month money (4.19 per cent p.a.) and 12-month money (3.47 per cent p.a.).

(c) What causes spot rates of exchange to change over time?

In fully efficient markets, each of these may also be answered by a rule based upon arbitrage operations. We saw in Section 3.3 that nominal rates of interest consist of two elements:

(1) the real rate of interest; and (2) the expected rate of inflation.

$$r \approx i - P^e \tag{3.15}$$

It follows that differences in expected inflation rates provide one cause of differences in international interest rates.

But what about real rates of interest? Ignoring the issue of exchange rate risk, and assuming perfect markets with perfect capital mobility and perfect information, theory tells us that capital should move from capital-rich countries in which the real rate of return on capital is low to capital-scarce countries with high real rates of return on capital and that this movement should continue until real rates of interest are equal across countries. This would be ensured by uncovered interest arbitrage. In practice, neither information nor international capital mobility is perfect and we have already noted the existence of default risk, exchange-rate risk, and political or sovereign risk which require interest rates of many countries to include risk premiums if they are to attract capital. Indeed, private capital barely flows at all to the poorest countries despite the existence of very high rates of interest. Nonetheless, we can say that if all the necessary assumptions did hold, and real rates of interest were equal across countries, international interest rates would differ only because of:

(a) expected exchange rate changes;
(b) differences in expected rates of inflation among countries.

We could use this (the Fisher effect) to help us explain the differences in interest rates between France and Italy noted above. We could say that, with real interest rates equal across countries and the foreign exchange market in equilibrium, the difference in nominal interest rates on francs and lire depends on the difference between the expected inflation rates in France and Italy. Treating France as

the domestic country (D) and Italy as the foreign country (F), we could write:

$$\frac{i_D - i_F}{1 + i_F} = \frac{P_D^e - P_F^e}{1 + \dot{P}_F^e} \tag{12.9}$$

This is sometimes known as the Fisher closed hypothesis. We have noted above that, if Italian inflation rates were expected to fall in the future relative to French rates, the differential between the two rates would be lower for transactions involving longer time periods.

12.3.3 The determinants of spot exchange rates – purchasing power parity

In the unlikely case that real interest rates were equal across all countries and that differences in nominal rates simply reflected differences in expected inflation rates, then in equilibrium, there would be no movements of capital internationally. The balance of payments balance would depend solely on the export and import of goods and services. Ignoring differences in product quality and continuing to assume perfect information, we could reach the position in which the only reason for preferring foreign goods to domestically produced goods or vice versa and hence the only cause of flows of currency from one country to another would be differences in price.

If, at the existing exchange rate, goods were cheaper in Italy than in France, French citizens would switch to Italian-produced *goods*. To do this they would sell francs and acquire lire, forcing down the value of the franc relative to the lira. This process of *goods arbitrage* would continue until prices in the two countries expressed in a common currency were equal. This is the essence of *purchasing power parity* (PPP). In this form – absolute PPP – spot exchange rates in equilibrium are a reflection of differences in price levels in different countries. Since we are generally interested not in absolute exchange rates but rather in changes from existing rates, PPP is usually expressed in relative terms: that changes in spot exchange rates reflect differences in inflation rates among countries. Using the direct quotation (E) of the exchange rate, this can be written:

$$\frac{\dot{P}_D^e - \dot{P}_F^e}{1 + \dot{P}_F^e} = \frac{E_{t+1}^e - E_S}{E_S} \qquad (12.10)$$

where $\dot{P}_D^e$ is the expected inflation rate in the domestic country (France), $\dot{P}_F^e$ the expected inflation rate in the foreign country (Italy), E_{t+1}^e the expected future spot rate of exchange at time $t+1$ and E_S the spot rate of exchange at time t. Assuming expected inflation rates in France of 2 per cent per annum and in Italy of 4 per cent per annum and a spot exchange rate FFr.03424 = L100 would give an expected exchange rate in one year's time on the basis of relative purchasing power parity of FFr0.3358 = L100. In other words, the franc would need to be stronger in one year's time if Italian goods were to maintain PPP, given the higher inflation rate in Italy. The formula for the same calculation in indirect quotation is:

$$\frac{\dot{P}_D^e - \dot{P}_F^e}{1 + \dot{P}_F^e} = \frac{S_S - S_{t+1}^e}{S_{t+1}^e} \qquad (12.11)$$

Using a spot rate of exchange of FFr10 = L2920.9, we obtain a future spot rate of exchange of FFr10 = L2978.2.

12.3.4 The determinants of spot exchange rates – putting the relationships together

Notice that we have now proposed that differences in expected inflation rates are equal to *both* the expected change in spot exchange rates (PPP) and the difference in interest rates (the Fisher closed effect). It follows that in equilibrium, differences in interest rates must equal the expected changes in the spot rates of exchange. This equality is sometimes known as the international Fisher effect or the Fisher open hypothesis and, from Equations 12.9, 12.10 and 12.11 we may write:

$$\frac{E_{t+1}^e - E_S}{E_S} = \frac{i_D - i_F}{1 + i_F} = \frac{S_S^e - S_{t+1}^e}{S_{t+1}^e} \qquad (12.12)$$

It can be seen that, maintaining our assumption of perfect markets, we have established a relationship between the forward rate of exchange (which is known in the present) and the future spot rate of exchange which is unknown. Covered interest parity establishes, remember, a link between interest rate differentials and forward rates of exchange. But the combination of purchasing power parity and the Fisher effect establishes a link between interest rate differentials and expected future spot rates of exchange. It follows that if people behave rationally and are perfectly informed and all the other assumptions of perfect markets hold, forward rates of exchange accurately predict movements in spot rates of exchange. We can see this by comparing Equations 12.4 and 12.7 with 12.12. This makes it clear that the interest rate differential is equal to *both* the forward exchange rate premium or discount (as expressed against the foreign currency in Equation 12.4 and against the home currency in Equation 12.7) *and* the difference between the future spot and the existing spot exchange rates (shown both against the foreign currency and against the home currency in Equation 12.12).

Of course, we cannot (even with all of the assumptions above) claim that forward rates of exchange predict future spot rates perfectly accurately. After all, news may come to the market which takes all market participants by surprise. Further, the notion of the forward rate of exchange being an unbiased predictor of the future spot rate implies that speculators are risk neutral. If speculators are risk averse, the forward rate must be a biased predictor – the future spot rate will not equal the forward rate because speculators demand a risk premium to allow for the risk associated with assuming an uncovered position in the market. In fact, of the relationships we have developed above, only covered interest rate parity performs well in empirical testing.

12.4   Exchange rate arbitrage

The interest rate parity theorem considered in Section 12.3.1 provided an example of interest rate arbitrage. *Exchange rate arbitrage* involves taking advantage of differentials in the price of a currency in different markets. Such arbitrage transactions may be classified in terms of the number of markets involved. Thus we may have transactions in two markets (two-point arbitrage), three markets (three-point arbitrage) or more. Two-point arbitrage operations are very simple, taking advantage of small variations in the one exchange rate in two markets. For example, if the spot exchange rate of the DM were DM2.73 = £1 in London and DM2.74 = £1 in Frankfurt, arbitrageurs could profit from the differential by buying DMs in Frankfurt and selling them immediately in London, forcing up the demand for DMs in Frankfurt, and causing the rate there to fall below DM2.74 = £1; and increasing the demand for sterling in London, pushing the London rate above DM2.73 = £1. The arbitrage operation would close the gap between the two rates. As always, the rates would not come exactly into line because of the existence of transactions costs, but the rates should move to being transactions-costs close – sufficiently close to remove any possible arbitrage profits.

Three-point arbitrage occurs where exchange rates among different currencies are mutually inconsistent. Arbitrageurs then attempt to profit from these inconsistencies and in the process eliminate discrepancies and establish mutually consistent exchange cross rates. Assume that the following three market rates applied in the Frankfurt market:

$US1 = SKr7.3588–7.3663
$US1 = DM1.6859–1.6865
DM1 = SKr4.3950–4.4030

We wish to consider the possibility that these rates are mutually inconsistent. Our first step is to take any pair of these market rates and use them to calculate the exchange cross rates consistent with them. We have already carried out this exercise for the first two rates in Section 12.2.1. There we discovered that the exchange cross rate for SKrs against the DM was:

DM1 = SKr4.3634–4.3694.

Thus, it is clear that the market price (DM1 = SKr4.3850–4.3930), *relative to the other pair of exchange rates*, is overvaluing the DM in terms of the SKr (the SKr is undervalued against the DM). In other words, the three market rates are mutually inconsistent and a profitable arbitrage opportunity exists. We could have arrived at the same conclusion by using the $/DM and DM/SKr rates to calculate the cross rate for SKrs against the dollar or by using the $/SKr and the DM/SKr rates to calculate the cross rate for DMs against the dollar.

To realize an arbitrage profit, it is necessary to follow two rules:

(a) buy cheap and sell dear;
(b) finish in the currency in which you started.

Assume we hold dollars. Our aim must be to organize our transaction to make sure that at some point we sell DM for SKrs, in order to take advantage of the inconsistency we discovered by calculating the cross rate (if we buy DM with SKrs, we shall make a loss). In order to be able to do this, we must take the following steps:

Step A: Sell $ for DM; *Step B*: sell DM for SKr; *Step C*: sell SKr for $.

At each step, we must make sure that we are using the correct rate (that is, the bid rate or the offer rate). The steps would be as follows:

Step A: Sell $ for DM at $1 = DM1.6859 (the market maker buys dollars and so the bid rate is applicable);

Step B: Sell DM for SKr at DM1 = SKr4.3950 (the market maker again buys the currency indirectly quoted, the DM, and again the bid rate applies);

Step C: Sell SKr for $ at $1 = SKr7.3663 (the market-maker sells dollars and the offer rate applies).

Make sure you understand each of these steps. You should then calculate the arbitrage profit on the assumption that you start with $1 million. If you don't finish up with a profit of $5,868.7, try it again. Exercise 12.2 provides other example for you to try.

Exercise 12.2

Imagine you are a British arbitrageur in the following example:

Actual exchange rates

£1 = $1.6188–1.6195
$1 = ¥122.780–122.840
£1 = £1 = ¥194.756–194.939

Start with £1,000,000.
(a) List the steps you need to take to make a profit.
(b) Calculate the rate of profit you will make.

(Answer in Box 12.5 overleaf)

The implied cross rate of ¥ against £ is: £1 = ¥198.756–198.939. Thus, in the market, the yen is overvalued against sterling and we must sell ¥ for £.

Thus:

Step A: Use £ to buy $; *Step B:* Use $ to buy ¥; *Step C:* Use ¥ to buy £.

Step A: Sell £ for $; market maker sells the foreign currency ($) at lower rate of $1.6188. This gives $1,618,800.

Step B: Sell $ for ¥; market maker sells the foreign currency (¥) at lower rate of 122.780. This gives ¥198,756,260.

Step C: Sell ¥ for £; market maker buys the foreign currency at the higher rate of £1 = ¥194.939 which gives £1,019,582.

Three things should be noted here. Firstly, the profit may seem small relative to the capital. However, this profit may be made in moments and the arbitrageur bears no risk of loss. He or she undertakes the above steps simultaneously and starts and finishes in the same currency. The profit would, in fact, be smaller in practice because of transactions costs.

Secondly, step A causes the price of $ in terms of DM to fall below 1.6859–6865; step B, the price of DM to fall below SKr4.3950–4.4030; and step C, the price of dollars to rise above 7.3588–7.3663. These changes continue until any possibility of profit from arbitrage is removed.

Thirdly, the same steps apply if we start and finish in a different currency from dollars, but the order of the steps is different. A German arbitrageur starting and finishing in DM would:

Step A: Sell DM for SKr ; *Step B*: Sell SKr for $; *Step C*: Sell $ for DM.

We could also re-work this example using direct quotation of exchange rates and then try it again using the $/DM and the DM/SKr rates to calculate the exchange cross-rate for SKr against the dollar. In each case the answer would be the same as above.

12.5 Foreign exchange risk and speculation

We have talked about the existence of foreign exchange risk. A market agent bearing risk is said to have an *open position in the market*. There are two types of open position – an agent may go *long* (take a long position) by having assets in a currency greater than his liabilities in the same currency. The risk then is that the currency will weaken, reducing the value of the position. An agent who goes *short* (takes a short position) has liabilities in a currency greater than assets. The risk is that the currency will strengthen, increasing the debt in that currency. The act of moving from an open position to a closed position in the market (that is, covering exchange rate risk) is known as *hedging*. Consider hedging more formally.

Consider the case of a German firm which expects to receive Pta1 million in three months. The anticipated sum is worth DM11,810 at a current spot exchange rate of DM1.181 = Pta100, but should the peseta be devalued to, say, DM1 = Pta100 before the end of this period, the German firm receives only DM10,000 and incurs a foreign exchange loss. If, however, it had initially contracted to sell pesetas forward at a rate of, say, DM1.16 = Pta100, it would have received DM11,600 and the loss would have been limited to the DM210 cost of the forward transaction. The existence of a long position (net foreign currency asset) and the failure to cover (hedge) this position exposed the German firm to an unfavourable and avoidable movement in the peseta spot exchange rate.

Take next the case of an Irish firm which must pay Fl50,000 in three months' time for goods from the Netherlands. At a present spot exchange rate of I£1 (Irish punt) = Fl2.995, this would cost I£16,694. If, however, the punt were to weaken against the guilder to, say, I£1 = Fl2.75 over the period, the firm would find itself paying I£18,182 and would suffer a foreign exchange loss of I£1488. This might be avoided by hedging through the forward exchange market: buying guilders forward at a rate of, say, I£1 = Fl2.98. In this case, the loss would have been limited to £85, the cost of the forward transaction.

How else might these firms cover themselves

against foreign exchange risk? In our second example, it would have been possible to pay three months ahead, that is, to *lead* the payment. The loss in this case would have been the loss of interest on I£16,994 for three months. Someone with a bill due now in a foreign currency which they feel will fall in value in the future may endeavour to pay late (to *lag* the payment). Again, foreign exchange risk can be covered using only the spot market. Thus, the Irish firm could buy guilders in the spot market, invest them in Netherlands securities for three months at Netherlands interest rates and then use the guilders at the end of the period to pay for the goods supplied. The German firm could borrow pesetas at the beginning of the period, convert them into DM at the spot exchange rate and use the pesetas received in three months' time to pay off the loan. The cost of this operation would have been the interest paid on the peseta loan.

The forward market, however, provides a more convenient way of hedging. In the German example, it would have been necessary to find someone in Spain willing to lend at reasonable interest rates. In the Irish case, either of the alternatives requires the firm to have funds now and to tie those funds up for three months. Other instruments useful for the hedging of risk, notably futures, options and swaps, are dealt with in Chapters 13 and 14.

Although the forward market was developed as a means of providing insurance against risk, it has come to be used principally as a means of speculation, which involves the taking on of risk (moving to an open position). Firms sometimes engage in speculation in an attempt to make additional profits to those produced by their normal activities. For example, the German firm may choose not to hedge against the exchange rate risk in the expectation that the currency in which it is long (the peseta) will strengthen, increasing the return on the transaction. Equally, the Irish firm may choose not to insure itself against forex risk in the hope that the guilder will weaken against the punt, allowing the firm to settle its bill at a lower cost in punts.

As well, a market agent may engage in speculation in a currency in which s/he has no other interest and may do this on either the spot or forward market. Most obviously, if a French speculator thinks that a currency, say Austrian schillings (Sch), is likely to strengthen against the franc, s/he may borrow funds in francs and use them to buy schillings spot, hold the schillings in the form of a liquid security and, if the schilling strengthens, cash in the security, reconvert the schillings to francs, and pay off the loan, leaving a profit. Alternatively, s/he may use the forward market, selling francs for schillings forward. Then, when the schilling strengthens, s/he buys francs for schillings at the new spot rate and sells francs to meet the requirement of the forward contract. This would again leave the agent with a profit. Of course, if the value of the schilling fell rather than rose, both strategies would produce losses. The use of the forward market does not require the speculator to have available or borrow the full amount of the transaction at the beginning of the period, although s/he will need to have sufficient funds available to persuade the market maker that s/he will be able to meet the forward contract when it falls due. Thus it is likely that acting through the forward market requires some of the funds needed for the transaction to be tied up for a shorter period than does acting through the spot market. This, in turn, means that the per annum rate of profit from a forward transaction is likely to be higher than for the equivalent spot market transaction.

You should next consider how a speculator might make use of the forward market to profit from a belief that his home currency, say Belgian francs (BFr), is likely to fall in value in the next month.

12.5.1 Attitudes to speculation

Speculators provide liquidity to a market. Thus, it is argued, their presence provides a benefit for agents who wish to use the market for normal business or insurance services. For example, in the absence of the activities of speculators, the number of people wishing to buy or sell a relatively minor currency forward may be so small that no market maker is prepared to offer forward contracts involving that currency. Again, if only a small number of a particular forward contract (involving, say, US dollars and Greek drachma) were sold, the risks to the market maker would be high and the bid/offer spread on the contract would be large. Thus, firms wishing to hedge against risks associated with holding Greek drachma would find it expensive to do so. The presence of speculators deepens the market, reduces the volatility of the exchange rates and leads to a lowering of the cost of using the market.

In addition, as we have already seen in Section 12.4 above, it is claimed that speculators act to ensure the efficient operation of markets, linking present and future prices of assets. This favourable view holds speculation to be stabilizing, always moving the market towards its equilibrium. Destabilizing speculators – those trying to bet against the natural direction of the market – would, it is argued, lose since market forces are so strong that it is not possible to act against them. For example, suppose market forces determine that the value of a currency must fall. Speculators make their profit by seeing this in advance of other people and selling the currency with the aim of buying it back later at a lower price. Thus their action forces the value down towards its new equilibrium value. Again, speculators who realize that a rise/fall from an equilibrium is likely to be only temporary act on the correct assumption that the exchange rate returns to its previous level after the effects of the temporary shock wear off. They sell/buy the currency when it has deviated sufficiently from its equilibrium value for the return to equilibrium to compensate them for the trouble and risk of engaging in the transaction. In doing this, they help to push the currency back to the original equilibrium position. Successful speculators thus are said to ensure that movements to new equilibrium positions occur more smoothly than otherwise would be the case and that equilibrium positions are stable. Since the aim of speculation is to make a profit, it follows that unsuccessful speculators quickly leave the market. Only successful speculators remain in the market. This support for speculation is an important part of the argument that markets left to themselves produce stable equilibrium exchange rates and thus is a major element in the case for floating rates of exchange.

Arguments against speculation claim that some speculators do lose – they are not the core of professionals in the market but a part of the large fringe of traders, tourists and central banks who take open positions in foreign exchange but to whom the activity is peripheral. If this is so, it does not follow that the outcome of speculation is always to move the market in the direction in which the market would otherwise have gone.

Of greater weight is the proposition that markets do not always work well and that this allows the possibility of profitable destabilizing speculation. Markets might, for example, fail because of time lags, different speeds of adjustment of different prices, lack of information or asymmetric information. In such circumstances, speculators might attempt to amplify price movements. This is more likely where trading volumes are low (thin markets) and market agents form expectations extrapolatively. For instance, speculators might be able to sell a currency sufficiently heavily to force its value down; others within the market observe the fall and assume it will continue. Thus, they also sell, pushing the price down further still. Speculators are then able to buy back in at the lower price, taking their profit.

We have also seen, in Section 12.4.5, the suggestion that even speculators may be risk averse, limiting the amount they bet on any economic outcome that is less than a sure thing. In such a case, their actions would not succeed, for example, in bringing into line forward and future spot rates of exchange.

12.6   Forecasting foreign exchange rates

A great deal of the activity in forex markets is based on expectations concerning future exchange rates. Consequently, much effort has gone into the development of models aimed at forecasting these rates. We have come across two approaches in this chapter – the use of market fundamentals and the application of the Efficient Market Hypothesis. We said, in Section 12.1, that fundamentalist models include important influences on the current and capital accounts of the balance of payments but this leaves matters very open. In fact, a wide range of fundamentalist models have been developed incorporating theories of the current and capital accounts of the balance of payments, the role of inflation, and theories of expectations formation. Fundamentalist models may be classified in a variety of ways.

One common classification is into *flow models*, those based on current account performance, and stock or *asset models* which stress the role of the capital account. Flow models incorporate relative prices (PPP), differences in the rate of productivity increase, and/or the relative rates of growth of domestic and world income. *Stock models* include relative interest rates and rates of growth of money supplies as well as exchange rate expectations and PPP among the market fundamentals. Most early fundamentalist models implied that real exchange rates should change relatively slowly over time. This left the major problem of explaining the volatility of exchange rates following the collapse of the Bretton Woods fixed exchange rate system of the International Monetary Fund in 1972.

One approach has been to attribute the volatility to the actions of governments and the intervention of central banks in the market. Governments, it has been argued, have often followed interventionist monetary policies which have kept exchange rates away from their equilibrium levels. Central banks have often bought and sold currencies (in effect acting as speculators) for political motives, attempting to influence the value of their own currencies or as part of a coordinated attempt to influence the values of important world currencies such as the dollar and the yen.

Another approach has been to incorporate time lags into models to explain why an exchange rate may not, once an equilibrium position has been disturbed, move directly and rapidly to a new equilibrium. One significant class of models of this kind has been the over-shooting exchange rate models (deriving from Dornbusch, 1976). These continue to assume the existence of long-run equilibrium rates of exchange and incorporate both covered interest rate and purchasing power parity. They also typically assume rational expectations and so market participants are assumed to make the best available use of all relevant information and to employ the best available model for forecasting future exchange rates. The result is that market agents are assumed to know what the long-run equilibrium exchange rate is. Nonetheless, despite this knowledge, exchange rates are held to overshoot their long-run equilibrium positions. That is, in the process of moving to a new equilibrium an exchange rate first shoots well beyond it in the opposite direction. This result is achieved by assuming that

different elements in the model adjust at different speeds. For instance, one might assume that the money market in an economy adjusts instantaneously but that the goods market is slow to adjust to new influences. An alternative is to assume that the prices of tradeable goods adjust quickly to international pressures but that the prices of non-tradeables change only slowly.

Unfortunately, all of the fundamentalist models have problems. Flow models assume either that capital is completely immobile or that prices are fixed or both. Simple stock models assume that domestic and foreign assets are perfect substitutes for each other and that a maintained interest rate differential produces a continual flow of capital. This does not happen in practice. PPP plays an important part in all stock models and we have noted that empirical evidence provides little support for PPP. Expectations are important in many stock models but there is uncertainty as to how to model them. None of the models do well in testing, many performing worse than a simple random walk model. One study (by Meese and Rogoff, 1983) tested the predictions over the late 1970s of three fundamentalist models (a monetary model; Dornbusch's over-shooting model; and a stock model which added current account factors to the Dornbusch model) together with those of a model stating simply that the exchange rate in the following period would be the same as in the current period. They found that the last model performed best! Models based on fundamentals faced particular difficulties in the first half of the 1980s as the dollar continued a prolonged increase in value (reaching its peak in February 1985) against all economic logic. This led to a number of developments in exchange rate theories.

Models were developed which attempted to explain sudden and apparently inexplicable jumps in the value of a currency through the phenomenon of *rational bubbles* (bubbles in which all participants know the correct model for the determination of the exchange rate but nonetheless the actual rate moves sharply away from equilibrium until eventually the bubble bursts – the phenomenon of bubbles in markets is discussed in Sections 5.5 and 11.1). Models which explain these jumps but which continue to assume that the market is characterized by rational behaviour, start in a disequilibrium position and show how rational decisions may cause the market to move further away from equilibrium rather than returning to it.

For example, in trying to explain the inexorable rise in value of the US dollar between 1981 and 1985, Dornbusch started with an overvalued exchange rate. Investors were assumed to be risk neutral, and so a strategy that has a risk of high losses if things go wrong but a potential for high profits if they go right is equivalent to one in which potential losses and profits are both low. Investors had to compare two probabilities: that the exchange rate would return to equilibrium and that it would go on rising. The further the exchange rate was currently above the equilibrium rate, the greater was the potential loss for investors if it fell back to equilibrium and the greater the required profits had to be if the rate kept on rising. To put it another way, the greater the risk of a crash, the faster the rate of appreciation had to be to compensate for potential losses. Investors were thus obliged to go on buying the currency, pushing the rate up further and further, although there was no economic justification for doing so.

Some models allowed for the existence of two kinds of forecasters in the market. In Goodhart's (1988) model, for example, dealers make their decisions on the basis of a weighted average of the forecasts of market efficiency theorists and modellers of fundamentals, with the weights determined by the relative past success of the two forecasts. Again the model starts with an overvalued exchange rate. In the absence of news, the market efficient forecast is for no change while fundamentalists predict that the exchange rate will fall to equilibrium. Assume next that a random shock forces it further away from equilibrium. Both forecasts will be wrong but the market efficiency forecast will be less wrong and in the next period the weights are changed to reflect this, causing the predicted fall in the exchange rate to be smaller. Dealers thus buy more of the overvalued currency, forcing the rate up yet further.

An alternative approach has been to reject rationality in its narrow economic sense. It is argued that much trading in forex markets is based on 'noise' rather than 'news' and that this results in excessive volatility. Frankel and Froot (1990) de-

veloped a model similar to Goodhart's, except that the bubble is not rational but speculative, being the outcome of self-confirming market speculations. Again there are two types of forecasters but this time they are fundamentalists and chartists. Fundamentalists (using an over-shooting model) forecast a depreciation of the dollar which would be rational if there were no chartists. Chartists extrapolate recent trends based on an information set that includes no fundamentals. Box 12.6 indicates some of the features of exchange rate behaviour of interest to chartists and the extent to which market practitioners often combine fundamentalism and chartism.

In Frankel and Froot's model, portfolio managers base their decisions on a weighted average of the forecasts of fundamentalists and chartists. Starting from an overvalued dollar (explained by over-shooting), fundamentalists forecast depreciation but are incorrect. Consequently, portfolio managers increase the weight they assign to the forecasts of the chartists. In doing this, they reduce their weighted-average expectations of depreciation, raise their demands for the dollar and thus bring about the dollar's continued appreciation. According to this view, in 1985 the dollar entered a new stage, with an ever-worsening current account deficit leading to the reversal of the overvaluation caused by the bubble. Frankel and Froot thus show how (non-rational but) sensible behaviour can generate not simply short-run volatility in exchange rates but also, and more importantly, large and cumulative exchange rate misalignments. More recent work has attempted to set such models within the framework of chaos theory in which very small changes in a system can produce dramatic results.

Speculators are also sometimes divided into those who think short-term (which in this context refers to one week or less) and those with long-run horizons (up to three months), with short-termers holding extrapolative expectations and long-termers regressive expectations. Much then depends on which group dominates the market at any particular time.

A number of special counter-examples have been developed to Friedman's (1953) argument, outlined above, that destabilizing speculators on average lose and are driven out of the market. Most of these involve heterogeneous actors, for instance 'suckers' who lose and 'sharpies' who win. In the simplest

---

Box 12.5   Forecasting foreign exchange rates with the use of charts

Forecasters who make use of charts of past foreign exchange rates are attempting only to forecast the very short term. They assume that current demand and supply conditions can best be understood by examining the way exchange rates have been moving. Forecasting is based principally upon three elements in the charts.

(a) Trends

Whether an exchange rate has been rising or falling and the gradient of the trend – relatively flat trends are regarded as being more sustainable; steep trends as more volatile and subject to change. Trends can be established by constructing a channel of two parallel lines which encompass all the exchange rate movements. If an exchange rate then breaks out of its current channel there is a suggestion that the present trend is about to be reversed. Analysis of trends can be supplemented by calculation of moving averages.

(b) Support and resistance levels

A support level is a rate at which the currency appears to be strongly demanded. Thus, it is difficult for the exchange rate to fall below this level. A resistance level is the reverse – a rate which it is difficult for the currency to rise above. Support and resistance levels thus establish the width of the current channel in which the currency is trading. It is usually felt that if support or resistance levels are breached, the currency will fall sharply below the previous support level or rise sharply above the prior resistance level.

(c) Pattern recognition

This is the recognition of visual patterns in the chart – either continuation patterns (including 'flags' and 'triangles') which suggest that the rate will continue to follow its current overall tendencies; or reversal patterns (such as 'head and shoulders').

In addition, chartists make use of information on momentum (the speed at which exchange rates change) and velocity (the rate of change of moving averages of exchange rates).

The example of financial journalism in Box 12.4 shows how ideas of market fundamentals may be combined with chartist views regarding support and resistance levels.

---

counter-example, based on the theory of rational speculative bubbles, each market participant loses if he does not go along with the herd.

12.7   Summary

The forex market is the market in which one national currency is traded for another. The market has grown hugely in recent years because of the rapid growth in international capital mobility and the volatility of exchange rates following the breakdown of the Bretton Woods fixed exchange rate system in the early 1970s. This volatility has greatly increased the need of firms to protect themselves against foreign exchange risk and has provided the opportunity to exploit exchange rate variations for profit.

Because exchange rates are prices of one currency in terms of another, they can be expressed in two ways – direct and indirect quotation. Currencies may be traded spot (for immediate delivery) or forward (delivery normally one month, three months or one year ahead). Exchange rate indices may be prepared expressing the average value of a currency against a basket of currencies or the real value of one currency against another, allowing for differences in expected rates of inflation.

If foreign exchange markets were perfect or dominated by perfectly informed arbitrageurs and speculators, both spot and forward exchange rates would adjust immediately to any new information received by the market and it can be shown that forward rates should be good predictors of future spot rates of exchange. This prediction can be established through the development of a number of important relationships – interest rate parity (showing the relationship between interest rate differentials and forward discounts and premiums), the Fisher effect (the relationship between expected inflation rates and nominal interest rates), and purchasing power parity (the relationship between relative inflation rates and future spot rates of exchange). Although these relationships are important in theory, the Fisher effect and purchasing power parity do not perform well under empirical testing.

Nonetheless, both arbitrageurs and speculators play important roles in the foreign exchange market. As well as helping to bring about covered interest rate parity, arbitrageurs act to ensure that exchange rates are mutually consistent through exchange rate arbitrage. The contribution of speculators is much more controversial. They make use of instruments (such as forward exchange rates) that were initially developed to provide protection against foreign-exchange risk to seek profits from outguessing the rest of the market. The fact that this is possible indicates that foreign exchange markets are, in fact, far from perfect. This is indicated also by the failure to develop reliable models for the forecasting of future rates of exchange.

Key concepts used in this chapter

Foreign exchange risk	Hedging	Interest rate parity
Indirect quotation	Speculation	Purchasing Power Parity (PPP)
Forward premiums and discounts	Chartism	Short versus long positions
	Direct quotation	Rational versus speculative
Effective exchange rate	Exchange cross rates	bubbles
Efficient markets hypothesis	Real exchange rate	Extrapolative expectations
Exchange rate arbitrage	Covered interest arbitrage	

Questions and problems

1 List as many items as you can of 'news' which would be likely to cause the value of your domestic currency to fall. Explain why in each case.

2 Explain the following terms in the context of the foreign exchange market:
 (a) Covered interest arbitrage
 (b) Long positions in a foreign currency
 (c) Hedging
 (d) Three-point foreign exchange arbitrage

3 Compare the Bank of England index for the pound sterling with the J P Morgan index for the dollar, as shown in the *Financial Times* and answer the following questions:
 (a) Why is a figure provided for the New Zealand dollar in the Bank of England index but not in the J P Morgan index?
 (b) Although Mexico trades a good deal with the United States, no figure is provided for the Mexican New Peso in the J P Morgan index. Why might that be?

4 In the 'Money Rates' column of the *Financial Times* of 22 February 1997, the three-month interest rate in Switzerland was quoted as 1.75 per cent; the three-month rate in the USA was given as 5.44 per cent. On the same day, the spot rate of exchange for the Swiss franc against the dollar was: $1 = SFr1.4656–1.4665. On the assumption of perfect interest parity what would one have expected the forward premium/discount on Swiss francs to have been? Why might the actual forward discount have been different from this?

5 (a) Describe the arbitrage operation that would produce a profit if the following set of spot exchange rates prevailed in a foreign exchange market, explaining how you arrived at your answer:
 $US1 = Pta142.680–142.780
 $US1 = DM1.6431–1.6439
 DM1 = Pta84.67–84.95

(b) What impacts would such an arbitrage operation have on the above set of exchange rates?

6 Examine the 'Dollar Spot Forward against the Dollar' table from any copy of the *Financial Times* and answer the following questions:
   (a) What information is being given by the columns headed: 'one month' and 'three months'?
   (b) In what way do the exchange rates given for the UK, Ireland and the Ecu differ from all the other rates in this table?
   (c) On which currencies is the bid–offer spread relatively large? Why might this be?

7 Explain the relationship postulated by the efficient markets hypothesis between forward rates of exchange and future spot rates of exchange.

8 You are given the following information:

   Spot exchange rate Fl1.8911–1.8916 = $1
   Expected Netherlands inflation rate for next year = 2.2%
   Expected US inflation rate for next year = 4.1%

Three-month money market interest rate for the Netherlands = 3.03%
Three-month money market interest rate for the USA = 5.44%

On the basis of these figures calculate:
(a) the real exchange rate of the guilder against the US dollar;
and
(b) the approximate three-month forward exchange rate of the guilder against the US dollar.

9 Explain and defend the argument that speculation in markets is desirable.

10 How might one use the spot markets to obtain protection against foreign exchange risk? What advantages do the forward markets have for this purpose?

11 Explain the following:
   (a) the relationship between spot and forward rates of exchange;
   (b) purchasing power parity;
   (c) the difference between a rational and a speculative bubble in the foreign exchange market.

Further reading

D Blake, *Financial Market Analysis* (London: McGraw-Hill, 1990) Ch. 7

A Buckley, *The Essence of International Money* (Hemel Hempstead: Prentice Hall, 1990)

R Dornbusch, 'Expectations and exchange rate dynamics', *Journal of Political Economy* 96, 1976, 1161–76

N Douch, *The Economics of Foreign Exchange* (Cambridge: Woodhead-Faulkner, 1989)

J A Frankel and K A Froot, 'Chartists, fundamentalists and trading in the forex market', *American Economic Review*, May, 1990, 181–5

M Friedman, 'The case for flexible exchange rates', in *Essays in Positive Economics* (Chicago: Chicago University Press, 1953, 157–203)

H D Gibson, *International Finance. Exchange Rates and*

Financial Flows in the International System (London: Longman, 1996) Chs 2 and 3

C A E Goodhart, 'The foreign exchange market: the random walk with a dragging anchor', *Economica*, 55, 1988, 437-60

C Paul Hallwood and R MacDonald, *International Money and Finance* (Oxford: Blackwell, 1994 2e) Chs 2, 3, 7, 11 and 12

R A Meese and K Rogoff, 'Empirical Exchange Rate Models of the Seventies: Do they fit out of sample?', *Journal of International Economics*, 14, 1983, 3–24

M Melvin, *International Money and Finance* (New York: HarperCollins, 1992, 3e)

K Pilbeam, *International Finance* (London: Macmillan, 1992)

K Redhead, *Introduction to the International Money Markets* (Cambridge: Woodhead-Faulkner, 1992) Ch. 2

CHAPTER 13

Derivatives – the financial futures markets

Box 13.1

What you will learn in this chapter:

- What derivatives are and why derivatives markets have grown so quickly
- What financial futures are and how futures exchanges are organized
- How to read financial futures information in the *Financial Times*
- What determines the pricing of financial futures in general
- How pricing rules may be applied to different types of financial futures

13.1 Introduction

One of the most striking developments in financial markets over the past quarter of a century has been the establishment and growth of financial derivatives markets. A derivative is a financial instrument based upon the performance of separately traded commodities or financial instruments. Many agricultural and mining products are traded on commodities markets by firms who are end users of those products. Equally, bond markets and foreign exchange markets allow end users to borrow or lend funds or to obtain foreign exchange. It is possible then to construct contracts which promise to deliver those products at some time in the future or give the right to buy or sell them in the future. These contracts may then be traded in markets different from the original commodities and financial markets (usually referred to as cash markets). Such contracts are known as *derivatives*. They are linked to the cash market through the possibility that a delivery of the primary commodity or instrument might occur. For example, if a trader is to carry out a promise to deliver an instrument in three months' time he will at some time during that three months need to buy the instrument in the cash market. It follows that the value of a derivative and hence its price varies as the price in the cash markets fluctuates. In practice, derivatives seldom lead to the exchange of the underlying instrument (referred to for short as the underlying). Instead, contracts are *closed out* or allowed to lapse before the delivery.

Derivatives, then, are instruments that allow market agents to gamble on movements in the prices of other instruments without being required actually to trade in them. Their initial purpose was to allow traders to hedge risks which they faced in the cash markets as a part of their normal business activity by offsetting one type of risk (resulting, for example, from being long in the cash market) with the opposite risk in a derivatives market. Clearly, however, these markets provide additional possibilities for speculators to take on risk in the expectation that they will be able to outguess the market. In the case of *financial derivatives*, the underlying instrument is financial: bonds, currencies, or stock exchange indices. Since commodity futures are also used for financial purposes, however, the difference between them and financial futures is of no great importance.

Although derivatives trading based upon commodities (agricultural products or minerals) has existed for well over a century, the need for financial derivatives markets was not seen until the early 1970s when the globalization of business, which had been proceeding apace for the previous 20 years, confronted the increased volatility of foreign exchange rates and increasing and fluctuating rates of inflation. As firms were exposed to increasing amounts of risk, risk management (or financial engineering) became a major concern of business. The most obvious form of *exchange rate risk* relates to current individual transactions (transactions exposure) – the possibility that apparently profitable activities will turn into losses because of unfavourable movements in exchange rates. More generally, the whole future trading performance of a foreign branch or subsidiary may suffer as a result of exchange rate changes, depending on the impact they have on factors such as relative inflation rates, government interest rate and other policies, and a firm's profit margins and market share (economic exposure). A different form of risk exists, however, for transnational firms with subsidiaries in other countries – the loss of value of foreign assets in the consolidated balance sheet of the parent company (translation exposure). In addition, the participation of firms in distant and foreign markets led not only to increased exchange rate risk but also to greater default risk and market risk and to sovereign risk.

Responses were many. To help counter foreign exchange risk, firms developed internal techniques relating to accounting systems and payment and invoicing procedures. Governments of developed countries became involved, providing exchange rate guarantees and other forms of insurance, in effect subsidizing the foreign activities of their exporting firms. Developments in international capital markets allowed firms to borrow more easily in foreign currencies against anticipated future payments in those currencies. The growth of Eurocurrency markets, in particular, allowed firms to obtain foreign currency overdrafts to offset long positions in major currencies. Forward foreign exchange markets developed and banks began to use them more imaginatively, offering, for example, optional date forward contracts in which a firm is given an option regarding the maturity date within a specified period and is charged the premium or discount that applies to the most costly of the settlement dates within the period.

These, and other activities, aimed to remove or reduce the risk faced by firms in particular transactions. An alternative approach in a generally risky environment is to oppose one form of risk to another and hence scope existed for the creation of new instruments which themselves carried risk but which firms could use to balance risks in other elements of their portfolios. More importantly, increases in the range of available instruments allowed firms to diversify their portfolios of assets further and we have seen the advantage of diversification in overall risk reduction in Section 2.3.

At the same time as firms were becoming increasingly international, they were merging or taking over other firms in different industries – the number of conglomerates was increasing. It was only a matter of time before large firms began to see trading in financial instruments as equivalent to any other part of their business. Risky situations came to be seen as opportunities for making profits which were equivalent to profits made from selling cars, chemicals or airline tickets. This great growth in financial activity was necessarily accompanied by a vast growth in international banking, with banks acting as guarantors, providing information and expertise and speculating on their own behalf in the new markets. Banks, seeking to manage the risk they were taking on in order to meet the needs of end users, increasingly engaged in transactions with other banks to the point where interbank transactions have come to make up a very high proportion of total financial activity.

The great growth in derivatives is indicated by the very rapid increase in the number of exchanges on which they are traded. The world market is still dominated by the big Chicago Exchanges which started life as commodities markets, the Chicago Board of Trade (CBOT) and the Chicago Mercantile Exchange (CME), but 46 new exchanges opened between 1980 and 1993 and derivatives are now traded on more than 60 exchanges worldwide, with almost all OECD countries possessing at least one such exchange. The Marché à Terme International de France (MATIF), which only opened in 1986, has become the leader in the European financial derivatives markets and the fourth-largest derivatives market in the world.

It is these relatively new instruments and markets that we need to explore in this chapter and the next. Although we shall come across many variants upon them, we shall follow the usual practice of dividing financial derivatives into three major groups –

futures, options and swaps. As we shall see, however, swaps are quite different in nature from the other two. We shall deal with futures in this chapter and in Chapter 14 shall consider options and swaps as well as making a comparison between the three types.

13.2 The nature of financial futures

Like any forward contract, a futures contract is an agreement to exchange a given commodity at a specified later date at a price established when the contract is signed. The buyer goes long in the cash market, that is s/he contracts to take delivery of the underlying in the future. The seller goes short, contracting to deliver the instrument in the future. Futures contracts differ from other forward contracts (such as in forward foreign exchange) in the form of operation of the market, the terms of the contract, and the likelihood of their leading to delivery of the underlying. Forward foreign exchange transactions are over-the-counter (OTC) business – that is, they are contracts between a bank and another market agent. The amount of the contract and its terms are determined by the two parties to it. Although most forward foreign exchange contracts are for the most common periods of one month, three months or one year, some flexibility is possible in the time period as well as in the amount. Crucially, a forward foreign exchange transaction does not produce a tradeable instrument which can be sold on to a third party and so forward foreign exchange contracts are not derivatives.

A futures contract, on the other hand, is tradeable and is sold on an exchange rather than being OTC business. Trading at a futures exchange takes place in trading *pits*, areas of the trading floor devoted to the trade of a particular contract. The direct method of trading between members, which allows all traders to hear every negotiated price, is known as *open outcry*. Some financial futures exchanges, for example the Swiss Options and Financial Futures Exchange (SOFFEX), have developed automated systems which allow screen-based trading.

To increase its tradeability, a futures contract is standardized in terms of both time period and amount. It specifies the quantity and quality of the underlying

instrument as well as the date of delivery and the agreed price at which delivery of the instrument will take place, should delivery actually occur. Thus, the Three Month Euromark futures contract offered by the London International Financial Futures Exchange (LIFFE) specifies an amount of DM1 million, while the Sterling Futures contract offered by the International Monetary Market (IMM) of the CME specifies an amount of £62,500. Interest rate futures specify the amount of the bond and its interest-rate coupon, for instance a $100,000 nominal 20-year Treasury bond with a 7 per cent coupon. As long as single contracts are for relatively small amounts, this does not reduce the flexibility of the market by much since it is always possible for a market agent to increase his or her exposure by buying or selling a number of contracts on the same underlying instrument for the same period.

Most financial futures contracts have four delivery dates per year. There are a number of very precise delivery details including lists of eligible assets which will satisfy the delivery requirements of a contract and methods of determining the final settlement price. However, as we said above, delivery does not usually occur as buyers and sellers of futures contracts are not normally end users of the underlying. Traders using futures to hedge against risk to which they are exposed in the cash market are seeking to lock into existing exchange or interest rates on future transactions. In such cases, the period for which the hedge is needed is unlikely to coincide with the time period of the futures contract. Once a firm has traded out of its open position in the cash market, it will no longer need the hedge in the futures market.

Financial futures may also be traded by speculators who wish to profit from the rises or falls they expect to occur in interest rates, exchange rates or stock exchange indices. Through futures, they can take a view about trends in cash markets without having to purchase the underlying currency or financial instrument. A speculator who felt that interest rates were likely to rise or a currency's value decline could go short in the relevant asset by selling a futures contract. Traders who are using the futures market to create an open position in this way usually close the position once they have achieved their profit objectives. If it does not seem likely that they will make the hoped-for profit, they will probably cut their losses before delivery is due. Investors wishing to cancel out the obligation to deliver or to accept delivery of the instrument can do so by entering into an offsetting (or reversing) contract. That is, if a market agent has entered into a contract to deliver a particular instrument, she can offset this by taking out another contract which requires her to take delivery of the same amount of the same instrument on the same date. Her obligations under the two contracts then cancel out. In some cases, such as futures based upon equity market indices or interest rates on short-term deposits, no delivery is possible and traders meet their obligations by making cash payments based upon the changes in the value of the index or interest rate in question.

To reduce default risk and hence to make futures more easily tradeable, futures exchanges make use of a *clearing house* which covers any default arising from a contract. Therefore, although all futures contracts involve a buyer and a seller, the obligation of each is to the clearing house, not to each other. That is, after the transaction has been recorded, the clearing house substitutes itself for the counterparty and becomes the seller to every buyer and vice versa. Therefore the only default risk faced by someone entering into a futures contract stems from any doubts about the creditworthiness of the clearing house itself. This is, in turn, reduced in a number of ways. Firstly, all transactions must take place through members of the exchange who act as brokers for anyone wishing to invest in the market. The number of members (or seats on the exchange) is limited. Seats on an exchange may be purchased from existing members but new members must demonstrate their creditworthiness to the exchange. In addition, the members of the exchange must keep with the clearing house special accounts (margin accounts) which are adjusted from day to day to ensure that they are always able to settle their debts to the clearing house. Investors must, in turn, maintain similar accounts with the members of the exchange. This is known as trading on margin, and futures positions are said to be margined on a *marked-to-market* basis. These rules should mean that the clearing house is able to guarantee the performance of every contract entered into on the exchange.

The first step in the system is that a member must, at the start of the contract period, pay into a margin

account a small percentage (the *initial margin*) of the value of the contract. The size of the initial margin is intended to reflect the maximum daily loss likely to arise on the contract and so will be related to the volatility of the price movements of that instrument. Initial margins are generally between one and five per cent of the value of the contract. Margin accounts must then be adjusted daily to reflect gains or losses on a contract over the day. Assume a contract has a commencing value of $10,000 with each counterparty paying an initial margin of $500 into their margin accounts with the clearing house. Assume next that during the first day's trading, the contract's value rises to $10,100, representing a loss for the seller and a gain for the buyer of the contract. The clearing house would then transfer $100 from the seller's margin account to that of the buyer. Should the price rise again the next day, a similar transfer would occur. If the balance in the seller's account fell below a specified level (the *maintenance margin*), she would be required to make additional payments into the account (the *variation margin*) in order to keep the account at or above an acceptable minimum balance. On the other hand, the buyer could, in this case, withdraw his daily profits from his margin account. Some exchanges (for example, LIFFE) set the maintenance margin at the same level as the initial margin.

Of course, should the value of the above contract fall below £10,000, the buyer's margin account would fall and he might be required to make additional payments. Failure to make such payments immediately would lead to the closure of the contract against the defaulting party. The system of marking accounts to market daily prevents losses from accumulating, and the holding of margins by the clearing house removes most default risk.

Daily gains and losses on contracts are determined by the settlement price which is set by the settlement committee of the exchange. It is normally the closing price for the day (the last price at which the contract has traded). However, if a contract has not traded for some time prior to the market's close, the committee may set a different settlement price in an attempt to reflect accurately the trading conditions at the close of the market. The freedom that the settlement committee has to fix the settlement price also allows it to protect the clearing house from the remaining default risk which might arise from very large daily swings in the price of a contract. They may do this by setting price limits – maximum movements up and down from the previous day's settlement price. If these limits would otherwise be broken, the market closes *limit-up* or *limit-down*. The aim is to prevent losses going above the amounts held in margin accounts, forcing or tempting losers to default. The hope is that the temporary closure of the market might lead traders to reassess their positions. However, the system of price limits has its disadvantages. As long as the market remains closed positions cannot be closed out and contracts become illiquid, destroying one of the major advantages of futures contracts, their tradeability. For this reason, many exchanges do not operate price limits during the delivery month of a contract.

The relative smallness of the margin requirements is responsible for another important aspect of futures markets – their high *gearing* (or leverage). If all goes well, the effective rate of profit on a futures contract can be very high. To see this, consider the following simple example. Assume that in June an investor buys a £62,500 contract on sterling for delivery in September at a price of £1 = $1.60. The contract value is $100,000. Assume an initial margin of two per cent ($2,000). Assume next that the value of sterling rises steadily over the contract period to £1 = $1.70 and the contract price rises in line with it. The value of the contract would have been rising steadily and no further margin payments would have been required. At the end of September, the investor takes delivery of the sterling at £1 = $1.60 and sells it spot at £1 = $1.70. The buyer of the contract makes a profit (and the seller a loss) of $6,250 (62,500 × $0.10) but has only had to outlay $2,000, giving a per annum rate of return of 850 per cent! Alternatively, he could take his profit by reversing the contract – taking out another contract to *sell* £62,500 in September at the now higher contract price.

Sadly, however, life is not quite as easy as this. In addition to making margin payments, investors must pay brokers a negotiated commission for executing orders. Commission (sometimes referred to as the direct cost of the contract) is charged on both the opening and the closing of a position and is normally payable either when the position is closed or when delivery takes place. More seriously, the value of

sterling may have fallen, requiring the investor to advance more margin. Suppose that the day after the contract was taken out, the value of sterling fell to £1 = $1.50. The value of the contract would have fallen to approximately $93,750 and (on the assumption that the maintenance margin was the same as the initial margin) a variation margin payment of $6,250 would need to be made. If sterling later rose in value, some of this variation margin could be withdrawn, but an investor would need to be fortunate not to have to make some variation margin payments over the life of a contract and thus the average amount held in the margin account over the contract period is likely to be above the initial margin. The possibility that additional margin payments may have to be made on a daily basis also requires an investor to keep a certain amount of his or her assets in a very liquid form. Of course, if the value of sterling did not rise again during the life of the contract, the investor would be required on the delivery date to buy sterling at $1.60 and would only be able to sell it spot for $1.50, producing a loss of $6,250. Again, the investor could avoid having to receive and then re-sell sterling by reversing the contract before the delivery date but this would not reduce the loss. Futures contracts, therefore, provide the prospect of high rates of return but involve considerable risks.

13.3   Reading the Financial Times

On the *Currencies and Money* page of the *Financial Times*, tables of a range of short-term interest rate and currency futures are provided. In Table 13.1, we present a number of short-term interest contracts offered by the London International Financial Futures and Options Exchange (LIFFE) and the International Monetary Market (IMM).

Other futures contracts on which information is provided by the Financial Times include the Three Month PIBOR (Paris Interbank Offer Rate) Futures of MATIF and Three Month Sterling Futures offered by the LIFFE. All the LIFFE contracts in Table 13.1 are contracts on three-month or one-month time deposits in the specified currencies. The buyer of such a contract would, on delivery, receive a time deposit at an eligible bank of the amount specified beside the title of the contract. The Three Month

Table 13.1

■ THREE MONTH EUROMARK FUTURES (LIFFE)* DM1m points of 100%						
	Open	Sett price	Change	High	Low	Est. vol	Open int.
Apr	96.84	96.82	-0.02	96.84	96.82	1101	5866
Jun	96.82	96.83	-0.01	96.84	96.82	22339	183982
Sep	96.76	96.75	-0.02	96.77	96.74	35818	150147
Dec	96.60	96.60	-0.03	96.62	96.59	18471	177580

■ ONE MONTH EUROMARK FUTURES (LIFFE)* DM3m points of 100%						
	Open	Sett price	Change	High	Low	Est. vol	Open int.
Mar	96.77	96.75	-0.04	96.77	96.74	267	18689
Apr	96.83	96.82	-0.04	96.83	96.82	452	4001
May	-	96.83	-0.04	-	-	0	3787
Jun	-	96.83	-0.04	-	-	0	430

■ THREE MONTH EUROLIRA FUTURES (LIFFE)* L1000m points of 100%						
	Open	Sett price	Change	High	Low	Est. vol	Open int.
Mar	92.91	92.87	+0.01	92.94	92.82	21935	84051
Jun	93.50	93.50	+0.05	93.53	93.44	22303	99379
Sep	93.84	93.82	+0.05	93.87	93.76	11302	48281
Dec	93.97	93.95	+0.05	94.00	93.89	7379	33411

■ THREE MONTH EURO SWISS FRANC FUTURES (LIFFE) SFr1m points of 100%						
	Open	Sett price	Change	High	Low	Est. vol	Open int.
Mar	98.20	98.28	+0.04	98.28	98.20	2159	30113
Jun	98.28	98.34	+0.05	98.34	98.27	4833	36436
Sep	98.21	98.25	+0.04	98.27	98.21	465	14517
Dec	98.04	98.09	+0.05	98.09	98.04	109	10395

■ THREE MONTH EUROYEN FUTURES (LIFFE) Y100m points of 100%						
	Open	Sett price	Change	High	Low	Est. vol	Open int.
Mar	-	99.44	-	-	-	0	n/a
Jun	99.42	99.42	-	99.42	99.42	286	n/a
Sep	99.35	99.35	+0.01	99.35	99.35	200	n/a

■ THREE MONTH ECU FUTURES (LIFFE) Ecu1m points of 100%						
	Open	Sett price	Change	High	Low	Est. vol	Open int.
Mar	95.87	95.86	-0.02	95.88	95.86	994	10623
Jun	95.92	95.92	-0.01	95.93	95.92	723	6114
Sep	95.92	95.92	-0.02	95.93	95.92	557	4033
Dec	95.88	95.88	-0.01	95.88	95.87	128	4874

* LIFFE futures also traded on APT

■ THREE MONTH EURODOLLAR (IMM) $1m per 100%						
	Open	Sett price	Change	High	Low	Est. vol	Open int.
Mar	94.50	94.51	-	94.51	94.50	35,560	389,811
Jun	94.39	94.40	-0.04	94.40	94.38	76,047	394,408
Sep	94.25	94.26	-0.14	94.27	94.24	79,854	301,028

■ US TREASURY BILL FUTURES (IMM) $1m per 100%						
	Open	Sett price	Change	High	Low	Est. vol	Open int.
Mar	95.04	95.03	-	95.04	95.03	434	5,547
Jun	94.94	94.94	-0.01	94.95	94.93	179	3,724
Sep	-	94.80	-	-	-	392	1,358

All Open Interest figs. are for previous day

Euromark contract is for a deposit of DM1 million; the One Month Euromark contract for DM3 million; the Three Month Euroyen contract for a deposit of ¥100 million and so on. The gamble in such contracts relates to changes in short-term interest rates (three-month or one-month) relative to those rates at the time the contract is negotiated. Beside the amount for each contract are the words *points of 100%*. That is, the price of the contract is quoted in the form of subtractions from 100 per cent – a price of 92.91 represents an annual interest rate of 7.09 per cent (100 − 92.91). The minimum price movement (or *tick size*) on most of these contracts is one basis point (0.01%). In the case of a DM3 million one-month time deposit, a change in the price of one basis point translates into a change in the value of the contract of DM25 (0.01

per cent per annum interest on 3 million DM for one month). This is known as the *tick value* of the contract. The tick value provides a simple way of quoting the profit or loss on a contract – a profit of 10-ticks on the One Month Euromark Futures contract is a profit of DM250; a 10 tick profit on the Three Month Euro Swiss Franc contract is SFr250.

Quoting the price as an index maintains the usual inverse relationship between the price of a financial instrument and the yield on it. As explained in Section 13.4 below, although the settlement price at the time of delivery is based on the spot interest rate on the last trading day of the contract, the interest rate implied by the futures price during the life of the future can differ from the interest rate on the underlying asset in the cash market. Some examples of the relationship between futures prices shown in Table 13.1 and spot market interest rates are shown in Box 13.2.

Down the left-hand side of each table are the delivery months. With the exception of the Euromark futures, delivery days are in March, June, September and December. Naturally, the One Month Euromark contract has a delivery date in each month. The delivery day on each contract is the first business day after the last trading day, and the last trading day is the third Wednesday of the delivery month. Each table shown in Table 13.1 has seven columns. These are as follows:

Open: The price of the contract at the beginning of business.

Sett price: The settlement price – the price at which contracts are settled at the end of the day.

Change: The change in the settlement price from the previous day – on some occasions this is not equal to the difference between the first two columns. For example, December Three Month Euromark futures have both an opening and settlement price of 96.60 (implying interest rates of 3.40 per cent) but a change of − 0.03 (− 3 basis points) is given suggesting that few contracts had changed hands the previous day and that the settlement price had been different from the opening price the following morning.

High: The highest price reached for the contract on the day.

Low: The lowest price reached for the contract on the day.

Est. vol: The estimated number of contracts entered into during the day.

Open int: Open interest – the number of outstanding contracts on the previous trading day.

Currency futures tables (as shown in Table 13.2) provide similar information except that prices here are quoted in exchange rates. For example, for D-Mark futures we are told that a contract is for DM125,000 and that the price is quoted *per DM*. That is, the price reflects the indirect quotation of the DM – how much DM1 exchanges for in US dollars. The settlement price shown in Table 13.2 for March delivery is DM1 = $0.5929. The settlement price for March delivery for sterling futures is £1 = $1.6172.

Long-term interest rate futures are to be found in the World Bond Price section of the *Financial Times*. They are typically based on notional government bonds. Table 13.3 shows a sample of these. The tables indicate at the top the name of the contract, the exchange on which it is traded – LIFFE, MATIF or MEFF (Mercado Español de Futuros Financieros) in these cases, and the value of the notional bond (£50,000 for notional UK gilt futures, DM250,000 for Notional German Bund futures). The form of the quotation is also given. As we pointed out in Section 9.1, interest rates in the UK and the USA are quoted in 32nds of one per cent with one tick being 1/32 of one per cent. Hence prices on notional UK gilt futures are quoted in 32nds of 100 per cent. 112-11 must be read as 112 11/32 and 111-27 as 111 27/32. In continental Europe, on the other hand, interest rates are quoted in decimals (100ths of 100 per cent), hence the settlement prices of 103.18 and 102.36 for German bund futures.

Note next that the settlement prices quoted in all of these tables is above 100, indicating that interest rates are now lower than the coupon rates on the notional bond.

Another important point stems from the fact that long-term bond futures are based on notional bonds since, in the unlikely event that the contract leads to the delivery of bonds, the seller of the contract is extremely unlikely to be able to deliver a bond with the exact characteristics of the notional bond. Thus, the exchange establishes a list of eligible bonds, any one of which may be used to effect delivery. For example, the notional bond may have a period to maturity of 20 years and a coupon rate of nine per cent while the eligible list established by the exchange might include bonds with periods of maturity between 15 and 25 years and coupon rates ranging from 6 to 12 per cent. This causes a complication at the point of delivery because the buyer of the contract must pay for the bond actually delivered whereas the final settlement price of the futures contract will be based on the notional price. To overcome this problem, the exchange publishes a *price factor* or *conversion factor* for each eligible bond which reflects the difference in value between the notional bond and the actual bond delivered. The final settlement price for the notional bond is multiplied by the price factor (which may be either greater than or less than one). This accounts for the very high settlement prices quoted for notional French bond futures and notional Italian government bond futures. The bonds available for delivery in these cases must have characteristics quite different from the notional bonds or very profitable arbitrage opportunities would exist between the bond market and the futures market.

Table 13.2

D-MARK FUTURES (IMM) DM 125,000 per DM

	Open	Sett price	Change	High	Low	Est. vol	Open int.
Mar	0.5949	0.5929	–0.0011	0.5958	0.5920	24,471	89,812
Jun	0.5986	0.5962	–0.0011	0.5991	0.5954	677	6,096
Sep	0.6016	0.5998	–0.0011	0.6016	0.6000	2	2,317

SWISS FRANC FUTURES (IMM) SFr 125,000 per SFr

Mar	0.6796	0.6810	+0.0020	0.6849	0.6782	16,792	50,988
Jun	0.6902	0.6873	+0.0020	0.6912	0.6864	1,042	2,961
Sep	0.6970	0.6940	+0.0020	0.6970	0.6935	381	1,695

JAPANESE YEN FUTURES (IMM) Yen 12.5 per Yen 100

	Open	Sett price	Change	High	Low	Est. vol	Open int.
Mar	0.8194	0.8137	–0.0042	0.8196	0.8133	29,026	76,872
Jun	0.8286	0.8241	–0.0042	0.8291	0.8238	994	3,947
Sep	–	0.8349	–0.0042	–	0.8359	32	676

STERLING FUTURES (IMM) £62,500 per £

Mar	1.6110	1.6172	+0.007	1.6204	1.6100	5,782	33,525
Jun	1.6074	1.6144	+0.007	1.6170	1.6074	118	2,813
Sep	1.6090	1.6108	+0.007	1.6130	1.6080	32	1,091

THREE MONTH STERLING FUTURES (LIFFE) £500,000 points of 100%

	Open	Sett price	Change	High	Low	Est. vol	Open int.
Mar	93.74	93.74	–0.01	93.75	93.73	3478	99180
Jun	93.57	93.58	–	93.59	93.56	9248	127264
Sep	93.40	93.39	–0.02	93.41	93.39	7288	86966
Dec	93.27	93.25	–0.02	93.28	93.25	4666	57610
Mar	93.17	93.15	–0.02	93.18	93.15	1265	39751

Also traded on APT. All Open interest figs. are for previous day.

Box 13.2   Short-term interest rate futures prices and short-term interest rates

Table 13.1 is taken from the *Financial Times* of 22 February 1997 and the settlement prices given are for the previous day. Delivery dates for the March, June, September and December contracts (the third Wednesday) were thus approximately one month, four months, seven months and ten months ahead. Thus, they do not correspond with the periods covered in the Euro Currency Interest Rates table on the same day. Nonetheless, they are sufficiently close for us to be able to make an interesting point. Consider the Three Month and One Month Euromark Futures tables shown in Table 13.1. From these, we can derive the following interest rates:

March 3.25%; May 3.17%; June 3.17%; September 3.25%.

Euromark interest rates on the same day were:

one month 3 5-16 to 3 1-16 (midpoint 3.19%)
three months 3 5-16 to 3 1-16 (midpoint 3.19%)
six months 3 5-16 to 3 1-16 (midpoint 3.19%)

Thus, although the two sets of rates are close, the rate given by the futures price varies whereas the spot market rates do not.

Of greater interest is the Eurolira futures table. Here the implied interest rates are:

March 7.13%; June 6.5%; September 6.18%; December 6.05%.

Eurolira interest rates on the same day were:

one month 7 13-32 to 7 5-16 (midpoint 7.36%)
three months 7 1-4 to 7 1-8 (midpoint 7.19%)
six months 7 to 6 7-8 (midpoint 6.94%)
one year 6 23-32 to 6 5-8 (midpoint 6.67%)

Although the time periods do not coincide, it is clear that the interest rate derived from the futures price is consistently below the spot interest rate – a condition known as *normal backwardation*. From inspection, can you think of a reason why this might be so? We discuss this case in Box 13.3 later in the text.

Exercise

1 US money market interest rates on 21 February 1997 were:

one month 5 5-16; three months 5 7-16; six months 5 1-2

Would you expect the US Treasury Bill futures price shown for September to be higher or lower than that for March?

Check your answer with Table 13.2.

2 What has happened to Italian interest rates since we finished writing this text?

Table 13.3

■ **NOTIONAL FRENCH BOND FUTURES** (MATIF) FFr500,000

	Open	Sett price	Change	High	Low	Est. vol.	Open int.
Mar	132.10	132.26	–	132.34	132.08	64,333	129,928
Jun	130.76	130.94	–	131.00	130.76	1,471	22,409
Sep	129.10	129.28	–	129.32	129.10	163	1,778

Germany
■ **NOTIONAL GERMAN BUND FUTURES** (LIFFE)* DM250,000 100ths of 100%

	Open	Sett price	Change	High	Low	Est. vol	Open int.
Mar	103.25	103.44	-0.06	103.47	103.17	129683	240913
Jun	102.45	102.61	-0.08	102.60	102.39	19071	59765

Italy
■ **NOTIONAL ITALIAN GOVT. BOND (BTP) FUTURES** (LIFFE)* Lira 200m 100ths of 100%

	Open	Sett price	Change	High	Low	Est. vol	Open int.
Mar	130.65	130.80	+0.24	130.94	130.59	50240	108375
Jun	129.95	130.18	+0.36	130.13	129.90	7875	24195

Spain
■ **NOTIONAL SPANISH BOND FUTURES** (MEFF)

	Open	Sett price	Change	High	Low	Est. vol.	Open int.
Mar	113.90	114.01	-0.09	114.18	113.88	49,506	62,205
Jun	114.32	114.25	-0.07	114.34	114.15	5,736	15,459

UK
■ **NOTIONAL UK GILT FUTURES** (LIFFE)* £50,000 32nds of 100%

	Open	Sett price	Change	High	Low	Est. vol	Open int.
Mar	113-10	113-10	-0-06	113-15	113-05	52365	192072
Jun	112-28	112-27	-0-06	112-29	112-22	5773	19702

US
■ **US TREASURY BOND FUTURES** (CBT) $100,000 32nds of 100%

	Open	Sett price	Change	High	Low	Est. vol	Open int.
Mar	112–27	112–30	–0–03	113–01	112–21	382,709	478,240
Jun	112–12	112–15	–0–03	112–18	112–06	10,612	55,787
Sep	112–00	112–01	–0–03	112–01	112–00	1,523	12,900

Japan
■ **NOTIONAL LONG TERM JAPANESE GOVT. BOND FUTURES** (LIFFE) Y100m 100ths of 100%

	Open	Close	Change	High	Low	Est. vol	Open int.
Mar	125.97	-	-	125.97	125.90	2052	n/a
Jun	124.57	-	-	124.57	124.52	636	n/a

* LIFFE futures also traded on APT. All Open interest figs. are for previous day.

Ecu
■ **ECU BOND FUTURES** (MATIF) ECU100,000

	Open	Sett price	Change	High	Low	Est. vol.	Open int.
Mar	98.10	98.18	+0.06	98.24	98.02	804	6,170

Another complication arises because, although both futures contracts and bonds trade at clean prices, bonds have accrued interest added on whereas futures contracts do not. Consequently, allowance has to be made for interest accrued between the date of the coupon prior to the delivery of the bond and the delivery date. These two modifications mean that the buyer of the contract must pay for the bond delivered to him, the final settlement price for the notional bond plus any unpaid interest accrued on the bond.

Of the bonds eligible for delivery, the seller always chooses the bond which is cheapest for him to deliver – the cheapest to deliver (CTD) bond. Delivery may take place on any day of the delivery month, although in practice it is always on either the first or the last day of the month. If the current yield on the bond which is to be delivered is greater than the money market interest rate, the seller will retain the bond until the last day of the month before delivering it. On the other hand, if money market interest rates are higher, he will deliver the bond on the first day of the month.

Stock exchange index futures are found on the stock exchange pages of the *Financial Times*. These provide information on two FTSE (Financial Times Stock Exchange Index) futures contracts as well as on a selection of contracts on the indices of other exchanges – the Swiss Options and Financial Futures Exchange (SOFFEX); the Tokyo Stock Exchanges Nikkei 225 index; and the Standard and Poor's (S&P) 500 index. Prices are quoted directly in terms of the index.

13.4   The pricing of futures

We have said above that very few, if any, end users of the underlying instrument use the futures market as a means of buying or selling that instrument. Thus, we have three principal types of agent – hedgers, speculators and arbitrageurs. For ease, hedgers can be assumed to be participants with open positions in the cash market who are using the futures market to offset their cash risk[1]. They may either be long in the cash market and wish to go short in the futures market or vice versa. Speculators, in effect, provide the insurance for hedgers by being prepared to take an open position. If hedgers in general wish to go short in the futures market, they can only sell contracts if speculators are prepared to go long and vice versa.

A major role in determining the pricing of futures is, however, played by arbitrageurs. The nature of their role can be seen by looking at forex futures. The existence of a forward market in forex (see Chapter 12) as well as forex futures contracts means that there are two markets in what is essentially the same product. Consequently, arbitrage is possible between the two markets and this should ensure that variations in the forward exchange rate of the DM should be reflected in changes in the price of a DM futures contract. If this did not occur, there would be a profit opportunity for arbitrageurs. Almost all forex futures contracts are priced in terms of dollars per unit of the other currency. Suppose the three-month forward value of the dollar per DM fell from DM1 = $0.5714 to DM1 = $0.6061 but the price of the equivalent futures contract did not change. Arbitrageurs would be able to buy DM futures contracts allowing delivery of DM in three months' time at an exchange rate of $0.5714 to the DM and, at the same time, sell DM three months forward at the higher exchange rate. At the end of the three months, they would take delivery of the DM under the futures contract and sell them under the terms of the forward contract, making a risk-free profit. The increased demand for the futures contract would force up the futures price while the sale of DM in the forward market would push down its forward exchange rate, changing its relationship with the spot rate and opening up possibilities for interest rate arbitrage. We would not return to equilibrium until the spot and forward exchange rates and the price of the futures contract had come into line and all arbitrage profit opportunities had been removed. This is not to say that prices in the futures, forward and spot markets move exactly together. We shall see that there is a

---

[1] In practice, hedgers could be using futures markets to diversify their portfolio and so reduce specific risk as part of a general risk management strategy.

financing cost associated with arbitraging between spot and futures markets; there are always transactions costs; and futures and forwards contracts while dealing in essentially the same product are not, as we have shown above, exactly the same. Among other things, futures contracts involve daily cash flow settlements while forward contracts do not.

Nonetheless, the prices of futures must be linked through arbitrage to the prices of the underlying instrument in the cash market. This link provides the basic theory for the determination of futures prices (the cost-of-carry model). It stems from the fact that buying the underlying and holding it for three months is always an alternative to buying a futures contract requiring one to take delivery of the instrument in three months' time. Equally, going short in the cash market is an alternative to selling a futures contract which may require its delivery in the future. Further, on the delivery date itself, the value of a futures contract is determined by the cash price of the underlying instrument.

13.4.1   The cost-of-carry model of futures pricing

According to the cost-of-carry model, futures prices depend on the price of the underlying instrument and the cost of holding it from the date of purchase to the delivery date. For financial instruments, the principal cost of carry is the financing cost. If a trader buys a financial instrument and holds it for three months, the financing cost (or cost of carry) is the interest paid or foregone on the funds needed to purchase the instrument less any yield obtained on it while it is being held. That is:

$$Cc = P_s(i - c) \tag{13.1}$$

where Cc is the cost of carry; P_s is the cash price of the underlying; i is the interest rate payable on the funds borrowed to purchase the instrument and c is any yield on the asset during the period in which it is held. The costs of borrowing in futures markets are usually low both because those borrowing are usually large financial institutions and because the purchased instrument may act as collateral for the loan. In our examples below, we shall assume that traders in the futures market are able to borrow at

money market rates and in any examples we shall use figures from the *Money Rates* or *Euro Currency* columns of the *Financial Times*.

The basic cost-of-carry rule for all futures is that the futures price, *in a perfect market*, must be equal to the cash price of the instrument plus the carrying charges necessary to carry the commodity forward to delivery.

$$P_f = P_s + Cc \tag{13.2}$$

and

$$P_f = P_s(1 + i - c) \tag{13.3}$$

where P_f is the futures price.

This is known as the *fair price* of futures and is the price that produces for the purchaser of a futures contract a risk-free rate of profit just equal to the costs of carry. This derives from the arbitrage opportunity which would exist in a perfect market if the futures price were different from the cash price of the instrument. If the futures price were greater than the cash price (including carrying costs), an arbitrageur could borrow and use the funds obtained to buy the instrument in the cash market while, at the same time, selling a futures contract promising delivery of the same amount of the instrument at the end of the period of the loan. On the delivery date, she would meet the requirements of the futures contract by delivering the instrument she had been holding and would use the funds received to repay her loan, leaving an arbitrage profit. No risk would have been involved in this 'cash-and-carry' operation. On the other hand, if the cash price were too high relative to the futures price, there would be a reverse cash-and-carry arbitrage opportunity. An arbitrageur could sell the instrument short, lend the proceeds of the short sale and buy a futures contract promising delivery at time t. At t, she would collect the proceeds from the loan (including interest) and pay for the instrument delivered under the terms of the futures contract. This would, in turn, be used to remove the short position in the asset, again leaving an arbitrage profit.

This example ignores the transactions costs that exist on both sides of the market, including fees to have orders executed (brokerage, commissions, exchange fees), any taxes payable, and the bid–offer spread found in all markets. Inclusion of these costs provides an area of indeterminacy for the futures price. If we were to assume that transactions costs were a fixed percentage, T, of the transaction amount and that these costs applied to the cash market but not the futures market, the above equation would become:

$$P_s(1 - T)(1 + i - c) \leq P_f \leq P_s(1 + T)(1 + i - c) \tag{13.4}$$

This equation defines the no-arbitrage band, outside of which there would be scope for arbitrage. If the futures price were to rise above the band, traders would buy the instrument in the cash market and sell the futures, forcing the futures price down and the cash price up, removing the arbitrage opportunity. With the futures price below the band, the reverse strategy would be profitable. In practice, transactions costs and hence the width of the no-arbitrage band vary amongst traders – a non-exchange member, for instance, faces much higher costs than a member. But for the market as a whole, the futures price should stay within or be rapidly forced back into the band set by the trader with the lowest transactions costs. With some financial futures, particularly stock exchange indices futures, attempting to arbitrage between cash and futures markets is not risk-free. This opens up a further possibility for differences emerging between cash and futures prices.

The next question we must ask is where, within the no-arbitrage band, the futures price will settle. In essence, this becomes a question of the price at which speculators will provide the insurance required by hedgers. From the point of view of the speculator, the important question is the relationship between the futures price and the future cash price of the underlying asset at the point of delivery specified in the futures contract. Thus, in order to decide what price she is willing to pay, a speculator needs to form an expectation of the future cash price. In a certain world, that expectation would always be correct and the futures would be priced to give the risk-free rate of return equal to the cost of carry. Under rational expectations and with risk-neutral speculators, the market average expectation of the future cash price would be correct and this expectation would determine the current futures price. Again only the risk-free profit in the cost-of-carry model would be received. The difference

between the futures price and the current cash price of the underlying asset (known as the *basis*) would be equal to the cost of carry.

If the cost of carry is positive (that is, $i > c$) and thus the futures price is above the cash price, the situation is known as a *contango*. In this case, the futures price is falling towards the cash price as the delivery day approaches since the amount of interest which must be paid to finance the holding of the underlying instrument is falling as the time to delivery shortens. If the futures price is below the cash price ($i < c$) we have what is known as *backwardation*. Then the futures price is rising towards the cash price as the delivery date approaches. These same ideas can be applied to a series of forward contracts for different time periods since again arbitrage is possible. Consider two three-month Euromark contracts, with June and September delivery dates respectively. Just as it is possible to go long by buying the instrument and holding it rather than buying a futures contract, it is possible to buy a June forward contract, take delivery, and then hold the instrument until September as an alternative to buying futures with a September delivery date. Thus, the relationship between the fair prices for a June futures contract (P_1^f) and a September contract (P_2^f) is given by the cost of carry:

$$P_2^f = P_1^f + P_1^f(i - c) \tag{13.5}$$

If the cost of carry is positive ($i > c$), contracts with more distant delivery dates will be trading at a premium to those with nearer dates. This is a *normal contango*. Where futures with more distant delivery dates are trading at a discount we have *normal backwardation*.

So far, we have been assuming risk-neutral speculators. But what if speculators are risk averse? Then they demand a risk premium and the current futures price varies from the cash price by more or less than the cost of carry, although it must always remain within the no-arbitrage band. The direction in which it varies will depend on the nature of the risk speculators are taking. If hedgers are long in the cash market and wish to go short in the futures market, speculators will need to go long in the futures market (buy the contract) if they are to provide the insurance hedgers are seeking. The risk for speculators would then be that the future cash price would be less than the futures price (they would have to sell the instrument when it was delivered to them at a lower price than they had paid for the futures). To reduce this risk, they would wish to pay a lower price for the futures than the expected future cash price. In other words, the risk premium built into the futures price would be negative and – as long as the risk premium were greater than any excess of i over c – we would have backwardation. If this were the normal state of affairs in the market, futures with more distant delivery dates would be trading at a discount and we would have normal backwardation.

For many years, dating back to Keynes (1930) and Hicks (1946), it was largely assumed that hedgers were firms that produced or utilized the underlying instrument and much of the research literature on futures markets (notably commodity futures) was based on the normal backwardation theory (Phillips and Weiner, 1994). It follows from this theory that if expectations are on average correct, speculators as a group receive a rate of return greater than the risk-free rate which would have been justified. That is, on average, speculators should gain and hedgers should lose. More recently, it has been demonstrated by Grossman and Stiglitz (1980) and by Kyle (1985) that differential information can affect prices and profits in financial markets. Shleifer and Summers (1990) have also developed a model based on asymmetrically informed market participants, with the less informed referred to as 'noise traders'. A literature has also developed based on portfolio theory (for example, the Capital Asset Pricing Model, explained in Section 2.6). Working on the assumption that forward and futures markets are perfectly integrated with markets for other assets, it has reached the conclusion that risk premia are not related to hedging, because speculators can costlessly enter forward and futures markets, and diversify the non-systematic risk assumed in these markets by combining them in portfolios with other assets. Hirshleifer (1988) has integrated the traditional theories of risk premia based on hedging with the portfolio approach and has shown that non-marketability of claims on profits, together with fixed costs of entering asset markets, yield predictions similar to those of the simple normal-backwardation model. In contrast, the asymmetric-information view of trader performance predicts that traders with better information gain at the expense of 'noise' traders. If traders who operate in the cash market have superior information about future supply and demand conditions, the prediction of the normal-backwardation model can be reversed.

Let us next apply the general approach outlined here to some specific types of financial futures.

13.4.2   Pricing interest-rate futures options

We begin by considering short-term interest rate futures. We assume initially a perfect market and ignore any special features of a futures contract. Assume that the contract is based on US Treasury bills as in the contract offered by IMM shown in Table 13.1. Thus, if the futures contract has 90 days to run to the delivery date and is for an eligible Treasury bill with a maturity on delivery of 90–92 days, a trader wishing to apply an arbitrage strategy would buy a 180-day bill so that it would have the correct properties on the delivery date 90 days hence. Because of this, the price of interest rate futures depends on forward-forward interest rates – interest rates for periods commencing at points of time in the future. Forward-forward rates are implied by the current rates for different maturities. Consider the following example.

In February 1997, the per annum rates of interest on three months' and six months' money in Italy were 7.13 per cent and 6.93 per cent respectively. The forward-forward rate three months' ahead is then the rate we would need to receive on funds deposited for three months in, say, June in order to ensure that funds invested in March for three months and then re-invested for another three months in June would produce the same return after six months as funds invested in March at the spot six months' rate. That is, the forward-forward rate compounded with the spot three months' rate must equal the spot six months' rate. Expressing interest rates in decimals, we can write:

$$(1 + i_f)(1 + i_s) = (1 + i_l) \tag{13.6}$$

where i_s and i_l are the spot interest rates on the shorter-term (in our case three months) and the longer-term deposits (in our case six months) respectively and i_f is the implied forward-forward interest rate s time periods ahead. From Equation 13.6, we can write:

$$i_f = \frac{(1 + i_l)}{(1 + i_s)} - 1 \qquad (13.7)$$

and using the Italian rates above, remembering to divide the per annum rates by four and two to find the yield for three months and six months respectively, we get:

$$i_f = (1.035/1.018) - 1$$

We can then calculate the forward-forward interest rate three months ahead as 6.68 per cent. It is entirely logical that in a case like this where the yield curve is sloping downwards the forward-forward interest rate should be less than both the three months' and six months' spot rates[2]. Exercise 13.1 provides some practice in calculating forward-forward interest rates.

Next, we need to see exactly why forward-forward interest rates (often referred to as the implied repo rate) are important for interest-rate futures prices. Consider the following set of actions of an arbitrageur:

Exercise 13.1   Forward-forward interest rates

Money market rates for the USA in February 1997 were:

one month 5.31   three months 5.44
six months 5.5   one year 5.81

(a) Calculate the forward-forward interest rates:
    (i)   for two months, one month ahead;
    (ii) for three months, three months ahead;
    (iii) for six months, six months ahead;
    (iv) for nine months, three months ahead.

(b) What general conclusions can you come to about the relationship between spot interest rates and forward-forward rates, by comparing your answers with the spot rates for the different time periods in the USA and with the Italian example in the text?

(Answers at end of chapter)

(a) He sells a futures contract requiring the delivery in three months' time of a bill maturing three months from the delivery date;
(b) To allow him to deliver the required bill in three month's time, he buys a 180-day Treasury bill (yielding i_l);
(c) To pay for the Treasury bill, he borrows in the money market for three months (at i_s).

No risk is involved here. At the end of three months, he settles the futures contract by delivering the Treasury bill he has been holding and uses the funds received to pay back his loan. All that is really going on here is the purchase of a 180-day Treasury bill which is re-sold three months ahead. In a perfect market and with no transactions costs, all that our arbitrageur should be able to ask for this bill in three months' time is the interest rate on three-month money three months ahead, that is, the three-month forward-forward interest rate three months from now. Since, in this example, the means used for carrying out the purchase and re-sale of the Treasury bill is the futures contract, that contract should be priced to yield the forward-forward interest rate. We have already seen that this is determined by the relationship between the spot rate of interest on money for six months and the spot rate of interest on three-month money. If the price of the futures contract were too high, yielding greater than the forward-forward rate, the arbitrage strategy above would produce a profit for the arbitrageur. On the other hand, if the yield on the futures contract were below the forward-forward interest rate, the reverse strategy would produce an arbitrage profit. Box 13.3 uses these rules to return to the question of the pricing of Eurolira futures raised in Box 13.2.

We can formalize the above argument as follows. From Equation 13.3, we have the price of a futures contract as:

$$P_f = P_s(1 + i - c) \qquad (13.3)$$

Since we are dealing here with a bill, there is no return on the bill while it is being held and $c = 0$. Thus we have:

$$P_f = P_s(1 + i_s.n_{sm}) = P_s + (i_s.n_{sm})P_s \qquad (13.8)$$

---

[2] We suggested some reasons why the Italian yield curve was sloping downwards during this period in Section 12.3.1.

Box 13.3 Pricing Eurolira futures

In Box 13.2 we reported that the implied interest rates on three-month Eurolira futures in February 1997 were March 7.13%; June 6.5%; September 6.18%; December 6.05%. We asked you to consider why these rates differed so much from spot Eurolira interest rates.

Using the formula in Equation 13.7, we can calculate the following forward-forward interest rates on the Eurolira using the mid-points given in Box 13.1 as:

Forward-forward rate:

for two months one month ahead $= 7.06\%$
for three months three months ahead $= 6.57\%$
for six months six months ahead $= 6.19\%$

You will see that these rates are now very close to the relevant futures interest rates. Thus, the gap between the spot rates of interest and the interest rates implied by the futures prices was largely a reflection of our rule that the *fair price* of a short-term interest rate future is given by the relevant forward-forward interest rate. There is still some difference between the last two rates, 6.19 per cent and 6.05 per cent, but then the forward-forward rate we really needed here was the rate for three months seven months ahead, not for six months six months ahead. Given the general fall in the Italian interest rate for longer periods, we should expect the forward-forward interest rate seven months ahead to be lower than 6.19.

---

where P_s is the spot price of the bill, i_s is the financing cost of holding the bill until the futures delivery date (three months in our example), and n_{sm} is the period to redemption expressed as a fraction of a year. We then need the expression for the spot price of the asset underlying the futures. This is the six-month bill, held for three months and then delivered to meet the futures contract with three months to delivery. The price of this bill, expressed in terms of the interest rate rather than the discount rate (see Section 9.2) can be written as:

$$P_s = \frac{M}{(1 + i_l.n_{sm})} \quad (13.9)$$

where M is the par value and i_l is the interest rate on the bill. Making use of Equation 13.6 above, we can write this as:

$$P_s = \frac{M}{(1 + i_s.n_{sm})(1 + i_f.n_{sm})} \quad (13.10)$$

where i_f is the forward-forward interest rate from s to l.

Substituting Equation 13.10 into Equation 13.8 gives us:

$$P_f = \frac{M}{(1 + i_f.n_{sm})} \quad (13.11)$$

and from Equation 13.7 above, we can write the fair price of our futures contract as:

$$P_f = \frac{\dfrac{M}{(1 + i_l.n_{sm})}}{(1 + i_s.n_{sm})} - 1 \quad (13.12)$$

You will notice that this is different from what we have done in Box 13.3 above where we have obtained a per annum interest rate implied by a futures price simply by subtracting the price from 100. This is, in fact, what futures exchanges do. Thus the expression for the fair price of futures becomes:

$$P_f = 100 - i_f$$

This may only be an approximation to Equation 13.12, but it does have the advantage of simplicity.

For a particular contract, say for three-month Euromark futures where the contract is for DM1 million, the fair price of the contract would be:

$$P_f = (100 - i_f).M/100 = (100 - i_f).DM1m/100$$

Of course, as in our general discussion above, the addition of transactions costs would introduce an element of freedom for futures prices. We would now have to say that the futures yield would have to be above or below the relevant forward-forward interest rate by more than necessary to meet transactions costs before arbitrage would be profitable. Also as in the general case, if we were to include a risk premium we could produce either backwardation or a contango.

To adapt this approach to long-term bond futures, we must allow for the coupon payments (thus c in

Equation 13.3 is positive rather than being zero as it is with short-term interest rate futures). This has the effect of lowering the net financing cost associated with an arbitrage operation although the amount paid for the asset will be higher than in the short-term interest rate futures case since the bond must be purchased at face value, rather than at a discount. We must also take into account the complications on delivery noted in Section 13.3. Suppose the futures contract has a delivery date three months ahead and is for a notional 20-year bond. The cash-and-carry arbitrage operation does not require the arbitrageur to buy now a bond which will, in three months' time, have 20 years to run to maturity. Rather, she will buy now the cheapest-to-deliver bond that will satisfy the contract. She must therefore borrow funds at money market rates to buy this bond and will pay the dirty price for it. The cost of carry will be given by the dirty price of the bond times the money market interest rate less the amount of accrued interest on the bond over the three months to the delivery which will depend on the coupon of the CTD bond. To establish the fair price of the notional bond, we must then divide by the price factor (PF) on the CTD bond. We can modify Equation 13.3 to:

$$P_f = \frac{P_s}{PF} + (1 + i.n_{sm} - c.n_{sm})\frac{P_s}{PF} \qquad (13.13)$$

Again, an actual futures price may vary from the fair price because of transactions costs and the incorporation of a risk premium.

13.4.3 Pricing currency futures

Establishing the fair price of currency futures is simply an exercise in covered interest rate parity which we considered in Section 12.3.1. Assume a US firm needs Swiss francs in three months' time (it is short in Swiss francs) and it wishes to lock in the existing SFR/$ exchange rate (hedging against the risk that the dollar would weaken over the following three months). It could do this by purchasing a futures contract on Swiss francs with a delivery date three months ahead (or it could buy Swiss francs forward). Alternatively, it could borrow for three months in US dollars at US interest rates, convert the funds borrowed into Swiss francs at the existing spot

exchange rate and invest the francs at Swiss interest rates for three months. At the end of the period, it would collect the Swiss francs from its investment and meet its obligations in Switzerland and repay its US$ loan.

These two strategies produce the same results and thus the fair price of the futures contract should depend on the spot exchange rate and the difference between interest rates in the USA and Switzerland. As we demonstrate in Box 13.4, we can write the fair price of the currency futures by rewriting Equation 12.4 as:

$$\frac{P_f - E_s}{E_s} = \frac{i_d - i_f}{1 + i_f} \qquad (13.14)$$

where P_f is the price of the futures contract. In our example above i_d, the domestic interest rate is the US rate, i_f the Swiss rate and E_s the exchange rate of dollars expressed in direct quotation.

This may be approximated as:

$$\frac{P_f - E_s}{E_s} = i_d - i_f \qquad (13.15)$$

Therefore the fair price of a currency futures contract is the same as the price of the equivalent forward contract under conditions of interest rate parity. As we have previously said, there will be differences between forward and futures prices when allowance is made for the margins payments under futures contracts and the interest foregone on margin payments. It must also be remembered, however, that traders wishing to buy foreign currency forwards from banks will be required to maintain deposits with the bank to insure the bank against default risk, and so the differences between forward and futures prices are likely in practice to be very small.

13.4.4 Equity index futures prices

The general rules apply also to the pricing of equity index futures and we could reproduce Equation 13.3, with c now being the dividend yield on shares held. However, a number of complications can be seen when the nature of the cash-and-carry arbitrage strategy is considered. Let us take the steps involved in the similar strategy for short-term interest rate futures listed in Section 13.4.1 and observe the differences.

Box 13.4   The fair price for currency futures and covered interest parity

Assume a US firm needs SFr125,000 in three months' time to pay for goods already ordered. It sets out to lock in the current exchange rate, using spot markets only as outlined in the text. Thus, it will need to invest in Switzerland: SFr125,000/(1 + i_{Sw}) where i_{Sw} is the spot interest rate in Switzerland. Assuming this to be 1.06 per cent, it will require SFr124,224.

To obtain this, it will need to convert into francs [$125,000/(1 + i_{Sw})].E$_S$ where E$_S$ is the spot exchange rate of the dollar in direct quotation. Assume this to be: SFr1 = $0.6780. That is, it will need to convert $84,224 into francs. It borrows this amount at US interest rates and at the end of the three months must repay this amount plus interest:

{[SFr125,000/(1 + i_{Sw})].E$_S$}. (1 + i_{US})

With US spot interest rates at 5.75 per cent, this

will amount to $85,403. Thus, the effective exchange rate obtained for the transfer of funds will be $85,403/125,000 = SFr1 or $0.6832 = $1.

We have omitted transactions costs here and so can assume that this should be the fair price of a currency future for the delivery of Swiss francs three months ahead. That is,

P_f = {[SFr125,000/(1 + i_{Sw})].E$_S$}. (1 + i_{US})

We may generalize the equation by letting: $i_{US} = i_d$; $i_{Sw} = i_f$ (domestic and foreign interest rates respectively) and SFr = 1 (contract). Then:

$P_f/E_S = (1 + i_d)/(1 + i_f)$

which we may rearrange and write as:

$(P_f - E_S)/E_S = (i_d - i_f)/(1 + i_f) = i_d - i_f$

which is the covered interest parity condition.

(a) The arbitrageur sells a futures contract requiring the delivery in three months' time of the stock exchange index. But an index cannot be delivered. Rather, stock exchange index futures are settled on the delivery date by cash payments reflecting the change in the value of the index over the period of the contract. Thus, the risk to the seller of the index is that the share price index will have risen during that time.

(b) To remove this risk of having to make a cash payment, the arbitrageur would need to construct, at the beginning of the period, a portfolio of all the shares in the stock exchange index in question, in the exact proportions used in the calculation of the index. The portfolio would be held until the delivery date of the futures contract and then sold in its entirety. The portfolio of shares would rise in value in the exact proportion as the index and the cash profit on the shares could be used to meet the required cash payments under the futures contract. The purchase of the shares would have the extra bonus that dividends would be received while the shares were being held and the fair price of the futures contract would be lower to this extent.

(c) to pay for the portfolio of shares, the arbitrageur borrows in the money market for the period of the contract.

Now consider the problems in step (b). Firstly, it would be impossible to construct the required portfolio instantaneously at the beginning of the period and thus prices might move against the arbitrageur while the portfolio was being constructed. That is, share prices might begin to rise, making it more expensive to acquire the required portfolio. Secondly, it is likely to be very difficult, if not impossible, to build up a portfolio exactly the same as that used in the calculation of the index. Given stock exchange rules regarding the minimum size of parcels of shares, a portfolio which exactly represented the index might need to be very large. To the extent that the portfolio held was different from the notional portfolio used to calculate the index, the level of systematic or market risk associated with the portfolio might be different from that of the index. Hence it is not possible to have a genuinely risk-free arbitrage strategy in the case of stock exchange indices. In addition, the transaction costs associated with acquiring the necessary shares would be likely to be much higher than they would be of purchasing a single bill or bond in the cash market. Therefore, the no-arbitrage band is bound to be much wider in the case of stock exchange index futures.

Finally, the dividend payments cause complications because, unlike bond coupon payments, they will not occur regularly throughout the period during which the shares are held and their size will be uncertain. This makes futures prices more volatile than the index itself. Suppose a number of dividend payments on the shares are bunched together. As soon as they are paid, the benefits of acquiring the representative portfolio of assets will fall (in terms of Equation 13.3, *c* will fall sharply) and the fair price of the futures will rise sharply. Meanwhile the index, which does not take dividend payments into account, will remain unaffected.

13.5 Summary

Risks facing firms have increased in a number of ways as they have become bigger and more international in nature and as exchange rates have become more volatile and future inflation rates more uncertain. To help counter these risks, new markets have grown up in financial derivatives – contracts to exchange based upon the performance of separately traded financial instruments. As part of this growth, financial futures markets have developed in which standardized contracts on short- and long-term interest rates, foreign exchange rates and stock exchange indices are traded on specialized exchanges. To reduce default risk and increase the tradeability of futures, clearing houses have been established which take over counterparty obligations on all contracts. Exchange members must keep accounts with the clearing house, which are adjusted daily to reflect profits and losses on all contracts. This system of margin payments means that futures are highly geared. Although very few exchanges of the underlying instruments actually occur under futures contracts, the possibility that delivery might be required ensures that the prices of futures will be closely linked (although not identical) to the prices on the cash markets through potential arbitrage strategies. These arbitrage strategies allow the fair price of futures – the price that provides the risk-free rate of profit – to be calculated. This rate of profit will always equal the net cost-of-carry, the net cost of holding the underlying instrument for the duration of the futures contract. In practice, transaction costs create a no-arbitrage band within which the price of the futures must lie and the actual futures price may vary from the fair price to include a risk premium. The basic fair pricing rule can be modified to suit the particular characteristics of the different types of financial futures.

Key concepts used in this chapter

Derivatives	Contango	Settlement price
Open outcry	Backwardation	Open interest
Initial margin	Normal backwardation	Cash and carry strategy
Marked to market	Financial futures	Basis
Price factor	Clearing house	Normal contango
Fair price	Variation margin	
Cost of carry	Limit-up/Limit-down	

Questions and problems

1 Explain each of the following:
   (a) the role of a clearing house in a futures market;
   (b) the potential advantages and risks of trading on margin in futures markets;
   (c) contango;
   (d) normal backwardation.

2 Outline the relative advantages and disadvantages of each of the following as instruments for providing protection against foreign exchange risk:
   (a) forward foreign exchange markets;
   (b) futures contracts in foreign exchange.

3 What are the characteristics of futures and futures exchanges which serve to increase the tradeability of futures?

4 Euro currency interest rates for Spain on 28 February 1997 were:

   one month 6.08   three months 6.06
   six months 5.77   one year 5.91

   Calculate the forward-forward interest rates:
   (i)   for two months, one month ahead;
   (ii) for three months, three months ahead;
   (iii) for six months, six months ahead;
   (iv) for nine months, three months ahead

5 You are given the following information:

   Spot German interest rates on three-month money: 3.125 per cent
   Spot US interest rates on three-month money: 5.50 per cent
   US$/DM exchange rate: $0.5923 = DM1

   (a) Calculate the fair price for a D-Mark futures contract with a delivery date three months ahead.
   (b) Why might the actual futures price differ from the fair price?
   (c) Describe the arbitrage strategy which would produce a profit if the actual futures price was (i) above the fair price, (ii) below the fair price.

   (d) Allow for transactions costs of 2 per cent of the value of the contract and calculate the no-arbitrage band for the futures price.

6 In Section 13.4.2 above, we write:

   If the price of the futures contract were too high, yielding greater than the forward-forward rate, the arbitrage strategy above would produce a profit for the arbitrageur. On the other hand, if the yield on the futures contract were below the forward-forward interest rate, the reverse strategy would produce an arbitrage profit.

   Outline the reverse strategy referred to here.

7 Assume that at the end of March 1997, three-month PIBOR futures offered by MATIF stood at:

   Jun   96.65   Sep   96.50   Dec   96.35

   What term would you use to describe this relationship between futures contracts of different periods? What is the opposite situation? What might the above set of figures imply that hedgers were using short-term interest rate futures to achieve?

8 You are given the following figures for the end of September:

   Spot dirty price of cheapest to deliver long-gilt = £97.25
   Price factor of cheapest to deliver long gilt = 0.9815625
   Sterling money market interest rate for 3 months = 6.25 per cent
   Coupon rate on the cheapest to deliver long gilt = 10 per cent

   Calculate the fair futures price for the December long gilt contract.

9 Why is so much attention given to the form of delivery of the underlying product on futures contracts when delivery hardly ever occurs?

Further reading

D Blake, *Financial Market Analysis* (London: McGraw-Hill, 1990) Ch. 8

S J Grossman and J Stiglitz, 'On the impossibility of informationally efficient markets', *American Economic Review*, 70, June, 1980, 393–408

J R Hicks, *Value and Capital* (London: Oxford University Press, 2e 1946)

D Hirshleifer, 'Residual risk, trading costs, and commodity futures risk premia', *Review of Financial Studies*, 1, Summer, 1988, 173–93

H S Houthakker and P J Williamson, *The Economics of Financial Markets* (Oxford: Oxford University Press, 1996) Chs 9 and 10

J M Keynes, *A Treatise on Money*, Vol. II (London: Macmillan, 1930)

R W Kolb, *Financial Derivatives*, (Oxford: Blackwell, 1996) Ch. 2

A S Kyle, 'Continuous auctions and insider trading', *Econometrica*, 53, November, 1985, 1315–35

G M Phillips and R J Weiner, 'Information and normal backwardation as determinants of trading performance: evidence from the North Sea Oil forward market', *Economic Journal*, 104 (436), 1994, 76–95

K Redhead, *Introduction to the International Money Markets* (Cambridge: Woodhead-Faulkner, 1992) Ch. 5

A Shleifer and L H Summers, 'The noise trader approach to finance', *Journal of Economic Perspectives*, 4, Spring, 1990, 19–33

J L Stein, *The Economics of Futures Markets* (Oxford: Blackwell, 1986)

R Vaitilingam, *The* Financial Times *Guide to Using the Financial Pages* (London: Pitman Publishing, 1996, 3e)

Answers to exercises

Exercise 13.1

(a) (i) 5.5; (ii) 5.49; (iii) 5.96; (iv) 5.85

CHAPTER 14

Options, swaps and other derivatives

Box 14.1

What you will learn in this chapter:

- The nature and uses of options
- How to read options tables in the *Financial Times*
- The factors determining options prices
- The nature and uses of swaps
- The advantages of different kinds of financial derivatives
- The advantages and disadvantages of financial derivatives in general

14.1 Introduction

Two other instruments whose use has grown rapidly in financial markets in recent years have been options and swaps. Both instruments help firms hedge risk but both have also become associated with speculation and spectacular financial disasters. In this chapter we look at the nature of these instruments and also at the advantages and disadvantages of derivatives generally. From Sections 14.2 to 14.5 we look at the use of and the pricing of options. Section 14.6 deals with swaps while Section 14.7 compares the different types of derivatives and Section 14.8 considers issues associated with derivatives generally.

14.2 Options

An option gives the right to buy or sell a given amount of a financial instrument or commodity at an agreed price (known as the *exercise* or *strike* price) within a specified time, but does not oblige investors to do so. Just as with futures, options contracts are drawn up between two counterparties, the purchaser and the writer (seller) of the option, and are registered with and traded through a futures and options exchange, generally using the same open outcry system employed in futures trading. Options contracts are offered both on cash securities (short- and long-term interest rates, exchange rates, equities of individual companies, and stock exchange indices) and on futures contracts. For options on cash securities (premium paid options), the buyer pays the full price or *premium* of the option at the time of purchase. For options on futures contracts (premium margined options), buyers and sellers are margined and marked to market in the same way as with futures themselves.

Banks may construct non-tradeable, custom-made options for their customers. These are known as over-the-counter (OTC) options and continue to make up a high proportion of the total value of options sold. Traditional options which are also not tradeable continue to exist in stock markets. As we have seen when dealing with futures, however, the major development in recent years has been the large increase in the number of specialized futures and options exchanges and the development of increasing numbers of traded options contracts.

The buyer of a *call* option acquires the right to buy the specified instrument. For example, an investor who thinks that the DM will rise against the US dollar could buy a DM/$ option, giving the right to buy DMs at a specified price, say $0.59 = DM1. The holder of the option then has the right to acquire DMs at that price at any time during the life of the option and is thus in a position to benefit from a rise in the spot price of the DM. If the spot exchange rate were to rise to $0.65 = 1DM, the option holder could acquire DMs at $0.59 under the terms of the option and sell them in the spot market at $0.65. The buyer of a call option thus assumes a long position in the underlying instrument (in this case DMs). As the price of the underlying instrument[1] rises, so too will the profit which can be made from exercising the option. Consequently, the premium which must be paid to acquire that option rises and this allows the holder of a call option to realize her profit by selling the option on, rather than by exercising it. If the option did not rise as the price of the underlying rose, there would be a profitable arbitrage opportunity. Box 14.2 provides a more detailed example relating to interest rate options.

The buyer of a *put* option acquires the right to sell and thus assumes a short position in the specified instrument. That is, the buyer of a put option stands to gain from a *fall* in the price of the underlying. Therefore, someone who buys a put option at $0.59 = DM1 will be hoping that the value of the DM will fall below that level. They will then be able to buy DMs in the spot market at, say $0.57 = DM1 and then exercise the option in order to sell the DMs at $0.59 each. In this case, as the DM falls, the profitability of a put option in DMs will rise and the premium that other investors are prepared to pay in order to acquire such an option will increase. As above, the holder of the put option may realize her profit by selling the option on, rather than by exercising it.

Just as in the futures market, the holder of an option sells it (closes out her market position) by entering into a reversing contract. That is, in the first case above in which we assumed that the DM was rising, a holder of a call option in DMs 'sells' the option by writing (that is, selling) a call option on the same instrument for the same expiration date, in effect cancelling her right to buy DMs. However, the increase in the price of the DM will have meant that the premium received for the sale of the call option

will be greater than the premium paid on the initial call option.

The example of a call option given above states that the option can be exercised at any time during its life up till (and including) the expiration date. Such an option is known as an *American option*. There exist also *European options* which give holders the right to exercise the option on the expiration date only. Most traded options are American options.

Like futures contracts, few options produce a delivery of the underlying because profitable market positions are generally closed out before expiration while unprofitable options are left to lapse, with the buyer losing only the premium. Therefore, the profit for most buyers of options is given by the change in the option premium between its purchase and sale. Options, then, like futures, give traders the opportunity to speculate on the likely direction of a market without actually trading in that market.

For hedgers who are short in the underlying, a call option establishes a maximum price for it:

- if the price in the cash market rises, the hedger may exercise the option at the lower strike price; or
- pay the higher price for the instrument in the cash market but set against this the profit obtained from selling the option.

However, if the spot market price falls, the hedger obtains the benefit of the fall and has only to set against this the premium paid for the option. Thus, the option provides protection from the spot price moving in one direction, without removing the profits which might arise if the price moves in the opposite direction. This is not the case in trading in either forwards or futures markets. The reverse arguments hold for hedgers who are long in the underlying. For them, a put option establishes a minimum price for the underlying. If the spot price falls, the premium of the put option rises and the holder may either exercise the option at the strike price (preventing a loss) or sell the underlying at the lower spot price and sell the option in order to offset

---

1 We have throughout the chapter used the term 'the underlying' to stand for the instrument, asset or commodity underlying an options contract.

Box 14.2   Arbitraging between the cash and options markets

Assume that the strike price of a three-month American option on a short-term interest rate (a three-month bank deposit) is 95; the premium is 0.25 per cent of the specified amount of the deposit which is £100,000. Thus, if the option is exercised, the writer of the option will pay the buyer interest on £100,000 for three months at a rate of 5 per cent p.a. (£1,250); the premium paid for buying the right to this payment is £250. The market rate of interest on the type of deposit specified is 5 per cent. The option is then said to be *at-the-money* – the value of the right granted by the option is equal to the market value of the underlying instrument. The current value of the option (the option's *intrinsic value*), the profit available from exercising it, would be zero. The buyer of the option could obtain from a prime bank exactly the same interest as is available from exercising the option.

Underlying deposit:	£100,000
Strike price:	95 (implying 5 per cent per annum interest rate)
Market rate of interest:	5 per cent per annum
Intrinsic value of option:	£0
Premium	0.25 per cent of underlying deposit = £250
Period to expiry:	Three months

Traders might still buy this option because the option grants the buyer more than the intrinsic value since interest rates might fall and the intrinsic value of the option rise before the expiry date. This right to benefit from a future rise in the price of an instrument is known as the option's *time value*.

Assume next that one month later (the option still has two months to expiry date), the current market rate of interest falls to 2 per cent but that the premium on the option does not change. The option holder could then exercise the option and receive £1,250 from the writer when a deposit of £100,000 with a bank (the alternative) would yield only £500. The option would be *in-the-money* – the value of the right granted by the option is greater than the market value of the underlying instrument and it would be profitable to exercise the option. We would have:

Underlying deposit:	£100,000
Strike price:	95
Market rate of interest:	2 per cent per annum
Intrinsic value of option:	£750
Premium:	0.25 per cent = £250
Period to expiry:	2 months

Clearly, large numbers of traders would wish to buy this option but no one would be willing to write it since a writer would have to pay a much higher rate of interest than was available to them on an equivalent deposit. The premium would have to rise *at least* to 0.75 per cent of the underlying deposit. Of course, it might rise higher because of the time value remaining to the option holder – the possibility that the market interest rate might fall further in the following two months.

Had the interest rate risen above 5 per cent in this case, an option with a strike price of 95 would have been *out-of-the-money*.

the loss incurred in the spot market. If the spot price rises, the holder of the option can benefit from the higher price in the cash market and allow the option to lapse. Thus, holding a long position in the cash market and buying a put option produces the same result as does buying a call option when the trader has no position in the cash market – in both cases, the holder of the option benefits from a rise in the price of the instrument in the cash market. For this reason the combination of being long in an instrument and holding a put option is sometimes known as a *synthetic call option*.

Whether a trader chooses futures or options will depend on what he thinks is likely to happen to the price of the underlying and on his attitude towards risk. A trader who has a long position in the cash market and who is convinced that the price of the instrument in question won't fall may well choose not to hedge at all. If he is certain that the price will fall, he may either sell the instrument or take an offsetting short position by selling futures contracts or, in the case of currency, selling forwards. This eliminates entirely his exposure to the price fall. The trader is only likely to choose options if he is uncertain in which direction the price will move. Even then, if he thinks that the price is more likely to

---

Box 14.3   Mixed strategies in options trading

It is possible to combine call and put options and the buying and writing of options to try to profit from expected conditions in the market. Some such options are:

A. Cases where a trader either buys or writes options but does not do both

Straddle – a call + a put at the same strike price and expiry date

Strangle – a call + a put for the same expiry date but at different strike prices

Strap – two calls + one put with the same expiry dates; the strike prices might be the same or different

Strip – two puts + one call with the same expiry date; again strike prices might be the same or different

In general, the buyer of these options is hoping for market prices to move sharply but is uncertain whether they will rise or fall. The buyer of a strap will gain more from a price rise than from a price fall; the buyer of a strip will gain more from a price fall. The writer in all four cases is hoping that the market will remain stable with little change in price during the life of the option.

B. Spreads: Combinations of buying and writing options

butterfly – *buying* two call options, one with a low exercise price, the other with a high exercise price + *writing* two call options with the same intermediate strike price **or** the reverse.

condor – similar to a butterfly except that the call options which are written have different intermediate prices.

Both a butterfly and a condor are *vertical* spreads – all options bought or sold have the same expiry date but diferent strike prices. *Horizontal* spreads have the same strike prices but different expiry dates. With *diagonal* spreads both the strike prices and the expiry dates are different.

Other mixed strategies have equally improbable names. They include: vertical bull call; vertical bull spread; vertical bear spread; rotated vertical bull spread; rotated vertical bear spread.

---

fall than to rise, financial futures are preferable to options. Options are preferable if the trader has no view or thinks that the price is more likely to rise than fall. Many mixed strategies are possible. Box 14.3 sets out some examples.

Options, like futures, are highly geared (leveraged) because the options price is only a small percentage of the price of the underlying. In the example in Box 14.2, the buyer of the call option may have made a profit of £750 for an outlay of only £250 in one month – a net per annum profit rate of 2400 per cent.

Although it carries a considerable risk, a trader may prefer to hedge or speculate by writing options rather than buying them. Writing a call option offers protection against a price fall since in this case the option will not be exercised and the writer will collect the premium on the option. In the same way, writing a put option offers protection against a price rise. Writing options is only effective, however, if the price changes are relatively small and it carries the risk that if prices go against the writer, the loss may become very large. For example, a trader who writes

a call option on the DM/$ exchange rate at a strike price of $0.595 agrees to sell DM at that price. If the DM increases in value and the writer is short in DM, she will need to acquire them in the spot market at the higher price and the amount she loses will depend on the size of the contract (DM62,500) and the amount the price rises. If the DM rose to $0.605, the loss would be $625 (62,500 × $0.01); if it rose to $0.655, the loss to the writer would be $3,750 (62,500 × .06) and so on. The writer cannot abandon a losing option in the way that the buyer can.

The trading of options contracts on organized exchanges guards against the risk that the writer of an option might default on it by not being able to deliver the underlying to the holder of a call option or to accept it from the holder of a put option. To buy an option, a trader must have an account with a brokerage firm holding a membership on the options exchange. The buyer pays for the option at the time of the trade and no other payments are required apart from a commission to the broker. However, because the writer of an option enters into an open-ended commitment, she may need large financial reserves to meet her obligations and the broker may require financial guarantees from option writers. A writer may write a *covered call* (the writer already owns the underlying and deposits it with the broker) or a *naked call*. In the latter case, the broker may require substantial deposits of cash or securities to ensure that the writer is able to meet her commitment. As in a futures market, the buyer and writer of an option have no obligations to a specific individual but to the clearing house of the exchange which manages the exercise process and the standardization of contract terms.

14.3   Reading the *Financial Times*

The *Financial Times* provides information on the trading of a number of different options contracts. Table 14.1 shows details of four different short-term interest rate contracts offered by LIFFE, all on the interest rates on short-term deposits in different currencies (Euromarks, Euro Swiss Francs, Eurolira and sterling). The size of the deposit underlying each contract is given at the top of each table (DM1 million, £500,000 and so on). The various strike prices are shown down the left-hand side of each table. The strike price is quoted in the same way as are short-term interest rate futures, with the interest rate offered on

Table 14.1

■ EUROMARK OPTIONS (LIFFE) DM1m points of 100%

Strike	CALLS				PUTS			
Price	Mar	Apr	May	Jun	Mar	Apr	May	Jun
9675	0.03	0.06	0.07	0.09	0.02	0.05	0.06	0.08
9700	0	0.01	0.01	0.02	0.24	0.25	0.25	0.26
9725	0	0	0	0	0.49	0.49	0.49	0.49

Est. vol. total, Calls 1579 Puts 3144. Previous day's open int., Calls 526023 Puts 313538

■ EURO SWISS FRANC OPTIONS (LIFFE) SFr 1m points of 100%

Strike	CALLS			PUTS		
Price	Mar	Jun	Sep	Mar	Jun	Sep
9850	0.01	0.06	0.11	0.23	0.23	0.33
9875	0	0.02	0.04	0.47	0.44	0.51

Est. vol. total, Calls 0 Puts 0. Previous day's open int., Calls 5935 Puts 3960

■ EUROLIRA OPTIONS (LIFFE) L1000m points of 100%

Strike	CALLS			PUTS		
Price	Mar	Jun	Sep	Mar	Jun	Sep
9250	0.61	0.61	0.94	0.03	0.10	0.18
9275	0.04	0.42	0.75	0.16	0.16	0.24
9300	0	0.28	0.59	0.37	0.27	0.33

Est. vol. total, Calls 15476 Puts 1488. Previous day's open int., Calls 156229 Puts 88849

■ SHORT STERLING OPTIONS (LIFFE) £500,000 points of 100%

Strike	CALLS			PUTS		
Price	Mar	Jun	Sep	Mar	Jun	Sep
9350	0.21	0.12	0.11	0	0.18	0.39
9375	0.03	0.04	0.05	0.07	0.35	0.58
9400	0	0.01	0.02	0.29	0.57	0.80

Est. vol. total, Calls 7928 Puts 7506. Previous day's open int., Calls 225898 Puts 188553

the deposit in question being subtracted from 100. Thus, traders interested in Euromark options were offered contracts on three different interest rates: 3.25 per cent, 3 per cent and 2.75 per cent respectively. With sterling, the Euro Swiss franc and the Eurolira contracts, the options relate to three-month deposits and the expiration dates are the same as the standard delivery dates for futures contracts – March, June, September and December. Euromark contracts are offered on one-month deposits with expiration dates in each month of the year. Premiums of call and put options (as a percentage of the contract value) are quoted for each strike price and time period.

In the case of short-term interest rate options, the option's price rises when the market interest rate falls since the exercise of the option would deliver to its holder a rate of interest higher than the market interest rate. Below each table the number of contracts traded the previous day and the total number of contracts outstanding (open interest) is provided. Exercise 14.1 asks you to consider the significance of some of the premiums quoted in Table 14.1.

Table 14.2 provides information on two currency options, both offered by the Philadelphia Stock Exchange – pound/dollar and DM/dollar.

All currency options are for the US dollar against a non-dollar currency and a call option gives the right to buy the non-dollar currency. Exercise prices are stated in US cents. Thus, the strike price of 0.590 on the DM/$ contract is an exchange rate of $0.590 =

Exercise 14.1

Consider Table 14.1 which relates to 28 February 1997. Three-month, six-month and one-year Eurolira interest rates on that day were 7.31, 7.14, and 6.94 per cent respectively.

1 Why were the premiums for September Eurolira calls so much higher than for puts?

2 Why were the premiums for September lira calls so much higher than for March calls?

3 What do the premiums on Euro Swiss Franc options tell you about Swiss interest rates on 28 February?

(Answers at end of chapter)

Table 14.2

■ PHILADELPHIA SE £/$ OPTIONS £31,250 (cents per pound)

Strike Price	CALLS Mar	Apr	May	PUTS Mar	Apr	May
1.600	3.20	3.79	–	0.24	0.91	1.57
1.610	2.46	3.11	3.74	0.45	1.23	1.94
1.620	1.77	2.51	3.16	0.76	1.61	2.36

Previous day's vol., Calls 571 Puts 366 . Prev. day's open int., Calls 34,564 Puts 50,967

■ PHILADELPHIA SE D-MARK/$ OPTIONS DM62,500 ($ per DM)

Strike Price	CALLS Mar	Apr	May	PUTS Mar	Apr	May
0.590	0.63	1.00	1.33	0.34	0.61	0.83
0.595	0.38	0.74	1.06	0.58	0.89	1.07
0.600	0.22	0.53	0.84	0.90	1.15	1.35

Previous day's vol., Calls 899 Puts 611 . Prev. day's open int., Calls 36,847 Puts 34,224

Table 14.3

■ LONG TERM FRENCH BOND OPTIONS (MATIF)

Strike Price	CALLS Mar	Apr	Jun	PUTS Mar	Apr	Jun
128	3.20	–	3.45	0.05	0.16	0.32
129	2.27	–	2.65	0.12	0.29	0.51
130	1.42	–	1.94	0.26	0.51	0.79
131	0.71	–	1.32	0.55	0.85	1.16
132	0.27	0.55	0.84	1.10	1.38	1.67

Est. vol. total, Calls 17,252 Puts 18,311. Previous day's open int., Calls 90,043 Puts 108,306.

■ BUND FUTURES OPTIONS (LIFFE) DM250,000 points of 100%

Strike Price	CALLS Apr	May	Jun	Sep	PUTS Apr	May	Jun	Sep
10200	0.80	1.11	1.33	1.37	0.44	0.75	0.97	1.86
10250	0.52	0.83	1.04	1.16	0.66	0.97	1.18	2.15
10300	0.31	0.59	0.80	0.97	0.95	1.23	1.44	2.46

Est. vol. total, Calls 31640 Puts 32218. Previous day's open int., Calls 142891 Puts 151062

■ ITALIAN GOVT. BOND (BTP) FUTURES OPTIONS (LIFFE) Lira200m 100ths of 100%

Strike Price	CALLS Jun	Sep	PUTS Jun	Sep
12700	2.22	2.85	1.97	2.75
12750	1.92	2.57	2.17	2.97
12800	1.66	2.31	2.41	3.21

Est. vol. total, Calls 2205 Puts 4031. Previous day's open int., Calls 59319 Puts 57386

■ LONG GILT FUTURES OPTIONS (LIFFE) £50,000 64ths of 100%

Strike Price	CALLS Apr	May	Jun	Sep	PUTS Apr	May	Jun	Sep
111	1-19	1-54	2-13	2-44	0-29	1-00	1-23	2-20
112	0-44	1-14	2-13	0-54	1-28	1-51	2-53	
113	0-20	0-54	1-12	1-50	1-30	2-00	2-22	3-26

Est. vol. total, Calls 3363 Puts 938. Previous day's open int., Calls 65721 Puts.23747

■ FTSE 100 INDEX OPTION (LIFFE) (*4308) £10 per full index point

	4150		4200		4250		4300		4350		4400		4450		4500	
	C	P	C	P	C	P	C	P	C	P	C	P	C	P	C	P
Mar	158½	13	111	22½	74	37	43½	57	22	87	8	124½	2	170½	1	220
Apr	178½	40½	140½	53½	108½	70½	77½	90½	55½	118	35½	150	21	185½	12	226
May	200½	60	163½	73	131½	90	101	109	77½	136	56	165	40½	199	26½	236
Jun	230	76½	197	93	165½	111	134½	131	109½	155½	83½	181	63½	213	46½	247
Dec†			302	147½			241	186½			191	236½			145	292

Calls 6,027 Puts 5,794

■ EURO STYLE FTSE 100 INDEX OPTION (LIFFE) £10 per full index point

	4125		4175		4225		4275		4325		4375		4425		4475	
Mar	170½	11	128	18½	89½	30	57	47	31	71	14½	104	5½	145	2	191
Apr	197½	37	160	49	125	63½	93	81½	65	102½	42½	129½	26	162½	14	200½
May	218½	52½	181½	64½	147	80	116½	99	90	122	67½	148½	49	179½	34	214
Jun	249½	73	214	86½	180½	102	148	119	119½	139½	94½	163½	73½	192	54	221½
Sept†	301	101½			235	132½			177	171½			126½	217½		

Calls 5,209 Puts 9,969 * Underlying index value. Premiums shown are based on settlement prices.
† Long dated expiry months.

DM1, the direct quotation of the dollar. FFr/$ options are quoted in tenths of a US cent while ¥/$ contracts are quoted in hundredths of a cent. The holder of a call option gains if the non-dollar currency rises in value. On 28 February (the day to which the tables refer) the spot exchange rate of the dollar against sterling was $1.6315 = £1 and options at all three strike prices quoted were in-the-money, accounting for the high call premiums. Where the premiums of both call and put options for the same strike price are both rising as the length of time to the expiration date is increasing, it is probable that many traders are uncertain about the direction of movement of the price of the instrument in question (the pound) and are following mixed strategies involving the purchase of both calls and puts, as explained in Box 14.3.

Table 14.3 shows details of bond options and bond futures options which give the right to buy or sell notional government bond futures rather than bonds themselves together with two stock exchange index options, one of which is a European option. Premiums of UK bond futures options are quoted in 64ths of a per cent: 1-54 for the May contract with a strike price of 111 is 1 54/64 = 1.84. All other quotations are in decimals. German and Italian strike prices are to two decimal places (12750 = 127.5 in the case of Italian government bond futures options). The stock exchange index options tables are both on the Financial Times Stock Exchange Index (FTSE) and are organized with the strike prices along the top and expiration dates down the left-hand side. The strike prices of the Euro-style option are all intermediate between strike prices offered on the more usual American option above it. As is to be expected, the premiums on the European option are generally below those on the American option because the European option may only be exercised on the expiration date.

14.4   The pricing of options

We have seen that the premium of an option on a given day consists of two elements: the *intrinsic value* – the profit that would be made by exercising the option on that day; and the *time value* – a measure of the chances that the option will become profitable before the expiration date. One element of the time value of an option is just the length of time that an option has to run to expiration since the longer that period is, the greater must be the chance that the price of the underlying will change, affecting the profitability of the option. Further, the chances of a change occurring in a price depend not only on the length of time but on the volatility of the price of the underlying. Where the price of the underlying normally changes frequently and by relatively large amounts (it has a high variance), the time value of an option will be greater for each period to expiration than where the price of the underlying is generally stable. It is true that a volatile price may fall sharply as well as rise sharply but falls in price are only relevant to the extent that they cause the option to be at-the-money at the time of expiration – greater falls in price will simply cause the option to be abandoned. It follows that sharp price movements up have a much stronger impact on the possible profitability of an option and that volatility will always be positively related to the premium.

It is also the case that intrinsic value and time value are related. If an option is presently deeply out-of-the money (it has no intrinsic value), the chances that (for any given time period and volatility of the cash price) a change in price will make the instrument profitable must be less than if the option is only just out-of-the-money or at-the-money. Equally, if an option is deeply in-the-money, the chances that the cash price will go on rising, continuing to increase the profitability of the option, are less than if the intrinsic value of the option is lower. We can put this more formally as: the further the strike price is from the prevailing spot rate (the deeper in- or out-of-the-money the option is) the lower will be its time value as the risk-adjusted probability of gain on the contract to the buyer declines.

The value of a call option and hence the premium on it will also be higher, the higher is the risk-free rate of interest. This arises because of the choice which is always available to buy the underlying in the cash market as an alternative to buying an option. One advantage of the option is that only the premium needs to be paid and thus the difference between the cost of buying the asset directly in the cash market and the premium paid on the option is available to be invested. If we wish to make the two strategies comparable, the investment of the amount made available for investment by buying the option should be invested in a risk-free form, hence the use of the risk-free rate of interest. It follows that increases in interest rates will cause options to become more attractive relative to a direct purchase in the cash market. The value of the option and the premium paid for it increase with increases in the rate of interest.

We can sum up this discussion by saying that the premium of an option will *ceteris paribus* be:

(a) positively related to the cash price (P_s) of the underlying since increases in P_s increase the intrinsic value of the option;

(b) negatively related to the strike price (P_x) since decreases in the strike price increase the intrinsic value of the option;

(c) positively related to the amount of time that the option has to run before expiration (n_m) since the longer this period is the greater the time value of the option is;

(d) positively related to the volatility of the cash price of the underlying since the greater the volatility of the cash price the greater is the chance that the cash price will rise to high levels before expiration (the higher the volatility, the higher the time value of the option); and

(e) positively related to the risk-free rate of interest (i_{rf}) since the higher is the rate of interest the more attractive the option is relative to a purchase of the underlying in the cash market.

The next step is to establish the band within which an options price must fall if there are not to be profitable arbitrage opportunities. Consider the premium of an American call option. Even if it is deeply out-of-the-money, a call option must always have a positive value before expiration because there must always be some chance that the cash price will change sufficiently to give the option intrinsic value by the expiration date. At the point of expiration, however, the option could have zero value, in which case it would lapse. Thus:

$$Pm^c \geq 0 \tag{14.1}$$

However, it is also true that the premium of an American call option must be at least equal to its intrinsic value at any time or the immediate exercise of the option would be profitable:

$$Pm^c \geq P_s - P_x \tag{14.2}$$

But by developing the argument in (e) above, we can develop another pricing rule. Compare two strategies: (i) buying the underlying in the cash market now and holding it for three months; (ii) buying a three-month European call option and exercising it at the strike price at expiration. The gain in following strategy (ii) is the difference between the present cash price and the premium. At the point of expiration, however, strategy (ii) will deliver only:

$$(P_s^2 - P_x) \geq 0$$

where P_s^2 is the cash price at expiration. Thus, the maximum loss associated with strategy (ii) will be the value of P_x in three months' time. To compare this with the present gain, we need to discount it back to the present and, since we might have invested the amount saved in the present from strategy (ii) at the risk-free rate of interest, we should use that rate of interest to discount back the strike price. Thus we have:

$$P_s - Pm^c \geq P_x e^{-i_{rf} n_m} \qquad (14.3)$$

where $P_x e^{-i_{rf} n_m}$ is the discounted value of the cash price and hence:

$$Pm^c \geq P_s - P_x e^{-i_{rf} n_m} \qquad (14.4)$$

That is, the premium of the call option must at least equal the present cash price minus the discounted strike price. This rule must also hold for an American option since an American option must be more valuable than a European option because it adds the time value of the option between the present and the expiration date to the intrinsic value of the option at expiration. Equation 14.4 also formalizes the argument above that an increase in the risk-free rate of interest must increase the premium of a call option since it will reduce the present value of the strike price at the point of expiration. Since the expression on the right-hand side of Equation 14.4 can become negative but, as shown in Equation 14.1, the option premium will never fall below zero, it is usual to combine Equations 14.1 and 14.4 into:

$$Pm^c \geq max\ (0, P_s - P_x e^{-i_{rf} n_m}) \qquad (14.5)$$

We can now use Equations 14.1, 14.2 and 14.4 to establish boundary conditions for the pricing of options as shown in Figure 14.1.

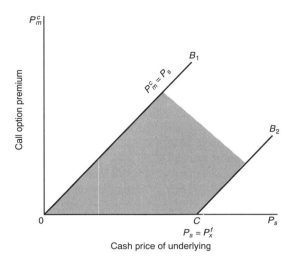

Figure 14.1 Option pricing limits.

Writing, $P_x e^{-i_{rf} n_m}$ as P_x^f for ease, we can interpret the diagram in the following way. Given the cash price of the underlying, the greatest value an option can assume will be where the strike price is zero. Then the call option premium will (from Equation 14.4) just equal the cash price. That is, the maximum premium for an option is shown along the ray from the origin $0B_1$ which is at 45 degrees to the horizontal axis. The minimum price of any option will be zero and this will occur where the cash price is less than or equal to P_x^f. For any given value of P_x^f, as P_s rises above P_x^f, the option premium will rise in line with the cash price (along the line CB_2). However, since P_x^f will change with changes in any or all of the strike price, the risk-free rate of interest, and the time to the expiration date of the option it is clear that the premium may fall anywhere in the shaded area between $0B_1$ and CB_2. Exercise 14.2 gives practice in the calculation of boundaries on call options prices.

Where any particular premium will fall will depend on the views of buyers and writers regarding the likely future value of the cash price since that is what will determine the profitability or otherwise of the option. We have seen that the expected volatility of the future cash price above the level where the cash price is greater than P_x^f is crucial here since that will influence the chances of the cash price reaching high levels. The usual assumption for the pricing of

Options, swaps and other derivatives   **285**

Exercise 14.2   Boundaries on £/$ options

Assume that March £/$ call options on the Philadelphia Stock Exchange in Table 14.2 contracts had one month to run to expiration and that the risk-free interest rate in the USA was the rate available for one-month money in the US money market (5.53 per cent). Thus, to discover the maximum call options premiums we discount back the various strike prices at a rate of 0.0553 for one month and subtract the figure we obtain from the spot price on the day ($1.6315).

Read example A below and then supply the missing figures for examples B and C.

A. Strike price $1.600

1   Discounting back $1.600 at 0.0553 for one month gives $1.593.

2   Subtracting $1.5926 from the spot price of $1.6315 gives $.0389.

   The premiums are, however, expressed in cents per £. Therefore, the maximum premium should be 3.89 US cents per £ and the premium should lie between 0 and 3.89. But we also know from Equation 14.2 in the text that the premium must be at least equal to the intrinsic value of the option. This was $1.6315 − $1.600 = $0.315 = 3.15 cents. Thus our rough calculations tell us that the option's premium should have been between 3.15 and 3.89.

We see from Table 14.2 that the actual premium for March contracts with a strike price of $1.600 was 3.20 cents. The market was thus attributing only a low time value to the option given the nearness of the expiration date.

B. Strike price $1.610

1   Discounting back $1.610 at 0.553 for one month gives (B1).
2   Subtracting (B2) from the spot price of (B3) gives (B4).
3   The premium for a call option at $1.610 should have been between (B5) and (B6).
4   The actual premium on this option in Table 14.2 is (B7).

C. Strike price $1.620

1   Discounting back $1.620 at 0.553 for one month gives (C1).
2   Subtracting (C2) from the spot price of (C3) gives (C4).
3   The premium for a call option at $1.620 should have been between (C5) and (C6).
4   The actual premium on this option in Table 14.2 is (C7).

D. Split the premiums in B7 and C7 into intrinsic value and time value.

(Answers at end of chapter)

---

options is that future volatility can be estimated from the past volatility of the cash price in question. Thus, the premium for a call option to buy DM (with dollars) will be influenced by the past distribution of the $/DM rate about its mean. The greater the variance of the rate in the past, the higher will be the option premium. This is the basis of the best known of the various theoretical models for pricing models, the Black–Scholes options pricing model which is based upon shares on which no dividends are paid.

The Black-Scholes model can be expressed in the following equations:

$$Pm^c = P_s N(d_1) - P_x e^{-i_{rf} n_m} N(d_2) \qquad (14.6)$$

where

$$d_1 = \frac{\ln(P_s/P_x) + [i_{rf} + (1/2)\sigma^2]n_m}{\sigma\sqrt{n_m}} \qquad (14.7)$$

and

$$d_2 = d_1 - \sigma\sqrt{n_m} \qquad (14.8)$$

In these equations $N(d_1)$ and $N(d_2)$ measure the cumulative weighted normal probability values (d_1 and d_2) of possible profit levels, given the past variance (σ) of the cash price of the underlying asset. The probabilities are derived from a log normal distribution of possible cash prices. The weighting takes into account the fact that low values of the cash price are of no significance since the option premium cannot fall below zero. In general, the greater is the expected volatility of the cash price and the longer the time to expiry, the more dispersed the distribution will be. The more dispersed the distribution, the higher will be the probabilities of relatively extreme values and the greater will be the weighted sum of potential profits to the buyer. Consequently, the higher will be the premium.

Similar principles may be used to calculate theoretical premiums for put options and for exotic options. Of course, the market is likely to use calculations from models such as the Black–Scholes options pricing model as a guide. If buyers and writers held rational expectations, they would take into account all the information that might affect future volatility, not just calculations based on the dispersion of past cash prices. In a market where expectations differ from one investor to another, speculators will be attempting to make profits by guessing better what will happen than the average investor. We have seen in Box 14.3 that investors use strategies which enable them to profit if they guess correctly that the market will be more or less volatile than the average investor believes. In Box 14.6 where we look at the collapse of the British bank, Barings, we see that the trader, Nick Leeson, was betting on Japanese share prices remaining stable, which had been the recent experience. In fact, they became very volatile.

14.5   Exotic options

There are many variations on the simple call and put options dealt with above. They are known as *exotic options*. We explain some of them here.

Barrier options are over-the-counter options designed to meet the particular needs of customers. They are also known as *knock-in* or *knock-out* options which means that they come into being (knock-in) or lapse (knock-out) when specified prices of the underlying are reached. There are four types of barrier options: calls and puts, each with a knock-out or knock-in feature.

A knock-in barrier option pays nothing at expiration unless it is first brought to life as a result of the price of the underlying reaching a specified level (the barrier). A knock-out option begins life as a standard option but is killed off if the cash price touches the barrier. Because they might never come into existence or might be killed off, they are much cheaper than conventional options. They are often used in the foreign exchange market by chartists (see Section 12.6 and Box 12.5) who feel strongly that

exchange rates will not fall below support levels or rise above resistance levels. Box 14.4 discusses the use of barrier options.

Credit risk derivatives were devised by banks to help manage their own credit risks but were then marketed to clients. The most popular has been the credit default option which protects the buyer against the default of a specific company or country. For example, an option might be taken out by a company which expects to be paid DM20m in three years' time when it completes a project in a foreign country. But since the country in question has defaulted on similar payments in the past, the company wants insurance against default risk. Hence it may take out an option with a bank which requires it to pay the premium in annual or semi-annual portions to the bank. In the event of a default, or a breach of other criteria agreed at the start of the option, the company will receive a payment.

The bank arranging the option will use outstanding bonds issued by the country concerned as a benchmark for setting the premium but since the bank will be hedging its own position by issuing bonds of a similar amount to investors, the company will have to pay above the yield on the outstanding bonds to attract buyers for the bonds backing the transaction. In the event of a default, there are various ways in which the size of the bank's payment may be calculated and the formula chosen by the company will influence the premium of the option. Credit risk derivatives are also sometimes bought by a fund manager holding, say, double-A rated bonds to compensate him if the securities were downgraded to single-A.

Other exotic options include:

- *Lookback options:* options that give the right to buy (lookback call) or sell (lookback put) at the lowest price reached by the underlying during the life of the option.
- *Asian options:* options whose intrinsic value is calculated by comparing the strike price with the average spot price over the period of the option.
- *Options on options:* an option that gives the right to buy an option.
- *Flex options:* options offered by the Chicago Board Options Exchange (CBOE) which allow an institutional OTC customer to choose any strike

Box 14.4   The use of a barrier option

A German company which imports oil, paying in US dollars, expects a bill for $1 million in three months' time. The current exchange rate is $0.61 = DM1. If the company is happy with that rate, it might buy a three-month DM call at that exercise price. This would protect the firm against the DM weakening and, if the DM strengthened, in the following three months the option could be allowed to lapse and the $1 million bought spot at a more favourable rate.

A *knock-out* DM call would give the same protection against the weakening of the DM (downside protection) but only until the exchange rate falls to a level below which the firm thinks it is unlikely to go. For example, a knock-out option with the same strike price and a barrier set at $0.57 = DM1 might cost much less than the standard option because the more extreme possibilities of loss to the writer would be cut off by the option being knocked out. If, at any time within the three months, the spot rate touched $0.55, and the option ceased to exist, the firm could buy the necessary DM in the spot market at that rate and put it on deposit until needed.

Barrier options are also used in investment products to enhance yield or to allow investors to express a view on two or more assets with a single instrument. For example, it would be possible to have a call option on a basket of French equities which knocked out if the French franc appreciated by more than a given percentage against the DM. This would be an example of an *outside barrier* – the barrier asset (the exchange rate) is different from the asset on which the basic option is written.

Another popular application during periods of low interest rates has been to use two knock-out options to create structured notes which pay high returns provided an underlying asset remains within a certain range. A typical example is a one-year dollar-denominated bond which yields 200 basis points more than conventional one-year paper provided the dollar/DM exchange rate remains within the ranges $0.56–$0.64 = DM1. The narrower the range and hence the more likely that the option would be knocked out, the greater the yield would be.

price and expiration date up to five years. Initially they applied to the CBOE's Standard and Poor's 100 and 500 Stock Index baskets and had an underlying value of $10m, much larger than the standard index options contracts.

■ *Warrants:* options to purchase or sell an underlying at a given price and time or series of prices and times. A warrant differs from a call or put option by ordinarily being issued for longer than a year. With covered warrants the shares that holders receive, if they exercise their warrants, already exist. Thus, the issuer of covered warrants is usually a bank which has bought up underlying shares. On the other hand, when companies issue warrants, usually in conjunction with bonds, it is generally a means of raising funds by creating new shares if the warrants are exercised.

14.6 Swaps

Swaps are exchanges of cash flows. They are attempts by firms to manage their asset/liability structure or to reduce their cost of borrowing. Cash flows generated by many different types of financial instruments may be swapped. Simple swaps such as interest rate and currency swaps are sometimes known as plain vanilla swaps. There are many variations on these.

An *interest rate* swap is an exchange of a cash flow representing a fixed rate of interest on a notional capital sum with that representing a floating rate on the same sum in the same currency. There is no exchange of the principal amount. They are potentially useful because the fixed and floating capital markets are distinct markets and firms wishing to borrow may not have equal access to both. For example, a firm may be quite large in a regional market and be able to borrow from regional banks at fine floating interest rates (that is, the rate at which banks themselves obtain their money – the basis rate or interbank rate – plus a small fixed rate spread). Nonetheless, it may be insufficiently well known to be able to launch a fixed interest rate bond without offering a high coupon because of the high risk premium which will be demanded in the bond market for holding bonds issued by a little known firm (because the firm is only regional it may be given a low credit rating by the international agencies).

Taking the floating rate loan, however, exposes the firm to the risk that interest rates may rise. The firm may be able to obtain better fixed interest rate terms in the national capital market on relatively short-term loans but will still face the interest rate risk if it wishes a long-term loan because the interest rate may change when it seeks to rollover the loan. The firm may be able to hedge the risk in a variety of ways. It could, for example, sell a long-term interest rate futures contract. Then, if the interest rate rises, the firm loses on its loan but this loss is offset by the profit made on the futures contract. Again, the firm could hedge by buying a put (or writing a call) option on long-term interest rates or interest rate futures.

Yet another possibility is for it to swap the interest rate payments it must make to its bank with a fixed interest rate flow of another firm which has been able to obtain a suitably priced fixed interest rate loan but would prefer a floating rate loan.

The default risk in a swap of future cash streams between firms is overcome in the swaps market by arranging the swap through a bank (the swap bank or hedge bank) which acts as a guarantor to both parties and charges a fee which takes into account the risk that one of the firms will default on their payments to the bank. This type of business has advantages to the bank because it earns a fee for its services without advancing any of its capital or using up any of its credit lines – it is off-balance-sheet business. Box 14.5 provides an example of how an interest-rate swap might work to benefit all parties.

Box 14.5   An interest rate swap

A major British defence industry supplier, Death Mines plc, wishes to borrow £1 million for 12 years at a fixed interest rate to finance a new investment project. It could do so by issuing a straight Eurobond but, as the international market has some doubts about the future of medium-sized arms suppliers, it would have to pay a coupon of 11 per cent which it regards as too high. The firm's own bank is willing to lend Death Mines the required amount via a one-year floating rate note at a rate of 1.5 per cent over the London inter-Bank Offered Rate (LIBOR), currently at 7 per cent, and rollover the loan annually.

The floating rate loan is much cheaper at the moment, but LIBOR could easily rise over the period of the loan to such a level that Death Mines will finish up losing on the project. Thus, it enters into a contract with a swap bank, Border International, to pay to it 8 per cent on the principal, receiving in exchange LIBOR.

The position of Death Mines now is:

Pays to its own bank	LIBOR + 1.5 per cent
Pays to Border	8 per cent
Receives from Border	LIBOR
Net position – fixed rate loan at	9.5 per cent

But what of Border International? It has taken on a risk that LIBOR will increase. To cover this, it must either find a counterparty that wishes to take the reverse action to Death Mines or hedge the risk through, perhaps, options or futures (this is known as warehousing). Let us assume that Border International finds a counterparty – a large US multinational, Babe Struth. Babe Struth is a prime borrower and so can borrow on the Eurobond market on the finest terms, but prefers a floating rate loan as it is willing to gamble on interest rates falling in the future. Thus, it issues a straight £500,000 Eurobond with a coupon of 7.375 per cent. Then it enters into a contract with Border International to pay Border LIBOR in exchange for a fixed return of 7.75 per cent.

The position of Babe Struth now is:

Pays on its straight Eurobond	7.375 per cent
Receives from Border	7.75 per cent
Pays to Border	LIBOR
Net position: floating rate loan at	LIBOR – 0.375 per cent

Border International's Position now is:

Receives from Death Mines	8 per cent
Pays to Death Mines	LIBOR
Receives from Babe Struth	LIBOR
Pays to Babe Struth	7.75 per cent
Net position – profit of	0.25 per cent (25 basis points)

This is an example where payments are swapped but receipts may also be swapped. Yet again, since the capital sums are only notional, it is possible to speculate on the possibility of an interest rate rise or fall through interest rate swaps. For example, a speculator might feel that interest rates are likely to fall and so offer a floating rate stream (which will fall as market interest rates decline) in exchange for a fixed rate stream which will not. If the speculator is right about the direction of interest rate change he will profit from the swap. The price of a swap (the charge made by the swap bank for its services) depends on the bank's estimate of the extent of default risk, the ease with which it can obtain a counterparty and the term structure of interest rates in the bond market.

A *currency swap* has three stages:

- an initial exchange of principal: the two counterparties exchange principal amounts at an agreed exchange rate. This can be a notional exchange since its purpose is to establish the principal amounts as a reference point for the calculation of interest payments and the re-exchange of the principal amounts;
- exchange of interest payments on agreed dates based on outstanding principal amounts and agreed fixed interest rates;
- re-exchange of the principal amounts at a predetermined exchange rate so the parties end up with their original currencies.

Again this may be done to hedge risk, to speculate on changes in exchange rates or to attempt to lower the cost of borrowing by borrowing in the currency in which the most favourable interest rates are available and then swapping into the currency that the firm needs to carry out its business. Whether this will be cheaper will depend among other things on the bid–offer spread.

There are many variations on simple currency swaps. In a *cross-currency basis swap* two floating-rate cash streams are swapped. This may be possible because the banks that have made the two loans are using a different basis rate for the calculation of their floating interest rates. The most commonly used basis rate in the London market is LIBOR (the London Inter-Bank Offered Rate). The US$ prime rate is also widely used. Thus, a basis rate swap may involve, for example, an exchange of a sterling cash stream representing a floating interest rate based upon LIBOR with a dollar cash stream representing a floating rate based upon the US$ prime rate.

A *cross-currency coupon swap* is a currency swap involving a fixed interest stream and a floating interest stream. In other words, it is a combination of an interest rate swap and a fixed rate currency swap – both the interest rate structure and the currency are exchanged.

Other types of swap include *equity swaps* which are agreements to exchange the rate of return on an equity or an equity index for a floating or fixed rate of interest. Equity swaps can be used as an alternative to futures and options for hedging but are most attractive to fund managers trying to outperform an index. The fund manager receives a stream of payments replicating the return of a direct investment in an equity index and makes in return a stream of payments usually based on LIBOR. An equity swap may increase a fund manager's ability to increase returns but because swaps, unlike futures, can run for up to 10 years, the default risk is greater, although exposure to it is limited by payments normally being made every three months and because there is no exchange of principal.

In a *commodity swap* the counterparties exchange cash flows, at least one of which is based on a commodity price or commodity price index. A high proportion of the market is made up of oil-related transactions. A *diff swap* (or *quanto swap*) is the exchange of the cash flows on an asset or liability in one currency for those in another. A firm making a diff swap separates foreign exchange and interest rate exposure, by paying interest rates based on one currency while taking the foreign exchange risk of another. For example, a company with US dollar liabilities, paying say 8 per cent interest, would prefer to be paying DM interest rates of 5 per cent but may not want to be exposed to the risk of changes in the value of the DM. Under a diff swap, the company agrees to receive dollar LIBOR and to pay a margin over DM LIBOR in dollars. The structure takes advantage of different-shaped yield curves to create immediate cost savings for the borrower and allows an investor to receive higher interest rates without changing currency exposure. Such an agreement typically runs from three to five years and so the risk for either borrower or investor is that the shape of one or both yield curves will change more quickly than expected, turning expected benefits into losses. Diff swaps became common when US and European interest rates diverged sharply. They involve *correlation risk* – an assumption that there will be a correlation between an interest rate movement and that of the currency. With a *LIBOR-in-arrears swap*, the borrower essentially takes a bet that implied forward rates are wrong by having LIBOR set, say, six months in arrears.

It is also possible to combine a zero coupon bond with an interest rate swap (known as a zero coupon swap). Then there are *swaptions* – options that give the right to enter into a swap within a specified period. Because swaps are off-balance-sheet business but carry risks for the swap bank there was a concern in the past that banks might take on more risk through swaps than was justified by the size of their capital backing. As a consequence, as we shall see in Chapter 24, the rules adopted by a number of countries (known as the Basle rules), which try to ensure that the capital backing of banks is adequate for the type of business in which they are engaged, make allowances for off-balance-sheet business. Because currency swaps involve both default risk and exchange rate risk, they require higher capital backing under the Basle rules and this has slowed down their expansion relative to interest rate swaps.

There are yet other derivatives which do not fit neatly under the futures, options and swaps headings. One such is *equity protected notes* – a zero-coupon, index-linked note allows investors to protect themselves against potential losses without giving up the possibility of gains. *Dynamic hedging* involves the buying and selling of forward contracts in the market in order to replicate options. It became popular in foreign exchange markets after the problems in the European Monetary System in 1992 (see Chapter 22) which caused options prices to rise sharply. *Safes* (synthetic agreements for forward foreign exchange) are forward contracts that do not require an exchange of principal. This means that banks need to devote less capital to them and are less exposed to default risk. There are two types of Safe: the Exchange Rate Agreement (ERA) which protects the purchaser against a change in the forward foreign exchange spread; and the Forward Exchange Agreement (FXA) which gives protection against a change in the spot rate as well as the forward spread. *Insurance risk contracts* are futures and options on catastrophe insurance, health, and homeowner's and reinsurance risk.

14.7 Comparing different types of derivatives

14.7.1 Exchange-traded derivatives versus OTC products

Exchange-traded derivatives have five principal advantages over over-the-counter options:

(1) the existence of the clearing house guarantees all trades and virtually eliminates the default risk present in OTC trades;
(2) price discovery is easier from exchange-based trading than in OTC markets because futures and options contracts are reported immediately and prices are widely distributed;
(3) markets for exchange-based derivatives are more liquid than bilateral OTC trades since there are many traders in each futures pit;
(4) exchange-based futures and options are highly tradeable because they are standardized whereas OTC options, being non-standard and redeemable only at the bank where they were bought, have a low resale value.
(5) exchange-based derivatives are lower in price than OTC derivatives since there will almost always be some irreducible residual risk that a bank is forced to take onto its own book, despite the fact that it will attempt to minimize its risks by arranging offsetting contracts with other customers/banks and/or by taking a position in exchange-traded options.

Against these, we must set the fact that OTC options are designed to meet the specific requirements of each customer in terms of size, strike price and expiration.

14.7.2 Forwards versus futures contracts

As we made clear in Chapter 13, there may be important cash-flow differences between forward and futures contracts because, whereas net profits on a futures hedge are accrued on a daily basis, the net profits on a forward hedge are only realized on the actual date of currency delivery (assuming the forward contract is not closed out prematurely). A different type of problem connected with the use of futures contracts to hedge an exposed currency position arises in cases where the lifetime of the futures contract continues beyond the intended date of currency delivery. This problem stems from the fact that the difference between the futures and spot rates may not tend uniformly towards zero as the delivery date for the futures contract approaches, which is the assumption that underlies calculations of the forward rate. Eventual convergence is certain, but in the meantime as the basis moves to compensate for changes in interest rate differentials between countries, so the futures hedge will tend to be in either profit or loss. Clearly, the further the anticipated date of actual currency conversion is from the futures delivery date, the less the natural tendency towards zero of the basis will dominate other factors and hence the less efficient the hedge.

14.7.3 Forwards and futures contracts versus options

Forward and futures contracts lock in an investor to a given exchange rate. Thus, the contract provides a hedge if the exchange rate moves in the direction which would have produced a loss, but there is an opportunity loss if the currency moves in the opposite direction. Currency options, on the other hand, do not lock in an investor to a particular exchange rate since the option does not have to be exercised.

14.8 The use and abuse of derivatives

We have seen that financial derivatives allow firms to hedge against erratic price and interest rate movements while also attracting speculators because of their high gearing. These two aspects of the market

have led to conflicting attitudes regarding their overall contribution to financial markets. Supporters of derivatives markets argue that they perform a number of important roles. They are said to:

- facilitate the hedging of risk through sophisticated risk management, and by so doing improve the productivity of investments;
- respond more quickly to new information than the cash markets and allow people who do not participate in derivatives trading, to forecast accurately what will happen to future cash market prices and use this information to make better consumption, pricing and investment decisions – this is known as the 'price discovery' role of derivatives;
- assist in the standardization of commodity or financial instrument contracts in the cash markets because derivatives contracts are highly standardized themselves;
- contribute to the integration of global capital markets, hence improving the global allocation of savings and fostering higher investment levels;
- help to combat the adverse effects of volatile commodity prices on the economies of developing countries because forward prices tend to be less volatile than spot prices, giving commodity producers an opportunity to reduce the volatility of the price of their output through hedging.[2]
- facilitate speculation which provides liquid markets enabling hedgers to protect themselves from risk in the most efficient way possible.

Doubts have been expressed about the price discovery role since it is dependent on the efficient markets hypothesis (introduced in Chapter 12 and dealt with in detail in Chapter 25). However, the main doubts expressed about the benefits of derivatives have centred on the role of speculation and the difficulties which the increasing complexity of derivatives products have caused for regulators. Support for the attack on derivatives trading has come from problems in markets as a whole and from examples of spectacular losses by individual companies and banks.

---

[2] This role was emphasized in a 1994 World Bank report which referred to a study of the oil futures market in the late 1980s where it was suggested that a producer routinely hedging 15 months in advance could cut price volatility by a half.

For example, derivatives trading was widely held to be partly to blame for the 1987 stock market crash. The argument was that stock market traders were pessimistic and expected a fall in the price of stocks when the exchanges opened after a weekend. Large orders to sell arrived at brokerage houses prior to opening and, as the market started falling, many traders automatically sold futures in the shares of the major corporations. This destabilized stock markets and contributed to the panic selling of stocks and shares. This view of the crash led to a general concern that high turnover in derivatives, particularly that involving large-scale arbitrage techniques, may contribute to the volatility of the cash market. This is strenuously denied by the derivatives markets themselves, but worries have been expressed at a high level. Towards the end of April 1994 finance ministers from the Group of 10 leading industrial countries agreed on the need to strengthen co-operation in gathering statistics and assessing the implications for the world financial system of the innovative segments of financial markets. There was also a call for improved disclosure requirements and sufficient capital adequacy standards among finan-cial institutions to underpin their risky activities.

Certainly there is some evidence that Wall Street equity prices have been affected by heavy activity in stock index contracts, especially around expiration dates, and there is a possible theoretical argument to support the view that derivatives trading makes the cash markets more volatile and nervy. This is that, in the past, people who thought prices in a market were becoming too high would speculate and express their bearish feelings by leaving the market. This would exert downward pressure on prices and help to stabilize them. Now, however, such firms stay in the market but protect themselves against risk using derivatives markets. No sale is made and bearish opinion loses its restraining influence on prices. Thus, although spreading risks through derivatives reduces risks for the individual, it increases risk for the system as a whole. This in turn provides big profit opportunities for the uninsured speculators but increases risks of bankruptcies.

Individual company losses through derivatives have in recent years become almost routine. The most spectacular was the collapse of the British merchant bank Barings in 1995. It is explained in Box 14.6.

Box 14.6   The case of Barings

The British merchant bank, Barings Brothers, were bankrupted in 1995, after losses of more than £860 million accrued on the Singapore and Osaka derivatives exchanges. The bank was the victim of its own star trader, Nick Leeson, and the absence of management controls to monitor his activities. Leeson was responsible for both trading and back office records of his deals at Simex. Between 1992 and 1995, he built up positions in futures and options contracts on the Nikkei 225 stock exchange index, which in the early years proved highly profitable for Barings.

Leeson bought futures positions on the Nikkei index and financed cash calls on them as they fell in value by selling put options on the contract, producing a straddle (see Box 14.3). He was thus betting against the volatility of the market. The contracts were bought through the Simex derivatives exchange in Singapore. He had been meant to run a hedged position in Nikkei index futures and make money by arbitraging different prices in Singapore and Osaka but he stopped hedging the purchases made in Singapore. The first purchase was made in early February. Further contracts were agreed in mid-February to provide cash for losses as the Nikkei index fell. At least 20,000 contracts were bought expiring in mid-March. During 1994, the Nikkei index had stayed within a narrow range. But in early 1995, the combination of a large earthquake in Kobe and a turn in investor sentiment against Japanese markets drove the Nikkei index sharply down. Each point of the Nikkei 225 futures contract carries a value of ¥1,000, and so with the Nikkei 225 trading at levels between 18,000 and 20,000 in the first few weeks of the year, each future would have had a value of some ¥18–20 million. With 20,000 contracts and a fall in price from ¥19.6 million to ¥17.6 million, losses would have amounted to ¥40 billion. The sale of the put options transformed an already highly geared trading strategy into a perilous double-or-quits game.

Most of Barings' employees were saved by Internationale Nederlanden Group which bought Barings and took on its losses for £1.

Another interesting case arose from the attempt made in the late 1980s by Hammersmith and Fulham local authority in London to profit from speculation in interest rate swaps, but they ran up huge losses instead. They entered the sterling interest rate swaps market on 1 December 1983. Council officers had visited LIFFE where the idea of using swaps to reduce the sensitivity of the council's borrowings to interest rate fluctuations was explained to them. An independent inquiry in 1991, however, showed that such was the level of the user's understanding that the leader of the council and the finance department were not clear whether they were interested in futures or options transactions. The council's activities in the money markets intensified in May 1987 when it began to become involved in swap options and other complex transactions, eventually totalling 550 transactions.

At the time, interest rates were falling and the local authorities gambled on their continued fall. Thus, in 1988 when the base rate of interest in the UK was 7.5 per cent, local authorities swapped fixed interest rate for floating interest rate loans of the same value with hedging banks. The only payments made were for the net liabilities on whichever was the higher – the fixed or the floating rate. Thus if interest rates had continued to fall the local authorities would have profited. Their aim was to pick correctly the trough in interest rates and at that stage to reverse the swap, moving back to a fixed interest rate, probably at a lower rate than their original interest payments.

However, the local authorities were taken unawares by the sharp jump in interest rates which saw the base rate of interest rise to 15 per cent in 1989. They were then, under the terms of the contract, required to pay large amounts to the banks – the difference between the now very high floating rates and the fixed rate on their original loans. Despite the volume of contracts and the size of the risk, there was never any monitoring system established to track the performance and possible dangers of their derivative business. But the ratepayers of the most indebted local authorities were rescued by the courts who ruled that it had been illegal for the local authorities to use their funds in this way and therefore that the contracts were unenforceable. The banks thus found themselves exposed to *legal risk*.

Another famous case was that of Metallgesellschaft (MG), the fourteenth largest industrial concern in Germany. The strategy of their US affiliate, MG Refinery and Marketing Inc., was to sell petrol, diesel and heating oil products to customers on fixed price contracts up to 10 years ahead. It then protected itself against price movements by hedging the full amount with futures and OTC swap contracts. Over the previous 10 years, spot prices had mostly exceeded near future prices (backwardation). This meant that hedging in short-dated futures would produce profits as each expiring contract yielded more than it cost. However, in 1993, a contango occurred, upsetting MG's calculations and shocking its banks. Every $1 fall in the spot oil price meant an extra $160 million of margin payments. Also complicating the question was the fact that MG was losing money every time it rolled over its oil futures contracts. On each rollover date, as it sold expiring futures contracts and bought new ones to carry the hedge forward, MG had to pay more for the new contracts than it received for the old ones because of the contango. This rollover cost amounted to $20–30 million in each of October and November and would have been $50 million in December. MG had to pay out over $900 million in the form of additional margin on its futures positions, and extra collateral to counterparties on over-the-counter swaps. This resulted in a severe liquidity crisis, leading to an emergency line of credit from banks and a forced unwinding of most of the company's derivative positions. Longer term hedging contracts would have been available – but at a higher price. It was the funding cost of the short-term hedging strategy that led to the heavy losses. Had winter come earlier (causing the spot oil price to rise), the crisis would have been averted, but there was no guarantee that it would not have arisen later. In January 1994, 150 German and international banks, headed by Deutsche and Dresdner Bank, mounted a DM3.4 bn rescue operation to save Metallgesellschaft from bankruptcy.

The large American firm, Procter and Gamble, was in 1994 required to make $102m after-tax charges on its profits arising from swap transactions losses. It later sued Bankers Trust, claiming that Bankers Trust did not 'accurately and fully' disclose information about the derivatives contract. Procter and Gamble had been using derivatives instruments to cut the cost of its borrowing and manage its exposure to interest rate and foreign exchange for years. However, the company took out two highly-geared swaps contracts, designed by Bankers Trust to allow Procter and Gamble to swap fixed interest rate loans for floating interest rate loans, on the assumption that US and German interest rates would stay low. When interest rates rose sharply, Procter and Gamble lost money on the contracts, which they later said were inconsistent with the company's internal policy on the use of derivatives. Bankers Trust were also sued at the same time on similar grounds by another American company, Gibson Greetings.[3]

Tokyo Securities lost ¥32 billion, one third of the firm's net assets, in 1994. Kashima Oil, a Japanese company, lost $1.5bn in foreign exchange derivative trading. The head of bond trading at the US securities firm, Kidder Peabody, was fired in 1994 for allegedly creating $350m of fictitious profits. The firm was broken up largely as a result. In 1991, another US securities firm, Salomon Brothers, had to pay several hundred million dollars in fines and compensation after its head of bond trading was found to have faked customer bids in Treasury auctions. The new management had to write off several hundred million dollars more early in 1995 for past bookkeeping errors. The Japanese car manufacturer, Mazda, lost ¥65 billion on its foreign exchange transactions in 1993/94.

On the other hand, the Italian clothing firm, Benetton, achieved a one-off gain of L50 billion from some well-timed currency hedges when the lira strengthened against the DM by almost 10 per cent in three months in 1993.

The Australian bank, Westpac, suffered from *tax risk* in 1992 when it was forced to pay an unexpected tax liability and penalties of nearly $80 million in the USA because of conflicting tax treatment of swaps and forward contracts in the USA and Australia. In 1991, Allied Lyons lost £150m in foreign exchange dealings, through writing currency options. This can lead to unlimited losses. This case is treated in Exercise 14.3.

A trader at Daiwa, one of Japan's largest and once

Exercise 14.3

Read the following extract from the *Financial Times* and answer the questions that follow:

'Allied-Lyons' losses of approximately £150 m, attributed to "abnormal foreign exchange exposures", arose because the company took a strong view on the direction of the dollar, and got it wrong. It is standard practice for companies with a large portion of dollar-based income from both operations and exports, as Allied-Lyons has, to hedge against adverse currency movements.

'But Allied-Lyons appears to have gone further, taking heavy positions on the expectation of dollar weakness. The company took positions in both derivative and cash markets, writing call options on the dollar, and selling the dollar short in the foreign exchange market, according to analysts....

'Although it is quite common for large companies to write call options, it is a practice approached with caution. In buying a call option, the option holder can only lose the nominal cost of the option ... Writing – that is, selling – a call option, on the other hand, leaves the writer with unlimited exposure ... '

Financial Times, 20 March 1991

Questions

(a) What is meant by 'hedging against adverse currency movements'? How might Allied-Lyons have hedged?
(b) What must they have done in order to go short in dollars?
(c) What is a call option in dollars?
(d) Under what circumstances will the writer of a call option in dollars lose?
(e) Explain why such losses may be unlimited.

(Answers at end of chapter)

---

3 For details of these cases see R Waters, 'US bank settles derivatives law suit' (*Financial Times*, 28 October 1994) and R Waters, 'P & G sues bank over big loss on derivatives' (*Financial Times*, 28 October 1994).

one of its most respected financial institutions, incurred losses of millions of dollars a week on the trading of government bonds. The total losses amounted to $1.1 billion. He hid those losses over 11 years by selling securities which the bank held but which belonged to its customers. To avoid suspicion, he continued to pay interest on those securities by forging bank statements. He confessed in July 1995 but the management then took steps designed to conceal the losses from the US authorities. The losses were not revealed to the world at large until September. Thus, in November, Daiwa was ordered by the US authorities to close its US operations and the company was accused of conspiring to defraud the United States by having lied to, misled and deceived US authorities. Specifically, Daiwa was accused of using its international treasury division in Tokyo to repurchase US Treasuries, making up for the missing ones sold by the trader and covering up what it was doing by preparing false documents including bank statements, internal records and a report issued to the Federal Reserve Board on 31 July, stating the bank's balance sheet.

14.9 Summary

Options are financial instruments that give the right to buy or sell an underlying financial instrument. Options are traded on exchanges and have many features in common with futures – they are also highly geared and are used by both hedgers and speculators. Options have advantages over futures in certain circumstances. In particular, they may be used to provide protection against the market moving in one direction without removing the prospect of gain if the market moves in the opposite direction. The price or premium of an option can be divided into the option's intrinsic value (the profit that would be made if the option were exercised immediately) and its time value (a measure of the possibility that the option's value might increase before the expiration date). Arbitrage possibilities between the cash market and the options market establish boundaries within which the option premium must lie but the actual premium depends on the market's estimate of the future volatility of the price of the underlying instrument.

Swaps are also widely used for hedging and speculation and for changing the structure of a company's balance sheet or reducing the interest it must pay on a loan. The most common form of swaps are exchanges of interest rate streams or cash flows in different currencies. There are very many variations on both swaps and options. Derivatives of all kinds perform a number of roles in financial markets and are strongly supported by many people. However, concern has been expressed about the effects of derivatives trading on the volatility of the underlying markets and the rapid growth of ever more complex derivatives trading has made life difficult for regulators and company managers alike. One consequence of this has been the very large losses regularly experienced by companies through the use of the derivatives markets.

Key concepts used in this chapter

Options	Synthetic call option	Interest rate swaps
Strike/exercise price	Covered/naked call	Currency swaps
Option premium	Intrinsic value	Cross-currency basis rate swaps
Call option	Time value	Cross-currency coupon swaps
Put option	Exotic options	Diff swaps
European option	Barrier options	Legal/tax risk
American option	Credit risk derivatives	

Questions and problems

1 Explain each of the following:
   (a) fixed rate currency swaps;
   (b) an 'in-the-money' option.

2 Explain the statement made by the Chairman of the Chicago Board of Trade (CBoT) in the following extract:

   'The Chicago Board of Trade will launch an oats futures options contract on May 1. Options on oats will provide a variety of hedging possibilities. The American Oats Association in Minneapolis said that producers were more likely to use options than futures. According to the CBoT chairman, by purchasing options a hedger can establish price ceilings and floors, and still benefit if cash prices change in his favor.'

3 Find out as much as you can about the activities and procedures of the international credit-rating agencies.

4 Answer the following questions concerning interest rate swaps:
   (a) Why might a borrower wish to enter into such a swap?
   (b) Why might such a swap be possible?
   (c) What risk does the guaranteeing bank run?

5 Consider Table 14.1 and answer the following questions:
   (a) Why do all Euromark options with a strike price of 9725 have premiums of 0?
   (b) Why do the premiums on put options increase as the strike price increases?
   (c) What do the premiums on Euromark options tell you about German interest rates on 28 February?

6 Find examples of companies having hedged through the use of derivatives products other than those mentioned in the text.

7 Find more information about some of the examples of company problems mentioned in the text.

8 You are given the following figures for Eurolira options contracts:

   Current rate of interest on short-term Eurolira deposits: 7.5 per cent

   Risk-free rate of interest: 7.25 per cent

   Calculate the minimum and maximum premiums of call options for the periods and strike prices below:

Strike price	Time to expiration		
	1 month	3 months	6 months
9250			
9275			
9300			

9 Find as many examples as you can of exotic options and variations upon plain vanilla swaps.

10 What factors are likely to influence the price that a swap bank will charge for participating in a currency swap?

11 Why do you think so many types of derivatives have been developed over such a short period?

Further reading

D Blake, *Financial Market Analysis* (London: McGraw-Hill, 1990) Chs 9 and 10

A Buckley, *The Essence of International Money* (Hemel Hempstead: Prentice Hall, 1990) Chs 9 and 11

H S Houthakker and P J Williamson, *The Economics of Financial Markets* (Oxford: Oxford University Press, 1996) Ch. 8

R W Kolb, *Financial Derivatives* (Oxford: Blackwell, 1996) chs. 3 and 4

K Redhead, *Introduction to the International Money Markets* (Cambridge: Woodhead-Faulkner, 1992) Chs 6 and 7

R Vaitilingam, *The* Financial Times *Guide to Using the Financial Pages* (London: Pitman Publishing, 1996, 3e)

Answers to exercises

Exercise 14.1

The prices quoted for Eurolira options contracts in Table 14.1 bear out the comments we have made about Italian interest rates in both Chapters 12 and 13.

1   The high price of 0.94 per cent for a September call option at a strike price of 9250 confirms the general market view at the beginning of March 1997 that Italian interest rates were likely to fall and thus the options' premiums rise. Because this seemed such a good bet, there was a strong demand for call options but few people wished to bet on the possibility that Italian interest rates would rise. Indeed, an option with a strike price of 9250 was already in-the-money and had intrinsic value. The market expectation that Italian interest rates would fall further also meant that it had a high time value also. A put option at a strike price of 9250 was, however, already out-of-the-money and the market expectation of a falling interest rate meant that its time value was low.

2   The expiry date of March calls was only three weeks ahead and so the prospect of Italian interest rates falling in this period was much less than for options with expiry dates in June and September. That is, the time value of March call options was very low and the main contributor to the price of March options was the intrinsic value. As we have noted above, those with a strike price of 9250 had intrinsic value whereas those with a strike price of 9300 were out-of-the-money. Traders were not willing to bet anything on the prospect of Eurolira interest rates falling sufficiently in the short remaining time to expiry to make these options profitable. Not surprisingly, the premium for puts was quite high at 0.37.

3   Puts were more expensive for both strike prices for all three expiry dates. Interestingly, however, the difference between call and put premiums was very little different for the three expiry dates. This suggests that the main element in the price was the intrinsic value. Since premiums for puts were much higher than for calls, the implication was that options

at both of these strike prices (implying interest rates of 1.5 and 1.25 per cent) were out-of-the-money on 28 February. This was confirmed by Euro Currency interest rates on that day – Euro Swiss Franc interest rates for one month, three months and six months were 1.625, 1.66 and 1.66 per cent respectively.

Exercise 14.2

B: 1. \$1.6026; 2. \$1.6026; 3. \$1.6315; 4. \$.0289; 5. 2.15 cents; 6. 2.89 cents; 7. 2.46 cents

C: 1. \$1.6125; 2. \$1.6125; 3. \$1.6315; 4. \$0.019; 5. 1.15 cents; 6. 1.90 cents; 7. 1.77 cents.

D. B7: intrinsic value 2.15 cents; time value 0.31 cents. C7: intrinsic value 1.15 cents; time value 0.62 cents.

Exercise 14.3

(a) Acting in financial markets to protect oneself against the risk of the value of a currency in which one is long falling in value **or** against the value of a currency in which one is short rising in value.

In Allied Lyons case they were initially long in dollars and thought the dollar would fall in value. They may have hedged by:
(i) selling dollars forwards;
(ii) selling futures contracts in dollars;
(iii) buying put options or writing call options in dollars.

(b) Acting as in (a) to a sufficient extent to reverse the existing long position, for example selling **more** dollars forwards than they expected to receive.

(c) A contract giving the right to buy dollars before or at the expiration date of the option at the strike price specified in the contract.

(d) If the value of the dollar rises.

(e) Because the writer must pay the excess of the spot price of the dollar over the strike price, no matter how high the dollar rises. The writer of the option has to meet their obligation to provide dollars to the buyer.

PART 5 Financial systems

An introduction to financial systems

15.1 Introduction

In Part 4 of this book we looked at a range of markets and the instruments traded in those markets. The instruments – bills, bonds, equities, futures and so on – are essentially the same from one country to another. They fulfil a common purpose and inevitably, therefore, they are priced according to the same principles wherever they are traded. Indeed, most of the instruments are internationally traded with the result, for example, that US equities are close substitutes for German equities in the portfolio of a French investor. Because they are close substitutes, changes in the price (or yield) of a given class of instruments in one country is often reflected in a similar change in those instruments across national boundaries. Indeed, when we looked at the *Financial Times's* commentary on equity price changes in Box 11.8 we saw examples of prices in all European markets following each other and following prices in

the USA. This means that the few differences that exist between *markets* in different countries amount to differences in size and differences in the institutional arrangements for the trading of instruments. These differences are neither large nor very important, but we picked out the main details in each of the market chapters.

However, it is not yet quite true that all financial *systems* are the same, even though under global pressures they may be growing increasingly similar. The differences lie in the institutions, rather than markets, and in approaches to the regulation of financial activity. In this part of the book, we provide a brief outline of the financial systems in Germany, France, UK, USA and Italy, concentrating upon the roles of the major financial institutions and on the regulatory framework.

To begin with, though, we look at different ways of classifying financial systems, an issue that has become complicated in recent years, and then we provide a summary of different types of financial institutions and their functions.

15.2 The classification of financial systems

If we go right back to basics (Section 1.2.1) we know that a deficit, and thus the need to borrow, arises only when saving is insufficient to finance investment. In Chapter 1 we noted that a function of a financial system is to channel funds between surplus and deficit units and to do this by creating assets and liabilities that are more attractive to lenders and borrowers than would be the case if they dealt with each other directly. If we aggregate units into sectors of the economy, we can say that households have traditionally constituted a surplus sector while firms have generally been a deficit sector. The traditional picture, therefore, is one in which the financial system, *in the aggregate*, channels funds from households to firms. One obvious way of classifying financial systems, therefore, is to look at the way in which this is done. Indeed, if we now make the assumption that households are the only, or at least the major, source of finance for firms (as must be the case in market economies), then the classification of financial systems requires only that we look at how firms are financed. This explains why the literature which tries to distinguish different 'types' of financial system concentrates on what looks like a much narrower question of corporate finance, namely, how do firms raise funds for investment?

One obvious answer is that they plough back profits, but remember that we are talking about financing a deficit, so 'internal' finance is taken for granted and our attention is focused on the manner in which funds get channelled from households to firms to cover the deficit. Essentially, there are two possibilities. Either households lend to firms via financial intermediaries, such as banks, or they do it via markets, for example by buying shares. Further refinements are possible: within 'market' finance, for example, we can distinguish those systems where households buy shares directly and those where they buy shares only indirectly by buying units in a trust or buying life insurance from a company that has large holdings of equities amongst its assets. However, *seen from the perspective of the firm*, such details are immaterial. In either of these cases, its finance comes from shares, and thus via markets, whoever holds the shares. Hence, the traditional practice has been to classify financial systems as *market-based* or *bank-based*, depending on whether firms in general get most of their finance from the issue of securities or loans. On this classification system, the UK and the USA have been regarded as market-based systems, while Germany and Japan have been regarded as bank-based, with other countries somewhere in between, but generally tending towards bank finance. It is thus easy to see that this system of classification results in a parallel distinction between 'Anglo-Saxon' and 'other' approaches to finance.

The distinction is important because on most conventional economic criteria, employment, growth, per capita income, inflation for example, the German and Japanese economies are regarded as having outperformed those of the UK, certainly, and the US, probably, and many commentators have been tempted to link the relative performance to the character of financial systems. Assuming for a moment that the 'bank-based' versus 'market-based' characterization is accurate (we shall question it later in this section), there are various ways in which financial structure could interact with economic performance. We take just two interrelated themes by way of example.

It is a criticism frequently made of the UK and the USA that the economic performance of firms suffers because of the 'short-termism' of their owners and because of the resulting instability of corporate control. Put briefly, the argument is that in the UK and USA equity issues form a large proportion of firms' financing. Thus there is often a clear division between ownership (in the hands of shareholders) and control (in the hands of managers) of firms. Ownership rests directly with financial institutions who look to their shareholdings to produce the maximum return over a short period. The market for products based upon these shareholdings is very competitive, characterized by performance and league tables as well as intensive marketing, and fund managers in financial institutions are often employed on an incentive system which specifies the short-run maximization of shareholder wealth as its objective. Shareholdings that look as though they are not going to produce the required return, *in the immediate future*, will be sold and replaced. This in turn reacts upon the management of firms, since sufficiently large-scale disposals of shares may result in change of ownership, with likely merger, at best much disruption, and at worst contraction or even closure of the firm. The extent to which firms' performance in the UK and USA has been affected by short-termism is a controversial issue and has been debated for many years. In the UK, the Wilson Committee looked at the question in 1980 and its *Report* is still worth reading. More recently, it has been debated by Ball (1991), Marsh (1990) and Williams (1991). The most recent, and the most detailed empirical work on the UK by Miles (1993), using data for about half of UK quoted companies for the period 1975–89, found that long-term future earnings were subject to excessive discounting when compared with earnings which accrued in the near term. Thus, '… cash flows which are not expected to come through for five years are discounted as if they did not accrue for nine years' (Miles, 1993 p. 1394). This does not *prove* the existence of short-termism, it may simply mean that investors attach very high (and variable) risk premia to long-term earnings. But if so, this requires explanation. While there is no explanation, and while an explanation looks implausible, then Miles's findings are *consistent with* the existence of short-termism in the UK market. The question of short-termism is part of the wider issue of financial market efficiency and we return to it in Chapter 25.

By contrast, in bank-based systems firms are more largely financed by borrowing, either from banks or by the issue of bonds. This means that *ownership* remains concentrated in very few hands – often the members of the founding family. There is very little trading of the shares that do exist and it is very difficult for ownership to change hands. (It also means that little household wealth is held in the form of equities.) Since banks provide a large part of firms' finance, either directly through loans or by buying and holding corporate bonds, it is common for them to have representatives on the supervisory boards. Banks are thus closely involved in the management of firms while the owners of firms, likely to hold shares for a lifetime, have an interest in the firm's *long-term* prospects.

Whether or not the UK and USA economies have been victims of 'short-termism' and (if so) whether that short-termism really does have its roots in a distinctive market-based system of finance are both important questions. But we need to note as well that whatever the truth may be, what people *think* it to be is also important. In Chapters 10 and 11, we commented on the way in which European securities markets were moving more closely together in their characteristics and methods of trading and in Chapter 20 we shall look in detail at the pressure and the plans for a single European financial system. Clearly, such standardization requires a set of rules and procedures on which to standardize and these are often a source of intense debate as each country looks to protect the strengths (as it seems to it) of its own system. There is a strong desire in creating a unified European financial system to do so along competitive lines and with the minimum of regulation. But there is real fear in some quarters that promoting the development of equity markets along UK/US lines will open up the ownership of firms, reducing the stakeholdings of banks in German firms, for example. This in turn may create a situation of corporate control like that in the UK and USA which is seen as responsible for low levels of long-term investment. 'If today you restrict or forbid stakeholding for German banks, the Federal Republic will become a sports arena for foreign banks, then you have Jimmy Goldsmith and other people here, and they will demonstrate to you how to buy, sell and strip industrial stakes in a market economy on the American model' (Siepp [Chairman of Commerz Bank], quoted in Story, 1995).

This view, that financial systems can be characterized as 'market-' or 'bank-' based, has come under review in recent years by Mayer[1] (1990), Corbett and Jenkinson (1994, 1996), Cobham *et al.* (1996) and Cobham and Serre (1996). The first critical point, made in most detail by Corbett and Jenkinson, is the very practical one that measuring the contribution of different types of finance is difficult since countries use different accounting conventions. Furthermore, it tends to be easier to get 'stock' data (that is, data showing the total accumulated financing by banks, bonds, equities and so on) than flow data (data showing how *new* or additional financing is carried out). The danger with the former is that the figures are heavily influenced by what has happened in the past. Thus, for example, if there has been a recent switch from bank to equity finance, stock data will still show that the bulk of firm finance consists of bank finance, even though for the last few years firms may have been entirely dependent on the stock market. Using 'sources and uses of funds' data from national flows of funds accounts and making appropriate adjustments to improve comparability, Corbett and Jenkinson make comparisons between

---

[1] C Mayer, 'Financial Systems, Corporate Finance and Economic Development', in R Hubbard (ed) *Asymmetric Information, Corporate Finance, and Investment*, (New York: National Bureau of Economic Research, 1990).

Table 15.1 Net sources of corporate finance, 1985–94 average (%)

	Germany	France	Italy[1]	Japan	UK	USA
Internal	71.8	92.1	83.7	71.2	81.2	109.8
Bank finance	16.9	22.8	20.9	19.5	0.2	−4.5
Bonds	−2.8	5.6	−6.4	2.1	6.3	10.4
New equity	−3.1	2.1	4.7	3.1	12.4	−4.2
Trade credit	2.1	−3.4	−6.5	0.9	1.0	−1.4
Capital transfers	−0.9	6.9	–	–	−0.4	–
Other	1.5	−24.7	−3.6	3.3	8.7	−6.1
Statistical adjustment[2]	6.3	−1.4	–	–	−9.4	−6.8

Notes: [1]1983–93 for Italy; [2] resulting from errors and omissions in the original data
Sources: France, Cobham and Serre (1996); Italy, Cobham, *et al.* (1996); others, Corbett and Jenkinson (1996)

the USA, the UK, Germany and Japan for recent years, basing those comparisons on the latest data but also comparing recent trends. (Cobham, with others, does similar analyses for France and Italy.)

We shall return to the findings later when we discuss each country but it is useful to look now at least at the picture as it appears for recent years, since it reveals why we have to be very careful about using the 'market-' versus 'bank-' based classification. Table 15.1 shows firms' net sources of finance for new investment each year, averaged over the years 1985–94.

The most striking figures are in the first row of the table. They show that for all five countries, most real investment was financed by firms' own savings, so that the financial deficit which had to be covered by transfers from the household sector were relatively modest in relation to the total amount of investment taking place. Japanese firms generated the lowest contribution from internal funds while for the USA the proportion was over 100 per cent of the total. But the market/bank classification of course is based on sources of external funds. However, this also contains some surprises (row 2). Bank finance is certainly important to most countries other than the UK and USA, though it is not especially large for Germany. Worse still (for the traditional classification) Japan derived finance from equity markets while for the USA the figures were actually negative.[2] The conclusion seems to be that market-

based sources of finance are always small. They are smallest (and negative) where firms are financed primarily from internal sources, increasing as external sources become more important. However, where external sources are really large, it is banks that dominate.

This reveals usefully, firstly that the contribution made to corporate finance by different components of a financial system can and does vary between countries; secondly, therefore, these differences may be a useful way of distinguishing between systems in a summary way; thirdly, however, it may not be so simple a matter as dividing systems into either bank- or market-based; and fourthly, and certainly, we need to be very careful about how we do the measuring.

15.3 Financial institutions

Although they are engaged in broadly similar activities, financial institutions come in many different shapes and sizes. In Sections 1.3 and 1.5 we introduced a distinction between *deposit-taking* and *other financial institutions* (OFIs). Banks are one obvious example of deposit-taking institutions but, depending on the country in question, the category also includes building societies, savings and loan associations and various savings institutions. By contrast, 'other' financial institutions is a category

2 Negative figures are possible because we are here dealing with *net* financing of fixed investment for a whole sector. Thus, negative equity financing means that firms may have issued new shares, but they also *bought* shares in other firms. The excess of purchases over new issues, divided by the value of investment in real capital goods, gives (roughly) the negative contribution of new equity issues. Gross new issues (of bonds and equity) are of course positive (see Corbett and Jenkinson, 1994, Table 2).

that includes insurance companies, pension funds, investment trusts and so on. We explained in Chapter 1 that the reason for this distinction is that the liabilities of deposit-taking institutions (their deposits) function in many cases as money, and even where the deposits are not included in official measures of money, they are very close substitutes.

But there are other differences too, particularly in the way in which funds flow into and out of institutions. Deposit-taking institutions are subject to a very large number of inflows and outflows in any given period of time. This is partly because the deposits are often being used as means of payment but it is also because the accumulation of deposits tends to be a *discretionary* act on the part of savers. 'Discretionary' here means that people decide on a day-to-day basis what deposits to hold. To some extent, therefore, changes in deposits absorb residual changes in financial wealth, after other commitments have been made. By contrast, OFIs have a high proportion of *contractual* inflows and outflows. 'Contractual' means that savers have made an agreement to contribute regular flows of funds as part of a contract. This is most clearly the case with pension funds and insurance contracts. And these differences are important because, as we shall see, they influence both the liabilities which institutions think it wise to attract and the assets which they think it appropriate to hold. And these decisions are decisions about the direction in which funds flow.

Finally, there is the question of regulation which also, usually, draws a distinction between different types of intermediary. This is because the liabilities of deposit-taking institutions form the means of payment, and the loss of a community's means of payment can have dire effects. As Goodhart (1989, Ch. 5) has pointed out the *external costs* of a bank's failure are far greater than those associated with the failure of, say, an insurance company. In the latter case, clients suffer a loss of wealth, incur some risk (while they are uninsured) and some inconvenience (while arranging new cover). None of these, however, is likely to cause people to make major adjustments to the rest of their portfolio. By contrast, in a bank failure, depositors lose means of payment.

This is more than a matter of inconvenience. It means that they are unable to pay bills or to make purchases and in these circumstances there are bound to be rapid and serious secondary effects as investors liquidate asset holdings in other institutions in order to restore their spending power. The externalities of bank failure lie in this risk of contagious liquidations, and therefore it is usually the case that deposit-taking institutions are subjected to more stringent regulation and, in return, have access to lender of last resort facilities at the central bank.

15.3.1   Banks

Banks are institutions whose liabilities consist overwhelmingly of deposits. These deposits are then typically pooled to make larger loans whose average maturity is longer than that of the deposit liabilities. Thus they are characterized by a high degree of 'maturity transformation'. In the UK, the personal sector banks almost exclusively with retail banks, which also operate the payments mechanism. Merchant (or investment) banks deal largely with the corporate sector and, in addition to providing loan and deposit facilities, provide a wide variety of corporate financial services, extending into securities markets. The absence of this distinction in Germany reflects the German tradition of 'universal banking': large banks provide all these services without distinction. The more important distinction in Germany is between the 'big three' – Commerz Bank, Dresdner Bank and Deutsche Bank – and the smaller, but still large, regional banks. In the USA, the tendency is towards 'universal' banks with an important distinction between banks being based upon whether a bank has opted for 'state' or 'federal' supervision and regulation.

Bank liabilities are overwhelmingly deposits, many of them convertible on demand or 'at sight'. Furthermore, all bank deposits are of fixed nominal value. For this reason, bank deposits function very well as means of payment[3] but less well as a form of long-term saving, especially in periods of rapid inflation.

---

[3] See Goodhart (1989) Ch. 5 for a very interesting discussion of the possibilty that a country's means of payment need not consist of fixed nominal value assets.

The nature of their liabilities has a large bearing on the assets that banks hold. These consist overwhelmingly of advances, or loans, to households or to firms, depending on the nature of the bank. These loans are also of fixed nominal value. For the most part, these advances are non-marketable. Thus banks are obliged as a matter of prudence to carry lesser-earning but more liquid assets which can be sold in the event of a need to raise funds to meet unexpected transfers or withdrawals. We shall see this in the following chapters.

15.3.2   Non-bank deposit-taking institutions

As we saw in Section 15.2, most countries apply quite strict regulations to banking activity because of the negative externalities that attach to bank failure. Thus it follows that these countries must have a very precise definition of what constitutes a bank. However, once one states precisely what constitutes banking activity, subject to banking regulations, one simultaneously identifies the boundary to those regulations and thus what is necessary to avoid them. As a result, most countries have intermediaries which accept deposits (and make loans) but are not classified as banks, usually because for some technical reason they fall outside the banking regulations. Building societies in the UK, for example, are 'friendly societies' – non-profit organizations 'owned' by their depositors. Their traditional function was to accept deposits only from persons and to lend to persons only for house purchase. Such was the position until the Building Societies Act, 1986, which permitted societies for the first time to make unsecured loans on a limited basis. In the USA, the nearest counterpart is the savings and loan association (S&L) which has very similar sources and uses of funds but may be either a mutual society or stock owned. In the USA, there are also 'non-bank' banks. These are even closer in function to commercial (state or national) banks but choose not to provide just one of the services which US banking regulations specify as defining a commercial bank; the purpose, of course, is to avoid the burden of some of the regulations. Credit unions exist in most countries but are significant, though still very small, in the USA. They function rather like the very

earliest building societies in that they are 'owned' by their depositors, and membership is restricted to people having some other common bond – membership of a trade union, church, housing development and so on. Their funds thus come entirely from persons (and individual deposits are very small) and they make small, fixed-term, personal loans.

15.3.3   Insurance companies

The principle behind insurance companies is that they offer clients the certainty of a slightly reduced income (reduced by virtue of the premiums that the company charges) in exchange for the possibility of a dramatic reduction in income as the outcome of some accident. Their products are thus grounded in the public's risk aversion. Strictly speaking, 'insurance', against events which are only probable, should be distinguished from 'assurance', against events which are certain, like death.

The main principle underlying the operation of insurance contracts is the pooling of risk and the '*law of large numbers*'. It is very difficult to tell in advance whether an individual is likely to incur a misfortune of a specified type, but it is comparatively easy to predict *what proportion* of people in a given population will suffer. If experience suggests a 10 per cent accident rate (for example) then, ignoring operating costs and the revenue from invested funds, cover can be provided for all policyholders if each pays a premium of 10 per cent of the sum insured. It is the job of actuaries to calculate the probability and frequency of insured events. However, insurance companies, like banks, are subject to problems arising from *asymmetric information* – the situation where buyers of insurance policies have better information about the risk to which they are exposed than does the insurance company. Asymmetric information gives rise to *moral hazard* and *adverse selection*. Moral hazard refers to the situation where policyholders, knowing they are insured against major loss, behave recklessly and thus incur additional risk. For example, a firm, knowing it has adequate fire insurance, may try to save on costs by cutting down on fire protection equipment and procedures. Adverse selection arises where the poorest quality customers are those which express the strongest demand. In the insurance context, this means that the riskiest clients will be the most eager buyers of insurance contracts, but because of information asymmetries the insurance company cannot tell which of its clients is the riskiest. The response to problems of asymmetric information is to operate a system of risk *screening*. For example, the study of past statistics may reveal that clients with particular characteristics are riskier than others and these can be charged *risk-based premiums*. Where screening is difficult, it is possible to discourage moral hazard by requiring the insured to bear some of the risk, by imposing an 'excess' or *deductible* amount which the insured has to pay for himself. The company can also impose *restrictive covenants* which make the insurance contract void if the insured behaves in an inappropriate way. All of these reactions to asymmetric information are commonplace in private motor insurance contracts where young drivers, and drivers with a poor accident record, are charged higher premiums; the policy pays only for claims in excess of a specified amount and it will also contain clauses invalidating the contract if the vehicle is used for anything other than private or 'domestic' purposes.

In most countries, a distinction has developed between 'general' insurance – of houses, cars, travel, property and so on, and 'long-term' or 'life' insurance. The latter provides cover against death, of course, but also against sickness and retirement. The reason for the distinction is that many governments have offered tax incentives to people to take out cover against these long-term eventualities. This in turn has made the policies into an attractive savings or investment vehicle, since the profits could be enjoyed free of, or at least at reduced rates of, tax. Eventually, the degree of insurance for some policies has become rather incidental to the main purpose which has become long-term tax-efficient saving. Clearly, an insurance company issuing this type of policy requires the risk assessment skills of a general insurance firm (the 'actuarial' skills) but it also requires the investment skills of a mutual fund manager. Because of their long-term liabilities, long-term insurance companies' prime investment requirement is security of long-term income. 'Security' here means an income flow which is known with certainty and which can reasonably be expected at least to match the rate of inflation. Hence, when compared with banks, for example, whose needs are quite different, insurance companies are major players in equity and long-term bond markets and have large holdings of these assets. While it is generally accepted that securities markets are dominated by 'capital risk averse' investors (as we saw in Section 10.5.2), long-term insurance companies provide an example of one group of investors which is 'income risk averse'.

15.3.4   Pension funds

Pension funds share many of their characteristics with long-term insurance companies. Indeed, in the UK pension funds are often managed by 'life assurance' companies and the two institutions are often bracketed together as 'life assurance and pension funds' (LAPFs) when it comes to studying financial institutions. The reason is that a pension fund is providing something very similar to a life contract – insurance against a long-term contingency which is virtually certain, namely retirement. The flows of funds for both LA and PFs are very similar – they are contractual – and their destination is very similar also. LAPFs are major holders of equities. Box 17.3 appears to show no pension funds in Germany. This is not strictly true, but Germany is a rather special case. This is because the tradition of pension provision has relied heavily upon the state, which finances pensions on a 'Pay-As-You-Go' basis from taxation. Even where firms provide an element of an ex-employee's pension, this is paid from the firm's current revenue. There is no tradition of 'funded' pensions whereby employees build up a fund which is invested in a wide variety of bonds and equities. However, a combination of rising unemployment and demographic trends means that the payment of pensions from general taxation has become increasingly difficult in recent years and there are plans to encourage the private provision of pensions on the UK/US pattern of building up a largely equity-based fund of savings. We return to this in Chapter 18. The nature of their liabilities is such that pension funds have similar asset requirements to those that we specified above for long-term insurance companies.

15.3.5 Mutual funds

Mutual funds are, strictly speaking, any funds in which investors savings are pooled, on an equal basis, for investment purposes. However, the term has acquired the rather specific meaning of a fund of savings collected in order to exploit the economies of scale that exist in the transactions costs associated with securities trading. In a mutual fund, small savings are placed with a fund manager who uses those funds to buy and sell securities with a view to achieving the objective set out in the 'Trust Deed'. The Trust Deed specifies a charge, usually an annual fee, ranging typically around 1 per cent of the investor's holding. Because the fund manager can use the pooled funds to make very large purchases of individual securities, the investor benefits from the much cheaper unit costs of each transaction. Diversification becomes possible at low cost. The securities may be money market ones, or longer-term bonds, or equities, or even, these days, various derivatives. These may be purchased within the country of origin of the fund or the fund may make a feature of buying an international spread or even claim to invest 'globally'. Trusts can be designed to achieve any one or more of a number of objectives: capital growth or income, for example, or they may invest in a particular sector of the market, enabling investors to back a hunch that shares are underpriced or are going to do particularly well in the near future. In the following chapters, when we look at the reporting of performance, we shall see that there are literally thousands of mutual funds each offering slightly differing characteristics to investors.

All these variations notwithstanding, it is common to distinguish two types of mutual fund, *open* and *closed*. A closed mutual fund is one that has a fixed number of shares in issue and is thus of fixed size. The funds raised from the initial share issue are used to buy shares in other firms. An increased desire to invest in a closed trust, therefore, means an increase in the demand for the shares. Since the fund is of fixed size and the number of shares is fixed, potential buyers can only buy from existing holders of the shares. This means that an increase in demand must bid up the price. Conversely, investors who wish to withdraw from a closed fund have to sell their shares to someone else, and a general desire to withdraw from the fund will push the share price down. The main examples of closed mutual funds in the UK are *investment trusts*.

Buying shares in a closed trust can be thought of as rather like buying shares in a firm whose business it is to hold shares. By contrast, when an open trust receives an inflow of funds, it can create shares (usually called *units*) and uses the inflow to buy more shares for its portfolio. In response to an outflow of funds it cancels units (in effect it buys them back from investors) and sells shares from its portfolio. In an open fund, therefore, an inflow or outflow of investors' money causes a change in the size of the fund, rather than in the price of the units. The value of the units changes with changes in the value of the securities held by the fund. In the UK, open mutual funds are usually called *unit trusts*.

15.4 Summary

As we saw in Chapter 1, a financial system consists of markets, institutions, end users and regulators. Markets and end users are similar the world over. Markets vary in size, and sometimes in trading arrangements, but the instruments that they trade are virtually identical and are becoming more so as end users expect to be able to lend and borrow across international boundaries.

Such differences as there are between financial systems are concentrated in financial institutions, rather than markets, and in the arrangements for regulation of financial activity, though these also are becoming increasingly standardized.

A traditional way of distinguishing between financial systems was to place them on a continuum which extended from 'market-based' to 'bank-based', the position to be decided by the extent to which firms raised funds from markets or from banking institutions. However, recent research has cast doubt on this approach, particularly on the way in which funds used by firms were measured. The picture now looks rather more complex and certainly does not consist of the UK and USA at the market end of the spectrum and everyone else towards the 'bank' end.

Nonetheless, there are differences between financial systems. We shall see more of these differences, and many similarities, as we look at each country in turn in the following chapters.

Key concepts used in this chapter

Market-based systems	Negative externalities	Asymmetric information
Bank-based systems	Contagious liquidation	Moral hazard
Sources and uses of funds	Non-bank deposit takers	Adverse selection
Short-termism	Credit unions	Pension funds
Ownership and control of firms	General insurance	Closed-end mutual funds
Discretionary inflows	'Life' assurance	Open-end mutual funds
Contractual inflows	Law of large numbers	

Questions and problems

1 What is meant by the distinction between 'market-based' and 'bank-based' financial systems? Why might this distinction be misleading?

2 Describe the main differences in the sources of funds available to (a) banks and (b) life assurance companies. How would you expect these different sources to affect their uses of funds?

3 Why is the failure of a bank likely to have a larger effect upon the community than the failure of a mutual investment fund of similar size?

4 Explain, and illustrate with examples, how an insurance company can limit its exposure to problems caused by asymmetric information.

5 Distinguish between open-end and closed-end mutual funds.

Further reading

J Ball, 'Short-Termism – Myth or Reality?', *National Westminster Bank Quarterly Review*, August 1991

D Cobham and J-M Serre, 'A Characterisation of the French Financial System', Dept. of Economics, University of St Andrews, mimeo (1996)

D Cobham, S Cosci and F Mattesini, 'The Italian Financial System: neither bank based nor market based', Dept. of Economics, University of St Andrews, mimeo (1996)

J Corbett and T Jenkinson, 'The Financing of Industry, 1970–89: An International Comparison', *Centre for Economic Policy Review*, Discussion Paper No. 948 (London: CEPR, 1994)

J Corbett and T Jenkinson, 'How is Investment Financed? A Study of Germany, Japan, UK and US', University of Oxford, mimeo (1996)

R Glenn Hubbard, *Money, The Financial System and the Economy* (Reading MA: Addison Wesley, 2e (1997), Chs 12-14

C A E Goodhart, *Money, Information and Uncertainty* (London: Macmillan, 2e, 1989)

P Marsh, *Short Termism on Trial* (London: International Fund Managers' Association, 1990)

D Miles, 'Testing for Short Termism in the UK Stock Market', *The Economic Journal*, 103 (1993), 1379–96

E H Neave, *Financial Systems: Principles and Organization* (London: Routledge, 1997)

J Story, 'The Politics and Markets of German Financial Services', *Institute for German Studies Discussion Paper*, No. IGS95/3 (Birmingham: University of Birmingham, 1995)

P Williams, 'Time and the City: Short-Termism in the UK, Myth or Reality?', *National Westminster Bank Quarterly Review*, August 1991

The UK financial system

16.1 Introduction

In this chapter, we look at the main characteristics of the UK financial system. As we said in the last chapter, the distinctive characteristics of a financial system lie largely in the institutions which comprise the system and the way(s) in which they are regulated. Accordingly, the chapter proceeds by examining in turn each of the groups of intermediaries briefly described in Chapter 15. Under each heading we indicate the scale of activity and the sources and uses of funds. We also outline the main features of the relevant regulatory regime.

There are various ways in which data can be used to compare the size and behaviour of financial intermediaries. Firstly, one can look at the use which is made each year of funds received from savers. For this, we require data on the *net acquisition of assets*. These are assets *purchased* during a period of time, *less* assets sold. This does not of course measure the

flow of new lending to ultimate borrowers, since many of the assets purchased will be assets already in existence; these are assets created by earlier lending, the institutions taking over the loan from a previous holder. Neither does it measure the total scale of trading in assets by any particular institution. In the course of a year an insurance company, for example, will buy and sell many assets of any given type. Its total sales and purchases of a given asset constitute the *turnover* in that asset while the net acquisition, as we said, is the difference between sales and purchases. Finally, we could compare stocks of assets currently held. This would involve looking at *balance sheet* data and that data would show the sum of net acquisitions cumulated over previous years. Comparisons made in this way would obviously be strongly affected by decisions made in the past.

For banks and building societies Tables 16.1 and 16.2 (respectively) give data on both stocks of assets and also changes in those assets in the most recent year for which data is available. Thus one can judge the size of banks and building societies either in terms of their accumulated wealth or in terms of the flows of funds which they are directing into new assets. One can also see the direction of those funds.

Our comparison of other (non-deposit-taking) financial intermediaries is based around Table 16.3 which shows data for net acquisitions and thus enables us to compare the scale of funds available for disposal by each institution and the way in which those funds were used in the most recent period for which data is available, and around Table 16.4 which shows stocks of assets. Using all four tables, comparisons can obviously be made between each type of intermediary. For non-deposit-taking institutions we also include a table (16.5) which shows the part played by each type of institution in the *turnover* of selected securities.

16.2 Banks in the UK

The banking sector in the UK has traditionally been highly segmented. In its February issue of the *Bank of England Quarterly Bulletin* every year the Bank of England lists all those banking institutions to whom it has granted a licence to operate as a bank in the UK. The list (of over 450) is divided into seven sections, distinguished sometimes by function and sometimes by nationality of ownership. As regards function, the major distinctions are between *retail banks, British merchant banks, other British banks* and *discount houses.*

The first group provides deposit and loan facilities to the household or personal sector, together with small and un-incorporated businesses. The retail banks together own the various payments mechanisms and money transfer is a major part of retail bank operations. In recent years, they have offered an increasing range of financial services, based on the marketing idea of 'one-stop shopping' so that it is now possible, within an individual branch, to buy and sell foreign currency, buy an insurance policy, open a personal pension fund, invest in unit trusts, and buy executor and other services. They have also diversified further by buying property agencies, merchant banks and securities dealing firms, though these are operated as separate, subsidiary firms, with different premises and, in the case of merchant banks and securities dealers, separate capital.

British merchant banks have a long history. Some predate the better-known retail banks and many remain independent of them. Their origins lie in the finance of overseas trade since this was the first activity that outgrew the ability of the owner-entrepreneur to provide his own capital. As firms and their capital requirements have expanded, so merchant banks have developed in step, providing a complete range of corporate financial services. These range from accepting deposits and making loans, to advising on alternative forms of finance, advising on risk management strategies, handling new securities issues and 'accepting' (that is, guaranteeing) bills issued by firms. Less well known than the retail banks with branches in every high street, the names of merchant banks often come to public attention in the event of major mergers or takeovers. This is especially true if the takeover is strongly contested.

Other British banks are banks which offer a range of banking services, but usually limited in some way. Although they may be subsidiaries of retail banks, they do not usually deal directly with the retail sector. Many of them grew out of what used to be called 'finance houses', providing funds for hire purchase deals. Much of their business now lies in buying and leasing equipment to firms and providing credit for retail sales, for which stores act in effect as the banks' agents.

Discount houses (just seven in number in 1996) perform a highly specialized and unique role in the UK financial system. They deal almost exclusively with other banks and with the Bank of England (as we saw in Sections 6.5 and 9.4). They accept surplus funds on a very short-term, often overnight, basis from banks and use the funds to buy and hold treasury and commercial bills. They thus provide the first source of liquid assets (after cash and central bank deposits) to the rest of the banking sector, so that any shortage or surplus funds are immediately reflected in discount houses' ability to buy bills, or need to sell them. As we saw in Section 9.4, the Bank of England adjusts banks' cash position on a daily basis by buying (or selling) bills to them at rates of discount which set the base rate for the rest of the banking system.[1]

Notice that all these banks accept deposits and make loans (though discount houses do so only to a very limited extent) and that deposits with all these institutions are included in the UK official measures of money and changes in the money stock occur as a result of net changes in lending by any of these banks.

We commented in Chapter 15 that bank liabilities were largely fixed nominal value deposits and that

---

[1] We noted also that the outright purchase of bills was to be replaced from 1997 by repo deals.

Table 16.1 UK bank assets 1995, £mn

	Stocks[1]	Changes[2]
Sterling assets		
Notes and coin	5,387	420
Balances at the Bank of England	1,795	-278
Market loans	188,719	23,994
Bills	21,653	-437
Repurchase agreements	–[3]	25,095
Advances	444,215	40,846
Investments	65,150	15,656
Other sterling assets	29,018	–1,266
Total sterling assets	755,937	104,028
Other currency assets		
Market loans	596,912	–20,008
Advances	217,620	15,572
Repurchase agreements	–[3]	109,813
Bills	14,429	2,784
Investments	162,982	20,829
Other assets	19,415	4,354
Total currency assets	1,011,358	133,344
TOTAL ASSETS	1,767,295	237,372

Sources and notes: Bank of England Quarterly Bulletin, June 1996, adapted from Table 3.
[1] At end 1995; [2] In year to end March 1996; [3] The reporting of sale and repurchase agrements began only from December 1995.

their liabilities consisted largely of advances, also of fixed nominal value. This can be seen from Table 16.1 which shows the combined assets of 'monthly reporting institutions' (the majority of banks operating in the UK). The table also shows the significant acquisitions/holdings of lower earning but highly marketable liquid assets, held against the possibility of unexpected withdrawals or transfers of deposits. These consist of treasury and commercial bills, as well as short-dated government bonds ('investments') and 'market loans' to the discount market and other banks. The table also shows how important are 'other currency' assets relative to sterling. If we were to look at the assets for different types of bank we should discover that this heavy weighting of non-sterling assets comes from the activities of merchant or investment banks, rather than retail banks or discount houses.

In the UK, the banking system is regulated by the Bank of England. The major relevant legislation at the moment is the Banking Act, 1987. This Act removed the distinction (which had operated since 1979) between 'banks' and 'licensed deposit takers'. Since 1987, every deposit-taking institution, except building societies (see below), has required a banking licence. Subject to banks meeting appropriate criteria, this is provided by the Bank of England and withdrawal of the licence is the ultimate sanction which can be used against institutions who fail to conduct their business in an appropriate manner.

The terms of the Act are broadly as follows. Firstly, the Act requires the Bank to certify that the directors of a bank are each 'fit and proper persons' for the purpose and lays down criteria whereby this may be determined. Secondly, it established a board of banking supervision to whom banks have to make regular and frequent disclosures of information about the conduct of their buseiness. It also requires a bank's auditors and accountants to divulge more information to the board than would normally be the case in the commercial relationship between client and auditor. This is reinforced by making it a criminal offence to 'knowingly or recklessly' provide false information to the supervisors and by giving the supervisors powers of entry to banking premises where a contravention of the Act is suspected. The Bank can also appoint its own accountants and consultants to report on the conduct of a bank's business and in particular its own monitoring and control procedures. Finally, the Bank has the power to veto the acquisition of shares in a bank which would take an individual shareholding over 15 per cent.

The criteria used by the supervisory board in order to judge that business is being conducted in a satisfactory manner are laid down (and periodically revised) in a series of additional papers. The key to the approach rests with *risk–asset* ratios as a means of judging a bank's capital adequacy. Prior to the 1987 Act, the tendency was to focus upon the gearing ratio, the size of a bank's capital relative to its liabilities. The risk–asset ratio, however, sets out to compare bank capital with total bank assets and, more significantly still, it applies differential weights to assets depending upon their apparent riskiness. The basic principle behind such a ratio is that the risks of carrying on a banking business should be borne by the shareholders (rather than the depositors, for example) and that the bank's capital should be adequate to absorb any losses that cannot be met out of current profits.

The risk weights currently given to different classes of assets are those proposed by the Basle Committee in 1988 (see Section 24.4). These were adopted as a basis for a common system of prudential banking control in all industrial countries in 1993. Cash, for example, has a weight of 0, while loans to the discount market are weighted at 0.1 and commercial loans at 1. The method of assessment, broadly speaking, is to multiply the market value of each asset by its risk factor and then to aggregate the risk-adjusted value. This is then compared with the bank's capital base, where the capital base is composed of 'tier 1' and 'tier 2' capital, with certain conditions applying to the overall composition. Tier 1 capital, for example, consists of equity, reserves and retained profits and should account for at least 50 per cent of total capital. The Basle Committee recommended a lower limit of 8 per cent for the ratio of total capital to risk-adjusted assets, though national bank supervisors have some discretion in applying this to different types of bank.

In recent years the risk-adjusted asset ratio has been applied to *off-balance-sheet activities*.[2] The method is the same as that used for on-balance sheet assets except that off-balance-sheet items are assigned an initial value which is normally some fraction of their market value, and the risk weightings are applied to this.

16.3 Building societies in the UK

As we shall see in a moment, the history, function and regulation of building societies distinguishes them quite clearly from banks. They are, however, deposit-taking institutions and since 1989, when M4 replaced M3 as the official measure of broad money in the UK, their deposits have been unambiguously 'money'.

'Unambiguously' is worth stressing. For most of the 1980s, the treatment of building society deposits was something of a problem. Undoubtedly depositors themselves saw the deposits as money. They could go into a building society branch and draw cash on demand. For larger purchases they could obtain, also on demand, a cheque signed by the manager payable to whomsoever they nominated. In the first case, though, it was the cash that was money while in the second case careful examination of the cheque would show that it was drawn on the building society's bank. It was the building society's *bank* deposit that was functioning as money, not a deposit with the society itself. As we shall see in the next section, competition between banks and building societies drove their products closer and closer together during the 1980s. Eventually, the Building Societies' Act, 1986, removed some of the formal distinctions. Most importantly it allowed building societies to issue cheque guarantee cards (so their own deposits became instantly acceptable as means of payment), and it provided for societies to 'incorporate' themselves as banks. At the time, building society deposits were included in a measure of 'liquidity', 'PSL2', but not in M3. After the 1986 Act this differential treatment of building society deposits became very difficult to sustain. A change was finally forced by the decision of the Abbey National Building Society, at the time the second largest society, to convert to banking status in 1989. This would have meant an overnight increase in M3 of about 11 per cent. This large break in the series persuaded the Bank of England to discontinue publication of the M3 measure and to treat M4, first published in 1987, as a replacement for PSL2, as the official measure of broad money. (A brief history of UK monetary aggregates was provided in Chapter 6). Thus, *from a monetary point of view*, the societies have become indistinguishable from banks.

Building societies began in the Eighteenth century as friendly or mutual societies, often with a local focus, into which members made periodic payments in order to finance the building of houses. Unlike banks therefore, a society has no shareholders; its members are the 'owners' and they lend to the

---

[2] 'Off-balance-sheet' activities are activities that earn income for banks without a corresponding asset (and liability) appearing on the balance sheet. Typical examples are the guaranteeing of commercial bills or the issuing of commercial paper. Such activities earn income in the form of fees, but the bills or paper are not owned by banks and so do not appear on the balance sheet. We discuss off-balance-sheet activity, and the reasons for its recent development, in more detail in Chapter 23.

society by, technically speaking, buying shares though these shares are, in effect, deposits. In the early days, it was quite common for building societies to be dissolved once their specific house building programme was completed. Some, however, became 'permanent' societies, adopting a continuous programme of housing construction and finance and it is these that have survived to today.

The history of the societies is important because it explains why, although in many respects it seems natural to treat them as a form of bank, they have been able to behave rather differently from banks and have been subject to different regulatory regimes. Because they were mutual societies, their regulation was for many years the responsibility of the Registrar of Friendly Societies. Because they were not companies their trade association, the Building Societies Association, was able for many years to operate a system of 'recommended' deposit and mortgage (interest) rates without contravening restrictive practices legislation. These were usually below market-clearing rates and thus provided comparatively cheap funds for house purchase but also created queues for mortgages and led to non-price rationing. The interest rate cartel broke up in 1983 following the entry of retail banks into the mortgage market.

Table 16.2 shows the distribution of assets and liabilities of UK building societies. It is immediately apparent that assets are still dominated by mortgage lending in spite of the freedoms granted by the 1986 Act. Class 1 lending is mainly lending to households for house purchase while class 2 lending is largely lending to firms, again secured on property. Unsecured lending is a subset of class 3 assets. The 1986 Act specifies limits for the balance between these classes and also for the balance of assets within each class. As with banks, we can see that assets other than loans are highly liquid and that this means relatively small holdings of securities and these concentrated at the short end of the maturity spectrum.

During the 1980s, building societies found themselves under increasing competitive pressure. There was competition within the industry following the ending of the interest rate cartel in 1983. But there was growing competition too from retail banks. Societies responded with a number of innovations. They introduced new types of deposits which paid

Table 16.2 UK building society assets, 1995 (£mn)

	Stocks[1]	Changes[2]
Liquid assets		
Cash	396	−51
Deposits (including CDs) with banks (including overseas banks)	32,558	2,295
Building society CDs	2,397	494
British government stock		
< 5 years to maturity	3588	−1,520
> 5 years to maturity	738	89
Treasury bills	2,707	2,809
Other liquid assets	9,473	110
Commercial assets		
Mortgage lending (class 1)	218,094	8,745
Mortgage lending (class 2)	8,697	1,029
Other lending (class 3)	14,139	6,267
Other	4,507	569
Total	297,294	20,836

Notes and sources: [1] At end 1995; [2] In the year to end Dec. 1995. Office for National Statistics, *Financial Statistics*, Jan. 1997, Tables 4.3a,b

premium rates of interest for regular contributions and for minimum balances. They introduced cheque book facilities and automated cash dispensers. Nonetheless, it was felt, firstly by the societies, but eventually by government, that the existing rules, dating from the Eighteenth century, put societies at a disadvantage, when compared with banks, and created an artificial segmentation of the loan/deposit market which inhibited competition. For example, the existing rules restricted societies to lending only on houses or similar property. They could not make unsecured loans and thus could not permit overdrafts. This in turn meant that thay could not issue cheque guarantee cards (since they would have been breaking the law if they had honoured the cheque of any customer who went overdrawn) and so their cheque book facilities were of limited use. The first change came in 1983 when the Finance Act enabled societies to pay interest gross on CDs and time deposits over £50,000. This, at last, meant societies could attract 'wholesale' deposits from firms, since firms were responsible for paying interest at whatever rate applied to their particular circumstance. Eurobond issues were permitted from 1985.

But the biggest changes came with the Building Societies Act, 1986. This broadened the assets in which societies were allowed to invest to include commercial assets and, crucially, allowed them to make unsecured loans, though both were limited to small fractions of total assets. Since unsecured lending, even in small amounts, meant that they could now provide cheque guarantee cards, building societies were able to offer means of payment facilities on an equal footing with banks. In Chapter 23, we shall see that this broadening of the competitive front between banks and building societies had important implications for a variety of financial developments.

The 1986 Act also gave the societies powers to seek 'incorporation', subject to their giving adequate notice of this intention and subject to a vote by their members. Incorporation meant that they would become limited liability joint stock companies with shareholders rather than members. It would also mean that an incorporating society would become a bank, subject to banking rather than building society regulations. As we saw above, the Abbey National Building Society was the first to take this step in 1989. Against expectations, there was no immediate rush to follow, but by 1997 several of the major societies, the Halifax and the Woolwich, for example, were queuing up to make the transition. The reason usually given for wanting to do so was that incorporation as a public company would enable the 'society' to raise large quantities of capital which would enable them to offer a wider range of services, at more competitive prices. These arguments were not always persuasive to building society members, some of whom protested vigorously by forming pressure groups. However, after the Abbey National flotation, other societies found that promising shares on generous terms to existing members would guarantee that formal votes would always go in favour of incorporation. The rush to incorporate coincided (in 1996–97) with research from a variety of consumer bodies suggesting that retail customers were generally better served by mutual societies than by plcs, receiving marginally higher interest payments on deposits and being charged less on loans. It remains to be seen whether this evidence will slow the rate of transition or perhaps lead to a more vivid demarcation between mutual deposit takers and banks as the former try to exploit this goodwill.

Since the 1986 Act, building societies have been subject to regulation by the Building Societies Commission. Its purpose is to determine whether the conduct of a society's business meets the intentions of the Act, particularly as regards the limits which still exist on the sources and uses of funds. In principle, the Commission's powers are considerable, permitting it as a last resort to withdraw a society's authorization to accept deposits.

16.4 Insurance companies

People take out insurance because they prefer a lower level of known income (their income minus the premiums) with the knowledge that they are protected against the possibility of catastrophic loss, to a higher known level of income with the possibility that their future wealth might be seriously damaged by accident, theft, ill-health and so on. This principle unites all types of insurance contract. However, there are major distinctions in the kinds of policy offered by insurance companies and in the types of risk covered. The distinction is so sharp that, although some of the larger firms deal in both, many specialize in one or the other. The distinction that is usually drawn is between *long-term* or *life* assurance, and *general* insurance.

We return to the distinctions in a moment, but we deal with the similarities first. The most obvious similarity is that insurance companies receive the bulk of their funds on a regular, contractual basis. This is because insurance against risk frequently involves a contract which extends over a period of time, sometimes many years, and clients pay a premium at intervals during the lifetime of the policy. The level of premium paid by clients depends, naturally, upon the probability of the event insured against occurring and the scale of compensation to be paid when it does. Alternatively, we may say that for a given level of benefit, the premium will be determined by the risk, or more briefly still, that the benefit:premium ratio is a function of risk. However, the payment of premiums creates a pool of funds at the companies' disposal, awaiting claims to be made against it. Provided sufficient funds are available or can be quickly recovered the remainder can be placed in earning assets by the companies to provide a further source of income. Thus their investment success is a second factor which influences the ratio of premium:benefit levels.

The principal legislation governing the conduct of insurance business in the UK is the Insurance Companies Act, 1982. This defines general insurance and divides it into 17 classes, and long-term insurance, divided into seven classes. The former includes accident and damage to property, vehicles, goods in transit, personal liability and so on. Classes of long-term insurance include life and annuity, permanent health, marriage and birth. An additional class of long-term business is pension fund management. This does not involve a company accepting an insurance risk but acknowledges that the skills required for the conduct of long-term insurance are largely investment skills and the same, therefore, as those required for pension fund management. Thus, over the years, many long-term insurance companies have taken on the management of pension funds on behalf of firms and other institutions. We can see why, if we consider more carefully the nature of long-term insurance contracts.

As we said earlier, long-term insurance contracts enable people to insure against such events as death or permanent illness or disablement. For obvious reasons, life- (that is, death-) related contracts dominate. These may be of various forms. A person can insure against death within a specified period, the policy paying nothing if the insured survives. This is known as *term insurance*. Alternatively, a *whole of life* policy insures against death at any time. An *endowment* policy pays a capital sum to the insured at a specified time in the future, or on death if earlier. This sum may be a guaranteed absolute amount, in which case the insured has a policy 'without profits', or there may be a guaranteed minimum plus an entitlement to share in the company's annual profits. On this 'with profits' type of policy, the share in the profits accumulates as a series of annual bonuses which are paid, with the guaranteed minimum, on termination of the contract. Increasingly, the proceeds from an endowment policy are linked to the value of units in a unit trust which may or may not be run by the insurance company itself. Under an *annuity* the company pays a regular income to the insured from a specified date until death. This may be paid in return for a lump sum payment, or the

annuity may be bought with the proceeds from an earlier endowment contract. As with other financial products, new types of insurance product are continually evolving, so this should not be treated as an exhaustive list.

It should be clear by now that the motivation behind many long-term 'insurance' contracts is essentially a desire to save for the future, either for one's own benefit or for the benefit of dependants. This means, of course, that while the products are distinct by virtue of their insurance element, life insurance contracts are in competition with a whole range of other products as a home for long-term saving.

The nature of these policies determines the risks to which long-term funds are exposed. Actuarial predictions of a country's mortality record are now very reliable and it is unlikely that a sudden change would find insurance companies struggling to meet the obligations on life policies. More probable is that changes in the products offered by competitors might cause an increase in terminations or 'early surrender' of policies. The most serious risk faced by long-term insurance companies, however, is that changes in future economic and financial conditions cause the yield on the asset portfolio to fall below expectations. This would be serious for the companies, since investment income amounts to about one-third of total (investment *plus* premium) income, and for investors who would share in reduced profits. During 1995 and 1996, several companies warned of lower yields in future, on the grounds that inflation was likely to be lower in the medium term than it had been in the 1970s and 1980s. This was a problem for some savers who had taken out with-profits or unit-linked life policies of a given projected value, as a means of repaying their mortgage at some point in the future. If inflation remains low, it seems possible that some of these policies may not yield a large enough sum.

We noted earlier that the major legislation affecting insurance companies dates from the 1982 Act. This makes it an offence for anyone to conduct insurance business without authorization and resulted from concern following the collapse of a number of (general) insurance companies in the 1970s. The power of authorization lies with the Department of Trade and Industry and is granted to each company with respect to particular classes of insurance business. In addition to providing authorization, the Department subsequently monitors the performance of companies, particularly with respect to solvency margins, and has the power to intervene in a number of ways. It may require a change in investment strategy, prevent the renewal of existing policies or the issuing of new ones. In the event that a company should fail, in spite of this scrutiny, policyholders have some degree of protection under the Policyholders Protection Act, 1975. The 1982 Act also imposes regulations on advertising and promotion of insurance products and provides for a 'cooling-off' period. The fact that so many insurance products involve a savings element brings them also within the scope of the Financial Services Act, 1986. We look at this, and at the issue of regulation generally, in Chapter 24.

The obvious contrast between long-term and general insurance companies in Table 16.3 is their size, the funds available to long-term insurance companies enabling them to spend some eight times the funds available to general companies. (In fact, a broadly similar picture emerges from balance sheet data in Table 16.4. Long-term companies had net assets worth £494bn in 1995, compared with £75bn

Table 16.3 UK Non-deposit-taking financial institutions, net acquisitions of selected assets, 1995 (£mn)

	PF	LTI	GI	IT-UT
Short-term assets	2,807	7,427	424	819
British government securities	8,177	6,858	582	−592
UK company securities				
ordinary	−6,494	4,029	691	3,625
other	280	2,512	130	524
Overseas securities				
company securities	−1,355	3,974	368	3,081
government securities	81	−341	739	−36
Loans and mortgages	−24	472	16	0
Unit trusts	3,137	650	−8	65
Property unit trust units	1	0	0	91
Other financial assets	863	562	221	0
Real capital assets	91	360	199	15
Total	7,564	26,503	3,362	7,592

Source: Office for National Statistics, *Financial Statistics*, January 1997, Table 5.3c

for general companies.) Compared with all other types of financial institution, long-term insurance companies were major investors in securities of all kinds, especially company shares, and their total asset acquisitions of £26.5bn dwarfed all other institutions.

16.5 Pension funds

In most developed countries, people expect to receive a pension after their retirement from employment. However, these come in various forms and only one strictly involves any degree of financial intermediation.

The essential distinction between pension arrangements is between those that are financed on a *Pay as You Go* (PAYG) basis and those that are *funded*. In a PAYG scheme, current workers pay the pensions of earlier, retired, workers. Current workers may *feel* that deductions from their wages or salaries are a form of saving for their own pensions, but this is an illusion. No fund is created, and current workers will be completely dependent upon future workers when their turn comes to draw a pension. Pensions paid by the state provide the obvious examples of PAYG schemes. Deductions are made from the wages of existing workers. In the UK these deductions are actually described as 'national insurance contributions' though they are in effect simply a form of direct taxation. The state retirement pension is then paid, like other social security benefits, from general taxation.

In addition to pensions provided by the state, however, many people (about 60 per cent in the UK) receive a pension from their previous employer, described as an *occupational pension*. In the case of state employees (teachers, civil servants, health workers and so on) occupational pensions are also generally financed from taxation on a PAYG basis. However, in the UK it has always been thought that PAYG was an unsatisfactory basis for private sector occupational pensions. In the public sector, the government can always call upon sufficient tax revenue to meet its pension obligations. Private firms, by contrast, might go bankrupt or they might find in a recession that their existing employees were too few to support the claims of a larger body of previously retired workers. Therefore, the practice in the private sector is for employers and employees to make contributions into a fund at a rate which, with judicious management of the fund, should be sufficient to meet obligations to current employees at some point in the future. In this sense, existing workers (and their employers) are funding their own pensions at a future date. Since the fund is kept separate from the firm's other assets, employees' pensions should remain secure even if the firm ceases trading. It is funded pension schemes that accumulate a stock of funds for investment and thus involve some element of intermediation.

From this description it should be obvious that a pension fund can be confident of the scale and source of inflows since these are a contractual obligation for employers and employees. The contract will also specify the future level of benefits for those currently contributing to the fund. For example, most schemes provide a pension based on some fraction of 'final salary'. 'Final salary' might then be defined as the average or the highest salary paid in the last three years of employment, and the contract will lay down some fraction, 1/60th or 1/80th for example, of this sum as an entitlement for each year of service. There will usually be some provision for index-linking or at least for periodic uprating. Given that the fund's future obligations per retired employee are known, its total obligations are a matter of actuarial calculation, involving the current size of the workforce, its age distribution, the average life expectancy after retirement, and other factors.

As with other intermediaries, the nature of the liabilities has some influence on the assets portfolio. If the purpose of the fund is to collect 'lifetime' contributions in order to pay a pension that is related to final salary, it is obviously a fundamental requirement that an employee's contributions be invested in a manner that keeps their value at least in line with rising earnings. In the normal course of events, this would mean a heavy investment in company shares, whose value and earnings would be expected to rise in line with nominal GDP. And if we were to look at stocks of assets accumulated in the past, we should see that in 1995 company securities constituted £261bn out of pension funds' total net assets of £507bn. Interestingly though, Table 16.3 shows that in 1995 pension fund managers on

balance turned away from company securities, being net sellers on balance, and bought large quantities of government securities instead.

The nominal value of UK pension funds has grown at about 14 per cent per annum in recent years. This reflects, of course, the increase in value of the underlying assets (approximately equal in the long run to the growth of nominal GDP) but also a net increase in contributions. In the UK pensions have been a very popular form of saving for many years. This is partly because occupational schemes involve a contribution from the employer as well as the employee but also because of favourable tax treatment. Pension contributions, up to a maximum of 15 per cent of salary, are deducted from salary before the calculation of income tax liability. Contributions to occupational schemes are generally much smaller than this but employees have been encouraged in recent years to make additional payments into 'free standing' pension schemes so as to take greater advantage of this tax subsidy. Benefits paid from the fund are taxed at the rate appropriate to the pensioner's circumstances.

When it comes to regulation, most pension funds are trusts. Their activities are therefore circumscribed by the terms of a trust deed and this deed itself must comply with legislation governing the conduct of trusts. To be exempt from taxation, the trust must meet Inland Revenue conditions relating to contributions and benefit entitlement.

This leaves pension funds with a very wide range of powers over the selection and management of investments and this has sometimes attracted adverse attention from time to time. An accusation frequently levelled at pension funds (and life insurance companies) is that they have been too willing to invest in overseas securities, channelling funds to the UK's competitors and, by implication, 'starving' UK industry of finance. This was one of the issues examined by the Wilson Committee in 1980, which found the case unproven though the argument rumbles on. More recently, questions of investment 'ethics' have been raised. Funds have been criticized for being too willing to invest in firms which engage in animal experimentation, or make tobacco products, or exploit the rainforests. In 1984, the National Union of Mineworkers fought an unsuccessful legal battle to prevent their pension fund managers from

Table 16.4 Non-deposit financial institutions, holdings of selected assets, end 1995 (£mn)

	PF	LTI	GI	IT-UT
Short-term assets	19,408	21,389	2,488	3,764
British government securities	52,409	81,590	14,363	2,971
UK company securities				
ordinary	255,047	199,172	12,282	78,505
other	6,136	35,209	4,243	4,412
Overseas securities				
company securities	86,177	59,950	4,422	58,432
government securities	12,049	8,793	6,511	2,421
Loans and mortgages	47	9,745	1,240	0
Unit trusts	15,466	38,173	354	302
Property unit trust units	2,511	0	0	0
Other financial assets	36,469	5,044	27,055	298
Real capital assets	21,509	35,596	2,100	137
Total	507,228	494,661	75,058	151,242

Source: Office for National Statistics, *Financial Statistics*, January 1997, Tables 5.1a (*LTI*), 5.1b (*PF*), 5.2a (*GI*), 5.2cd (*IT-UT*)

investing in alternative, that is, competing, energy sources. The difficulty that such protests face is that the trust deed invariably requires the managers to invest in the best interest of beneficiaries of the fund (not animals or the environment) and their best interest is usually interpreted by the courts in a fairly narrow way to mean 'pecuniary' interest.

16.6   Unit trusts

The purpose of a unit trust is to accept funds from individuals or companies and to invest those funds in a wide variety of assets. Contributors to the trust then have a share in the income and capital appreciation of the underlying assets. As we said at the beginning of this chapter, UK unit trusts are examples of open-ended trusts. To understand the implications of this, we need to understand the concept of a *unit*.

Imagine that a newly formed trust advertises for funds offering units in exchange. The units are offered at a price, let us say £1 for convenience. Setting the price determines the number of units created for a given inflow of funds. The advertisement will state the broad objective of the trust. This may be capital growth, or income, or investment in emerging economies, or any one of many others. If the trust receives £10m in subscriptions, then, ignoring expenses, it will create 10m units, allocating them to subscribers on the basis of the amount subscribed. The funds received will be invested in securities corresponding to the trust objective and the subsequent value of the units will depend upon the performance of those underlying securities. If, again for the sake of convenience, the securities double in market value, then the outstanding 10m units will have a value of £2 each. The trust is open-ended in the sense that if new investors offer to invest in the fund, new units will be created, at the going market price, the managers will buy additional securities and the fund will expand. Notice that the new inflow of funds has no effect on the unit price. That remains based upon the total value of the underlying securities.

The attractions to investors are several. Firstly a 'small' saver is able to reduce risk by investing quite cheaply in a much wider portfolio of assets than would be the case by buying securities directly. The unit trust company, in other words, is exploiting the market imperfection which is the economy of scale available in securities trading. Secondly, holdings can be liquidated very quickly. In Chapter 11 we saw that securities trading in the UK is divided into fortnightly account periods and accounts are settled only after the end of each period. By contrast, the holder of units in a trust can sell the units back to the managers and receive payment, normally within ten days. Notice that units can only be traded between the investor and the trust manager. There is no secondary market.

Each trust is always the responsibility of two companies. Firstly, there is the company responsible for day-to-day management of the trust (the trust manager). This may be a specialist unit trust management company or it may be part of some larger financial grouping. We saw in Section 16.2, for example, that retail banks have their own unit trust management companies. The management company makes the detailed investment decisions, issues certificates of ownership, pays income to investors and so forth.

In addition, each trust has a *trustee*. These are mainly specialist subsidiaries of major banks. The job of the trustee is to see that the fund is managed within the terms of its trustee deed. This deed specifies the objective of the trust and lays down broad conditions governing the management of the funds. The trustee company is acting to some degree as guardian of the investors' interest.

There are of course expenses involved in the running of unit trusts: the management company and the trustees are entitled to reward for their services. For the management company, income comes from two sources. Firstly, there is the 'spread', the difference between the *bid* (the trust's buying) and *offer* (the trust's selling) prices. Unit trusts are permitted to operate a spread as wide as 15 per cent of the fund's net asset value. In our example, the bid price could be as low as 92.5p while the offer price could be 107.5p. However, competition between management companies keeps the spread closer to 6–7 per cent (97–103p). In addition the management company is entitled to charge an annual management fee of 0.5–1 per cent of net asset value. This is normally deducted from the fund's investment income before deciding upon the distribution to be made to unit holders. The trust company receives an annual fee, normally calculated as a very small proportion of the trust's net asset value.

Box 16.2 shows data for the group of unit trusts managed by AXA Equity & Law. The data was taken from the *Financial Times* of 25 January 1997. Reading from the top, it shows the name of the management company and its address and telephone number. It also shows, in the expression '(1200)F', the time of day at which the units in the fund are revalued and indicates that the managers will normally deal 'at forward prices', that is to say at the prices which prevail at the *next* valuation. The first column gives the abbreviated name of each trust, which tells investors something about the objective of the trust or the geographical area in which it invests. The first column of figures shows the

---

Box 16.2   UK Unit Trusts – prices and yields.

AXA Equity & Law Unit Tst Mngrs (1200)F
Equity & Law Hse, Corpn St, Coventry   01203 553231

General Inc	5	590.50	628.20	−2.70	2.48
General Acc	5	707.40	752.60	−3.20	2.35
UK Growth Acc	6	490.70	522.10	−2.30	2.48
UK Growth Inc	6	317.60	337.90	−1.60	2.48
Higher Inc Acc	6	877.30	933.30	−4.20	3.87
Higher Inc Inc	6	467.30	497.20	−2.20	3.87
Gilts/Fxd Int Acc	5½	215.90	228.00	−0.40	5.36
Gilts/Fxd Int Inc	5½	94.54	99.85	−0.15	5.36
Nth America	6	377.50	401.60	+0.20	0.00
Europe	6	381.30	405.70	−0.10	0.15
Brit Excell	6	97.13	103.40	−0.40	2.58
Brit Fndmtls Acc	6	123.70	131.70	−0.80	4.33
Brit Fndmtls Inc	6	82.81	88.10	−0.44	4.33
Global Opps	6	103.20	109.80	+0.10	0.00
Balanced Acc	6	65.82	70.03	−0.27	2.42
Balanced Inc	6	61.46	65.39	−0.25	2.42
Japan Tst Acc	6	36.77	39.12	−0.10	0.00
Pacific Basin Tst Acc	6	412.90	439.30	−3.40	0.80

---

management company's initial charge (the spread in percentage terms). The next two columns show the latest bid–offer prices and the next column shows the change in value of the units since the previous day's valuation. The final column shows the gross yield (dividend (or coupon) divided by price).

Table 16.3 shows how strongly, in relation to their total investible funds, unit (and investment) trusts are concentrated in equities. Understandably, therefore, the growth of unit trust funds has been erratic, reflecting both the public's perception of the benefit of equity investment and the underlying performance of the equities in which they invested. Thus the creation of new units virtually ceased after the crash of 1987, but has since recovered. Growth in the 1990s has averaged about 18 per cent per annum, but even this included a year of negative growth in 1994. Total assets at the end of 1995 were £112bn.

16.7   Investment trusts

Investment trusts differ from all the other institutions we have discussed in this chapter in a number of significant ways. The chief of these is that while all previous intermediaries are 'open-ended', investment trusts are 'closed'. By open-ended we mean that any number of savers can lend any volume of funds to the intermediary at any time. Any increase in the demand for the liabilities of open-ended intermediaries means that more funds are made available to ultimate users.

In the case of investment trusts, however, what savers buy is shares in a trust which is, in effect, a firm whose business it is to own stocks and shares. At any moment, the number of shares in the trust is fixed. Thus new savers can buy shares only from existing shareholders and so when we speak of a flow of funds into investment trusts we must recognize that extra funds do not go into the trust at all. There is no increase in lending by the trust to ultimate lenders. All that happens is that the market price of the shares rises.

The fact that an increase in the demand for an investment trust's shares does not mean that more funds are made available to ultimate borrowers raises the question of whether investment trusts should be considered as intermediaries at all. The reasons for doing so are twofold. Firstly, there must once have been a flow of funds from savers to the trust and on to borrowers when the trust was first established. Also, of course, a trust is at liberty to raise new capital by the issue of new shares or debentures. Futhermore, when investment trust shares are popular and their price is high, this makes the cost of new capital to the trust comparatively cheap (see Chapter 11). Thus a flow of funds 'into' investment trusts which pushes up their price may be the prelude to issue of new shares and a genuine flow of new funds into the securities market.

Secondly, even with only sporadic injections of new funds, investment trusts may still be active traders in securities markets. Even without an inflow of funds from savers, trusts have income from dividends and interest on their assets and from capital gains. After the deduction of operating costs and payments to shareholders, this is put to reserve. From this reserve and from the immediate disposal of existing assets, trusts can make acquisitions of new assets. Investment trusts are generally very active in the market for new issues of shares and in this respect they are channelling new funds to ultimate borrowers. Remember also, as we saw in Chapter 11, that active trading in *existing* stocks makes them more liquid. This makes them more attractive to investors and thus lowers the dividends that their issuers have to pay to induce people to hold them.

The more liquid the market, *ceteris paribus*, the lower the cost of capital to firms.

Investment trusts are not trusts at all in the strict sense of the word, and this is reflected in the regulations governing their activity. As we have now said several times, investment trusts are firms, whose business is shareholding. Thus, like other publicly quoted firms they are subject to the Companies Acts and to the conditions that the Stock Exchange imposes upon firms wanting a stock exchange listing. Finally, the Inland Revenue 'approves' investment trusts for purposes of tax treatment (principally their exemption from capital gains tax on their sales of securities). Total assets at the end of 1995 were £44bn.

16.8 Summary

A financial system consists of a set of markets, institutions and their ultimate users. As a result of competition, improving communications technology and a general movement towards deregulation of economic and financial activity, systems are becoming increasingly homogeneous. However, some differences still remain and these are reflected rather more in institutions than in markets.

A common practice is to divide institutions into those that take deposits (often included in official measures of 'money') and those that do not. In the UK, we need further to divide deposit-taking institutions into banks and building societies. In their main activities, there are considerable similarities between retail banks and building societies, though the former have greater freedom in both sources and uses of funds. Partly for this reason, some larger building societies are considering converting to banks and becoming subject to banking rather than building society regulation.

Bank (and building society) assets consist overwhelmingly of non-marketable loans supplemented by a small proportion of short-dated, highly liquid government securities. The bulk of company securities, and of longer-dated government bonds, are held by non-deposit-taking (or 'other') financial institutions. This is because (with the exception of general insurance companies) their liabilities are held

Table 16.5 Turnover of securities by non-deposit-taking financial institutions, 1995, (£m)

	PF	LTI	GI	IT-UT	Total
Listed UK ordinary shares	71,799	66,935	5,713	66,321	210,767
Other listed UK company securities	5,331	27,036	2,821	4,205	39,393
Overseas ordinary shares	60,429	46,155	3,031	79,702	189,317
Other overseas company and government securities	30,435	28,368	17,238	8,667	84,708

Source: Office for National Statistics, *Financial Statistics*, January 1997, Table 5.3a

largely as long-term savings products by the public who want protection from inflation and a share in the real growth of the economy. For this they are prepared to accept some degree of risk that their savings will fluctuate in value over time.

Given these figures, it is easy to assume that the non-deposit-taking institutions are the main channel of funds from savers to firms. But if we remember what we saw in Chapter 15 then we know that one can tell very little about the net financing of firms simply from looking at the scale of activity in which intermediaries engage. Let us take it a step at a time. Firstly, we need to distinguish 'turnover' from 'net acquisitions'. Table 16.5 shows that the former is huge in relation to the latter, but turnover figures tell us nothing about new finance. They do tell us something about the speed with which the ownership of existing securities changes hands and may therefore indicate something about the market for corporate control, but that is a different matter. Secondly, when we compare the annual change in bank assets with those for all other intermediaries, we see that it far exceeds that for any other group of

financial intermediaries, banks' addition to assets in 1995 of £237bn being nearly 10 times that of long-term insurance companies (at £26.5bn) and more than 10 times that for building societies (at £20.8bn). And remember that while they may not make large purchases of new securities, banks (and to a lesser extent building societies) lend to firms under the heading of 'advances'. Thirdly, none of this data on intermediaries' asset acquisitions allows us to tell how important intermediaries are in making a net contribution to firms' financing of real capital investment. The data in Table 15.1 tell us that UK firms have been largely self-financing in recent years with banks contributing about 16 per cent of net funds raised externally. In spite of all the activity in equities, documented in this chapter, they actually made a negative net contribution to the financing of real investment, meaning that firms actually bought more securities than they issued. Bonds made a net positive contribution and given the data in Table 16.3 (for 'other' company securities) it is a reasonable supposition that for 1995 at least, the funds came via *LTIs, UT-ITs, PFs* and *GIs* in that order.

Key concepts used in this chapter

Net acquisitions	Off-balance-sheet activities	Fully funded
Turnover	Mutual society	'Pay as you go'
Stocks held	General insurance	Trust manager
Retail banks	Long-term insurance	Trustee
Merchant banks	Term insurance	Open-ended fund
Discount houses	Annuity	Closed-end fund
Risk–asset ratios	Endowment	

Questions and problems

1 Distinguish between the main sources and uses of funds for retail banks and other banks in the UK.

2 Identify the main distinguishing features of UK discount houses.

3 Explain how deposit-taking institutions vary from other financial institutions in their sources and uses of funds.

4 Distinguish between a 'mutual' and a 'joint stock' corporation. List some of the potential advantages of a mutual to stock conversion.

5 Distinguish between a 'funded' and a 'pay-as-you-go' pension plan. How would you expect the market for ordinary company shares to be affected by a general switch from PAYG to funded schemes?

6 Explain how favourable tax treatment can encourage particular types of saving.

7 Distinguish between the 'net acquisition of assets', 'turnover in assets' and 'holdings of assets at end of period'.

Further reading

A: General

Bank of England Quarterly Bulletin, 'Risk Measurement and Capital Requirements for Banks', 35 (1995) 177–81.
M Buckle and J Thomson, *The UK Financial System* (Manchester: Manchester U P, 1995) Ch. 17
C A E Goodhart, *Money, Information and Uncertainty* (London: Macmillan, 2e 1989) Ch. 5
P G A Howells and K Bain, *Financial Markets and Institutions* (London: Longman, 1994) Ch. 3

B: Sources of data

Bank of England Quarterly Bulletin (every issue), 'Financial Market Developments'
Office for National Statistics, *Financial Statistics* (monthly)
Stock Exchange Quarterly (London: London Stock Exchange)
Stock Exchange Quality of Markets Fact Sheet (quarterly) (London: London Stock Exchange)

The US financial system

17.1   Introduction

We saw in Section 15.2 that the US financial system is often grouped with that of the UK as a market-based system, indicating that the finance of firms comes largely from the issue of securities, and thus via markets. However, Table 15.1 showed us that, between 1985 and 1994, the net contribution of bond and equity issues to corporate finance was only 6.2 per cent, very little different from in Japan (regarded as having a bank-based financial system) and considerably lower than in the UK. Nonetheless, it remains true that Wall Street (the location of the New York Stock Exchange) is central to the US financial system both psychologically and in terms of its influence on economic policy.

The psychological importance of Wall Street stemmed in part from the role of securities markets in the financing of firms during the period of the USA's most rapid growth; but in part also from the image which the USA had of itself as a young, confident, risk-taking nation in which almost anyone could become rich overnight. The stock market became the focus of one element of the American dream. The sharp price rises on Wall Street in the 1920s and the crash in 1929 are widely accepted as indicators of the economic boom and the subsequent worldwide depression of the 1930s. We also saw in Chapter 13, that commodities markets first developed in the USA, as did trading in futures, financial futures and options. US markets in these instruments remain the world's largest. The 'get rich' aspect of financial markets has remained important as shown, for instance, by the junk bonds scam of the 1980s (discussed in Box 17.3).

Although the role of securities markets in providing finance to industry has declined, the actual importance of the stock exchange in the lives of average Americans has increased since the 1970s with the growth of mutual funds and the development of pension funds. This, in turn, was caused partly by the limitations imposed by law on the US banking system (discussed in Section 17.2) and partly by the increased volatility of inflation and interest rates in the world economy in the 1970s. Banking laws and the attitudes that gave rise to them have thus played an important role in the development of the system as a whole and, like all national financial systems, that of the USA is, in reality, highly individual. Comparisons can, of course, be drawn and there are ways in which the US system has more in common with that of the UK than with that of, say, Germany. One example of this is the strength of securities houses which concentrate on business lending and investment activity. However, there are many ways in which the US system is dramatically different from that of the UK.

The importance of the US financial system to economic policy is also not recent. For example, it is widely held that the contractionary policies of the US Federal Reserve System in 1928 contributed significantly to the onset of the Great Depression. These contractionary policies were introduced specifically to curb stock market speculation. There was an echo of these policies in December 1996 as the Governor of the Board of the Federal Reserve, Alan Greenspan, commented unfavourably on speculative activities in financial markets, prompting fears among market practitioners of increases in interest rates.

The size of the US economy and the continued dominance of the dollar in international transactions has meant that the US financial system has become central not only to the US economy but also to the global economy. Financial markets in all countries pay great attention to the ups and downs of the Dow Jones index[1] (see Case Study 2).

17.2 Deposit-taking institutions in the USA

The US banking system has a number of characteristics which distinguish it from those of other countries. Firstly, there are a very large number of banking organizations. Although the number of banks has fallen sharply in recent years, particularly through mergers and acquisitions, there remained at the end of June 1996 a total of 9670 commercial banks. Secondly, until recently, legislation limited the growth of US banks and their ability to expand from their home states to other states within the country. The restriction on expansion within the USA was one of a number of reasons (discussed in Section 9.5) for large banks from the financial centre, New York, choosing from the 1960s on to establish branches offshore, and playing a major part in the development of the Eurocurrency markets. Thirdly, there is a dual system of control with banks being chartered by both

the federal government and individual states. Fourthly, for a significant part of this century, other restrictions on the operation of banks have been in force, limiting interest payments on deposits and providing for a strict separation of investment banks from commercial banks. Finally, a central bank was not established until 1913 – although there had been two much earlier attempts to do so. The central bank which was then established was not a single institution but a system of 12 Federal Reserve Banks overseen by a Board in Washington DC.

Most of these characteristics can be explained by two major fears within the USA – the fear of centralized authority and the fear of domination by moneyed interests. These fears reflect the origins of the US nation state – settlement from Europe had been by separate, relatively small groups often fleeing from religious or political domination. The first significant united action by settlers was the struggle against the distant authority of Britain. The two fears combined to produce a determination to prevent the financial system being controlled either by large institutions in the financial centre of New York or by political forces concentrated in Washington. This led to severe geographical restrictions on the development of US banking, to the extent that banks were not permitted to have branch offices. The result of this was the continued existence of a very large number of banks, most of them small. It has only been in the 1970s and particularly the 1980s and 1990s that this structure has begun to change.

The limitations on the development of banks, together with a general distrust in the population of financial institutions, left the system vulnerable to *bank runs* on individual banks. These frequently developed into *multi-bank panics*. Fourteen such panics have been identified in the years between 1800 and 1933, 11 of which led to widespread restriction of convertibility of deposits into currency. This strongly influenced the nature of bank legislation and this, in turn, had a marked impact on the way in which the system developed. Laws passed during the 1930s sought to restrict what was seen as damaging competition among banks, to prevent firms from engaging in a mixture of banking and

---

[1] The Dow Jones Industrial Average index is the most quoted index of equity prices on the New York Stock Exchange (see Chapter 11).

non-banking business, and to provide a system of insurance of bank deposits. Ironically, the system which had been developed to limit the number of bank failures and to provide greater security for depositors has been held by many to be largely responsible for a new wave of failures in the 1980s and early 1990s.

17.2.1 The Classification of US depository institutions

Classification of the US banking system is complicated by a number of the system's features. Firstly, there is the dual nature of the chartering system with banks being granted licences to operate either by individual states (*state-chartered banks*) or by an agency of the federal government (*national banks*). States used their power to charter banks to restrict the ability of banks to open branches even within their own states and virtually to prevent cross-border activities of banks by not allowing those chartered in other states to open within their borders. National banks were prevented from opening branches until the *McFadden–Pepper Act* of 1927 when they became subject to the banking restrictions that applied to state-chartered banks in the state in which they were operating.

A second distinction arises because of the deposit insurance provisions of banking law. Although the first insurance fund to protect depositors was set up by New York state as early as 1829, the present, nationwide system of deposit insurance was established by *The Banking Act* of 1933 (widely known as the *Glass–Steagall Act*). In reaction to three banking panics between 1930 and 1933, the Glass–Steagall Act set up the Federal Deposit Insurance Corporation (FDIC) to implement the federal insurance of deposits. Participation in the scheme was mandatory for all Federal Reserve member banks. Other banks could participate if approved by the FDIC. A very high percentage of banks currently participate in the scheme although there remain some small uninsured credit unions and a few uninsured banks.

The Glass-Steagall Act was also responsible for a third distinction through the restrictions it placed on the operations of insured banks. These included the strict separation, mentioned above, between invest-

ment and commercial banks. Commercial banks were, in effect, prohibited from originating, trading or holding securities other than those of the federal government or general obligations of state and local governments. In contrast to the UK, US investment banks are non-depository institutions.

A fourth distinction still represented in bank statistics is that between independent banks and *bank holding companies* (BHCs) – companies which have controlling interests in one or more US banks. The ability to form a bank holding company has existed for more than a century but it became a popular form of organization only after World War II. Forming a bank holding company provided a way around some of the restrictions imposed on banks by legislation. This was particularly true of restrictions on the formation of bank branches both within and between states since a bank holding company could form separate banking subsidiaries in other parts of its home state or in other states. Up until 1956, bank holding companies could also have controlling interests in companies engaged in activities other than banking. This led to fears that bank assets would be used to finance the losses of non-banking subsidiaries, increasing the riskiness of banks. Thus, the *Bank Holding Company Act* of 1956 prevented multi-bank holding companies from engaging in non-banking activities which were not, in the judgement of the Federal Reserve, closely related to banking. Multi-bank holding companies were also limited to owning banking subsidiaries in their home states, unless other states expressly permitted their entry. Since no state permitted such entry prior to 1975, the 1956 act ruled out the possibility of multi-bank holding companies engaging in interstate banking. In 1970 the law was extended to cover the activities of one-bank holding companies.

Fifthly, there is the classification of depository institutions into *banking organizations* or commercial banks (consisting of bank holding companies and independent banks) and thrift institutions. *Thrifts* are subdivided into *savings and loan associations* (S&Ls), savings banks and credit unions, although credit unions, which are on average much smaller than S&Ls and savings banks, are often regarded as forming a separate category from the other thrifts. Thrifts have longer-term assets and liabilities than commercial banks. Their assets principally consist of long-term bonds or house mortgages. Until the early 1980s, mortgage advances were required to be fixed-interest loans. Their liabilities are almost exclusively savings and time deposits.

S&Ls are primarily involved in real estate and housing finance. They can be traced back to the early 1830s when they began to be set up as credit co-operatives to provide housing finance and to act as a safe repository for small savers. They became the second largest type of financial institution in the USA, behind only commercial banks, but have

declined both in number and asset size following the savings and loans crisis of the 1980s (discussed in Box 17.2). Most S&Ls were organized as mutual associations (owned by their members rather than by stock-holders). Indeed, in the majority of states they were required by law to be mutual associations. Their very rapid growth in the Nineteenth and early Twentieth centuries can be seen as a reflection of the fear of 'moneyed interests' mentioned above. The collapse of house prices in the great depression of the early 1930s led to the failure of nearly 2000 S&Ls

---

Box 17.2   The Savings and Loans crisis of the 1980s and 1990s

The 1933 Banking Act had introduced federal deposit insurance through the FDIC. This was extended to S&Ls by the setting up of the Federal Savings and Loan Insurance Corporation (FSLIC) in 1934. The schemes required the payment by members of flat-rate premiums unrelated to the riskiness of assets. The Act also prohibited interest payments to owners of FDIC-insured demand deposits and authorized the Federal Reserve System (FED) and the FDIC to set limits for rates paid on insured savings deposits of various maturities. This was implemented by the Fed under Regulation Q. Although these interest rate ceilings were not extended to thrifts until 1966, their imposition on banks allowed thrifts also to raise funds at low cost without fear of competition for deposits from the banks. S&Ls flourished during the 1950s and 1960s as housing became a national priority. Mortgage-lending tripled in the 1950s and in the 1960s the assets of S&Ls again doubled.

However, commercial banks began to find their way around the limitations through the use of Certificates of Deposit, placing increased pressure on S&Ls. The Fed responded by using powers granted to them in 1966 to allow S&Ls to offer interest rates on deposits half-a-point higher than the limit on banks. But in the 1970s, inflation rates became more volatile and the Fed met increased inflationary pressure by tight monetary policy which forced market interest rates well above Regulation Q ceilings. Money market mutual funds (see Section 17.4.3) developed in the mid 1970s to offer savers higher rates of return, putting both banks and thrifts under severe competitive pressure for deposits.

In 1980, interest rate ceilings were removed, allowing banks and thrifts to compete for deposits, but the problem continued until 1982

when they were allowed to offer an unregulated deposit account directly competitive with the money market mutual funds. But the higher interest rates sharply increased costs and, since S&Ls were still largely invested in much lower-yielding fixed-rate mortgages, most thrifts lost money. Net worth declined to what would have been crisis levels in the absence of federal deposit insurance.

No action was taken since it was assumed that the problem would disappear when interest rates again fell. Indeed, S&Ls were encouraged to expand and their capital requirements were lowered from five to three per cent of assets. Informally, the standards were lowered even further by the introduction of less stringent accounting principles and a cut in the number of examiners of thrifts.

Variable rate mortgages were allowed in 1981 but there was considerable consumer resistance to them. Congress expanded the lending activities permitted to thrifts to allow them to diversify their portfolios but this only made things worse as S&Ls sought to return to profit by engaging in very risky activities, including the purchase of junk bonds (see Box 17.3), secure in the knowledge that they were covered by the FSLIC. The number of loan defaults began to rise and S&Ls to fail.

Problems during the period were intensified by poor management of S&Ls and by fraud which was uncovered in many of the loans when institutions were taken over by FSLIC. The resources of FSLIC came under great pressure as it sought to dispose of the assets and liabilities of failed S&Ls. The FSLIC became insolvent and in 1989 its duties were transferred to the new Savings Association Insurance Fund (SAIF) at the FDIC.

(out of a total of just under 13,000) and to two important pieces of legislation – the Federal Home Loan Bank system (1932) which provided a central credit facility to lend to troubled institutions, and the introduction of deposit insurance with the establishment of the Federal Savings and Loan Insurance Corporation (FSLIC) in 1934. This was similar to that provided for commercial banks by the FDIC. Problems began to arise, however, in the late 1960s and 1970s.

Savings banks were first set up in the early Nineteenth century as mutual philanthropic institutions aimed to encourage the poor to save. They grew rapidly throughout the century, although they remained heavily concentrated in the north-east and middle Atlantic regions of the country. They, too, engaged in mortgage lending while also holding large quantities of government and corporate bonds. Savings banks have always been safer than other depository institutions. During the depression only eight of the 598 savings banks failed and they also performed much better than S&Ls during the 1980s crisis. This was partly because they responded more flexibly to the changing economic and financial circumstances than did S&Ls and, from the late 1960s on, began diversifying their assets away from mortgages towards securities. Recently, a number of surviving S&Ls have converted to savings banks to escape the S&L name. Regulatory changes since World War II have, however, eroded the boundaries between savings banks and other financial intermediaries. All savings banks are now federally insured and many of the larger banks have shed their mutual status, although a higher proportion of savings banks have remained mutuals than has been the case with S&Ls.

Credit unions deal primarily in small, fixed-term, personal loans. Their funds come entirely from persons (and individual deposits are very small). As is shown in Table 17.1, the average deposits in 1984 of S&Ls and Savings Banks was $272.3m, that of credit unions only $5.6m. As mentioned in Section 15.3, credit unions too were established as mutuals. Under the *Federal Credit Union Act*, their membership was limited to groups having a common bond of occupation or association. They were thus essentially local in nature. Although, unlike commercial banks and other thrifts, they were not legally prohibited

from operating across state lines, the common bond requirement restricted the interstate activities of credit unions to a few large institutions serving the armed forces or large multinational corporations. However, in 1982, the regulator of federally chartered credit unions, the National Credit Union Administration (NCUA), ruled that in some cases a single credit union could serve more than one unrelated group, each of which shared a common bond. Much freer interpretations of the term 'common bond' have followed, resulting in credit union mergers. In 1991, the NCUA also allowed credit unions to share branches, giving them an inexpensive way of expanding geographically. Table 17.1 provides a comparison of the numbers of different types of federally insured depository institutions at the end of 1984 and at the end of 1994. The changes between these dates are discussed in Section 17.2.2.

Finally, there is the relationship between banks and the Federal Reserve System (widely known as the Fed). Under the *Federal Reserve Act* of 1913, all national banks were required to become members of the Federal Reserve but membership was optional for state-chartered banks. Membership gave access to Federal Reserve services but imposed obligations such as reserve requirements designed to guarantee the liquidity of banks. The *Depository Institutions and Monetary Control Act of 1980* extended the Fed's benefits and obligations to all depository institutions but state banks may still be classified as member or non-member banks of the Federal Reserve System.

17.2.2 Changes in the structure of depository institutions

The volume of federally insured deposits is very large ($3,321bn at the end of 1994) and increased by 26 per cent over 1984–94. However, the rate of increase of total US financial assets was much greater. Insured deposits are a product of declining importance to the US economy. As Table 17.1 shows, in the 10 years between 1984 and 1994, the total number of federally insured depository institutions fell by over 25 per cent to 21,883. The

Table 17.1

Type of institution	1984					1994				
	Number of firms	Percent of total	Deposits (billions of dollars)	Percent of deposits	Mean deposits per firm (millions of dollars)	Number of firms	Percent of firms	Deposits (billions of dolars)	Percent of deposits	Mean deposits per firm (millions of dollars)
Banking organizations	11,342	38.0	1,613.7	61.4	142.3	7,898	36.1	2,382.7	71.7	301.7
Independent banks	5,698	19.1	209.9	8.0	36.8	2,634	12.0	170.0	5.1	64.5
One-bank holding companies	4,926	16.5	467.7	17.8	94.9	4,464	20.4	523.0	15.7	117.2
Multibank holding companies	718	2.4	936.1	35.6	1,303.7	800	3.7	1,689.6	50.9	2,112.1
Thrift institutions	3,414	11.4	929.8	35.4	272.3	2,058	9.4	684.5	20.6	332.6
Savings & loan associations	2,882	9.6	697.5	26.5	242.0	776	3.5	147.2	4.4	189.7
Federal savings banks	264	9	121.6	4.6	460.6	756	3.5	357.5	10.8	472.9
State savings banks	268	9	110.7	4.2	413.0	526	2.4	179.8	5.4	341.8
Credit unions	15,126	50.6	84.1	3.2	5.6	11,927	54.5	254.0	7.6	21.3
Total	29,882	100.0	2,627.6	100.0	87.9	21,883	100.0	3,321.2	100.0	151.8

NOTE: The data in this table are, to the extent possible, aggregated within categories. Thus, banks that are part of the same multibank holding company are aggregated into one banking organization. Banking organizations and thrift institutions that are affiliated are counted separately, as there are any combinations of the three different types of thrift institutions that are under common ownership.

"Chain banking" organizations – banks owned by an individual or a group of individuals but not legally affiliated – are not consolidated, owing to data limitations.

Data is as of year-end. Components may not sum to totals, and calculations may not yield the percentages shown, because of rounding.

Source: D F Amel, 'Trends in the structure of federally insured deposit institutions, 1984–94', *Federal Reserve Bulletin*, 82, 1996, p.5

most spectacular fall was in the number of Savings and Loan Associations which fell from 2882 to 776 in the period. The conversion of many of the failed S&Ls into Savings Banks is reflected in the high percentage increase in the numbers of both Federal and State Savings Banks.

The number of banking organizations also fell by more than 30 per cent to 7898. Within that decline, there was a considerable shift away from independent banks to bank holding companies, with the number of independent banks declining by over 50 per cent. Increased concentration within the system can be seen in the increase in the average size of the deposit base of banking organizations which rose from $142.3m to $301.7m. Although the numbers of multi-bank holding companies rose only from 718 to 800, their average deposits more than doubled to $2,112.1m, causing the percentage of the deposits of all depository institutions held by multi-bank holding companies to rise from 35.6 to 50.9. Table 17.2 provides information on the assets of US banking organizations for October 1996.

Average deposits of S&Ls fell from $242m to $189.7m and their deposit share plummeted from 26.5 per cent to 4.4 per cent. The average size of credit unions nearly quadrupled over the decade, although credit unions remain much smaller than other types of depository institutions. Over the

period, institutions controlling less than $5 billion in deposits tended to lose market share while those controlling more than $5 billion gained share, from about 30 per cent to more than 50 per cent.

Amel (1996) identifies five reasons for the considerable structural changes within depository institutions:

- mergers and acquisitions;
- legislative changes affecting interstate expansion;
- legislative changes affecting expansion by branching;
- changes in credit union membership regulations;
- failures of depository institutions.

Table 17.2 USA banking organizations assets, average for October 1996[1], $bn

Cash assets[2]	222.6
Advances	2667.5
Interbank loans	199.7
Investments	968.4
Other assets	250.9
Total assets	4334.9

Sources and notes: Federal Reserve Bulletin February 1997, adapted from Table 1.26 [1] seasonally adjusted; [2] includes vault cash, cash items in process of collection, balances due from depository institutions, and balances due from Federal Reserve Banks.

Merger activity among healthy banks rose to record levels during the 1980s as banks sought to reduce costs, partly as a result of increased competition from non-depository institutions. This was spurred by technological change which broadened access to the commercial paper market and reduced the role of commercial banks in lending to large corporations. Technological change also probably reduced costs for large firms relative to small firms. From an average of about 200 in the years between 1970 and 1980, the number of bank acquisitions jumped to a total of around 5300 during the 1980s. Whereas acquisitions in the 1970s were principally of small banks, banks merged or taken over in the 1980s included larger institutions. Of the 200 largest depositories at the end of 1984, only 99 existed 10 years later; of the 100 largest, only 57 survived as independent firms; nine of the largest 25 were absorbed by competitors during the decade. A major element in the increased number of acquisitions was the changed attitude of the US government and of federal agencies towards mergers in the finance industry. Under US law, any bank wishing to acquire another bank must obtain approval from the appropriate federal bank regulator and from the Department of Justice, which is the primary authority for administering US competition laws. From 1980 onwards, the administration of President Reagan spoke out strongly in favour of bank mergers in general and found few that it believed should be challenged.

These changed attitudes were also reflected in legislation and in the interpretation of legislation. Many individual states liberalized their banking laws to allow greater geographic expansion within their borders and interstate banking began to get under way as an increasing number of states passed laws allowing entry by banks from some or all other states. The first step towards allowing out-of-state bank holding companies to own banks was taken by Maine in 1975, although this only applied to banks from other states which granted similar rights to Maine bank holding companies. By 1983, however, all of the New England states had enacted similar reciprocal laws and by the end of 1994, every state but Hawaii had introduced laws allowing some degree of interstate banking. On 29 September, 1995, bank holding companies were given the right to purchase banks throughout the USA for the first time since the passage of the *Bank Holding Company Act* of 1956. The *Riegle–Neal Interstate Banking and Branching Efficiency Act* of 1994, which permitted the expansion, will also, by June 1997, allow banks to branch across state lines. This overrode all remaining restrictions on bank holding company expansion, including the state laws in Hawaii.

Legal interpretations by federal agencies led to the reduction of restrictions on state-chartered banks. In many states, the laws restricting intra-state branching had not applied to thrift institutions. The Office of the Comptroller of the Currency (OCC) argued that national banks were in competition with state-chartered thrifts and thus ruled that national banks could branch to the same extent as thrifts. This would have put state-chartered banking organizations at a disadvantage relative to national banks and states responded by relaxing their restrictions on intrastate branching by state-chartered banks.

The OCC also took advantage of a long-standing rule which allowed national banks to move their head offices up to 30 miles and retain the previous head offices as branches. In 1985, the OCC ruled that a national bank that had an office within 30 miles of a state line could make that its head office and then branch into the adjacent state. The ruling had little effect until 1994 when it began to be used by bank holding companies for branching across state lines against state laws. A few bank holding companies merged banks in more than two states by repeatedly moving their head offices near a state border, then across the border, then across the new 'home state' to within 30 miles of another state border and so on. This practice encouraged some states to allow interstate branching by state banks before the 1997 date set by the Riegle–Neal Act so that state-chartered banks were not at a disadvantage to national banks that branched interstate. Both the OCC rulings mentioned here survived a number of court challenges.

Federal agency interpretation was also important in breaking down the separation of securities and banking business. The Banking Act of 1933 (Glass–Steagall) had allowed banks to carry out securities business through separate subsidiaries provided they were not engaged principally in such non-banking activities. From the early 1980s on, the Fed and the OCC began to interpret this provision more liberally, allowing banks to expand in a small way into new markets – first commercial paper, then mortgage-backed bonds, corporate debt and equities. In 1982, the OCC authorized several national banks to conduct discount brokerage businesses through subsidiaries and in 1983 the Fed permitted the then second largest US bank holding company to acquire the largest US discount brokerage company. In 1986, the Fed ruled that a bank holding company subsidiary, until then doing only a discount brokerage business, could provide customers with investment advice. The OCC then authorized brokerage subsidiaries of national banks to provide investment advice. After 1986, some bank holding companies were able to extend their underwriting activities considerably.

The final factor in the consolidation of US depository institutions was the large number of failures in depository institutions in the 1980s and early 1990s. Between 1984 and 1994, 1276 banks, 1129 thrifts (predominantly S&Ls) and 987 credit unions failed. The crisis had an impact on interstate expansion by thrift institutions as the federal regulators sought to sell the failing firms at least cost to the thrift deposit insurance fund. In 1986, the Federal Home Loan Bank Board proposed that buyers of failing thrift institutions be allowed to branch into any three states of their choice. In 1990, a Federal appeals court upheld the right of the organization set up specially to dispose of failing thrifts to allow purchasing banks to convert failed thrifts[2] into branches, even if this violated state branching laws. In May 1992, the Office of Thrift Supervision, the successor agency to the Federal Home Loan Bank Board, acted to allow nationwide branching by all thrift institutions.

17.3   The Federal Reserve System

The *Federal Reserve System* (the Fed) was created by the Federal Reserve Act of 1913. Unlike most central banks in Europe, the Fed had not evolved into a central bank from an ordinary bank of discount, deposit and note issue. The Fed was a compromise between two central banking traditions – that of the corporate central bank, chartered by the state but owned wholly or in great part by private investors, and that of having the government's fiscal authority (the US Treasury) act also as the central bank. The first was tried with the First Bank of the United States (1791–1811) and the Second Bank of the United States (1816–36) but both were strongly opposed on the grounds that a large and privileged corporation with a monopoly of the federal government's banking business was incompatible with America's democratic ideals. Neither charter was renewed. In 1840–1 and from 1846 to 1914, the federal government acted as its own banker, establishing a number of sub-treasuries in major cities. Treasury officials gradually realized that funds might be added to or withdrawn from the private sector on a discretionary basis to prevent financial panics and as an element of macro-economic policy. However, this led to a widespread fear of political control of money and finance, particularly that the Treasury would have a long-run bias towards 'easy money' and inflation and that it would favour some financial, geographic and economic interests over others. A financial panic in 1907 led to the setting up of a commission of enquiry and its report led to the 1913 Federal Reserve Act.

This gave both bankers and the Treasury a voice in central bank policy formulation but aimed to prevent control of policy by either New York bankers or Washington politicians. The system consists of 12 regional *Federal Reserve Banks*, each having authority in a specific geographical area, and a co-ordinating Federal Reserve Board in Washington DC. The capital stock of each of the regional Reserve Banks was subscribed by the member banks in its district. Member banks received a fixed dividend on their capital contribution with any profits in excess of these dividends going to the Treasury. They also received the right to participate in electing six of the nine directors of their Federal Reserve Bank. The other three directors of each Bank were appointed by the Federal Reserve Board in Washington. The regional Reserve Banks were given a monopoly (originally only partial) of the nation's note issue, became fiscal agents of the government, banks of rediscount and reserve for member banks, and lenders

---

2 The Resolution Trust Corporation (RTC)

of last resort in their districts. Each Bank set its own discount rate and engaged in its own open market operations. It was hoped that this decentralized structure would ensure a sufficient supply of credit in each region.

Member banks held legally prescribed reserves as deposits in their Reserve Banks and in return were entitled to rediscount their eligible commercial paper at the Banks when in need of temporary liquidity – use the Fed clearing facilities including electronic funds transfers and the currency and information services of the Banks. The original Federal Reserve Board comprised five members appointed to staggered 10-year terms by the US president, and the Secretary of the Treasury and the Comptroller of the Currency as *ex-officio* members. The Fed was intended to be independent of:

(1) private financial business interests;
(2) duly constituted government authorities (executive and legislature); and
(3) partisan political interests.

The job of the Federal Reserve Board was to oversee and supervise the operations of the Reserve Banks, co-ordinate their activities, handle the System's relations with the federal government, bring about a uniform banking and monetary policy in the USA, and participate in the regulation and supervision of the banking system. It was given little authority to initiate policies. Its late appearance meant that the Fed had to share regulatory and supervisory duties with already established federal agencies and state banking authorities. Under the present division of responsibilities, the Fed oversees bank holding companies, foreign banks and state-chartered banks which belong to the Federal Reserve System. The FDIC monitors other state-banks at the federal level and runs the fund guaranteeing depositors in the event of failure.

The Office of the Comptroller of the Currency (OCC) oversees nationally chartered banks while the Office of Thrift Supervision oversees S&L institutions.

The Fed's responsibility for all bank holding companies has meant that, as BHCs have become more popular, it has come to be the primary federal overseer of banks, now holding about 90 per cent of the nation's deposits.

It is widely held that the Fed performed badly in the Depression. Friedman and Schwartz (1963), for example, blame it for not suspending convertibility until it was too late. Part of the blame was placed on the decentralized structure of the system since during the depression, serious disagreements had arisen over monetary policy both among the Federal Reserve Banks and between the Banks and the Board. The Federal Reserve Bank of New York and, somewhat later, the Board, favoured policies to stimulate the economy, but several other regional Banks had sufficient power to resist such policies.

In the Glass–Steagall Act of 1933 but particularly in the Banking Act of 1935, Congress moved to centralize authority in the renamed *Board of Governors of the Federal Reserve System*, led by a Chairman with enhanced powers. All seven members of the new Board were directly appointed by the President with the advice and consent of the Senate. The Federal Open Market Committee (FOMC) was set up and the Board was given the authority to adjust reserve requirements of its member banks. The FOMC comprised the seven members of the Board of Governors, the president of the Federal Reserve Board of New York and four other Reserve Bank presidents, serving on a rotating basis. This gave the Board members a permanent majority on the Committee and ensured a unified monetary policy.

The Chairman of the Board of the Federal Reserve is now widely regarded as one of the most powerful economic policy makers in the world. Nonetheless, a potent distrust of the Fed remains in American society. This is strongly reflected in Greider (1987) who sees the Fed as a non-elected body with an anti-inflationary bias that restrains economic growth in order to preserve the value of financial assets, most of which are owned by wealthy people.

17.4 Non-depository Institutions in the USA

Non-depository institutions in the USA consist of investment banks, insurance companies, mutual funds, pension funds and finance companies.

17.4.1 Securities firms

Securities firms engage in a variety of activities, most of which can be classified as investment banking or brokerage. The securities industry is overseen by the Securities and Exchange Commission (SEC) which regulates the issue of securities, and the various securities exchanges. There is also self-regulation of the industry through the National Association of Securities Dealers (NASD) and the Federal Reserve Board has some regulatory influence through determining the credit limits or margin requirements in securities markets. There are around 5000 securities firms in the USA. In recent years the large US securities firms have spread throughout the world. At the same time, although foreign banks have not made major inroads into US retail banking[3], foreign-owned institutions, notably the very large Japanese banks, have made considerable inroads into wholesale banking and the securities industry in the USA.

Securities firms come to the attention of the public principally when there is a major collapse or court case. For example, in the 1980s, the US securities industry was perhaps best known in relation to the issue of junk bonds. This is dealt with in Box 17.3. Other well-known cases include that of Kidder Peabody, where the head of bond trading was fired in 1994 for allegedly creating $350m of fictitious profits. This led to the demise of the firm. In 1991, Salomon Brothers had to pay several hundred million dollars in fines and compensation after its head of bond trading was found to have faked customer bids in Treasury auctions. New management had to write off an additional several hundred million dollars early in 1995 for past bookkeeping errors. The US problems of Daiwa were discussed in Section 14.8.

17.4.2 Insurance Companies

There are over 2000 life insurance companies and more than 3000 general insurers in the USA. In the 1970s and 1980s, life insurance companies ran into

---

Box 17.3   The growth of junk bonds

Junk bonds are corporate debt instruments that the credit-rating agencies regard as 'below investment grade' because they judge that the issuing companies might not be able to meet interest or principal payments. In the late 1970s the market consisted largely of debt securities of companies that had been successful in the past but had run into difficulties ('fallen angels'). However, from 1984 onwards, Michael Milken, of the securities firm Drexel Burnham Lambert, transformed the market by selling high-yield bonds as a means of raising finance for corporate raiders and shell companies without earnings or assets to undertake leveraged buyouts. The bonds yielded an average of 350–450 basis points more than Treasury bonds of similar maturities, but with a very wide range. For instance, bonds issued by a steel company, LTV, which sought legal protection from its creditors in 1986, yielded around 35 per cent. Milken found a ready home for the bonds among insurance companies and thrift institutions which were seeking to diversify away from fixed-interest lending and were willing to take risks to maintain returns, pension plans, the mutual funds and even the public directly. In 1980 there had been 46 issues of junk bonds for a total of $1.38bn. By 1986 this had grown to 210 issues for a total of $29.83bn.

Drexel charged very high commissions to the issuing firms (up to three or four per cent of the principal) and paid very high bonuses to their traders. In 1987 Milken received $550mn for his services. However, in 1989 Drexel was heavily fined for mail and securities fraud and the following year Milken was heavily fined and later jailed for securities violations which included cheating some customers and helping others to break securities law. The value of most junk bonds declined sharply in late 1989 and S&Ls were required under the *Financial Institutions Reform, Recovery and Enforcement Act* of 1989 to sell their junk bond holdings. Drexel Burnham Lambert went bankrupt in February 1990.

---

3 The percentage of insured US deposits held by foreign organizations increased from 4.5 per cent of all deposits only to 5.3 per cent over the 10 years from 1984 to 1994.

the same disintermediation difficulties as the S&Ls. At the beginning of the 1970s the assets of life insurance companies were long-term fixed interest (usually acquired years before when interest rates were low). Liabilities were very largely whole life policies. As market interest rates rose in the 1970s and as money market mutual funds developed offering much higher returns than were available on life policies, the competitiveness of the life insurance industry was much reduced.

Life insurance policies in fact consist of two elements – the insurance element and one of saving and accumulation. Policyholders found that they could unbundle their policies by taking out short-term life policies and undertaking the accumulation element in other ways. Between 1970 and 1984, premiums on life policies fell from 3.12 per cent to 1.99 per cent of disposable income while whole of life policies declined from 82 per cent to 22 per cent of new policies written. Lapses and surrenders of both old and new policies doubled to 12 per cent of all policies in force in 1984. Attempts by US companies to follow the UK practice of acquiring claims to real streams of goods and services (such as the earnings of industrial and commercial enterprises or holdings of real estate and property) were restricted by state regulations covering the types of assets life offices could hold. Nonetheless, they diversified as much as possible, often into riskier products with higher rates of return including junk bonds and doubtful commercial real estate loans. The sharp downturn in the junk bond market in 1989 (discussed in Box 17.3) caused problems for a number of, mainly small, life insurance companies. Forty-three companies failed in 1989, another 30 in 1990 and more in 1991, including some rather larger companies. The industry self-regulation authority, the National Life Association of Insurance Commissioners, promoted nationwide standards for capital adequacy and for state guarantee funds.

Insurance companies also responded to the pressure on their profits in the 1970s and 1980s by seeking to market more flexible types of policies and to enter new product markets. Some companies began to offer certificates of deposit or cash management accounts in direct competition with commercial banks while others which have merged with brokerage firms have begun to offer a wide range of securities-related services. Insurance companies have also begun to offer mutual funds to investors.

17.4.3 Mutual Funds

Mutual funds (the equivalent of unit and investment trusts in the UK) are investment companies that invest pools of money into a number of investment options. They have been in existence since the 1920s and are regulated by the Securities and Exchange Commission (SEC) under the *Investment Company Act* of 1940. The Act sets fiduciary standards as well as reporting and disclosure requirements. Funds usually specialize in particular types of investment, including growth stocks, income-producing stocks, small-firm stocks, short- or long-term bonds, tax-exempt bonds, precious metals or international stocks. We have seen that the development of money market mutual funds (MMMFs) from 1975 onwards had a profound effect on banks, thrifts and insurance companies. They specialize in high-grade, short-term securities that offer market returns on cash-equivalents, and permit cheque-writing privileges. Thus they were able to offer rates of return that reflected the higher rates of short-term interest produced in the late 1970s by world economic events and the Fed's response to them. Between the beginning of 1979 and the end of 1982, the assets of money market mutual funds jumped from $12bn to $230bn.

17.4.4 Other non-depository institutions

Other non-depository institutions include finance companies and pension funds. Finance companies specialize in the provision of short- and medium-term credit to firms and households. Some are subsidiaries of bank holding companies or insurance companies or themselves have subsidiaries which offer banking or commercial services. Funds are raised mainly through bank loans or the issue of commercial paper or bonds, although some states allow finance companies to seal customer deposits under particular circumstances. Finance companies are for the most part regulated by the states and regulations vary between states. There are generally, however, limits placed on the size and the maturity of loan finance companies can make and on the interest rates they can charge.

Pension funds have developed in much the same way as in the UK. The performance of their portfolios is very susceptible to market conditions. Criticisms of the operation of pension funds led to the *Employee Retirement Income Security Act* of 1974 (revised in 1989) which introduced rules regarding the length of membership of the fund needed before a pension would be paid and about transfers from one fund to another. It also stipulated that contributions should be invested in a prudent manner. Pension funds are also subject to state regulation.

17.5 Summary

The US financial system is highly individual, having developed to reflect two major concerns present since the early days of the country – the fear of moneyed interests and the fear of being controlled either by large institutions in the financial centre of New York or by political forces concentrated in Washington.

This led to a complicated dual system of regulation and to state and federal laws limiting the ability of banks to open branches and to engage in interstate banking. This ensured that there would be a large number of small banks and that, in turn, contributed to the tendency of the system to suffer from bank runs and multi-bank panics.

This led to legislation which aimed to restrict the activities of banks and to insure their deposits. The result was a large reduction in the number of bank failures from the 1940s to the 1970s. However, with changes in the international economic environment in the 1970s, problems arose and the 1980s saw a new burst of bank failures especially among Savings and Loan Associations. This, together with the effects of technological change and a number of legislative changes at both federal and state levels, has produced a major consolidation of the US banking system which seems bound to continue. In recent years, banks have become increasingly free to open branches and to engage in interstate banking. In addition, the barrier erected between commercial and investment banking in the 1930s has begun to be eroded.

The US central bank (the Federal Reserve System) is also quite different from other central banks and the form it has taken also owes much to long-lived attitudes and to historical developments. There have also been a number of important developments among non-depository financial institutions, not least with the establishment of Money Market Mutual Funds in the 1970s.

Key concepts used in this chapter

Bank runs
State-chartered banks
The Glass–Steagall Act
Banking organizations
Savings & Loan Associations
Federal Reserve Banks
Multi-bank panics

National banks
Bank holding companies
Thrifts
Federal Reserve System
Board of Governors of the Federal Reserve
System

Questions and problems

1 Why are US financial markets so important to the rest of the world?

2 Consider the relationship between US bank legislation and the structure of the banking industry in the USA.

3 Discuss the advantages and disadvantages of a banking system with large numbers of small, independent banks.

4 Why was investment banking separated from commercial banking in the USA? Do the arguments which were used for doing this in the 1930s still apply today?

5 Are there advantages in having a regionally-based central bank? Compare the structure of the Federal Reserve System with that of the Bundesbank.

6 What did S&Ls and insurance companies have in common in the 1970s? Why did that cause them problems?

Further reading

D F Amel, 'Trends in the structure of federally insured depository institutions, 1984–94', Federal Reserve Bulletin, 82, 1996, 1–15

M Friedman and A Schwartz, *A Monetary History of the United States, 1867–1960* (Princeton: Princeton University Press, 1963)

W Greider, *Secrets of the Temple: How the Federal Reserve Runs the Country* (New York: Simon and Schuster, 1987)

M Kohn, *Financial Institutions and Markets* (New York: McGraw-Hill, 1994)

J Madura, *Financial Markets and Institutions* (St Paul: West Publishing, 1992) 2e

P Newman, M Milgate and J Eatwell (eds), *The New Palgrave Dictionary of Money and Finance* (London: Macmillan, 1992)

R Sylla, 'The Autonomy of the Monetary Authorities: The Case of the US Federal Reserve System', in G Toniolo (ed.), *Central Banks' Independence in Historical Perspective* (Berlin: Walter de Grayter, 1988)

The German financial system

18.1   Introduction

In the past 30 years the German economy has emerged as the strongest in Europe and its financial system has acquired an outstanding reputation for stability. For example, in Chapter 21 we note that other countries have tried, in various ways, to link their currency to the Deutschmark in order to acquire some of the 'credibility' which it enjoys as a currency with a low risk of depreciation.

The strength of the Deutschmark is often said to be the result of certain institutional features of the German financial system, in particular the independence of the central bank, the Bundesbank. This is not the whole story, as we shall see in the next section. A more fundamental explanation takes us back to Germany's economic and financial history. More than any other European country in the

Twentieth century, Germany has suffered the effects of violent currency fluctuations.

The first and most spectacular of these had its origins in the financing of Germany's 1914–18 war efforts, when the Reichsbank, the central bank, had provided finance to the government by accepting large quantities of treasury bills. This is as close as it is possible to get to financing a budget deficit by 'printing money' in a modern financial system. The government issues its own treasury bills and the central bank credits the government account with corresponding deposits. As government deposits were spent, the broad money supply increased by a corresponding amount and, naturally enough, notes and coin increased in step as some of the deposits were converted to cash. An indication of the rate of expansion is given by the fact that notes and coin in circulation increased by 50–60 per cent per year, 1917–1921. After 1920, punitive reparations payments imposed by the allies made matters worse. The payments had to be made in US dollars and the only means of paying for these dollars, given the state of the German economy, was to buy them with Marks created by selling treasury bills to the Reichsbank. While war finance was the cause of the emergency, the Reichsbank occasionally protested at the unorthodox methods of finance but once the cause of the deficits was seen to be 'unfair' reparations imposed by the allies, the Reichsbank gave up and agreed that "… it would continue to take into its reserves all the treasury bills the government wished to issue' (Marsh, 1992 p.99). Predictably, the Mark fell rapidly in value against other currencies and, in an attempt to end the process, in 1922 the allies forced the passage of a law making the Reichsbank independent of government. It made not the slightest difference and the episode is thus an interesting illustration of the limited power of independence. Independent central banks succeed in the pursuit of low inflation because the community wants them to succeed. Where there is a view that inflation has some merit (as a means of undermining unfair reparations) central bank independence can achieve very little. Consumer prices rose at an exponential rate. At the worst, in 1923, prices rose nearly 2 billionfold. When stabilization finally occurred in November 1923[1] the exchange rate was M4.2 trillion per US dollar.[2] At inflation rates of this magnitude, conventional payment systems, based on money, collapse and exchange takes the form of barter, with all the inefficiencies and disruption that follow. Savings in the form of financial wealth, especially where the assets are of fixed nominal value, are also destroyed.

The hyperinflation of 1922–3 is now more than 70 years away. But there was a more recent reminder of its effects, particularly upon savings, in the conversion of the Mark in another post-war setting, in 1948. The Reichsmark, as it had by then become, was virtually worthless and, under allied supervision, the Bank Deutscher Länder, forerunner of the Bundesbank, embarked on a process of converting Reichsmarks into Deutschmarks. Current payments, including wages and salaries, were converted at a one-for-one basis in June 1948. But savings, when converted in October 1948, were converted at the rate of DM6.50 to RM100. Once again, financial wealth was drastically reduced.

It is this experience that has made *all* German institutions and administrations strongly inflation averse (and also perhaps more risk averse) than those of other countries. These aversions predate the Bundesbank's success. They explain *why* the Bundesbank was established with such a high degree of independence and they explain why the Bundesbank has had a comparatively simple task in maintaining low rates of inflation: it has enjoyed widespread support throughout German society. The aversions and the low inflation record also explain

some other characteristics of the German financial system which we shall touch on in this chapter, particularly the low levels of equity holdings in household portfolios and the correspondingly low levels of equity finance in German firms.

In the rest of this chapter we shall look at German banks and other deposit-taking institutions (in Section 18.2); at non-deposit-taking institutions (in Section 18.3) and at the use of bond and equity markets by institutions and households (in Section 18.4).

18.2   Banks and other deposit-taking institutions[3]

The central bank in Germany is the Bundesbank. It was formally established in 1957 with a constitution that made the stability of the currency its principal objective. Its constitution also stresses its independence from government, though the Bundesbank is technically owned by the central government, which has the power to appoint the president and and other members of the directorate. The Bundesbank is organized along federal lines. Each state (Land) has a central bank (effectively regional offices of the Bundesbank) and each of these has one representative on the governing body of the Bundesbank. So far as the mechanical aspects of central banking are concerned, commercial banks hold operational balances with the Land central bank, which maintains balances with the Bundesbank in Frankfurt. Intra-regional payments are thus reflected in banks' balances at the Land central bank while net tranfers between banks in different regions will be reflected in changed Land central bank balances at the Bundesbank. Unlike the Bank of England, the Bundesbank is not responsible for supervision of the banking system. This is the job of the Federal Banking Supervisory Office, although the data required for monitoring bank behaviour is collected and published monthly by the Bundesbank as part of a whole series of banking statistics (see Deutsche Bundesbank *Banken Statistik* (monthly)).

---

1 By linking the note issue to the value of agricultural and industrial land, a commodity in (relatively) fixed supply. See Marsh (1992) Ch. 4 for details.
2 1 trillion = 1,000 billion.

3 The data relating to different types of German banks in this section comes mainly from Deutsche Bundesbank, *Monthly Report*, January 1997, Table IV(3).

Its constitution obviously gives the Bundesbank an overwhelming responsibility for the conduct of monetary policy. In this it is often portrayed as an institution firmly committed to a rigid policy of tight money where tight money corresponds to strict control of the money supply along the lines of a textbook exposition of monetarism. As we saw in Table 9.2 the Bundesbank certainly has published monetary targets for longer than any other European central bank, and it has certainly had more success in achieving them. However, there has been a great deal of pragmatism in Bundesbank policy over the years. Firstly, targets are set only for one year at a time. Longer-term targets have always been dismissed as unrealistic – an interesting contrast with the UK government's experiment with medium-term targets. Furthermore, the money supply and inflation targets are set in the light of what seems reasonable. There is no attempt to use monetary policy to combat 'unavoidable inflation'. If, in the course of the year, other inflation indicators conflict with the money supply figures, the money supply targets may be overwritten. Above all the approach '... underlines the Bundesbank's conviction that control of the money supply for the sake of combating inflation and ensuring steady economic growth can only be successful if the policies and behaviour of public authorities, enterprises and trade unions are guided by the same objectives'. Banks are subject to mandatory reserve ratios but the system uses lagged reserve accounting – reserves today must match deposits at an earlier date – and thus the Bundesbank makes no attempt to control reserves directly. Like other central banks it provides reserves on demand to ensure the stability of the financial system. Also like other central banks, the Bundesbank varies short-term interest rates to influence the *demand* for reserves (and thus the rate of monetary growth).[4]

Unlike the UK, USA and Japan, Germany has a tradition of *universal banking*. This means that any recognized bank is able to provide a full range of banking services and many other services that elsewhere would be called financial rather than banking services. Thus they can offer the usual range of retail banking services but also engage in wholesale and investment banking. They can even buy and sell securities on behalf of customers. In the UK and USA it often appears that a single bank offers this range of services but strictly speaking it does this only by creating separately capitalized subsidiaries with names similar to the parent. Switzerland also has a tradition of universal banking while Spain, France and the Netherlands lie somewhere between the universal and the segmented traditions.

That said, it does not follow that banks are *obliged* to offer a full range of services with equal emphasis. Box 18.2 lists the categories of banking institutions recognized by the Federal Banking Supervisory Office. Banking statistics are published by the Bundesbank using these categories and a summary of recent figures appears in Table 18.1.

Using the concept of universal banking it is possible to divide the list of institutions into two groups: universal banks and specialist credit

---

Box 18.2   The classification of German banks

Universal banks

Commercial banks
   The 'Big 3' banks
   Regional banks and other commercial banks
   Branches of foreign banks
   Private bankers

Regional giro institutions

Savings banks

Regional institutions of credit co-operatives

Credit co-operatives

Specialized credit institutions

Mortgage banks

Credit institutions with special functions
   Deutsche Postbank AG
   Building and loan associations
   Instalment credit banks
   Other specialist banks

---

4 This passage is based on evidence given by representatives of the Bundesbank to the UK Treasury and Civil Service Select Committee in November 1980. The evidence is particularly revealing of just how limited the Bundesbank feels its power to be and how heavily it relies on pushing in the direction that public opinion in general wishes to go.

Table 18.1 Selected assets and liabilities of German banks, November 1996 (DMmn)

Institution	Number	Volume of business	Assets					Liabilities					Total assets
			Cash & balances with central banks	Bills	Other securities	Advances	Other	Sight deposits	Time deposits	Savings deposits	Capital	Other	
Big 3	3	760	9	14	114	561	54	211	272	87	55	127	752
Regional and other commercial banks[1]	193	1,061	7	12	137	803	60	198	403	61	62	194	1,018
Branches of foreign banks	72	110	<1	3	18	82	6	25	69	0	2	16	109
Private banks[2]	63	53	<1	1	6	42	2	17	20	4	8	3	38
Savings banks	607	1,585	26	9	398	1,069	51	253	363	575	63	299	1,553
Regional giro institutions	13	1,500	2	5	174	1,175	70	180	616	20	49	561	1,426
Credit co-operatives	2,513	925	16	5	182	667	30	143	247	324	44	142	900
Regional institutions of credit co-operatives	4	302	<1	2	76	189	16	76	143	0	11	54	284
Mortgage banks	34	1,113	<1	<1	31	1,036	39	18	382	<1	26	680	1,107
Other specialist credit institutions	18	779	6	<1	92	602	16	143	324	58	25	167	

Source: Based upon data in Deutsche Bundesbank, *Monthly Report*, January 1997, table IV(3). Notes:[1] includes private banks which are not sole proprietor or partnerships; [2] excludes private banks which are not sole proprietor or partnerships

institutions. Universal banks in turn comprise the commercial banks, the saving banks and the credit co-operatives, while remaining banks comprise the specialist category. When we go into more detail in a moment we shall see that the reason for distinguishing between commercial banks, savings banks and credit co-operatives is not because their functions differ – their names may suggest this but since they all offer 'universal' services this cannot be the case – but because their ownership structure is very different. Commercial banks are private sector institutions; savings banks are public sector institutions while credit co-operatives are 'mutuals'. We look first at the universal group and then at the specialized institutions.

Commercial banks are privately owned banks, ranging in size from the 'Big 3' (Dresdner, Commerz- and Deutscher Bank), through regional banks, branches of foreign banks to private banks. The Big 3 (the *Großbanken*) all date from the beginnings of the unified German state in the 1870s. As universal banks they offer retail, wholesale and investment banking though, by comparison with other universal banks, their business is concentrated especially in investment banking, the financing of firms, and foreign trade. Only in recent years have they made a major effort to compete for retail deposits. The Großbanken account for approximately 10 per cent of all banking business in Germany.

Smaller, but still significant among commercial banks, are some regionally based banking groups such as the Bayerische Veriensbank and the Berliner Handels und Frankfurter Bank (the *Regionalbanken*). Their description as 'regional' banks is a reference to their geographical origin and the fact that their branches are still concentrated in the region of origin. They have branches throughout Germany (and abroad), however, and they are joint stock limited companies in the same way as the Big 3.

Much smaller in aggregate, though more numerous, are the branches of foreign banks (*Zweigstellen ausländischer Banken*) and private banks (*Privatbankiers*). The German financial system has always been fairly open to foreign participation and currently some 70 foreign banks have branches in Germany, mostly operating in Frankfurt. At the end of 1996 there was a similar number of private banks, though the trends for the two groups are very different with more foreign banks coming to Germany, while the number of private banks has been in steep decline since 1939 (when there were over 500). Private banks are mainly concerned with the issue of and dealing in securities. In that sense they are similar to investment banks in the UK, though they are much smaller. Those that are independent of the Big 3 and the large regional banks are mainly private limited companies or partnerships.

Savings banks (*Sparkassen*) constitute the second category of universal banks. In 1996 they numbered over 600 with about 20,000 branches. Many date from the Nineteenth century when they were founded by local and regional government authority. Their function was to provide finance for local and regional infrastructure and to make loans to disadvantaged groups in the local population. This was done by attracting small retail deposits from households and firms. Thus it was the savings banks that were in the strongest position to develop a cheque payment system which they did after 1900 by associating themselves with a regional 'girobank' which conducted the clearing operations. The regional girobanks developed later into what are often called the *Landesbanken* which became large universal banks (while savings banks have maintained their emphasis on retail deposit taking). The *Westdeutsche Landesbank-Girozentrale* indeed is the fourth largest bank and, together with the *Byerische Landesbank Girozentrale* and the *Hesse Landesbank Girozentrale*, it offers a full range of banking services including international banking. The solvency of savings banks is guaranteed by the owning public authority which imposes some restrictions on bank business, steering them away from the riskiest activities. In return they are subject to lower capital adequacy requirements than commercial banks.

Co-operative banks (*Kreditgenossenschaften*) constitute the third category of universal banks and are, as their name implies, mutual organizations owned by their members. Their origin was often linked to particular trades and professions, deposits being taken from members of the profession and loans being made to enterprises in that field, the objective being to further the interests of the profession. Such banks are quite common in continental Europe. The biggest and best known – with obvious origins – is France's *Crédit Agricole*. In Germany there are over 2500 with some 16,000 branches. There are many similarities between the savings and co-operative bank sectors. The individual co-ops have, for example, remained committed largely to retail deposit business on the liability side while making loans to a regional co-operative bank on the asset side. As with the *Landesbanken*, it is these regional co-operatives (called *Genossenschaftliche Zentralbanken*) that are the genuinely universal banks.

The universal banking sector of the German financial system therefore consists of three categories of bank, distinguished by type of ownership – private, public and mutual. We turn next to the specialist credit institutions. These, obviously, are classified by function; we shall find various patterns of ownership within each category.

Germany has both *mortgage* banks (*Hypotheken-banken*) and *building and loan associations* (*Bausparkassen*). Both accept deposits but also finance their lending by the sale of bonds known as Pfandbriefen. Legally, the Hypothekenbanken are usually private companies while the Bausparkassen are owned by public authorities or are mutuals. The function of both is to provide finance for construction though the mortgage banks have also taken up considerable holdings of general government debt. Rather like the UK building society sector, the Bausparkassen have benefited from the increasing aspiration of people to own their own homes and from tax incentives which encourage borrowing for home purchase.

The instalment credit banks are mostly sub-sidiaries of the biggest commercial banks. Their lending consists largely of overdrafts to customers who also hold deposits with the bank and have their main income credited to an account held at the bank.

The remaining specialized credit institutions are institutions established by the state for some specific purpose, often linked to post-war reconstruction problems. They include the Equalization of Burdens Bank (*Lastenausgleichsbank*) whose main function was to settle claims for damages and to help with restitution claims by refugees. The Reconstruction Loan Corporation (*Kreditanstalt für Wiederaufbrau*) was founded in 1948 to administer public funds for reconstruction purposes and now handles much of Germany's aid to developing countries. There are also specialist institutions dealing with the requirements of forestry and agriculture. There is also a Post Office Savings Bank (*Deutsche Postbank*) which holds personal sector deposits and operates a payments mechanism.

18.3 Non-deposit institutions

When we compare the German financial system with that of the UK or the USA, the first striking feature is the *presence* of 'universal' banks which we discussed in the previous section. The second is the *absence* of pension funds. In both the USA and the UK, pension funds constitute a major division of the 'institutional' investors and the importance of their behaviour, in securities markets in particular, is considerable. In Germany, however, the major provider of pensions is the state which operates a

---

Box 18.3 Financial assets of German non-bank institutional investors

End-of-year figures

Item	1970	1980	1990	1995
Insurance enterprises DM billion				
With banks[1]	11.6	81.1	297.9	493.3
In shares	7.8	15.9	114.9	209.4
In debt securities	16.6	56.2	121.9	204.6
In investment fund certificates	0.7	9.0	71.2	162.9
In other forms[2]	48.9	121.2	218.9	261.7
Total	85.6	283.3	824.8	1332.0
Percentages				
With banks[1]	13.6	28.6	36.1	37.0
In shares	9.0	5.6	13.9	15.7
In debt securities	19.6	19.8	14.8	15.4
In investment fund securities	0.8	3.2	8.6	12.2
In other forms[2]	57.1	42.8	26.5	19.6
Total	100	100	100	100

Item	1970	1980	1990	1995
Investment funds DM Billion				
With banks[1]	0.9	3.7	26.1	32.2
In shares	5.0	12.4	44.5	127.0
In debt securities	4.2	27.9	153.0	330.0
In other forms[3]	.	.	4.3	40.0
Total	10.1	44.0	228.0	529.2
Percentages				
With banks[1]	8.9	8.4	11.4	6.1
In shares	49.5	28.2	19.5	24.0
In debt securities	41.6	63.4	67.1	62.4
In other forms	.	.	1.9	7.6
Total	100	100	100	100

[1] Primarily time deposits, including registered debt securities and claims on banks arising from borrowers' notes.
[2] Mortgages, claims arising from borrowers' notes and book-entry securities as well as participating interest in non-banks.
[3] Primarily loans against borrowers' notes.
Source: Deutsche Bundesbank

pay-as-you-go (as opposed to a *funded*) system in which pensions are paid out of current taxation; no investment fund is created. Where companies operate a pension scheme, they retain contributions within the firm as working capital so that pension payments are a charge on the firms' profits. For savers who wish to make further provision for old age, there are tax incentives to do so by subscribing to life insurance policies and, as we shall see, insurance companies have grown rapidly in recent years. In common with other European countries, Germany now has a rising proportion of retired to working population which is beginning to cause problems for the state scheme. It seems likely, therefore, that the future will see increasing private sector provision of pensions but that in itself does not necessarily mean the growth of a 'pension fund sector'. It may simply mean the further expansion of insurance companies.

The two major non-bank groups of financial institutions in Germany therefore are the insurance companies, which function as we described for insurance companies in Section 15.3, and the investment funds which function broadly as closed-end mutual funds. They occupy a similar position to unit trust companies in the UK, though the instruments held by savers are known as 'certificates' rather than 'units'.

Box 18.3 gives some impression of the recent rates of growth of the two groups of institutions. It also shows the distribution of their asset holdings.

The difference in size is immediately apparent (the combined assets of UK insurance companies converted at the current exchange rate would amount to approximately DM1600bn). Rapidly though insurance companies have grown, starting from a much smaller base investment companies have grown rather faster. Looking at the distribution of asset holdings, it is apparent that investment funds hold much higher proportions of securities. The 15 per cent holdings of equities and bonds by German insurance companies is very small by comparison with Anglo-Saxon life companies. Although equity holdings are much larger as a proportion of

investment fund assets, that proportion is small too compared with UK unit trust exposure to equities. The striking feature of investment fund asset portfolios is the importance of bond holdings. These have increased, relative to equity holdings while for insurance companies the trend has been in the opposite direction, with equity holdings catching up with bonds.

18.4 The use of bond and equity markets in Germany

Universal banks and the lack of a pension funds sector are just two of the distinctive features of the German financial system. Others, which we shall discuss in this section, are:

- the limited use of equity finance by firms;
- the small size of equity markets relative to GDP;
- the small number of publicly quoted firms;
- the portfolio preference amongst households for deposits and bonds over equity;
- the dominant role of bank intermediation in channelling funds from surplus to deficit units.

Notice that most of these statements refer to *stocks* of assets and liabilities. In other words they refer to the position as it has built up over the years. This contrasts with the magnitudes that we discussed in Chapter 15. There we were concerned with *flows* (of financing) in recent years.

Plainly, these characteristics are interrelated: if firms have historically avoided equity finance it follows that households must hold alternative assets. Nonetheless, we take each in turn.

As in other countries, there are two main forms of corporate ownership in Germany: public, limited liability joint stock companies (AGs)[5] (which separate ownership and control) and private limited companies (GmbHs)[6]. The latter outnumber the former in Germany by nearly 100 to 1 (400,000 to 4000). Indeed, through the 1960s and 1970s the number of AGs actually declined though this was reversed in the 1980s. This picture is confirmed in

---

5 *Aktiengesellschaft.* Equivalent to plc in the UK or corporation in the USA.

6 *Gesellschaft mit beschränkter Haftung.* (Private) limited company or 'Ltd' in UK terms.

Box 18.4   The financial structure of German firms

End-of-year figures

Item	1970	1980	1990	1995		Item	1970	1980	1990	1995
DM billion						Percentages				
Bank loans[1]	263.8	652.2	1,224.9	1,764.4		Bankloans[1]	46.8	51.4	47.8	48.5
shares in circulation	155.0	244.5	604.2	980.2		Shares in circulation	27.5	19.3	23.2	26.9
Pension commitments	26.0	89.4	197.3	252.6		Pension commitments	4.6	7.0	7.6	6.9
Total	563.3	1,268.3	2,604.2	3,638.6		Total	100	100	100	100

Outside funds including volume of shares in circulation according to the financial assets and liabilities account; from 1990 onwards Germany as a whole.
[1] From domestic and foreign banks.

Source: Deutsche Bundesbank

the figures in Box 18.4 which shows the historic dependence of enterprises on bank finance and the dip in shares in circulation between in the 1970s.

Three reasons for the unpopularity of AG status for many years were the relatively high rates of corporation tax in Germany which gives a large subsidy to (tax-deductible) interest payments on bonds; the legal requirement of a two-tier management board structure which requires worker representation; and a long tradition of family ownership and control of firms in Germany, which can be preserved as a GmbH. The latter has developed in recent years into a fear of the short-termism and instability of corporate control alleged to be characteristics of Anglo-Saxon economies where AG (plc) status is the norm for large firms. We discussed this issue in Section 15.2.

If firms do not issue shares, households cannot hold them. The table in Box 18.5 shows this clearly. In 1995, German households held more than 40 per cent of their financial assets in bank deposits. This is a significant reduction on the position in 1970 but it is notable that bank assets have been replaced by bonds and by investment fund certificates. Direct shareholdings have actually fallen, though most of the fall occurred in the 1970s. Remember too that investment funds are small and shares form only 24 per cent of their portfolios, so it is difficult to argue

that households have replaced direct shareholdings with indirect ownership. As we said in the opening to this chapter, part of the reason for these preferences lies in the risk aversion of the German public following an exceptionally turbulent financial history. That turbulence has led to a widespread anti-inflation consensus and with sustained low inflation rates one of the main incentives to equity holding disappears. Taxation has also worked against household equity investment for part of the period, subjecting shareholders to double taxation (taxation of the company's profits and then taxation of the dividends paid to shareholders) and high rates of capital gains tax.

The effect of all this is shown in Box 18.6 where we can see that the German equity market is comparatively large, so long as we focus only on the value of shares in issue. Once we compare the value of those equities with the size of the economy (measured by GDP), Germany plunges down the league table.

In recent years, governments have tried to tip the balance further towards equity financing and shareholding. Tax reforms in 1977 abolished the double taxation of dividend income and introduced a capital gains tax exemption for gains on shares held for more than six months. More recently, in 1994, the Companies Act was amended to simplify the

Box 18.5 Financial assets of households*

End-of-year figures

Item	1970	1980	1990	1995	Item	1970	1980	1990	1995
DM billion					Percentages				
With banks[1]	314.3	886.9	1,553.7	2,024.8	with banks[1]	59.9	59.8	48.7	43.6
With insurance enterprises[2]	77.8	246.2	646.6	988.6	with insurance enterprises[2]	14.8	16.6	20.3	21.3
In shares	53.6	61.7	175.0	245.6	in shares	10.2	4.2	5.5	5.3
In debt securities	35.8	152.8	450.7	741.1	in debt securities	6.8	10.3	14.1	15.9
In investment fund certificates	10.1	29.5	132.9	353.4	in investment fund certificates	1.9	2.0	4.2	7.6
Total	524.3	1,483.5	3,187.6	4,647.6	Total	100	100	100	100

*Including private non-profit organisations; from 1990 onwards Germany as a whole
[1] Including building and loan associations.
[2] Including pension funds.

Source: Deutsche Bundesbank

formation of an AG and also removed employees' rights of co-determination, for AGs with fewer than 500 employees. When Deutsche Telekom was privatized in November 1996 the flotation was designed, like UK privatizations in the 1980s, with features to appeal to personal shareholders. It remains to be seen whether this, and other planned privatizations, do much to fire an enthusiasm for

Box 18.6 Equity markets compared: Market capitalization in selected OECD countries

End November 1996

Country	Shares in circulation in DM billion[1]	Market capitalization coefficient[2]	Country	Shares in circulation in DM billion[1]	Market capitalization coefficient[2]
United States[3]	13,354	122	Italy	386	23
Japan[4]	4,881	63	Sweden	357	103
United Kingdom	2,544	152	Spain[6]	332	39
Germany	1,002	27	Belgium	180	44
France	892	38	Denmark	105	40
Canada[5]	756	88	Finland	90	47
Switzerland	624	135	Norway	85	38
Netherlands	555	93	Austria	48	14

[1]Market value of domestic listed shares
[2]Shares incirculation as % of the 1995 nominal gross domestic product
[3]New York Stock Exchange and NASDAQ
[4]Tokyo Stock Exchange
[5]Toronto Stock Exchange
[6]Madrid Stock Exchange

Source: Deutsche Bundesbank, Fédération Internationale des Bourses des Valeurs and own calculations.

equity investment. But it may be worth noting that the Federal Government disposed of holdings in several major undertakings during the 1960s and did so on terms designed to attract broad groups of shareholders. The initial sales of these *Volksaktien* were initially successful but within a few years most had found their way to institutional investors – a story rather similar to that of the UK in the 1990s.

18.5   Summary

The German financial system is one which, historically speaking, has been dominated by banks. Consequently, financial flows have been channelled through credit institutions rather than through markets. The result is that firms' balance sheets show high levels of bank finance, followed by bond finance, with equity finance in a minority role. This has further consequences: Germany has relatively few public limited companies, and security markets, although absolutely large by comparison with some countries, are small relative to the German economy as a whole. Inevitably, therefore, households' asset portfolios are dominated by bank instruments, with equities, held directly or indirectly, playing a very small part.

The reasons for this are partly historical, resulting from Germany's turbulent financial history which has created strong inflation aversion, making fixed interest and fixed nominal value assets relatively attractive. Pension funds, major participants in securities markets elsewhere, are largely absent in Germany because existing pension arrangements make them unnecessary. Additionally, there is a corporate culture which has favoured private ownership and the private conduct of business generally. Until recently, public limited liability status was also discouraged by tax and other regulatory measures. These have diminished in recent years and it may be that the immediate future will see an increase in market mediation, particularly if there is a change towards 'funded' pension arrangements.

Key concepts used in this chapter

Universal banking	Specialist credit institutions
Commercial banks	Pay-as-you-go pension scheme
Großbanken	Funded pension scheme
Regional banks	AG
Private banks	GmbH
Co-operative banks	

Questions and problems

1 Why has the Bundesbank placed such strong emphasis upon maintaining low rates of inflation? Comment on the significance of

(a) 'independence' of the Bundesbank; and

(b) popular support in helping to achieve that objective.

2 Explain what is meant by 'universal banking'.

3 Distinguish between 'commercial banks', 'savings banks' and 'co-operative banks'.

4 Why does Germany have a very small pension fund sector?

5 How would you explain the comparatively small role historically played by equities in the financing of German firms and in German household asset portfolios?

Further reading

Deutsche Bundesbank, *Monthly Reports* (Frankfurt am Main: Deutsche Bundesbank)

Deutsche Bundesbank, *Banken Statistik* (Frankfurt am Main: Deutsche Bundesbank)

J Edwards and K Fischer, *Banks, Finance and Investment in Germany* (Cambridge: Cambridge U P, 1993)

L Größl, 'Banking Groups in the Federal Republic of Germany and their Relationships with Industrial Companies', *Research Papers in Banking and Finance*, No. 90/27 (Bangor: Institute of European Finance, 1990)

H-H Francke and M Hudson, *Banking and Finance in West Germany* (London: Croom-Helm, 1984)

D Marsh, The Bundesbank (London: Heinemann, 1992)

J Story, 'The Politics and Markets of German Financial Services' *Institute for German Studies Discussion Paper*, No. IGS95/3 (Birmingham: University of Birmingham, 1995)

N Walter and R Von Rosen (eds), *German Financial Markets* (Cambridge: Woodhead Publishers Ltd) Chs 3–6

CHAPTER 19

The French and Italian financial systems

Box 19.1

What you will learn in this chapter:

- The main features of the French and Italian banking systems
- The size and significance of non-depository institutions
- The comparatively small use made of equity finance by French and Italian firms in the past
- The role of social and political influences upon the past development of the systems
- Some comparisons and contrasts with the financial system of Spain

19.1 Introduction

For many years there has been a tradition of describing France as an '*overdraft economy*'. This term originated in the work of J R Hicks in 1974 and describes an economy in which the flow of funds between surplus and deficit units takes place largely through intermediaries, that is, banks rather than through markets. In simpler language, we might say that such economies rely on 'indirect' rather than 'direct' finance. It is essentially the same distinction that we first met in Chapter 15 where we distinguished between 'bank-based' and 'market-based' financial systems.

Recall that in Chapter 15 we issued some words of warning about this distinction, based on recent research which showed that if we looked at the flows of funds going to finance firms' investment in recent years, it is difficult to make the market–bank distinction. However, we need to remember that creditors' (debtors') portfolios comprise assets (liabilities) which have accumulated as the result of past patterns of financing so that when we look at firms' balance sheets, or households' financial savings, there may be very considerable differences between what we find in one country and another even though current patterns of financing may be converging. Thus, while the market–bank distinction may not be very helpful in describing current patterns of corporate financing it may still be useful when it comes to looking at balance sheets and at the structure of the financial system. Both of these depend to a great extent on what has happened in the past.

Until the 1970s it certainly was reasonable to describe France as a bank-based or overdraft economy, whether one focused on stocks or flows. However, since the 1970s there have been numerous changes (which we note below) which have moved the French financial system more towards the use of markets. In this respect, there are similarities between the French and the German systems (as we saw in the previous chapter). As in Germany, the French financial system is dominated by banks, and securities markets are (relative to the UK, USA and Japan) underdeveloped. Correspondingly, firm and household balance sheets are still dominated by bank instruments, but the picture is changing quickly.

Another characteristic of the French financial system is that historically it has always been highly centralized and regulated. We shall see later that most major banks are still nationalized. Furthermore, the changes that have taken place in recent years have been much more closely connected to decisions by the French state to change the regulatory framework than is generally the case in other countries where

---

> ## Box 19.2 Credit institutions in France
>
> ### Short-term deposit takers
> - Major banks, members of the *Association Français des Banques*
> - Mutual and co-operative banks
>   *Crédit Muteul*
>   *Crédit Coopératif*
>   *Crédit Maritime Mutuel*
>   *Crédit Agricole Mutuel*
>   *Crédit Populaire*
> - Savings banks, *Caisses d'Epargne*
> - *Crédit Municipal*
>
> ### Specialist 'credit institutions'
> - Financial companies
> - *Crédit Foncier de France* (land bank)
> - *Crédit National* (industry and service)
> - *Comptoirs des Entrepeneurs* (housing finance)
> - *Crédit Local de France* (local authorities)
> - *Société Française d'Assurance du capital-risque des PME*
> - *MATIF* (futures and options markets)
> - *Société de Développment Régional* (regional and overseas aid)
> - Licensed money brokers
> - Securities houses

they have been spontaneous responses on the part of the private sector to changed financial conditions.

Between 1945 and 1984 French banking regulation favoured the specialization of banking institutions. This contrasts with the German tradition of 'universal' banking which we looked at in the previous chapter. However, by the early 1980s three things were apparent. Firstly, the increasing trend toward a single European market was opening the French financial system to competition. Secondly, banks in other European countries, subject to lighter regulation, were better placed to exploit economies of scope. Thirdly, plans to encourage the development of French securities markets might cause a rapid switch of bank clients to deal directly in markets if the banking system remained compartmentalized and required agents to deal with several banks at once. The result was the Banking Act of 1984 which, in spite of its title, has implications for almost all financial institutions and even for markets.

This defines 'credit institution' as one which engages in *any one* of the following:

- issuing means of payment;
- deposit-taking;
- extending loans.

The first thing that we should note is that 'credit institution' means something much wider than 'bank'. The Act covers non-deposit institutions and even includes organizations responsible for operating securities markets in France. Thus, within this broad

category we can distinguish between those institutions that accept sight and short-term deposits, the nearest to 'banks' in the conventional sense, and 'others' with more specialized functions which stretch away into non-deposit business. Within 'banks' again there is a further division we can make, based sometimes on function but sometimes on ownership patterns. Box 19.2 makes all this clearer.

Broad as the institutions covered by the 1984 Act are, there are some obviously credit institutions which are excluded. These are:

- The Trésor Public
- The Banque de France
- Postal financial services
- The Caisse de Dépôts et Consignations

In the rest of this chapter we shall look firstly, in Section 19.2, at the structure and operation of the banking sector. This will include those institutions listed in Box 19.2 as 'short-term deposit takers' together with most of the institutions we have just listed as excluded from the Banking Act 1984. We then turn, in Section 19.3, to specialist and non-deposit institutions (the lower part of Box 19.2). Then in Section 19.4 we look at financial markets and their importance.

In Sections 19.5 and 19.6 we move on to look at the Italian financial system which definitely remains bank-based. It contrasts, however, with the French system in that one part of the securities market has become highly developed – the market for public sector debt. Corporate finance has come almost entirely from retained earnings and borrowing from banks. Having identified key features of the Italian system, we consider the possibility that it is similar to that of Spain which in many ways has a similar economy. A brief view of the Spanish financial system in Section 19.7 shows that it is different from that of Italy in a number of ways, confirming the view that national financial systems are highly individual. The one thing that all the financial systems we have looked at have in common is that they have been subject to great change in recent years. As usual, the final section, 19.8, summarizes.

19.2 The French banking system

As with other banking systems, it is reasonable to begin our review by starting with the most central organizations and then to work down to local institutions. The *Banque de France* is France's central bank. (It is one of just three institutions we discuss in this chapter which falls outside the terms of the Banking Law.) Founded in 1800, the *Banque* was nationalized in 1945. It was made 'autonomous' from government by legislation in 1993 but it remains a limited company whose capital is 100 per cent owned by the state. It is headed by a Governor and two deputies, appointed by the government for a term of six years, renewable once. The 1993 Act protects them from being dismissed except by reason of criminal acts. The main decision-making bodies within the Banque are the *Conseil de la Politique Monétaire* and the *Conseil Général*, the former having responsibility for monetary policy and the latter looking after day-to-day administrative matters. The government also makes appointments to these bodies for fixed terms but with similar protection. As the central bank, the Banque de France manages the government accounts, the foreign exchange reserves and holds the operational deposits of commercial banks. It is also charged with overall responsibility for the regulation and stability of the banking system though its regulatory functions in practice are delegated to three other national bodies.

The first of these is the *Comité des Etablissements de Crédit*. This is chaired by the Governor of the

Banque de France and is largely concerned with the issuing of banking licences and the allocation of licence holders to one of the categories listed in Box 19.2. It also has powers to intervene when change of ownership of a bank is proposed.

The *Comité de Réglementation Bancaire* (chaired by the Minister of Finance) is responsible for specifying liquidity, capital and solvency ratios. It also approves banks' internal supervisory arrangements.

The *Commission Bancaire* (chaired by the Governor) is responsible for monitoring compliance with regulations laid down by the other two bodies and has extensive powers to impose sanctions in cases of violation.

A fourth central body, the *Conseil National de Crédit*, has an advisory or consultative role relating to the operation of the financial system and the conduct of monetary policy. It is best known for the annual report that it produces on each of these.

The major banks in France are members of the *Association Française des Banques*. (For purposes of statistical reporting their aggregated data often appears under the heading 'AFB banks'). This group includes famous names like *Crédit Lyonnais*, *Banque National de Paris* (BNP), *Banque Paribas* and *Société Générale*. Since 1945 all the major French banks have experienced periods of state ownership. A wave of nationalization was justified in 1982, by a socialist government, on the grounds that small and medium-sized firms were at a persistent disadvantage and that the banks were reluctant to finance sections of industry which the government saw as being of strategic importance. The results were disappointing and since 1986 the movement towards private ownership has been justified by the need for banks to be able to raise more capital and have more freedom to compete in the emerging single market. Even so, the state has retained large stakes – directly or indirectly – in the privatized banks. Freedom of behaviour does not necessarily follow ownership, however. The Banque de France and the Ministry of Finance have always exercised considerable influence over the French banking system by the use of 'moral suasion'. Since the 1984 Act, AFB members have functioned more or less as universal banks, offering retail, investment and wholesale banking services and a money transmission mechanism. The AFB has about 400 members, a figure which has been fairly stable since the 1950s. In recent years they have been under great pressure from the mutual and co-operative banks and the savings banks (see below) for deposits.

Mutual and co-operative banks have broadly similar origins, structures and functions. They are owned by their 'members', usually their depositors. Their origins lie in the Nineteenth century when their purpose was to provide a source of credit for people with limited income. Because they did not need to earn a profit for shareholders, their lending rates would be comparatively low. The rates paid to members were also comparatively low but were nonetheless attractive to members who were mainly small depositors and not welcome at the larger private banks. So far as structure is concerned, we can take the *Crédit Mutuel* as typical of the group of mutual banks. At the base of the pyramid, there are local offices grouped into several co-operative companies. Each of the local offices is a member of a regional federation (22 in all). The function of the regional offices is to provide clearing facilities between local offices, to pool and on-lend their surpluses and to make loans to local offices where necessary (creating in effect an interbank market for mutuals). There are two national organizations: the *Caisse Centrale de Crédit Mutuel* and the *Cofédération Nationale de Crédit Mutuel*. The former acts as a bank to the regional organizations while the latter is a more 'political' body, speaking on behalf of the movement and representing their common interests.

The other co-operative and mutual banks are organized upon similar pyramid lines – local branches, regional offices and a national organization. Their objectives are also similar, taking deposits from and lending to members who tend to be households or local public bodies or co-operative and mutual organizations. As the names of the organizations suggest, their members tend to be drawn from a particular field of activity – fishing, agriculture and so on. The *Crédit Agricole* has been particularly succesful in competing for deposits with the large AFB banks.

Table 19.1 lists the 10 largest French banking companies (in descending order of balance sheet size) in 1994.

Table 19.1 The ten largest French banks (in descending order, by size of balance sheet) in 1994

1	Caisse Nationale de Crédit Agricole
2	Banque Nationale de Paris
3	Société Générale
4	Crédit Lyonnais
5	Banque de France
6	Caisse des Dépots et Consignations
7	Banque Paribas
8	Crédit Foncier de France
9	Crédit Local de France
10	Banque Indosuez

Source: INSEE, *Images Economiques des Entreprises au 1.1.94*, vol III (Paris: INSEE, 1996) p. 370

The *Crédit Populaire* was created in 1917, originally to provide credit to the small firm sector. They now function as universal banks. There are 33 regional institutions and two central ones, the *Chambre Syndicale des Banques Populaires* and the *Caisse Centrale des Banques Populaires*, whose functions parallel those of the two central bodies for the Crédit Mutuel.

The *Caisses d'Epargne*, savings banks, are also co-operative institutions providing a full range of services for retail depositors, with the distinctive features, however, that loans must not be for commercial and trade purposes and interest on deposits is tax-free up to a maximum threshold (Ffr 90,000 in 1994). Like the other financial networks, the savings bank have a regional layer of organization (the SOREFIs) and two national bodies. The *Centre National des Caisses d'Epargne et de Prévoyance* represents the interests of the movement and provides regulatory oversight while the *Caisse des Dépôts et Consignations* (CDC) manages the funds collected by the savings bank network.

The CDC is another institution whose activities fall outside the 1984 Banking Law provisions. It occupies a central role in the French financial system and participates extensively in the long-term securities markets. Although it takes deposits (indirectly via the Caisses d'Epargne) its activities are so extensive that we discuss it in more detail in the next section.

Municipal credit banks, collectively known as the *Crédit Municipal*, are established by local authorities. They accept deposits from the general public, again with an emphasis upon personal savings, and make loans to public sector employees and organizations. They also provide a home for the local authority's spare funds. Since each is created by its own local authority, each *Crédit Municipal* is independent of the others, but there is a national organization, the *Central Union des Crédit Municipaux*, which represents their common interests.

Finally, before leaving this list of deposit-taking, 'banking' institutions, we should note that the French postal service also offers money transmission services, clearing cheques drawn on generally small, retail deposits. It is not allowed to make loans. It also collects savings for the National Savings Fund, one of many funds managed by the CDC.

Table 19.2 gives some indication of the comparative size of these components of the French banking system.

We noted in the introduction to this chapter that the French financial system has traditionally been highly centralized and highly regulated. Both of these characteristics, as applied to the banking system, require further comment. With the development of a single market there is an inevitable tendency towards homogenization of systems, products and procedures. It is thus a common theme in the recent development of most European financial systems that rapid change has been necessary to meet the threat of competition posed by more lightly regulated institutions with a background in the UK (or even in the USA). France, Italy and Germany have all had to give more freedom to their banking systems in recent years. In France, for example, lending rates were controlled by the Banque de France until 1967. The legislation which liberalized lending rates also lifted restrictions on the opening of bank branches with the result that many

large banks opened new branches, one form of non-price competition, to the point where some areas of France became 'over banked'. Since 1986, banks have been closing branches in an attempt to cut costs and restore profits.

The deregulation of deposit rates has, however, been more gradual. The 1967 act actually prohibited interest payments on sight deposits, a state of affairs which was defended by banks for many years on the grounds that it enabled them to provide 'free' services on current accounts. The continuing controls on deposit rates was a major reason for the outbreak of *non-price* competition in the 1970s. Such restrictions create fertile ground for financial innovation to sidestep the controls. (See, for example, the development of US money market mutual funds in Chapter 23). By 1996 deposit rates and bank commissions, and fees generally, were deregulated. This was partly a response to circumventory innovations but also to the development of a single market, in which banks from most other countries paid market-determined rates on all deposits, and also to a desire to see greater clarity in the pricing of banking services, with explicit prices for each service and less cross-subsidization.

19.3 Specialist and non-deposit institutions

We look firstly at the institutions listed in the lower part of Box 19.2.

The term 'financial companies' covers a broad range of institutions engaged in a variety of financial activities. Most of these activities involve the renting or leasing of property and equipment or financing credit sales. In this respect, they are rather similar to the 'finance houses' that were a feature of the UK financial system in the 1960s and 1970s. As a rule (imposed by the *Comité de Réglementation Bancaire*) they are not allowed to take deposits.

The next group of institutions in the list can be best described as banks providing wholesale banking services to specialist sectors of the economy. The sectors concerned are generally clear from the title of the institution.

MATIF and the *Sociétés des Bourses Françaises* are the bodies responsible for the operation of the

Table 19.2 The French banking system (1994 data)

Type of bank	Number of firms	Turnover[1]
Central bank		477
AFB banks	478	593,804
Mutual and co-operative banks	2682	26,441
Savings banks	37	61
Other banking institutions	6	8

Source: Adapted from INSEE, *Images Economiques des Entreprises au 1.1.94*, vol III (Paris: INSEE, 1996) p.368.
[1] FFrmn.

futures and options markets and the stock market, respectively, while licensed money brokers are intermediaries operating in the interbank market.

Securities houses manage portfolios on behalf of clients in a manner similar to that of UK stockbrokers prior to 'Big Bang' in 1986. A similar service is offered by the major banks and both, banks and securities houses, provide mutual investment facilities through closed-end funds, known in France as SICAVs (*Sociétés d'Investissement à Capital Variable*).

Towards the end of the last section, we noted some of the activities of the *Caisse des Dépôts et Consignations*. The CDC is one of France's major institutional investors. We have seen that it collects funds from local savings banks and via the postal network. It also manages a number of public funds for the financing of specific activities such as the *Fond de Soutien des Rentes* (Pension Support Fund) and the *Caisse Nationale des Autoroutes* (National Motorways Fund). It also manages the National Provident Fund, a major source of life assurance for French savers. These activities make it a major participant in bond and equity markets.

In our classification of non-deposit-taking institutions in Chapter 15, we listed insurance companies, pension funds, unit trusts and investment trusts. These all have their counterparts in France (and, we shall see, in other countries too). But there are some differences of detail. The major insurance companies in France are major participants in securities markets, as they are in other countries but, as we have just seen, many people hold life insurance policies with the publicly owned CDC. Table 19.3 lists the major French insurance companies (life and general) in descending order of balance sheet size in 1994.

With pension funds, we meet a characteristic which is even more pronounced in the case of Germany. The size of pension fund activity depends, naturally enough, on the extent to which savers build up funds during their working life in order to draw an income in retirement. This in turn depends to a large degree upon government social policy. In Germany and in France there has been a long tradition of state pension provision and in state schemes it is common for those currently retired to draw pensions paid for directly from the taxes and other contributions of those in work. Such schemes are known as 'pay-as-you-go' schemes and consist of straightforward transfers. No fund is accumulated and financial markets and institutions, consequently, are by-passed. The basic state pension in the UK functions in a similar way, but in the UK, because the state pension is paid at a very low level, many people belong additionally to an employers' pension scheme and recently some have paid into private pension schemes of their own choosing. In both these cases contributions during working life accumulate in a fund which can be invested in long-term financial assets. To a considerable degree, therefore, the development, size and importance of markets for long-term securities like equities and bonds depend upon whether pensions are provided largely by the state (and therefore usually 'unfunded') or privately. In France, Germany and Italy where the tradition of state pensions is strong, the pension fund sector is comparatively underdeveloped. This is a situation that is slowly changing because of demographic pressures. The feasibility of a pay-as-you-go scheme depends critically upon the age structure of the population. If, say, seven or eight workers are paying taxes to support one retired person, the individual tax burden is acceptable; it may not be acceptable if the population as a whole 'ages' and each pensioner has to be supported by only three or four working taxpayers. Ageing populations are a characteristic particularly of Germany, but also at the moment of France and Italy. The introduction of tax-free equity-based savings schemes by Prime Minister Bérégovoy (see the next section) was a first step towards encouraging the private funding of pensions.

Table 19.3 Ten largest French insurance companies (in descending order by balance sheet size)

1	Union des Assurances de Paris Vie
2	Prévoyance Dialogue du Crédit Agricole
3	CNP Assurances
4	Assurances Générales de France Vie
5	Abbeille Vie
6	Gan Vie-Cie Française Assurances Vie
7	Groupama Vie
8	Nato Vie
9	Ecureil Vie
10	Les Assurances Fédérales-Vie

Source: INSEE, *Images Economiques des Entreprises au 1.1.94*, vol III (Paris: INSEE, 1996) p. 377

Table 19.4 French non-bank financial institutions (1994 data)

Institution	Number of firms	Turnover[1]
Finance companies	428	96,289
Securities houses	5057	21,201
Specialist credit institutions	556	91,663
Life assurance	187	311,529
General insurance	353	246,979
Pension funds	6	79
Reinsurance	44	28,700
Other	166	4,199

Source: Adapted from INSEE, Images Economiques des Entreprises au 1.1.94, vol III (Paris: INSEE, 1996) pp. 368 and 375.
[1] FFr mn.

Table 19.4 gives some indication of the comparative size of the non-bank components of the French financial system.

We have already noted that the French variant of the open-ended mutual fund is the SICAV (*Société d'Investissement à Capital Variable*). The equivalent of the closed-end fund is the FCP (*Fonds Communs de Placement*). As in the UK and USA, such mutual funds are popular methods of investing in long-term securities, though it is notable that in France there are many more SICAVs and FCPs which invest in short-term money market instruments than one finds in the UK. This reflects the rapid progress that was made in modernizing and expanding the French money markets in the 1980s (see below) and also the below-market rates paid on deposits until recently.

19.4   Financial markets in France

The high degree of regulation to which the French financial system was subject until recently affected financial markets as well as institutions. This regulation helped to maintain sharp segmentation between institutions and limited the development of securities markets. (Before 1985, there were no money market securities and the French 'money market' was, in effect, simply an interbank market.)

Several consequences naturally followed. Firstly, financial assets available to the general public were highly liquid, consisting either of 'money' or of savings deposits. According to Cobham and Serre (1996) money and short-term liquid savings accounted for 85 per cent of total financial assets available to savers as recently as 1978. From this in turn, it followed that banks and other financial intermediaries played a more important role (compared to markets) in the French financial system and that they had to perform a higher degree of maturity transformation than intermediaries in systems where securitization was commonplace.

Financial liberalization broadly defined was begun in 1966–67, with the deregulation of lending rates. But liberalization, applied to financial markets, began with the Barre Plan (1976–81) and continued through the 1980s with two related strands. The first was to encourage the setting up of new markets and the modernization of existing ones. Trading in money market securities began in 1985, with CDs (see Chapter 9); this was followed in 1986 by the futures market, MATIF[1]; the options market, MONEP[2], opened in 1988; while at the same time the French stock market was opened up to French and foreign banks, acting in dual capacity in the style of post-Big Bang London (see Chapter 10). The second strand sought to encourage the flow of new savings towards securities. The SICAVs developed after the Monory Law of 1978 encouraged investment in French company shares (the earliest UK unit trusts by comparison date from the 1930s) and received a boost from the development of money market securities after 1985. Money market funds have since become very popular, helped by a ceiling placed on wholesale term deposits in 1981. In Chapter 11 we referred to 'Balladur bonds' as an incentive to private investors to buy company shares; other finance ministers – Delors and Bérégovoy – also launched initiatives to encourage private shareholding.

There were several reasons for these changes. Firstly, during the 1970s the French budget moved into permanent deficit. If this was not to be financed by monetary means – with risks for inflation – then there had to be a rapid development of long- and short-term government securities and markets in which a wide range of savers would be encouraged to buy them. Secondly, regulation imposed costs which had ultimately to be borne by borrowers who found increasingly that they could borrow more cheaply in other countries. We noted in Chapter 11 that the fear of competition from the London capital markets after 'Big Bang' was a powerful stimulus to reform of many continental stock exchanges. Thirdly, the European Union had adopted a policy of liberalization and unification of financial markets which was bound to increase competition between all European financial centres.

Despite all these changes, however, the balance sheets of French firms still show a heavier reliance upon bank-intermediated finance than their counterparts in the UK and USA. Consequently, the savings of French households are still concentrated in bank liabilities, though money market assets, held indirectly via mutual funds, have taken an increased share in recent years. We shall see that equity and bond (direct plus indirect) holdings play a larger role than they do in Germany but they are unlikely to reach UK and USA proportions until funded pension schemes become the norm.

Table 19.5 shows the size, growth and composition of security market activity in recent years.

Table 19.5 Security market activity – selected indicators (Ffr mn)

	1992	1993	1994	1995
Market capitalization (Paris Bourse)				
Equities	1,809	2,692	2,415	2,445
Bonds and preference shares	3,194	3,877	3,756	4,125
New issues, including the second market				
Equities	50	67	76	37
Bonds (net)	205	339	190	na
Mutual funds (outstanding value)				
Fonds communs de placements	708	844	889	951
SICAVs	1,804	2,212	1,776	1,603

Source: INSEE, *Revenus et Patrimoine des Ménages*, No.5, 1996 (Paris: INSEE, 1996) p. 164

19.5 The development of the Italian financial system

The Italian financial system is clearly bank-based rather than market-based (see Section 15.2). This was borne out in Table 15.1 which showed that, over the period 1985–94, firms raised only 4.7 per cent of their funds through the issue of new equity while bond issues did not contribute at all – indeed, firms had been net purchasers of bonds. In this sense, the Italian system was in line with the other systems of continental Europe. Despite this, the system remains highly individual and has a number of features in common with that of the USA.

As with the USA, the basis for the development of the system for the following 50 years was laid in the 1930s. Italy had only become a united country in 1870 and, by the standards of Northern Europe, much of it was economically underdeveloped. Its social and economic history had left it with a shortage of private capital willing and able to engage in banking. Prior to the 1930s there had been a succession of bank failures and financial crises and the position deteriorated during the economic crisis of the 1930s. The Italian response was strikingly different to that of the USA in that public intervention frequently followed and, as a result, most of Italy's banks became state-owned, either directly or under the control of charitable, non-profit-making foundations which were themselves government supervised.

However, the *Banking Act of 1936* derived from the same determination to ensure the stability and security of the system which we saw to be the driving force behind the 1933 Glass–Steagall act in the USA (see Section 17.2) – and it followed much the same approach. The law created a rigid demarcation between financial institutions in providing corporate finance. Commercial banks (standard credit institutions) were only allowed to conduct short-term (up to 18 months) deposit and lending business while medium- and longer-term financing was to be provided by investment banks (special credit institutions). This distinction existed nowhere else in Europe. Commercial banks were given slightly more freedom than this suggests since they could grant medium-term loans not exceeding eight per cent of their deposits as long as loans to any one institution did not rise above 15 per cent of capital, but any such loans had to be individually authorized by the central bank, the *Banca d'Italia*. Banks were also prohibited from acquiring participating interests in industrial companies and the development of branch networks was discouraged by the Banca d'Italia which demanded evidence that there were valid economic reasons for any such expansion.

The banking system which developed was one with a very large number of small local banks which faced very little competition. As a consequence, banks became very bureaucratic and did not provide a high level of service. Savings products provided by the banking system were few and unsophisticated. In the larger public sector banks, as in most parts of the Italian state, appointments of top officials became highly politicized and the banks had little chance of raising share capital.

The structure of Italian capitalism also contributed to the way in which the financial system developed. The family remained central to the operation of capitalism much longer than in comparable countries. The average size of firms remained small and many of the larger firms continued to be essentially privately owned. This is still true of firms such as Fiat, Pirelli, Olivetti, Benetton and Gucci. Many other large Italian firms were owned either directly or indirectly by the state. Under these circumstances there was very little call for an equity market and, although it has been strengthened over the past 10 years, its contribution to the growth of the Italian economy has been very small.

Following the formation of the EU in 1957, the Italian economy grew very rapidly. However, when growth rates in all Western economies turned down in the 1970s, much of the burden in Italy fell upon the Italian state, especially since much of the country's heavy industry was state-owned. Continuing regional problems and public attitudes made it difficult for the government to finance increased expenditure through high taxation and Italy embarked upon a series of large budget deficits. Savings ratios in Italy were high and, given the unsophisticated nature of savings vehicles provided by the banking system and the existence of exchange controls which made it difficult for capital to leave the country, the government was able to finance its deficits through the domestic sale of securities, although at an increasing cost in terms of interest rates and payments. The bond market became entirely dominated by government debt.

Firms seeking capital either provided it themselves through retained earnings or entered into special relationships with investment banks. One such bank, Mediobanca, a government-controlled bank in Milan, became central in financing operations and oversaw the development of close relationships among a number of the country's largest private firms. This was in part a response to the lack of development of bond and equity markets but contributed to the continued slow development of those markets.

It was not until the late 1980s that things began seriously to change. The pressures for deregulation which we have noted in all other countries gradually came to be felt in Italy. Pressure for reform came also from the Italian employers' association, Confindustria, which argued that inefficiencies in Italian banking threatened the long-term viability of Italian manufacturing. The Italian Bankers' Association drew attention to unsystematic *ad hoc* lending criteria and undisciplined loan-monitoring procedures. The Banca d'Italia acted in a number of ways to try to bring Italian banking practices into line with the rest of Europe. The requirement that commercial banks needed special authorization from the Banca d'Italia to grant medium- or long-term loans was removed. Administrative controls and regulations on the investment of banks' funds in government securities began to be revoked from 1984 on. As soon as the law allowed, the central bank fostered competition by encouraging the merger of smaller credit institutions and, after May 1990, it discontinued the policy of limiting and controlling branch networks.

The gradual reduction in restrictions on capital outflow under the terms of the Single European Act, culminating in the removal of the final foreign exchange control by the end of June 1990, had profound effects. Italian financial institutions now had to compete for the funds of Italian savers with foreign savings products; foreign banks increased their presence within Italy. This occurred first in investment banking with Italian government bond trading becoming dominated by foreign houses including J P Morgan, Morgan Stanley and Salomon Brothers. Later, Deutsche Bank and other EU banks began to make inroads into the retail market. Italian banks sought to diversify by granting medium- and long-term loans through special subsidiaries and by engaging in near-banking business such as leasing and factoring. Agreements between commercial and investment banks and insurance companies provided for the marketing of the financial products of other institutions.

It was clear that the 1936 Banking Act had to be replaced. A bill to reform the act was tabled in parliament in 1989 but the new Banking Act was not passed until 1 September 1993, coming into force on 1 September 1994. This law, however, incorporated a number of legislative and administrative changes which had been made from 1990 on. Perhaps the most significant of these was the *Legge Amato* (Law no. 218) of 30 July 1990 which authorized the transformation of public banks into limited companies, establishing the full legal parity of public and private financial intermediaries, on the principle that all banks are business firms. In May 1993, banks were allowed participating interests in industrial companies up to the limit of 15 per cent of their own funds. The 1993 *Banking Act* removed the distinction between short-term and medium- and long-term lending. It also introduced a separation between the banks themselves (now all private law limited companies) and the public foundations owning shares in those banks. The foundations were allowed to sell or exchange shares, leading to increased concentration. The law thus led to the existence of bank holding companies with subsidiaries providing medium-term lending, insurance and other financial services. It was hoped that this would result in four or five large financial institutions able to compete internationally.

This became more urgent with the translation into Italian law of the EU's *Second Banking Directive* towards the end of 1995. This was followed by a rush of notifications of intent to offer banking services in Italy from banks based in other EU countries. There were 68 such notifications from nine EU countries within the following 12 months.

19.6 The current position of the Italian financial system

19.6.1 The banking industry

Although there are still very many banks, mergers and acquisitions have reduced their number from 1060 in 1992 to 970 at the end of 1995. As Table 19.6 shows, this reduction in number is the net result of a significant number of new registrations (53 in 1995) and cancellations of licences (77 in 1995).

The change in the banking law allowing the formation of bank holding companies has resulted in 212 of the 970 banks operating at the end of 1995 being owned by 91 registered banking groups which also owned between them 173 auxiliary companies and 451 financial companies. The 212 banks owned by banking groups generally represent the larger banks in the system. This is shown by the fact that independent banks accounted for only 16 per cent of the total assets of the banking system. Thus, the formation of financial conglomerates can be seen to be well under way. Table 19.6 also shows another international tendency in that the biggest loss in banks was of mutual banks whose numbers fell from 643 to 619 in 1995. Twenty-eight of the 64 mergers and acquisitions which occurred in 1995 (the highest number for 10 years) involved mutual banks.

Following the removal of restrictions on the development of branch networks, the total number of bank branches has been increasing steadily, rising by 981 in 1995 to a total of 23,440 and to 24,014 by September 1996. This was almost double the number of bank branches (12,174) in existence in 1980. The increase in concentration in the industry is shown by the activity of the seven leading banking groups[3] which, over the five years to the end of 1995, increased their total number of branches by 4252 with 56 per cent of the increase coming from acquisitions of other banks and the rest from internal expansion. This increased the proportion of total Italian branches held by the seven groups from 24 to 35 per cent while their share of the deposits market grew by more than

[3] San Paolo di Torino, Cassa di Risparmio di Roma, Cariplo, Banca Nazionale del Lavoro, Monte dei Paschi di Siena, Credito Italiano and Banca Commerciale Italiana.

Table 19.6 The Italian banking system

	At end -1994		Changes in 1995[1]		At end -1995	
	Number of banks	Number of branches in Italy	New registrations	Cancellations	Number of banks	Number of branches in Italy
Limited company banks accepting short-term funds	170	16,073	12	19	163	16,621
Limited company banks accepting medium and long-term funds[2]	35	96	2	3	34	95
Co-operative banks (*banche popolari*)	95	3,938	8	7	96	4,239
Mutual banks (*banche di credito cooperativo*)	643	2,254	23	47	619	2,379
Central credit and refinancing institutions	6	28	–	–	6	28
Branches of foreign banks	45	70	8	1	52	78
Total	994	22,459	53	77	970	23,440
In the process of opening	8	661			6	600

[1] Includes changes due to the creation of new banks, mergers and changes in institutional category.
[2] The item includes *Astituto per ilcredito sportivo*.
Source: Banca d'Italia, *Annual Report* 1995. Table 4.5

10 percentage points and of lending by more than eight points. Despite this increased concentration, many very small banks remain. In terms of size, Italian banks are officially classified into five groups: maggiori (very large), grandi (large), medie (medium), piccole (small) and minori (very small). The eight banks classed as maggiori had at the end of September 1996 a total of 7019 branches while the 799 banks classed as minori had only a total of 4581 branches (that is, 84 per cent of the banks had a total of only 19 per cent of all bank branches).

Table 19.7 shows the principal assets of Italian banks at the end of 1995 and the percentage changes in them between 1990 and 1995.

The apparently large increase in assets is only in nominal terms. In 1995, banking activity contracted in real term as the result of the restrictive monetary policy stance of the central bank and substantial corporate self-financing, especially by exporting firms. In relation to GDP, the volume of outstanding bank loans fell in both 1994 and 1995.

Despite the changes which have occurred in recent years, Italy's banks remain the least profitable in Europe with a very low return on equity (ROE) compared with European competitors. At the end of

Table 19.7 Principal assets of Italian banks 1995, billions of lire

	Stocks[1]	% Change[2]
Bank reserves	79,169	–38.6
Interbank loans	150,479	58.4
Securities	352,273	59.0
Equities[3]	51,446	95.3
Repurchase agreements	14,772	191.1
Advances to residents	1,073,410	38.4
Interest-bearing external assets	231,535	99.4
Provision for bad debts	110,134	172.0
Total assets	2,063,218	46.5

Sources and notes: adapted from *Banca d'Italia Economic Bulletin*, February 1996, Table a33 and Annuario Statistico 1995, Table 16.9. [1] at end 1995; [2] percentage change from end of 1990; [3] includes azioni (shares) and partecipazioni (participating interests)

1995, the average ROE for European banks was 12.8 per cent but average ROEs for individual countries ranged from 21.1 per cent in the UK through 12.6 per cent in Spain, 11.7 per cent in the Netherlands, down to 6.2 per cent in France and 4.13 per cent in Italy. Several reasons are advanced for this low profitability. Italian banks still depend heavily on traditional loan income with only small amounts of revenue coming from commission or other fee-based income. Although bank staff declined in number for the first time in 1989 and have continued to fall, Italian banks are held to be severely overstaffed and this, together with high salaries, causes staff costs to be a high (even if declining) percentage of banks' gross income. The continued fragmentation of the industry (despite the movement towards increased concentration discussed above) and the direct or indirect state control of many banks are also blamed. There have been a number of high profile privatizations in the finance industry since December 1993 when IRI, the large government-owned holding company, sold its 64 per cent stake of ordinary stock in Credito Italiano. Later part or full privatizations included Banca Commerciale Italiana, IMI, a Rome-based banking and financial services group, and the investment bank, Mediobanca. Nonetheless, the withdrawal of the public sector from control of the industry has been slow in comparison with programmes of privatization elsewhere.

In recent years, the capital bases and the profitability of banks have declined. The decline in capital bases has in part been caused by poor earnings retention. The ambitious strategy of expansion has affected both capital bases and profit margins because of the poor state of many of the banks acquired. The low profitability and weak capitalization have had an adverse effect on credit ratings.

The performance of the Italian banking industry is influenced by the strong North–South difference. The weak economy of the South has led to crisis in the credit system in recent years with bad debts up to three times higher than in the North. Two of the largest banks in the area, the Banco di Napoli and Sicilcassa, ran into serious trouble. The Banco di Napoli had to be rescued from a liquidity crisis with huge loans from the Deposits and Loans Fund and from leading banks. In addition, Parliament authorized the Treasury to subscribe additional increases in the bank's capital. Sicilcassa was taken into special administration. Other smaller banks in the South have also found themselves in trouble. Many interventions by the supervisory authorities have aimed at avoiding interruption to the supply of financial services in the areas concerned and at transferring sound credit positions to other banks. This has often led to banks located in the South being taken over by banking groups whose parent companies are based in the Centre and the North.

19.6.2   The banking authorities

The Banca d'Italia is, like the Bank of England, both the bank of issue and the government's principal banker. Together with the Ufficio Italiano dei Cambi (UIC), it is responsible for exchange rate policy. It was founded in 1893 and is formally owned by the public sector banks. It derives its primary role as responsible for monetary stability from article 47 of the 1947 Italian constitution. This is a vaguely worded article which does not mention the Banca d'Italia by name but talks of encouraging savings and controlling credit.

Until 1992, the Banca d'Italia was far from being independent of government. The Comitato Interministeriale per il Credito e il Risparmio (CICR) was responsible for monetary policy issues and bank supervision policy. It was made up of the Treasury, Finance and other economic ministers, with the governor of the Banca d'Italia only being present at meetings in an advisory capacity. The Minister of Finance, together with the Minister for Trade, was responsible for all foreign exchange policy decisions and appointed or dismissed presidents of public banks in consultation with the political parties. The problem of financing the government's large budget deficits led to regular conflicts between it and the Banca d'Italia. Until 1981 the Banca d'Italia was required to take into its own portfolio any government securities not taken up by the market. Although this requirement was annulled, the government continued to make constant use of a cash advance facility which obligated the Banca d'Italia to provide up to 14 per cent of projected budgetary expenditure. In January 1983 the Banca d'Italia made use of a

1948 legislative decree under which, when the Treasury persistently exceeded the limits of the cash advance facility, it could suspend its payments to the Treasury and force Parliament to resolve the conflict between the central bank and the Executive. Parliament responded by approving legislation requiring the Banca d'Italia to grant the Treasury extraordinary additional finance.

Government influence on the Bank has also been possible through the method of appointment of its top officials. The Banca d'Italia's executive directorate is composed of the governor (who has no fixed term) and three other members all of whom are chosen by the governing council on which sits the Bank's 13 regional office chairmen. Appointments must, however, be confirmed by the Italian President in consultation with the government. An example of conflict over bank appointments was seen in 1994 when the government used its power to veto the appointment of Tommasso Padoa Schioppa to the executive directorate of the bank but could not then enforce the selection of its own preferred candidate. Instead, the Banca d'Italia was able to appoint a substitute for Padoa Schioppa from within its ranks.

As in most other countries, steps have been taken to increase the power of the central bank relative to that of elected governments. In February 1992, the authority to determine the discount rate was transferred from the Minister for Finance to the central bank and in June 1994, the Banca d'Italia assumed responsibility for determining minimum reserve policy.

19.6.3 The securities industry

The potential for securities markets in Italy has been high for a long time because Italian savings have been second in volume only to those of Japan. However, as we have noted above, Italian savings products have until recently been unsophisticated and only a small proportion of Italian savings has been professionally managed.

The large budget deficits of the 1970s and 1980s led to securities markets being dominated by the market for public debt. From 1980 to 1991, that debt grew almost six-fold; relative to national income it rose from 59 per cent to 102 per cent. By 1996,

General Government Gross Debt was 123.4 per cent of GDP. This limited the development of the equity market and accentuated the corporate sector's preference for bank or internal sources of financing. The Italian government debt market is now the third largest in the world in nominal terms behind those of USA and Japan. Most of the relatively small number of private bonds have been issued by publicly owned companies such as public banks or the Italian state railways. Bonds directly issued by the corporate sector represent only a tiny proportion of the total amount outstanding. At the end of 1995, of a total stock of outstanding bonds and government securities of Lire 2,048,038bn, 88.2 per cent consisted of public sector bonds or bills. Banks had been responsible for the issue of 10.5 per cent of the stock and firms for only 1.5 per cent.

The securities issued by the Treasury are of standard types ranging from Treasury bills to floating rate issues. Denominations are small enough to allow private investors to participate in the fortnightly auctions through financial intermediaries. The result is that over three-quarters of the public debt consists of securities placed in the domestic market with the greater part held by households, firms and institutional investors. Investment in government securities has spread to all the different components of society: around 40 per cent of pensioners hold government securities as do more than 35 per cent of white-collar households and nearly 25 per cent of blue-collar households.

The market was reformed in 1988, with a group of institutions becoming market makers quoting bid–offer prices on various bonds as in the UK and USA. Previously, Treasury bonds had been sold by banks forming a consortium and subscribing to a whole issue even if at prices below the equilibrium level. There had been government arm-twisting of financial intermediaries to ensure the sale of bonds. The market was reformed in part because of the perceived need to attract foreign investors following the removal of exchange controls which increased the possibility of Italian savings flowing abroad. In fact, the foreign holdings of Italian assets remained relatively modest. In 1996, non-residents owned only about 15 per cent of all Italian treasuries. In 1988 also an efficient screen-based secondary market for government securities was established.

Table 19.8 Institutional investors: net assets as a percentage share of households' financial assets (end of period data)

	1989	1990	1992	1993	1994	1995
Investment funds	2.7	2.3	2.5	4.0	4.5	4.2
Portfolio manage-ment services	3.0	3.2	4.0	5.1	6.2	6.3
Insurance companies[1,2]	3.4	3.7	4.1	4.3	4.3	4.9
Pension funds[2]	...	0.6	3.1	3.1	3.3	3.5
Securities firms[3]	–	...	0.0	0.3	0.2	0.2
Total	9.1	9.8	13.7	16.8	18.5	19.1

Notes: [1] Technical reserves, excluding securities entrusted to portfolio management services [2] The figure for 1995 is estimated [3] Securities firms' own trading portfolios.

Development of the equities market was also hindered in the past by factors other than the size of the market for public debt. Although the equity market grew in the 1980s, with the market capitalization of listed shares rising from six per cent to 13 per cent of GDP, progress was slowed by the way in which the stock exchange operated. A 1913 law had given a monopoly over transactions to brokers. They were meant to be pure brokers, acting only as agents. However, the market did not work well in the late 1980s. No one was compelled to use the stock exchange and only 20 per cent of transactions went through the exchange; the average availability of a company's share capital on the

market was very small. The official market was thus thin and speculative and was a market for insiders. There were no rules of conduct or investor protection. Specifically, there was no law on insider trading and no rules requiring public takeover offers. This all led to many complaints that share deals were frequently rigged by big groups, that small investors were cheated and that the market was characterized by secret pacts and the atmosphere of a private club. A new bill was presented to Parliament in 1989 requiring transactions in equities to go through authorized intermediaries on the official market. The distinction between brokers and market makers disappeared. New firms became market makers, brokers, and fund managers with Chinese walls being required.

19.6.3 Institutional investors

The late 1980s and 1990s has seen a marked growth in the professional management of savings. Table 19.8 shows the steady growth in the net assets of institutional investors as a percentage of household's financial assets.

The growth of investment funds is indicated by the existence at the end of 1995 of 54 operational open-end fund management companies (UCITs) managing a total of 459 funds, compared with only 354 at the end of the previous year. Two closed fund management companies (SICAVs) also began operating in 1995. Table 19.9 shows the net assets of Italian investment funds. The domination of the

Table 19.9 Net assets of Italian investment funds (billions of lire)

	Net fund-raising		Dividends paid		Capital gains/losses[1]		Net assets[2]		
	1994	1995	1994	1995	1994	1995	December 1993	December 1994	December 1995
Bond-based	4,071	–3,223	1,758	1,211	–1.049	7,734	72,029	73,293	76,593
linked to current accounts	324	–1,100	47	55	709	2,251	28,051	29,037	30,133
Mixed	3,376	–3,817	30	10	1,290	1,278	13,467	18,103	15,554
Share-based	18,008	–3,450	...	...	–3,832	–668	24,597	38,773	34,665
Total	25,455	–10,490	1,788	1,221	–3,591	8,344	110,093	130,169	126,802

Notes: [1] Including coupons and interest received and subtracting management costs
[2] The change in net assets is equal to the sum of fund-raising and capital gains (losses) minus dividends paid.
Source: Banca Italia *Annual Report* for 1995. Table 34.

Table 19.10 Assets of Italian portfolio management
services, end 1995 (billions of lire)

Italian govt securities	129,422
Other domestic bonds	18,763
Italian equities	8,521
Foreign currency bonds	13,227
Foreign currency equities	1,930
Total portfolio	179,612
Total assets	192,438
of which:	
banks	135,551
securities firms	38,029
trust companies	18,858

Source: Banca d'Italia, *Annual Report* for 1995, Table 35

securities market by bond-trading is also indicated
here, with purely bond-based funds accounting for
60.4 per cent of the total assets of the sector at the
end of 1995.

As well as the investment funds there were 272
operational securities firms and trust companies
engaged in portfolio management services along
with banks. There were also 259 registered financial
companies, most of which grant specialized forms of
credit, although a small number of them offer a range
of financial products. Table 19.10 shows the assets of
portfolio management services and their division
among banks, securities firms and trust companies.

Table 19.11 Main assets of Italian insurance
companies, end 1992 and end 1995 (billions of lire)

	1992	1995
Life insurance		
Securities	58,507	91,351
Deposits and cash	2,050	2,219
Loans and annuities	2,766	1,620
Real estate	9,407	12,156
Total assets	99,492	169,562
General insurance		
Securities	41,554	60,076
Deposits and cash	2,324	2,812
Loans and annuities	976	186
Real estate	10,822	12,356
Total assets	94,463	118,112

Source: Banca d'Italia *Annual Report* for 1995, Table 36

The Italian life insurance industry has also been
relatively underdeveloped until recent years and
pension funds have been slow to develop largely
because of the generous state pension provision.
However, as Table 19.11 shows, the total assets of
life insurance companies have grown very rapidly
over the past four years.

There has also been a strong tendency towards the
concentration of the industry and several mergers
involving foreign insurance companies. Pension
funds have started to grow as state pensions have
come under pressure as part of the government's
attempt to reduce the public sector deficit in the hope
of qualifying for membership of the European
Monetary Union (see Chapter 21). Table 19.12 sets
out the principal assets of Italian pension funds at the
end of 1995.

Table 19.12 Main assets of Italian pension funds, end
1994 (billions of lire)

Cash and deposits	15,535
Government securities	25,257
Corporate bonds	4,446
Equities	1,730
Foreign currency securities	770
Loans and other financial assets	11,737
Real estate	–
Total assets	59,475

Source: Banca d'Italia, *Annual Report* for 1995, Table 38

19.7 A comparison between the financial systems of Italy and Spain

We have seen throughout the last four chapters just
how different national financial systems can be.
There are very few rules that can be applied to
explain why systems have developed in particular
ways. For example, we have seen that the Italian
financial system has had some features in common
with that of the United States – the large number of
small banks and the separation of commercial
banking activities from those of investment banks.
These features appear to have arisen in both
countries because of the history of financial crises

and the strong attachment to the importance of local independence. In the United States, the smallness of local banks contributed to the regularity of financial crises. In Italy, the crises were partly a reflection of an underdeveloped real economy. It was this that ensured the large role of the public sector in the banking industry, something that certainly did not occur in the United States. A failure to appreciate the range of determinants of the nature of financial systems might lead one to suspect that other Mediterranean economies might have produced similar financial systems to that of Italy. Spain would be an obvious candidate for testing this hypothesis.

What, however, do we find? It is true that Spain has a large number of mutual and co-operative savings banks (Cajas de Ahorros) and that these give the banking industry a stronger regional focus than many countries with a small number of relatively large private banks such as the UK. On the other hand, in the period after the Spanish Civil War the Spanish commercial banking system came to be dominated by a small group of large joint stock banks which operated a cartel, dividing the market up between them. As in Italy and the United States, restrictions applied in Spain on the formation of new branches but when these were removed in 1974, the cartel members competed largely through the formation of new branches. The result was almost certainly an overbanked economy in contrast with Italy in which the number of branches has been heavily restricted until very recently.

Traditionally, the joint stock banks were universal banks in the German fashion. Some still have large industrial holdings. The state has certainly played a role within the system and there existed a number of official banks, some of which dated back to the last century. In 1991 these were placed under a single holding company which then sought private capital. Nonetheless, the role of the state was much smaller than in Italy. The savings banks were either non-profit-making institutions without shareholders' capital or credit co-operatives. Despite this, some (such as Caja-Madrid and La Caixa) are large. Although the market for public debt is important in Spain, the country's General Gross Government Debt is currently only 67.8 per cent of GDP – a much lower percentage than in Italy. But Spanish saving rates have been considerably below those of Italy and

thus the financing of government deficits has often required high interest rates as in Italy. Nonetheless, our hypothesis that the financial systems of Italy and Spain should have much in common has little to support it. Spain merely adds to the strength of the argument that the development of financial systems is inextricably intertwined with political, economic and social features and are hence extremely difficult to classify.

The one feature that all financial systems appear to have in common is the extent of change over the past 15 to 20 years. In Spain, as elsewhere, mergers and acquisitions have become increasingly both common among the joint stock banks and the mutuals. As with mutuals in other countries, increased competition in recent years has seen a move towards the abandonment of mutual status among Spanish savings banks in search of increased capital. Non-bank financial intermediaries have grown. Fierce competition in the banking sector in the late 1980s and early 1990s led to the emergence of new financial products that caused a sharp lift in household portfolios.

The insurance industry which has been traditionally weak in Spain has been expanding under the influence of the large banks. A 1987 law set up a modern regime to organize pension plans and to encourage households to make their own retirement plans, giving fiscal benefits which made their after-tax return higher than that on regular savings assets. Banks have responded by acting as promoters organizing pension plans for their customers, acting with subsidiaries as managers of the funds and becoming the depository of assets held by the funds.

Investment funds began in Spain in the early 1970s, but recent changes in their tax treatment made them much more popular. Funds may be closed-end funds with fixed or variable capital or general open-ended funds similar to UK unit trusts. Some open-ended funds specialize in short-term money market assets and are thus equivalent to the money market mutual funds in the USA. The stock market has been reformed and has moved to electronic trading and futures and options markets developed from the late 1980s. Foreign competition is increasing in most sectors. Change will continue with increased integration in Europe. We shall see in Section 20.3.3 that a 1988 report estimated that

Spanish consumers have a great deal to gain from increased competition which should result from the development of a single European market in financial services as Spanish prices across much of the industry are high by the standards of other European countries. We can thus be certain that change will continue.

19.8 Summary

Until the 1970s, France could certainly be regarded as having an overdraft economy – one with a bank-based financial system. The system has also been highly centralized and regulated. Many changes have taken place in recent years although these have largely occurred as a result of deliberate decisions made by the French state rather than being a private sector response to changed financial conditions.

The changes introduced by the state were made in response to the movement towards a single European market which was opening the French financial system to competition. The result was the Banking Act of 1984 which had implications for almost all financial institutions. In 1993, as part of the preparation for a move to European Monetary Union (discussed in Chapter 21), the Banque de France, France's central bank, was made autonomous from government. As with Germany, however, securities markets, and particularly the market for equities, have been less important in providing corporate finance and assets four households than US and UK markets have been for their savers and borrowers. In both cases this is partly the result of the small pension fund sector, itself a product of generous state pensions financed on PAYG principles.

Italy is different again. Its banking system is highly segmented. Its securities markets are also less developed than those of the UK and USA, though it has a very large bond market – the result of persistent large government deficits. What this study of financial structures shows us is that while there may well be a tendency under the development of a single European market for financial systems to become more homogeneous, the current structures still show the importance of historical, political and social influences.

Key concepts used in this chapter

Overdraft economy	Fonds Commun de Placement
Mutual and co-operative banks	Government borrowing requirement
Savings banks	Debt ratio
SICAVs	Return on equity

Questions and problems

1 Explain what is meant by an 'overdraft' economy.

2 Distinguish between the functions of the *Comité des Etablissements de Crédit*, the *Comité de Réglementation Bancaire* and the *Commission Bancaire*.

3 Give three examples of steps taken to stimulate the development of securities markets in France in recent years.

4 Why have French governments taken these steps?

5 What does the Italian financial system have in common with that of the United States? In what ways are the two systems strikingly different?

6 Why has the Italian financial system remained bank-based?

7 How important for the development of financial systems are the existence of large regional inequalities?

8 Why might one expect similarities between the Italian and Spanish financial systems?

9 On the basis of the discussion of national financial systems in Chapters 16 to 19, what features might one expect in the systems of:
   (a) Greece;
   (b) Sweden;
   (c) Austria
   (d) Portugal?

10 What important changes have taken place in the financial system of your own country since early in 1997 when this book was completed?

Further reading

C de Boissieu, 'France: Monetary and Financial System', in P Newman, M Milgate and J Eatwell, *The New Palgrave Dictionary of Money and Finance* (London: Macmillan, 1992)

D Cobham and J-M Serre, 'A Characterisation of the French Financial System', Dept. of Economics, University of St. Andrews, mimeo (1996)

Conseil National du Crédit, *Annual Report* (Paris: Conseil National du Crédit)

G Durieux, M Serieyssol and P Stephan, *French Financial Markets* (Cambridge: Woodhead Publishers Ltd, 1995) Ch.1

E P M Gardener and P Molyneux, *Changes in Western European Banking* (London: Routledge, 1990)

R Henderson, *European Finance* (London: McGraw Hill, 1993)

J R Hicks, *The Crisis in Keynesian Economics* (Oxford: Blackwell, 1974)

INSEE, *Revenus et Patrimoine des Ménages*, No.5, 1996 (Paris: INSEE, 1996)

INSEE, *Images Economiques des Entreprises au 1.1.94*, vol III (Paris: INSEE, 1996)

INSEE, *Bulletin Mensuel de Statistique* (Paris: INSEE, 1996)

D K R Klein, *The Banking Systems of the EU Member States* (Cambridge: Gresham Books, 1995)

P Moore, 'The quest for a Risorgimento', *Euromoney* (Sept 1996, pp. 356–60)

P Newman, M Milgate and J Eatwell (eds), *The New Palgrave Dictionary of Money and Finance* (London: Macmillan, 1992)

Current issues

The single European market

20.1 Introduction

Although the early history of the European Union was concerned largely with the removal of tariffs among member states and the establishment of a common commercial policy towards the rest of the world, the Treaty of Rome had required nothing short of a single European market (SEM) in all goods and services. To this end, the 1957 Treaty had specified the dismantling of all non-tariff barriers to the free movement of goods among members. The progressive abolition of all restrictions on the freedom to supply services, such as banking,

insurance and communications services, across frontiers was also sought and this was to be accompanied by the free movement of labour and capital. All discrimination based on nationality was to disappear.

Progress in the removal of tariffs was quite rapid but, although the European Commission battled constantly towards the goal of a single market in all areas of production, the gains throughout the 1970s and early 1980s were small. The first stage of integration was complete by the mid-1980s but many of the other objectives of the Rome Treaty had not been achieved. Indeed, non-tariff barriers within the EU had almost certainly increased between 1975 and 1985, partly as a response to the removal of tariffs among members. Advances had been even slower in services, notably transport and financial services, than in other sectors of the economy. At the same time, there was increasing concern over slow rates of growth in much of the EU in comparison with apparently more dynamic economies elsewhere. Consequently, it was felt that a new drive was needed to deepen the integration among member countries. Thus, the 1986 Single European Act (the SEA) was intended to achieve both the removal of non-tariff barriers to trade and the free movement of labour and capital by the beginning of 1993.

In Section 20.2 we look at the objectives and achievements of the SEA and progress made towards the full achievement of the SEM. Section 20.3 looks specifically at the attempt to achieve a single European financial market while Section 20.4 looks at specific sections of the financial services industry from this point of view. Section 20.5 summarizes.

20.2   The objectives and achievements of
the Single European Act

Objectives were set by the SEA in relation to three
main types of non-tariff barriers to trade and factor
mobility.

In regard to *physical barriers* created by customs
formalities and controls, this included the simplification of administrative checks and their movement
away from borders, the elimination of all internal
frontiers and controls on people and capital as well as
on goods and services and the development of a
common transport policy.

In relation to *technical barriers* such as different
technical specifications of products, it was intended
to harmonize regulations or, failing this, to have
mutual recognition of each other's standards; to
remove exchange controls; and to establish the
equivalence of qualifications.

Under the heading of *fiscal barriers* came the
much more difficult to achieve goal of the harmonization of taxation rates and systems, especially in
the fields of indirect and corporation taxes.

The SEA also stressed the desirability of opening
up each country's public purchasing to competition
from other member states; ensuring a firmer
application of competition policy; and incorporating
the social charter. However, there were no credible
plans for dealing with differences in external trade
policy and the Commission's attitude towards
subsidies was unclear. There was also uncertainty
over the degree to which harmonization could give
way to mutual recognition in the completion of the
single market.

The European Commission argued that the
movement to a single market would produce gains of
a number of types for the EU:

(1) It would extend the static gains attributed to the
removal of tariffs between countries – net trade
creation. This is a measure of trade creation
minus trade diversion. *Trade creation* is the
replacement of high-cost domestic output of one
member state by the lower-cost output of another
member state. *Trade diversion* is the diversion of
output from low-cost outside sources of supply to
a higher-cost source within the integrated area. It
was held that the gains from the removal of non-

tariff barriers might be even greater than from the
removal of tariffs because governments had no
revenue from non-tariff barriers to lose. Further,
trade diversion was likely to be less since the
removal of some non-tariff barriers (such as
different product standards and definitions)
would be helpful to outside producers as well as
to those in EU member states.

(2) It would produce many dynamic gains in the
form of economies of scale, increased competition resulting in reductions in X-inefficiency and
international price discrimination, and an
increase in the variety of products available
across the market.

(3) Any gains made under (1) and (2) would lead to
increased investment both from within and
without the EU, further adding to the increase in
welfare attributable to the single market.

Just how large the gains would be, however, was
extremely difficult to say. A major attempt was made
to estimate the possible gains from the single market
in a report, running to 16 volumes, prepared for the
European Commission on the 'Costs of non-Europe'
(Cecchini *et al.*, 1988; Emerson *et al.*, 1992).
Unsurprisingly, the estimates in this report have been
subject to much discussion and criticism.

The study approached the problem from both
microeconomic and macroeconomic angles. The
microeconomic analysis focused, sector by sector, on
three types of benefits:

- *direct* gains of the removal of trade barriers;
- *indirect* gains of increased market integration
  from the removal of barriers to competition such
  as those connected with public purchasing and
  technical standards;
- *efficiency* gains from the greater exploitation of
  economies of scale and the reduction of
  X-inefficiency.

The welfare effects on each sector of industry were
estimated within a partial equilibrium framework in
which, importantly, it was assumed that employment
would remain constant. Thus, it was being assumed
that workers displaced from inefficient firms would
be able to move quickly and easily into other jobs.
The welfare gains were estimated at between 4.3 per
cent and 6.4 per cent of GDP for the EU as a whole.

These were said to be cautious estimates, implying that the true effects could be yet higher.

From a macroeconomic angle, the estimated gain was 4.5 per cent of EU GDP. However, it was argued that these gains would help to ease pressures on the macroeconomic management of the economy and hence allow further gains. Taking this into account, one estimate put the likely once-and-for-all medium-term gain at 7.5 per cent of EU GDP, together with the creation of five million jobs.

These estimates were criticized as over-optimistic by several writers. It was argued, in particular, that the Cecchini gains assumed that all members would implement all directives and accept the unpleasant consequences of intensified competition without resorting to subsidies and hidden discrimination; and firms would compete and not collude or merge to avoid the extra competitive pressures. It also assumed that the Commission would be able to enforce the competition rules and that Court of Justice rulings would be obeyed by all. Many thought that all of this was unlikely.

There was criticism, too, that the report failed to take full account of the costs of the restructuring which would be needed in many economies if the SEA was to achieve its objectives. It was assumed that any resources made unemployed by the 1992 process would be fully re-absorbed by the end of 1992. Grahl and Teague (1990) and Culter *et al.* (1989) argued that some parts of the EU could experience a downward spiral in employment as a result of the SEA programme as some companies lost market share to more efficient producers in the 'core' of the EU. Cecchini ignored this possible regional effect of the SEM programme. The possibility of regional problems arising from the single market programme was, however, taken seriously and both the SEA and the Maastricht Treaty talked of the need for economic and social cohesion to overcome problems of regional imbalance within the Union. Despite these concerns, there was widespread support for the move to a single European market even from people who were

later much more sceptical about the possibility of gains from the movement to European Monetary Union (see Chapter 21).

20.2.1 Progress towards the SEM

Frontier controls were abolished and most of the proposed legislative changes had been adopted by the Council of Ministers by the target date of 1 January 1993. However, in some areas, notably financial services, major pieces of legislation had been adopted rather late. For example, the directive to allow for cross-frontier trade in life insurance only came into force in July 1994. Another problem, pointed out by the Sutherland Report (1992), was the slowness in the implementation of some of the directives into the national laws of the member states. Concern was still being expressed in 1996 about the slowness of some members in adopting laws aimed at creating the single market. The worst performers included Germany, Greece and Austria.[1] Denmark, the Netherlands, Sweden and Spain had the best records, all with higher than 95 per cent implementation rates, in comparison with the average rate of 93.4 per cent. Progress had been particularly slow in areas such as public procurement, insurance, the free movement of people, and intellectual and industrial property rights.

Infringement proceedings were pending against a number of member states for failure to implement directives on time or for implementing them incorrectly. The worst areas were in public procurement; the right of residence, both generally and for students in particular; intellectual and industrial property rights where the average level of adoption of laws was only 73 per cent; and mutual recognition of professional training and education, which had been adopted by only five member states. In 1995, the European Commission issued 1016 warning letters to governments over infringements of single market legislation.[2]

There was also growing concern that laws

---

[1] Although, to be fair, Austria had only joined the EU from the beginning of 1995.

[2] This is the first step in a three-step procedure against infringements. If the letter of warning fails to produce an adequate response, the Commission sends a reasoned opinion stating in detail what a member is doing wrong and what needs to be done to rectify the position. If this fails, the member state is taken by the Commission to the European Court of Justice.

governing the single market were not being applied equally and effectively in all member states. Penalties for breaking the laws are much harsher in some countries than in others. It is one thing to implement the laws, another to enforce them.

A completely different worry was that small and medium-sized firms and consumers appeared to have little knowledge of the new laws and this raised the possibility that the mutual recognition of technical regulations would not be widely respected. This would undermine the expected change in trade flows and limit the process of restructuring the SEA was meant to engender. The Sutherland Report had argued that consumers' rights (for example, in relation to products that did not meet acceptable standards) needed to be more clearly specified if they were to buy goods and services from companies in other member states.

20.3 The single financial market (European Financial Common market – the EFCM)

To achieve a single market in financial services, it was necessary to ensure:

- the free mobility of capital;
- the right of establishment by firms in other member states;
- the right to supply cross-border services;
- the acceptance of common supervisory regulations; and
- the harmonization of taxes.

Fully mobile capital, in turn, could only be achieved with the removal of all exchange controls, ideally the disappearance of exchange rate uncertainties and the full acceptance of the rights to raise capital and to invest in all EU markets. It was clearly always going to be difficult to meet all or even the majority of these requirements. This was especially so because the financial services industry has always been politically sensitive and had been highly regulated everywhere. The principal reason for this was the fear of *systemic risk* – the fear that, because of the crucial importance of confidence to the industry, problems within one firm or segment of it might endanger the whole system. This magnified the importance of the question of which regulatory regime should apply when a firm opened branches in other countries or sold services across borders – the regulations of the home country of the firm or those of the host country in which the firm was locating.

National regulatory authorities preferred to oversee the prudential standards of all firms in the market, whatever their country of origin. Further, with home-country regulation, firms operating in one country might face regulations of differing degrees of severity, producing competitive distortions between different nationalities of banks. Again, since financial services are seen as having a central role in the economy, governments and regulatory authorities have been reluctant to allow national markets to be dominated by foreign institutions. This has led to action to prevent foreign institutions from competing with domestic financial institutions. Finally, purchasers of financial services are often thought to need high levels of consumer protection and this is assumed to be better provided by host governments.

On the other hand, national regulation created different regulatory regimes in all member states and this raised barriers to competition. Host-country regulation also made it easy for governments to discriminate against firms from other countries and limited foreign firms to providing the same range of services as domestic firms were allowed to offer under domestic law. Thus, host-country regulation tended to reinforce other tendencies towards a fragmented and inefficient financial services industry.

Governments worried about foreign competition for their own financial institutions had found it relatively easy to limit that foreign competition because firms generally need to locate in a country in order to provide financial services within it. This allowed governments to reduce competition by placing barriers against the establishment of branches or the takeover of domestic institutions by foreign firms. Cross-border trade from outside a country, while possible, is much less important in finance than in trade in goods. The outcome of these various forces was that although competition and integration had become international in some areas of finance such as wholesale banking, other areas such as retail banking and insurance had remained fragmented. Even for corporate business, EU national financial systems were, by the 1980s, far from integrated with differences remaining between them in regulation, taxation, the competitive environment, and the role of the state.

20.3.1 The Treaty of Rome and the single financial market

The reluctance on the part of governments to give up control of financial firms operating in their national markets explained why resistance to a single European financial market was greater than in most areas of production. This reluctance was in evidence even in the Treaty of Rome itself. It is true that among the Treaty's many objectives were:

- the right of establishment – the freedom of firms to locate anywhere in the market;
- the freedom of firms to supply services across national borders; and
- the free movement of capital.

However, Article 67 of the Treaty which expressed the objective of the free movement of capital implied that this was of secondary interest, being required only to the extent needed to ensure the proper functioning of the common market. In any case, much of the force of the objectives was lost by the inclusion in the Treaty of general exceptions which ensured that the freedom to supply financial services across borders remained, in practice, limited. For instance, Article 73 of the Treaty included an escape clause allowing governments to place restrictions on capital mobility during balance of payments crises. In any case, the Treaty only specified the liberalization of payments in connection with current transactions and did nothing towards the achievement of the other requirements for a common financial market listed above.

The chances of a movement to a single financial market were reduced still further by a ruling of the European Court of Justice that governments could impose specific regulatory requirements on cross-border suppliers of services provided that, among other things, the rules were objectively justified by the general interest and that the host country was unable to apply other, less restrictive, measures to achieve the same end (the principle of proportionality).

The first Council of Ministers directives on finance appeared in 1960 and 1962. These made some progress towards the goal of capital mobility by introducing a limited degree of liberalization of payments in connection with capital transactions. Capital movements were divided into four groups, for two of which unconditional liberalization was required. These covered transactions related to foreign trade or to foreign direct investment and operations in listed securities. A third category, including the buying and selling of unit trusts, and unlisted securities, long-term commercial credits and medium-term financial credits were granted conditional liberalization. On the other hand, governments were free to impose any restrictions they chose on the fourth category which included dealings in money market instruments, short-term financial credits and transactions in bank deposits. Even in areas where freedom from restrictions was specified, the directives had very little impact. Although they were binding on member governments, the choice of method of achieving the end result was left to individual governments and this allowed scope for many differences in interpretation and practice.

Nonetheless, there was extensive liberalization of financial markets in the 1960s regarding direct investments, commercial credits and the acquisition of securities on foreign stock exchanges. Yet the 1970s saw this trend reversed in several member states, notably France and Italy, largely because of the turmoil in international currency markets in that decade. Consequently, the advance towards capital mobility was, until 1980, moderate, especially in comparison with the increases occurring in intra-Union trade in goods. In 1979, the UK removed all capital controls and in the following few years, Germany, the Netherlands and Luxembourg followed suit. Then, as the foreign exchange markets calmed down and, in the middle 1980s, the stability of the EMS increased, exchange controls were eased in most other member states.

As we pointed out above, however, exchange controls were only one of the barriers to free capital mobility and it was only one of the barriers to a single market in financial services. Despite the relative stability among exchange rates in the second half of the 1980s, significant interest rate differentials remained among member states and exchange rate uncertainties were to return in the 1990s. The free flow of capital was also hindered by differences in tax regimes among countries, particularly relating to the taxation of profits. The intra-EU mobility of capital was also restricted by differences in capital markets. For example, the takeover of firms was more difficult in Germany than in the Netherlands or the UK. This was held to be partly because of the role of the major banks as shareholders and as the holders of proxies for other shareholders in Germany. Differences in investor and consumer attitudes may also have been important as in the widely held, though disputed, view that institutional shareholders in the UK had a short-run attitude towards their equity investments. Such differences between the structures in the member states tended to maintain the fragmentation of the market.

Other important barriers to financial integration in Europe in the 1970s and 1980s were the limitations placed on cross-border trade in financial services and barriers to the free location of financial institutions and other suppliers of financial services. For example, although only Spain imposed limits on their establishment, formal authorization was needed everywhere for the setting up of branches by foreign institutions and, in all countries except the UK, dedicated capital had to be provided. Further, regulators and governments had placed restrictions on the acquisition by foreigners of domestic financial firms, especially where major domestic banks were the target of foreign purchase. To this end, most countries required the notification of anything more than minor shareholdings in banks. Although some progress had been achieved in specific segments of the financial services industry in the 1970s, especially in relation to the right of establishment, much remained to be achieved.

20.3.2 The Cockfield Report, the SEA and the change of strategy

The approach to be taken in the SEA towards the financial services industry was developed in the Cockfield Report, prepared for the European Commission in 1985. The aim was to move towards complete mobility of capital and to the integration of banking, insurance and securities trading.

The report saw the removal of restrictions on international capital mobility as an integral part of the full development of a common market in financial services but also as essential for the completion of the internal market in all its dimensions. This was argued on three grounds:

(1) that freedom of capital was necessary for the achievement of totally integrated markets for all goods and services and also for promoting the free movement of labour across borders;
(2) that freedom of capital would provide a powerful incentive for governments to adopt macroeconomic policies which would lead to price and exchange rate stability; and
(3) that opening up the capital market would widen the freedom of choice for European investors and contribute to a more efficient allocation of savings.

The report also tackled the question of home country versus host country regulation. Prior to the Cockfield Report, the Commission had operated on the basis of Article 100 of the Treaty of Rome which implied that a common market in financial services could not come about until regulatory arrangements had been harmonized between members. Harmonization requires that all countries agree precisely on a common set of laws and can only take place with a spirit of compromise and much good will. However, the Treaty of Rome had also indicated that regulation would be based on host country and national principles and this gave each national authority an incentive to attempt to impose its regulatory system on other member states. Under these circumstances few were prepared to make any concessions regarding their own arrangements. The Cockfield Report argued that if a single market in financial services was to be achieved by 1992 a change of strategy was needed.

The report thus proposed the drawing of a clear distinction between what had to be harmonized and what could be left to mutual recognition of national regulations and standards. Mutual recognition had become important within the European Union as a result of a ruling by the European Court of Justice in 1979 which denied Germany the right to ban the import of *Cassis de Dijon* from France on the grounds that its alcoholic content was lower than that required by German law. The force of this ruling was that failure to meet a national law was not, in itself, sufficient reason for refusing to import a good or service from another member state. This, in turn, meant that full harmonization of national laws was not needed for the movement to a single market – all that was required was acceptance (or recognition) of each other's laws. A refusal to recognize the laws of other member states required a demonstration that to do so would cause a threat to public health or the rights of the consumer, or would damage fiscal supervision or the fairness of commercial transactions. Mutual recognition of national laws was clearly much easier to achieve than the harmonization of them.

The Cockfield Report further proposed that in cases of mutual recognition, regulation would be based on *home-country requirements*. In other words, if two members had different regulations in an area in which the Commission decided that harmonization was not needed, the regulations of the country in which the financial institution was registered or licensed would apply to it no matter where it was doing business. This accepted the principle of freedom of establishment and the cross-border provision of services within the Union since an institution authorized in one country would be deemed to be similarly authorized in all other member states.

The requirement to indicate areas where harmonization was necessary meant that, for each harmonization initiative, the Commission would decide whether or not national regulations were excessive and constituted a barrier to trade. In the banking sector, for instance, it was agreed that harmonization of regulation was needed in the following areas: authorization criteria; minimum capital requirements; the definition of own funds (equity capital); large exposure limits; deposit-protection arrangements; control of the major share-holdings in banks; limits on banks' involvement in non-bank sectors; and the quality of accountancy and internal control mechanisms. Anything else could be left to mutual recognition.

20.3.3 The Cecchini Report and the financial services industry

The Cecchini report foresaw a number of benefits from the movement to a single market in financial services including:

- lower prices of financial services resulting from the measures needed to complete the single market;
- an increase in general efficiency in the economy arising because financial services are a major input into industry;
- increased access to a wider range of markets, instruments and services, allowing increased portfolio diversification and raising welfare by improving the risk/return combination (see Section 2.3);
- more efficient allocation of capital, conveying generalized benefits to the economy as a whole.

The potential gains to consumers seemed to be substantial given the wide disparities in prices between member states for apparently standardized financial products. According to Cecchini, prices were likely to fall furthest in Belgium, France, Italy and Spain. The report discovered particularly wide price differences in motor vehicle insurance, home loans, consumer credit, foreign exchange drafts and most securities operations. The study considered eight countries (the original six members of the EU plus Britain and Spain) and estimated that across these countries the single market would produce an average price reduction in financial services of 10 per cent (ranging from 4 per cent in the Netherlands to 21 per cent in Spain). The potential price falls in the Cecchini Report are shown in Table 20.1. The increased competition, producing the reduced price dispersion, would, the report claimed, increase the value added in financial services by the equivalent of 0.7 per cent of GDP.

There are three types of objection to the Cecchini estimates. Firstly, there are doubts about the way existing price differences were measured. The calculations were based on identifying standardized financial products. Each country's prices for these products was then compared with the average of the four lowest prices for the product and the discrepancies were converted into potential price

Table 19.1 Cecchini Report estimates of potential price falls

	Belgium	Germany	Spain	France	Italy	Netherlands	UK
Banking							
Consumer credit	−41	136	39	105	*n/a*	31	121
Credit cards	79	60	26	−30	89	43	16
Mortgages	31	57	118	78	−4	−6	−20
Letters of credit	22	−10	59	−7	9	17	8
Foreign exchange	6	31	196	56	23	−46	16
Travellers' cheques	35	−7	30	39	22	33	−7
Commercial loans	−5	6	19	−7	9	43	46
Insurance							
Life	78	5	37	33	83	−9	−30
Home	−16	3	−4	39	81	−17	90
Motor	30	15	100	9	148	−7	−17
Commercial, fire, theft	−9	43	24	153	245	−1	−27
Securities							
Private equity	36	7	65	−13	−3	114	123
Private gilts	14	90	217	21	−63	161	36
Institutional equity	26	69	153	−5	47	26	−47
Institutional gilts	284	−4	60	57	92	21	n/a
Theoretical, potential price falls							
Banking	15	33	34	25	18	10	18
Insurance	31	10	32	24	51	1	4
Securities	52	11	44	23	33	18	12
Total	23	25	34	24	29	9	13

Source: 'The Economics of 1992', study by Price Waterhouse for the European Commission, in *European Economy* (1988)

falls. These were then scaled down to produce figures for expected price falls in each country, making some allowance for the fact that price differences might arise from factors other than a lack of competition. But it was arguable that this scaling down was insufficient. In practice products cannot easily be standardized. For instance, price differences in insurance markets may reflect differences in risk. Again, for many products the prices charged by banks reflect a customer's total business with the bank (relationship pricing). Thus, there are many cross-subsidies, making it difficult to isolate the price of one financial product from others. It may also be argued that the benchmark prices used for computing the potential price falls were artificial prices which existed in no one country of the union.

Secondly, the estimates implicitly assume that observed price differences are accounted for principally by lack of competition. But wide price differences may arise also because of differences among countries in the efficiency of financial systems, regulatory taxes, the competitive environment and the extent to which economies of scale are exploited. In principle, these differences should all be attacked by increased competition but this may be limited by location, information and transaction costs. These latter are, in turn, influenced by exchange rate uncertainties. In addition, there may be different structures of cross-subsidies within banks and other financial institutions. Although some cross-subsidies may reflect differences in competitive conditions between markets, not all do so. Significant price differences are bound to remain for specific financial products within countries despite an increase in competition resulting from the removal of regulatory and other barriers.

Thirdly, the report assumes that the 1992 arrangements will raise competitive pressures in financial systems. But entry costs, scale constraints and imperfect information may mean that markets remain partially segmented.

We have already noted the possible impact of

national differences in the structure of capital markets. It may be the case that national or regional differences in consumer tastes are less pronounced in the field of financial services than in other products. On the other hand, the importance to people of many single financial decisions and the consequent fear of loss may increase consumer loyalty to local firms.

Thus, although there was no doubt that the changes introduced in the SEA and the subsequent directives would compete away some existing restrictive practices and collusive agreements and overcome some protective regulatory arrangements, the Cecchini figures for gains to consumers were optimistic.

20.3.4 The EFCM and the periphery

Just as there has been a general concern about the impact of the move to a single market on the peripheral (poorer) members of the EU, particular worries have surfaced with regard to the movement to a European Financial Common Market. With regard to the peripheral countries, it has been argued that the movement to a single financial market across Europe may produce either of two outcomes. The relatively low profits of peripheral country banks may discourage the restructuring of the European banking system (Grilli, 1989), leaving peripheral banking systems relatively underdeveloped with many banks remaining essentially regional. This would accentuate the differences between core and peripheral countries and could increase the financial fragility of the peripheral countries since banks with a narrow base will be more at risk from external shocks because of their inability to diversify.

Alternatively, restructuring may occur with core country banks taking over banks within the periphery (Gibson and Tsakalotos, 1993). This may have a variety of consequences for the periphery, including the reduction of specialist regional advice and service within the periphery as the 'over-branched' peripheral banks are slimmed down in search of efficiency gains and better profit performance. The accompanying centralization of bank administration and decision making may also lead to a large reduction in available knowledge of the riskiness of potential borrowers. This too may increase the risks of financial fragility or

may produce credit rationing, making it more difficult for small entrepreneurs to obtain funds for investment. In either case, banking developments could contribute to a widening of real income differences between rich and poor member states.

However, none of these worries have led the poorer countries to oppose the movement to the EFCM. They have obtained derogations with regard to a number of directives to allow them to delay implementation for some years but have generally put their faith in enhanced regional policies and the new concern for economic and political cohesion in the EU.

20.4 Progress towards the EFCM

20.4.1 Freedom of capital movements

The Single European Act (1986) set the end of 1992 as the date for removal of all controls and in 1985 and 1986 liberalization rules were agreed which removed all restrictions from the third category of capital movements under the 1960s directives, such as the buying and selling of unit trusts and unlisted securities. The *Capital Liberalization Directive*, adopted in June 1988, then completely liberalized all capital movements. Eight of the then 12 member states were given until July 1990 to achieve this. Spain, Portugal, Ireland and Greece were allowed until the end of 1992 to meet the terms of the directive, with Greece and Portugal permitted to apply for a further extension to 1995. Despite some reinstatement of controls following the EMS crisis in 1992, progress continued to be made in these four countries and the addition of Sweden, Finland and Austria to the union caused no further problems in this regard. Under the *Treaty on European Union*, the old capital mobility articles of the Rome Treaty were scrapped. The new provisions prohibit all restrictions on the movement of capital and on payments between member states. The safeguard clauses which had been retained in the Capital Liberalization Directive were removed and even restrictions on capital movements and payments between member states and non-member states were prohibited. Only one escape clause remains and this only relates to movements of capital to and from non-member states.

The complete freedom of capital movements is by no means an unmixed blessing and arguments have been made in recent years for taxing the international movement of capital in an attempt to restore to governments some control over their macro-economic policies. However, if one views capital mobility strictly in terms of the movement to a single European market in financial services, it had to be regarded as essential. Clearly, a major element in it has now been achieved. However, following the problems with the European Monetary System in 1992 and 1993 (discussed in Chapter 21), a good deal of exchange rate uncertainty remains as shown by interest rate differentials among member states. In March 1997, Eurocurrency interest rates were between 3 and 4 per cent in Belgium, Denmark, Germany, the Netherlands and France but remained between 3 and 4 per cent higher in Spain, Portugal, Italy and the UK while being still higher in Greece. Much in this regard will depend in the next few years on progress, or lack of it, towards European Monetary Union.

20.4.2 The Banking Industry

The banking industry was one of the most highly regulated industries in the EU and operated with widely varied regulatory practices. In general, barriers to the supply of cross-border services were more of a problem than those related to location. In some countries laws and regulations restricted the right of non-resident banks and financial institutions to conduct business with residents.

Prior to the SEA, there had been two major directives relating to the banking industry: the *First Banking Directive on Coordination of Regulations Governing Credit Institutions* of 1977; and the 1983 *Directive on the Supervision of Credit Institutions on a Consolidated Basis*.

The First Banking Directive required member states to establish systems for authorizing and supervising banks and other credit institutions that take deposits and lend money. It required such institutions to be licensed. Once licensed, they would be allowed to conduct business in other member countries provided they were authorized to do so by the host government and complied with the conditions and supervision applied to local banks. To be authorized, a credit institution was required to have separate capital from its owners, to meet an initial capital requirement, and to have at least two directors and a reputable and experienced management. However, authorization could not legally be withheld on the sole ground that the head office was in another member state. As we have seen, the host country principle on which the directive was based meant that a German bank in Spain, for example, could only do what Spanish laws allowed its own banks to do in Spain.

The Directive on the Supervision of Credit Institutions on a Consolidated Basis (1983) established the common principle that bank activities were to be supervised on the basis of their worldwide activities. Thus, capital requirements were to relate to their global balance sheet position, preventing banks from seeking to avoid capital requirements by arranging business through less strictly regulated financial centres. This derived from the growing international concern with the solvency of banks, particularly at the commencement of the international debt crisis of the developing countries.

Since the SEA, there have been a series of directives on the banking industry, most notably the *Second Banking Coordination Directive* of 1989 (SBCD). This was based on the Cockfield Report strategy of home country regulation and mutual recognition. It gave the right to banks to establish branches and to trade in financial services throughout the EU on the basis of a single licence obtained from the home-country authorities. The directive included some exceptions to home-country control. Host countries retained the right to control bank liquidity for monetary policy purposes and had to comply with host-nation consumer protection and similar laws in the public interest. There was some ambiguity in relation to the scope of the consumer protection qualification. However, the directive eliminated the requirement for branches of foreign banks to maintain dedicated capital for their local operations.

The directive covered much else. It set out a detailed list of bank activities to which the directive applied. This, as is shown in Box 20.2, was very broad and included much of what is generally

---

Box 20.2 What a Universal Bank might do

According to the EU's Second Banking Directive, EU banks may engage in all of the following activities:

1 Acceptance of deposits and other repayable funds from the public
2 Lending to include consumer credit, mortgage credit, factoring, financing of commercial transactions (including forfaiting)
3 Financial leasing
4 Money transmission services
5 Issuing and administering means of payment (for example credit cards, travellers' cheques and bankers' drafts)
6 Guarantees and commitments
7 Trading for own account or for account of customers in:
   (a) money market instruments (cheques, bills, CDs, and so on)
   (b) foreign exchange
   (c) financial futures and options
   (d) exchange and interest rate instruments
   (e) transferable securities

8 Participation in share issues and the provision of services related to such issues
9 Advice to undertakings on capital structure, industrial strategy and related questions, and advice and services relating to mergers and the purchase of undertakings
10 Money broking
11 Portfolio management and advice
12 Safekeeping and administration of securities
13 Credit references services
14 Safe custody services.

Source: The Second Banking Directive 89/646/EEC (*Official Journal* of the EC, L386, Vol. 12, 30 December 1989, Annex).

In short, banks may participate in all activities considered in this book (with the exception of central banking) and a good deal besides.

---

included under the heading of securities or investment business in addition to activities more widely considered as banking. This accepted the principle of universal banking on which the German banking industry was organized.

The directive established the right of banks with head offices in other EU countries to pursue all the listed activities in a host country, including those that host-country laws might forbid to local banks. Essentially, banks were allowed to participate fully in securities business either directly or through subsidiaries. Nonetheless, despite the apparently comprehensive nature of the list, difficulties of interpretation remained. For example, Davis and Smales (1990) raised the question of variable-rate mortgage lending which was legal in the UK but not in Belgium. If this were regarded as a technique, Belgium would be required to allow UK banks to market the product in Belgium. On the other hand, if it were regarded as a basic activity, Belgium could prevent UK banks from marketing it under the consumer protection exception since it was not listed separately from mortgage lending. This is a difficulty associated with any listing which attempts to be comprehensive, especially in a period of rapid change and innovation. Difficulties associated with the regulation of banks engaged in both banking and securities business are discussed in Chapter 24.

The directive included rules regarding the exchange of information between home and host country regulators and harmonized minimum standards of authorization and prudential supervision. This included setting minimum requirements for the size of own funds (equity capital) – credit institutions were required to have initially and to maintain capital of at least Ecu5 million. The authorities in all countries were given the right to supervise ownership and control to prevent cross-financing and conflicts of interest. Hence, disclosure of the identity of a bank's most important shareholders was required and limits on banks' shareholdings in other financial and non-financial companies were harmonized.

A number of other directives, ancillary to the Second Banking Directive, were approved in 1989 and later years in order to meet the harmonization requirements for banking indicated above. Box 20.3 lists these directives.

Box 20.3   EU banking directives

The principal ancillary banking directives to the Second Banking Coordination Directive 1989 have been:

> Own Funds Directive of 1989 (89/299) (OFD)
> Bank Solvency Ratio Directive of 1989 (BSRD)
> Second Consolidated Supervision Directive of 1992 (SCSD)
> Large Exposures Directive of 1992 (LED)
> Deposit Guarantee Directive of 1994 (DGD)

They aimed at providing a common regulatory framework for banking.

The OFD and the BSRD, together with the Second Banking Directive, came into force at the beginning of 1993. They were concerned with the adequate capitalization of banks. The OFD harmonizes the definition of the minimum capital base of credit institutions. The BSRD harmonizes the minimum prudent solvency ratio for banks. Both directives follow the principles and figures set out in the Basle capital adequacy rules of the Bank for International Settlements, discussed in Chapter 24. The LED strengthened the capital

adequacy provisions in the other directives by requiring credit institutions to report annually on all large exposures to individual borrowers amounting to more than 15 per cent of their own funds (equity capital) or of the largest exposures, even if less than 15 per cent. The DGD requires members to establish deposit guarantee schemes, financed by banks, to protect depositors in the event of a credit institution's financial collapse.

There have also been two directives on bank accounts, both of which came into force on 31 December 1990. One described the layout, nomenclature and terminology for bank balance sheets, profit and loss statements and consolidated accounts of banks and greatly improved the comparability of bank accounts across member states. The second laid down the accounting obligations of bank branches of foreign banks in member states.

In 1990 there was a recommendation on transparency of banking conditions relating to cross-border financial transactions which aimed to prevent money laundering.

20.4.3   Securities markets

A genuine single financial market across the EU needed to apply much more broadly than to banking. It was accepted that if competition were to be fair for all firms across the EU, free access was required to all sources of capital. It was also accepted that if savings were to be utilized as effectively as possible, investors should have free access to all investment products irrespective of their country of origin. With the very rapid development of financial markets and the great increase in new financial products from the early 1970s onwards, the securities (or investment) industry (which covers securities trading, unit trusts, broking and market making, portfolio management, underwriting and investment advice as well as issues related to the access of companies to foreign stock exchanges and the quotation of securities on foreign stock exchanges) was becoming increasingly significant. However, it was also an area in which markets developed much more rapidly in some member states than others. This caused anxiety in some countries that increased competition across the

EU would damage, if not destroy, their under-developed markets and institutions. Under these circumstances, progress towards a single market was bound to be slow.

Nonetheless, strong efforts were made in some segments of the industry from the late 1970s on, notably in regard to the harmonization of the different regulations of the member states on the admission of securities to stock exchange listing and the information provided to investors. In 1979, the *Directive Coordinating the Conditions for the Admission of Securities to Official Stock Exchange Listing* set out the minimum conditions to be met by issuers of securities, including minimum issue price, a company's period of existence, free negotiability, sufficient distribution, and the provision of appropriate information to investors. Member states were free to impose stricter requirements. This was the first of four directives (the others followed in 1980 and 1982) which were designed to make it easier for companies to list their shares or raise capital on other EU stock exchanges. Directives concerned with information to investors covered the disclosure of large shareholdings in companies, the provision of information in prospectuses and insider dealing.

The new Cockfield Report and SEA principles of minimum harmonization, mutual recognition, a single passport and home-country regulation were applied in two directives on the marketing of unit trusts in 1985 and 1988. These allowed a unit trust which had been approved in one member country to be sold anywhere in the EU without further authorization provided it met investor protection requirements in force in the host country.

The first major securities industry directive based on Cockfield principles was the *Investment Services Directive* (ISD) which came into force in June 1992. It extended the single passport principle to non-bank investment firms generally. This extension was essential because the SBCD had given this right to banks carrying out securities business but did not grant it to non banks in this area. There was a particular problem because, as we have noted, the banking industry in some member states had traditionally been organized on universal banking principles whereas in other member states (notably the UK), the two forms of business had been separated. Thus, if the ISD had not been agreed, banks engaged in securities business would have been given a competitive advantage over non-bank firms. The ISD thus provided for the removal of barriers to both the provision of cross-border securities services and the establishment of branches throughout the EU for all firms. It also liberalized the rules governing access to stock exchanges and financial futures and options exchanges.

The difference in the organization of banking and securities industries among member countries led to problems in relation to capital adequacy. If capital adequacy rules had not been extended to cover non-bank securities firms, then they, in their turn, would have been given a competitive advantage over banks engaged in securities business who were required to meet capital adequacy rules. However, as we explain in Chapter 24, it was widely argued that the same rules should not apply to both forms of business. This ultimately led to the *Capital Adequacy Directive* (CAD) of 1993 which applied to both investment firms and to the securities activities of banks.

20.4.4 Insurance Services

As with other financial services, the insurance industry has typically been highly regulated. There are particular reasons for this in the nature of some kinds of insurance. Firstly, specifically in the area of life insurance, contracts are very long term with the consequence that a policyholder faces a significant default risk, especially since the insurance companies themselves face major problems in the assessment of risk and maturity transformation. But information on the ability of a company to meet its financial obligations many years ahead is difficult to come by and expensive.

Secondly, the risks being insured may be very large relative to other aspects of a policyholder's annual or even lifetime income. Few people are sufficiently wealthy to be able to afford not to have their house or even their motor vehicle insured. Third-party payments on motor vehicle accidents is potentially so large that insurance against it is a legal requirement for drivers. The failure of a pension or superannuation fund can make a very great difference to the comfort of people in old age.

Thirdly, the nature of the product is far from transparent. The complexity of the risks being insured and of the terms of settlement of contracts means that the problem of 'the small print' in contracts is of more importance in insurance than in most mass consumer industries and that open and honest professional advice is a crucial element of the industry. Consumer protection is thus a very important issue in insurance.

It is not surprising, then, that there has always been a tendency to regulate the insurance industry quite tightly. The special features of insurance have also, until quite recently, favoured local insurance companies. Consumers have, on balance, felt more confident in assessing the reliability of local companies. Equally, until insurance companies became very large and began to act entirely on the basis of probability, there were advantages for domestic over international companies. The result of all of this has been that legal barriers have strongly reinforced other factors in the fragmentation of insurance into a number of relatively isolated national markets. With the exception of reinsurance, which deals with very large and often international risks, the insurance industry has, in all EU countries other than the UK, been well protected from foreign competition.

From the beginning, the European Commission acknowledged the additional problems associated with the long average length of contracts in life insurance by the issuing of separate directives for life and non-life insurance. Hence, 1973 saw the promulgation of the *First Non-Life Insurance Directive*. The *First Life Insurance Directive* followed in 1979. Both of these directives followed the principle of host-country regulation. They established the right for companies to operate in other member states but harmonization of regulations across the EU was very slow. Several members strongly resisted attempts to open up their insurance markets to greater competition. In Germany, for example, non-German firms were required to have a local establishment and were taxed at rates which the European Commission considered discriminatory. In 1986 the European Court of Justice made a ruling that the restrictions imposed on insurance companies from other member states by Germany, France, Ireland and Denmark were partly illegal. In particular, the Court attacked the practice of requiring establishment and local authorization before a company could participate in the co-insurance of large risks situated outside of its home country.

The court ruling, together with the increased role for qualified majority voting introduced in the Single European Act, encouraged the European Commission to attempt to incorporate the home-country regulation principle into insurance directives. They were, however, inhibited from replacing the requirement of full harmonization of the rules regarding the authorization of companies by mutual recognition because of the sensitivity of the consumer protection issue in a significant part of the insurance industry. Consumer protection was, remember, one of the areas which, under the 1979 *Cassis de Dijon* court ruling, could be used to justify the rejection of the standards applied by other member states.

The Commission tackled the problem by following the 1986 Court of Justice ruling which had made a distinction between the insurance of large risks (including all marine, transport and aviation risk) and small commercial risks and personal insurance. Whereas host-country regulation was preserved for the latter category, the Commission felt able to apply the home-country regulation principle to the former category on the grounds that large companies or people responsible for insuring large risks are much better able to collect and assess information about insurance companies than is the average consumer.

Thus, in the *Freedom of Services Directive for Non-Life Insurance*, for small-risk business the regulations of the country in which the policyholder resides apply while for large-risk business the regulations of the country in which the company is licensed apply. Large-risk business was defined to cover policies for companies with more than 500 employees or more than £15 million turnover. Motor insurance was brought within the scope of the Non-Life directive by the *Motor Insurance Services Directive* of 1990.

The distinction between large and small risks could not be made in the *Second Life Assurance Directive* and so a different distinction was made to bring in an element of home-country regulation. Host-country regulation applied except where the initiative for a cross-border policy came from the policy-holder rather than the company – then the home-country regulation principle applied. Should the initiative for a cross-border policy come from the insurance company, on the other hand, host-country rules would apply and the provisions applicable would be those of the country in which the risk was situated. Host countries also retained responsibility for the regulation of branches of foreign companies, although 'well-established' companies covering large risks were, under the terms of the directive, simply required to notify the host authorities of their intention to provide services in the host country.

Despite continued resistance from some members and problems over the distortion of competition by different tax relief treatment on premiums, the Commission pushed ahead and in July 1994 the *Third Non-Life Insurance Directive*, the *Third Motor Insurance Directive* and the *Third Life Assurance Directive* came into force, introducing the full single passport, home-regulation regime to the insurance industry, although derogations giving extra time for implementation, ranging from the end of 1995 to the end of 1998, were granted to Spain, Portugal and

Greece. Although the home-country regulation will apply, a role will remain for host institutions. In practice, most insurance companies will establish a local presence because of the need to provide follow-up customer sales and service. Local rules on sales techniques and advertising will apply but cannot be used to discriminate against foreign companies. In certain circumstances, host states can exercise control over particular products, for instance mandatory third-party motor insurance. Finally, policyholders will be protected by the application of domestic contract law.

20.4.5   Progress – an overview

With regard to the five requirements for a single European financial market, it is now arguable that the European Commission has done almost all that it can do in terms of having legislation accepted at an EU level. There are, however, exceptions to this. The Commission has, for example, made no progress on the removal of national restrictions on the investment of pension funds. In 1996, having failed to persuade the Council of Ministers to act, it issued a non-binding communication calling on member states to ensure that their national legislation does not restrict the freedom of pension funds to select a manager based in another EU country nor prevent them from investing all their funds in the interests of their beneficiaries. This, however, can be seen as an act almost of desperation. The Commission also sees unfinished business in insurance, notably with regard to cross-border taxation especially on products related to pension schemes. It is further arguable that there will be no end to required EU legislation as action must be taken to cope with fast-changing products and structures. Under this heading, we shall deal with recent attempts to incorporate new international agreements on the regulation of risk in Chapter 24.

Other issues of concern relate to the movement to a single currency (discussed in Chapter 21) and the harmonization of taxation. Both of these are difficult, if not intractable areas. The initial acceptance of VAT as the common form of general indirect tax for the Union was a major step forwards, but since then progress on tax harmonization has been slow and, everywhere, grudging. Some progress has been made in limiting the ranges of VAT applied by member countries and in July 1996, the Commission announced a three-year timetable for the presentation of final proposals for an EU-wide VAT structure, based on the country of origin principle, in which domestic and cross-border transactions are subject to the same taxation. This would, however, require a reallocation of revenues based upon consumption statistics, agreement on a single standard rate of tax, and harmonization of the number and scope of reduced rates and exemptions currently in operation. Many battles loom for the Commission in both the Council of Ministers and the European Parliament in these areas. Much also remains to be done with regard to the taxation of profits.

Further, it will only be possible to claim that the EFCM has been established when more progress has been made on implementation. The Commission continues to face severe problems in this regard. In 1996, it was necessary to take Italy to the European Court of Justice before the country was willing to transpose the Investment Services Directive (ISD) into national law. The Commission has had many problems also with other member states in the implementation of both the ISD and the Capital Adequacy Directive into their national laws. Finally, the Commission has become seriously worried about the way in which some directives are being implemented. For example, they fear that inconsistencies in the way member states have implemented the banking directives have been a deterrent to banks seeking to take advantage of a single banking licence.

Beyond the formal rules, a single financial market only comes about through the behaviour of suppliers and consumers. Recent years have seen a number of takeovers in the finance industry across Europe, notably in merchant banking and insurance. Within countries, mergers have also been common, in part as a response to the additional competitive pressures from other member states which the SEA has engendered. However, it will be some years yet before we can hope to see the sort of gains in the financial industry that were foreseen in the Cecchini Report.

20.5 Summary

Progress towards a fully integrated European economy had begun to slow down by the early 1980s. Although tariffs among member states had been removed, there were still many barriers to intra-EU trade. The removal of these barriers would increase competition and allow the fuller exploitation of economies of scale, leading to increased efficiency, lower costs, and higher levels of investment and rates of economic growth. The Single European Act of 1986 thus sought to deepen integration through the removal of all non-tariff barriers to trade in both goods and services and to the mobility of capital and labour.

Estimates were made of considerable welfare gains which would accrue to Europe through the movement to the single market and these were published in the *Cecchini Report*. Criticisms followed that the estimates were overly optimistic and that regional and structural problems might result. Nonetheless, there was widespread acceptance of the single market programme.

The removal of barriers to trade within financial services and to the mobility of capital had been even slower than in other areas of the European economy.

One major reason for this lay in the unwillingness of national regulatory authorities to cede control of activities in their own national markets. This had led to progress in the harmonization of regulations across the EU being very slow. To speed up the movement to a single financial market, a change of strategy was incorporated in the Single European Act. The objective of complete harmonization of regulations was replaced with the much more easily attainable mutual recognition of national standards and regulations. A second major change was the move from host-country regulation of the firms of other member states within a country to home-country regulation. This allowed a company to operate anywhere within the EU on the basis of a single licence obtained from the regulatory authorities in its home market.

These new principles were incorporated in directives aimed at the creation of a single market in the three categories of financial services – banking, the rapidly growing securities market and insurance. However, there is still much to be done in terms of further directives, the implementation into national law of all existing directives, and the enforcement of single market laws at a national level before the gains foreseen from a European Financial Common Market can begin to come through.

Key concepts used in this chapter

Single/internal market	Harmonization	Fiscal barriers to trade
Physical barriers to trade	Single passport	Single financial market
Technical barriers to trade	Relationship pricing	Host-country regulation
Costs of non-Europe	Single European Act (SEA)	Mutual recognition
Home-country regulation	Single European Market (SEM)	Cross-subsidies

Questions and problems

1 What disadvantages do you see in the movement to the SEM?

2 List as many technical barriers to trade as you can think of.

3 Why is the measurement of gains from the movement to a single market so difficult?

4 What was special about the financial services industry which led progress towards the harmonization of national laws to be so slow?

5 List the arguments in favour of host-country regulation and discuss them. Why did the European Commission favour home-country regulation?

6 Have you seen examples in your town or region of the development of a single European financial market?

7 What is meant by systemic risk in connection with the banking industry?

8 Why is consumer protection such an important issue in insurance?

Further reading

R E Baldwin, 'On the growth effects of 1992', *Economic Policy*, 1989, 9, 248–81

P Cecchini *et al.*, *The European Challenge 1992: the benefits of a single market*, Report of the Cost of Non-Europe Steering Committee (Aldershot: Wildwood House, 1988)

T Culter, C Haslem, J Williams and K Williams, *1992 – The Struggle for Europe* (London: Berg, 1989)

E Davis and C Smales, 'The integration of European financial services', in J Kay (ed.), *1992: Myths and Realities* (London: London Business School, 1990), 205–41

R Dixon, *Banking in Europe: the Single Market* (London: Routledge, 1991)

M Emerson *et al.*, *The Economics of 1992* (Brussels: Commission of the EC, 1988)

H D Gibson and E Tsakalotos, 'European Integration and the Banking Sector in Southern Europe: Competition, Efficiency and Structure,' *Banca Nazionale del Lavoro Quarterly Review* (1993, September), 299–326

J Grahl and P Teague, *The Big Market* (London: Lawrence and Wishart, 1990)

V Grilli, 'Europe 1992: Issues and prospects for the financial markets,' *Economic Policy*, 1989, 9

N M Healey (ed.), *The Economics of the New Europe* (London: Routledge, 1995) Ch. 7

R Henderson, *European Finance* (London: McGraw Hill, 1993)

G U-M Nielsen, H Heinrich and J D Hansen, *An Economic Analysis of the EC* (London: McGraw-Hill, 1991) Ch. 4

P Sutherland *et al.*, *The Internal Market after 1992: Meeting the Challenge*, Report to the European Commission by the High Level Group on the Operation of the Internal Market (1992)

D Swann D (ed.), *The Single European Market and Beyond* (Routledge: London, 1992) Ch. 5

CHAPTER 21

The European Monetary System and European Monetary Union

Box 21.1

What you will learn in this chapter:

- The background and early history of the EMS
- The plans for EMU in the Maastricht Treaty
- The principal reasons for the ERM problems in the early 1990s
- The issues concerning the prospects of EMU happening by 1999
- The post-EMU problems for members' and non-members' influence over interest rates

21.1 Introduction

The European Monetary System (EMS) was established in 1979 for a mixture of economic and political reasons. The central element in the system was the Exchange Rate Mechanism (ERM), a fixed exchange rate arrangement which sought to restrict the extent to which volatile exchange rates interfered with fair competition among EU producers. From an economic viewpoint, fixed exchange rates became essential once the International Monetary Fund's fixed exchange rate system had started to come under pressure in the late 1960s. Under the IMF system, the exchange rates of EU countries could vary against each other by a maximum of ± 2 per cent.[1] However, in August 1969, the French franc was devalued by

11.11 per cent and later the Deutschmark was revalued by over 9 per cent. In December 1971, the band which each currency had to maintain against the dollar was increased to 2.25 per cent, widening the allowable variation in the value of one European currency against another to ±4.5 per cent. The combination of the wide band and possible changes in the exchange rate parity was thought to interfere too much with the fairness of competition among producers in different EU states and to raise the possibility of countries acting to push down the relative values of their currencies in order to improve the competitiveness of their industries.

Volatile exchange rates also caused a specific problem for the Common Agricultural Policy (CAP) of the EU. The policy had been designed in the 1960s on the assumption that the exchange rates among the EU currencies would remain unchanged. Prices in the CAP were fixed in terms of the EUA – the European Unit of Account, the forerunner of the Ecu. A fall in the value of the franc, say, against the dollar and the EUA meant that farm prices in France would rise in terms of French francs but remain the same elsewhere. This would give French farmers an advantage over other farmers within the Union and encourage them to increase production, adding to the already strong incentives for European farmers to over-produce. In 1971 a formal system of levies and subsidies (known as MCAs – Monetary Compensatory Amounts) was introduced. This established a dual system of exchange rates – the actual market

---

[1] All currencies were required to remain within a band *against the US dollar* of ±1 per cent, which meant that all non-dollar curriencies could vary against other non-dollar currencies by

±2 per cent: with at times currency A being 1 per cent above its parity with the dollar and currency B being 1 per cent below its dollar parity; while at other times the reverse might apply.

Box 21.2   The Exchange Rate Mechanism of the EMS

The ERM was based on a *parity grid* which tied each currency to every other currency in a system of mutually agreed and consistent rates. Under a *parity grid*, whenever a currency diverges from parity, all other exchange rates also diverge from the agreed rate. Hence, all countries must respond to bring about the re-establishment of parity. It was thus intended that the burden of maintaining the fixed exchange rate system would be shared equally among all members; those with strong and weak currencies alike. Central rates (parities) in the EMS were established against the European Currency Unit (Ecu), a weighted average of the value of the currencies of all EU members.

As the system operated from its inception in 1979 until the collapse early in August 1993, each of the currencies in the ERM had to stay within a band either of ± 2.25 per cent (narrow band) or ± 6 per cent (broad band) around its central rate against the Ecu (at the time of the collapse, the peseta and the escudo were the only two of the nine currencies within the broad band). In August 1993, the band for all members was widened to ± 15 per cent, although Germany and the Netherlands agreed separately to retain the old narrow band for the relationship between their currencies.

The parity grid, showing the required relationship of each country against every other currency in the mechanism, was derived from the central rates of each currency against the ECU. In addition to being required to stay within its band against the Ecu, each currency has to stay within the same band against every other currency. In practice, currencies under pressure within the mechanism fall out of their bands against individual currencies before they fall out of their bands against the Ecu.

Intervention points are calculated at 75 per cent of the permitted divergence of a currency from its central parity against the Ecu. When a currency reaches an intervention point, the central bank in question is required to intervene in the market, buying or selling its own currency in order to keep the currency within its band. Adjustments to central parities were allowed from time to time, although these were meant to stop under Stage II of the EMU process.

---

rate and the Green rate of exchange which was used to convert farm prices set in EUAs into national currencies. Countries whose market exchange rates fell below their Green rates would pay MCAs, those whose market rates rose above their Green rates would receive MCAs. Although MCAs adjusted to some extent for the exchange rate changes in terms of fairness, these modifications to the CAP meant that there was no longer a system of common prices throughout the Union.

Although the Treaty of Rome had contained nothing about monetary integration, there had always been considerable support on political grounds for the idea that monetary integration should eventually occur. Proposals for steps to be taken towards a single currency and single monetary policy were made as early as 1961. Serious discussion of monetary integration began at The Hague summit in December 1969 and this was followed in 1971 by the Werner Committee report which recommended the achievement of European Monetary Union by 1980. Any possibility that this might happen was removed by the volatility of exchange rates following the complete breakdown of the Bretton Woods system in 1972.

This also destroyed any chance of success for the system of fixed exchange rates, known as the Snake in the Tunnel, which was established in Europe in April 1972 and struggled on until March 1979, when the EMS replaced it. The Snake attempted to limit the freedom of European currencies to move against each other to ± 2.25 per cent around the established central rates – half the freedom which had been possible under the modified IMF arrangements. However, only Benelux, West Germany and Denmark remained members of the Snake for the seven years of its existence. At various times, France, the UK, Sweden, Norway and Italy all entered and left. The 'fixed' parities were altered 31 times.

Details of the exchange rate mechanism of the EMS are provided in Box 21.2.

As can be seen from Box 21.2, an attempt was made to allow for the problems of particular countries by requiring those that had not survived within the Snake to maintain the value of their

---

Box 21.3   Central parity changes in the ERM

(All figures are percentage changes in central rates against the ECU)

Period One – 1979 to 1983: the early problems

13 Mar 1979	ERM comes into operation
24 Sep 1979	DM +2; krone −2.9
30 Nov 1979	Krone −4.8
23 Mar 1981	Lira −6
5 Oct 1981	Lira, Fr franc −3; DM, guilder +5.5
22 Feb 1982	Bel/Lux franc −8.5; krone −3
14 June 1982	Fr franc −5.75; lira −2.75; DM, guilder +4.25
21 Mar 1983	Fr franc, lira −2.5; DM +5.5; punt −3.5; Bel/Lux franc +1.5; krone +2.5; guilder +3.5

Period Two – 1983 to 1987: settling down

22 Jul 1985	Lira −6; all others +2
7 Apr 1986	Fr franc −3; DM, guilder +3; krone, Bel/Lux franc +1 krone +1
4 Aug 1986	Punt −8
12 Jan 1987	Bel/Lux franc +2; DM, guilder +3

Period Three – 1987 to 1992: stability

1 Jun 1989	Peseta joins ERM
5 Jan 1990	Lira's band narrowed from ±6 to ±2.25, implicitly changing central rate by −3.7
8 Oct 1990	Sterling joins ERM
6 Apr 1992	Escudo joins ERM

Period Four – 1992 to 1996: renewed disturbance

14 Sep 1992	Lira −3.5; all others +3.5
16 Sep 1992	Sterling suspended from ERM
17 Sep 1992	Lira suspended from ERM; peseta −5
23 Nov 1992	Peseta, escudo −6
30 Jan 1993	Punt −10
13 May 1993	Peseta −8; escudo −6.5
2 Aug 1993	Bands widened to ±15
1 Jan 1995	Schilling joins ERM
6 Mar 1995	Peseta −7; escudo −3.5
14 Oct 1996	Markka joins ERM
25 Nov 1996	Lira rejoins ERM

---

currency within a very wide band of ±6 per cent around the central rates which were established against the ECU.[2] Despite this attempt at increased flexibility, the mechanism faced many early problems and seven adjustments were made to central rates in the first four years. After much talk in 1982 and early 1983 of French withdrawal and of the system's virtual collapse, things began to settle down and there were only three further realignments prior to the general realignment of January 1987. Towards the end of this period of relative exchange rate stability, talk began to be heard again about the possibility of a movement to monetary union. Box 21.3 summarizes this last section by showing the changes in central parities in the ERM between 1979 and 1995.

The period up until September 1992 was one of capital liberalization and a determined attempt to achieve exchange rate stability as a step towards monetary union. The only change in central rates in over $5\frac{1}{2}$ years was a small reduction in the central rate

of the lira to allow it to move from the ±6 per cent band to the ±2.25 per cent band. There was growing evidence of inflation rates among members converging on the lower rate of inflation experienced by Germany. For several countries, this convergence of inflation rates was accompanied by large increases in unemployment but most governments seemed prepared to accept this as a necessary cost of lower inflation. In 1990, the EMS was generally held to have been a success because it had reduced the variability of members' bilateral exchange rates.

The second half of the 1980s also saw a renewed political push towards monetary integration. In 1985, when member countries adopted the Single European Act, they increased the need for the progressive development of EMU. In June 1988 the Council of Europe set up a committee under Jacques Delors, the President of the European Commission, to study and make proposals regarding the necessary stages for the achievement of EMU. The result, submitted in April 1989, was The *Report of the Committee on*

---

2 Only Italy accepted this offer at the beginning, although later Spain (1989), the UK (1990) and Portugal (1992) all accepted the 6 per cent band on joining the ERM.

Economic and Monetary Union, also known as the Delors Report. It set out the goal to be reached, the reasons for it and its possible implications, as well as specifying the desired stages leading up to EMU. The Delors Report was accepted as the basis for the debate at the European summit held in Madrid on 26 June 1989. Its principal recommendations were then incorporated into the Treaty on European Union, agreed upon at Maastricht in December 1991.[3]

21.2 The Treaty on European Union and the plans for EMU

The Treaty on European Union set out the nature, functions and constitution of the new central banking system which would manage the single currency, monetary policy and foreign exchange in EMU (discussed in Chapter 22). It also explained how fiscal and budgetary policy would be managed and set out the stages through which EMU would be reached. The first stage was seen retrospectively as having commenced in July 1990 with the liberalization of capital flows and the integration of financial markets under the single market programme. During this first stage, all EU countries were to become full members of the ERM in the narrow band. There was to be an increase in the coordination of national monetary policies and the pooling of 10 per cent of national foreign exchange reserves to allow intervention in currency markets.

Stage 2 was to begin in January 1994 with the establishment of the European Monetary Institute (EMI) which would have the task of preparing the way for EMU. During Stage 2, responsibility for the execution of monetary, exchange rate and fiscal policy would still rest with the member states. However, the EMI would plan monetary policy, monitor the policies of member states, and advise member governments. Changes would only be allowed to central exchange rates in the ERM under exceptional circumstances.

The EMI would be replaced at the beginning of Stage 3 by the European Central Bank (ECB) which, together with the central banks of the member states,

would form the European System of Central Banks (ESCB). In Stage 3 exchange rates would be irrevocably fixed and national currencies would eventually be replaced by a single EU currency. The ECB would take over from the EMI, and would assume responsibility for exchange rate and monetary policies. A decision was required before the end of December 1996 as to when Stage 3 would commence. If, however, no date had been set by the end of 1997, the third stage would start on 1 January 1999.

With regard to membership of EMU, the Treaty set out a number of convergence conditions, which EU member states would need to meet to be allowed to join. Membership would require:

(1) demonstration that the country's inflation rate had converged on the lowest rates of inflation within the union – to be judged specifically by whether the average rate of inflation, observed over a period of one year before the decision regarding membership was within 1.5 percentage points of the average of the three lowest national rates;

(2) evidence that the inflation convergence was durable – to be shown by a long-term interest rate within two percentage points of the average of the long-term interest rate of the three countries with lowest inflation;

(3) a sustainable government financial position defined as (i) a general government budget deficit no greater than 3 per cent of GDP at market prices and (ii) a ratio of gross public debt to GDP at market prices no greater than 60 per cent – unless this debt ratio is falling 'at a satisfactory pace';

(4) observance of the normal fluctuation margins provided for by the ERM of the EMS for at least two years with no devaluations against any other member currency.

In addition, the Commission and the EMI were required to take account of development of the Ecu, the results of the integration of markets, the situation and development of the balances of payments on current account, and the development of unit labour costs and other price indices.

---

[3] Although it was agreed upon at Maastricht, the Treaty on European Union was not signed until 7 February 1992 and did not come into force until 1 November 1993, following slowness in ratification of the Treaty by many countries.

A majority of the member states were required to be economically fit for EMU if the currency union were to go ahead from December 1996 but no such 'critical mass' was required for the union to be established on 1 January 1999 (with membership being determined before 1 July 1998).

The specific numbers included in the convergence conditions had nothing in particular to recommend them. At the time of the signing of the Treaty on European Union, they looked to be achievable targets for many EU member states while appearing sufficiently tough to hope to persuade financial markets that the monetary policies pursued after 1999 would be strong, anti-inflationary policies.

21.3   The problems of the 1990s

At the beginning of 1992, everything seemed to be going well for the EMS and hopes were high of meeting the deadlines of the Treaty on European Union for the formation of EMU by 1997 or by 1999 at the latest. Yet by September of that same year, two major currencies (sterling and the lira) had been forced out of the ERM while three others (the peseta, the escudo and the punt) had devalued. Three more currencies (the French franc, the Danish krone and the Belgian franc) remained under severe pressure at various stages in the following months and in August 1993, the allowable band around central rates within which countries were required to keep their exchange rates was widened to ±15 per cent in order to preserve the central rate of the French franc and to make life more difficult for speculators.

What had gone wrong? Almost inevitably, both economic and political factors contributed to the crisis. Part of the problem was that by 1992 exchange rates were well out of line following the prolonged period without adjustment of central rates. Although inflation rates had converged to a considerable extent, the differences that remained had meant that a number of countries had become seriously uncompetitive at the existing exchange rates. This seemed clear in the case of the UK because the current account of its balance of payments remained firmly in deficit despite the country being in a deep economic recession. The standard response of increasing

interest rates to counter a deficit was, for political reasons, not available in the middle of a recession.

The economic problem of misaligned exchange rates was added to by popular concerns regarding the increased speed of integration of the EU. In Britain's case this was nothing new. The British government's doubts had been expressed at the Maastricht conference by its insistence that Britain be given the right to opt out of membership of EMU. In other member states, uncertainty about the future had clearly increased and this was shown by the narrowness with which the referendum held in France to approve the Treaty on European Union was passed and the loss of the first referendum held in Denmark on the same question. The increase in doubt about the future of the EU expressed itself in foreign exchange markets through a weakening of currencies already weakened by worries about competitiveness.

The final element was the increased freedom which speculators had to exploit the difficulties of weak currencies because of the capital liberalization which had occurred under the Single European Act. Speculators knew that if they sold weak currencies in large quantities for sufficient periods of time, currencies were very likely to be forced either to devalue or to leave the ERM. In the second case, once weak currencies floated outside the ERM they would be very likely to fall sharply. In either event, speculators would be able to buy the weak currencies back at much lower rates than they had sold them for, thus making very large per annum rates of profit. Because central banks could no longer impose capital controls and because the capital movements were so very large, central banks were in no position to resist the downward pressure on weak currencies. Where they tried and failed, as with the Bank of England, they experienced very large losses.

There were two apparent solutions. The first was that interest rates should be generally lowered across the EU to help countries in recession. This would have required the Bundesbank to lower its interest rate. This it was unwilling to do for two reasons – one local and one related to the aims of the EMS as a whole. The local, if very large, problem which Germany faced was the absorption by West Germany of the very weak East German economy following German unification in 1989.

The German government had, for internal economic and political reasons, exchanged Deutschmarks for the East German currency, the Ostmark, at equal value. This had increased the total German money supply much more than total German production had increased as a result of unification and raised fears of increasing inflation. These fears were augmented by the promise of the government not to increase taxation rates during the unification process. Public expenditure and budget deficits inevitably increased.

The Bundesbank's natural response was to raise interest rates, rather than to lower them as the UK wanted. This made sense in terms of the system as a whole, if one accepted (as many appeared to do) that a major advantage of the EMS was that it allowed inflation-prone countries to lower their rates of inflation by linking their currencies to that of low-inflation Germany. This possibility would have disappeared had inflation rates in Germany climbed very sharply.

The solution from the German perspective was then for the weak currency countries to accept a realignment within the EMS. The devaluation of those currencies would, however, have increased inflationary pressures and caused doubts to arise about their future determination to fight inflation. Thus the UK, in particular, was unwilling to countenance an organized, ordered devaluation. The increase in tensions between the Bundesbank and the British government caused further doubts in the foreign exchange market and led to more downward pressure being exerted on sterling. Italy was also thought to be uncompetitive at the existing central rates and speculators spread their attack to the lira. Spain and Portugal were able to contain the pressure to some extent both because they were still in the 6 per cent band of the EMS and because they were able to reintroduce controls over the flow of capital.[4] Until the changes of August 1993, speculators were able to go on attacking weak currencies with very little risk of loss.

This period of exchange rate turmoil marked the beginning of a long period of doubt about both the prospects of EMU occurring in 1999[5] and the countries likely to qualify to join at its beginning. Doubts were intensified as it became clear that most EU members would have grave difficulty in meeting the convergence conditions laid down at Maastricht. Worse, it began to seem possible that Germany itself might not be able to do so. The principal difficulty related to the requirement of a sustainable government financial position. European economies experienced deep recessions in the early 1990s and this inevitably led to budget deficits in most countries well beyond the limit of 3 per cent of GDP.

As we said above, there was no particular reason for choosing 3 per cent as the target in the first place but once the target had been set, it took on a life of its own. Any attempt to increase the figure to allow more countries to qualify for membership ran the risk of being interpreted as a weakening of anti-inflationary resolve. The fear then was that markets would assume that inflation rates would be higher after EMU, calling the value of the EMU single currency against the dollar and the yen into doubt. That would lead to a higher risk premium being built into interest rates on the single currency and into the long-term interest rates of all EU members during the run-up to EMU.

In addition to the problems over government finances, the exchange rate disturbances of 1992 and 1993 had made the achievement of the fourth convergence condition very difficult. To begin with, by March 1997, the UK had not rejoined the ERM and Greece and Sweden were still to become members. The narrow band had all but been destroyed and, with bands of ±15 per cent, the phrase 'observance of the normal fluctuation margins provided for by the ERM' had very little meaning. The exchange rate changes had also interfered with the convergence of inflation rates.

---

[4] As we mentioned in Chapter 20, Spain and Portugal had both been given until the end of 1992 to remove all capital controls under the SEA.

[5] It was fairly quickly realized that there was little serious possibility of EMU starting by the earlier date of 1997 allowed in the Maastricht Treaty.

Table 21.1 EU members and the convergence criteria – 1996

(All figures in percentages)

Country	Inflation rate (a)	Long-term interest rate (b)	Genl govt borrowing (c)	Genl govt gross debt (d)
Belgium	1.6	6.7	3.3	130.6
Denmark (e)	2.2	7.4	1.4	70.2 (f)
Germany	1.3	6.3	4.0	60.8
Greece	8.4	15.1	7.9	110.6
Spain	3.8	9.5	4.4	67.8
France	2.1	6.6	4.0	56.4
Ireland	2.1	7.5	1.6	74.7 (f)
Italy	4.7	10.3	6.6	123.4
Luxembourg	1.3	7.0	0.9	7.8
Netherlands	1.2	6.3	2.6	78.7
Austria	1.7	6.5	4.3	71.7
Portugal	3.0	9.4	4.0	71.1
Finland	0.9	7.4	3.3	61.3
Sweden	1.6	8.5	3.9	78.1
UK	3.0	8.0	4.6	56.3

Average inflation rate of three lowest-inflation countries 1.13%
Average long-term interest rate of three lowest-inflation countries 6.7%

(a) Annual average inflation rate September 1996
(b) Annual average long-term interest rate September 1996
(c) As percentage of GDP: European Commission estimates autumn 1996
(d) As percentage of GDP: European Commission estimates autumn 1996
(e) General government gross debt figures are not adjusted for the assets held by the Danish Social Pension Fund against sectors outside general government nor for government deposits at the central bank for the management of foreign exchange reserves
(f) In 1994, 1995 and 1996 Ireland was not the subject of an European Council decision under article 104c(6) of the Treaty that an excessive deficit exists; in 1996 this was also the case for Denmark

Source: European Monetary Institute

21.4   Current prospects for EMU

By 1997 doubts about EMU had risen to the extent that postponement of the 1999 starting date seemed increasingly likely. As shown in Table 21.1, few countries seemed likely to meet all convergence criteria by July 1998.

Ten countries were meeting the inflation convergence target of 2.63 per cent or less. All of these plus the U.K. were meeting the long-term interest requirement of 8.7 per cent or less. However, only Denmark, Ireland, Luxembourg and the Netherlands were meeting the requirement that General Government Borrowing be no more than 3 per cent of GDP. Of these four, only Luxembourg and Denmark[6] strictly qualified on the General Government Gross Debt criterion. Ireland, too, effectively was qualifying since it had been judged for three successive years to be moving sufficiently quickly

6 Although Table 21.1 shows its General Government Gross Debt as 70.1 per cent of GDP, the possible adjustments to that figure mentioned in note (e) of the table allowed Denmark to qualify.

towards the required 60 per cent. Optimistic forecasts suggested that one or two other countries might qualify by 1998. The big worries were France and Germany.

The governments of France and Germany remained strongly committed to EMU on political grounds but faced increasing doubts from their own populations. France had for some time been in favour of EMU as the only sure way of tying Germany firmly to the rest of Europe. Ever since the unification of Germany, the German chancellor, Kohl, had appeared to share the French fear that, in the event of a loosening of European ties, Germany could become more introspective and nationalist and more concerned with the position of German minorities in other European countries. EMU was thus as much a symbol of European integration as it was an economic arrangement.

France, however, had unemployment of over 12 per cent and had experienced both social and industrial unrest. There was a strong feeling that the high unemployment was at least partly the result of the *Franc fort* policy of maintaining the value of the franc in terms of the German mark in order to keep alive hopes of EMU. This had required constant downward pressure on government expenditure but yet more cuts in expenditure would be needed to push government borrowing below 3 per cent of GDP. The extreme right-wing political party, the National Front, had gained considerable strength partly on immigration and racist issues but partly on the basis of its anti-EU rhetoric. Meanwhile, Germany had high unemployment also, although this could still be seen to a significant extent as one of the costs of unification. Of more concern to the German supporters of EMU were the widespread fears that the replacement of the Deutschmark by the Euro, the name accepted for the EMU single currency, would mean higher inflation.

In an attempt to counter these fears and, at the same time, to persuade the financial markets of the anti-inflation credibility of post-EMU monetary policy, the German government had, in December 1996, obtained acceptance of a stability pact[7] which set out rules for government borrowing of EMU members after January 1999. These rules converted the 3 per cent of the Maastricht agreement into a ceiling which should only be breached under exceptional circumstances. 'Exceptional circumstances' were defined to cover a natural disaster or a fall in GDP of at least 2 per cent over a year. Such a severe recession is not at all common, having occurred only 13 times in any of the 15 EU members in the past 30 years. In cases where GDP has fallen between 0.75 per cent and 2 per cent, EU finance ministers will have discretion on whether or not to impose penalties, taking into account factors such as the abruptness of the downturn. Members who broke the 3 per cent barrier in other circumstances would be required to make heavy non-interest-bearing deposits with the European Central Bank. Continued failure to return below the 3 per cent limit would see these deposits converted into fines. From an economic point of view this made little sense since the fines would make it even more difficult for the governments in question to get their borrowing back down below 3 per cent of GDP. But this was beside the point. The stability pact was an attempt to enhance the anti-inflation credibility of post-EMU monetary policy in the eyes of the German population.

The doubt was whether Germany itself would be able to achieve the 3 per cent target by 1998. In March 1997, the German Finance Minister argued that the achievement of the convergence conditions was more important than the timing of convergence. This added to the feeling that Germany might be willing to accept a postponement of the 1999 commencing date for EMU. The German fear, as we have seen, was that any weakness on the entry criteria would be taken badly by both the markets and the German population. Further, in October 1993, the German constitutional court had attached conditions to Germany's ratification of the treaty on European Union which specified that Germany could not be committed to an 'unclear, automatic and uncontrollable mechanism leading to currency union'. This meant that the court retained the power to prevent Germany's entry to EMU if the conditions for monetary union in the Maastricht Treaty were not adhered to. Although this

---

7 The pact was formally called 'the stability and growth pact' although it had much more to do with stability than with growth.

seemed unlikely, the court ruling added to pressure on the German government to ensure that the full achievement of the Maastricht convergence conditions remained the test of entry to EMU. Stressing the inviolability of the convergence conditions was also a way of discouraging the increasing push of Spain, Italy and Portugal to be allowed to join from 1999. Their presence in the first wave of EMU membership would have greatly added to the feeling that the post-EMU single currency would be weak and the EMU inflation rate much higher than most Germans seemed prepared to accept.

Yet the risks associated with delaying the start of EMU seemed rather high, particularly for countries on the fringe of joining. Interest rates in countries such as Spain and Italy had fallen sharply in anticipation of EMU as the markets judged that all potential candidates for membership would be working hard to meet the entry conditions. Delay in the start would reopen the possibility that countries, particularly those with high unemployment, would come under increased domestic pressure to ease their economic policies, leading to higher inflation and a fall in the value of their currencies. In anticipation of this, the markets would demand higher risk premiums for holding their currencies and interest rates would rise. This would increase the cost of financing their existing government debts and would make it less likely that they would be able to meet the convergence conditions in the future.

In any case, there was no provision in the Treaty on European Union for delay: 1 January 1999 was the compulsory date for the start of EMU. To delay the start would require a formal renegotiation of the Treaty with all 15 members agreeing on the change and with the change needing to be ratified by each member, through either national parliamentary approval or popular referendum. Another possibility would be for EMU to go ahead on time but with the European Council ruling that no countries had met the convergence criteria. EMU would be left as an 'empty shell' waiting for later activation. But this would increase the risks associated with delay since it would leave the possible date for the later commencement of EMU completely uncertain. This would be much more difficult for countries to cope with than would the substitution of a stated new date for the existing one. Also, the 'empty shell' option

would require manipulation of the rules since, as we have seen, at least three countries – Luxembourg, Denmark and Ireland – seemed likely to qualify fully for membership. The only way to make these countries ineligible would be to suspend the ERM for a few hours so that no country could meet the requirement of two years of uninterrupted ERM membership.

Under these circumstances, it was best in March 1997 to treat Germany's not very veiled warnings of the possibility of delay as a continuation of its determination to stress the importance of the convergence criteria and to bet that EMU would indeed commence in some form or other on 1 January 1999. But many problems other than the initial membership of the monetary union remained. These included the relationship which would be maintained between the currencies of EMU members and those of the EU countries outside of EMU as well as the likelihood of those countries excluded from EMU at the beginning later being able to meet the conditions of membership.

21.5 Post-EMU problems for EMU members and non-members

The principal danger for EMU members would come from the values of the currencies of non-members falling sharply following the beginning of EMU, damaging the competitiveness in trade of EMU members. The extent of this danger can be well illustrated by the events following the departure of the lira and sterling from the ERM in September 1992. Both currencies, the lira in particular, depreciated sharply, increasing the competitiveness of Italy and Britain and making life much more difficult for producers within the countries that remained within the ERM. The way in which it was hoped to avoid this problem after EMU was to require all EU members who are outside of EMU to join a new version of the EMS (EMS II) which would maintain fixed exchange rates among its members *and* with the single currency of the EMU. This would have an advantage also for aspiring EMU members since it would assist them in achieving the convergence necessary for later entry.

However, this scheme almost certainly underestimated the strength of the currency markets. It seemed very likely that the currencies of countries excluded from the first wave of EMU membership would come under very great selling pressure and that there would be, at the least, a once-and-for-all devaluation of several currencies. It was probably also the case that downwards pressure would remain on EMS II member countries after EMU, especially if it appeared that their chances of becoming members of EMU were not strong.

We have already mentioned the principal problems for non-EMU members after EMU. Initial devaluations of their currencies might well be beneficial for trade and employment but would make future convergence on the lower inflation rate within EMU more difficult. The attempt thereafter to maintain a fixed exchange rate with the single currency would almost certainly require higher interest rates, reducing the chances of achieving the government finances conditions. Later entry would become yet more difficult if the EMU members succeeded in applying the rules of the stability pact (see Section 21.4 above) for then the EMU members might wish to apply a tighter test for future membership than that specified in the Maastricht convergence conditions.

21.6 Summary

There have always been strong political and economic motives behind the desire to move to European Monetary Union (EMU). The need for closer monetary integration only became urgent,

however, with the breakdown of the fixed exchange rate Bretton Woods system from the late 1960s on. Plans to move to EMU by 1980 came to nothing and the fixed exchange rate system established in 1972, the Snake, failed. The European Monetary System (EMS) was established in 1979 to attempt to limit exchange rate uncertainty within the EU. After some difficult years, the system appeared to be settling down. This, together with the passing of the Single European Act in 1986, encouraged hopes for a renewed attempt to move to EMU. The Delors Report recommended a three-stage process for achieving EMU and this was confirmed at the Maastricht conference in December 1991, with 1 January 1999 being set as the latest date by which EMU must occur.

Optimism about EMU was badly dented by the major currency disturbances of 1992 and 1993 which led to sterling and the lira being suspended from membership of the exchange rate mechanism of the EMS and to the bands within which currencies were allowed to move within the mechanism being dramatically widened. Despite this, a strong determination to achieve EMU remained on the part of the European Commission and of several governments. As the starting date became closer, however, doubts arose about the ability of many governments, most importantly those of Germany and France, to meet the conditions for EMU membership laid down at Maastricht for membership of EMU. At the time of the writing of this book, it remained uncertain whether EMU would commence at the beginning of 1999. It was also very unclear as to which countries would join EMU in the first wave, were it indeed to start on time.

Key concepts used in this chapter

Exchange Rate Mechanism (ERM)	Parity grid
Snake in the Tunnel	Central rates
Convergence	European Monetary Union (EMU)
European Monetary Institute	Government financial position
Stability pact	Anti-inflationary credibility

Questions and problems

1 Explain the reasoning behind each of the Maastricht convergence conditions.

2 What are the economic reasons for wanting monetary integration in Europe?

3 Consider the argument that EMU is a necessary extension of the European single market.

4 Why is it more difficult to achieve the convergence conditions for EMU membership when a country is in recession?

5 Why is it important that Germany should be a member of EMU?

6 Bring the account in this chapter (written in March 1997) up to date.

Further reading

D Cobham (ed.), *European Monetary Upheavals* (Manchester: Manchester University Press, 1994)

M Crawford, *One Money for Europe? The Economics and Politics of Maastricht* (Basingstoke: Macmillan, 1993)

P De Grauwe, *The Economics of Monetary Integration* (Oxford: Oxford University Press, 1994, 2e)

C Johnson and S Collignon (eds), *The Monetary Economics of Europe: the Causes of the EMS Crisis* (London: Pinter, 1994)

C Taylor, *EMU 2000? Prospects for European Monetary Union* (London: Royal Institute of International Affairs, 1995)

CHAPTER 22   The European Central Bank and post-EMU monetary policy

Box 22.1

What you will learn in this chapter:

- The possible forms of determining monetary policy in a monetary union
- The arguments for and against central bank independence
- The reasons for concern about the size of the budget deficits of EMU members
- The Maastricht Treaty rules regarding the European Central Bank and its policy
- The nature of the questions to be resolved concerning post-EMU monetary policy

22.1   Introduction

In a currency area with completely fixed exchange rates *and* full freedom of capital flows, there must be a common monetary policy. Imagine that each member of such an area tried to operate its own monetary policy. Suppose that one member decided to have a tighter monetary policy than the rest. As soon as it raised interest rates, capital would flow into the country from other member states. This must happen since, with completely fixed exchange rates, there would be no foreign exchange risk and so no distinction between covered and uncovered interest parity (discussed in Chapter 12). Capital would move until interest rates were again the same in all member states. Exactly where the common interest rate finished up would depend on the monetary policies and relative strengths of the member states, but there would be only one interest rate for the area as a whole (we shall see an exception to this in Section 22.3).

But how should the common monetary policy be determined? There are two possible models:

(1) the *asymmetric leadership model*: one country's monetary policy dominates those of other members and effectively becomes the monetary policy for the entire area;
(2) the *joint-decision model*: governments or central banks of member countries meet together and decide upon the common monetary policy through discussion and compromise.

This leaves us to ask who becomes the leader in the asymmetric leadership model. Again there are two possibilities:

1   that the system is organized around one currency which thus necessarily becomes the leader – this was the case with the US dollar in the Bretton Woods fixed exchange rate system;
2   that a currency becomes the leader because the market and other governments feel that it is most likely to retain its value – this is likely to be the currency which is thought likely to have, over a run of years, the lowest average rate of inflation since, within a fixed exchange rate system, higher rates of inflation will quickly make a country's goods uncompetitive in international markets.

If exchange rates are not fully fixed and/or if there are effective controls on the flow of capital, member countries may be able to determine their own monetary policies to a considerable extent. We have seen that, apart from the five years between 1987 and 1992, the EMS has not been a fully fixed exchange rate system. Even between 1987 and 1992, the possibility of changes in central rates was sufficiently powerful that there was very little change over the period in foreign exchange risk premiums. Equally, up until 1990, many members still had capital controls in place. Thus members had some freedom over their own monetary policies. Nonetheless, it is generally accepted that the Deutschmark has been the leading currency within the system and that German monetary policy has had a quite strong influence on the policies of other countries. Why has this been so?

Firstly, Germany had, over a long period, built up a reputation as a low-inflation country. It was also the biggest and most powerful economy in the system. Secondly, it was believed that its institutional arrangements were such that it would go on delivering low inflation into the future. That is, its monetary policy was run by its central bank, the Bundesbank, which was constitutionally independent of the democratic political process. Further, the control of inflation was the major, although not the only, objective set down in the Bundesbank's constitution.

The importance given to this institutional arrangement was seen in the period immediately after German unification. As mentioned in Chapter 21, the way in which the West and East German monetary systems were unified, combined with the unwillingness of the German government to raise tax rates to pay for the inevitable increase in government expenditure following unification, led to a temporary increase in inflation above the levels normally associated with Germany. Given the severe difficulties faced by the inefficient industry of the old East Germany, there would have been a strong temptation for any government in control of monetary policy to run an easy, low-interest-rate policy to encourage investment and expansion. The financial markets were confident, however, that the Bundesbank would not follow such a policy. Thus, although French inflation was lower than German inflation for some time, there was no great switch of funds from DMs to French francs. The markets held to the view that the DM was still the more trustworthy currency in the medium to long term.

The general argument about the relationship between the independence of central banks and the rate of inflation is summarized in Box 22.2.

A full monetary union with a single currency must, *a fortiori*, have a common monetary policy since the possibility, which must continue to exist in any fixed exchange rate system, that exchange rate parities might be changed, is completely removed. The question still remains as to how that monetary policy will be determined. It is possible, although not essential, to place the operation of policy in the hands of a single, supranational central bank, but this does not determine what the central bank's monetary policy should be. That policy could be decided either by member governments or by central bankers or by a combination of both. For a country such as Germany, used to both low inflation and a politically independent central bank, there was a serious concern here – that the inclusion in the monetary union of countries which have a record of high inflation and/or have current economic problems which would provide incentives to operate a loose monetary policy would lead to any monetary policy decided by discussion and compromise being weaker and more inflationary than the existing German policy.

One solution, discussed in Chapter 21, was to apply strict entry conditions designed to keep such countries out of the union *and* to introduce rules which would carry those strict conditions through into policy after the formation of the monetary union (the stability pact). But even this might not suffice for two reasons. Firstly, the EMU has never been intended to be merely an economic arrangement. The case for it is at least as strongly political as it is economic and it might not make political sense to restrict membership to a small number of low-inflation countries. Secondly, a recession that spread across several countries might persuade a majority of governments, whatever their past inflation performance, to ease monetary policy. The obvious answer to this was to model the European Central Bank on the Bundesbank, making it independent of all member governments and establishing for it a constitution which stressed the objective of low inflation. As we shall see in Section 22.3, this was what was proposed in the Maastricht Treaty.

Before looking at the nature of the proposed European Central Bank, however, we need to consider rather more closely the problems that this structure was meant to counter.

Box 22.2   The independence of central banks and the rate of inflation

In recent years, it has been widely argued that there is a close association between the degree of independence of central banks and low rates of inflation. The argument depends on a number of contentious theoretical and empirical points.

FOR

(1) Democratic political systems are inflationary because they do not take the long-run costs of expansionary policies fully into account because:
    (a) politicians aim to maximize votes;
    (b) voters believe that expansionary policy reduces unemployment;
    (c) there is no long-run trade-off between inflation and unemployment.

(2) Independent central bankers can precommit themselves credibly to a low-inflation policy rule in the way that governments cannot because:
    (a) central bankers do not face re-election;
    (b) it is known that governments benefit from inflation through seigniorage – the gains which accrue to the issuer of a currency because it obtains real resources in return for non-interest-bearing, non-repayable debt.

(3) Empirical evidence appears to show a relationship between the degree of central bank independence and low rates of inflation.

AGAINST

(1) The apparent empirical relationship is suspect because it depends on a subjective assessment of the degree of independence of central banks.

(2) Even if there is a statistical relationship, this does not prove causality. Other factors may be responsible for low inflation. Thus, low German inflation may be due to:
    (a) the system of universal banking which is lending-based rather than securities-based;
    (b) the separation of prudential supervision of the banking system from monetary policy;
    (c) the federal system of government;
    (d) Germany's historical experience of high inflation;
    (e) the form of organization of labour markets in Germany.

(3) Removal of the control of monetary policy from the democratic system has income redistribution effects: favouring those who benefit from low inflation, notably the financial sector, at the expense of the rest of the population.

(4) Central banks cannot effectively control the money supply which is endogenous – independent central banks merely appear to validate deflationary policies.

22.2   Inflation, exchange rate risk and default risk in EMU

The concern with inflation had a number of sources. One stemmed from conventional economic theory. The majority of economists had, by the early 1980s, come to accept a model of the economy in which government attempts to expand the economy through monetary and fiscal policy would lead both to higher inflation and, in the long run, to increased unemployment. Low inflation was thus seen as a prerequisite for future economic growth. The evidence for this proposition was weak but it was the case that the most successful European economy, that of Germany, had low inflation over a long period. Thus, it was felt that, although there might be high short-run costs in terms of higher unemployment in getting inflation down, these would be outweighed by the long-run benefits of low inflation.

The current economic theory also taught that the most important element in becoming a low-inflation economy was to establish anti-inflation credibility – that is, to convince the markets that the government was serious in its determination to reduce inflation and to keep it low. If a government could do this, it was held, the short-run costs of producing low inflation would be much reduced. One way of trying to achieve this anti-inflation credibility was to link the economy to low-inflation Germany in a fixed-exchange rate system dominated by German monetary policy. This explained the significance of the determination expressed in the Maastricht conditions for convergence on a *low* rate of inflation.[1]

At least two other elements entered the picture as seen by Germany. The first was historical. Even in the 1990s, the folk memory of the economic, social and political devastation wrought by the very high German inflation of the early 1920s appeared to be quite strong (see Section 18.1). Probably of greater importance, however, was the understandable fear of savers in a low-inflation economy that the real value of their savings would be rapidly eroded by high future inflation. This fear was given apparent credence by the behaviour of the financial markets which assumed that post-EMU monetary policy would be weaker than the existing German policy. From the early 1990s, this assumption was built into long-term German interest rates, with the yield curve rising sharply for maturities beyond 1999. Thus, for Germany, the crucial economic issue became the external value of the single currency (the Euro) after 1999.

The third Maastricht condition (see Section 21.2) regarding the government financial position was, in part, related to the desire to produce and maintain low inflation since there was concern that heavily indebted governments would have an additional incentive to push for an expansionary common monetary policy, since a low interest rate would reduce the interest burden upon them and a higher inflation rate would reduce the real value of their debt. However, there was an extra question – the possibility of individual governments attempting to act as free riders. The potential difficulty arose because a monetary union does not necessarily require a common fiscal policy. Indeed, to have a fully common fiscal policy requires a high degree of political as well as economic integration. Even federal states, such as the United States, allow some local tax raising and some freedom in the construction of local budgets. There was certainly little prospect of any imminent move by the EU to a form of political organization that would allow a common fiscal policy.

Members of EMU would thus be free to set their own budgets and determine their own budget deficits. With monetary policy in the hands of the European Central Bank they would not be able to finance those deficits by borrowing from their own central banks as in the past; but they would still be able to issue and sell their own government securities. Post-EMU, the bulk of these securities would be denominated in Euros. With a single interest rate across EMU, the prospect arose of heavily indebted countries being able to sell their debt at a lower interest rate than would have been the case previously. Prior to EMU, when, for example, Italy issued lira-denominated securities, it needed to offer an interest rate sufficiently high to take into account the market assessment of the foreign exchange risk associated with holding the lira. The removal of that foreign exchange risk opened up the possibility of Italy being able to borrow at lower interest rates.

Individual countries in a large monetary union might then think that they could increase government expenditure and the budget deficit and finance this by selling additional government securities without causing interest rates to rise. A previously existing constraint on fiscal policy would have been removed. But if several countries behaved in this way, the outcome would be a significant increase in the total amount of the government debt of EMU countries on the market, with the consequence that interest rates across the EMU would be forced up. Governments with tight fiscal policies would have to accept part of the burden of their more freely spending partners in the form of higher interest rates or support an easier monetary policy from the European Central Bank, with the associated risk of higher inflation.

---

1 After all, from the point of the requirements of a single market, all that was needed was convergence of inflation rates. For competition among single market members not to be affected, it would not matter whether that convergence was on a low or a high rate of inflation.

There was yet another issue. Prior to EMU, the interest rate on a country's government securities reflected default risk as well as foreign exchange risk. Indeed, where governments attempted to remove the element of foreign exchange risk by denominating their debt in a foreign currency, the credit-rating agencies often attached a lower credit rating to the debt, signalling to the market that the interest rate paid on that debt should reflect a higher default risk. Thus, there was a second constraint on government fiscal policy. If they allowed their indebtedness to grow too large, the credit agencies would lower the credit rating of the government and force the government to pay higher interest rates on their debt, making it more likely that total indebtedness would continue to grow. It was possible to construct a model in which a country's total government debt might grow explosively and become totally out of control.[2] Governments could, thus, not afford to allow the market's assessment of their default risk to become too high.

But what would happen to default risk after EMU? It was arguable that prior to EMU an Italian default on part of its public debt would have very little impact on any other country. On the other hand, the default of a member of a monetary union on debt payments in the single currency might easily be seen as having a spillover effect on market confidence in other Euro-denominated debt. Hence it was widely assumed that the European Central Bank would not be prepared to allow any of the monetary union members to become, in effect, bankrupt – that it would be bound to step in and bail out the country in trouble with a consequent increase in the money supply and the risk of greater inflation. The impact of a country believing that it was bound to be bailed out would be to remove also the constraint on its spending imposed by default risk. If the markets believed that any member would be bailed out by the European Central Bank, the relevant credit rating for any Euro-denominated debt would be the credit rating of the European Central Bank itself.

This would give free-spending governments total freedom to go on spending and it might also lower the credit rating of the European Central Bank, again causing interest rates on all Euro-denominated debt to rise. EMU would give governments a clear incentive to operate expansionary fiscal policies. Any country which chose not to do so would not obtain the benefits of increased public expenditure but would incur costs as a result of the expansionary policies of other member governments. This possibility explains the importance attached to the government financial position in the Maastricht convergence conditions and to the stability pact relating to post-EMU policy which was insisted upon by Germany. It also explains some of the detail of the Maastricht Treaty which we consider below.

22.3 Monetary institutions and policy in the Maastricht Treaty

Under the Maastricht Treaty, monetary policy after EMU will be conducted by the European System of Central Banks (ESCB), consisting of the European Central Bank (ECB) and the national central banks of the member states. The ESCB will be governed by the Governing Council and the Executive Board of the ECB. To ensure the independence of the ESCB from both the European Commission and the governments of the member states, the national central banks, although continuing to be owned by their governments, are also required to become independent of the political process in their own countries.

Article 105(2) of the Treaty on European Union sets the ESCB four basic tasks:

(1) to define and implement monetary policy of the Community;[3]
(2) to conduct foreign exchange operations;
(3) to hold and manage the official foreign exchange reserves of the member states; and
(4) to promote the smooth operation of payments systems.

---

2 This, admittedly unlikely, set of events was first modelled by T Sargent and N Wallace, 'Some Unpleasant Monetarist Arithmetic', Federal Reserve Bank of Minneapolis, *Quarterly Review*, 1981

3 Although we have generally used the term European Union (EU)

throughout this book, direct reference to the Treaty on European Union must use the term European Community (EC) because, according to the Treaty, the Economic Community is the economic and monetary pillar of the three-pillared European Union, the other two of which relate to common foreign and security policies.

Article 105(1) of the Treaty established the primary objective of the ESCB as the maintenance of price stability. It is also enjoined, without prejudice to the goal of price stability, to support the EU's general economic policies and to act in accordance with the principle of an open market economy with free competition, favouring an efficient allocation of resources. The general economic policies of the EC are stated in Article 2 of the Treaty as being 'to promote throughout the Community a harmonious and balanced development of economic activities, sustainable and non-inflationary growth respecting the environment, a high degree of convergence of economic performance, a high level of employment and social protection, the raising of the standard of living and quality of life, and economic and social cohesion and solidarity among Member States'. Article 3a further requires that in attempting to achieve all of this, member states and the Community should comply with the guiding principles of stable prices, sound public finances and monetary conditions, and a sustainable balance of payments. This gives the ESCB a set of objectives similar to those of the Bundesbank which is obliged by law to safeguard the currency while supporting the general economic policy of the German federal government.

Although pursuit of general economic policy objectives is not meant to prejudice the achievement of price stability, there is clearly scope for interpretation under circumstances in which an apparent conflict exists between tightening monetary policy and one or more of the general objectives. 'Price stability', after all, does not necessarily mean the lowest possible level of inflation. Indeed, with a central bank composed of people from a number of countries with different economic conditions and problems, one might expect a range of interpretations of price stability. Nonetheless, control of inflation is clearly intended to be central. Further, the objective of low inflation is statutorily protected since the ESCB's objectives will only be able to be changed by the unanimous decision of the Council of Ministers. The European Parliament will have no influence on the objectives of monetary policy.

The possibility of the system's objectives being interpreted in different ways makes the issue of the composition of the ECB extremely important and raises the question of how it is possible to ensure the political independence of the decision makers within the system. Box 22.3 set out a number of factors widely accepted as relevant to the degree of political independence of a central bank which may be compared with the Maastricht framework below.

The ECB does generally very well on the criteria listed in Box 22.3.

The Executive Board of the ECB, which will run the bank, will comprise a president, vice-president and four other members to be appointed by the Heads of State on a recommendation from the European Council after consultation with the European Parliament and the Governing Council of the ECB. All six members are required to be 'persons of recognized standing and professional experience in monetary or banking matters'. In other words, they will be representatives from the world of finance, making it very likely that their interpretation of 'price stability' will be conservative.

The term of office for Executive Board members is to be eight years and is to be non-renewable. Members of the Executive Board may be compulsorily retired but only for 'misconduct' which is defined to include the taking of instructions from a

---

Box 22.3 Features important in determining the independence of a central bank

1 Statutory guarantees of independence or non-interference
2 The existence of statutory objectives for the central bank and the nature of those objectives
3 The methods of appointment and removal of the governor, senior officers and the board of directors
4 The length of the governor's term of office
5 The presence or absence of government officials on the bank's board

6 The extent to which the bank is bound by instructions from the government and the range of instruments at the bank's disposal
7 The limits on central financing of the government
8 The ease with which any of the above features can be altered by government

member government. Compulsory retirement can only be achieved through the European Court of Justice on the application of the ECB Council or the Executive Board. Governors of national central banks must be appointed for at least five years and may end their terms prematurely only for serious cause, notified either by themselves or the ECB council. That is, they cannot be removed by their own national governments. The long and non-renewable term is meant to reduce the possibility of Board members following the wishes of governments in the hope of being reappointed to their positions. Of course, Board members who have pleased the governments of the member states may still find themselves being offered other attractive positions at the end of their period of office. Equally, Executive Board members whose attitudes and policies meet with the approval of financial markets (generally accepted as favouring very low rates of inflation) may also receive offers of attractive private sector positions at the end of their terms of office.[4] Thus, no set of rules can remove all possibility of external influences on Board members.

The Governing Council will consist of the Executive Board plus the governors of the national central banks. Voting, on all issues except those related to the bank's capital, is to be on a one-person one-vote basis, with decision by simple majority. The significance of this will depend on how many countries are able to join EMU in 1999. Clearly, if more than six countries join EMU, then the representatives of the national central banks will be able to outvote the Executive Board members on the Governing Council. It might also be possible for the smaller members of EMU to outvote large members such as Germany on all issues other than those related to the ECB's capital. This provides an extra reason for countries concerned that the EMU follow strict monetary policies to insist on strict adherence to the Maastricht convergence condition in determining membership.

Where the bank's capital is involved, voting power will be proportional to the member states' subscribed capital and the Executive Board will have no votes.

The subscribed capital, in turn, is to be determined by equal weighting of (1) the member states' shares of the population and (2) GDP at market prices, averaged over the previous five years. Subscriptions are to be revised every five years.

The ECB is to be responsible for the note issue, open market operations, the setting of minimum reserve requirements and other aspects of monetary control. However, the ECB is unlikely itself to conduct open market operations or intervene directly in the markets in other ways, at least in the early years of the EMU. Rather, it is thought likely that it will make use of the national central banks to carry out operations.

The ECB may supply liquidity to the banking system subject to the availability of 'adequate collateral' (Statute, Article 18). However, in an attempt to overcome the potential problems discussed in Section 22.2 above, the ESCB will not be permitted to lend to governments except through the acquisition of their paper in the secondary market. Overdraft or other credit facilities by the ECB or national central banks to any EU or member state public body are explicitly prohibited by Article 104 of the Treaty.

To strengthen the control of high-spending member governments, the Maastricht treaty forbids excessive government deficits and the 'bailing out' of indebted member governments by EU governments or institutions. If this is carried through, member governments will again face default risk with the consequence that bond issues of different governments will continue to carry different rates of interest after EMU to reflect the market's assessment of the default risk associated with each government's debt issue. Indeed, given that post-EMU all the debt of EMU members will be denominated in what will effectively be an external currency, the risk of default will be higher than it currently is. Consequently, it was being suggested in bond markets in early 1997 that the formation of EMU might see the dramatic downgrading of the debt of countries such as Belgium, assuming that Belgium became a member of EMU.

Further, the European Council will monitor

---

[4] It is of interest in this regard that the 1913 act of the US Congress which set up the Federal Reserve system required it to be independent of private financial business interests as well as of the government and partisan political interests.

economic developments in each of the member states. Where it finds economic policies of a member state that 'risk jeopardizing the proper functioning of economic and monetary union' (Article 103), the Council may make recommendations to the member concerned and may publish them. In all areas other than that of fiscal deficits, members need not accept these recommendations. However, Article 104c forbids member states to have excessive governmental deficits and charges the European Commission with the task of monitoring the budgetary situation and the stock of government debt of member states 'with a view to identifying gross errors'. The Commission may report to the Council that an excessive deficit exists. The Council may then make policy recommendations which the member state in question is *obliged to follow*. Failure to do so may ultimately lead to the imposition of financial sanctions in the form of a non-interest-bearing deposit or a fine. We have already seen that the stability pact agreed upon in December 1996 is an attempt to add detail to this clause.

The Treaty separates the operation of monetary policy from the prudential supervision of credit institutions and the stability of the financial system. The latter is to remain the responsibility of the member states, although the ESCB is expected to ensure the smooth conduct of policies relating to prudential supervision and the ECB may, with the unanimous approval of the European Council and the approval of the European Parliament, be given specific tasks in this area (Article 105.6). In general, this conforms to the German model in which prudential supervision is not carried out by the Bundesbank but by the separate Aufsichtsamt (the Federal Banking Supervisory Office), while preserving an element of the British system which gives to the Bank of England the role of ensuring the financial probity and soundness of individual banks and the banking sector as a whole and hence the role of guarantor of the degree of public confidence in the system.

Any attempt to place significant power in the hands of an unelected body, as the ECB will be, raises the question of the accountability of that body to governments and, ultimately, to the citizens of the member states. Accountability under the Maastricht Treaty is weak as seems bound to be the case where

the aim is to prevent as far as is possible the contamination of the central bank by the attitudes and policies of the democratic political system. What accountability there is takes a number of forms. Firstly, the ECB will be subject to audit and under the jurisdiction of the Court of Justice. Secondly, the President of the European Council and a member of the European Commission will be allowed to attend meetings of the Governing Council of the ECB but will not be allowed to vote. Thirdly, the ECB will be required to report annually on its activities to the Council and the European Parliament and the President and other members of the Executive Board will be heard by the relevant committees of the parliament at either side's request.

The general view of all of these regulations is that the Treaty has succeeded in creating a strongly independent central bank. Indeed, it is likely to be more politically independent than the Bundesbank itself. One argument given for this view is that when the Bundesbank and the German government hold different views regarding economic policy, the Bundesbank has a single and united opponent which is able to point to its electoral support. Within the EMU, the counterpart of the German government will be a group of governments which may have different political persuasions and whose countries may be experiencing different economic problems. Consequently, there is unlikely to be a single united political view to contrast with that of the Executive Board of the ECB.

In addition, the Bundesbank central council includes the 11 presidents of the German Länder (regions) and it is argued that this regional representation keeps the Bundesbank more in touch to some extent with the real problems of the economy than is likely to be the case with the General Council of the ECB where the equivalent of the Land central bank presidents will be the national central bank governors of the member states.

And yet, despite all of the attempts to preserve the political independence of the ECB, to enforce strict convergence conditions for membership and forbid loose budgetary policies, the view of both the financial markets and leading economists in late 1996 and early 1997 was that the Euro, in the long term, would be a weak currency. One basis for this view was that the high proportion of intra-EU trade of prospective members of EMU would mean that the EMU would, like the USA, be a substantially closed economic area with its external trade possibly making up considerably less than 20 per cent of GDP. This, it was held, would cause the ECB[5] to be less concerned about the external value of the Euro than the Bundesbank currently is about the DM and more likely to behave like the US Federal Reserve – pursuing internal price stability but being largely indifferent to the impact of the exchange rate on foreign trade. This would make it more open to pressures for weaker monetary policy in order to stimulate economic growth, particularly given the slow growth and high rates of unemployment in much of the EU. A supporting argument was that the Euro, as a broader-based reserve currency than the Deutschmark, would be less likely to be driven artificially high on occasions. In addition, there remained great scepticism about the threat that the ECB would never bail out member states that would otherwise be forced to default on their debt.

22.4   The operation of monetary policy in EMU

Although, as we have seen, the Treaty on European Union contains a good deal of institutional detail concerning the nature of the ECB and its responsibilities, very little is said about the operation of policy or about its division between the ECB and the national central banks. Several issues relating to the operation of policy need to be settled in advance of 1999 and this was one of the tasks given to the European Monetary Institute during Stage II of the path to EMU. As we suggested in Section 7.5, there are two principal issues: the choice of an intermediate objective and of policy instruments.

Given that the final objective is price stability and that the likely instrument is the control of short-term interest rates, the first question with regard to the choice of an intermediate objective is whether it makes sense to target some measure of the money supply. This has the advantage that the time lag between adjusting short-term interest rates and

changes in the objective are shorter than if the objective is nominal GNP or the rate of inflation itself. Further, despite difficulties which many central banks have had in controlling the money supply, there are fewer exogenous influences upon it than is the case with a GNP or inflation target. However, the use of an intermediate money supply target only makes sense if there is a stable short-run demand function for money. For this reason, where the short-run money demand function has been manifestly unstable over the past 20 years, as in the UK, the use of a single money supply target has been abandoned. Germany, on the other hand, continues to use a target for broad money and continues to recommend the use of a similar target for the ECB, despite the fact that, as we suggested in Box 7.5, it is arguable that in practice they have in recent years paid as much attention to the rate of inflation itself as to the broad money target.

Rejection of an intermediate money supply target is supported by the possibility that the German demand function may be starting to become unstable as a result of financial liberalization and increased financial innovation in Germany. Further, financial liberalization has made it harder for central banks to control the money supply because it has become harder to influence relative interest rates between money and other financial assets. In response to this, it has been suggested that the demand for money function for the whole EMU may be more stable than that for any one country. This view is based upon the theory that one of the reasons for unstable demand for money functions has been the possibility of currency substitution among EU currencies – switching from one currency to another. Thus, attempts to tighten monetary policy by pushing up interest rates might attract a flow of capital into a country, pushing up the country's money supply and seemingly interfering with the relationship between interest rates and the short-run demand for money. It is claimed that the replacement of a number of currencies by a single currency under EMU necessarily reduces the possibility of currency substitution and thus helps to remove one of the causes of instability. However, the empirical

---

[5] In any case, as we have seen, exchange rate strategy will rest with the European Council, not with the ECB.

evidence on this issue is uncertain and the theoretical argument is not strong since currency substitution will remain possible between the single currency and non-EMU European currencies as well as the dollar, yen and other non-European currencies.

Certainly, it appears clear that there are sufficient uncertainties to make it inadvisable in the early years of EMU to depend on a single measure of the money supply as an intermediate target. Such a target could be set on the basis of past relationships between the money supply and inflation or on the basis of a model of the economy of the EMU but there would be a serious possibility that it would prove to be of little use and such a failure would merely add to the already existing uncertainty regarding the strength of monetary policy within EMU. It would seem more advisable either to set an inflation target or to make use of a range of indicators to guide policy.

The major question with regard to the choice of policy instrument is whether to support the control of short-term interest rates with the requirement that banks hold mandatory minimum reserve ratios (see Sections 6.4 and 6.5). This is practised in the majority of EU member countries in the belief that this allows the central bank more easily to manage short-term interest rates by creating a predictable demand for reserves at the central bank under circumstances in which bank balance sheets are growing rapidly in response to increased demand for credit. Because the reserves which must be held at the central bank do not pay interest, the ratios act as a tax upon banks and as they grow will push banks into pushing up interest rates on loans to restore their overall rates of profit. This in turn will put downward pressure on the demand for credit.

On the other hand, it may be argued that minimum reserve ratios are not required in financial markets which are deep and liquid where the central bank can achieve its objectives through open market operations. In addition, the use of minimum reserve ratios may be seen to conflict with the Maastricht Treaty requirement that policy should be conducted in accordance with the principle of an open market economy with free competition, favouring an efficient allocation of resources. Other technical questions which need to be resolved include the method to be used for relieving liquidity shortages among banks.

As we saw in Section 9.4, the method currently favoured in most EU countries is for the central bank to conduct repo operations in short-dated money market instruments. Until 1 March 1997 the Bank of England was the one exception, but it has now fallen into line.

22.5 Summary

In a currency area with completely fixed exchange rates *and* full freedom of capital flows, there must be a common monetary policy. Such a policy could be determined by a single leader or on the basis of a joint decision by governments or central banks. The EMS has never had both fully fixed exchange rates and fully mobile capital but the Deutschmark had been the strongest currency in the system partly because of Germany's reputation for low inflation and partly because the political independence of the Bundesbank was seen as a guarantee that low inflation would continue. For EMU, a supranational central bank, the European Central Bank, will be established to conduct the common monetary policy but the question remains as to how that policy will be determined.

Many of the decisions made about the European Central Bank in the Treaty on European Union can be explained by a consideration of the fears that prospective members had about the operation of the system. Above all, there was the fear that the common monetary policy might be inflationary. This was thought possible to the extent that the policy became a compromise among countries with different attitudes towards inflation. More importantly, it was thought that the existence of the single currency and the conse-quent removal of exchange rate risk would remove one of the constraints on the fiscal policy of countries prone to high spending and deficit finance. Worse, it was thought that if the European Central Bank was to come to bail out member governments who were in danger of defaulting over payments on their govern-ment debt, another constraint would be removed. Thus it was thought necessary to design a set of institutions which would overcome these potential problems.

The Maastricht Treaty thus modelled the European

Central Bank on the Bundesbank and included many rules aimed to prevent member countries from running excessive government deficits. Despite all of this, financial markets still tend to think that the Euro will, in the long term, be a relatively weak currency.

Although the Maastricht Treaty contains many institutional details, it says little about the operation of monetary policy. Issues such as the choice of an intermediate objective and the form of monetary instruments to be used remain to be resolved.

Key concepts used in this chapter

Currency area	Asymmetric leadership
Common monetary policy	To bail out a bankrupt country
ECB	ESCB
Price stability	Excessive government deficits
Prudential supervision	Accountability
Currency substitution	Minimum reserve ratios

Questions and problems

1 Explain the conflict between a low-inflation policy and a weak Euro.

2 Why might a European Monetary Union with many members be more inflationary than one with only a few members?

3 Why do you think credit-rating agencies currently rate a country's debt denominated in its own currency more highly than its debt denominated in a foreign currency?

4 Discover what you can about the degree of independence of the Japanese central bank and consider why the Japanese case presents a problem for the argument that the independence of the central bank is necessary for the control of a country's inflation.

5 Why might it be undesirable for all the members of a monetary union for one member to default on its government debt?

6 Does it matter if a country's central bank is only weakly accountable to the country's political institutions?

7 Compare and contrast the organization and objectives of the Bundesbank with those of the European Central Bank.

8 Why might interest rates differ in different countries, even within a monetary union?

Further reading

C H Church and D Phinnemore, *European Union and European Community. A Handbook and Commentary on the Post-Maastricht Treaties* (Hemel Hempstead: Harvester Wheatsheaf, 1994)

M Crawford, One Money for Europe? *The Economics and Politics of Maastricht* (Basingstoke: Macmillan, 1993)

P De Grauwe, *The Economics of Monetary Integration* (Oxford: Oxford University Press, 1994, 2e)

A Duff, J Pinder and R Pryce, *Maastricht and Beyond. Building the European Union* (London: Routledge, 1994)

European Monetary Institute, *Annual Reports*, (Frankfurt am Main)

C Johnson and S Collignon (eds), *The Monetary Economics of Europe: the Causes of the EMS Crisis* (London: Pinter, 1994)

C Taylor, *EMU 2000? Prospects for European Monetary Union* (London: Royal Institute of International Affairs, 1995)

Financial innovation

23.1 Introduction

One function of a financial system is to channel funds between the end users of the system, that is to say from surplus to deficit units. In so doing, the components of the system – markets and institutions – provide a range of services for which ultimate lenders and borrowers are prepared to pay. Some measure of the value end users place upon the facilities can be gained from the commissions, fees and spreads charged by providers of the services. As with any other profit-driven economic activity, suppliers are looking continually for products which can be differentiated (or at least presented as differentiated) from those of their competitors and for ways of finding competitive cost advantages. The result is a continually evolving menu of financial products and processes.

However, not all new products and processes survive. This leads some commentators (for example, Finnerty, 1992) to distinguish between 'trivial' and 'non-trivial' innovations. The latter are those that continue to supply a need even after the original stimulus to their development has disappeared. The fact that there seems still to be a place for lasting innovations is often taken as evidence that financial markets are still 'incomplete'.

Financial innovation, therefore, is no more a novelty of the 1990s than is innovation in consumer durables. Indeed, financial innovation is not even confined to recent times. In Chapter 6 we noted that money today consists largely of bank deposits – the liabilities of private firms working for profit – and that this poses considerable difficulties for the authorities who often wish to control the growth of money. From a monetary point of view, therefore, the developments which replaced precious metals and then notes and coin with bank deposits were amongst the most important and these took place in the sixteenth and nineteenth centuries. Partnerships and lotteries are two more examples of what were once upon a time 'innovations', designed to help raise finance for firms and for the state respectively.

Continuous as the process of financial innovation may be, however, the innovations of the 1980s and 1990s can be seen as the latest stage or phase of a longer wave of rapid change which dates from the mid-1960s. Sametz (1992), for example, identifies the first stage running from 1965 to 1972 when a combination of regulatory inflexibility and rising inflation and interest rates produced the first certificates of deposit and money market mutual funds. The second phase ran from 1973 to 1982 when the increased volatility of interest, inflation and exchange rates combined to produce hedging instruments such as options and futures contracts. The third phase, running from 1982, has been driven by increased volatility in security prices, of which the 1987 crash is the most conspicuous example, and by increased merger and acquisition activity.

In this chapter we shall look firstly at some of the theories which try to explain why financial innovation takes place. There is no completely satisfactory theory of financial innovation. As we have just seen, different 'causes' are likely to appear at different times. Then, in Section 23.3, we shall look at two cases, off-balance-sheet activity and retail liability management, which illustrate the interaction of regulation, technology and the economic environment as 'causes' and show how they in turn produce new dilemmas for the regulatory authorities. These are only two of many innovations. Many of the others, particularly where they involve the development of new products in new markets, are treated in detail elsewhere in this book and we shall make cross-references to them as appropriate. In Section 23.4 we look at the impact of retail liability management on the demand for money and the conduct of monetary policy. This section, therefore, returns us to some of the important issues raised earlier in Chapters 6, 7 and 8. Section 23.5 summarizes.

23.2 Theories of innovation

The immediate cause of innovation is the prospect of profit. It is driven by the desire, on the one hand, of financial firms to increase profit and by the desire on the other of lenders and borrowers to be able to carry out their lending and borrowing on terms which offer them the prospect of a greater increase in their wealth for a given level of risk than was available previously. But this rather basic statement of economic motivation does not take us very far. It merely raises the subsequent question of why the possibilities of profitable innovation occur when they do and in particular why they seem to occur more at certain times than at others. The answer to this must be that profitable opportunities arise with changes in the economic environment. It is when we try to identify the relevant changes that the picture becomes complicated. What sort of changes in the economic

environment are important in stimulating financial innovation?

When it comes to explaining the burst of innovative activity since the 1960s three most frequently cited influences are: *regulation* (and *deregulation*), *technology* and *volatility*. The economic environment has been changed by all three of these over the past 30 years or so, and all three are undoubtedly relevant but they interact in a continuous and complex way and so the challenge becomes one of imposing some sort of order. This can be done either by chronology in which one influence dominates at a particular time (as with Sametz above); or by treating some as acting upon demand (for example volatility) and others (for example, technology) upon supply; or by treating some as originating outside the financial system itself, volatility and technology being the most promising candidates, in that order, while others are seen as originating within the financial system initially as a response to the other disturbances but then helping to carry the developments forward. Following this approach, one can distinguish between 'exogenous' and 'endogenous' factors. The brief survey here is organized chronologically. We look firstly at regulation as something that has always been present in financial systems and has always been an inducement to innovation; then we look at volatility and technological change which are amongst the circumstances peculiar to the 1970s and 1980s, Stametz's second and third waves. But, before we begin, we take a look at Table 23.1 which tries to impose some order on what is a very complex picture. Notice that it is divided into three columns. The first of these is headed 'causes' and contains the three most relevant environmental changes that we have just listed. In the second column, we have listed the innovations (products and services) for which each of these causes was largely responsible. This is a simplification, since most innovations were influenced by more than one cause, but it is reasonable to argue that in most cases there was a principal cause, more important than the other two. The third column we have headed 'consequences'. This is because we want to emphasize the broader significance of these innovations. Each innovation has its own justification in providing a product or service that consumers regard as an improvement on

Table 23.1 Financial Innovation

Causes	Results	Implications
Regulation and deregulation	Eurodollar markets	Money substitutes
	Money Market Mutual Funds	New monetary instruments
	CDs	Evade quantity controls
	'Bill leak'	Rise in money's own rate
	Off balance sheet activity	Money's own rate market related
	Increased competition	Liability management
Volatility	Swaps	Risk reduction
	Options	Loan demand less interest-elastic
	Futures	
	Variable rate lending	
Technology	Globalization	Economies in cash holding
	24hr markets	Larger debit and credit positions
	Programme trading	(fall in velocity)
	Derivatives	Liability management
	ATMs	
	EFTPOS	
	Credit checking	
	Cheaper intermediation	
	Cheaper entry (contestable markets)	

what went before. But some innovations have a wider significance for monetary and financial economics. This is often because they change agents' behaviour in a major way which in turn forces us to change our view of how a modern monetary economy works. Quite often, this change in behaviour causes problems for the authorities who find that their monetary and financial policies, based on old patterns of behaviour, are less effective than they were. As the table shows, not all new products and services have this wider significance.

We turn now to the argument that regulation has long been central to the process of financial innovation. This is most strongly associated with Kane (1981, 1984, 1988) who coined the term *regulatory dialectic* to describe the continuous interaction between financial firms who seek to minimize the burden of regulation and the authorities who modify the rules of regulation in response to the latest products and practices of financial firms. Kane's thesis was based largely upon US experience and the circumstances surrounding the growth of Eurodollar deposits, the growth of repurchase agreements and money market mutual funds. The first developed after 1966 while the others took off in the 1970s. All were a response to *Regulation Q* which limited banks'

ability to pay interest on deposits. The regulation was circumvented in the first case by overseas US banks whose deposits were outside US jurisdiction; in the second case by repurchasing at a loss securities lent for a specified period (the loss amounting to interest); and in the third case by pooling retail deposits and investing them in short-term money market instruments (which became technically the source of the interest) while allowing withdrawals on demand. In the UK, an obvious parallel was the 'bill-leak' which occurred at intervals in the 1970s when the 'corset' or supplementary special deposits scheme was in operation. Under the corset, banks were limited to target rates of growth in their interest-bearing liabilities (roughly, interest-bearing deposits) and were subject to financial penalties on a scale which increased steeply with the degree of overshoot. Like all direct controls, the corset frustrated both sides of the market with the predictable effect that eventually both sides would collude in circumvention. Circumvention began with large corporations borrowing in the money markets by issuing their own commercial bills but developed rapidly when firms discovered that the discount on the bills (the cost of funds) would be much smaller if the bills carried the guarantee of a major bank. The advantage to banks was that the fee income from these 'acceptances' partly replaced the interest income foregone on the loans they were prevented from making. This incident introduced UK banks to the advantages of 'off-balance-sheet' activity which developed rapidly in many directions thereafter. Chapter 13 discusses banks' involvement with 'swaps', another example of off-balance-sheet activity, and Chapter 24 discusses some of the regulatory issues that are raised by banks engaging in business which is not represented in the structure of assets and liabilities in their balance sheets.

Both Hester (1981) and Silber (1983) similarly emphasize the role of regulation. Hester also focused on innovations in the US after 1960. Many of these, he concluded, were the result of monetary policy decisions and the outcome of most was beneficial since regulation led to inefficiency. A feature of Hester's argument, however, was the simultaneous emphasis upon the underlying conditions which made innovation worthwhile. These included high and variable interest rates (which determined the 'cost' of Regulation Q) and the progress in information technology which lowered the cost of circumventory action. In Silber, regulation appears as a special case in a more general theory of innovation. Financial firms are assumed to maximize utility (essentially profit) subject to a balance sheet constraint. Innovation is thus a profit-oriented response to some externally imposed constraint. Innovation is usually a response to *changes* which may either force a reduction in the utility of the firm or increase the cost of adhering to the constraint. Within this framework, a new regulation reduces utility while changing conditions (such as higher interest rates) may make compliance more costly.

Financial innovation also occurs at times and in places where regulation is not an obvious burden to intermediaries. Indeed, some of the most far-reaching (in their effects) innovations in the UK in the 1970s and 1980s came about during periods of overt slackening of regulation. *Competition and Credit Control* (*CCC*) facilitated the first stage of liability management while legislation in 1983 and 1986 to put banks and building societies onto a more equal footing took it a stage further (as we shall see in Section 23.3). For this reason alone, some attention to the underlying economic conditions is required. As we have seen, both the level and

volatility of interest rates have been cited as instrumental in the inducement to innovate, either in conjunction with regulation (by determining the cost of compliance) or alone (by increasing the level of financial risk).

We saw earlier that Sametz regards *financial volatility* as central to the innovation process since the 1970s. Balance of payments surpluses and deficits have been both absolutely larger and larger also in relation to their respective GDPs than at any earlier period. Commodity prices have shown larger swings and nominal interest and exchange rates have also been extremely volatile. Recall (from Chapter 10) that a doubling in nominal interest rates will almost halve the value of a long-dated fixed interest bond and interest rates often doubled and halved in the 1970s and 1980s. Relevant information about future price movements thus became increasingly expensive, if not impossible to obtain, and accordingly (on this view) it has been markets and intermediaries that have been able to develop practices and products that help to manage the risk associated with price and rate fluctuations that have prospered. It is no coincidence that the most rapid growth in the 1970s and 1980s has taken place in financial futures (Chapter 13), interest rate and currency swaps, and traded options markets (Chapter 14). The growth of variable rate lending in US banking is another obvious response to volatility. This increase in the instability of financial and economic conditions, as we have seen, is generally recognized even in quarters where other stimuli are also thought to have been critical. Both Goodhart (1986) and Lewis (1988) have given it particular emphasis.

Whether it comes as a response to the frustrations of regulation or in response to increasing risk, financial innovation takes place only when it seems likely to be profitable. The role of technology in financial as in other activity is to lower the costs of production and possibly also the costs of entry. We take firstly the costs of production.

Conventional banking operations were once very labour intensive. Furthermore, those activities that required the storage and transmission of information were limited by the speed with which paper and people could be moved from one place to another. The development of ever more powerful and compact computers and more importantly the simultaneous development of communications networks allowing remote operators virtually instant access to centrally stored information has widened the range of services financial firms can offer. It has also increased the speed with which those services can be supplied, lowered their cost, changed dramatically the conditions (and locations) of work for those employed in the industry and changed the relationship between the supplier and consumer of financial services.

At one extreme, one thinks of the high speed and low cost with which firms based in London can transact business in Tokyo or New York, through their local subsidiaries. Indeed, the existence of local subsidiaries is itself dependent upon the cheap and instant interchange of information between the subsidiary and head office. The globalization of money and capital markets would simply not have been possible without these developments. As the recent trials of the exchange rate mechanism of the European Monetary System have demonstrated, there are important implications here for exchange rate stability and for governments' and central banks' powers of intervention.

Equally, the development of new instruments and their markets would not have been possible without the facility of 'real-time' computer access. The pricing of options, currency futures and derivative instruments generally is a non-trivial arithmetic exercise which requires appropriate computer software and, again, instant access.

Seemingly less glamorous, but with effects which we shall see later are just as far-reaching, technology has had its effect upon retail consumers. Cash dispensing automated teller machines (ATMs) first appeared in the mid-1970s and have spread rapidly ever since. In the 1980s rival institutions have combined their ATMs into networks to give customers even easier access to their accounts. In the 1990s, the same technology is being extended to electronic funds transfer (EFT) with the result that stores can provide cash withdrawal facilities. Two processes are at work here. Firstly, the electronic handling of transactions is much cheaper than paper-based transfer, not just in labour but also in its requirement for premises. For years banks defended bank charges and later the non-payment of interest on

checkable deposits on the grounds that they needed the endowment effect to subsidize the high cost of the money transmission system. One of the reasons that UK banks have been able to pay interest on sight deposits since 1983 is that the unit cost has fallen.

Another sense in which technology has contributed to cost reduction is through the lowering of the costs of entry into the provision of financial services, making financial markets more *contestable*. Building societies have been able to enter the money transmission business because electronic transfer of funds merely requires an extension to their existing computing capacity where previously it would have required prohibitive expenditure on labour and premises. The case of retail stores provides an even clearer illustration. Once computer terminals had been installed at checkouts, originally to improve the management of stocks, it required only software modifications, and a secure link to cooperating banking institutions, to enable the same equipment to debit a customer's account for the purchase of goods. Debiting the account for cash was an obvious next step. The cost of entering the cash management part of banking business is now so low for any nationwide organization which has a large number of retail outlets linked to a central computer that it is difficult to see where this development will end. In the opening months of 1997, the hot news in the UK was the competition between major food retailers to provide further banking services, including current accounts with overdraft facilities. Box 23.2 describes the latest moves in this direction in February 1997.

The cost-reducing potential of technology has a number of implications for monetary economics. Firstly, a reduction in transactions costs lowers the costs of intermediation generally. Other things being equal, people will be willing to hold larger simultaneous debit and credit positions leading to a larger money stock and lower velocity than hitherto. Pushing in the opposite direction, as we see in Section 23.3, however, the reduction of transactions costs and the ability to access current balance information more quickly and cheaply may encourage people to hold fewer precautionary balances and to economize on cash holdings in particular, with whatever consequences that may have for the ratio of bank deposits to monetary base.

Box 23.2   Supermarkets becoming banks?

The following extract is taken from the *Financial Times* for 22 February 1997

Supermarkets at war

Sainsbury's salvo

Sainsbury's Bank, a joint venture between supermarket giant J. Sainsbury and Bank of Scotland, this week launched the first items in its long awaited range of financial products.

The flagship is a highly competitive instant access account which pays 5.75 per cent on all balances – a market-leading rate for anyone saving less than £5,000. It will be available nationally over the next few weeks.

The launch sounded the bell for the start of round two in the heavyweight battle between Sainsbury and Tesco to win market share by making attractive financial offers.

Tesco struck first, in June last year, with its Clubcard Plus savings account. Clubcard Plus, which has 180,000 savers, now pays 5.5 per cent – a fraction less than Sainsbury's Instant Access.

Safeway, another supermarket chain, plans to launch its ABC bonus card in March. This

will pay 5 per cent on balances up to £600, but only 1 per cent thereafter. Safeway does not want big savings deposits.

The chart below shows just how competitive these supermarket accounts are. Those with instant access from Sainsbury and Tesco pay better rates than the best 90-day high street bank savings accounts below £10,000. (So does Safeway, but only for savings up to £600.) They also offer better rates than the telephone services, First Direct and Direct Line.

The only accounts which offer better interest for savers depositing around £5,000 are old-style building society postal accounts. Northern Rock pays 6.35 per cent on deposits over £5,000 – but you are allowed only three withdrawals a year.

Below £5,000, Sainsbury and

Tesco win hands down against all competition. Even at much bigger sums, they beat the high street banks. Both pay more interest on £1 (instant access) than Barclays, Midland, Lloyds or NatWest pay on £50,000 in a 90-day account.

Sainsbury's account is essentially a copy of Clubcard Plus, with some practical differences.

If you want to open an account with Tesco or Safeway, you must set up a monthly standing order from your current account or your salary. Sainsbury does not require this.

You can pay a lump sum into a Tesco account by visiting a branch of NatWest bank which,

| A competitive instant access account heads a package of financial products announced this week. **Krishna Guha** reports

for the time being, manages the Clubcard Plus accounts. Tesco branches do not accept deposits. But Sainsbury does not accept deposits via a bank although it will set up paying-in boxes in its stores.

Clubcard Plus savers can withdraw up to £50 a day without notice from a Tesco store and a similar amount from one

of NatWest's 8,500 cash machines. Sainsbury account-holders can withdraw up to £250 a day from any of the UK's 10,000 Link cash machines, some of which are already in stores.

A handful of Sainsbury's Bank cash machines will be installed, too. But you cannot withdraw cash from a Sainsbury store itself.

Tesco offers a highly competitive overdraft, equal to your monthly standing order, which charges 9.5 per cent interest with no fees. Sainsbury and Safeway do not offer overdraft facilities.

Tesco, however, is soon to transfer account management from NatWest to Royal Bank of Scotland, which could cause disruption. Royal Bank has fewer branches and cash machines than NatWest in England, although it has more in Scotland.

Sainsbury and Tesco accounts feature debit cards which can be used only instore. But Safeway's ABC bonus card can be used as an Electron debit card in 70,000 outlets, and it can be used to withdraw up to £250 a day from any Link machine.

Alongside its instant access account, Sainsbury this week launched a much less appealing "Christmas saver" account. This pays less interest than the instant access rate – and requires you to lock up your money until November.

Sainsbury also launched a pair of Classic and Gold Visa cards, tied to its loyalty programme. But both have an annual fee – £10 and £25 respectively – even though these are waived in the first year and in subsequent years if you use the cards often.

If you do not always pay off your balance in full, there are much better-value cards on the market.

People's Bank of Connecticut and RBS Advanta charge no annual fees and less interest than Sainsbury.

Comparing the rates

	Acc name	Type	£1	£500	£2,000	£5,000	£10,000
Supermarket accounts...							
Sainsbury	Instant Access	Instant	**5.75**	**5.75**	**5.75**	5.75	5.75
Tesco	Clubcard Plus	Instant	5.5	5.5	5.5	5.5	5.5
Safeway	ABC bonus	Instant	5.0	5.0	1.0[(1)]	1.0[(1)]	1.0[(1)]
...offer high savings rates than 90-day notice accounts...							
Halifax	Solid gold	90-day	–	3.0	3.0	3.25	4.0
Abbey National	Investment	90-day	–	3.05	3.05	3.3	4.0
Barclays	90 day savings	90-day	–	–	3.9	3.9	4.0
Midland	Exchequer	90-day	–	–	–	4.0	4.35
...and instant telephone or high interest cheque accounts...							
First Direct	High interest	Instant	3.25	3.25	3.75	3.75	3.75
Portman	Instant access	Instant	–	4.7	4.7	4.7	4.7
Kleinwort Benson	HICA	HICA	–	–	5.2	5.2	5.2
...but on big sums postal accounts are best.							
Northern Rock	Select instant	Postal	–	–	–	**6.35**	6.35
Birmingham Midshires	First class	90-day postal	–	–	–	–	**6.55**

Bold numbers denote best interest rate for a given deposit
(1) Safeway pays 5% interest up to £600 and 1% interest thereafter, and is competitive only up to £600   *Source: Moneyfacts*

23.3   Two case studies

As we saw in the last section there are many points of contact between policy and innovation. There are times, for example, when monetary policy imposes constraints upon agents within the financial system and upon the end users. Innovations are a rational response to these constraints when the costs of compliance, often affected by the prevailing economic conditions, exceed the cost of innovation, often affected by technological change. Some innovations produce consequences that affect the outcomes of policy makers' plans and raise the question of re-regulation.

Two significant innovations which illustrate this process at work, and also have potentially interesting monetary consequences, are the switch towards 'off-balance-sheet activities', including securitization, by banks; and a variety of new products and practices developed by UK banks and building societies as *de*regulation threw them into direct competition in the 1980s – a package of developments we shall call 'retail liability management'. Other examples of innovations, not discussed here but treated elsewhere in this book, are Eurocurrencies (in Chapter 9), Eurobonds (in Chapter 10), futures (Chapter 13) and options and other derivatives (Chapter 14). Readers making a comprehensive study of financial innovation should consult the relevant sections as well as reading what follows here.

23.3.1   Off-balance-sheet operations

'Off-balance-sheet' operations are activities that generate income for banks without creating assets or liabilities which normal accounting procedures would place in their balance sheets. Once again, it is worth noting that there is nothing very remarkable in this. Firms search continually for new services and products to offer to customers. Their success or failure shows in the profit and loss account. We would not expect to see new activities directly reflected in balance sheet changes: the effect on assets and liabilities could be very large or very small. So what is so remarkable about banks engaging increasingly in activities which are only indirectly reflected in balance sheets? The interest

that attaches to off-balance-sheet operations by banks stems from a traditional, and rather limited, model of bank behaviour which sees bank income and profit generated more or less exclusively by the maturity and risk transformation that banks carry out specifically by mismatching their assets and liabilities. On this view, an expansion of traditional bank business necessarily requires a corresponding increase in (on-balance-sheet) assets and liabilities.

This still risks an overstatement of the novelty of off-balance-sheet activity, however. One of the earliest functions of UK banks was the guaranteeing or 'acceptance' of commercial bills; trustee work, executorships and financial advice generally, also have a long tradition. As with most other innovations, the interest in off-balance-sheet operations lies not in their novelty but in their recent rapid expansion and increasing variety. A recent survey (Lewis, 1988) listed some 60 off-balance-sheet activities. These were divided roughly equally between 'financial services' and those giving rise to 'contingent claims'. The former included activities such as tax and financial planning, investment advice, portfolio management, insurance broking, credit/debit card services and (most recently) estate agency. The latter included the issuing of guarantees of many kinds, securities underwriting, market making in securities and arranging swap and hedging transactions. One of the themes running through the growth of off-balance-sheet operations, and much discussed in the financial innovation literature, is *securitization*. This refers both to the increasing use by ultimate lenders and borrowers of capital markets, in preference to bank intermediation, and to the practice by banks themselves of selling off loans from their asset portfolio, by turning them into marketable securities – shifting them off the balance sheet.

The securitization of bank loans has developed furthest in the USA where there is a highly developed market for *mortgage-backed securities*. The tradition of mortgage lenders transferring the original loan to a second investor has its origin in the 1930s when the Federal government began offering insurance for mortgages made to certain disadvantaged social groups. Because the mortgages were guaranteed, investors were prepared to take them over from the originator. However, the development of an active secondary market in securities dates from the 1970s when the Federal government reorganized the Federal National Mortgage Association (FNMA or 'Fannie Mae') and established two new agencies – the Government National Mortgage Association (GNMA or 'Ginnie Mae') and the Federal Home Loan Mortgage Corporation (FHMLC or 'Freddie Mac'). Their purpose was to issue securities backed by both insured and uninsured mortgages. The basic security is the *passthrough*. The agency puts together a pool of mortgages and sells *shares* in the pool to investors who earn a corresponding share of the payments (of interest and principal) made by the borrowers. The principle of the passthrough, although it originated in the securitization of mortgages, is now a commonly adopted securitization technique and is therefore worth considering in a little detail. Figure 23.1 illustrates the steps.

The source of the loan is any financial intermediary, say a bank or savings and loan, which makes secured loans. In the short run, until sufficient new loans have been created to justify pooling, the loans stay on the intermediary's balance sheet. At intervals, however, a collection of loans is pooled and placed with a trust, administered by a trustee. The trust issues securities which are then passed to an underwriter who distributes them to the general

public in the normal way. The proceeds of the sale return to the source of the loan. If, as we have assumed, the source is a private commercial organization it may purchase a guarantee for the loans which naturally enhances the attractiveness of the ultimate securities. (When the source is one of the government agencies this step will be omitted.) Throughout the life of the loan the borrower makes payment to the originator of the loan in the usual way and the intermediary passes the income to the trustee. The trustee deducts its own expenses and those of the original lender (in continuing to collect and monitor the payments) and distributes ('passes through') the income to the investors.

We have described the passthrough as a share. This is because it has many of the characteristics of an ordinary company share. In particular, the income associated with it may fluctuate as a result of *prepayment*. This arises when borrowers choose to repay the loan before its scheduled terminal date. This has the effect of boosting investors' income now but lowering it for the remaining life of the security. For the lender, the attractiveness of securitization has always been greatest for fixed rate loans (as US mortgages usually are) since such loans are subject to interest rate risk – the lender suffering when interest rates rise. Securitization has the advantage for the lender that the interest rate risk is moved to the holders of the securities. Recall that borrowers are paying a fixed rate of interest. When interest rates fall, it becomes attractive to prepay the loan and to replace it with another loan at the new, lower, fixed rate. If this happens on a sufficiently large scale, the holders of the security find that they receive all their income early and then face reinvestment risk – the risk that they will not be able to reinvest their funds for the period that they originally intended at the original rate of return.

Reinvestment risk is a particular problem for life assurance and pension funds for whom security of long-term interest is essential (see Section 15.3). For these institutions, passthroughs are less attractive than bonds which offer a fixed return for a fixed period. Where the loan-backed security takes the form of a bond, however, the prepayment risk remains with the trustee (and thus with the originator of the loan). For this reason, the yield on passthroughs is usually greater than the yield on bonds.

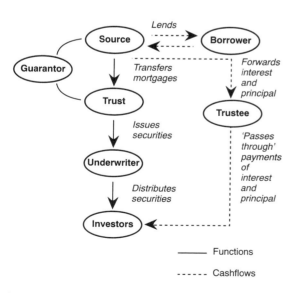

Figure 23.1 The securitization process.

Clearly, at an institutional level, one can view this growth of off-balance-sheet activities as representing a significant change in banking operations. On a more theoretical level, however, one should take seriously the argument that off-balance-sheet activities are essentially the same as the 'traditional on-balance sheet lending and borrowing operations of banks [which] can be seen to be packages of information and risk-sharing (or insurance) services' (Lewis, 1988, p. 396). By taking a customer's deposit a bank (traditionally) creates a very secure, very liquid asset, repayable at par, and turns it into a long-term liability for a borrower. The bank protects both from risk by its superior information and by its size. The interest rate 'spread' is the price that lenders and borrowers pay for this service. Nothing is fundamentally different when a bank accepts a bill or issues a standby letter of credit. The holder of the bill (or letter) enjoys a transfer of risk to the bank for which s/he pays by accepting a lower interest rate on the loan than would have been the case without the bank's guarantee; the borrower pays a fee to the bank for the benefit of the lower interest charge required by the market. Furthermore the bank is willing to accept the risk in the guarantee because it has information which enables it to make a reasonable assessment of the individual default risk and to price it bearing in mind the average default rate on the total pool of guarantees.

When it comes to identifying the consequences, actual and potential, of the expansion of off-balance-sheet activity, one can say, as with the growth of Euromarkets, that by supplying services that customers want, banks are helping to mobilize funds which might otherwise have lain idle and are generally adding to the liquidity of the financial system. Similar implications can be traced in the case of off-balance-sheet activity. In the last section, for example, we observed that one consequence of the 'corset', which penalized the growth of interest-bearing deposits in the UK in the 1970s (and thus reduced the attractiveness of lending), was the 'bill-leak'. Banks found it more profitable to accept commercial bills issued by their clients. Corporate borrowers were thus still able to borrow, on terms very close to those that would have prevailed on a bank loan. Spending, presumably, grew at much the same rate that it would have done without the corset,

thwarting the authorities' intentions and at the same time removing whatever useful information may until then have been contained in the growth rates of the monetary aggregates. The growth of off-balance-sheet operations, just like the growth of Eurocurrency business, widens the scope for disintermediation to follow as a response to any form of monetary control that targets banks' balance sheets.

Other possible consequences of concern to the authorities involve questions of efficiency and stability. Firstly, there is a question of *moral hazard*. This arises from the regulatory authorities in most countries being also the lender of last resort. It may be, for example, that banks' willingness to offer guarantees of various kinds relies itself upon the banks' knowledge that they have access to liquidity support services offered by central banks and, furthermore, that guaranteed access to this support might encourage more reckless excursions into new activities than would otherwise be the case. For reasons of efficiency regulators wish to see that banks are not operating with unfair advantage. They wish to see equal opportunities available to all market participants and not just to banks enjoying access to lender of last resort facilities.

Moral hazard arises also from the widespread availability of deposit and other forms of customer insurance in developed financial systems. Indeed, one of the arguments sometimes advanced for the specific off-balance-sheet innovations is the *moral hazard hypothesis* – banks know that their customers are protected and are thus encouraged to take greater risks. This is often combined with the *regulatory tax hypothesis* that argues that off-balance-sheet activity develops specifically to avoid capital, reserve and other regulatory requirements designed to make the system stable. Viewed from this perspective, the regulators' main concern is to control banks' exposure to risks which banks have been encouraged to take on as a result of earlier actions by the regulators themselves.

Clearly, off-balance-sheet activity exposes banks to many types of risk (as does on-balance-sheet business). Most of the regulators' attention has focused upon credit or default risk which banks incur mainly through guarantees and acceptances. The approach has been to try to incorporate off-balance-sheet commitments as part of total assets in calculating a ratio of capital to (risk-adjusted) assets. The details are discussed in Chapter 24.

The growth of Euromarkets and off-balance-sheet activity both owe something to the constraints imposed on traditional banking business by regulation. We turn now to a group of developments where interest lies rather more in their effect on the operation of monetary policy.

23.3.2   Retail liability management

To the consumer of financial services in the UK, one of the most visually obvious features of the 1980s has been the diversification of financial institutions and the breakdown of traditional demarcations. Retail banks have become mortgage lenders, market makers in securities, unit trust companies, insurance agents and, with a sense of timing paralleled only by their judgement of the merits of Third-World lending, estate agents. Building societies have become banks (virtually in most cases, literally in some). They too have taken on insurance and estate agency and the provision of legal services. *Within* banking, traditional divisions have become blurred as retail banks join others in raising funds in wholesale markets and moving away from their traditional function of 'direct' lending, to advising commercial clients on a wide range of financial matters, offering acceptances and guarantees and other off-balance-sheet facilities as we noted above.

A further breach of traditional demarcations has developed with major stores establishing their own financial subsidiaries, firstly to market credit accounts to the store's customers and later to offer interest on positive balances on credit accounts which involved regular customer payments. In 1988 Marks and Spencer launched its own unit trust, and selected branches of Tesco began to provide cash withdrawal facilities at checkouts in the 1990s.

Looking at developments from the point of view of the retail consumer, the first, and potentially the most far-reaching development of the 1980s was the entry of banks into the mortgage market in 1981. From this stemmed the break-up of the building societies' interest rate cartel in 1983, the rise in building society deposit and advances rates to market clearing

levels and the consequent demise of mortgage rationing. As building societies moved onto the offensive, they dabbled in money transmission services by issuing chequebooks (of limited attraction without the benefit of cheque guarantee cards) and set about lobbying the government for a change in the Building Societies Act, 1962, which limited their sources of funds to retail deposits on which interest had to be paid net of tax and restricted their lending to first mortgages secured on property.

Pushing on an open door where deregulation was concerned, the societies were quickly rewarded with the *Building Societies Act, 1986*, which broadened both the sources and destinations of societies' funds. In particular, large societies were permitted a limited amount of unsecured personal lending. This apparently minor change had momentous results. Since societies could now legally permit customers to be overdrawn, they could, for the first time, issue cheque guarantee cards. This made building society cheque accounts indistinguishable from those of banks except for the considerable advantages that societies paid interest on all positive balances, stayed open longer and were generally seen as more user-friendly by the public. The change in building society regulation, therefore, ensured that banks which had, since 1983, grudgingly paid interest on selected cheque accounts with restricted use, would have to follow. The first announcement came from Lloyds Bank in December 1988. The increasing tendency to pay interest on sight deposits has a number of possible consequences. If it narrows the spread between lending and deposit rates, it is one way by which the cost of bank intermediation may fall. Borrowing to finance spending becomes cheaper relative to using existing liquid assets; at the same time, money's own rate increases relative to other assets. In short, money and bank debt both become more attractive. We look briefly at the implications for the demand for money in the next section.

The willingness to hold higher levels of bank (and building society) debt relative both to income and to other liquid assets and liabilities was quite likely further encouraged by a reduction in the *non-pecuniary costs of borrowing* for many people. The unsecured personal bank loan (as opposed to overdraft) is a product strictly of the 1970s when it became available to established bank customers in exchange for the prior completion of an application form requesting extensive personal information. In the 1980s the forms got shorter and the development of credit-rating agencies using computer data files removed the delay. What once involved an interview with a bank manager became available on demand from high street stores. Furthermore, a combination of advertising, unsolicited postal offers of credit and unrequested increases in established credit limits not only made borrowing easier, but transformed its image. The stigma of 'debt' was eventually replaced by the status of 'credit'.

Furthermore, the increasing tendency to pay interest at rates that move with the general level of market rates made it increasingly difficult to engineer changes in *relative* rates for monetary control purposes. The cheapening of bank and building society debt and the loss of control over interest relativities are both related to the general issue of monetary control, an issue to which we turn next.

23.4 The demand for money and monetary policy

In the early chapters of this book we repeatedly stressed that the successful conduct of monetary policy, especially where that policy includes targeting monetary growth rates, relies heavily upon a stable demand for money function. An obvious comment to make about financial innovation, therefore, is that it must surely make it more difficult to operate monetary policy and in particular to operate any monetary policy, such as following a money growth rule, which relies upon a stable demand for money function (see Chapter 7). In this section we explore numerous ways in which changes in the financial system can lead to changes in the demand for money. We begin by suggesting a number of ways in which one could imagine this happening in principle. The purpose of this is to emphasize the large number of channels through which institutional changes might work and the difficulty of judging *a priori* which of several contradictory results a given innovation is likely to have. Even so, our list is not exhaustive. Towards the end of the section, we make brief reference to recent empirical work on the demand for money which has

tried to identify and incorporate the impact of one or more aspects of financial innovation.

Interest rates.   As we saw in Chapter 7, which rate of interest should be chosen to represent the opportunity cost of holding money has been a perennial problem. What is and what is not a close substitute for money changes over time. Furthermore, the 'closeness' of substitutes varies with the definition of money, something which itself varies as innovations in very liquid assets take place. In a study of UK households' demand for money, for example, one might have taken some measure of building society share and deposit rates up until 1989 when M3 (which excluded building society deposits) was replaced by M4 (which included them). Even with a constant definition of money, however, the closest substitutes will change through time. Taking the 1980s again, it would be interesting to know whether the aggressive marketing of National Savings instruments, including new products paying more closely market-related interest rates, made NS rates more relevant than, say, bond rates. For firms, the development of the CD and the interbank market from the end of the 1960s explains the appearance of those rates of interest in money demand studies. The Eurocurrency markets offer a new, possibly relevant, set of rates. Furthermore, while theoretical considerations may dictate the relevance of, say, long rather than short rates the appropriate choice in practice requires knowledge of institutional detail. In this case the obvious choice might seem to be the rate on long-dated gilts, and this would be correct in a financial system where secondary trading was thin and costly and where securities were generally held to maturity. The growth and development of the secondary gilts market, however, and the changes especially since 'Big Bang' have made all gilts extremely liquid. As we noted in Chapter 11, long gilts like shorts can be sold cheaply and easily for cash in 24 hours.

Whether or not absolute changes in the rate(s) on non-money assets represent changes in the opportunity cost of money depends, of course, on what is happening to money's 'own rate'. In a world where bank deposits do not pay interest, money's explicit own rate is zero and absolute changes in rates on non-money assets necessarily indicate changes in opportunity cost. An intermediate situation applies where deposits pay interest but at rates which are probably low but above all are very sticky. This was a situation which prevailed in the UK until the changes in *Competition and Credit Control* in 1971. Once deposits begin to pay market-related rates then changes in money's own rate mean that it is changes in the 'spread' or differential between the rate on money and the rate on other assets that indicate a change in opportunity cost. Furthermore, where some deposits (and notes and coin) still pay no interest and where banks offer premium rates for differing terms and conditions, theory suggests that money's own rate should be indicated by a weighted average of deposit rates.

In theory at least, the spread between money's own rate and the rate charged on bank lending should also influence the demand for money since spending in excess of income can be financed either by running down liquid assets or by borrowing. It has been pointed out by Goodhart (1984) that when the rate on overdrafts and the rate on deposits are equal, the demand for overdrafts will become infinite. The significance of this observation is widely recognized in studies of the demand for bank lending. It is less frequently recognized that there is also an implication for the demand for money since the attraction of overdrafts when this spread approaches zero arises from a reluctance to run down liquid assets. Clearly, the growth of interest-bearing deposits and the resulting changes in money's own rate is involved here as well. Furthermore, financial innovation may be implicated in changes in the other part of the spread, the cost of bank lending. As we shall see in the next section competition between banks and building societies to lend for house purchase in the 1980s led households in the UK to build up their holdings of floating rate debt. This altered dramatically the composition of their bank debt as the share made up of personal loans and overdrafts diminished while the share of mortgage debt rose. Until the fall in property prices began in 1990, mortgage lending was charged at rates very close to base rates with the result that at any given level of interest rates the average cost of bank debt, weighted by its components, was falling. The attractiveness of borrowing from banks while building up liquid assets was possible further reinforced by the increasing ease with which bank credit became obtainable – a decline in the non-pecuniary costs of borrowing. Again, the next section details the rise in personal sector indebtedness and its consequences; it should be remembered that this was the counterpart to a steady rise in the demand for money relative to income and to the dramatic decline in income velocity.

Velocity and the scale variable.   As we noted in Chapter 7, when economists today refer to velocity, they are almost always referring to *income* velocity, that is to say GDP/M, or PY/M – in contrast to Irving Fisher's use of transactions velocity, PT/M. The most commonly expressed reason for this seems to be that since we are ultimately concerned with money's influence on *output* (or the price of output), PY is more relevant than PT. As we shall see shortly, this runs the risk of ignoring links that may run in the other direction – from spending to money.

Limiting our discussion to income velocity for the moment, it is clear that velocity can change in any direction, depending on the precise form that innovations take. The more traditional view, which associates innovation with the development of near-money substitutes, would lead us to expect a fall in the demand for money relative to GDP. As the need for asset balances declines, the existing money stock is able to finance more (income) transactions. On this view, innovation is associated with rising velocity. On the other hand, and this is a compelling argument given developments in the UK in the 1980s, if innovation leads to the development of increasingly close money substitutes that bear interest, then this may be followed by a rise in money's own rate relative to other rates which *increases* its attraction as a liquid asset. This is simply restating the earlier interest rate argument in velocity rather than demand terms.

There may, however, be much more subtle connections between innovation and velocity which we can explore only if we go back to the idea of transactions velocity, PT/M. Total transactions are larger than 'income' transactions by an amount which reflects, *inter alia*, the volume of intermediate transactions involved in the production process (itself a reflection of the degree of integration in production), the volume of financial transactions and the volume of transactions in existing assets or 'secondhand goods'. The latter of course includes a very large proportion of total house sales/purchases. In adopting PY rather than PT the point is often made that total transactions are likely to be stably related to income transactions and that the distinction between the two is, therefore, unlikely to matter. This is certainly convenient, but not very compelling. Clearly Fisher did not think it probable and Keynes explicitly denied its likelihood in the first volume of the *Treatise*. Various attempts have been made in recent years to develop a PT series and to compare its movements with PY or GDP. Following Keynes and using cheque and electronic payments data, Bain and Howells (1991) constructed a PT series which showed a dramatic upward divergence from GDP, from a multiple of approximately two to three between 1979 and 1989. Interestingly, this study deliberately omitted all transactions through the CHAPS and 'Town Clearing' systems. These are 'same day' payments mechanisms used predominantly by financial firms but also in the settlement of housing transactions. Including CHAPS and Town Clearing data not only makes the PT/PY multiple much larger but also increases dramatically the divergence over time. It seems at least worth considering the possibility, therefore, that financial innovation could have a fairly direct effect upon *transactions* velocity by causing a rise in financial and 'secondhand' transactions relative to those involving newly produced goods and services. Howells and Hussein (1997) found that the demand for UK broad money is much better explained by PT, represented by the Bain/Howells series, than by PY, where PY includes only GDP transactions.

This distinction between income and transactions velocities and the possibility that financial innovation may somehow be implicated, raises another interesting possibility although it is more strictly related to supply and only indirectly to the demand for money. The endogeneity argument, as we saw in Chapter 6, is based upon (deposit-creating) advances being demand-determined. The demand for bank lending originates ultimately from the expenditure needs of deficit units. The desire to spend in excess of one's income can reflect a desire for newly produced goods or services or for financial

assets or for secondhand goods. There seems no good reason, therefore, why GDP rather than PT should appear in bank lending equations. Indeed, theory suggests the reverse. Suppose now that the demand for bank lending were shown to be sensitive to PT rather than to GDP. Bank lending follows total transactions and grows more rapidly than if it were closely linked to GDP. Bank lending and the money supply grow more rapidly than income and income velocity must fall. Financial activity thus not only affects transactions velocity but is causally implicated in the fall in income velocity. Of course, in equilibrium, the resulting deposits must be held. It would be interesting to see the effect of using a PT series as the scale variable in demand for money studies.

Transactions costs. Since Baumol and Tobin brought inventory-theoretic considerations to bear upon transactions demand it has been recognized that brokerage charges (for changing bonds into money), or the 'shoe leather cost' of going to the bank to change deposits into cash or non-money assets into deposits, should play some part in determining the quantity of money people wish to hold and the form in which they wish to hold it.

Such charges, explicit and implicit, are amongst the costs most likely to be reduced by technological innovation in the banking and payments systems. Firstly, we should note that electronic communication and ATMs lower the cost of entry into some areas of banking activity. Where competition increases we should expect a narrowing of spreads and a desire to hold both larger deposits and larger debts than hitherto. More specifically, where extensive (and expensive) specialist labour and premises would previously have been required, cash deposit and withdrawal facilities can now be offered by retail stores whose computer networks already allowed for payment by credit and debit cards. Three obvious consequences could follow from this. Firstly, there is an opportunity to economize on non-interest-bearing cash and an increased desire to hold deposits, giving banks command over a greater proportion of monetary base. Secondly, the virtual automatic access to credit lines provided by plastic cards raises the theoretical question of whether this unused credit should be included in a 'truer' measure of money and at the same time reinforces the point we made above that easier credit makes it more attractive to hold both debit and credit positions simultaneously. On the other hand, ATMs, which typically offer current balance statements and more especially on-screen home banking services, could reduce considerably the need for significant holdings of precautionary balances by making it easier for people to manage their money balances with precision.

Predictably, attempts to incorporate the effects of financial innovation in empirical work have been most marked with respect to interest rates and a recognition that variations in money's own rate, where the demand for broad money is at issue, could be significant. The own rate can be entered implicitly as an element in the differential between *money's own rate* and the rate on other assets or explicitly with the rate on other assets appearing independently. Adam (1991), for example, estimated long and short-run equations from quarterly data for UK real M3 1975–86 using a weighted average own rate on money, with the weights and interest rates reflecting each of the components of M3. Other, opportunity cost, interest rates were the yield on bonds (including capital gains) and on Eurodollar deposits (adjusted for expected depreciation of sterling), recognizing thus the 'innovations' of Euromarkets and the abolition of exchange controls. Both money's own rate and the rate on foreign assets were significant in the long-run equation.

In Chapter 7 we noted that empirical work on the demand for money had employed a variety of scale variables in an attempt to capture the effect of, variously, income, wealth or transactions. This variety is driven more from the controversies which still surround the motives for holding money, however, than by a recognition that financial innovation has changed the appropriate variable. If, as we have said several times, the boom in financial activity in recent years has caused non-income transactions to rise as a proportion of total transactions then it would be interesting to see the effect of using a *PT* rather than *PY* series as the scale variable. A recent comparison of the demand for broad money in the UK and Germany (Biefang-Frisancho Mariscal *et al.*, 1995) found the coefficient on real GNP for Germany was close to unity, while for the UK it was nearly 1.7. The latter is what one

would expect if the demand for money were following a *PT* series which was growing more rapidly than *GNP*. It may not be coincidence that *PT* has diverged from *PY* in the UK since the mid-1970s while it has not done so in Germany.

Most explicit attempts to include the effects of institutional change on the demand for money have focused upon long-run changes, rather in the spirit of the quantity theory that while velocity may change it does so only in the long run and as the result of institutional factors. Institutionally related variables used in studies have included bank offices per head of population, the proportion of the labour force employed outside of agriculture, and the ratio of currency to total money stock and of nonbank to bank financial assets. Other efforts have involved the inclusion of past peak levels of interest rates on the grounds that the incentive to innovation, as we saw in Section 23.2, comes from changes in costs of which interest rates are an important part. The argument is then that an innovation, once adopted, is not usually reversed even when interest rates fall. Clearly, however difficult it may be to measure the effects empirically, the scope for financial innovations to modify the demand for money, in various contradictory ways, are considerable. Consider the following:

- liability management affects money's own rate and thus the opportunity cost of holding money;
- a change in financial transactions relative to GNP transactions may make GNP an inappropriate scale variable;
- a reduction in transactions costs may reduce the demand for precautionary balances but may also lead to more borrowing and larger debit and credit positions;
- by creating ever closer money substitutes, innovation may lead to an increase in velocity;
- cheaper access to cash may reduce the demand for cash and thus reduce a, the public's cash ratio, with implications also for money supply;
- better access to balance sheet information may reduce the demand for precautionary balances;
- better access to financial innovation generally may make agents more sensitive to interest rate differentials leading to more frequent switching between components of broad money.

From this, one can theorize *a priori* virtually any effect one chooses upon the demand for money. Figure 23.2 shows five money demand curves. The rate of interest is an absolute rate on alternative assets and money is assumed (for the moment) not to pay interest. Let M_d^0 be the 'original' curve. Consider firstly the possible effects of liability management where this results most notably in money starting to pay market-related interest rates. If the demand curve in Figure 23.2 shows the demand for broad money, then the increasing practice of liability management, leading to an increase in the proportion of money that pays interest, shifts the curve outward from M_d^0 to M_d^1. More money is demanded at any rate of interest. If, however, the figure depicts the demand for narrow money, while liability management results in interest being paid only on the components of the broader aggregates, then M_d^0 will shift to the left, to M_d^2. Similar effects follow from any of the innovations which lead to an economizing on money holdings.

Now consider the effect of a rise in interest rates. We start on curve M_d^1. When money does not pay interest, a rise in the general level of interest rates from i_0 to i_1 moves us up M_d^1 in the normal way. When money's own rate is market-related, however,

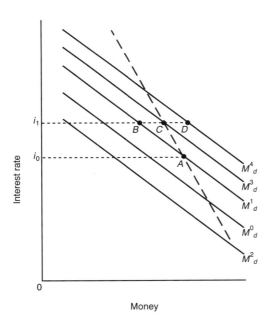

the rise in interest rates on non-money assets is accompanied by a rise in money's own rate and the demand curve *shifts out*, reflecting the increase or improvement in money's 'services'. In Figure 23.2, the demand curve shifts to M_d^3 and the quantity of money demanded is reduced from A to C rather than to B. If we plot the change in quantity against the change in price, we trace out the false demand curve shown by the long-dashed line. It is this that presumably leads to the oft-made but strictly incorrect assertion that liability management makes the demand for money less interest-elastic. If we were to redraw Figure 23.2 with the genuine opportunity cost under liability management, that is, the bond rate minus own rate *spread*, on the vertical axis then the confusion is clearly exposed. Liability management delivers a smaller change in the spread and so we move a smaller distance along a *given* demand curve. In the case where money's own rate moved perfectly with the bond rate, there would be no change at all in the spread and we would stay at one point on the curve. In Figure 23.2 as drawn with a simple, absolute, rate on the vertical axis, this would be shown by a rightward shift of the curve to M_d^4, sufficient to offset completely the movement up it A to D.

Remember that in Chapter 6, where we discussed the history of monetary targeting and techniques of monetary control, we saw that the rationale for monetary targets is a stable relationship between money growth rates and the rate of growth of spending – a stable velocity. Furthermore we noted that the main instrument that central banks have at their disposal for influencing monetary growth is changes in short-term interest rates. Ideally a change in official dealing rates would cause a change in *relative* interest rates. When official rates are increased (for example) the return on non-money assets rises in relation to the return on money. Money becomes less attractive and people hold fewer deposits. The rise in rates also increases the cost of borrowing. The flow of new loans diminishes and the money supply expands more slowly. The reduction in the demand for loans will be further reinforced if the switch from deposits to non-money assets makes it cheaper for firms to borrow by issuing liabilities which are taken up in preference to deposits. But all this begins with, and depends upon, the central

Figure 23.2 Financial innovation and the money demand curve.

bank's ability to change *relative* rates when it changes its official dealing rates. This becomes increasingly difficult as money pays interest and as the rate that it pays moves in line with changes in other rates. At the same time, sharp changes in the interest-bearing proportion of money, such as that witnessed in the UK in the 1980s, mean that the average 'own rate' on money changes. When this happens, people hold more (or less) money relative to spending. Velocity is no longer stable.

23.5 Summary

Innovation is a natural and continuous process in a competitive economic environment. However, it is stimulated by changes in the economic environment and these changes are more pronounced at some periods than others. Typically relevant changes are those involving regulation, technology and volatility of financial flows. Each of these has played a major role in stimulating groups of financial innovations during the past 30 years.

Examples of financial innovation are scattered throughout this book, but in this chapter we looked at two particular forms of innovation, which are both widespread and significant either for the regulatory authorities or for the conduct of monetary policy. The first of these is the development of off-balance-sheet activity. This originated as a response to regulation but has blossomed – particularly in the form of securitization of loans – as a response to reducing the risk exposure of institutions which make fixed rate loans in periods of volatile interest rates. The second is retail liability management. This began in response to deregulation and has had major impacts on the demand for money and on the ability of the authorities to control monetary growth.

Key concepts used in this chapter

Regulatory dialectic	Securitization	Non-pecuniary costs
'Competition and Credit Control'	Moral hazard hypothesis	Relative interest rates
	Regulatory tax hypothesis	Money's own rate
Financial volatility	Passthrough	Income velocity
Regulation Q	Prepayment	Transactions velocity
Contestable markets	Retail liability management	Transactions costs
Off-balance-sheet operations	Building Societies Act, 1986	

Questions and problems

1 Why does financial innovation occur?

2 Explain, using examples, how regulation, technological change and volatility can encourage financial innovation.

3 Why has financial innovation been such a feature of the past 25 years?

4 Explain what is meant by 'off-balance-sheet operations' and give three examples.

5 Explain the basic principles underlying the creation of loan-backed securities.

6 What are the characteristics of a 'passthrough' security? Why might these characteristics limit the attractiveness of this type of security for some types of investor?

7 What is meant by 'retail liability management'? Explain how it has been encouraged by deregulation.

8 Discuss the impacts, potential and actual, of liability management on the demand for money.

9 Why has retail liability management made control of the money supply more difficult?

Further reading

C S Adam, 'Financial innovation and the demand for M3 in the UK 1975–86', *Oxford Bulletin of Economics and Statistics*, 53, 1991

K Bain and P G A Howells, 'The income and transactions velocities of money', *Review of Social Economy*, XLIX, 1991

I BiefangFrisancho Mariscal, HM Trautwein, P G A Howells, P Arestis and H Hagemann, 'Financial Innovation and the Demand for Money in the UK and in West Germany', *Weltwirtschaftliches Archiv*, June 1995

T R Boemio and G A Edwards, 'Asset Securitization: A Supervisory Perspective', *Federal Reserve Bulletin*, October 1989

J D Finnerty, 'Financial engineering', in Newman P, M Milgate and J Eatwell (eds), *The New Palgrave Dictionary of Money and Finance* (London: Macmillan, 1992)

C A E Goodhart, *Monetary Theory and Practice: The UK Experience* (London: Macmillan, 1984)

C A E Goodhart, 'Financial Innovation and Monetary Control', *Oxford Review of Economic Policy*, 2 (4), 1986

D D Hester, 'Innovations and monetary control', *Brookings Papers on Economic Activity*, 1, 1981

P G A Howells and K A Hussein, 'The Demand for Money in the UK: Transactions as the Scale Variable', *Economics Letters*, 1987

E J Kane, 'Accelerating inflation, technological innovations and the decreasing effectiveness of banking regulation', *Journal of Finance*, 36 (2), 1981

E J Kane, 'Technological and regulatory forces in the developing fusion of financial services competition', *Journal of Finance*, 39 (3), 1984

E J Kane, 'How market forces influence the structure of financial regulation' in Haraf W S and R M Kushmeider (eds), *Restructuring Banking and Financial Services in America* (Washington DC: American Enterprise Institute, 1988)

M Kohn, *Financial Institutions and Markets* (New York: McGraw-Hill, 1994) Ch. 20

M K Lewis, 'Off-Balance Sheet Activities and Financial Innovation in Banking', *Banca Nazionale del Lavoro*, 1988

L S Ritter and W L Silber, *Principles of Money, Banking and Financial Markets* (New York: Basic Books, 1991) Ch. 11

A W Sametz, 'Financial innovation and regulation in the United States', in Newman P, M Milgate and J Eatwell (eds), *The New Palgrave Dictionary of Money and Finance* (London: Macmillan, 1992)

W L Silber, 'The process of financial innovation', *American Economic Review, Papers*, 73 (2), 1983

The regulation of financial markets

24.1 Introduction

As we noted in Section 20.3, the financial services industry has always been politically sensitive and, consequently, heavily regulated. The political sensitivity of the industry stemmed from its origin in money-lending which many religions have equated with usury.[1] The rejection by Christianity of usury up until the early years of the Renaissance led to money-lending being dominated by non-Christian outsiders which, in turn, intensified the distaste for it, even while the services of money-lenders were becoming increasingly demanded. Shakespeare's *The Merchant of Venice* shows a society which accorded moral superiority to the shipping of goods from one country to another over the lending of money even though the former depended on the latter.

There have also been more specific reasons for concern about the practice of the industry. Up until the past quarter of a century or so, the term 'financial services' referred principally to the banking and insurance industries. The specific reasons for the demand for regulation of these two industries have been rather different. For the banking industry, the basic problem has been its reliance on public confidence. The fractional reserve banking system – the holding of only relatively small reserves against deposits – vastly increases the potential profitability of banks but, at the same time, leaves them at risk from loss of public confidence which may cause a run on their deposits. The risk of collapse is made greater by the contrast between the liquid nature of bank liabilities (deposits) and the illiquid nature of their assets (loans). Further, the assets of a bank are likely to have a significantly lower value when the bank is in liquidation than when it is a going concern. Consequently, a collapse will generally result in a heavy loss to creditors.

There are two principal areas of concern in relation to bank collapse. The first is the prospect of *contagion* – the collapse of one bank leading to the collapse of others with the possibility of damage occurring to the whole financial industry. This, in turn, might have very serious consequences for the real economy. Contagion might arise to the extent

---

[1] It is the strict Islamic rejection of usury that has led to the quite rapid development in recent years of Islamic banking which eschews the taking of interest.

that a failure of one bank causes a loss of confidence in banking in general. Thus, a run on a bank may occur because it becomes known that it is in a difficult financial position – perhaps it has made a number of dubious loans which are not likely to be repaid. This could either lead the public to become more discriminating in their choice of bank, in which case there would be no danger for soundly managed banks, or it could lead to many depositors wishing to withdraw their funds from the banking system in general, causing problems for all banks. A second possible source of contagion is the very high level of interbank dealings which is a common feature of modern finance – the collapse of a large bank might create a significant quantity of bad debts for other banks. It is possible as well that the default of a major borrower might encourage other borrowers to default also. This was one of the fears in the early years of the international debt crisis of the developing countries which started in 1982 with the decision by Mexico to default on debt repayments.

The second concern with regard to possible bank collapse relates to consumer protection. As we saw in Section 1.5, the efficiency of a modern economy is greatly enhanced by the development of the financial system and thus it is desirable that as many people as possible participate in that system. It follows that collapses of financial institutions within a sophisticated financial system are bound to affect large numbers of people, small savers as well as large. As a further consequence, many people who take part in financial transactions have very little knowledge of either the products or the processes of the system. In addition, as we have pointed out in Sections 5.5 and 11.4.2, prices in financial markets depend heavily on expectations and can thus move very sharply as a result of market optimism or pessimism. This means that large profits (and losses) can, on occasions, be made with great rapidity. It is hardly surprising, then, that greed, chicanery and gullibility are present to a greater extent in financial markets than in many others. A recent example with grave political and social consequences was the collapse of the pyramid savings schemes in Albania in early 1997.

In markets where the potential losers may be thought to be people with ready access to financial resources and information, it may seem reasonable to follow the principle of *caveat emptor*.[2] It would, however, take a bold politician to ignore the plight of small savers threatened with the loss of their life savings. The safest response is to attempt to regulate the market in the hope of preventing such situations from occurring and/or to provide insurance where they do arise. Box 24.2 considers some contrasting British cases from this point of view.

As we pointed out in Section 15.3, deposit-taking institutions have been subject to heavy regulation because their liabilities form the means of payment. Thus, bank regulation aims to guarantee the integrity of the transactions medium and to prevent the process of financial intermediation from failing.

We have already, in Section 20.4.4 considered special features which explain the high level of regulation of the insurance market, notably the very long term of some contracts, the size of many of the risks being insured relative to policyholders' incomes, and the lack of transparency of many of the products. Until quite recently, in other financial markets – for equities, bonds, bills, derivatives – only the funds of professional investors were at risk. Now, however, many people have a small, if indirect, interest in the performance of such markets through unit trusts, investment trusts and pension funds managed for them by professional fund managers. More of us than ever before have a reason for wishing financial markets to be sound and transparent.

24.2   The difficulties of regulation

The case for regulation can be put in more technical terms than we have done above. Regulation is necessary, we could say, because of *market failure*. Market failure might arise for any number of reasons – because of the presence of elements of monopoly or oligopoly; because confidence in the financial system is a social benefit which will not be adequately valued by individuals in the market;

---

2 Let the buyer beware

Box 24.2 Attitudes towards losers in financial markets

1 *Lloyd's of London names*

Lloyd's of London is an insurance market organized into 400 syndicates supplying a range of insurance services. Syndicates are backed by 'names' who guarantee to meet any syndicate losses from their personal wealth on a basis of unlimited liability. In profitable years 'names' do not have to provide funds and thus earn a rate of return on money which can also be invested elsewhere. However, in the late 1980s and early 1990s, several syndicates experienced years of large losses and 'names' backing these syndicates were called upon to pay large sums. Although it was claimed that some losses were the result of manipulation by professionals in the market and the market felt obliged to provide some compensation to losers in order to try to salvage its own reputation, there was very little public sympathy for 'names'. It was widely believed that they were happy to accept the high returns without being prepared to accept the accompanying risk.

2 *Barlow Clowes*

Barlow Clowes was a firm of investment fund managers which had been licensed by the British government despite warnings from both the Bank of England and the London Stock Exchange. Barlow Clowes operated a number of funds, claiming to invest in UK gilts. Some were UK funds, others were operated from Gibraltar to provide a tax shelter for investors. Clients were offered a very high rate of return. In fact, a good proportion of the money had gone to support the extravagant life style of the firm's directors. That part which had been invested had gone into riskier investments than gilts in an attempt to make up for the shortfall. In May 1988, the firm was closed by the industry regulators and subsequent investigation discovered a deficiency of around £100 million. In December 1989, the government accepted responsibility and established a compensation fund to meet the claims of investors because it was argued that the licence provided by the DTI had given investors false information about the reliability of the firm.

3 *UK private pensions*

In the early 1990s, new legislation opened up the possibility of people taking out private pension plans. Large insurance companies saw this as a major new market and set about persuading large numbers of people to switch from their existing pension schemes operated by their employers to private pension plans. In many cases people were misled by the insurance companies into believing that they would be better off with a personal pension plan when, in fact, the reverse was the case. When it became clear that this had occurred, there was widespread public and political anger and the industry regulators required that compensation be paid. Although the form of compensation had not been agreed by April 1997 (some two years after the problem had come to light), it seemed likely that the insurance companies would ultimately face a bill of between £2 billion and £4 billion in compensation.

---

because of the lack of perfect knowledge and so on. A particular form of the lack of perfect information is *asymmetric information* – the ignorance of consumers relative to producers in highly technical markets. Although not all the arguments are convincing, there is a firm basis of support for some level and form of regulation of financial markets. We do, however, face a number of difficulties.

Firstly, regulation can cause problems as well as solve them. This has been at the base of the strong demand over the past quarter of a century for *deregulation* – for greater freedom from government control – in all areas of the economy, not least in financial markets. These demands have been supported by the development of the 'economic theory of regulation' which stresses a number of undesirable features of regulation. The theory[3] derives from the idea of *agency capture* – that the regulatory process will inevitably be captured by producers and used in their interests rather than in the interests of consumers. The theory of regulation points to four major failings of regulation:

---

[3] The theory was developed in G J Stigler, 'The theory of economic regulation', *Bell Journal of Economics and Management Science*, 1971, 2, 1, 3–31.

- Regulation creates *moral hazard*. That is, it causes people to behave in a counter-productive way. For example, a belief that the government will ensure the safety of deposits with all financial institutions leads savers to deposit their money without giving thought to the behaviour of the company with whom they bank. This, in turn, allows dubious organizations to survive. Equally, the belief that they will always be rescued from collapse causes financial institutions to take greater risks in their lending policies in search of higher returns. Moral hazard is discussed in Section 23.3 in relation to off-balance-sheet activity. A much-quoted example of moral hazard in operation was the risky behaviour of Savings and Loans Associations in the USA in the 1980s (see Box 17.2).

- The regulatory process is likely to be captured by producers since the activities of regulators are much more important to each of the relatively small number of producers than to each of the much larger number of consumers. Further, the next career move of regulators is often into the industry they have been regulating and so they may not wish to offend producers and/or regulators may be ex-practitioners who share the judgements and values of the producers.

- Regulation creates *compliance* costs (the costs of adhering to the regulations) for producers. The effects of such costs depend on the degree of competition in the industry and the nature of the costs. If producers are able to pass the costs on to consumers, the result is higher prices and lower output. On the other hand, fixed compliance costs will have no impact on marginal costs and, in a genuinely competitive industry, will not affect output. Complying with regulations may also have benefits for firms. They might, for example, be required to keep better records than they would have chosen to do voluntarily and might later discover advantages in having done so.

- The need to comply with regulations increases the costs of entry into and exit from markets. This helps to preserve monopoly positions and make cartels more stable.

Combining the last two arguments produces the proposition that regulation inhibits competition and thus reduces the efficiency with which financial markets help to allocate the economy's scarce resources (see Section 1.5.3). However, even if we accept that regulation restricts competition, it is by no means the only factor in financial markets that does so and there is no guarantee that a reduction in regulation will lead to increased competition. The deregulation argument may work in two ways.

- Regulation keeps out new entrants who, if they could enter, would force existing firms in the market to be more efficient and would compete prices down, removing monopoly rents.

- Regulation prevents mergers and acquisitions and allows small inefficient firms to remain in business. Thus, deregulation would lead to mergers which would result in economies of scale, economies of scope and the replacement of poor management by superior management.

With regard to the first of these, the benefits of lower prices which might arise from deregulation have to be weighed against costs such as possible reductions in the stability of the system and increased risk of loss for consumers. Unfortunately for the second proposition, studies of the very considerable merger activity which took place in US banking in the 1980s and 1990s have produced no convincing evidence of increased efficiency or profitability.[4] On the other hand, if there were significant economies of scale, and mergers occurred to take advantage of them, it would become difficult for new entrants to come into the market, even in the absence of regulation.

It therefore seems that none of the criticisms of regulation provide sufficient reason to reject all regulation, though they all point to matters which must be taken into account in decisions as to how much regulation there should be and what form it should take.

With regard to the form of regulation, we must first ask who should carry out the regulation – the government or a government agency, or the industry itself (*self-regulation*). The argument for self-regula-tion has two elements. Firstly, the industry has a

---

4 See S A Rhoades. 'Banking acquisitions', in P Newman, M Milgate and J Eatwell (eds), *The New Palgrave Dictionary of Money,* *Banking and Finance* (London: Macmillan, 1992).

commercial incentive to protect its own reputation and so members will be prepared to pay to achieve this, thus overcoming one of the principal market failure arguments for government regulation. Secondly, practitioners understand the needs of the industry and are likely to interfere less with its efficient functioning. This counters a common complaint against public regulatory bodies that, because they will be heavily criticized over the collapse of firms but not praised for actions which lead to lower prices, they will always impose excessive safety standards, raising the cost of regulation to both producers and consumers.

The assumption then is that self-regulation is almost certain to be lighter than regulation by an external body. There is a danger, however, that self-regulation may turn out to be an awkward halfway house. To begin with, it must be supported by some government regulation at least to the extent that firms are legally required to join the industry regulatory scheme. Otherwise, an incentive would be created for some firms to act as free riders, hoping to benefit from any increase in reputation of the industry resulting from the behaviour of firms within the regulatory organization without paying the costs of membership.

More importantly, self-regulation will only create less moral hazard than public regulation to the extent that it leaves an element of risk for both consumers and producers. The problem is that once an element of risk exists, the degree of risk has to be assessed to allow a judgement to be made of the risk/return profile of an investment. This should cause no worries to professionals, but the general public faces two types of difficulty. Firstly, it may be time-consuming and costly to acquire the necessary knowledge to assess risk accurately. Secondly, the ability of non-experts in a field to assess risk is notoriously poor. There is a strong tendency for people to respond to risk by adopting one or other extreme position. They may, as responses to food scares show, eschew a product or activity completely as soon as an element of risk is made clear. Alternatively, they may, as people's behaviour as car drivers and smokers attests, believe that risk only exists for other people. Thus, the possibility of consumers assessing risk at all accurately is remote, especially in markets which are characterized by asymmetric information and where

producers have both the incentive and the capacity to mislead consumers.

Further, the existence of consumers who are, in the field of finance, risk takers or who underestimate the true level of risk ensures that dubious firms will continue to survive despite the apparent reduction of moral hazard. On the other hand, those who are risk averters or who overestimate the true risk may be driven away from products from which they might have benefited.

Nor does self-regulation perform particularly well in terms of the other complaints about regulation. By definition, self-regulation places regulation in the hands of the producers. Indeed, it places it in the hands of *existing* producers and provides an incentive for them to use regulation to increase barriers to entry to the industry. Thus, it may lead to a lowering of some kinds of compliance costs, but not necessarily all.

Many of the problems of self-regulation can be illustrated by a consideration of the operation of the UK's *Financial Services Act* of 1986. The Act set up a regulatory system for the City of London with the aim of creating a flexible system of self-regulation which inspired confidence in both market practitioners and investors. It established a new principal regulatory authority, the Securities and Investment Board (SIB), which recognized three types of organization: a number of self-regulatory organizations (SROs) which were composed of investment practitioners and which were given the responsibility of regulating their own segment of the industry; a group of recognized professional bodies (RPBs) whose task it was to maintain the standards of the lawyers, accountants, insurance brokers and actuaries who participate in the market; and a number of exchanges. The exchanges were divided into two groups – recognized investment exchanges (RIEs) located in the UK, and designated investment exchanges (DIEs) located either outside the UK or in both the UK and other countries.

The Act covered all financial services. This had the effect, as mentioned in Section 16.4, of making the insurance industry subject to the Act as well as to the Insurance Companies Act of 1982. An initial problem was with the classification of the industry for the purpose of defining membership of the SROs. This is far from easy because of the overlapping of activities. For example, life assurance firms, as we have seen, not only provide insurance but also run pension funds, have an interest in housing finance, engage in fund management and provide investment advice. Banks also participate in a variety of fields and overlap with insurance companies in some ways. This problem increased with the *functional integration* of financial services firms. A single firm may now[5] be engaged in banking, insurance and securities business.

The argument that self-regulation is desirable because practitioners understand best the needs and working of an industry requires that regulation should be undertaken by experts. The complexity of the various elements of the industry, in turn, means that the regulatory needs of the various activities will be different and that there should be a number of SROs each dealing with a precise segment of the industry. Yet this is bound to produce some overlap among the SROs. It follows that if the legal requirement is for firms to join only one regulatory organization, some will have a choice as to which organization to join and the separate SROs may find themselves competing for members.

This introduces the possibility of *competitive laxity* with those regulating authorities that try to maintain high standards losing out to those that choose to reduce standards in the interests of their members. In this way, the regulating authorities might act as trade associations, looking after the interests of their members, and underplaying the role of consumer protection. Some regulators may attempt to maximize membership by keeping subscriptions low, reducing their ability to supervise the behaviour of members. A case in point in Britain in the early 1990s was FIMBRA (the Financial Intermediaries, Managers and Brokers Regulatory Association), one of the original SROs set up by *The Financial Services Act*. FIMBRA kept its subscriptions low and as a result soon ran into financial problems. It then had to be rescued by loans from its larger members, causing it to be heavily dependent on a small number of members who could transfer to other associations if the actions of FIMBRA did not suit them. One of the consequences of this weakening of the regulatory system in this way was the Maxwell pension fund scandal which is set out in Box 24.3.

In addition, as the Chairman of Britain's Securities and Investment Board (SIB), Andrew Large, admitted in 1993, self-regulation is often seen to equate with self-interest. This was particularly true of the City of London self-regulatory system as a result of the uncovering of a large number of illegal activities and institutional collapses in the late 1980s and 1990s.

It was possible to give the system the benefit of the doubt for some years, arguing that a complex system needed time to settle down. However, still in 1997, 11 years after the Financial Services Act, the industry was struggling to cope with issues such as the failure of agents to seek the best prices for clients and the giving of unsuitable investment advice. Attempts, to overcome a general lack of confidence in a self-regulatory scheme, such as compulsory investor compensation schemes, may cause compliance costs for prudent firms to be higher than they would need to be under a system that was more trusted.

If regulation is to be left to the government or a government agency, there is a choice between *direct regulation* which prescribes the activities that a financial institution can undertake and *indirect regulation* which tries to persuade a firm to behave in a socially desirable way by offering incentives to them to do so. In theory, indirect regulation should interfere less with the activities of firms and impose less of a burden. Consequently, it has become more popular in recent years. However, it has been argued by Boot and Greenbaum (1992)[6] in relation to proposals for changes in US banking regulation that indirect regulation might impose a huge informational burden on regulators and may ultimately lead to intrusive and arbitrary supervision.

We have mentioned above problems for regulators arising from functional integration in financial markets. Other recent developments have also added

---

5 A significant amount of functional integration has always existed in countries such as Germany and Austria in which banks have been universal – able to provide a wide range of banking and securities services (see Box 20.2). On the other hand, self-regulation has not been practised in those countries.

6 A W Boot and S I Greenbaum, 'American banking legislation, recent', in P Newman, M Milgate and J Eatwell (eds), *The New Palgrave Dictionary of Money and Finance* (London: Macmillan, 1992).

Box 24.4 Maxwell and the pension funds

On 31 October 1991 the body of the newspaper tycoon, Robert Maxwell, was discovered floating in the sea off the Canary Islands. During the subsequent unravelling of the affairs of the Maxwell group of companies, including Maxwell Communications Corporation (MCC) and Mirror Group Newspapers (MGN), massive fraud was discovered relating to the pension funds of the Maxwell companies.

Two types of problems were uncovered. The first was the management of the pension funds in the interests of the Maxwell family rather than the investors in the fund. When Maxwell had taken control of the MGN fund in 1985, investments were largely in UK blue chip equities. By April 1990, more than half of the 20 largest investments in the fund's portfolio were in companies with which Maxwell had a connection or in his own private interests. This was clearly contrary to general trust law which lays down three obligations for trustees:

- to diversify investments;
- to avoid exposing beneficiaries to undue risk;
- to act reasonably.

However, much worse was to follow. During 1991, Maxwell siphoned off up to £1 billion from the pension funds of his companies in the form of unsecured loans for his own use in defending his seriously troubled empire. When the Maxwell companies collapsed, this money was lost, leaving several of the funds unable to meet their obligations to pay pensions to employees and former employees.

How could this have happened?

Pension funds (as mentioned in Chapter 4) are required by law to be kept separate from company accounts. A Board of 'independent' Trustees is appointed to oversee the running of the fund. However, Maxwell was able to appoint his own trustees and did so to good effect. There was a gradual erosion of representation of employees on the board and most trustees appeared to know little of what was being done in their name. Maxwell managed the funds through his own private management firm, Bishopgate Investment Management (BIM). It was subject to inspection by auditors and to regulation by one of the SROs, IMRO (the Investment Management Regulatory Organization).

A report compiled by the House of Commons social security select committee later described the events as a 'spectacle to make even Pontius Pilate blush' as everyone in the City seemed mainly concerned to deny blame. The report concluded that if the regulators had 'acted with the proper degree of suspicion ... and if professional advisers' care had been commensurate with their fees ... then the Maxwell pension funds would have been secure' (*Financial Times* 10/3/1992 page 8).

The report particularly criticized the accountancy firm, Coopers & Lybrand Deloitte, which had detailed serious shortcomings in the way BIM managed the pension funds as early as February 1991 but had reported this only to the pension fund manager and only rarely attended meetings of the trustees of the funds. IMRO was also heavily criticized. It had investigated BIM only five weeks before Maxwell's death but had claimed to find nothing wrong. They had failed, said the select committee, to spot stealing on a massive scale. *Self-regulation*, said the committee, was little short of tragic comedy.

---

to the difficulties faced by regulators. One such development has been the *globalization* of financial markets. In the period since 1980 there has been a very rapid growth in the stock of cross-border bank assets and cross-border securities transactions. A quarter of stock market trades worldwide involves either a foreign security or a foreign counterparty. Between 1989 and 1995, estimated global turnover in foreign exchange more than doubled (see Table 12.1). Both the sheer size and the interdependence of markets now pose problems. In its 1995 annual

report, the Geneva-based Bank for International Settlements (BIS) warned that essentially local events might have disruptive implications for the whole international financial system.

Globalization has also caused fears of competitive laxity among national regulatory authorities. A national authority may feel that too strict regulation may leave its own country's firms at a competitive disadvantage in comparison with firms based in countries with less stringent rules. For example, Japanese authorities have been particularly strict with the result that Japanese equity purchasing fees are up to eight times higher than other financial centres. Since much of the financial services industry is footloose, strict regulation in one country may cause firms to move their operations to other countries, possibly resulting in a considerable loss of income and employment to the country attempting to operate a responsible regulatory regime. As a result of the costs on firms of the Japanese regulatory system, much trade has shifted offshore to cheaper and less regulated centres. Initially, tight regulation of derivatives trading at the Tokyo exchange led to a substantial part of the market moving to Osaka and then from Osaka to Singapore. To the extent that regulations are loosened everywhere and/or that firms do move to more poorly regulated areas, the level of systemic risk through contagious financial disorders may be increased.

We have seen, in Chapter 20, the problems faced by the EU in its attempt to ensure fair competition among firms from different member states. The principle of *home* regulation which the EU has chosen must tempt firms to locate their head offices in the member states with the most producer-friendly regulations. One way of attempting to remove the consequent dangers of competitive laxity among member governments is through the harmonization of regulations aimed to reduce cross-border systemic risk. However, as Dale (1996) notes, the decision made by the European Commission as to which regulations must be harmonized appears to have had more to do with competitive than with systemic concerns – the principal motivation of the *Investment Services Directive* and the *Capital Adequacy Directive* seems to have been to ensure competitive equality between universal banks and non-bank investment firms.

Financial innovation and rapid technological change in the financial services industry have posed yet more major problems for regulators. The development of screen-based trading systems, securitization and the rapid growth in the availability of new, sophisticated derivatives have all complicated the job of the authorities. Especial concern has been expressed over the growth of off-balance sheet risk and the risk posed by fast-changing on-balance-sheet positions. The traditional regulatory, accounting and legal framework for financial organizations which

depended on the regular scrutiny of balance sheets has been left behind by such developments. We look at these questions in Section 24.4 below.

We can sum up by saying that regulation of financial services faces many serious problems and may, under certain circumstances, make matters worse. We have seen, however, that self-regulation does not provide a simple remedy for such problems. We shall see in Section 24.4 that government regulators have no choice but to work with the industry itself in the operation of regulatory regimes, but there remains a strong case for regulatory bodies which are external to the industry. Certainly, the difficulties of regulation do not justify complete deregulation of the industry. It has been frequently argued by those in favour of deregulation that financial markets are not different in kind from other markets but only in degree and so should not be treated any differently. However, large differences in degree are equivalent to differences in kind. Financial markets are of great importance to the economy as a whole and to a large number of individual consumers. Views about their regulation cannot satisfactorily be derived from the treatment of non-financial markets.

24.3   Banking regulation

We have mentioned two regulatory issues in banking:

- the possibility of contagion as the result of a run on one bank turning into a *panic* which might lead to a serious reduction in liquidity for the system a a whole;
- the need for consumer protection, given the nature of the banking industry and the cost and difficulty of acquiring knowledge.

We have added to these the need to cause as little moral hazard as possible, to keep compliance costs low and to interfere as little as possible with competition either by creating barriers to entry or exit or by favouring some institutions over others within the market.

A common approach to ensuring the stability of the banking industry has been to prevent banks from participating in the more risky aspects of finance by limiting them to deposit creation and lending functions. Thus, we have seen in earlier chapters that in both the United States and Italy, legislation passed during the 1930s rigidly separated commercial banking from investment banking and other financial activities. Since banks could provide a wider range of financial services not just in their own name but through the acquisition of other companies, this had to be supported by legislation that restricted the ability of banks to acquire non-banking firms and vice versa. In the United States, for example, the *Bank Holding Act* of 1956 sought to prevent companies owning banks from being allied with insurance companies, securities firms and commercial enterprises. Such a separation fitted well with the British and American model of banking in which the various kinds of banking business were typically by different types of banking organization. In particular, deposit-taking banks concentrated on short-term lending. This contrasted with the universal banking model common in northern Europe (see Section 15.3).

Other approaches to ensuring the stability of banks have included guaranteeing the liquidity of the overall banking system by giving the central bank the role of lender of last resort to the system (see Section 6.4), seeking to prevent runs on individual banks by introducing some form of deposit insurance scheme, placing limitations on interest payments on deposits to prevent competition for deposits (liability management), and establishing barriers to entry also with the intention of limiting competition among banks.

We have seen that all of these restrictions have come under challenge in recent years. High and variable inflation and interest rates put pressure on traditional specialized savings institutions. In the United States this was magnified by legal restrictions on rates of interest payable on retail deposits. As financial services became an increasingly international industry, governments became concerned about the competitiveness of their domestic financial industries hobbled by tight regulation. In a world of increasingly mobile capital firms found their way around existing restrictions and sooner or later forced legislative changes which gave them greater

freedom. Diversification of asset bases provided benefits in an increasingly risky environment and firms sought to benefit from economies of both scale and scope. The financial conglomerate was born. All of this was fostered by an anti-government mood in the worlds of both business and finance.

Regulation aimed at ensuring the stability of the banking system has, as a result, been reduced almost entirely to rules regarding the capital adequacy of banks – rules specifying the proportion of bank assets which a bank's own capital must comprise. These rules, discussed in Section 16.2 in relation to the UK, have, in turn, been complicated by the need to cope with both the globalization of financial markets and by financial innovation.

24.4 Issues in international regulation

24.4.1 The impact of globalization and financial innovation – the Basle Committee

The globalization of the banking industry led to a great increase in international interbank lending and increased dramatically the possibility that the collapse of a bank in one country could cause serious losses for banks in other countries. Regulators became strongly aware of this danger with the collapse in 1974 of both the Franklin National Bank in New York and the Herstatt Bank in Germany. At the same time, there was increasing worry over the gravitation of banks to the least regulated national jurisdictions with resulting competition in regulatory laxity between financial centres. One outcome of these concerns was the setting up of a standing committee of bank supervisors under the auspices of the Bank for International Settlements (BIS). The committee comprised representatives of the bank supervisors of the 11 Group of Ten countries[7] together with Luxembourg. Its formal title was the Committee on Banking Regulation and Supervisory Practices but it has become known as 'the Cooke Committee' after its chairman from 1977 to 1988 or

---

[7] USA, UK, Japan, Germany, France, Italy, Canada, Netherlands, Belgium, Sweden and Switzerland.

the Basle Committee. It sought to link together the different regulatory regimes in different countries in order to ensure that all banks were supervised according to certain broad principles.

The initial concern of the committee was to establish guidelines for the division of responsibilities among the national supervisory authorities and this led to the signing of the Basle Concordat in December 1975 by the central bank governors of the Group of Ten. This distinguished between 'host' and 'parent' authorities and between branches and subsidiaries of foreign banks. Under the Concordat, the supervision of foreign banking establishments was to be the joint responsibility of parent and host authorities. Host authorities were to be responsible for the supervision of the liquidity of foreign banks. Solvency was to be the responsibility of the parent authority in the case of foreign branches and of the host authority in the case of foreign subsidiaries. Great stress was laid upon the exchange of inform-ation between host and parent authorities.

The Concordat was voluntary but all countries represented on the committee adopted its rules. However, it soon became clear that there was a good deal of confusion over the interpretation of the rules. The confusion increased following the adoption in 1978 of a rule that the international business of banks should be conducted on a consolidated basis to limit the opportunities for regulatory evasion since this appeared to conflict with the earlier granting of responsibility for the solvency of foreign subsidiaries to host authorities. A second problem was that the different supervisory standards among countries led some countries, notably the USA, to be more reluctant than others to share or delegate supervisory responsibilities. The collapse of Banco Ambro-siano's Luxembourg subsidiary in the summer of 1982 caused particular concern as neither the Luxembourg nor the Italian authorities would accept responsibility for either supervision or emergency support of the bank, in part because the Luxembourg subsidiary was technically a holding company rather than a bank. In an attempt to overcome the various problems, the Concordat was revised in 1983 with the revision being based upon the principle of consolidated supervision and provisions designed to ensure adequate supervisory standards. The aim was to encourage national authorities to lock out foreign banks originating from permissive jurisdictions and to prevent their own banks from conducting their international operations from poorly regulated centres. The adoption of the principle of consolidated supervision was intended to make the solvency of foreign subsidiaries a joint responsibility of parent and host authorities. Foreign bank subsidiaries were to be required to be financially sound in their own right, while also being supervised as integral parts of the group to which they belonged. Responsibility for the supervision of liquidity of both foreign branches and subsidiaries was to remain with host authorities. The new agreement also introduced more precise guidelines for the supervision of holding companies.

Despite the changes in the revised Concordat, problems remained and these were highlighted by the pressure placed on the international banking system by the debt crisis of the developing countries during the early 1980s. When, early in 1982, the Mexican government declared a moratorium on debt repay-ments, there was a potential crisis for international banks which had lent Mexico vast amounts over the previous eight years and possibly for the whole international financial system. Several banks had lent to Latin American countries (especially Mexico, Argentina and Brazil) considerably more than their total capital. In 1982, claims of selected US banks on five major Latin American debtors ranged from between 140 and 260 per cent of the paid-in capital of the banks. In many cases, loans to a single country were more than half the bank's capital. Thus, if Mexico had continued to default on its repayments and if other countries had followed suit, a number of banks would have been wiped out. This possibility raised the spectre of the contagious bankruptcy of many other banks. The IMF, the World Bank and the USA combined to help banks out of these particular problems, but the view took hold that a degree of harmonization of supervisory standards was needed among national regulatory authorities.

The principal outcome of this was the Basle minimum capital adequacy guidelines for inter-national banks approved in July 1988. As explained in Section 16.2, these established common prudential risk-adjusted ratios for banks to apply from the beginning of 1993. It also made allowance for off-balance-sheet credit exposures which are converted into balance sheet equivalent amounts using a formula that takes account of the likely extent of the default risk involved.

This involved a two-tier classification of capital:

Tier I capital: equity and disclosed reserves at the bank's free disposal and thus readily available to cushion losses;

Tier II capital: funds available but not fully owned or controlled by the institution, such as subordinated loans.

Tier II elements could not make up more than 50 per cent of an institution's own funds. Solvency ratios must maintain shareholders' funds at not less than 8 per cent of risk-weighted assets. The agreement sought both to strengthen the soundness and stability of the international banking system and to ensure competitive equality among international banks. The accord incorporated capital requirements for over-the-counter derivatives (see Chapters 13 and 14), with the capital adequacy requirement being determined by estimates of current and potential credit exposure, taking into account the nature of the counterparty.

Other developments followed. In April 1990 an addendum to the Basle Concordat aimed to encourage more regular and structured collaboration between supervisors, with provision being made for supervisory consultations at the authorization stage. In the same year, the Committee tried to deal with the single most important cause of bank failures, excessive concentration of default risk. It did this by recommending common definitions and procedures related to large exposures, recommending maximum limits on single exposures of 25 per cent of the capital base.

That serious problems remained, however, became clear with the forced closure of the Bank of Credit and Commerce International (BCCI) in July 1991. BCCI's corporate structure was based on a non-bank holding company in Luxembourg which owned two separate banking networks incorporated in Luxembourg and the Cayman Islands. The holding company was unregulated and so consolidated supervision of the group was not possible, allowing BCCI to hide its problems by shifting assets between national jurisdictions. The Basle Committee responded to the BCCI affair by issuing a set of minimum standards for supervision of international banks.

But other problems were coming to the fore, particularly with the very rapid growth in derivatives

trading worldwide. The speed at which the risks of derivatives can be transformed and the complexity of the transformation process result in a loss of transparency. This makes risk assessment much more difficult and, it was argued, weakened both market discipline and regulatory oversight, leading to greatly increased systemic risks. Risk was increased also, it was thought, because end users frequently did not understand how derivatives worked and the management of banks and securities houses often did not understand what their dealers were doing. This last problem is magnified to the extent that pay systems reward traders hugely for success in achieving profits and provide them with little incentive to follow cautious strategies. We have also considered in Section 14.8 the argument that derivatives trading increases the volatility of financial asset prices. Finally, there were concerns over the concentration of derivatives trading among a few major financial institutions, with the possibility that the failure of a large derivatives dealer could both inflict large losses on counterparties and also damage the liquidity of the derivatives market.

One approach to the potential increase in default risk has been to encourage the use of *netting agreements* which create a single legal obligation covering multiple transactions between two counterparties, allowing them to reduce both the amount and the number of payments in comparison to settlements on a gross basis. In the USA, the International Swap Dealers Association (ISDA) drew up a master agreement which allows an intermediary to reconcile all of its transactions with a defaulted counterparty and come up with a final net payment, permitting the amount of capital set aside to support the business to be reduced by 50 per cent since the capital adequacy rules only have to be applied to the net value of transactions payments. In line with this, the Basle Committee amended the 1988 Accord by reducing the capital that must be held against derivatives credit exposures which are subject to bilateral netting, subject to banks being able to demonstrate to their supervisors the legal enforceability of netting arrangements in all relevant jurisdictions. Regulators have also acted to include derivatives transactions in large exposure limits, along with conventional on-balance-sheet exposures.

This still left market risk, not treated at all in the

1988 Accord, to be dealt with. In April 1993[8] the Basle Committee published proposals for minimum capital requirements to cover banks' exposure to market fluctuations. Derivatives were to be converted into positions in the relevant underlying asset and become subject to capital requirements designed to capture specific and general market risk. However, this was criticized on the grounds that static capital adequacy rules cannot capture the risk profiles of individual institutions. It was argued that a much more sophisticated approach was needed which made use of the complex risk management models used by the major derivatives dealers with regulators acting to validate the models and set the risk parameters used in the estimate of the overall value-at-risk against which capital must be held.

In July 1994[9], the Basle Committee and the International Organization of Securities Commissions (IOSCO) produced a joint policy statement on the oversight of the risk management process by senior management; the measurement, control and reporting of risk exposures; and the internal controls and audits regarding risk management. In April 1995, following the collapse of Barings (see Box 14.6), the Basle Committee agreed to allow banks to use their own computer models to assess the risks arising from market volatility, rather than complying with standardized measures of volatility and risk for particular financial instruments. Also, for the first time, capital charges were required to cover commodities risks. The Committee later supported a number of steps to improve the quality of risk management. These included *stress tests* which examine the overall impact of a worst case scenario (such as a repeat of the 1987 stock market crash) on a bank's capital base. In addition, it supported the separation of the trading and settlement arms of banks' trading divisions.

There are still worries about the reliability of the computer models with regard to the more complex derivatives products and about the ability of regulators to evaluate the models. It is also feared that the use of the models will greatly reduce the transparency of financial markets because only banks and regulators will know the basis on which risks have been measured.

The European Commission has followed developments in the Basle Accord. In May 1996 it proposed the amendment of the First Banking Directive, the Solvency Ratio Directive and the Capital Adequacy Directive (see Chapter 20) to change supervisory rules for banks to introduce more sophisticated capital requirements for default risks involved in OTC derivatives in line with the Basle Committee changes. The Solvency Ratio Directive was also amended in 1996 to encourage bilateral netting agreements, allowing the offsetting of mutual claims and liabilities from OTC derivatives contracts.

24.4.2 The regulation of universal banking in the EU

A particular problem related to the regulation of banking arose in the EU because of the different banking traditions of its members. We have seen that a significant proportion of German banks engaged in a wide range of securities operations as well as in the narrow banking activities of deposit-taking and making commercial loans. Thus, when the European Commission put forward its proposals for the regulation of EU-wide banking in the *Second Banking Coordination Directive* of 1989, regulatory authorities in a member state were allowed to grant their home banks a licence to offer a wide variety of services throughout all member states (see Box 20.2 for the list of these activities).

In its attempt to ensure the stability of the EU banking system, the *Second Banking Directive and the Bank Solvency Ratio Directive* of 1989 adopted the Basle capital adequacy ratios discussed above. This, however, left non-bank securities houses, notably those in the UK, unregulated at EU level – neither guaranteed a single passport to trade freely across the EU nor subject to capital adequacy and solvency rules. The former left the British financial

---

[8] Basle Committee on Banking Supervision (1993), *Supervisory Recognition of Netting for Capital Adequacy Purposes*, Consultation Proposal, Geneva: Bank for International Settlements, April.

[9] Basle Committee on Banking Supervision (1994), *Risk Management Guidelines for Derivatives*, Geneva: Bank for International Settlements, July.

industry at a serious competitive disadvantage relative to that of Germany and made the *Investment Services Directive* which came into force in June 1992 essential, extending the single passport principle to non-bank investment firms generally. The latter then placed German banks and their subsidiaries engaged in securities trading at a competitive disadvantage relative to the British non-bank securities firms. To overcome this, the *Capital Adequacy Directive* (CAD) of 1993 had to apply to both investment firms and to the securities activities of banks.

But the argument for official protection of investment firms is less clear than for banks. Dale (1996) advances several reasons for this:

- Investors are typically not small market agents who can be assumed to have little knowledge; this makes the argument that consumer protection is needed less strong.
- In any case consumer protection can be provided in other ways, through, for example, requiring investment houses to segregate investors' cash and securities in special accounts.
- It is argued that the principal risk for securities houses is market risk whereas for banks it is default risk.
- Investment firms are well placed because of their liquid assets to arrange secured financing which does not give rise to full default risk exposure.
- The assets of securities houses consist largely of marketable securities, making them much less vulnerable than banks to contagious liquidity and solvency crises. Thus, there is much less chance than in the case of banks that they will cause systemic problems and their associated social costs.

Systemic problems may, of course, arise for banks within a financial market regime characterized by increasing integration of banking and securities business to the extent that banks engage in securities business directly or through a subsidiary or lend to investment firms. This, however, does not provide a justification for the regulation of separate investment firms. Further, if both banks and securities houses are to be regulated, Dale argues that different techniques should be applied since they have different object-ives. The emphasis should be on solvency for banks

but on liquidity for securities houses. This should, in turn, mean that different measurements of capital should be used for the purpose of calculating capital adequacy ratios: the capital of banks should be permanent to support the institution as a going concern; while that for securities houses may only need to be temporary because of their fluctuating need for capital resources and because of the ease with which they can respond to problems by scaling down their activities. Again, there may be less need for consolidated supervision in the case of securities houses because they are thought to be less vulnerable than banks to cross-infection from a troubled parent or affiliate. Finally, investment firms do not need access to a lender of last resort.

The solution chosen by the EU in the Capital Adequacy Directive was that where banks engage either directly or indirectly in securities activities or trading, those activities should be subject to a capital adequacy regime separate from that of the banking business. This approach is known as the *trading book model* since the bank is being required, for the purposes of capital adequacy, to keep its trading business separate from its banking business. This ensures competitive equality between the securities arms of universal banks and separate investment firms, but in doing so it assumes that banks engaged in securities business can genuinely prevent problems in one part of its activities from spreading to the other. In Dale's view, the approach puts competitive equality before that of the soundness and stability of the system.

24.5 Summary

The financial services industry has always been heavily regulated. This has been particularly true of banking because of the vulnerability of banks to a loss of public confidence. The collapse of a single bank arouses fears that it might be contagious, causing problems for the banking industry as a whole and hence for the provision of the economy's medium of exchange. Important consumer protection issues also arise in the failure of banks.

The case for regulation is based upon the existence of various types of market failure, notably the existence of asymmetric information, while strong arguments against regulation are centred on the ideas of moral hazard, agency capture and compliance costs. Regulation increases the costs of entry and exit for new firms and thus may inhibit competition. In some circumstances, regulation may even increase the instability of an industry. A compromise position is to support regulation but to argue in favour of self-regulation on the grounds that practitioners have an interest in maintaining the reputation of their industry and are in the best position to understand the impact of regulation on the industry. Nonetheless, several problems have emerged in self-regulatory schemes.

Financial markets have been greatly influenced by globalization and financial innovation, both of which have caused particular problems for regulators. Globalization has led to the need for coordination of activities among bank supervisors and for the development of common regulatory standards to avoid competitive laxity among the supervising authorities. As the EU financial services directives have shown, however, it is not easy to devise common regulatory standards among countries with differently organized financial systems.

Key concepts used in this chapter

Asymmetric information	Indirect regulation	Functional integration
Deregulation	Trading book model	Direct regulation
Self-regulation	Agency capture	Netting agreements
Competitive laxity	Compliance costs	

Questions and problems

1 Why might the existence of asymmetric information lead bankers to be conservative in their lending policies?

2 How does asymmetric information produce a role for credit-rating agencies? What dangers might there be in the financial services industry becoming too dependent on credit-rating agencies?

3 How important is moral hazard as a determinant of people's behaviour? Provide examples of moral hazard related both to everyday life and to the financial services industry.

4 Under what circumstances might regulation decrease rather than increase the stability of an industry?

5 Discuss the view that self-regulation cannot cope with the problem that what is good for the industry as a whole may not be good for individual practitioners.

6 Why has globalization of the financial services industry made the problems faced by regulators more difficult?

7 Explain the basis of the distinction between two types of capital in the Basle Concordat.

8 Why is it thought that simple capital adequacy ratios are insufficient as a basis for supervising the activities of firms engaged in securities trading?

9 What aspects of the regulatory problem were highlighted by the collapse of Baring's Bank in 1995?

Further reading

Bank of England Quarterly Bulletin, 'Financial Regulation: Why? How? and by whom?', February 1997.

R Dale, *Risk and Regulation in Global Securities Markets* (Chichester: Wiley, 1996)

D Gowland, *The Regulation of Financial Markets in the 1990s* (Aldershot: Edward Elgar, 1990)

M J B Hall, *Handbook of Banking Regulation and Supervision* (London: Woodhead-Faulkner, 1993, 2e)

H S Houthakker and P J Williamson, *The Economics of Financial Markets* (Oxford: Oxford University Press, 1996), Ch. 11

A Seldon (ed.), *Financial Regulation – or Over-Regulation* (London: Institute of Economic Affairs, 1988)

Financial market efficiency

25.1 Introduction

It is perhaps appropriate that the final chapter of this book should take us back to where we began. In Chapter 1 we explained that a fundamental purpose of a financial system is to help funds to move from those with a financial surplus to those with a financial deficit. In Section 1.5 we discussed the many benefits that would flow from this, amongst which should be a higher level of saving and investing and a higher rate of economic growth.

These are large potential benefits and so it seems reasonable to ask questions about the efficiency with which financial systems work. One such question we met in Chapter 15 when we saw that some critics feel that the UK and US so-called market-based financial systems encourage 'short-termism'. Understandably, therefore, a substantial amount of effort has gone into investigating financial market efficiency.

In these investigations 'efficiency' has been defined quite narrowly. In saying that any market is efficient, one could mean any one of several things. Firstly, one might mean that the market is *operationally efficient*. This would mean that trading is carried out quickly, reliably, and at minimum cost. If one were interested in this kind of efficiency, one might look back at the chapters in Part 5 of this book where we saw that most financial systems have very high levels of activity and turnover in relation to the net flows of funds actually channelled between lenders and borrowers. On the other hand, one might ask whether a market was *allocationally efficient*. This would mean that the resources being allocated, 'funds' in the present case, were going to their most productive use. If one were interested in this kind of efficiency one would certainly want to know whether firms with long-term projects found funds unreasonably expensive to raise compared with firms with short-term projects: the short-termism hypothesis. Finally, one might ask whether a market was *informationally efficient* in the sense that prices were based on the best information available. If one were interested in this kind of efficiency, one would want to see whether it was possible to seek out information that enabled one to make better predictions of future prices than those that the market made for itself. Notice that in order for a market to be allocationally efficient, it must also be informationally efficient since allocation decisions are made in response to prices. Thus prices must be 'correct' in the sense that they incorporate all information. Indeed, allocational efficiency imposes an even stricter condition which is that the information in question must relate wholly and exclusively to 'fundamentals'. We shall see the significance of this in a moment.

In practice, the financial market literature is concerned with pricing efficiency. 'Efficient', when applied to financial markets, means quite simply that:

security prices fully reflect all available information.

Since we know that, all other things given, the price fixes the return on assets and vice versa, it is immaterial whether we write the definition in terms of prices or rates of return.

Notice that, as we have written it, the definition is impossibly broad. It cannot be the case that security prices reflect literally *all* information. Nor does efficiency require it. It requires that prices reflect all *relevant* information. But this then raises a further question. 'Relevant to what?' Well, relevant to the pricing of securities, obviously. But we already know that security prices could be driven by a range of quite different factors. The best place to look is in Sections 5.4 and 5.5. In Section 5.4 we introduced models of asset valuation involving a risk-adjusted discount rate, the current income payment and an earnings forecast. These, we stressed at some length, are often described as an asset's fundamentals. On the other hand, we said in Section 16.5 that asset prices *might* be driven by other things, including the belief, in a boom for example, that there is always someone prepared to pay a higher price whatever the fundamentals may be. The definition that we have given of an efficient financial market, even if we add the word 'relevant', is strictly agnostic as to what information it is that should be incorporated. As we noted above, if we want markets to be allocatively efficient, we want them to be informationally efficient but we also need to know that the relevant information that is playing its part is information about the asset's fundamentals, since it is these fundamentals that are linked to productivity and social rates of return.[1] The situation where markets are informationally efficient *and* the information involved relates to fundamentals is described by Elton and Gruber (1995) as *market rationality*. We shall follow this practice but it is fraught with danger because the lesser question of whether markets are informationally efficient (regardless of the information source) hinges upon whether traders form their expectations

rationally. Clearly, these are references to two quite different 'rationalities': that of agents in using information to form expectations, and that of markets in choosing a pricing model which relies only on fundamentals. We must be very careful not to confuse the two. With this in mind, we shall take the issue of informational efficiency first and turn to market rationality at the end.

Thus, in the next section we set out the efficient market hypothesis (*EMH*) formally and we distinguish between different 'levels' at which it may operate. In Section 25.3 we look at the implications of the hypothesis and in Section 25.4 at ways of testing the hypothesis and at some of the evidence. In Section 25.5 we turn to the question of market rationality, looking at the implications and the evidence in the one section. As usual, the final section provides a summary.

25.2 The efficient market hypothesis

As we noted above, the hypothesis states that the current price of securities incorporates all available information or, equivalently, that securities yield rates of return which incorporate all available information.

Looking at rates of return first, we know from Equation 5.3 that the total return on a security is the sum of its dividend yield (dividend divided by price) plus any capital appreciation (or loss). Thus, where K is the rate of return, P_0 is the purchase price, D_1 is the dividend paid during the holding period and g is the rate of capital appreciation:

$$K = D_1/P_0 + g \qquad (25.1)$$

Recall then that the rate of capital appreciation is merely the change in price divided by the price paid, then:

$$K = \frac{D_1}{P_0} + \frac{P_1 - P_0}{P_0} \qquad (25.2)$$

where P_1 is the price in the next period.

Imagine a security, a company share say, where

---

[1] If this has been forgotten or remains obscure, a glance at Section 5.4 might be useful.

the next dividend, D_1, is known.[2] Then the rate of return, $\hat{K}$ *expected* at the beginning of the period, is uncertain by virtue of the fact that we do not know, but can only form *expectations of*, P_1. Thus:

$$\hat{K} = \frac{\hat{P}_1 - P_0 + D_1}{P_0} \qquad 25.3$$

Since efficient market theory argues that people use all available information in forming expectations of future events, then $\hat{K}$ is an *optimal forecast* of K, and since making an optimal forecast of K requires that we make an optimal forecast of P_1, then $\hat{P}_1$ must be an optimal forecast of P_1. Thus:

$$\hat{K} = K^{of} \text{ and } \hat{P}_1 = P^{of}_1$$

where the superscript ^{of} stands for optimal forecast.

The efficient market hypothesis is persuasive at first sight since it is merely an application of the basic economic proposition that people act as rational maximizers.[3] We have made the assumption throughout this book that agents are risk-averse, wealth maximizers. If they do not form expectations of the future in the optimal way, then they will be foregoing wealth maximizing opportunities: 'irrational' expectations are costly. Suppose, for example, that when directors sell shares in their own companies this is generally followed by announcements of lower than expected earnings. We know (from Chapter 11) that lower than expected earnings will cause a share's price to fall and the holders of that share will suffer a reduction in wealth. However, if there is a regular observable pattern of directors' sales followed by poor earnings announcements, agents who are genuinely wealth maximizers and genuinely rational will seek out this information[4] and incorporate it into what they think shares are worth. Thus a director's disposal will itself act as a signal to sell as well-informed ('rational') investors try to avoid a capital loss, and the subsequent reduced earnings announcement will have no effect on the price which will already have incorporated this information.

Another way of looking at the forces pushing agents to make optimum forecasts based on all information is to think of 'equilibrium' prices or returns. By 'equilibrium' we mean those prices which produce rates of return that are just equal to what people require (again, for the moment we say nothing about the origin of this valuation). Let us call the equilibrium return[5] K^* and the corresponding equilibrium price P^*. Then it follows that if an optimal forecast of K exceeds $\bar{K}$, informed investors will wish to buy the corresponding asset in order to benefit from the abnormally high return. Buying the share will of course cause the price to rise and the forecast return to fall until the optimal forecast just equals the required or equilibrium return. Conversely, if the optimal forecast of returns is that they are below what investors require, then well-informed investors again will try to benefit, this time trying to avoid a capital loss, by selling the corresponding asset. Its price will fall until, again, the optimal forecast return rises to that required by the market. Using our symbols, we can summarize:

$$\text{If } K^{of} > \bar{K}, P\uparrow \rightarrow K^{of}\downarrow$$

$$\text{If } K^{of} < \bar{K}, P\downarrow \rightarrow K^{of}\uparrow$$

We turn now to what the *EMH* does *not* imply. This is important since finding that the implications of the *EMH* are not confirmed in practice is one way of casting doubt upon it. But if the implications themselves are incorrect, this rejection will be unjustified.

Firstly, the *EMH does not say that prices will always be correct*. It merely says that the expectations that people form are the best possible forecasts in the prevailing situation. Thus, it will frequently be the case that our forecast of price in the next period, $\hat{P}_1$, will be:

$$\hat{P}_1 = P_1 + \varepsilon \qquad (25.4)$$

where ε is an error term. What the *EMH does* say is that there is nothing in the behaviour of the error term which enables us to improve our forecast. If, for

---

2 In many cases of course it will not be known but this makes little difference to the analysis. We should simply have to assume that the forecasts of D_1 also use all available information.

3 The efficient market hypothesis is just one application of the 'theory of rational expectations' first set out in 1961 by John Muth.

4 The Saturday issue of the *Financial Times* lists the major sales (and purchases) by directors of shares in their own company.

5 Defined as the required rate of return, K^* is simply equivalent to $\bar{K}$ which was the symbol we used in Chapters 5 and 11.

example, ε were always positive this would mean that our forecast of the price was always too high. In these circumstances, we could improve the forecast by adjusting it downwards. In this example, the error term is *systematically* positive. In fact, we can always improve the forecast if the error term behaves in any way that suggests a systematic connection with the forecast. We simply have to find out how the error term behaves and make the appropriate adjustment. This leads to an important conclusion which is best stated formally. If our forecasts are to be *optimal* forecasts (and the *EMH* holds) then it must be the case that the forecast errors have a mean value of zero and that they have zero covariance with the forecast. Thus, a market can make forecast errors of future prices (and yields) and still be efficient, provided that there was no way of doing anything better. Box 25.2 provides an interesting example of the UK money markets failing to make correct forecasts of movements in short-term interest rates; notice, however, that the errors were soon corrected!

Secondly, *the EMH does not require people to use all information in forming their expectations*. This would be realistic only if information were costless. We noted above that one of the forces that drives markets towards efficiency is the motivation of traders in those markets. Their incentive to trade efficiently is the desire not to forego profitable opportunities. But an opportunity in which it costs more to acquire the information than could possibly be lost by making a second-best forecast is not a profitable one. Since information costs are generally positive, we should better say that the *EMH* implies that prices reflect all that information whose marginal cost is less than the marginal benefit from incorporating it in the decision.

Lastly, the *EMH does not require everyone to behave as well-informed*, rational, risk-averse wealth maximizers. The fact that we can always find some trader somewhere who makes a 'silly' or at least highly questionable decision does not disprove the *EMH*. Market prices are determined by the actions of the majority. Provided that there numerous well-informed traders looking for unexploited profit opportunities, market prices will be driven to the

point where they reflect all profitable information.

Since Fama (1970) it has been standard practice to identify three *levels* at which the *EMH* can be said to hold,[6] where each level is distinguished by the stringency of the demands which it places on the information to be incorporated in the price. The first is the *weak* form, in which all information contained in the past behaviour of the asset's price is included. This amounts to saying that studying past trends tells us nothing about the next price movement because any useful information in those past trends has already been exploited. The price has already moved. In the *semi-strong* form, all publicly available information is incorporated in the current price. This amounts to saying that studying current publicly available information – about the growth of retail sales or a firm's latest earnings, for example – is no guide to future movements and for the same reason. Any information that could be extracted is already in the price. In the *strong* form, all information – public and private – is incorporated. This makes the most stringent demands on information since it says that even the information available only to those closely concerned with the firms has already been taken up and incorporated in the price.

This distinction between 'levels' of the EMH is important. Firstly, in the next section, we shall see that each level of the EMH has different implications for financial markets and investors' strategies, and in Section 25.4 we shall see that different empirical tests are required for each level.

25.3 Implications of the *EMH*

The main or the fundamental implication of the *EMH* is that if markets are efficient then it is impossible for investors to exploit information in order to earn excess returns over a sustained period of time. 'Excess' here means in excess of the equilibrium or required rate of return, howsoever that is determined. In these circumstances it is sometimes said that the process determining security prices makes for a *fair game*. Based on the information available at time *t*,

---

6 The definition of each was modified slightly in a more recent paper (Fama, 1991).

Box 25.2   UK money markets get it wrong

The following report is taken from the *Financial Times*, 12 January 1997. Its central theme is that the UK money markets made at least two sequential errors in forecasting the movement in UK short-term interest rates. Notice, firstly, that the errors are quickly corrected and also that the errors are said to have arisen because markets were dealing with novel information which they were having to interpret for the first time. This is the case of the Governor of the Bank of England and the Chancellor of the Exchequer disagreeing *in public* about the next change in rates.

Money markets miss the target on base rates

Brokers suggest too much notice was taken of media coverage and the Bank of England's views

It is rare for a market to be completely wrong twice in three months. But that is what happened to the sterling money market.

"It has been consistently wrong most of the way through" says Mr Robin Aspinall, chief economist at National Australia Bank in London. Mr Philip Shaw, chief economist at Union Discount, admits: "It's sometimes difficult to see exactly why financial markets are pricing in what they are pricing in."

The money markets trade interest rate futures, with dealers in effect betting on how high UK base rates will be at certain dates. For the last three months, the markets seem to have grossly overestimated future rate levels.

Just over a fortnight ago, the March 1997 sterling futures contract stood at 93.26. That meant the market was expecting interest rates of 6.74 per cent (100 minus 93.26) for March and to some extent the following three months. Base rates are currently 6 per cent.

Then Mr Kenneth Clarke, the chancellor, shocked the market by leaving interest rates unchanged on January 16, the day after his monetary policy meeting with Mr Eddie George, governor of the Bank of England.

On the same day, UK inflation figures emerged far tamer than forecast. And this week soft retail sales figures for December appeared, confounding press reports that had suggested a bumper Christmas for shops.

Interest rate expectations have collapsed. The March contract closed at 93.61 yesterday, implying a rate rise of just a quarter of a percentage point this spring.

The belief that base rates would soar in the run-up to a general election was the market's second mistake. On October 30, when Mr Clarke did raise rates, it had also been taken by surprise.

Short sterling

March '97 future contract, bid price

Source: Datastream

So why has the sterling money market proved so poor at forecasting the one decision that moves it most: whether Mr Clarke will change interest rates?

The director of one money market broker blames the media's coverage of the UK economy. There has been much talk of a British boom, he says, whereas in fact the economy has been growing at about its trend rate.

Furthermore, brokers say, traders listened too much to the Bank of England's calls for higher rates. After all, Mr George does not set rates – he merely advises Mr Clarke, who often disregards the advice. Mr George's view that rates should rise was well known, yet each time he repeated it, sterling futures contracts fell, pricing in higher expected rates.

The brokerage director also blames market analysts, "who have probably got an economics O-level and sit in banks and talk". But that is unfair.

In the run up to this month's monetary meeting, most City economists were forecasting no change in rates. The money market, with its forecast of a rise, was out on a limb.

"There's an emotion in the marketplace that sometimes gathers", says the chairman of another money broker. "That emotion is not prevalent as much in an economist's office." Any rational investor listening to mainstream predictions could have made a killing in the market by betting that rates would not rise.

Mr Aspinall points to another reason why the market was pricing in too many rate rises. Most UK companies are net payers of interest. A rise in base rates would therefore add to their debt payments, and many hedge themselves against that. They buy interest rate swaps, and these purchases in themselves send the money market yield curve upwards, to price in unrealistically high base rate expectations.

Most banks and brokers trading in the money markets therefore expect lower rate levels than the yield curve suggests. So the banks and brokers tend to buy contracts, while the companies sell. That means that the collapse in rate rise expectations, which sent sterling futures contracts upwards, did little damage to money market traders.

Nor were the corporate players hurt, as the rate rises they feared have not materialised.

Mr Aspinall says many traders were saved by last week's dive in expectations. Those who had mistakenly bet in October that rates would stay unchanged saw the market at last move back in their direction.

Simon Kuper

an investor makes an estimate of what an asset's return will be between t and $t+1$ (or between 0 and 1 in our examples above). As we saw in the last section, an investor will compare this expectation with the equilibrium or required return for an asset of that type. The estimate may be higher or lower than equilibrium and the investor will accordingly buy or sell. Sometimes the eventual outturn will show that the return was correctly estimated; sometimes it will show the estimate was too high and sometimes too low. If prices are determined by a fair game process, there should be no relationship between the investor's estimates of deviations from the required return and the actual deviation from the required return as it turns out to be at $t+1$. As we have said all along, systematic errors can be corrected and the *EMH* says that, in general, they will be.

It is sometimes said that if the EMH holds then returns follow a *random walk*. As we shall see in a moment, the random walk model is a restricted version of the fair game model, but the origin is the same. If past information is already incorporated in the price, the only information that can cause a price change is *news*, and news by its nature is unpredictable. Sometimes the news will be good and sometimes it will be bad. Prices (or returns) which respond to this news will thus follow a random pattern. Strictly speaking, a random pattern of returns means that each return is independent of the one before. Furthermore, the returns are identically distributed over time: they are drawn, in other words, from a constant distribution of returns. This condition need not apply in the fair game model and indeed for many shares one would not expect it. A firm with a large investment programme aimed at changing its core business, for example, may be entering markets with a higher risk/return combination. In this situation, successive returns will not be independent but will be increasing. Even so, the information about the firms's change of direction cannot be used to earn excess returns since its risk is also increasing and the returns will follow a fair game process even though they do not follow a random walk.

We shall see shortly that there are all sorts of practical, subsidiary implications that follow from the fundamental point that information cannot be used to extract excess returns, but first we need to note that each of the three forms of the *EMH* carry this implication for different types of information. We consider the implications of each form in turn.

Firstly, if the market is weak-form efficient then it will be impossible to earn consistent excess returns by using any information extracted from the past behaviour of asset returns (or prices). Imagine the case of a share whose price and dividends have increased steadily over the past few years, giving a consistent rate of return. *If* there is any information in this trend that suggests that it will continue, then this is already built into the price that people are prepared to pay for it. Equally, any useful information that might be conveyed by the price of a share which recently declined sharply and is now recovering is already incorporated in today's price. Investors could, if they wished, construct portfolios based on shares of either type. Thus a naive, risk-averse investor, believing that the past is a good guide to the future, might be tempted to invest in shares of the first type, turning her back on shares whose returns may fall again shortly. However, the message of the weak-form *EMH* is that neither strategy, investing in 'steady growth' or in 'recovery' shares simply on the evidence of past price movements, will yield a return which is consistently above that required by the market for shares of each risk class.

Secondly, if the market is semi-strong-form efficient, then it is impossible to earn excess returns from the exploitation of current, publicly available information. According to this view, the investor who studies firms' announcements about earnings, sales, new products, changes in capital structure and so on, will be no more able to buy shares at a price which yields excess returns than he would if he bought those shares that gave him the desired combination of risk and return at any time that suited him. The effect of any announcements that have been made is already incorporated in the price. If it were possible to devise 'rules' or 'clues' that allowed announcements to be anticipated, then these rules and clues would also be exploited in order to anticipate the announcement and again the effect on the price would already have occurred by the time our investor could act. The same goes for market-wide information. We know, for example, that a change in interest rates causes bond prices to change in the opposite direction. But bond prices do not wait for the change in interest rates to occur. This is because changes in rates are to some degree predictable on the basis of what we know the government's objectives to be, we know the model of the economy that it is using in order to achieve those objectives and we can see the present direction of the economy. Thus, if we know that the government is following a strict money supply rule (as it did in the UK from 1980 to 1985) then the rapid growth of bank lending becomes a leading indicator of interest changes and so bond prices responded to information about bank credit. In this situation, the semi-strong version of the EMH says that no excess returns can be made from studying bank lending trends since any information which is known to be interest relevant will already be incorporated in bond prices.

In its strong form, the *EMH* says that even information available only to privileged groups of investors is incorporated in the price. Consequently, this information is also unhelpful as a source of excess returns. This is clearly the most demanding of the three forms of the *EMH* and looks implausible at first glance. It seems obvious to most people that someone working in a large corporation, for example, could become aware of profitable information even before the directors. Imagine a drug or biotechnology company whose profits are extremely sensitive to scientific breakthroughs. Common sense suggests that it must be possible for researchers to become aware of a major breakthrough before this is known to managers who cannot understand the research data until it is interpreted. Someone in such a position must surely be able to earn excess returns. In most countries he will also earn a spell in gaol since *insider trading*, trading on information available only to those inside the firm, is illegal. Undoubtedly it is possible to earn excess returns by breaking the law, in financial markets just as much as in other walks of life. The question addressed by the strong form of the *EMH* is whether this can be done by legally exploiting information available only to the few. In practice, as we shall see shortly, this usually means 'is it possible for professional analysts to earn excess returns by studying the characteristics and behaviour of individual firms?'.

Notice that what is at issue in all these forms of the *EMH* is the speed with which the particular category of information is incorporated into the price. If markets are informationally efficient, it is the speed with which information (of whatever category) is used that prevents investors from earning excess returns. The possibility that markets might be so efficient that investors cannot profit from exploiting information of any kind itself has further implications. We have space to discuss only limited examples.

If the *EMH* says that it is impossible for investors to exploit information so as to earn excess returns for any sustained period of time, then this suggests that there is little point in expending effort in searching for *bargains*. There are no bargains. There will be 'cheap' securities and 'expensive' ones (that is, securities with high yields and low yields respectively) but this will be because of the degree of risk that attaches to them or to some other characteristic(s) on which the market bases its valuation. 'Bargains' are anomalies. But if the market is informationally efficient, all relevant information is incorporated in the price by the time the investor comes to buy it. In these circumstances, the best investment strategy is to buy a portfolio of shares and to hold them for a long period in order to minimize transaction costs. A portfolio (rather than a single asset) is necessary in order to diversify risk and it is tempting to say that the investor should assemble a portfolio of shares that matches his risk/return preferences. But if we remember the discussion in Section 2.5, we recall that there is at least a theoretical case that the 'best' combination of risk and return comes from holding part of one's wealth in a portfolio that replicates the whole market of risky assets and allocating the rest to a risk-free asset. In practice, this reasoning gives rise to the *index tracker funds* marketed by most unit trust or mutual investment funds. Investors' funds are used to buy units in a portfolio of shares which matches, if not the whole market portfolio, at least the portfolio of shares that make up some representative index. Having assembled that portfolio, the fund managers have little to do but adjust the portfolio on the comparatively rare occasions that the composition of the index changes. In other words, they pursue a 'buy and hold' strategy on behalf of investors. Since this absorbs little management time and effort, compared with all the research and analysis that goes into trying to pick 'winners', charges on tracker funds are much lower than on actively managed funds. In the UK at least, investors' returns from index tracker funds have been in the top quartile of unit trusts ranked by return over the last five years. This performance, combined with low charges, has made them a popular recommendation from consumer organizations though they remain a small proportion of the whole range of funds available. One might say that their success is some evidence in favour of the *EMH*, but the investing public appears to remain sceptical and is prepared to pay for specialist advice which it thinks can beat the market. Box 25.3 suggests that the picture is rather similar in the USA.

If the *EMH* calls into question the wisdom of investors trying to select assets that beat the market, it also calls into question the wisdom of paying for specialist advice in order to make the selection. If the market is strong-form efficient and prices incorporate *all* relevant information, regardless of its source, then *no one* has an informational advantage and so paying for advice is a waste of money. However, if the market is only semi-strong efficient, then it might be possible that professional research, conducted by analysts who concentrate on just one sector of the market or just one narrowly defined set of assets, *might* succeed in uncovering bargains. The question then for investors is 'does the superior information generate excess returns, greater than the cost of acquiring it?'. As we shall see in the next section, one of the tests of the strong-form *EMH* involves looking at the returns to investors generated by actively managed mutual funds *after* their charges have been deducted. On the face of it, financial markets throughout the world appear to accept some degree of informational inefficiency. If the market were strong-form efficient there could be no superior alternative to 'buy and hold'. However, we saw in Chapter 16 that turnover figures for securities of all kinds were many times greater than the net acquisitions made by investment institutions on behalf of investors. Securities markets are very active and this must, to some degree, represent a view that superior returns can be made by moving, and moving frequently, between assets. Furthermore, investors clearly are prepared to pay for professional advice and those that offer it can earn substantial salaries. In January 1997, the UK media were briefly fascinated by a story of a female fund manager who had been sacked from a

post in which she had reportedly been earning over £1m p.a. More interestingly, from our point of view, however, is the background to the story in which it was alleged by her employers that she had been preparing to move to a rival firm and had been encouraging selected colleagues to move with her. The extensive commentary which accompanied these events made it clear that investment institutions supported an active transfer market for successful and very highly paid fund managers.

The fact that some professionals are particularly sought after for their apparent ability to beat the market seems to suggest that the market is to some degree at least inefficient. Indeed, one might ask whether the mere existence of so much financial analysis and financial advice is evidence of inefficiency. If an efficient market is one in which investors cannot beat the returns from a 'buy and hold' strategy, then devoting considerable resources to looking for bargains seems pointless. But we need to be careful with this evidence. Firstly, the fact that a lot of skilled work goes into researching firm-specific and whole market conditions is one of the reasons why financial markets possess whatever informational efficiency they do possess. There is a paradox here. If the market is efficient, the research is unnecessary but without the research the market will not be efficient. Secondly, remember that market efficiency does not require that *all* investors make the best use of available information. Many will; these are the 'information traders' whose role we discussed in Section 10.6. But we also identified 'noise traders', those who buy and sell in response to their own view of how a security's price is going to move. Noise traders, whether they realize it or not, behave *as if* the market is inefficient and provide a ready market for advice, tips and so forth.

The *EMH* has implications for corporate finance as well as private investment. Recall (from Chapter 11) that the market value of a firm is the market value of the securities in issue. Furthermore, the dividends paid on equities and the interest paid on any bonds are components of the firm's cost of capital. If, as we said above, there are no bargains for shareholders – prices accurately reflect the market's valuation of the securities' characteristics – then there is nothing that firms can do to influence the price of their own bonds and shares. This could be important in a variety of

Box 25.3 US index tracker funds

The following report is taken from the *Financial Times*, 11 January 1997. Its central theme is that the majority of funds failed to match the S and P 500 index in 1996, in spite of their expert management. By comparison, tracker funds did well. Notice also their small role in the mutual funds market and their low charges. The article ends by saying that specialist funds under active management *can* sometimes do better. But the question posed by the EMH is 'can they do it *consistently*?'.

Wall Street
Mutuals manage to miss the track
Beating the index proves too difficult for most. **John Authers** examines why

American mutual funds, the equivalent of unit trusts, which now manage $3,500bn on behalf of small investors, seem to be missing the track. As analysts started to pick through the records, and identify the winners and losers from 1996 – a year when the industry attracted more funds than ever before – one fact became painfully clear: the vast majority of mutuals, in spite of being paid for their expert investment management, failed even to match the market index.

According to Morningstar of Chicago, one of the nation's leading investment analysts, the average US equity growth fund returned 18.82 per cent, while the average return for "aggressive growth" funds was only 13.67. The return on the Standard & Poor's 500 index, accepted generally as the fairest benchmark of Wall Street's performance, was 22.95 per cent.

Only one of the 10 biggest funds, in terms of the total assets they manage, successfully beat the index last year. Most tellingly, the diversified sector which performed best had funds which made no attempt to beat the market. According to Lipper Analytical Services, another leading analyst, funds in the S&P 500 Index sector, which merely attempt to replicate the performance of the index, gained 22.3 per cent.

These funds have a higher proportion of large companies in their portfolios than most of their rivals, which goes some way to explaining their success in a year in which the market rally was led by blue chips.

Unfortunately, underper-

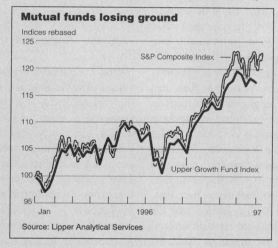

Mutual funds losing ground
Indices rebased
S&P Composite Index
Upper Growth Fund Index
Jan 1996 97
Source: Lipper Analytical Services

forming the index seems to be a regular habit. According to Lipper, about 25 per cent of diversified US equity funds managed to match the S&P, which meant the industry had done significantly better than in 1995 when only about 16 per cent managed to match it.

Small investors are now moving towards conservatively managed funds. It seems that the fund to attract the most new net cash last year (final figures are not yet available) was Vanguard Index 500, which has total net assets of $30.31bn. This makes it the third largest of all mutual funds. It is also by far the most successful of the 56 index tracker funds which, in total, have $65bn under management.

A comparative figure from the UK puts their staggering commercial success into context. Last year, the largest UK index unit trust, run by Legal & General was worth £422m, or about $715m at present exchange rates.

Vanguard is a name that could become much more familiar. It is selling a lot of mutual funds; new investments exceeded redemptions by $26.1bn in the 11 months to November last year, putting it comfortably ahead of everyone else in the industry. And it embodies a realistic approach to investment which is becoming increasingly popular.

John Bogle, Vanguard's founder, once tracked the performance of funds after they had performed well enough to appear on the "honour roll" published by Forbes magazine. They underperformed both the market and the average for the industry thereafter, the message being that successful active management cannot be expected to persist.

Vanguard makes a policy of boasting more about its costs than its investment performance. There are no sales charges on its index fund and the annual management charge last year was 0.2 per cent of assets.

It puts its philosophy this way: "If you don't have a high return, you either have to lower your costs or increase your risks. Costs are something you can control much more than risks."

Are there problems with passive management? An obvious complaint is that trackers look good when they chase the index up, but less so when they follow it straight back down again. It is also harder to replicate exactly the performance of an index than it might seem. All the S&P funds came fairly close to target last year, but the total range in performance was from 23.06 to 20.24 per cent – a difference that would look more significant in a bad year.

Last year's data shows that picking a sector, and getting it right, still pays dividends. Natural resources funds gained 32.74 per cent, which real estate funds gained 30.8 per cent. And if a fund outperforms the index for a few years, compound interest gives it a spectacular return.

Take Fidelity's much abused Magellan, for example. It had a terrible year in 1996, gaining only 11.69 per cent. But it is still the nation's biggest fund and still has the best performance over the past 20 years. Vanguard's index fund grew by 1,311 per cent in that period – an admirable backbone to any portfolio. But Magellan gained 7,445 per cent.

Dow Jones Ind Average	
Monday	6567.18 + 23.09
Tuesday	6600.66 + 33.48
Wednesday	6549.48 – 51.18
Thursday	6625.67 + 76.19
Friday	6703.79 + 78.12

contexts. In a contested takeover, for example, it is advantageous to both sides to maximize the value of their shares since, for the target, this makes it more expensive for the predator to buy, while, for the predator, a high share price means that fewer of its own shares have to be offered in any deal with the shareholders of the target company. A firm wishing to raise capital via a new issue of shares will also find a high share price advantageous since, for the current level of dividend payments, each new share brings in more funds than would be the case if the price were low: a high share price means a low cost of capital. In both these (and other) cases, firms might be tempted to manipulate information in order to raise their share price – bringing forward 'good' information and suppressing 'bad', for example. But if the market is strong-form efficient this should not work. There is no inside information which only the firm can exploit. Any 'news' that it tries to create is already in the price. The market must be only semi-strong-form efficient if this type of operation is to succeed. So far as one can judge from their behaviour, firms are divided in their views. Many bitterly contested takeovers are fought out with expensive public relations techniques designed to influence investors' perceptions of firms' value by suggesting that the share price does not incorporate all relevant information. On the other hand, the infamous Guinness takeover battle for the Distillers company resulted in the Guinness chairman and associates being sentenced to prison for organizing an illegal share support operation. Essentially, this involved paying inducements to selected investors to encourage them to buy Guinness shares in the hope that this would push up the price and so strengthen Guinness's position. This suggests a belief on the part of the Guinness side that the market was so efficient that there was nothing they could do to strengthen their position by manipulating information. The only way to move their shares' price was to pay others to buy them.

25.4   Testing the *EMH*

In its weakest form, the *EMH* says that returns (or price changes) cannot be predicted from information

about the past behaviour of returns (or prices). As we saw in the last section, this amounts to saying that events in the next time period are unrelated to those in the last. Tests of the weak form of the *EMH* therefore consist of tests for the absence of correlation between returns (or prices) in successive time periods. Two commonly used tests which do this directly are (regression) tests for serial correlation and 'runs' tests. A less direct approach is to see whether traders can make abnormal profits by adopting a trading rule based on past data patterns. We look at each in turn.

25.4.1   Regression tests for serial correlation

'Serial correlation' simply means that successive values of a variable are related. Thus the value of the variable today is to some extent determined by yesterday's value. As we have seen, the *EMH* denies this since any information available in yesterday's price would already have been exploited in determining today's price. It is quite easy to test for serial correlation using the standard regression techniques employed to test many hypotheses in economics. If we make today's return, K_t, the dependent variable, our question is 'is K_t dependent, in any significant, way upon K_{t-1} or K_{t-2} … etc?'. If we simply test for dependence upon the previous period's price then we estimate the equation:

$$K_t = a + bK_{t-1} + \varepsilon_t \qquad (25.5)$$

If the *EMH* holds, then b should be zero, or at least it should not be significantly different from zero when subject to standard tests of significance. However, since the explanatory variable, K_{t-1}, is simply the lagged dependent variable, estimating the value of b is equivalent to estimating the correlation coefficient between K_t and K_{t-1} and many of the studies which use this approach prefer to report their results in terms of correlation coefficients. The reported correlation coefficients in most studies are extremely small (though not actually zero), typically less than 0.1 per cent. (Less than one tenth of one per cent of the variation of today's return is explained by yesterday's return. See Elton and Gruber, 1995, Ch.17.)

25.4.2 Runs tests

'Runs' tests are another way of examining successive price (or return) *changes*. If the *EMH* holds then successive changes should be unrelated. This lack of a relationship sets a limit to the number of days on which a 'run' of consecutive price rises (for example) can occur. Too many in succession is more than coincidence. Thus, a large number of short runs tends to favour the *EMH*; a small number of long runs does not.

The tests are done by examining the behaviour of a price series over time and identifying each day's price as a '+' (a rise), a '−' (a fall) or a '0' (no change). A succession of days with the same sign is a run and so our price series will be divided into a series of runs. Notice that the shorter the runs, the more runs there must be in a given series. (If each sign were always followed by a different sign, the runs would all have the value 1, and the number of runs would equal the number of observations in the series!) Fortunately, we can be reasonably precise about the number (and length) of runs that we would expect if successive changes turn out to be the same only by chance. Firstly we calculate the total number of '+'s, '−'s, and '0's and we note the number of runs, which we might denote v. Appropriate statistical tables will give us the critical value of v, given the number of '+'s, '−'s and '0's. Such critical values are usually given for a five per cent level of significance. Remember that more runs indicates less association. Then if, for example, our table tells us that $v_{crit} = 11$, while our data gives us a total of seven runs, we know that there is only a five per cent chance of such a small number (long length) of runs occurring by chance. By contrast, there is a 95 per cent probability that the runs indicate some degree of association between successive changes.

The evidence of large-scale runs tests is that actual runs are often slightly fewer than one would expect from probability tables and this suggests some very slight evidence for positive correlation. But it is very slight: in many cases the actual runs are almost identical with the expected value and the closeness becomes very striking when the change is measured over longer periods, weeks say, rather than days.

25.4.3 Filter tests

The tests that we have so far described are tests for a linear relationship between current returns and past returns. As we have seen, there is little evidence of serial correlation. However, finding that price changes and returns are not related in a linear manner does not mean that there is no relationship. It might be that they follow a more complex pattern. If this were true, then it might still be possible to earn excess returns by exploiting this more complex pattern and this possibility can be explored by formulating a trading rule based on the assumption of some pattern and comparing the resulting investment returns with a policy of simple 'buy and hold'. This argument forms the basis of 'filter rules' (and of some aspects of 'chartist' or 'technical' analysis).

Let us suppose, as seems reasonable, that the price of a security, instead of being rigidly fixed at a point, oscillates from day to day within fairly narrow bands around its equilibrium. The price breaks out of these bands only when genuinely relevant news arrives and the price moves towards a new equilibrium. Investors who buy when the price breaks through the upper band (or sell when the price falls through the lower band) will benefit. The trick, of course, is to identify the bands and this done by formulating a 'filter rule' which says, for example, 'buy when the price rises by 5 per cent from its previous low and sell when it declines by 3 per cent from its previous high'. Here the filters, 5 per cent and 3 per cent, are being used to identify an usually large price change which marks progress to a new equilibrium level (rather than a day-to-day fluctuation). In theory, the numerical value of the filter could be anything. It is simply a question of what (if any) filter works and that involves repeated testing.

Perhaps unsurprisingly, given the outcomes from regression and runs tests, filter tests do not suggest that there are past patterns of behaviour which can be profitably exploited. Certainly this is true when we allow for taxes and transactions costs.

A market that fails the tests for weak-form efficiency cannot be semi-strong or strong-form efficient. The converse, though, is not true and thus, since many tests suggest that markets are at least weak-form efficient, economists are naturally curious to know whether that efficiency extends in any cases to the semi-strong or even, possibly, the strong form. We look at one common way of testing each form.

The semi-strong form of the *EMH* says that publicly available news is so quickly incorporated in security prices that no advantage can be gained from studying this information. One way of testing whether or not this is true is to study the behaviour of prices with respect to public announcements of news. The methodology of *event studies*, as these are known, is fairly straightforward and can be described in a series of steps:

(1) Identify a sample of firms which experienced a major public announcement.
(2) Identify the announcement day and number it 'zero'.
(3) Define a period (say 30 days) either side of day zero.
(4) For each firm, compute the actual return on each day.
(5) Compute a 'normal' return for each day. Practice varies here but one common approach is to average the actual return on each day of other (unselected) firms in the same sector.
(6) Compute the 'abnormal' return on each day by comparing the actual return with the normal return calculated in (5).
(7) Some studies cumulate the abnormal return, but the crucial step is:
8) Examine the abnormal return (or the cumulated abnormal return) with respect to time.

If the market is semi-strong-form efficient then most of the abnormal return will be earned before or on the day of the announcement and it will not be possible, after the announcement, to use the news in order to earn abnormal returns. These tests, which were very popular in the 1970s and 1980s, generally found that the UK and US equity markets were semi-strong-form efficient and that information was incorporated in prices too rapidly for investors to be able to make subsequent excess returns.

If markets are strong-form efficient, then even private information is incorporated sufficiently quickly that it cannot be exploited to make consistent excess returns. Remember (from the last section) that what we are interested in here is the question of whether it is possible *legally* to benefit from the use of

private information. In practice, this comes down to the question of whether 'private' information can be purchased legitimately at a price which allows above average returns to be earned and that in turn means that the tests of the strong-form *EMH* are usually tests of the performance of fund managers who have access to professional analysis and research. We might think it reasonable that analysts who follow closely the behaviour of a small number of firms or a particular sector, and who enjoy occasional briefings by firms' financial managers, might well acquire useful information before it is available to the general public. If there is an advantage (and the market is thus strong-form *in*efficient) then managed funds should outperform a simple buy and hold strategy which could be proxied by a broad-based stock market index.

There have been many tests of managed fund performance over the years. However, many suffer from what is known as 'survivorship bias'. That is to say, the very unsuccessful ones tend to last only for short periods with the result that studies that look at the performance of a sample of funds over a long period of time are looking at a sample of funds which, *by definition*, have a better average performance than the whole population of managed funds. Even so, the evidence from most of these studies does not suggest that there is much advantage to be gained from buying specialist information. The costs of that information are passed on to investors through bid–ask spreads and management charges and it is not generally the case that, once these are allowed for, investors would have done better than by buying and holding a portfolio selected (by themselves) based upon an index. Indeed, Elton and Gruber (1995, p. 437) cite studies where, with survivorship bias removed, managed funds perform worse than an index and, furthermore, where the underperformance is *positively* related to the scale of the management charges. In these circumstances, the apparent lack of interest in index tracker funds (noted above) is all the more surprising.

25.5   Market rationality

So far, we have been concerned with whether or not financial markets incorporate information into the pricing of assets sufficiently quickly that no one can have an informational advantage. We can pose this question about three different types of information and this gives rise to the three forms of the *EMH*. But we have not yet said anything about what information is relevant nor anything about *how* it is incorporated. All our tests so far tell us is that whatever information drives security prices and howsoever it is seen to be relevant to those prices, it does not seem possible to obtain this information in order to earn excess returns.

And yet much more is often claimed for the *EMH*. For example, it is often implied (and sometimes stated) that if the *EMH* holds then assets will be priced according to their fundamentals and funds will (with a few additional assumptions) be subject to optimum allocation. This does not strictly follow from the *EMH* alone. Markets could be informationally efficient in the sense of making optimal forecasts on the basis of current information but 'optimal' only means that those forecasts are on average correct and cannot be improved upon. What it is that is driving prices is unspecified. It may be that markets are responding (super-efficiently) to information which drives prices but which economists cannot see to have any rational connection with prices whatsoever. The question of what information is relevant, and the model which links it to prices, is a separate question from the one of informational efficiency. Nonetheless, it is undoubtedly the case that many who would like to feel that the *EMH* holds would like also to feel that financial markets are efficient at directing limited funds to those uses that are in some sense better than others and so it is worth considering the additional conditions that are necessary.

To do this, we need only look back, quite briefly, to Section 5.4 where we discussed the 'fundamentals' of asset valuation. In Section 5.4 we were arguing that the capital asset pricing model gave us a *rational* explanation of how security prices were determined. The CAPM says that prices will adjust until the asset yields just that rate of return required by investors and then goes on to explain how that required rate is determined. The required rate of return is explained throughout as the result of attempts to maximize returns, subject to constraints, by rational investors. Furthermore, by establishing the required return as a rational process, the model then in effect imposes that

return as the *cost* of capital to firms. Only those firms who have real investment projects which match this cost will have access to the funds. The ability of those investment projects to match the cost of capital depends upon the physical productivity of capital and the revenue for which its output can be sold. This in turn depends upon consumers' willingness to pay and this, as all first year economics students know, is carried to the point where the satisfaction from the marginal unit consumed is just equal to its price. *If prices (and returns) are driven by the process described by the CAPM, then the pricing of financial assets is just one small part of a grand rational process in which everyone is doing the best they can to maximize their own wellbeing subject to constraints.* If financial markets are informationally efficient, and prices are determined by the CAPM, then the informational efficiency is indeed important to an efficient and benevolent allocation of funds. But none of our tests so far shed any light on this question. We need something different.

The major challenges to the view that the market prices securities rationally, as well as efficiently, consist of volatility tests and the examination of major market movements such as the 1987 crash.

Volatility tests compare the actual variance in share prices with the variance in theoretical prices. Theoretical prices are those that one would have expected had securities been priced according to fundamentals in a model such as the CAPM. These can be calculated, *ex post*, using actual changes in dividend discount rates (resulting from changes in interest rates and/or in the market risk of an asset) and actual changes in dividends. The most famous of these tests was carried out by Shiller (1981) and it shows that long runs of US stock prices show much greater volatility than could be accounted for by the changes in fundamentals that actually occurred.

The other obvious challenge to the proposition that markets always produce rational valuations of securities comes from the spectacular booms and slumps that have occasionally hit asset markets. These range, chronologically, from the Dutch Tulip Mania of the sixteenth century to the stock market crashes of October 1987 and include the 1929 Wall Street crash and the eighteenth century South Sea and Mississippi bubbles. The argument of critics here again is that prices changed too far and too fast to be justified by any change in fundamentals. In the 1987 crash, for example, both the London and New York markets saw prices fall by 25 per cent in one day. *Ex post*, it is difficult to see any news that could have caused investors to reappraise either the discount rate, the current level of expected dividends or the earnings growth rate by an amount sufficient to cause a price change of this magnitude (but see Case Study 3 for a discussion of the required change in earnings growth). However, it is worth looking at the symposium of papers collected by Stiglitz (1990) to see just how careful one needs to be in looking at historic information through the eyes of those who had to interpret it at the time. What might look to us in retrospect to be evidently foolish interpretations of information may not have been without foundation for those trying to understand it at the time.

25.6 Summary

Markets can be efficient in a number of ways, but the term 'efficient markets' is usually understood to refer to informational efficiency and this in turn refers to the speed with which markets react to information. If markets are informationally efficient then prices adjust so quickly to new information that it is impossible for any agent to exploit information in order to make consistent excess profits. The degree of informational efficiency is distinguished by reference to the type of information to which markets respond quickly. If current security prices incorpor-

ate all the information contained in past price behaviour, they are said to be 'weak-form' efficient. Markets which are 'semi-strong-form' efficient incorporate all publicly available information too quickly for any trader to exploit it profitably while markets which are 'strong-form' efficient react quickly even to information which is not universally available.

Tests of the *EMH* tend to support the hypothesis in its weaker forms. The evidence is not quite so convincing for the strong form of the hypothesis though it still seems unlikely that investors can derive sufficient advantage from private information to make consistent excess profits after allowing for the cost of acquiring the information.

The *EMH* only says that investors use information to make the best possible forecast of future prices and/or yields. In this respect, it assumes that investors behave 'rationally' by learning from any past mistakes. Thus the *EMH* assumes that investors apply their information to the 'best' model of security pricing, where 'best' means the one that the market appears to use. What this model may be is a separate issue. It could be that the market values assets according to their 'fundamentals', in the manner described by the CAPM. If that is the case, then fluctuations in security prices and returns should reflect fluctuations in these fundamentals and we could then describe markets as behaving 'rationally'. However, the evidence for market rationality is not so convincing as the evidence for the *EMH*.

Key concepts used in this chapter

Operational efficiency	Optimal forecast	Bargains
Allocative efficiency	Weak-form EMH	Index tracker funds
Informational efficiency	Semi-strong-form EMH	Serial correlation
Pricing efficiency	Strong-form EMH	Runs tests
Relevant information	Fair game model	Filter tests
Market rationality	Random walk	Event studies
Rational expectations	Insider trading	

Questions and problems

1 Distinguish between the meanings which can be attached to 'efficiency' when applied to financial markets.

2 What forces tend to make financial markets informationally efficient?

3 Distinguish between the different forms of the efficient market hypothesis?

4 How might an investment strategy appropriate for a market which is informationally efficient differ from one appropriate for a market which is inefficient.

4 How might you test for 'weak' and 'semi-strong' efficiency?

5 You suspect that directors' purchases/sales of shares in their own firms are an indicator of future share price movements. How would you test whether such information could be profitably exploited?

6 Explain what is meant by 'market rationality'.

Further reading

D M Cutler, J M Poterba, and L H Summers, 'What Moves Stock Prices?', *Journal of Financial Economics*, (1989), 4–12

E J Elton and M J Gruber, *Modern Portfolio Theory and Investment Analysis* (New York: Wiley, 5e 1995)

E Fama, 'Efficient Capital Markets: A Review of Theory and Empirical Work', *Journal of Finance*, 25 (2), (1970), 383–417

E Fama, 'Efficient Capital Markets II', *Journal of Finance*, 26 (5), (1991) 1575–1617

P Garber, 'Famous First Bubbles', *Journal of Economic Perspectives*, 4 (2), (1990) 35–54

A W Lo, *Market Efficiency* (Aldershot: Edward Elgar, 1997) 2 vols

B Malkiel, *A Random Walk Down Wall Street* (New York: Norton, 1973)

J Muth, 'Rational Expectations and the Theory of Price Movements', *Econometrica* 29, (1961), 315–335

R J Shiller, 'Do Stock Prices Move too Much to be Justified by Subsequent Changes in Dividends?', *American Economic Review*, (1981), 421–36.

G Stiglitz (ed.), 'Symposium on "Bubbles"' in *Journal of Economic Perspectives*, 4 (2), (1990).

CASE STUDY 1   UK interest rates rise

On Thursday 31 October 1996 the London *Financial Times* reported a rise in UK interest rates, brought about by the joint decision of the UK chancellor of the exchequer, Kenneth Clarke, and the governor of the Bank of England, Eddie George.

The background to the decision is that the setting of short-term interest rates in the UK has always been the joint responsibility of the central bank and the ministry of finance (the UK Treasury). Which of the two institutions exercised the greater power was for many years kept secret but, since the Bank of England is owned by the state and since the governor is appointed by the government, it was widely assumed that the Bank was usually following instructions from the political power. Thus, in the terms of the debate about central bank independence which developed after 1990 (and which we discuss in Section 22.1) the UK's central bank was generally seen as lacking independence and thus lacking some degree of credibility in its repeated anti-inflation promises. In 1994 the significant step was taken of announcing that the chancellor and the governor would meet monthly, on a date which was well publicized, and that the minutes of the meeting would be published. The argument behind this was that the central bank would gain in power and independence because financial markets would be more inclined to accept the judgement of professional bankers than elected politicians. Thus, if it became clear through the minutes of the meeting that politicians were repeatedly rejecting central bank calls for an increase, say, in interest rates, there would very likely be a negative market reaction. Investors would start to sell sterling assets, causing yields to rise regardless of central bank action and causing the sterling exchange rate to weaken. The latter, especially, was seen as a big threat to any UK government. In actual fact, the minutes of meetings during the summer of 1996 had suggested that the Bank was beginning to favour a rise in interest rates while the chancellor wanted to wait and see. Fortunately, the inflation indicators continued to be sufficiently ambiguous through the summer for financial markets to accept the chancellor's desire to delay. In particular, the indicators for manufacturing industry suggested very low levels of recovery from recession even though consumer spending was clearly rising.

It is against this background that financial markets were taken by surprise. The *Financial Times* emphasizes this surprise in the opening paragraph of its report but also makes it completely unambiguous in its opening sentence that the 'chancellor ... raised UK base rates'. This is typical of the evidence to which we referred in Section 3.4. Textbooks may theorize about 'loanable funds' and 'liquidity preference' but observers of the real world believe that interest rates are 'administered' by some combination of central bank and government. The report contains no details of the way in which interest rates were raised; it merely says that base rates were raised by a quarter-point. Base rates are rates used by UK banks as the basis for calculating many of their other, lending and deposit, rates. However, base rates are set in relation to those money market rates that represent banks' marginal cost of funds. We explained this in Section 9.5. The most relevant rates are the 7-day treasury bill rate and interbank rate.

Pound strengthens as Chancellor acts to curb inflation pressures

Clarke surprises City with rise in bank base rates

By Robert Chote, Andrew Taylor and Robert Peston

Mr Kenneth Clarke, the chancellor, unexpectedly raised UK base rates by a quarter-point to 6 per cent yesterday, leaving the financial markets expecting further increases in the run-up to the general election.

The Bank of England, which opposed Mr Clarke's last rate cut four months ago, welcomed the move and said it had improved the chancellor's chances of keeping within his inflation target of 2.5 per cent in the medium term.

"Moving now to moderate the accelerating pace of the economic upswing is likely to mean that we will need to tighten policy less than we would otherwise," said Mr Eddie George, governor of the Bank of England.

Mr Clarke said the economy was set to grow by more than 3 per cent next year and that a rise in rates was now desirable: "Experience has shown that by increasing rates early, as I did in 1994 and am doing today, possible inflation can be nipped in the bud."

A close colleage said the rise – the first for 20 months – was a pre-emptive strike to avoid the risk that interest rates would go up nearer the election, which the chancellor said in the Commons would take place "next spring".

However, short-sterling futures contracts point to a further quarter-point rise in rates by Christmas and almost half a point by spring.

The strength of the economy was underlined by a survey from Business Strategies, the economics consultancy, showing consumers are more optimistic about the economy and household finances than at any time since before the last recession.

The move also prompted speculation about the chancellor's intentions in next month's budget. Mr Michael Dicks, economist at Lehman Brothers, said Mr Clarke's display of prudence would make it easier to cut taxes. "He is likely to reduce the tax burden on households significantly."

But a minister cautioned against expectations of "substantial reductions in the basic rate of income tax", indicating that a 1p reduction to 23p was the most likely option.

British Chambers of Commerce expresssed alarm at the rate increase, noting that exporters would be hard hit as it made an already strong pound even stronger.

The pound closed at 90.2 per cent of its 1992 value against a basket of currencies, its highest point for over two-and-a-half years.

"We are worried that this may snuff out the very recent recovery in manufacturing, and their investment plans," said Mr Ian Fletcher, economist at the BCC.

The three largest mortgage lenders said they had no immediate plans to raise borrowing costs, but builders feared an upset to the housing market recovery.

Shares reacted badly. The FT-SE 100 index fell 29.6 points to 3,963.9. Gilts, which sometimes benefit from monetary rectitude, fell with the benchmark 10-year issue dropping a quarter point.

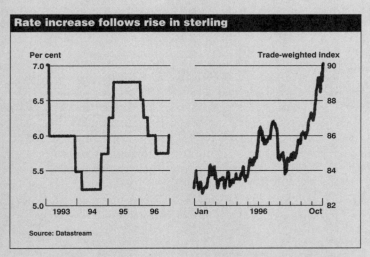

Rate increase follows rise in sterling

Per cent

Trade-weighted index

Source: Datastream

Given that markets were surprised, the question obviously arises of *why* the change came when it did. The article offers two pieces of evidence, one 'economic', the other 'political'. The former is the survey of consumer and household confidence which suggests that this had reached a particularly high level (reported in paragraph 8). Given that figures for credit growth and consumer spending were already known to be growing quite quickly, the survey might be cause for thinking that the consumer boom would develop too strongly if not checked. The other piece of evidence is particularly interesting in the light of what we said in Sections 3.4 and in 22.2 about economic policy having to be conducted with a view to what financial markets will accept. At the time of this increase, the UK government faced a general election within six months, which most evidence suggested it would lose. One of the few instruments whereby electoral support might be recovered was the budget statement due in November. Conventional wisdom in Conservative Party circles has always been that tax cuts attract votes in elections. However, with the size of the UK budget deficit exceeding the Maastricht criteria, there was no obvious economic case for tax cuts and there was a real possibility that financial markets would react adversely, in the manner described above. The suggestion is made in paragraph 9 of the *Financial Times* report that being seen to be 'tough' on interest rates in October might make it easier to be 'generous' with tax cuts in November.

Most importantly for many readers, the *Financial Times* reports the effect on security prices. In the last paragraph, it says 'Shares reacted badly …' This is exactly what we would expect from our discussion of asset valuation in Section 5.3 and, in more detail, in Box 10.3 and Section 11.4. When the authorities raise short-term rates, they are, in effect, raising the risk-free rate, K_f, in the capital asset pricing model. If we assume that the market risk premium remains constant (there is certainly no reason to suppose that it *falls*) then the required rate of return increases. Since the required rate appears in the denominator of all the

UK GILTS PRICES

Shorts" (Lives up to Five Years)

Notes	Yield Int	Yield Red	Price £	+ or –	52 week High	52 week Low
Conversion 10pc 1996	9.99	6.42	$100\frac{1}{8}$	$-\frac{1}{32}$	$103\frac{19}{32}$	$100\frac{1}{8}$
Treas 13¼pc 1997#	13.05	6.23	$101\frac{1}{2}$	$-\frac{1}{16}$	$107\frac{3}{4}$	$100\frac{1}{2}$
Exch 10½pc 1997	10.36	6.02	$101\frac{3}{16}$	$-\frac{1}{16}$	$107\frac{3}{16}$	$100\frac{7}{16}$
Treas Cnv 7pc 1997#	6.96	6.22	$100\frac{19}{32}$	$-\frac{1}{8}$	$101\frac{19}{32}$	$100\frac{15}{32}$
Treas 8¾pc 1997#	8.58	6.28	102	$-\frac{5}{32}$	$107\frac{22}{32}$	102
Exch 15pc 1997	13.86	6.33	$108\frac{7}{32}$	$-\frac{7}{32}$	$115\frac{13}{32}$	$102\frac{21}{32}$
Exch 9¾pc 1998	9.40	6.48	$103\frac{3}{4}$	$-\frac{1}{4}$	$106\frac{7}{8}$	$100\frac{1}{32}$
Treas 7¼pc1998#	7.18	6.51	$101\frac{1}{32}$	$-\frac{3}{16}$	$109\frac{19}{32}$	$100\frac{5}{8}$
Treas 15½pc '98#	13.42	6.71	$115\frac{1}{2}$	$-\frac{3}{16}$	$123\frac{1}{32}$	$115\frac{1}{2}$
Exch 12pc 1998	10.93	6.77	$109\frac{25}{32}$	$-\frac{7}{16}$	$114\frac{5}{8}$	$109\frac{25}{32}$
Treas 9½pc 1999#	9.01	6.79	$105\frac{7}{16}$	$-\frac{9}{32}$	$108\frac{9}{16}$	$105\frac{13}{32}$
Treas Fltg Rate 1999	–	–	$99\frac{31}{32}$	$-\frac{1}{32}$	$100\frac{5}{16}$	$99\frac{7}{8}$
Exch 12¼pc 1999	10.96	6.84	$111\frac{25}{32}$	$-\frac{5}{16}$	$116\frac{21}{32}$	$110\frac{19}{32}$
Treas 10½pc 1999	9.70	6.88	$108\frac{9}{32}$	$-\frac{5}{16}$	$112\frac{3}{16}$	$108\frac{9}{32}$
Treas 6pc 1999#	6.13	6.82	$97\frac{29}{32}$	$-\frac{11}{32}$	$99\frac{1}{4}$	$95\frac{5}{8}$
Conversion10¼pc 1999	9.42	6.97	$108\frac{27}{32}$	$-\frac{11}{32}$	$112\frac{17}{32}$	$108\frac{13}{32}$
Conv 9pc 2000#	8.50	6.99	$105\frac{7}{8}$	$-\frac{9}{16}$	$108\frac{27}{32}$	$103\frac{29}{32}$
Treas 13pc 2000	10.94	7.09	$118\frac{7}{8}$	$-\frac{9}{16}$	$124\frac{15}{32}$	$118\frac{7}{8}$
Treas 14pc 1998–1	12.64	6.61	$110\frac{25}{32}$	$-\frac{9}{32}$	$117\frac{1}{16}$	$110\frac{3}{4}$
Treas 8pc 2000#	7.75	7.06	$103\frac{1}{4}$	$-\frac{7}{16}$	$105\frac{7}{8}$	$101\frac{3}{32}$
Treas Fltg Rate 2001	5.70	–	$99\frac{27}{32}$	–	$99\frac{7}{8}$	$99\frac{3}{4}$
Treas 10pc 2001	9.07	7.17	$110\frac{1}{4}$	$-\frac{9}{16}$	114	$100\frac{23}{32}$

Five to Fifteen Years

Notes	Yield Int	Yield Red	Price £	+ or –	52 week High	52 week Low
Treas 7pc 2001 #	7.06	7.21	$99\frac{3}{32}$	$-\frac{19}{32}$	$101\frac{1}{32}$	$96\frac{1}{2}$
Treas 9¾pc 2002	8.77	7.34	$111\frac{3}{16}$	$-\frac{17}{32}$	$114\frac{5}{8}$	$106\frac{7}{8}$
Treas 8pc 2003#	7.73	7.33	$103\frac{7}{16}$	$-\frac{1}{2}$	$105\frac{23}{32}$	$99\frac{31}{32}$
Treas 10pc 2003	8.79	7.39	$113\frac{23}{32}$	$-\frac{17}{32}$	$117\frac{3}{32}$	39
Treas 11½pc 2001–4	9.94	7.26	$115\frac{11}{16}$	$-\frac{17}{32}$	$121\frac{5}{8}$	$114\frac{9}{16}$
Funding 3½pc 1999–4	4.21	6.33	$83\frac{7}{32}$	$+\frac{5}{32}$	$84\frac{21}{32}$	$78\frac{3}{4}$
Conversion 9½pc 2004	8.50	7.51	$111\frac{3}{4}$	$-\frac{3}{8}$	$114\frac{9}{16}$	$107\frac{15}{16}$
Treas 6¾pc 2004#	7.06	7.48	$95\frac{19}{32}$	$-\frac{11}{32}$	$97\frac{7}{32}$	$91\frac{9}{16}$
Conv 9½pc 2005	8.49	7.56	$111\frac{7}{8}$	$-\frac{3}{8}$	$114\frac{23}{32}$	$108\frac{1}{32}$
Treas 12½pc 2003–5	9.82	7.44	$127\frac{11}{32}$	$-\frac{13}{32}$	$131\frac{3}{8}$	$123\frac{15}{16}$
Treas 8½pc 2005#	8.01	7.55	$106\frac{3}{32}$	$-\frac{9}{32}$	$108\frac{21}{32}$	$101\frac{7}{8}$
Treas 7½pc 2006#	7.55	7.59	$99\frac{9}{32}$	$-\frac{9}{32}$	$101\frac{23}{32}$	$94\frac{13}{16}$
Treas 7¾pc 2006#	7.69	7.62	$100\frac{27}{32}$	$-\frac{1}{4}$	$103\frac{1}{4}$	$96\frac{9}{16}$
Treas 8pc 2002–6#	7.86	7.51	$101\frac{25}{32}$	$-\frac{3}{16}$	$104\frac{11}{32}$	$97\frac{7}{8}$
Treas 11¾pc 2003–7	9.70	7.42	$121\frac{3}{32}$	$-\frac{17}{32}$	$125\frac{3}{32}$	$118\frac{15}{32}$
Treas 8½pc 2007 #	8.02	7.65	$106\frac{1}{32}$	$-\frac{9}{32}$	$108\frac{27}{32}$	$101\frac{9}{32}$
Treas 9pc 2008 #	8.18	7.69	$110\frac{1}{32}$	$-\frac{9}{32}$	$112\frac{13}{16}$	$103\frac{11}{32}$
Treas 8pc 2009	7.84	7.75	$102\frac{1}{16}$	$+\frac{1}{8}$	$104\frac{1}{2}$	$96\frac{31}{32}$
Treas 6¼pc 2010#	7.22	7.84	$86\frac{17}{32}$	$-\frac{3}{16}$	$88\frac{3}{16}$	$81\frac{3}{4}$
Conv 9pc Ln 2011 #	8.18	7.83	$110\frac{1}{16}$	$-\frac{3}{16}$	$112\frac{13}{16}$	$104\frac{5}{8}$

Over Fifteen Years

Notes	Yield Int	Yield Red	Price £	+ or –	52 week High	52 week Low
Treas 9pc 2012#	8.17	7.86	$110\frac{3}{16}$	$-\frac{1}{8}$	$113\frac{3}{16}$	$104\frac{23}{32}$
Treas 5½pc 2008–12#	6.83	7.64	$80\frac{9}{16}$	$+\frac{7}{32}$	$82\frac{3}{4}$	$75\frac{7}{8}$
Treas 8pc 2013#	7.90	7.86	$101\frac{1}{4}$	$+\frac{1}{32}$	$103\frac{13}{16}$	$75\frac{7}{8}$
Treas 7¾pc 2012–15#	7.83	7.87	$98\frac{31}{32}$	$+\frac{9}{16}$	$101\frac{13}{32}$	$93\frac{13}{32}$
Treas 8pc 2015#	7.89	7.86	$101\frac{3}{8}$	$+\frac{13}{32}$	$104\frac{9}{32}$	$95\frac{11}{16}$
Treas 8¾pc 2017#	8.07	7.91	$108\frac{15}{32}$	$+\frac{3}{16}$	$111\frac{5}{8}$	$102\frac{1}{2}$
Exch 12pc 2013–17	8.68	7.88	$138\frac{5}{16}$	$+\frac{3}{16}$	$141\frac{19}{32}$	$130\frac{13}{16}$
Treas 8pc 2021#	7.89	7.86	$101\frac{7}{16}$	$+\frac{1}{2}$	$103\frac{3}{8}$	$95\frac{27}{32}$

Undated

Notes	Yield Int	Yield Red	Price £	+ or –	52 week High	52 week Low
Consols 4pc	8.12	–	$49\frac{9}{32}$	$+\frac{1}{4}$	$50\frac{31}{32}$	$46\frac{3}{8}$
War Loan 3½pc#	7.93	–	$44\frac{9}{32}$	$+\frac{1}{32}$	$45\frac{9}{16}$	$41\frac{3}{16}$
Conv 3½pc '61 Aft	5.77	–	$60\frac{11}{16}$	–	$62\frac{1}{4}$	$58\frac{9}{16}$
Treas 3pc '66 Aft	8.18	–	$36\frac{11}{16}$	–	$38\frac{1}{16}$	$34\frac{9}{16}$
Consols 2½pc	7.98	–	$31\frac{5}{16}$	$-\frac{1}{8}$	$33\frac{1}{8}$	$29\frac{5}{8}$
Treas 2½pc	8.00	–	$31\frac{1}{4}$	$+\frac{1}{4}$	$32\frac{3}{16}$	$29\frac{1}{2}$

Index-linked

	Notes (b)	Yield (1)	Yield (2)	Price £	+ or –	52 week High	52 week Low
4⅝pc '98#	(135.8)	0.49	2.32	114	$-\frac{5}{32}$	$114\frac{3}{8}$	$111\frac{3}{16}$
2½pc '01	(78.3)	2.61	3.18	$185\frac{7}{32}$	$-\frac{11}{32}$	$185\frac{25}{32}$	$176\frac{1}{4}$
2½pc '03	(78.8)	2.87	3.30	$181\frac{3}{16}$	$-\frac{3}{8}$	$181\frac{3}{4}$	$171\frac{27}{32}$
4⅜pc '04#	(135.6)	2.97	3.35	$118\frac{9}{32}$	$-\frac{3}{8}$	$118\frac{23}{32}$	$112\frac{31}{32}$
2pc '06	(69.5)	3.13	3.42	$190\frac{1}{8}$	$-\frac{11}{16}$	$191\frac{1}{8}$	$179\frac{13}{32}$
2½pc '09	(78.8)	3.25	3.50	$170\frac{27}{32}$	$-\frac{13}{16}$	172	$161\frac{1}{32}$
2½pc '11	(74.6)	3.32	3.54	$176\frac{17}{32}$	$-\frac{7}{8}$	$177\frac{29}{32}$	$166\frac{7}{16}$
2½pc '13	(89.2)	3.38	3.58	$145\frac{1}{16}$	$-\frac{25}{32}$	$146\frac{13}{32}$	$136\frac{7}{32}$
2½pc '16	(81.6)	3.44	3.62	$154\frac{3}{8}$	$-\frac{27}{32}$	$155\frac{23}{32}$	$145\frac{1}{16}$
2½pc '20	(83.0)	3.50	3.65	$147\frac{13}{16}$	$-\frac{7}{8}$	$149\frac{7}{16}$	$138\frac{15}{16}$
2½pc '24#	(97.7)	3.50	3.64	$122\frac{27}{32}$	$-\frac{13}{16}$	$124\frac{13}{32}$	$115\frac{3}{16}$
4⅛pc '30	(135.1)	3.50	3.64	$120\frac{29}{32}$	$-\frac{13}{16}$	$122\frac{15}{32}$	$113\frac{21}{32}$

Prospective real redemption rate on projected inflation of (1) 10% and (2) 5%. Figures in parentheses show RPI base for indexing (ie 8 months prior to issue) and have been adjusted to reflect rebasing of RPI to 100 in February 1987. Conversion factor 3.945. RPI for February 1996: 150.9 and for September 1996: 153.8.

Other Fixed Interest

Notes	Yield Int	Yield Red	Price £	+ or –	52 week High	52 week Low
Asian Dev 10¼pc 2009	8.69	7.94	118	$-\frac{9}{32}$	120	$111\frac{31}{32}$
B'ham 11½pc 2012	9.09	8.45	$126\frac{1}{2}$xd	–	128	$119\frac{1}{2}$
Ireland Cap 8½pc '10	8.04	–	$105\frac{3}{4}$	–	$105\frac{3}{4}$	$105\frac{3}{4}$
9pc Cap 1996	8.65	–	104	–	104	104
13pc '97–2	11.72	–	$110\frac{7}{8}$	–	$110\frac{7}{8}$	$110\frac{7}{8}$
Leeds 13½pc 2006	10.11	–	$133\frac{1}{2}$	–	$136\frac{1}{2}$	129
Liverpool 13½pc Imed	8.97	–	39	–	41	33
LCC 3pc '20 Aft	9.09	–	33	–1	36	$32\frac{1}{2}$
Manchester 11½pc 2007	9.39	8.33	$122\frac{1}{2}$	–1	$124\frac{1}{2}$	117
Met. Wtr. 3pc 'B'	3.80	7.10	79	–	80	$70\frac{1}{4}$
N'wide Anglia 3⅞pc 2001	–	4.21	$143\frac{7}{8}$	$-\frac{3}{16}$	$144\frac{1}{16}$	133
4¼pc IL 2024	–	4.33	$138\frac{3}{4}$	$-\frac{3}{16}$	$140\frac{5}{8}$	$130\frac{1}{2}$
Utd Mex States 16½pc 2008	12.22	–	135	–	$136\frac{1}{2}$	120

● 'Tap' stock. # Tax-free to non-residents on application. E Auction basis. xd Ex dividend. Closing mid-prices are shown in pounds per £100 nominal of stock.
Prospective real Index-Linked redemption yields are calculated by HSBC Greenwell from Bank of England closing prices.

pricing formulae, prices must fall. The same reasoning applies to bond prices. The risk-free rate represents a threshold. The rate of return *required* on a relatively safe fixed interest bond consists of the risk-free rate plus a mark-up. If the threshold is raised, and the mark-up unchanged, the required rate must rise and prices will fall. We reproduce here the table of UK gilt prices and a table from the *Financial Times* front page summarizing changes in a variety of prices, yields and exchange rates. The former shows falls in gilt prices spread throughout the spectrum.

It is interesting though to make an informal inspection of the yield curve on the 31st and compare it with the curve shown in Box 10.5 (for 26 October 1996). The yield curve still slopes upward. But the rise in short-term rates had a bigger effect at the short end. Yields on bonds with more than 15 years to maturity were hardly changed, leaving the curve less steep. This is not difficult to rationalize. Let us suppose that the original yield curve was upward sloping because markets expected future short-term rates to be higher than they were at the time of publication (the 'expectations hypothesis' which we discussed in Section 10.5.1). The rise in short-term rates causes people to expect future short-term rates to be higher in the near future than they previously did (so the early section of the later yield curve lies above the earlier one). But recent events have little if any effect on what people expect short-term rates to do, 15 years and more in the future. The change in the shape does not lend much support to the term premium hypothesis (Section 10.5.2). If there were a stable term premium, the whole curve would have shifted upward in a parallel way.'

Notice that the rise in interest rates was *unexpected*. This is central to the impact on prices. We stressed the importance of unanticipated events in Box 10.3 and in section 11.4. Asset prices respond to 'news'. As we explained in section 25.4.3, even if markets are only semi-strong efficient, information available to the public (as official interest rates obviously are!) is already incorporated in the price. If the market had been expecting the interest rate rise, we should have seen security prices falling *in anticipation*. The fact that they did not, and that the market was taken by surprise, is some evidence that, on this occasion at least, the authorities made an independent decision to change rates; they were not just following what the market was already dictating.

■ STOCK MARKET INDICES		
FTSE 100:	3,963.9	(−29.6)
Yield	3.94	
FTSE Eurotrack 100	1,754.97	(−3.17)
FTSE All-Share	1,952.02	(−0.6%)
FT/S&P-A World Index	216.48	(unchngd)
Nikkei	20,681.67	(−276.41)
New York:		
Dow Jones Ind Ave	5,993.23	(−13.79)
S&P Composite	700.89	(−0.61)
■ US RATES		
Federal Funds:	$5\frac{5}{16}$%	$(5\frac{3}{8}$%)
3-mo Treas Bills:	5.134%	(5.124%)
Long Bond	$100\frac{19}{32}$	$(100\frac{27}{32})$
Yield	6.698%	(6.678%)
■ LONDON MONEY		
3-mo Interbank	$6\frac{3}{16}$%	$(5\frac{31}{32}$%)
Liffe long gilt future	$Dec109\frac{17}{32}$	$(109\frac{25}{32})$
■ NORTH SEA OIL (Argus)		
Brent Dated	$23.165	(23.27)
■ GOLD		
New York Comex (Dec)	$381.3	(381.6)
London	$380.2	(381.5)

■ STERLING		
New York:		
$	1.63305	(1.61035)
London:		
$	1.6324	(1.6101)
DM	2.4604	(2.4316)
FFr	8.3115	(8.2233)
SFr	2.0395	(2.0214)
Y	185.892	(183.707)
£ Index	90.2	(89.1)
■ DOLLAR		
New York:		
DM	1.51135	(1.51055)
FFr	5.101	(5.1127)
SFr	1.25525	(1.256)
Y	114.125	(114.35)
London:		
DM	1.5073	(1.5103)
FFr	5.0918	(5.1075)
SFr	1.2494	(1.2555)
Y	113.88	(114.10)
$ Index	97.0	(97.3)
Tokyo open Y	113.825	

This was a feature of our discussion in Section 3.4.

A rise in short-term interest rates, other things being equal, will cause the value of the domestic currency to rise relative to others. (The table from the front page shows sterling rise against all other currencies.) As report says (paragraph 1) sterling had been rising in value against other currencies and some, with an interest in exporting, reacted the interest rate rise with a worry 'that exporters would be hard hit'. However, paragraph 6 tells us that 'short-sterling futures contracts point to a further quarter-point rise in rate'. From our discussion in Sections 12.2 and 12.3 we know that these futures contracts are actually telling us that the value of sterling will be higher in future and the *Financial Times* is reporting that practitioners in the sterling futures market are calculating that the implied future value of sterling is consistent with interest rates being a quarter-point higher. This is similar information to that which comes out of the flattening of the yield curve. In the near short run, short rates are going to be higher.

Questions for discussion:

1 Explain the mechanism(s) whereby 'possible inflation may be nipped in the bud' by a rise in interest rates.

2 What other effects would you expect an increase in interest rates to have upon people?

3 How would you expect security prices to have reacted if the rise in rates had been fully anticipated?

Case Study 2   Share prices fall sharply

On Thursday evening 5 December 1996, Alan Greenspan, chairman of the United States Federal Reserve Board, made a speech in which he raised the possibility that equity prices in the USA were perhaps unjustified. The extract from the *Financial Times* on 7 December shows how equity markets reacted during the next 24 hours. We look firstly at how and why these remarks caused share prices to fall, drawing as far as possible on what we learned in Chapter 11. We then draw together a number of interesting points that the report illustrates.

First of all, notice that we are looking at a change in equity prices spread across a number of markets and recall that we said in Section 11.4.1 that market-wide movements must always be explained by market wide events and that this usually means changes in interest rates, exchange rates and/or inflation rates. The key to the markets' chain of reasoning lies in the second paragraph. The chairman's remarks were taken to contain a possible threat of higher interest rates. In Section 11.4 we made two further important points that are clearly illustrated here. The first of these is that an event need only be *expected* in order to have an effect on asset prices. The reaction here is not a reaction to a change in interest rates but a reaction to an 'implied threat'. The second point is that anticipating what is likely to happen to interest rates involves an appraisal of the government's current policy thinking and objectives. To put it more formally, it involves guessing the government's (here the Fed's) 'reaction function'. The report does not make clear exactly what indicators the Federal Reserve is using in deciding how to set interest rates, but the rate of inflation is bound to be one of them and it is clear from the report that Greenspan's remarks were made in a context of anxiety about inflation developments. However, paragraph six is particularly interesting. It is suggesting that asset prices, *in themselves*, are being used as one indicator of the stance of monetary policy: 'Assessing movements in asset prices ... had to be an "integral part" of monetary policy.' We suggested that this had recently become the case with some governments in our discussion surrounding Table 9.2. Given then that we are dealing with the threat of higher interest rates, we can understand the downward movement in share prices by reference to the terms D, $\bar{K}$ and g. If interest rates rise, holders of all assets will require a higher return and so $\bar{K}$ will increase. For most firms, there is also the real prospect that g will fall since the rise in interest rates raises the cost of capital (and future investment) as well as depressing consumer demand.

Notice, though, that while it is easy to rationalize the direction of share price movements, it is not possible, without some guessing of the size of the interest rate change, to tell whether or not the *scale* of the price falls is reasonable. The report makes it clear that the markets had some rapid second thoughts. Paragraphs 3–5 detail the immediate reaction, pointing out that these spread around the world following the sequence of time zones. Notice that price movements are measured by reference to one or more share price indices, since we are dealing with whole market movements, and that the change of so many points in each index is helpfully converted into a percentage change. It really makes no sense to write headlines which scream 'Footsie lose 200 points' or '£5bn wiped off London share prices' (though it is often done in less reputable newspapers) since it is impossible to judge these absolute magnitudes. Movements in the Nikkei-225 always look very dramatic (as they do here) but that is because the index number is very large in the first place, standing at over 20,000. The report then goes on to say that the Dow (index) recovered a substantial part of its original loss as the US market considered other inflation indicators and decided that the threat of higher interest rates was not quite so immediate as they first thought.

Paragraph 10 then reports the recovery as it spread to European markets. Paragraphs 3–5 and 10 illustrate another theme on which we have touched repeatedly (see Box 11.8 for example). This is the 'internationalization' or 'globalization' of markets. The chairman of the Federal Reserve makes a significant remark at about 02:00 hrs UK time, and when UK dealers get to work (about 08:00) 'Asian markets were "on their knees"...'. Then in the course of the European day there is time for European share

Frantic day on world markets

Big falls as Fed charman's remarks lead to rate rise jitters

By Phillip Coggan in London, Gerard Baker in Washington and Lisa Bransten in New York

World financial markets suffered a "frantic Friday" yesterday as comments by Mr Alan Greenspan, the Federal Reserve chairman, about "irrational exuberance" in asset markets unsettled traders and investors.

The implied threat behind the comments was that the Fed might, at some point, have to raise rates to cool such sentiments and to head off inflationary pressures.

Asian markets were the first to take fright, with the Nikkei 225 average in Tokyo falling 667.2 points, or 3.2 per cent to 20,276.7, its biggest one-day decline since April 1995. Hong Kong, which because of its link to the US dollar is closely tied to US interest rates, also suffered, with the Hang Seng index dropping 2.9 per cent. Europe followed suit. At their worst, the German and French stock markets were down 4.7 per cent and 4.9 per cent respectively while Amsterdam dropped 6.2 per cent. In London, the FTSE 100 index was 168.5 points, or 4.2 per cent, lower at its worst.

The sell-off carried over into the US where, just after

Asian markets were "on their knees" when traders got to their desks in London yesterday, Steve Thompson writes.

The immediate response of marketmakers was to turn the screens red, chopping 50 points off the Footsie to discourage sellers. There was no real panic in the London market, according to dealers.

"We have seen this sort of thing too many times now since 1987, when virtually all the marketmakers were

Wall Street opened, the Dow Jones Industrial Average shed more than 145 points. But US payroll data eased fears of inflationary pressures and the Dow recovered some ground to close 55.16 points lower at 6,381.94.

Mr Greenspan made his remarks in a speech on Thursday evening on developments in US monetary policy. He suggested the central bank was paying close attention to the recent surge in US equity markets. Assessing movements in asset prices, he said had to be an "integral part" of monetary policy. "How do we know when irrational exuberance has unduly escalated asset values, which then become subject to unexpected and prolonged contractions?"

The Fed has not changed

carried out feet first. We all learned some very painful lessons then and we have not forgotten them," said one seasoned market campaigner.

The consensus was that selling by institutional investors had been limited. Nevertheless, "it was very messy for a while", said one trader.

"The first 50-point fall was down to the marketmakers chopping their dealing levels, which headed off any early sellers. The next 50 points saw

short term interest rates since it lowered them at the start of the year, as inflation has remained low and wage pressures slight. But some officials have been concerned about the implications of the rising stock market for the economy.

It was the Labor Department's employment report for November, showing a jump in unemployment, that eased investors' fears a little.

Over the past three months payroll gains have averaged 113,000 per month, less than half the pace earlier in the year. The figures were in line with other recent evidence that suggested growth has slowed to a more sustainable rate than was achieved in the first half of 1996.

The Dow's revival allowed European markets to rebound.

Frankfurt finished 2.1 per

some selling develop and the next 50 points represented a real scramble by marketmakers to get out of the way," another trader said.

Mr Martin Lupton, head of marketmaking at Kleinwort Benson, said "If Greenspan puts the word out that caution is needed I cannot believe we have seen the worst of the market so far. Although Wall Street has rallied, it has not gone far enough. The dangers lie on the downside."

cent lower, Paris lost 2.3 per cent and Amsterdam 1.9 per cent. In London, the Footsie closed with a loss of 88.2 points at 3,963.

Analysts said the markets may have read too much into Mr Greenspan's remarks. "It is an indication of just how nervous the markets are after a good run this year," said Mr Keith Skeoch, chief economist at James Capel, "but I think the markets have over-reacted and it will turn out to be a storm in a teacup."

US commentators viewed the equity sell-off as healthy given that the Dow had rallied more than 900 points since August.

One said that in coming weeks the market should consolidate before resuming its upward trend.

prices to fall sharply and then to recover after New York opened (13:00 European time) and had first and then second thoughts.

A further point which we might consider is what model of share price valuation the chairman of the

Fed might have been using for his assessment of US share prices. The only clue that we have is the reference to his words 'irrational exuberance'. This might be taken to mean that his own view was based upon fundamentals and that he was not persuaded that the fundamentals any longer justified the current level of share prices. This suggests that he was conducting some sort of mental experiment, putting 'normal' values for $\bar{K}$ and g, together with recent values for D_0 into Equation 11.6 and finding that calculated prices were a good deal lower than those which actually prevailed. This is of course possible but it is unlikely. An easier way of forming a judgement would be to look at the information contained in one or more of the tables of share price indices in the *Financial Times* or the *Wall Street Journal*. Looking at movements in the index over a period of time would allow us to calculate an annual percentage rate of growth, which we might then judge as 'reasonable' or 'unsustainable' in the light of long-run historical trends. Even more effective might be to look at movements over time in the *P/E* ratio associated with each share price index (see Section 11.5.3). Remember that the *P/E* ratio tells us the price that has to be paid in order to secure a claim on firms' earnings. Provided that we have a notion of some long-run normal value for a broadly based *P/E* ratio, we can form some judgement about whether the price that investors are paying is 'too high' (historically speaking) or 'too low'.

Finally, it is worth taking a brief look at the insert in the report which describes the way in which dealers reacted to falling prices. Recall that the London Stock Exchange is a 'quote-driven' continuous market (see Figure 10.7 and Section 11.5). This mean that dealers are obliged to buy (and sell) at the prices they quote and thus to add stocks to their own inventories (or to run down those inventories). In a situation where bad news develops overnight, it is reasonable to guess that if the market opens quoting share prices unchanged from the previous day's close (before the bad news) there will be an avalanche of 'sell' orders and very few buyers. Dealers will then have to take up all the shares offered for sale and hold them on their own books, while prices subsequently fall. This is what seems to have happened in the 1987 crash before market makers were fully aware of the implications of the system. As a result, 'virtually all the marketmakers were carried out feet first'. As the report says, dealers have learnt from experience and this time reduced prices by an equivalent of 50 points on the FTSE-100 before trading started.

Questions

1 What proportion of their original losses did most markets subsequently recover? How would you explain the original 'overshooting' of the apparent equilibrium price level?
2 Explain the risk that market dealers were trying to avoid by cutting prices by the equivalent of 50 points before trading began. How do you think events would have unfolded in an 'order-driven' trading system?
3 Why does a fall in US share prices cause prices in the Europe and Asia to fall as well?

Case Study 3 Earnings forecasts have dramatic effects

On 21 March 1997, the shares in Eastman-Kodak, a US photographic products company fell sharply. The *Financial Times* of 22 March reported this in the article opposite. The report illustrates a number of issues that we have touched on in this book.

Notice firstly the explanation given for the price fall: '… its sales growth had halted in the first two months of this year'. This poor sales performance is in turn explained largely by currency fluctuations. The appreciation of the US$ made Kodak products in overseas markets more expensive even though, it seems, Kodak lowered its selling prices. At the same time the depreciation of the yen enabled Fuji, a major competitor, to sell more cheaply outside Japan, and Fuji seems to have gained an extra 3 per cent of the market. This underlines the importance of exchange rate fluctuations to the real economy – a point we made in Chapter 12.

Now look at the scale of the price fall: 'Shares in Eastman Kodak fell by 11 per cent … wiping $3bn from its stock market value.' If we were looking at this incident from our efficient markets perspective, the first thing we have to say is that the halt in sales growth was clearly 'news' to the market, and the

Kodak shares fall on "flat sales"

By Richard Waters in New York

Shares in Eastman Kodak fell by 11 per cent yesterday morning, wiping $3bn from its stock market value, as the US photographic products company revealed that its sales growth had halted in the first two months of this year.

The news comes as Wall Street is monitoring the general profits outlook for US companies, thanks in part to recent comments by Mr Alan Greenspan, chairman of the Federal Reserve.

Mr Greenspan said this month he did not believe US share prices were too high, provided companies could match the expectations for profits this year.

Kodak, one of the 30 companies in the Dow Jones industrial average, did no predict what effect the sales slowdown would have on its earnings. But its shares plunged by $9\frac{5}{8}$ to $78\frac{5}{8}$ by lunchtime as analysts abandoned their expectations of the company's earning per share continuing their double-digit growth of the past two years.

The company said sales in the first two months of this year were "essentially flat" compared with the year before, because of the rise in the US dollar and lower selling prices.

Also, growth in the emerging markets, where sales of Kodak film have been rising at more than 10 per cent a year, had "moderated considerably".

Mr Harry Kavetas, chief financial officer, said the unexpected drop-off in sales would not change the company's "fundamental operating plans and objectives".

The news appeared to reflect a successful onslaught by Fuji, Kodak's arch-rival, on photographic film markets, said Mr Alex Henderson, an analyst at Prudential Securities in New York. Fuji's push, helped by the yen's fall against the dollar, appeared to have enabled it to seize an extra 3 percentage points of film sales in the US recently, he added.

The dollar's appreciation has also eaten into Kodak's reported sales from outside the US – an effect that will be echoed by other US-based multinational companies when they report first-quarter earnings.

Mr Charles Hill, research director of First Call, which monitors earnings expectations aid that despite some recent profits warnings from other US companies, there had been less negative news on earnings than was normally the case just before a quarterly reporting season.

price reacted very quickly ('yesterday morning'). But the size of the fall also raises the question of market *rationality*. Is it possible that so large a fall can be explained by changes in 'fundamentals'? Can a two-month halt in sales growth be incorporated in a rational value formula to generate a change in price even approximately equal to 11 per cent? Unfortunately, the report does not contain enough information for us to see exactly which fundamentals have changed and by how much. But combining the facts in the report with other information about Eastman-Kodak shares elsewhere in the same *Financial Times*, we can create a sufficiently detailed picture to see whether an 11 per cent price fall is a *plausible* response to changes in fundamentals. As we make our estimates, we must check at each stage that they seem at least believable.

We begin with the constant growth model of share valuation where $P_0 = D_1 / K - g$. Looking at this formula and the information in the report, the most obvious fundamental change appears to involve a reduction in the earnings growth rate, though the report strictly refers to sales. The question then is: does the report suggest that g might have changed by an amount sufficient to cause the price change which we observe? This involves making a calculation of the change in g required to bring about a $7 price

change and then considering whether its order of magnitude seems reasonable or not. The difficulty that we face is that much of the information that we need. We know that P_1 is $78.625 and since ΔP is $7.625 it follows that P_0 was $88.25. What we do not know are the values of D_1, K and g! However, from the US stock prices page in the same issue of the FT we know that the dividend yield (at the new, lower price) is 2.2 per cent. This enables us to calculate the last dividend, D_0, to be $1.73 per share (= $78.625 × 0.022). K and g however pose bigger problems. Firstly, we do not know what previous earnings growth was or what new growth rates are forecast. We are only given information about sales. These had been growing 'more than 10 per cent'. Forecasts of future sales growth 'have moderated considerably.' Let us make the reasonable assumption that sales and earnings grow together. The question now is what values do we adopt for g, old and new. The report implies that it had been more than 10 per cent and we could err on the side of caution by setting the original value for g at 0.1. Making all these assumptions, we can now find the value of D_1, expected at the old share price in 'good' trading conditions, and the value of K. We can do this as follows:

$$\$88.25 = \frac{1.73(1 + 0.1)}{K - 0.1} = \frac{1.903}{K - 0.1}$$

Rearranging to find K, we have:

$$K = \frac{1.903}{88.25} + 0.1 = 0.1216$$

Checking for plausibility, does a required rate of return of 12.16 per cent on Eastman-Kodak shares seem reasonable? Recall (from Chapters 2 and 5) that K, in this model, comes from the *CAPM*. It is found by adding a risk premium, based on the *relative* riskiness of the shares, to a risk-free rate. On 21 March 1997 the risk-free rate in the USA was 5.25 per cent. Bearing in mind the US market risk premium at the time and Eastman-Kodak's relatively low risk rating ($\beta \approx 1$), $K = 12.16$ does not seem wholly unreasonable.

A reasonable reconstruction of the position before the bad news, using our constant growth model, therefore looks like this:

$$\$88.25 = \frac{1.903}{0.1216 - 0.1}$$

We are now in a position to see what effect follows from lowering the value of g, leaving the last dividend and the required rate of return unchanged. Suppose that we lower our earnings growth forecast from 10 to 9 per cent. Then:

$$P = \frac{1.72975\,(1 + 0.09)}{0.1216 - 0.09} = \frac{1.8854}{0.0316} = \$59.66$$

The result is dramatic. Merely by lowering the earnings forecast by one percentage point, we cause a price fall of over 30 per cent. As we said above, we do not *know* that the original earnings growth forecast was *actually* 10 per cent per annum or that the required rate of return was *actually* 12.16 percent. But these are not unreasonable figures and what our little experiment shows is that any sort of reduction at all will have quite a sharp effect on prices. So far as the report in the *Financial Times* is concerned, therefore, we do not have to read anything terribly dramatic into the implied reduction in the earnings growth forecast. (Enthusiasts may wish to use the last equation to find the value of g necessary to cause the price fall quoted in the report – it is approximately 9.75 per cent, a cut of just 0.25 percentage points.)

As far as market rationality and the *EMH* are concerned, therefore, we can see that quite large price changes can be generated by events which cause a change in earnings growth forecasts. Seeing what we have seen here, the 30 per cent price falls seen in stock market values on 19 October 1987 do not seem so irrational. However, we should not forget that a market-wide price change requires a market-wide revision of earnings growth forecasts. These will always be happening for individual firms, but will not be so easy to explain for the market as a whole.

Question for discussion

Given the information in the *Financial Times* report and our analysis of it above, provide a detailed explanation of how you would expect Kodak's share price to be affected by a reduction in US interest rates, other things being equal.

Case Study 4 Only 'news' moves prices

The following report appeared in the *Financial Times* on Monday 28 April 1997. It illustrates a number of themes that we have met scattered through several chapters in this book. The background to the article is that over the preceding year the exchange rate against other currencies of both the pound and the US dollar had increased by about 20 per cent and 30 per cent respectively. A few days before, the G7 finance ministers had held a meeting at which they expressed concern about the continuing rise in the dollar, and in the UK attention was focused upon a general election which the Labour Party was expected to win for the first time in 18 years.

Traditionally, UK financial markets have reacted adversely to the possibility of Labour governments. This reaction was based partly on the historic

Traders calm at prospect of victory for Labour

This could be a big week for the forex market. The pound and dollar in particular could find new direction.

The US currency, which trod water last week as traders awaited yesterday's Group of Seven meeting, could start moving again from today.

And on Thursday the UK goes to the polls for its general election. The markets have priced in a Labour victory, and after 18 years of Conservative rule they seem calm about the prospect. Only an unexpectedly close

vote, creating a hung parliament or a very narrow Labour majority, would be likely to hit UK assets and the pound. A Conservative victory would be expected to cheer sterling.

If Labour does win, the market has to decide whether Mr Gordon Brown, the party's proposed chancellor, would raise interest rates sharply. The markets have priced in a 50-basis point rate rise virtually immediately after a Labour win. By December, they expect base rates of about 7 per cent, a

percentage point above today's levels.

However, such sharp rate rises would boost the strong pound even further, dealing further blows to suffering manufacturers. It seems increasingly possible that Mr Brown, if he became chancellor, would raise taxes instead, increasing interest rates only modestly. The pound could suffer if he did signal early that he was going to concentrate on taxes to slow the fast growing consumer sector.

There is also a wealth of

US data out this week. Many expect the Federal Reserve to raise rates after its Open Market committee meeting on May 20, given recent signs that inflation may be appearing on the horizon. The most important data are Tuesday's employment cost index, the final gross domestic product figure for the first quarter on Wednesday and non-farm payrolls and average hourly earnings on Friday. Most of the data are expected to emerge strong.

association of left-wing governments with high inflation; partly on such governments' commitment to the redistribution of income and wealth which meant higher taxes for people with large holdings of financial assets; and partly on the tendency of such governments to strengthen the bargaining power of workers at the expense of company profits. However, with four days to go to a likely Labour victory we are told that currency markets were 'calm about the prospect'. The reason comes in the same paragraph where we are told that 'markets have priced in a Labour victory', meaning that the signs of a change in government had been apparent long enough for markets already to have adjusted. The prospect of a Labour win was no longer 'news' and so, as we saw in Chapter 25, there was no need for prices to change.

Interestingly, the report identifies two possible outcomes in which prices might change. The first is the situation of a 'hung' parliament – one where no party has an overall majority – and therefore one in which any government is unlikely to have a stable future. It will be continually negotiating support with other parties and may need to call another election at short notice. First of all, since such an outcome is unexpected, it would be 'news' and asset prices would be bound to react. Furthermore though, as the report makes clear, the news would be bad news and asset prices would fall. This is because such a situation would increase the level of uncertainty and

risk in financial markets. As we have said throughout this book we normally expect higher risk to be compensated by higher yields and higher yields mean lower prices. The other possibility must also be unexpected. This is the possibility of a Conservative victory. Traditionally, Conservative governments have been sympathetic to the interests of finance and capital and thus such an unexpected outcome 'would be expected to cheer sterling'.

Notice also that the report speaks very confidently of what markets expect to happen after the election. 'The markets have priced in a 50-basis-point rate rise virtually immediately after a Labour win.' It even goes on to say that (bank) base rates will be 7 per cent by December. From Chapter 9 we know that 50 basis points is equivalent to one-half of one per cent. The report does not tell us the source of these predictions but from Chapter 10 we can be sure that these higher interest rates are being derived from the current shape of the yield curve. The report is, in effect, drawing our attention to the fact that current interest rates on (say) one-month deposits are higher than they are on overnight money and thus that investors expect overnight rates to rise over the next month by sufficient to yield an average return equal to the one-month rate. Markets are observing an upward-sloping yield curve and applying the expectations theory of the term structure that we discussed in Chapter 10.

The report goes on to suggest that raising interest rates in the present situation might, however, have inverse side-effects. Higher rates woud be likely to increase the pound's exchange rate even more, 'dealing further blows to suffering manufacturers'. An alternative way of trying to restrain the growth of consumer spending and reduce inflationary pressure would be to increase taxes. If the present value of the pound suggests that a rise in interest rates is already 'priced in' to the pound's value, a rise in taxes rather than interest rates would come as a surprise, as 'news' and the pound 'could suffer'.

Finally, notice that the report draws our attention to forthcoming events in the USA. As always for smaller economies, what happens in the USA could be the most important factor in determining asset prices and yields.

Questions for discussion

1 Why does a rise in interest rates, *ceteris paribus*, cause the value of the domestic currency to rise?
2 Why do financial markets generally prefer 'conservative' goverments?
3 At the end of the report we are told that 'Most of the (US) data are expected to emerge strong'. What does this mean and what effect is it likely to have on US interest rates and the value of the US\$ if it turns out to be correct?

Case Study 5

The accompanying article appeared in the *Financial Times* on 19 March 1997. It highlights a number of important features of bond markets and illustrates the importance of psychology in the politics of international finance.

In March 1997, Italy entertained strong hopes of joining EMU at its planned start in January 1999 despite its almost certain failure to achieve some of the Maastricht convergence targets required for membership. As we saw in Box 13.3, financial markets were assuming that Italy had a good chance of being allowed to join with the result that its yield curve had turned down. Germany was (as mentioned in Section 21.4) very worried about the prospect, fearing that Spanish and Italian currency markets would cause higher inflation and a weaker Euro. Both securities and currency markets were vulnerable at the time to claim and counter-claim regarding Italy's likely membership. The Markets Report in the *Financial Times* of 19 April 1997 contained the following statement:

Several peripheral European currencies also suffered from some turbulence against the core European currencies. Reports of a secret deal between France and Germany to thwart Italy's participation in European monetary union swept the market. The Finnish markka, the Portuguese escudo and the Italian lira were all volatile against the D-mark during the day. The D-mark ended trading against the Italian lira at L987.5, a rise of two lira.

We have seen in Section 19.5 that Italy's very large public debt required it to make large bond issues. Although most of Italy's debt was sold at home, a significant amount, in volume terms, had to be sold abroad, especially after 1990 when all foreign exchange restrictions were removed. In issuing debt to be sold abroad Italy had the choice of issuing bonds denominated in lira, in which case the interest rate would be high to reflect the risk premium attached to the lira, or bonds denominated in strong foreign currencies. In the latter case the interest rate could be lower but involved the risk for Italy that any devaluation of the lira would increase the cost, in

Italy is first country to issue bond in euros

By Edward Luce

The Italian government yesterday stepped up its drive to be a founding member of the European single currency by becoming the first country to issue a bond denominated in euros.

The 1bn euro (£720m) issue, which is only the second bond offered in the single European currency, was bought up quickly by mostly European investors after its launch.

"This is a strong statement by Italy that it is committed to the European single currency," said a syndicate official at Paribas which jointly managed yesterday's deal with SBC Warburg. "After the success of this, we

expect a flood of other debut euro issues in the next few months."

Syndicate officials said the launch was also designed to be reduce the costs of servicing Italy's debt. Italy's domestic lira bonds are trading at more than 200 basis points over French bonds compared with just 18 basis points in yesterday's euro launch.

A basis point is a hundredth of a percentage point.

The Italian bond is expected to become a benchmark for the pricing of issues in the single currency by other European borrowers.

Traders said that the bond, which will pay interest in euros when the currency comes into being, was

unaffected by the lacklustre mood of Europe's bond markets.

The euro will have the same value as the ecu – a currency derived from a basket of European currencies. "Italy priced this bond quite cheaply probably to ensure that nothing could possibly go wrong," said one analyst. "There is a lot of kudos from being the first country to issue in euros."

The euro-denominated bond will be serviced in the single currency regardless of whether Italy qualifies for the first round of monetary union. It follows a 1bn euro issue earlier this year by the European Investment Bank.

Syndicate officials said the level of investor appetite for

euro-denominated debt overcame general bond market pessimism in advance of a possible increase in UK interest rates at the US Federal Reserve meeting next week.

The bond, priced to yield just 18 basis points more than seven-year French ecu bonds, narrowed by 17 basis points over French debt in secondary market trading reflecting strong demand for the paper.

"The euro-denominated debt market will probably become the second largest bond market in the world within the next two years," said one official in London. "There is therefore a lot of appetite out there for euro debt."

domestic currency, of interest payments and of the eventual repayment of the face value of the bond. Thus, an issue of bonds in a strong foreign currency was equivalent to a statement by the Italian government that in its view devaluation of the lira were not very likely and thus that the risk premium built into the Italian rates was overestimating the likelihood of a lira devaluation.

The Italian government thus took advantage of this possibility to assure the markets of their own confidence that Italy would be allowed into the EMU (a failure to become a member would almost certainly result in a substantial devaluation of the lira). At the same time Italy stressed its European credentials by choosing the Euro as the currency of denomination (rather than the DM or the dollar), thus expressing confidence that the whole EMU project would go ahead.

This was clearly a clever move. As the article demonstrates, the market for bonds denominated in Euros is likely to grow very rapidly and this strong potential demand for bonds of this type meant that the bond would be in strong demand and hence could be priced favourably from the point of view of the Italians

(bearing an interest rate only 18 basis points above 7-year French Ecu bonds). This was in comparison with the 200 basis point premium require on lira bonds. Thus, *as long as the value of the lira does not fall*, the Italian government will reduce the cost of financing its public debt through issues of this kind.

As the market showed, the 18 basis point premium was actually a higher interest rate than had been needed (the bond had been priced quite cheaply and the bond price rose on the secondary market) but this had obviously ben difficult to calculate in advance and the Italian government had been principally concerned that the issue should be a success.

Questions for discussion

1 Consider the factors likely to influence the risk premium on the Italian lira.

2 What reasons can you advance in support of the proposition above that the failure to become a member would almost certainly result in a substantial depreciation of the lira?

3 Why should there be a strong potential demand for bonds denominated in Euros?

Case Study 6

The statement from Mr Wim Duisenberg, reported in the *Financial Times* on 22 March 1997, raises the question of the relative importance of what the authorities say they are going to do and what they actually do. In Section 7.5 it was pointed out that any instability in the demand for money function made it difficult to accept money supply targets as an intermediate objective of monetary policy. One alternative considered was to base monetary policy decisions on a range of indicators including money stock and monetary base figures, the rate of inflation, the level of unemployment and the exchange rate. Mr Duisenberg suggests both a positive and a negative reason for using monetary targets. The positive reason is that 'recent research' suggests that the demand for money in Europe is sufficiently stable in several EU countries to allow the use of monetary targeting. The problem with this is that what is needed, given that the same monetary policy is to apply to all member countries, is that the demand for money function for the whole EMU needs to be stable. A stable demand for money in 'several countries' is not enough unless one accepts the possibility raised in Section 22.4 that the replacement of a number of currencies by a single currency under EMU will reduce the possibility of currency substitution with the result that the demand for money function of the EMU countries considered together is more likely to be stable than that of individual countries.

Even if one were to accept this, there would be very great uncertainty surrounding the question of what the monetary targets of the EMU should be, especially given the differences in the definitions of money currently in use across the EU (see Chapter 6). More to the point, the decision has yet to be made as to which countries will become members of the EMU. It is possible, of course, that there is a hidden

Future EU central bank looks set to adopt monetary targeting

Duisenberg backs German model

By Wolfgang Münchau,
Economics Correspondent

The likely president of the future European Central Bank (ECB) yesterday came out in favour of Germany's approach to monetary policy, rejecting the UK method as lacking in transparency.

Mr Wim Duisenberg, head of the Dutch central bank, said the ECB should use monetary targeting, rather than inflation targeting, to determine interest rates.

His comments, in a speech in Maastricht, are the clearest indication yet of how Europe's central banking establishment will react when confronted with choosing between the two systems in 1998.

The European Monetary Institute, forerunner to the ECB, tried to strike a balance when it recently refused to endorse one method over the other.

Under monetary targeting, a central bank looks at broad money supply as an indicator of future inflation. With inflation targeting, it forecasts rates by a variety of indicators, and sets interest rates to keep inflation within an agreed range.

Mr Duisenberg said yesterday that "the explicit use of a variety of indicators poses a threat to the transparency and credibility of monetary policy, because there is then no immediate way of knowing which information has prompted interest rate decisions".

Most central banks use a combination of both methods in practice, but they usually adopt one as their official policy.

The targeting of broad money is thought to have worked well in Germany – at least until unification. In the UK, however, broad money targeting was blamed for the deep recession in the early 1980s.

After sterling's exit from the exchange rate mechanism, Britain moved over to inflation targeting, a method also used by central banks in Sweden, Finland, Spain and Australia.

In his speech Mr Duisenberg pointed towards recent research suggesting that the demand for money in Europe was sufficiently stable in several EU countries to allow the use of monetary targeting.

Such a method would have the additional advantage of being the preferred method of the German central bank. Mr Duisenberg said "The continuity of monetary policy in Europe would be best served by monetary targeting, the strategy applied for several decades already by the most successful central bank in Europe, the Bundesbank."

His comments reflect a preference in Germany, but also in the Netherlands, to have the future ECB modelled as closely as possible on the Bundesbank to maximise goodwill in financial markets.

The ECB itself is due to take key policy decisions next year on how it operates. The policies set then will also apply to countries that chose to join the single currency at a later stage.

assumption in Mr Duisenberg's statement – that EMU membership should be restricted to those countries with a relatively stable demand for money. One extra problem raised in Section 22.4 is that a system of targeting measures of the money supply almost certainly needs to be supported by a set of mandatory minimum reserve ratios. This raises resource allocation questions and may be interpreted as being in conflict with the Maastricht Treaty requirement that policy should be conducted in accordance with the principle of an open market economy with free competition.

The negative reason is that the alternative possibility 'poses a threat to the transparency and credibility of monetary policy'. There is no doubt that a system employing a number of indicators is less transparent than one using a single indicator *as long as policy changes are clearly based only on that single indicator*. The credibility argument follows since any system that gives greater freedom to the authorities raises the possibility that their decisions will be based on political rather than economic imperatives. There is, however, a second part to the credibility argument mentioned – that, in effect, the markets trust the Bundesbank and therefore they are more likely to rust eh ECB if it does exactly what the Bundesbank now does.

The only problem with this is that, as we pointed out in Box 7.5, the Bundesbank in practice operates pragmatically and certainly at times appears to adjust monetary policy in accordance with what is happening to inflation, not simply on the basis of money supply figures. Thus, the Bundesbank is in reality one of those central banks that 'use a combination of both methods in practice' while adopting one as their official policy.

This raises the interesting question of why financial markets should be persuaded by the nature of the official policy, *even when they know that that policy is not being followed in practice*.

Questions for discussion

1 Discuss the relationship between the stability of the demand for money function and the usefulness of money supply targets.

2 Why might currency substitution occur? Consider whether currency substitution is indeed less likely with a single EMU currency than it is now.

3 Why might financial markets be persuaded by the nature of a country's official monetary policy, even when they know that policy is not being followed in practice?

Index

IMAGES OF
ABERDEEN

IMAGES OF
ABERDEEN

Raymond Anderson

*Evening***Express**

breedon **books**
PUBLISHING

First published in Great Britain by
The Breedon Books Publishing Company Limited
3 The Parker Centre, Mansfield Road, Derby, DE21 4SZ.
1994
Second impression 1995
Softback edition 2004.
Reprinted 2008

ISBN 978-1-85983-664-4

Printed and bound by Cromwell Press, Trowbridge, Wiltshire

Contents

Acknowledgements

Thanks for help in the compilation of this book are due to a number of colleagues. Charlie Flett, Photographic Manager of the *Evening Express*, not only helped me trace old glass plates and organised their printing, but also actually took some of the more memorable images. Photographers Gordon Bissett and Jack Cryle also helped me date and identify prints used.

Duncan Smith, Ken Mackay, and Bob Stewart in the *Aberdeen Journals* library were endlessly helpful and patient in the face of sore provocation and unreasonable demands; and the promptings of Susan Mackay of our Retail Sales Unit were never other than tactful.

Thanks are also due to His Majesty's Theatre, Mrs Diane Mackie, and Mrs Min Clark.

Introduction

IN compiling this photographic collection from the archives of *Aberdeen Journals*, I first had to decide when history 'stopped' – at which decade was the patina of time sufficiently developed to consider the images worthy of inclusion?

I reluctantly decided to draw the line at the beginning of the 1970s. More than 30 years of rapid change have passed since then and it seemed appropriate to halt this record at the 1960s, a decade which changed so much. One small regret was that this self-imposed discipline meant the exclusion of so many of Aberdeen FC's victories.

In choosing the pictures it has been attempted to capture something of the uniqueness of Aberdeen and the Aberdonians. The dry humour, natural reserve and thriftiness born of hard times has often been misinterpreted as aloofness or misrepresented as meanness by those from outwith the area. Hopefully the pictures in this collection tell the true tale of honest endeavour, deep sense of community and, above all, a pride in the sturdy grey granite city.

Times of celebration are recorded as are the darker days of the city's dramas and the war years. And it wouldn't be Aberdeen if there wasn't a section on extremes of weather.

Royalty also command a section. The Balmoral connection has made the Royal Family the most regular of visitors to Aberdeen since Queen Victoria's days. A particularly charming set of photographs come from the days when the young Prince Charles and Princess Anne regularly went by train to London from Aberdeen's Joint Station.

But perhaps the strength of the book lies in the photographs of an Aberdeen now disappeared. It is certainly those seemingly mundane scenes which create the greatest interest when they are featured in the *Evening Express* Flashback series. To many these pictures are pure nostalgia, invoking many memories.

The chapter on the Changing Face of the city shows how it outgrew its Victorian boundaries and the large new housing areas began to spring up. Photographs, many taken from the air, show these areas when they were rolling green fields.

Few parts of the city have seen as dramatic change as the harbour … from the herring boats under sail, to the steam and diesel trawlers, to oil rig supply boats.

This book doesn't claim to be comprehensive – much photography that is significant is in private hands and many of the plates of Aberdeen's photographic pioneer George Washington Wilson are in the University of Aberdeen collection. The images in this book will be of more interest to the ordinary Aberdonian than the scholar.

This then is the folklore of Aberdeen captured by the camera. Moments in the history of a singular city.

Raymond Anderson, Aberdeen
July 1994

The Changing Face

Union Street in 1936 with horse and cart sharing the road with tram, bus and car. The Palace Hotel is on the left and across the intersection is the 'Monkey House', the entrance to the Northern Assurance Company Limited which became a popular meeting place for young men and their girlfriends.

Aberdeen's most famous street still echoing to the rattle of the tramcar in 1950.

The Castlegate in 1949 with the narrow entrance to Lodge Walk and the police station on the left. The Salvation Army Citadel dominates the eastern end of Union Street.

Holburn Junction, the west end of Union Street which was known as Babbie Law after a shop owner who was one of the areas worthies. This was taken in 1947.

The Aberdeen Beach buses on the Promenade in 1937. In the background the Beach Baths.

A 1930s-style traffic hold-up on Union Street near Market Street.

Bustling St Nicholas Street in August 1943. The tram for Woodside has attracted a long queue.

A 'Moving time for a Queen'. It is January 1964 and time for Queen Victoria to make an undignified move from St Nicholas Street to Queen's Cross where she can gaze in the direction of her beloved Balmoral.

Queen Victoria rises
from her plinth on
the corner of St
Nicholas Street.

Work on the North Breakwater pier in the early 1900s. Note the undeveloped beach area beyond Fittie.

Looking down on old Torry in 1875. A dirt track runs down to the Free Kirk. This was before Torry Dock or the Victoria Bridge were built.

A general view of Aberdeen from Balnagask showing a skyline pierced by the Town House and church steeples.

The first houses being built at Kincorth in 1947.

The city centre of Aberdeen in 1961. The Kirk of St Nicholas is prominent on the left of the picture and the Green is at bottom left. Marischal College on the right overlooks an area soon to see dramatic change.

The Bridge of Dee area in 1947.

Ferryhill from the air in the 1930s, looking towards Craiginches and Tullos.

Northfield and the Cummings Park area in 1948.

Garthdee and Kaimhill begin to take shape in 1955.

An early aerial view of the Woodside area looking north in the 1930s.

The widened Bridge of Don sweeps cars to the beginnings of the massive development of the area.

Shops under construction at Union Bridge in 1963, controversially obstructing the view from the bridge.

Bare-footed Torry children follow the band along Victoria Road at the turn of the century.

The Mansefield Dairy, a feature in Victoria Road, Torry, for many years.

The now vanished Lemon Tree Bar in St Nicholas Street. It carried the name of an ancient hostelry which is now borne by a popular centre for the arts.

The old Meal Mill, Bridge of Don.

The corner shoppie serving a small area was a fine tradition in Aberdeen as elsewhere before shopping habits changed. This example stood on the corner of Park Street and Jasmine Terrace.

Demolishing the once grand Northern Club, Union Street, in 1963.

Middle-class Edwardian ladies showing their new won freedom by taking up cycling.

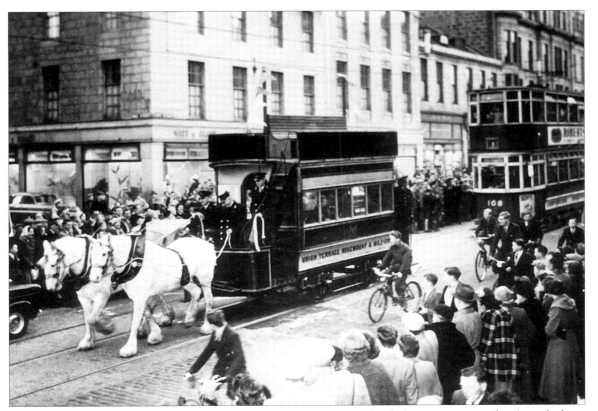

The Aberdonian affection for the tramcars which served them well for so long showed in the huge turn-out to see them in cavalcade on Union Street in 1958.

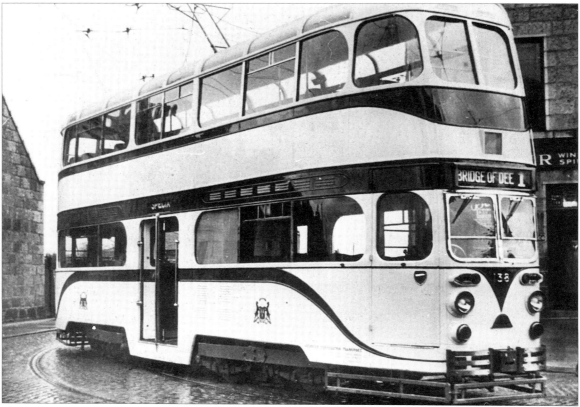

The double-bogie Pickering No.138 whose curves were a familiar sight on Aberdeen streets.

Salting the points at the Bridge of Don.

A Bridge of Dee tram in the 1920s with one of the earliest conductresses or 'clippies'.

During World War Two 'clippies' took over due to the shortage of manpower.

One of the electric trams first introduced on the Woodside route in 1899. The new tram stands alongside one still drawn by horses.

The last tram journey in Aberdeen was from the Bridge of Dee to the Bridge of Don in 1958 and was followed by this spectacular fire at the beach terminus.

Bidding fond farewells on the Deeside Subbie line which operated for 40 years, opening Aberdeen's suburban areas to commuters. The last Subbie ran on April 1937.

Ready for the off. The last train from Aberdeen to Ballater on 27 February 1966, bringing to an end a railway line whose associations with Royalty stretched back to Queen Victoria.

The impressive wooden booking office at Aberdeen Station which was demolished and replaced by a new travel centre in the 1970s.

The Harper Motor Co garage at Union Glen in 1961.

A gleaming new, early sports car at the Claud Hamilton garage in Union Row.

The proud Aberdeen owners of a new 1907 Argyll Tourer. A car of Scottish manufacture.

The Loch Street
Shopping Arcade, once
the headquarters and
main shopping centre
of the Northern Co-
operative Society,
bustling with shoppers
in 1961.

The tearoom in the Loch Street Arcade in the 1930s.

A salesman entertains the Loch Street Arcade shoppers as he tries to sell his wares.

The abandoned and decrepit Loch Street arcade in the 1970s. Eventually the fountain was restored and can still be seen today at the Scottish Co-op's Berryden superstore.

One of the Northern Co-op's mobile shops which were popular in the 1960s.

The Gallowgate in the 1930s.

Broad Street of old ... now many of the buildings crowding around Marischal College are gone.

Sinclair Road, Torry, in 1901.

Concert Court before
entrance to it from
Broad Street was
blocked off.

The Wallace Tower, Netherkirkgate, in 1954.

Beattie's Tower, a now demolished landmark in the Guestrow.

The Guestrow, Aberdeen, with gas light and the distinctive pawnbroker's sign.

The Union Street end of
Broad Street in the 1930s.

The west side of Broad Street which was demolished. This street had many courts – Cruden's Court, Ogston's Court, Huxter's Row and Longacre – all now long lost.

The Spa Bar in the Upper Denburn in 1970 just before redevelopment.

The Denburn area in 1952.

Cobbled streets and gas lamps are still evident in this 1956 picture of the Denburn.

On the left the tall granite Black's Buildings and on the right the smaller houses of Mutton Brae which were demolished to make way for Rosemount Viaduct, completed in 1889. In the foreground the Den Burn.

The Friday market in the Green in the 1930s. The Mannie in the Green fountain which was situated there from 1852 to 1958 is now back on its original site in the Castlegate.

An early photograph of The Mannie in the Green.

Congestion on the narrow Bridge of Don in September 1956.

Widening work on the Bridge of Don well under way in 1958.

The popular city bus tours of the 1950s and 1960s left from this stance in the Castlegate.

Guild Street and the Tivoli Theatre in its heyday.

The Guild Street bus station opening ceremony in 1963.

The gas lamps give way to electric lighting in 1966.

Enter the traffic wardens. All smiles on their first day on patrol in 1966.

Aberdeen at Work

Herring boats make a fine sight as they sail into Aberdeen Harbour.

Sailing down the channel.

The paddle tug *Granite City* tows fishing boats into Aberdeen Harbour at the beginning of the 20th century.

Herring drifters tied up in Aberdeen in the 1930s. Torry is in the background.

Preparing for a sea trip. Fishing boats take on coal and ice at Albert Quay.

Trawlers berthed side by side at Aberdeen Harbour in 1964.

Baskets of fish are swung across to the fish market porters from steam trawlers.

The Aberdeen Harbour ferry at work around 1910.

Teams of women hard at work gutting in an Aberdeen fish house in 1946.

The herring section of the
fish market in 1964.

Both horse and motorised transport waiting for their loads of fish in 1928.

The staff of Aberdeen shipbuilders Alex Hall & Co stand proudly before two ships under construction in 1862.

The *Thermopylæ* at Blaikie's Quay, Aberdeen Harbour. This is not the famous Aberdeen-built tea run clipper but a steamer of the Aberdeen and Commonwealth Line. She was built in 1891 and sank off Cape Town, South Africa, in 1899.

The gates of the Hall Russell shipyard open for a stream of homeward bound shipworkers in the 1950s.

The first of the
Aberdeen
prefabricated
trawlers under
construction at
Hall Russell in
1959. It was
built in only 29
days.

Another trawler is launched from the John Lewis yard. The year is 1961 and the trawler is the *Carency*.

The giant shadow of the Thameshaven is cast over Footdee as the largest ship built in Aberdeen takes shape in the Hall Russell yard in 1970.

The 10,500-ton Thameshaven after months of work. A section of York Street had to be fenced off to allow completion.

An early Aberdeen lifeboat attracts some interest at the dockside.

The Aberdeen motor lifeboat of the 1930s is admired by the men on the quayside.

The 1937 *St Clair* is towed from Aberdeen Harbour on her way to the pontoon dock for a final overhaul before going to sea. The same vessel was later renamed *St Magnus* and made her last run to the northern isles in 1950. She was the second *St Clair* and fourth *St Magnus*.

The new *St Ola* leaves Aberdeen Harbour for the first time in May 1951 on her first run to Orkney.

It's August 1959 and the *St Clement* passes young fishers as she starts another trip to Kirkwall.

The sturdy elegance of the dining salon of the *St Clair* in the 1940s.

The *St Magnus* leaving Aberdeen Harbour in 1965.

The Aberdeen-built three-masted schooner *Malcolm Miller* sails out to the bay for sea trials in 1968.

The *Malcolm Miller* lies over in a fresh breeze during her sea trials.

An Aberdeen docker with a hand barrow at Jamieson's Quay in 1965.

Unloading at Aberdeen deep water berth in 1959.

Coal arrives in Aberdeen and is loaded on to a lorry in 1963.

A load that became familiar at Aberdeen Harbour from the close of the 1960s . . .a load of pipes on an oil supply boat at Atlantic Wharf.

Coopers at work on wine and whisky barrels in Aberdeen.

Wrights and coopers at work loading barrels for Speyside distilleries at Gorrods, Regent Quay, in 1966.

Aberdeen City Fire Brigade and their horse-drawn fire tender in 1875.

Aberdeen's first motorised fire appliance.

A 1930s fire appliance with the National Fire Service insignia at a tenement fire.

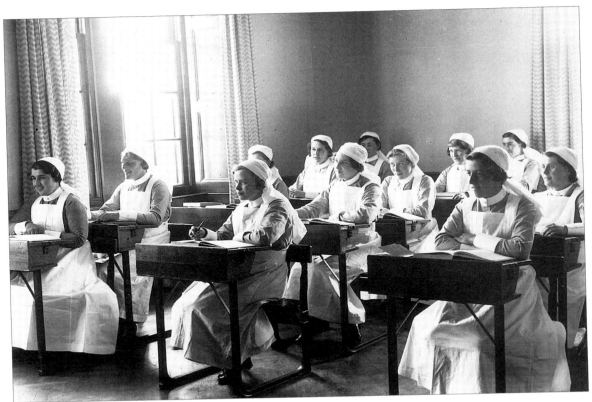

Nurses at a class in Aberdeen Royal Infirmary, Foresterhill, in 1936.

An ambulance enters Aberdeen City Hospital in 1964.

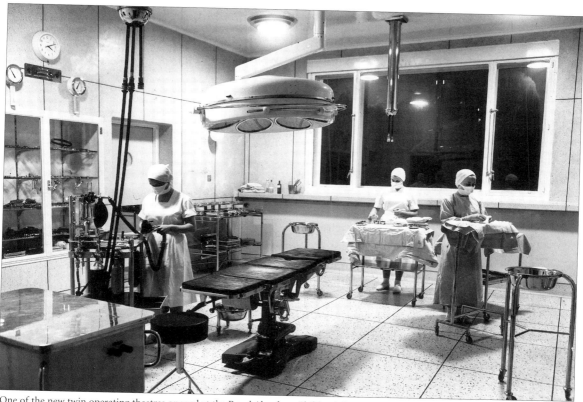

One of the new twin operating theatres opened at the Royal Aberdeen Children's Hospital in 1960.

The Wire Room at Aberdeen Journals offices, Broad Street, in 1948. This was where news was received from around the world.

Typesetting machines which continued to produce the 'hot metal' Evening Express until 1979.

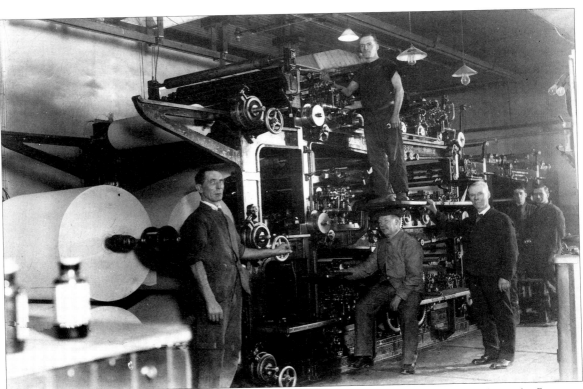

A printing press at Broad Street. What is notable is the size of this press compared to the giants which now print the Evening Express and Press and Journal.

The news of the D-Day landings hits the streets.

A lighthouse lamp cleaner going about his important work.

At work in the Seaton Potteries in 1936.

The Stoneywood paperworks complex in 1948.

At work in the Stoneywood Mills in 1935.

The Overhauling Dept at Stoneywood in 1966 when it was controlled by Alex Pirie and Sons.

A giant bobbin machine at
Grandholm Mills.

The burling room at Grandholm Works, the final stage in preparation of the cloth when it is picked and brushed clean.

Preparing the world-famous Crombie cloth at Grandholm Works.

The weaving shop at Grandholm in 1965.

At work in Ogston & Tennant's soap factory in the Gallowgate.

Men stacking and packing soap and candles at 'Soapie' Ogston's.

The employees of Devanha Brewery all dressed up and posing for a souvenir picture before setting out on their annual staff outing.

A large crowd of farm servants and farmers at the 'Muckle Friday' Feeing Market in the Castlegate on 21 May 1936.

A young man is fee-ed to a farmer at the 'Rascal Friday' Castlegate Feeing Market in May 1936. The deal done this farm servant was tied to work for the farmer for the next six months.

Onion Johnnie
Nicol Farnco
arrives in the
North-East in
1960

A group of Onion Johnnies from Brittany arrive in Aberdeen in 1953 with their cargo.

Rubislaw Quarry in 1882, seven years after granite was first taken from a 60-foot hill on the site.

At the end of its life as a worked quarry in 1970, Rubislaw is the biggest man-made hole in Europe.

No longer constantly
pumped, Rubislaw Quarry
has now filled with water.

A 30-foot solid granite roller – the
longest produced by the Pittodrie
Granite Turning Co – is prepared for
export in 1966.

The giant roller, made in Aberdeen from Swedish granite, is loaded on a ship to be taken to Stuttgart to be installed on a paper-making machine.

A conveyor belt carries letters to be sorted by hand at Aberdeen General Post Office in 1968.

Parcels and packets are stamped
by hand before being sorted into
out-going bags in 1968.

Shore Porters premises
on Shore Lane.

The Shore Porters present-day fleet of vehicles proudly bear the inscription 'Founded in 1498'. On the right is Mr John Beattie in the old Shore Porters' uniform and also pictured is a 160-year-old bogie which was used by the company.

SHORE PORTERS SOCIETY

SHORE PORTERS SOCIETY ABERDEEN. ESTABLISHED 1498

PHO

The drawing office at Hall & Co in the 1960s with models of the firm's schemes for Kincorth in the foreground.

A van equipped as a mobile
laboratory by the Rowett Research
Institute in 1966.

Staff line up outside the Northern Co-operative Society's Commerce Street shops at the beginning of the century.

Fresh milk delivered to the door in Midstocket Road in 1900.

The Northern Co-op milkmen and their carts outside the dairy at Berryden in 1927.

This milk cart photographed in Woodside was one of the last in Aberdeen.

Filling the milk bottles at the Berryden dairy in 1961.

A new giant oven at the Northern Co-op Berryden Road bakery in 1959. It is 46 feet long, heated by 100 gas jets and could turn out 1,344 loaves an hour.

Aberdonians find out about a new kind of shopping after the opening of the Fine Fare superstore at the Bridge of Dee in 1970.

The 12.40 for London is flagged off at Aberdeen Station. A scene from 1955.

The large bustling railyard at Kittybrewster in 1959.

Keen interest at the Kittybrewster auction ring in 1955.

Aberdeen at Play

Getting into the swing of things at a turn-of-the-century picnic at the Bay of Nigg.

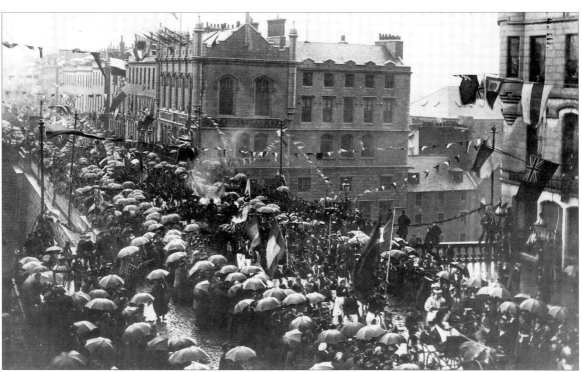

The procession to mark the opening of the Duthie Park on 27 September 1883. The gift of Miss Elizabeth Duthie to the city, the park was officially opened by Queen Victoria's youngest daughter, Princess Beatrice. More than 5,000 people took part in the parade.

Model boats sailing on the Duthie Park pond in 1900.

The old Winter Gardens at the Duthie Park about to be bulldozed in 1969.

Going … going … soon to be replaced by the new Winter Gardens.

The West Lodge of the Duthie Park in 1938. It was taken down and rebuilt in Rubislaw Den South.

Croquet being played at the Duthie Park by women well protected from the sun by hats and parasols.

The Westburn Park being kept in good trim by a team of gardeners.

Seaton Park is the scene of this well supported horse race meeting in 1937.

The Kittybrewster fairground in 1929. This photograph of the Codona Brothers Carnival was taken from the high dive tower on an Aberdeen May holiday.

The carnival site at the beachfront in the 1940s.

Large crowds at Empire Air Day, Dyce, in 1938.

Listening to the band at the Queen's Links in the 1930s with trams waiting at their terminus in the background.

One of the first buses to operate in Aberdeen. It ran from the Bathing Station at the beach to Market Street. This is the oldest known photograph of a bus in Aberdeen. It is a pre-1910 solid-tyred model, possibly a Daimler.

Crowds at the last Timmer Market in the Castlegate in 1934. This annual autumn fair became popular for its timber (or timmer) goods – spurtles, stools, cradles and suchlike as well as the toys which made it such an attraction for children.

The Timmer Market's first day on its new stance off Justice Street in 1935.

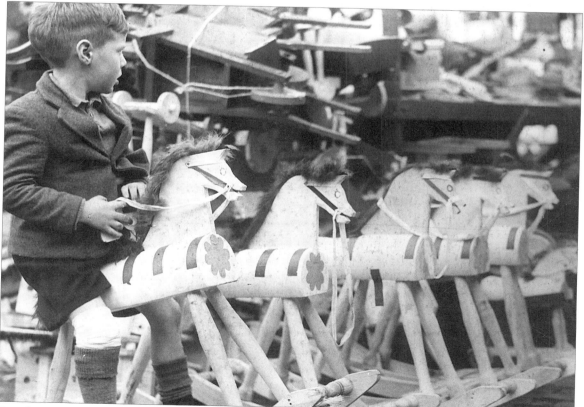

A wee boy is spoiled for choice at the Timmer Market in 1946.

Aberdeen Navy Reserve at the ready for a parade, probably part of Queen Victoria's Jubilee celebrations in 1887.

Aberdeen Beach packed with sunseekers during a heatwave in 1946.

Throwing themselves into the spirit of rock 'n' roll in 1956.

Waving farewell to a tradition at the end of the last show at the Tivoli in 1963. Calum Kennedy (centre) and Joe Gordon (right).

The Tivoli "Theatre of Varieties" advertises Jack Radcliffe and his show in the 1950s.

The interior of the Tivoli Theatre in 1938.

The original plaster work at His Majesty's Theatre being created in 1906 by the staff of James Scott and Sons.

A souvenir picture of the staff of His Majesty's Theatre taken at Christmas 1923.

Billy Smart's Circus in town, June 1966, and the elephant parade proves a big attraction.

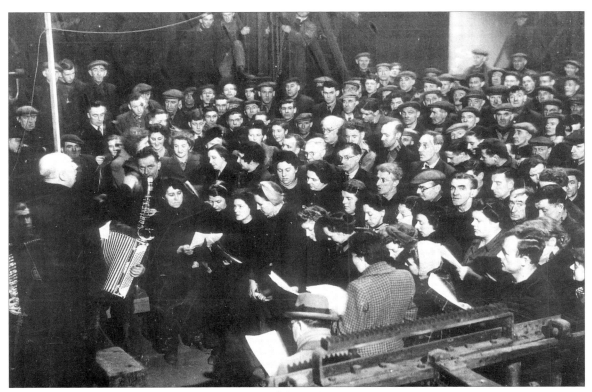

The shipyard workers at Hall Russell take part in a service on Christmas Eve, 1943.

Listening to the Salvation Army carol singers who gave a recital outside the Citadel during a Watchnight Service in 1952.

The Salvation Army
Citadel packed out
for the Citizens'
Carol Singing
Service in 1963.

The Aberdeen Greyhound Stadium, Garthdee, in 1956. It opened in 1933 and closed in 1969.

A driver, well wrapped in fur to keep warm, waits for his lady passenger to be helped aboard the car outside the prestigious Palace Hotel in Union Street.

The giant locomotive *Bittern* is the centre of attention as the record-breaking A4 Pacific Class engine makes its last official passenger run in 1966.

The coffee stall at the Joint Station in 1938. For a number of years it provided travellers with hot food and drink.

Aberdonians queueing up at the Joint Station during the July Trades holiday in 1950.

Rail enthusiasts from all over Britain travelled to the city for a trip on the Aberdeen Harbour Commissioners' track around the harbour in 1967 as part of Aberdeen Joint Station's centenary celebrations.

The Globetrotters basketball show drew large crowds to Pittodrie. Meadowlark Lemon runs rings around an opponent.

A sea of bunnets marching towards Pittodrie for a game against Celtic shows the popularity of football in the 1940s. The orderly, good humoured crowd also highlights the social change that has occurred.

The winning Aberdeen goal at the 1945-46 season League Cup Final. The Dons beat Rangers 3-2 at Hampden.

The victorious 1945 League Cup team are welcomed home at Aberdeen Joint Station.

Dons' skipper Frank Dunlop holds aloft the Scottish Cup at Aberdeen Station in 1947 as the history-making team who beat Hibs 2-1 at Hampden return home to a tumultuous reception.

Lord Provost Graham congratulates the 1954-55 Scottish League champions. It was the first time the Dons had won the League in their 52-year history. Paddy Buckley is shaking hands with the provost.

The victorious Dons show the Scottish Cup to their fans after winning it for the first time on 19 April 1947.

The 1954-55 League champion's flag is unfurled at Pittodrie.

It's 1955 and Dons' skipper Jimmy Mitchell holds the League Cup for goalkeeper Fred Martin to fill with champagne as Dave Caldwell, Jim Clunie, Bobby Wilson, Harry Yorston, Jackie Hather and Paddy Buckley (obscured) look on. The Dons beat St Mirren 2-1 in the Final.

ons captain Jimmy
itchell holds the League
up as he is chaired to the
am bus on their return
Aberdeen.

The high-wire students get their message across.

Daredevil students perform a spectacular rag week stunt at
Rubislaw Quarry in 1966.

The Casino Cinema in Wales Street. Opened in 1916, closed 1959, demolished 1971.

The Torry Cinema ... opened 1921, closed 1968.

The Queen's Cinema, Union Street ... opened as the first Advocates Hall in 1838, later became a cinema which closed in 1981.

The Playhouse Cinema pictured here in 1959. The Union Street cinema opened in 1915 and closed in 1974.

The Odeon cinema on Justice Mill Lane which replaced the Regent Cinema on the same site. It is now Cannons Health and Fitness Centre.

The Palace Cinema, originally built to house a circus, became a dance hall in 1959.

The Majestic, Union Street, which closed in 1973 after 50 years as a cinema.

The Kingsway on Frederick Street
which became a bingo hall in 1962.

The Grand Central, George Street, opened in 1921, closed in 1981.

Bright lights at the
Gaumont in 1956. The
cinema closed in 1973
after 59 years.

The Gaumont on Union Street in 1957 with a long queue waiting to see one of the Doctor series of films.

The News Cinema in
Diamond Street became the
Cosmo 2 and had a time as an
alternative cinema in the
1970s but closed in 1977.

The Cinema House on Skene Terrace closed 1970.

The City Cinema in George Street was the largest in Aberdeen with 2,300 seats.

The Astoria in Kittybrewster which opened in 1934 and closed in 1967 after four months as a bingo hall.

The noted cinema organ at the Capitol, Union Street, which entertained audiences for nearly 50 years.

The ABC cinema on Union Street in the 1980s. It had previously been The Regal. In more recent years it was The Cannon, The Lighthouse, and then Vue.

The War Years

It's April 1939 and these stony-faced men are at a recruiting drive for what became known as the Fish Troop.

Outside the fish market on Albert Quay the recruiting sergeant has his say.

The Royal Army Medical Corps march across Union Street in 1939 on their way to the war.

A reassuring smile and a look of concern from the platform as Gordon Highlanders set off from Aberdeen on 17 April 1940.

Painting the edges of the pavements to aid pedestrians and drivers during the blackouts.

An infant respirator is demonstrated in 1938
when the fear of gas attacks was very real.

An Aberdeen policeman
prepared for a new role.

Working the Aberdeen
telephone exchange w
gas masks being worn
1939.

The Boys' Brigade with a good haul as it does its bit collecting salvage for the Aberdeen war effort in 1939.

The Women's Voluntary Service HQ in 1940 with a big collection of aluminium pots and pans, which were collected to be used for plane production.

The John Lewis Shipyard Home Guard on the alert in 1940.

A smoke bomb is exploded in Union Street in 1941 during an Air Raid Patrol test to ensure everyone carries – and wears – their mask when necessary.

The crowded camaraderie of the air raid shelter. This one was in Tullos.

A head count for evacuees as they arrive in the North-East.

Who are you? A newly-arrived
evacuee has his label read in
1939 at the railway station.

An ARP warden helps two
Aberdeen youngsters
collect a small bundle of
belongings from their
bomb-blitzed home after
a 1940 air raid which hit
Wellington Road, Torry.

The Women's Land Army
parades down Union Street
in 1941.

An elderly
woman walks
from her home
with a few
salvaged
possessions after
the Menzies
Road, Torry, raid
in August 1941.

Clearing up Menzies Road after the 1941 raid.

Czech pilots (and their mascot) scramble to their Hurricanes at Dyce in 1941. They were the first Czech Squadron to be formed in Britain as a part of the RAF.

King Street after a raid on 25 April 1942 which killed a child and a man.

Bomb damage at Porthill Church, Gallowgate, following the 25 April air raid.

The search for survivors after a
bomb hit McBride's pub and
tenement home, Loch Street
on 13 February 1941.

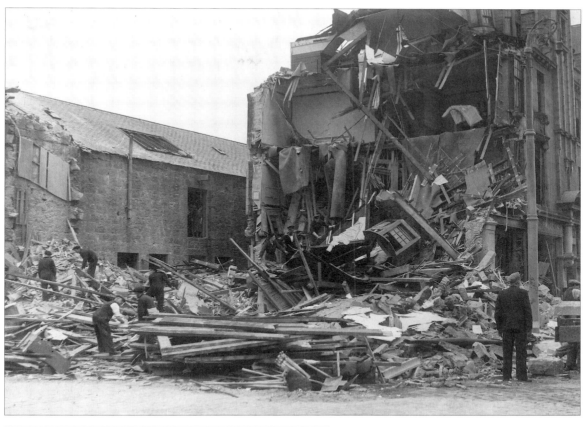

Bomb damage on South Market Street, 7 August 1942.

St Mary's Episcopal
Church, Carden Place
(the Tartan Kirkie) after
the 21 April 1943, air
raid. It was the worst
Aberdeen suffered.

Causewayend Church stands open to the
street following the 21 April raid.

Causewayend Church can be seen behind the rubble of Charles Street.

Bomb damage in Cattofield after the air raid which claimed 97 lives, men women children and babies.

A man salvages furniture from his wrecked home in Hilton Terrace.

A tenement in Stafford Street which was gutted by fire in the April 1943 raid.

The ruins of Middlefield School is surveyed by a group of children.

People stand in silent tribute as the funeral cortege for some of the victims of the 21 April air raid approaches Trinity Cemetery.

Dad's Army on parade …
the third birthday parade of
Aberdeen Home Guard,
May 1943.

There's a war and it's raining but a bonny baby competition can always raise a smile. A popular event during the Stay at Home holidays of the war years.

An open-air dance attracts a big crowd in July 1944, but there's not enough men for dance partners.

Stay-at-Home fun during the Eightsome Reel at Hazlehead Park during the Summer of 1942.

Prisoners-of-war at work repairing roads in Aberdeen in 1945.

Evening Express newsvendor Patsy Gallacher gives out the news of the Normandy landings to an excited crowd in June 1944.

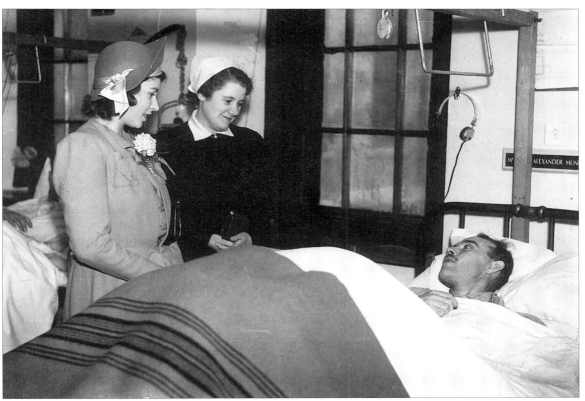

Princess Elizabeth visits war wounded at Aberdeen Royal Infirmary, Foresterhill, in October 1944.

Putting out the flags for VJ Day in August 1945.

It's 15 August 1945, and a huge crowd gather around the Town House to listen to the Lord Provost.

Happy cheering crowds on VJ Day.

The victory parade on Sunday, 19 August 1945.

The streets are alive with excitement at the news of victory.

More victory celebrations.

Austerity days and Aberdonians queue for a consignment of bananas just arrived at Peglers on Union Street, 11 May 1946.

The Royal Connection

King Edward VII's Coronation procession at Queen's Cross in 1902.

The Prince of Wales lays the foundation stone for Aberdeen Royal Infirmary in 1928.

Uniformed nurses line up to honour the Prince of Wales after the foundation stone ceremony.

Excitement on Union Street as people crane to see the Prince of Wales during his 1928 visit.

The official opening of the new Royal Infirmary in 1936, but it was the Duke and Duchess of York who performed the ceremony not the new King Edward VIII whose attachment to Mrs Wallis Simpson was growing. He chose to continue his holiday at Balmoral.

The Duke of York opens the door of the new Aberdeen Royal Infirmary. A long cherished dream of Aberdonians is realised.

Queen Mary arrives at Ballater in 1925 after travelling from Aberdeen on the Deeside line.

King Edward VIII and the Duke of York arrive at Ballater Station on 19 September 1936, as they travel to Balmoral.

The Royal brothers inspect the Guard of Honour at Ballater . . .only months before Edward abdicates to marry Mrs Simpson on 10 December 1936.

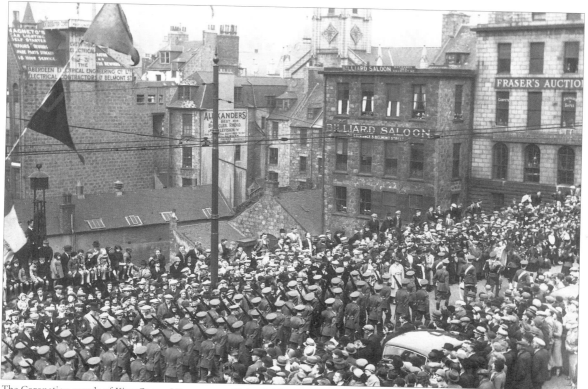

The Coronation parade of King George VI passes over Union Bridge in 1937.

Aberdeen celebrations for the Coronation of King George VI.

August 1938, and King George VI, Queen Elizabeth, Princess Elizabeth and Princess Margaret arrive at Aberdeen by sea.

The Royal party is greeted by the Lord Provost and councillors.

Queen Elizabeth opens the King George VI Bridge over the River Dee in 1941.

Princess Margaret at her first public engagement, inspecting local youth organisations at the Rose Review at Dyce on 16 September 1945.

A young Prince makes an uncertain entrance. Prince Charles looks back for reassurance as he arrives at Ballater after the rail journey from Aberdeen on 18 September 1950.

Nurse Helen
Lightbody with
Prince Charles and
the infant Princess
Anne as they arrive
at Aberdeen Joint
Station to travel
south. The year is
1950.

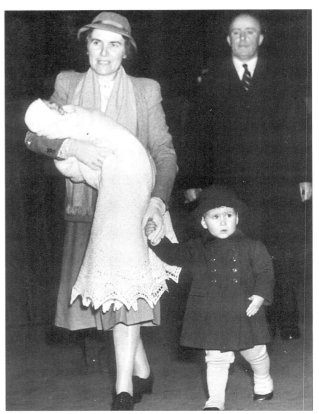

The King and Queen with Prince Charles and Princess Anne at the start of their Balmoral holiday in August 1951.

The Royal children with Nurse Lightbody at Aberdeen, October 1951, before returning to London.

Prince Charles and teddy at the window of the Royal Train, Aberdeen, October 1951.

A cuddle for sister Anne as the Royal youngsters wait for the train from Aberdeen to set off.

Left: Princess Anne shows off a corgi to the onlookers at Aberdeen Station, August 1954, and right: Prince Charles gets the corgi to show a paw.

Ready for bed. The Royal children in their pyjamas at the railway station in 1956.

The Queen Mother after opening the refurbished Provost Skene's House in 1953. She took a personal interest in the restoration of this ancient house.

President Eisenhower waves
to the crowds at the gates of
Balmoral Castle during his
stay in 1959.

The Royal Yacht *Britannia* leaves Aberdeen in 1965 watched by large crowds.

Aberdeen Dramas

The crowd wait silently for the fateful moment outside Craiginches prison on the morning of 15 August 1963. Within the prison, at one minute past eight, Henry Burnett was hanged for murder.

Aberdeen's luxurious Palace Hotel ablaze on 31 October 1941.

The burned out shell of the Palace Hotel. Six people lost their lives in the blaze which started in the grill service room. One of a chain of LNER hotels, it was built in 1874.

A bus poised over a basement flat in Holburn Street after crashing in 1959.

How the *Evening Express* reported the Aberdeen typhoid epidemic in May 1964.

Sign in an Aberdeen shop window during the typhoid outbreak.

Typhoid put Aberdeen in the media spotlight and Medical Officer of Health Dr Ian MacQueen (right) became a well-known face on television and in the newspapers as he gave out the latest information.

A child quarantined in Aberdeen's City Hospital during the outbreak can see his family only through a window.

Rising to the occasion to see a typhoid patient in June 1964.

The Queen symbolically signalled that the typhoid epidemic was over and Aberdeen was no longer a beleaguered city when she visited Lord Provost Norman Hogg.

Grateful crowds of Aberdonians acknowledge the Queen's dramatic visit to the city.

The crowds outside the Town House rejoice as the weight of the typhoid epidemic is lifted.

A spectacular view of the blaze at Aberdeen Combworks, Gallowgate, 1969.

Fighting the blaze at
Middleton's the printers in
Rose Street, May 1968.

The skeleton of the new zoology building in 1966.

The dramatic scene after the zoology building collapsed, killing five men.

The *Ben Screel* which ran aground on the rocks at Girdleness in 1933.

The grounded *Ben Screel*
which missed the Aberdeen
Harbour entrance in fog
on 18 January 1933.

The *Luffness* scuttled off Cove in 1958 after being grounded in Aberdeen navigation channel.

Coastguards fire a line to the Aberdeen trawler *Ben Gulvain* grounded at Balgownie. January 1976.

Rescuers look on anxiously as a crewman is winched off the *Ben Gulvain* while others cluster at the prow.

Firemen tackle the blazing Hamlyn grain warehouse in Aberdeen in 1967.

A workman holds his head in horror as a building being demolished in Broad Street in 1964 falls the wrong way.

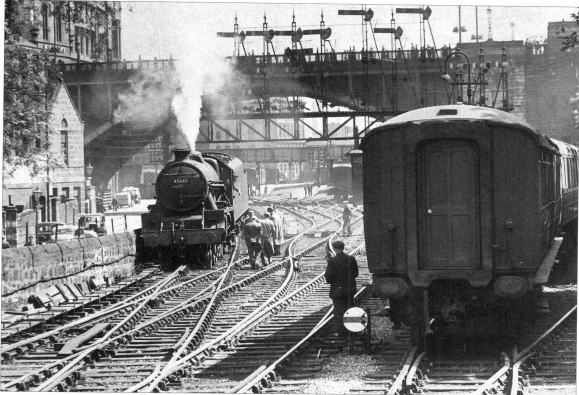

A steam train derailed in 1954.

Strikers pointedly ignore a mounted police patrol on Union Street during the General Strike in 1926.

Weel Kent Faces

Right: Lord Byron, one of the most famous residents of Broad Street. Far right: Mary Slessor, famous for her work as a missionary, is usually associated with Dundee but was in fact born in Aberdeen in 1848 in Mutton Brae and spent her early years in the city before the family moved to Dundee.

No.64 Broad Street (right of the turreted building) where the poet Byron lived in the 1790s while attending the Grammar School. These buildings were swept away at the beginning of the century to build the Marischal College façade.

A fashionable couple on Union Street at the turn of the century.

One of the last of the fishwives who sold hard fish at The Green negotiates with a potential customer. The year was 1947.

Fire at Hunter's premises (now Rosemount Square) in 1937.

A rare picture of cocky Hunter who was born in 1868 in Water Lane off Virginia Street. He opened the first of a number of shops in 1903 and built up a reputation of being prepared to buy or sell anything.

Cocky Hunter's store in Castle Street which was famous for its chaotic jumble of different goods. The building was previously a children's hospital.

Aberdeen's only organ
grinder Benedetto
Suave in 1938.

Benedetto's familiar hand cart and organ
attracts a small group of listeners in 1938.

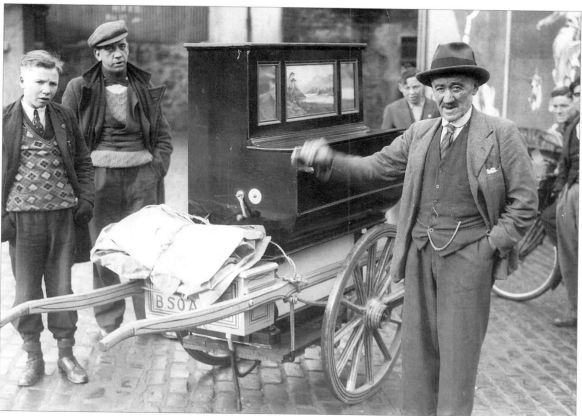

Hot chestnut man Fool (or Foul) Friday heating the nuts at his Castlegate stance in the 1930s.

Long serving Aberdeen North MP Hector Hughes still taking his regular dip at Aberdeen Beach in his 80s.

Famous Aberdonian comedian Harry Gordon and his wife at Aberdeen Joint Station in 1955, and right: Harry Gordon steps out on Union Street in his ENSA (Entertainments National Service Association) uniform in 1945. He was soon to travel to the Continent to entertain troops.

Harry Gordon still joking with the nurses after a heart attack in 1955. He spent much of his time in hospital answering mail from concerned fans.

Mary Garden the
opera singer who
was world
famous
throughout the
world in her
heyday. She
returned to
Aberdeen in her
later years and
died in 1967.

Harlaw Academy pupil
Annie Lennox, aged 16.

Annie and The Tourists receive a silver disc from Lord Provost William Fraser in the old council chamber at Aberdeen Town House. World fame is just around the corner.

Youthful Rolling Stones Mick Jagger, Keith Richards, Charlie Watts, Brian Jones and Bill Wyman with youthful reporter Julie Davidson in 1965 when the group took Aberdeen by storm.

Scotland the What? learned
their stage craft in Aberdeen
students' shows and went on
to become the foremost
exponents of the gentle
humour of the North-East.
Here Buff Hardie, Steve
Robertson and George Donald
poke fun at the *Evening
Express*.

Complete with Nicky
Tams Andy Stewart, a
frequent and popular
visitor to Aberdeen,
in full flow in 1959.

Andy Stewart with wife Sheila (left) and Hal Dyer who stood in at the last minute to take parts in an Aberdeen production of *Aladdin* in 1959.

It's 1960 and the most expensive footballer in Britain is getting a hard time from young fans as they have a kick-about outside his Woodside home. The boys took the game too seriously and Denis Law, just transferred to Manchester City for a record British fee of £53,000, feared he would have to limp back to his team.

Stormy Days

A trawler enters Aberdeen Harbour in stormy weather in 1969.

Two young men with bicycles are caught as huge waves break over Aberdeen's North Pier in 1950.

The Great Gale of 1953 left the North-East bruised and battered … .it even flattened forests like this one at Crathes.

An aerial view of what the winds did to this forest at Ballogie in January 1953.

Snow swept Union Street in the 1950s with Queen Victoria surveying the wintry scene at the corner of St Nicholas Street.

January 1960, and the snowbound Aberdeen to Kintore road is littered with abandoned vehicles.

Children struggle though five-foot drifts in Northfield during the winter of 1968.

Battered by a snowstorm – Union Street, 1969.

One brave traveller waits for a bus on Provost Fraser Drive as cars slither through the blizzard in 1969.

Christmas 1970 and the buses have stopped running because of the road conditions. This small huddle of shoppers is waiting for a taxi.

The weather in Aberdeen can be fierce, but it can also be beautiful, like this scene from January 1970 with the sun reflecting on the ice-covered river below the old Bridge of Dee.